Reuss, Jeremias [illegible]

Das gelehrte England, oder Lexikon der jetzlebenden Schriftsteller

in Großbritannien, Irland und Nordamerika (A-K)

Reuss, Jeremias David

Das gelehrte England, oder Lexikon der jetzlebenden Schriftsteller

in Großbritannien, Irland und Nordamerika (A-K)

Inktank publishing, 2018

www.inktank-publishing.com

ISBN/EAN: 9783747703052

DAS

GELEHRTE ENGLAND

ODER

LEXIKON

DER JEZTLEBENDEN

SCHRIFTSTELLER

IN

GROSSBRITANNIEN, IRLAND UND NORD-AMERIKA

NEBST EINEM

VERZEICHNISS IHRER SCHRIFTEN

VOM JAHR 1770 BIS 1790.

NACHTRAG UND *FORTSEZUNG*

VOM JAHR 1790 BIS 1803.

VON

JEREMIAS DAVID REUSS,

HOFRATH UND PROFESSOR DER PHILOSOPHIE, MITGLIED DER KÖNIGL. GESELLSCH. DER WISSENSCH. UND UNTER-BIBLIOTHEKAR BEY DER UNIVERSITÄTS-BIBLIOTHEK ZU GÖTTINGEN.

TH. I. A—K.

BERLIN UND STETTIN,
bey FRIED. NICOLAI.
1804.

Dignum laude virum Musa vetat mori.

Horatius, Lib. IV, Od. 8.

Vorrede.

Vor dreyzehn Jahren habe ich es gewagt, ein Handbuch der neueren Brittischen und Amerikanischen Litteratur von zwey Jahrzehenden, unter dem Titel: Das gelehrte England oder Lexikon der jeztlebenden Schriftsteller in Grossbrittannien, Irland und Nord-Amerika, nebst einem Verzeichniss ihrer Schriften; vom Jahr 1770 bis 1790. Berlin u. Stettin. 1791. herauszugeben. Dieser erste Versuch ist von Freunden der Litteratur so günstig aufgenommen worden, dass ich mir es sogleich zur Pflicht machte, alles was zur Verbesserung des ersteren und zur Fortsezung desselben seit jenem Zeitpunct beytragen könnte, mit Fleiss zu sammeln. Ein solches Unternehmen erfordert eine eigene Gedult und Aufmerksamkeit; einen Zeitaufwand, zu welchem nur eine besondere uneigennüzige Vorliebe den Muth geben kann; aber auch diese würde den Nachtrag nicht zu Tage gefördert haben und meine Sammlung wäre wahrscheinlich in meinem Pult verschlossen geblieben, wenn nicht der um die Ausbreitung der Litteratur in Deutschland so sehr verdiente Herr *Nicolai*, in Berlin, zur Bekanntmachung derselben die Hand geboten hätte.

Gern hätte ich es, in mancher Rücksicht, gesehen, wenn auch diese Fortsezung in einem mäßsigen Band, so wie der erste Versuch, hätte geliefert werden können; da ich aber mich nicht blofs auf die neuen Schriftsteller, welche seit dem Jahr 1790 angefangen haben zu schreiben, allein einschränken durfte, sondern, um vollständig zu seyn, auch das Verzeichnifs der Schriften, welche die älteren Schriftsteller in dem Zeitraum vom Jahr 1790–1803 oder bis an ihren Tod, geliefert haben, fortsezen mufste; da ich aufserdem, so wie im ersteren Versuch auch hier, alle kleinere Abhandlungen eines Mannes, welche in den Gesellschafts- und periodischen Schriften zerstreut vorkommen, mit möglichstem Fleifs zusammenstellen wollte, so liefs sich dieses nicht in einen Band zusammenfassen.

Den Freunden der Englischen neuern Litteratur, welche nicht allein den litterarischen Fleifs eines Mannes kennen lernen oder die Geisteswerke, welche er geliefert hat, mit einem Blick übersehen wollen, sondern auch Nachricht von seiner Ausbildung, seinem Wirken auf andere, seinem häuslichem Leben u. dergl. zu lesen wünschen, wird es nicht unangenehm seyn, dafs ich bey Lebenden und vorzüglich bey verstorbenen Schriftstellern die Werke angezeigt habe, welche Nachrichten von ihrem Leben enthalten.

Die

Die Schriftſteller, welche in dieſer Fortſezung zum erſtenmahl erſcheinen, habe ich mit einem Sternchen (*), vor ihrem Namen, bezeichnet; die andern Artikel ohne Sternchen, enthalten die litterariſchen Arbeiten ſolcher Schriftſteller, welche in meinem erſten Verſuch ſchon vorgekommen ſind.

Die Berichtigungen und Zuſäze zu dem erſtern Werk, die dieſer Nachtrag enthält, habe ich, zur Erſparung des Raums, nicht jedesmahl ausdrücklich bemerkt, weil ſie ein jeder, bey angeſtellter Vergleichung, leicht ſelbſt finden kann.

Seit dem Jahre 1790 ſind zwey Schriftſteller-Verzeichniſſe von lebenden Engliſchen Gelehrten erſchienen; Das eine mit dem Titel:

> Literary memoirs of living Authors of Great-Britain — in two volumes. London. 1798. 8.

das andere:

> A new catalogue of living English authors — Vol. 1. London. 1799. 8.

Dieſer Band enthält die Buchſtaben A-C, Sechs Bände ſollten das ganze Werk beſchlieſsen, allein noch iſt nicht der zweyte Theil erſchienen. Erſteres iſt ſehr unvollſtändig und wenig genau; etwas beſſer iſt das zweyte; allein beyde ungenannte Verfaſſer haben die lebenden Gelehrten und ihre angeführten Schriften groſsentheils mit einer partheyiſchen, öfters bittern und inhumanen Characteriſtick begleitet, welche nicht zur Würdigung ihrer litterariſchen Bemühungen gehört.

Auch diesesmahl kostete es mich nicht geringe Mühe zu erfahren, ob ein Schriftsteller noch lebt und in welchem Jahr er gestorben ist; bey mehreren habe ich deswegen ein Frage-Zeichen (?) beygesezt, wo ich gefunden habe, dass eine Abhandlung nach seinem Tode erst gedruckt worden ist; aber dass ich nicht manchen, der längst gestorben ist, noch unter die Lebenden gezählt habe, kann ich nicht verbürgen. Ich wiederhohle daher meine Bitte mich mit Berichtigungen und Beyträgen zu unterstüzen;

Möchte ich eben das Glück, wie Herr Professor *Ersch* in Halle, geniessen und solche Berichtigungen und Beyträge aus England selbst erhalten, wie der achtungs-würdige Litterator des Gelehrten Frankreich's sie so reichlich aus Frankreich selbst erhielt!

Erklärung der Abkürzungen.

American Museum. *(Matthew Carey)* The American Museum, or, repository of ancient and modern fugitive pieces, prose and poetical. Vol. 1-11. Y. 1787 — Y. 1792. Part 1. Jan. - June. Philadelphia. 8.

Arch. Archaeologia; or Miscellaneous Tracts relating to Antiquity; published, by the Society of Antiquaries of London. Vol. 10-13. London. 1792-1800. 4.

Asiatic Miscellany. The Asiatic Miscellany, consisting of translations, imitations, fugitive pieces, original productions and extracts from curious publications by *W. Chambers* and Sir *W. Jones* — Calcutta. 1787. 8.

Asiat. Res. Asiatick researches; or, transactions of the society instituted in Bengal, for inquiring into the history and antiquities, the arts, sciences and litterature of Asia. Vol. 2-4. Calcutta. 1790-1795. 4. Vol. 5. 6. London. 1799. 1801. 8.

Bath Agric. Soc. Letters and papers of agriculculture, planting etc. selected from the correspondance-book of the society instituted at Bath for the encouragements of agriculture, arts, manufactures and commerce. Vol. 1. Ed. 3. Bath. 1788. Vol. 2. 3. Ed. 2. 1788. Vol. 4-9. 1788-1799. 8.

Coll. of Massachusetts H. S. Collections of the Massachusetts historical society for the Y. 1792-1801. (Vol. 1-8.) 8.

The *Columbian Magazine*, or monthly miſcellany. Vol. 1-7. (Y. 1786. Sept. — Y. 1790. June.) Vol. 8-11. The Univerſal Aſylum and Columbian Magazine. (Y. 1790. July — Y. 1792. June.)

Comm. and Agric. Mag. The commercial and agricultural magazine for the Y. 1799 - Y. 1802. April. Vol. 1-8. London. 8.

Comm. to the B. of Agr. Communications to the board of agriculture on ſubjects relative to the husbandry and internal improvement of the country. Vol. 1. Vol. 2. Vol. 3. Part 1. London. 1797-1802. 4.

Duncan's M. C. *Duncan's* Medical Commentaries for the Y. 1791-1795. Dec. 2. Vol. 6-10. Edinb. 8.

Duncan's A. of Med. *Duncan's* Annals of Medecine for the Y. 1796-1800. (Vol. 1-6.) Edinb. 8.

The *Evangelical Magazine* for the Y. 1793-1800. Vol. 1-10. 8.

Gentleman's Magazine Y. 1790-1803.

The *Maſſachuſetts Magazine*; or monthly muſeum of knowledge and rational entertainment. Boſton. 8. Vol. 1. for 1789. (Jan.-Dec.) Vol. 2. for 1790. (Jan.-Dec.) Vol. 3. for 1791. (Jan.-Dec.) Vol. 4. for 1792. (...May-Dec.) Vol. 5. for 1793. (Jan.-Dec.) Vol. 6. for 1794. (Jan.-Dec.) Vol. 7. for 1795. (...Apr.-Dec.) Vol. 8. for 1796. (...March-Aug.)

M. C. Medical communications. Vol. 2. London. 1790. 8.

M. P. of M. S. Medical papers, communicated to the Maſſachuſetts medical ſociety — publiſhed by the ſociety. Numb. 1. Boſton. 1790. 8.

M. Rec. and Reſ. Medical records and reſearches, ſelected from the papers of a private medical aſſociation. London. 1798. 8.

The *Medical Repoſitory*. Vol. 1-3. New-York. 1798-1800. 8.

Mem.

Mem. of B. A. Memoirs of the American Academy of Arts and Sciences. Vol. 2. Part 1. Boston. 1793. 4.

Mem. of M. Memoirs of the Litterary and Philosophical Society of Manchester. Vol. 3-5. 1790-1802. 8.

Mem. of M. S. of L. Memoirs of the medical society of London instituted in the Y. 1773. Vol. 3-5. London. 1792-1799. 8.

The *Monthly Magazine* and British register for 1796-1802. Vol. 1-14. Y. 1803. Jan.-April.

N. A: Nautical Almanac for the Year 1790-1802. 1804. 8.

The *New-York Magazine*, or literary repository. Vol...2. (Y. 1791. Jan.-Dec.) Vol. 3. (Y. 1792. Jan.-Dec.) Vol. 5. (Y. 1794. Jan.-Sept.....) Vol. 6. (Y. 1795. Jan.-Dec.) New series Vol. 1. (Y. 1796. Jan.-Dec.) Vol. 2. (Y. 1797. Jan.-May.....)

Nicholson's Journal of natural philosophy, chemistry and the arts, illustrated with engravings. Vol. 1-5. London. 1797-1801. 4. Vol. 1. 2. (Y. 1802. Jan.-Aug.) Vol. 3. (Y. 1802. Sept.-Nov.) 8.

Phil. Transact. Philosophical Transactions of the Royal Society of London for the Y. 1791. — 1802. 4.

Public Characters of 1798-1799. Ed. 3. London. 1801. of 1799-1803. London. 1799-1803. (Vol. 1-5.) 8.

(Simmons) Medical Facts and Observations. Vol. 1-8. London. 1791-1800. 8.

Tilloch's Philos. Magaz. The philosophical Magazine comprehending the various branches of science, the liberal and fine arts, agriculture, manufactures and commerce by *Alexander Tilloch.* Vol. 1-15. Y. 1798 — Y. 1803. April.

Tr. of A. S. Transactions of the American philosophical society held at Philadelphia for promo-

promoting ufeful knowledge. Vol. 3-5. Philadelphia. 1793-1802. 4.

Transactions of the Society of the Antiquaries of Scotland. Vol. 1. Edinburgh. 1792. 4.

Tr. of Dublin Soc. Transactions of the Dublin Society. Vol. 1. P. 1. 2. for the Y. 1799. Dublin. 1800. 8.

Tr. of E. S. Transactions of the Royal Society of Edinburgh. Vol. 3. Vol. 4. Vol. 5. Part 1. Edinb. 1794-1799. 4.

Tr. of the Soc. for the E. of A. Transactions of the fociety inftituted at London for the encouragement of arts, manufactures and commerce; Vol. 1-19. London. 1783-1801. 8.

Tr. of Highland Soc. Prize effays and Transactions of the Highland Society of Scotland. Vol. 1. Edinb. 1799. 8.

Tr. of J. A. The Transactions of the Royal Irish Academy. Vol. 3-8. Dublin. 1790-1802. 4.

Transact. of L. S. Transactions of the Linnean Society. Vol. 1-6. London. 1791-1802. 4.

Transactions of a Society for the improvement of medical and chirurgical knowledge. Vol. 1. 2. London. 1793-1800. 8.

Tr. of Phyf. of Philad. Transactions of the College of Phyficians of Philadelphia. Vol. 1. Part 1. Philad. 1793. 8.

Young's A. of Agr. *Arthur Young's* Annals of agriculture and other ufeful arts. Vol. 1-38. Nrb. 1-217. Bury St. Edmund's. 1784-1802. 8.

---

* ABBOT,

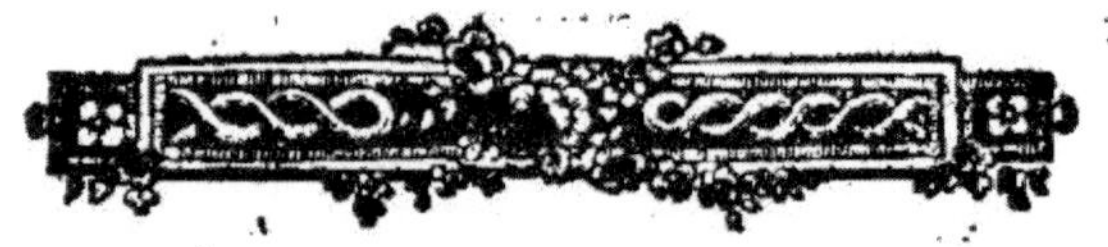

*ABBOT, [Charles] *Esq. M. P. LL. D. F. R, A. S. Barrister at law, and Clerk of the rules in the court of King's Bench.*

*Rules and orders on the plea side of the court of King's Bench; beginning in easter term 1731 and ending in trinity term 1795, with preface and index. 1795. 8. (2 sh. 6 d.) Jurisdiction and practice of the court of great sessions of Wales, on the Chester circuit; with preface and index. 1795. 8. Hints relative to the population bill. (*Young's* A. of Agr. Vol. 36. p. 455.) A treatise of the law relative to merchant-ships and seamen; in four parts. 1802. 8. (9 sh.)

*ABBOT, [Charles] *M. A: F. L. S: Vicar of Oakley Raynes in Bedfordshire.*

Flora Bedfordiensis; comprehending such plants as grow wild in the county of Bedford, arranged according to the system of *Linnaeus*; with occasional remarks. 1798. 8. (6 sh. 6 d.)

*ABBOT, [John] *Resident in Georgia.*

The natural history of the rarer lepidopterous insects of Georgia; Including their systematic characters, the particulars of their several metamorphoses, and the plants on which they feed. Collected from the observations of *John Abbot* by *James Edward Smith*. Vol. 1. 2. 1797. fol. (21 L.)

*ABBS, [Cooper]

Observations on the remarkable failure of haddocks, on the coasts of Northumberland, Durham and Yorkshire. (Phil. Transact. Y. 1792. p. 367.)

*ABDY, [Thomas Abdy] *Rev.*

On the culture of potatoes and their use in fattening cattle. (*Young's* A. of Agr. Vol. 10. p. 324.) On the Essex dairies. (Ib. Vol. 11. p. 122.)

Reuss G. E. Suppl. A ABER-

Benj. Goosequill and Peter Paragraph. 1790. 8. (5 sh.) (The anecdotes relate to *Makittrick*, who has lately called himself *Adair*; see Critical Review. Y. 1790. Nov. p. 579.) A candid enquiry into the truth of certain charges of the dangerous consequences of the Suttonian or cooling regimen, under inoculation for the small-pox. 1790. 8. (1 sh.) Curious facts and anecdotes, not contained in the memoirs of *Philip Thicknesse* Esq. — by *Benj. Goosequill* and *Peter Paragraph*. 1790. 8. (2 sh.) Two sermons, the first addressed to Seamen, the second to the British West-India slaves. 1791. 8. The history of three cases of phthisis pulmonalis, treated by cuprum vitriolatum and conium maculatum; two of which terminated favourably. (*Duncan's* M. C. Dec. 2. Vol. 7. p. 473.) An essay on regimen. 1799. 8.

*ADAIR, [Robert] *Esq. M. P.*

Part of a letter from *Robert Adair*, Esq. to the R. Honor. C. *J. Fox*, occasioned by Mr. *Burke's* mention of Lord *Keppel* in a recent publication. 1796. 8. (1 sh.) The letter of the R. Hon. C. *J. Fox* to the Electors of Westminster Jan. 1793. with an application of its principles to subsequent events. 1802. 8. (3 sh. 6 d.)

*ADAIR, [William] *Esq. Surgeon-General to the Garrison of Gibraltar.*

An account of the successfull treatment of a case in which the brachial artery was divided. (*Simmons's* Medical Facts and observations. Vol. 4. p. 21.) übers. Repertor. Chir. u. Medic. Abhandl. B. 2. S. 3. An account of the effects of oil of turpentine in a case of internal haemorrhage. (Ibid. Vol. 4. p. 25.) A case of imperforated anus. (Ibid. Vol. 4. p. 27.) übers. Repertor. Chir. u. Mediz. Abhandl. B. 2. S. 6.

ADAM, [Alexander] *LL. D. Rector of the high School of Edinburgh.*

Roman antiquities; or, an account of the manners and customs of the Romans. 1791. 8. Ed. 2. 1792. (7 sh. 6 d.) übers. von *Joh. Leonh. Meyer*, Th. 1. 2. Erlangen. 1794. 1796. 8. A summary of geography and history both antient and modern — 1795. 8. (9 sh.) Classical biography, exhibiting

biting alphabetically the proper names, with a short account of the several deities, heroes and other persons, mentioned in the ancient classic authors —. 1800. 8. (6 sh.)

ADAM, [James] *Esq. Architect.*
born . . . . . died. 20 Sept. 1794.
See Gentleman's Magaz. Y. 1794. Nov. p. 1056.
On ploughs and particularly the Rev. Mr. *Cooke's* new swing plough. (Bath Agricult. Soc. Vol. 5. p. 428.)

ADAM, [Robert] *Esq. F. R. S. F. S. A. Architect.*
born at Kirkaldy in the County of Fife 1728.
died 3 March. 1792.
See Gentleman's Magaz. Y. 1792. March. p. 282.
Neue Bibl. der Sch. Wissensch. B. 53. S. 108.
Allg. Litt. Zeit. J. 1792. ItBl. Nro. 80.

***ADAM**, [William] *Esq. Of Lincoln's Inn: a King's Counsel and formerly a Member of Parliament.*
Speech in the House of Commons March 10. 1794. on the moving for the production of certain records and for an adddress to the King, to interpose the Royal justice and clemency in behalf of *Thomas Muir*, Esq. and the Rev. *Thomas Fyshe Palmer*, 1794. 8. (2 sh. 6 d.)

***ADAMS**, [Daniel] *A. B.*
An inaugural dissertation on the principle of animation 1799. 8.

***ADAMS**, [Francis] *Esq. One of his Maj. Justices of the Peace and Deputy Lieutenant for the County of Sommerset.*
A plan for raising the taxes impartially and almost free of expence in war; and in peace for paying of the national debt at the same time that the wealthy shall receive interest for their money and the poor be eased of taxes. 1798. 8. (1 sh. 6 d.)

ADAMS, [George]. *Mathematical Instrument-maker to his Majesty and Optician to his Roy. Highness the Prince of Wales.*
born . . . . 1750. died 14 Aug. 1795.
See Gentleman's Magazine Y. 1795. Aug. p. 708.
Allgem. LitteraturZeitung J. 1796. ItBl. Nro. 56. S. 459.
Essay on vision — Ed. 2. 1792. 8. übers. mit Zus. u. Anmerk. von *Fr. Kries*. Gotha 1794. 8.

Aufl. 2. Gotha 1800. 8. Lectures on natural and experimental philosophy, considered in it's present state of improvement; describing in a familiar and easy manner, the principal phaenomena of nature and shewing, that they all co-operate in displaying the goodness, wisdom and power of God. Vol. 1-5. 1794. 8. (1 L. 10sh.) übers. von *I. G. Geissler* Th. 1. 2. Leipzig. 1798. 1799. 8. Geometrical and graphical essays, containing a general description of mathematical instruments used in geometry, surveying; 1791. 8. (13 sh.) New edition, corrected and enlarged with illustrating plates by *William Jones*. 1798. 8. (14 sh.) Lectures on natural and experimental philosophy; Ed. 2. with additions. Vol. 1 - 5. 1799. 8. Essay on comets. (Massachusetts Magaz. Y. 1791. June p. 361.)

*ADAMS, [Hannah]

A summary history of New-England from the first settlement at Plymouth to the acceptance of the federal constitution. 1799.

*ADAMS, [James] *S. R. E. S.*

The pronunciation of the english language vindicated from imputed anomaly and caprice; in two parts, with an appendix. 1799. 8. (4 sh.)

ADAMS, [John] *LL. D. President of the United States of America.*

History of the principal republics in the world: a defence of the constitutions of government of the United States of America, against the attack of Mr. *Turgot*, in his letter to Dr. *Price* dated the 22 of March 1778. Ed. 2. Vol. 1-3. 1794. 8. (1 L. 1 sh.) Original letters, written by him, during the American revolution in the Y. 1776. (Columbian Magaz. Y. 1792. Vol. I. p. 157. 219. 313. 314.) A view of universal history from the creation to the present time; Including an account of the celebrated revolutions in France, Poland, Sweden, Geneva &c. Vol. 1-3. 1795. 8. (18 sh.) Authentic copies of the correspondence of *Charles Cotesworth Pinckney*, *John Marshall* and *Elbridge Gerry* Esq. Envoys Extraord. and Ministres Plenipotent. to the

the Republick of France, as presented to the house of Congress April 3. 1798. — 1798.

*ADAMS, [John] *Esq. F. L. S. of Pembroke.*
born . . . . he unfortunately fell into the sea and was drowned 1798. Nov.
See Gentleman's Magaz. Y. 1798. Dec. p. 1087.
Allg. Litt.Zeitung ItBl. J. 1800. S. 655.
The specific characters of some minute shells discovered on the coast of Pembrokeshire, with an account of a new marine animal. (Transact. of L. S. Vol. 3. p. 64.) Descriptions of actinia crassicornis and some british shells. (Ibid. Vol. 3. p. 252.) Descriptions of some minute shells. (Ib. Vol. 5. p. 1.) Descriptions of some marine animals found on the coast of Wales. (Ib. Vol. 5. p. 7.)

*ADAMS, [John] *Esq.*
An answer to *Paine's* rights of man. 1793. 8. (1 sh. 6 d.) übers. Copenhagen. 1793. 8.

ADAMS, [John] A. M. *Schoolmaster of Putney.*
The English parnassus, being a new selection of didactic, descriptive, pathetic, plaintive and pastoral poetry, extracted from the works of the latest and most celebrated poets. 1789. 12. Modern voyages: containing a variety of useful and entertaining facts, respecting the expeditions and the principal discoveries of *Cavendish, Dampiere; Spilbergen; Anson; Byron; Wallis; Carteret; Bougainville; Dixon; Portlock* and others. Vol. 1. 2. 1790. 8. (6 sh.) Curious thoughts on the history of man; chiefly abridged or selected from the celebrated works of Lord *Kaimes*, Lord *Monboddo*, Dr. *Dunbar* and the immortal *Montesquieu*. 1790. 8. (3 sh.) Curious anecdotes, bons mots and characteristic traits. Vol. 2. 1792. 12. (4 sh.) The death of his most Christian Majesty Louis XVI. considered. 1793. 8. (6 d.) A view of universal history, from the creation to the present time. Vol. 1-3. 1795. 8. The elements of useful knowledge: comprehending amongst other interesting particulars, short systems of astronomy, mythology, chronology and rhetoric; with a brief account of the trial and execution of Louis XVI. and of the late trans-

actions in France. —. 1795. 8. (3 sh. 6 d.) Ed. 2. 1799. 8. (3 sh. 6 d.) Elements of reading; being select english lessons in prose and verse, for young readers of both sexes. Ed. 3. much enlarged. 1800. 12. A new history of Great Britain; from the invasion of Julius Cesar to the present time —; 1802. 12. (4 sh. 6 d.)

*ADAMS, [John] *Riding-Master.*
Analysis of horse manship, teaching the whole art of riding, in the manege, military, hunting, racing or travelling system; Together with the method of breaking horses and dressing them, to all kinds of manege; with plates. Vol. 1. 1801. 8. (12 sh.)

*ADAMS, [John] *Teacher of the Mathematics at Edmonton, Middlesex.*
An historical account and description of an artificial horizon for determining the apparent altitudes of the sun, moon, or a star, with *Hadley's* quadrant or sextant. (Tr. of the Soc. for the E. of A. Vol. 4. p. 204.) Paper on subdivision of a nonius invented by him. (Ibid. Vol. 8. p. 175.)

*ADAMS, [Joseph] *Esq. M. Dr. Physician in the Island of Madeira.*
Observations on morbid poisons, phagedaena and cancer; containing a comparative view of the theories of Dr. *Swediaur*, *John Hunter*, *Foot*, *More* and *Bell*, on the law of the venereal virus. And also some preliminary remarks on the language and mode of reasoning adopted by medical writers. 1795. 8. (5 sh.) übers. Breslau, 1796. 8. A short account of the climate of Madeira; with instructions to those who resort thither for the recovery of their health. 1801. 8. (1 sh.) Observations on cancerous breast, consisting chiefly of original correspondance between the author and Dr. *Baillie*, *Cline*, *Robington*, *Abernethy* and *Stokes*. 1801. 8. (3 sh. 6 d.)

*ADAMS, [William]
The republican minister; or, thoughts tending to disclose the real motives of Mr. *Pitt* in the persecution of the present war with the republic of

of France. 1797. 8. (6 d.) Thoughts on the antimonarchical tendency of the measures of the British minister. 1796. (1 ſh.)

*ADDINGTON, [Henry] *Chancellor of the Exchequer.*

See Public Characters of 1801–1802. p. 1. Speech — 12 Febr. 1799. relative to an union with Ireland. 1799. 8. (1 ſh.) Speech in the Committee of ways and means Dec. 10. 1802. 8. (1 ſh.) Speech — on the budget. 1803.

*ADDINGTON, [John] *Surgeon.*

Practical obſervations on the inoculation of the cow-pox: to which is prefixed a compendious hiſtory of that diſeaſe and of its introduction as a preventive of the ſmall-pox. 1801. 8. (1 ſh. 6 d.) überſ. mit Anmerk. von *Fried. Gotth. Frieſe.* Breslau. 1802. 8.

ADDINGTON, [Stephen] *DD. late Paſtor of a Congregation of Proteſtant Diſſenters in Miles's-lane, Cannon-ſtreet*; born .... died 6 Febr. 1796.

See Gentleman's Magaz. Y. 1796. March. p. 255. Apr. p. 348.

A ſyſtem of arithmetick. 8. Maxims religious and prudential, with a ſermon to young people. 12. An enquiry into the reaſons for and againſt incloſing open fields. 8. Reſignation, the duty of mourners, a funeral diſcourſe on Job IX. 12. 8. The importance of early attendance on public worſhip. 12. (3 d.) A collection of pſalm tunes for public worſhip. 8. A collection of Anthems; 8. The divine architect, on laying the firſt ſtone of a building for the uſe of Middleſex ſociety for educating poor children in the Proteſtant religion; 8. A ſermon on lying the foundation of a Meeting houſe for Proteſtant Diſſenters at Chelmsford. 8. A people periſhing for lack of knowledge, a ſermon. 8.

ADDINGTON, [William] *Sir. Knt. One of the Juſtices of the public office at London.*

An abridgment of penal ſtatutes, which exhibits at one view the offences and the puniſhments or penalties in conſequence of thoſe offences, the mode

A 5 of

of recovering and application of the penalties, the number of witnesses and the jurisdictions necessary to the several convictions, and the chapters and sections of the enacting statutes, including the fifth session of the 17th parliament 1795. Ed. 4. with large additions and annotations. 1795. 4. (14 sh.)

*ADDISON, (......)
Interesting anecdotes, memoirs, allegories, essays and poetical fragments, tending to amuse the fancy and inculcate morality. Vol. 1-4. 1796. 8. (1 L.)

*ADOLPHUS, [John] *F. S. A.*
Biographical memoirs of the French revolution. Vol. 1. 2. 1799. 8. (16 sh.) The British cabinet: containing portraits of illustrious personages, engraved from original pictures with biographical memoirs. Vol. 1. 1799. 4. (2 L. 2 sh.) The History of England, from the accession of King George III. to the conclusion of peace in the year 1783. Vol. 1-3. 1802. 8. (1 L. 11 sh. 6 d.) Reflections on the causes of the present rupture with France. 1803. 8. (3 sh. 6 d.)

*AGNEW, [James] *A. M.*
On perspiration. Philadelphia. 1800. 8.

*AGUTTER, [William] *M. A. Chaplain and Secretary to the asylum for female orphans, near Westminster-bridge.*
Christian politics; or the origin of power and the grounds of subordination; a sermon. 1792. 8. (6 d.) An address to every British subject on the late important victories. 1798. (6 d.) The faithfull soldier and true christian and miseries of rebellion, considered in two sermons. 1798.
(Several single sermons.)

*AIKIN, [A....]
and C.... R.... *Aikin*, syllabus of a course of lectures on chemistry. 1799. 8. (1 sh.)

*AIKIN, [Anna Laetitia]
See *Barbauld*, Mrs.

and

*AIKIN, [Arthur] *Esq.*

Journal of a tour through North-Wales and part of Shropſhire; with obſervations in mineralogy and other branches of natural hiſtory. 1797. 8. (4 ſh.) Geological obſervations on North-Wales. (*Nicholſon's* Journal. Vol. 1. p. 220.). An account of the great copper works in the isle of Angleſey. (Ibid. Vol. 1. p. 367.) The natural hiſtory of the year; being an enlargement of Dr. *Aikin's* (father) Calendar of nature. 1798. 12. (3 ſh.) Travels in upper and lower Egypt — by *Vivant Denon* - translated from the original. Vol. 1. 2. 1802. 4. (4 L. 4 ſh.) Another edition, with the ſame plates, in octavo Vol. 1-3. (2 L. 2 ſh.) Deſcription of the ſchieferſpath. (*Tilloch's* Philoſ. Magaz. Vol. 14. p. 293.)

*AIKIN, [C.... R....] *Member of the Roy. College of Surgeons in London.*

A conciſe view of all the moſt important facts which have hitherto appeared concerning the cow-pox. 1800. 8. (2 ſh.) Ed. 2. 1801. 8. überſ. von *J. Hunnemann*, Hannover 1801. 8. überſ. von *F. G. Frieſe*, Breslau 1801. 8. überſ. von *** Berlin. 1801. 8.

*AIKIN, [G....]

Proof that rooks are not entirely carnivorous. (Monthly Magaz. Y. 1802. May. p. 316.)

*AIKIN, [J....] *M. Dr.*

Heads of inquiry for the deſcription of a country. (*Young's* A. of Agr. Vol. 21. p. 374.)

AIKIN, [John] *M. Dr. Phyſician at Great-Yarmouth in the County of Norfolk.* (Brother to Mr. *Barbauld.*)

Obſervations on the external uſe of preparations of lead; 1771. 8. Thoughts on hoſpitals; 1771. 8. *Cn. Julii Agricolae* vita, ſcriptore *C. Cornelio Tacito*, with a tranſlation. 1774. 8. A ſpecimen of the medical biography of Great-Britain. 1775. 4. A manual of chemiſtry, tranſlated from the French of *Baumé* 1778. 8. Biographical memoirs of medicine in Great-Britain, from the revival of literature to the time of *Harvey*. 1780. 8. England delineated; or a geographical de-

ſcription

ſcription of every county in England and Wales —; 1788. 8. (4 ſh. 6 d.) Poems. 1791. 8. *Lewis* materia medica. Ed. 4. 1791. 8. (13 ſh.) A view of the character and public ſervices of the late *John Howard*, Esq. LL. D. F. R. S. 1792. 8. (3 ſh. 6 d.) überſ. von *Joh. Chriſt. Fick*. Leipzig. 1792. 8. Caſe of haemorrhage and purple ſpots, without fever or previous illneſs. (Mem. of M. S. of L. Vol. 3. p. 393.) Letters from a father to his ſon, on various topics, relative to literature and the conduct of life. Vol. 1. 1793. 8. (5 ſh.) Vol. 2. 1800. 8. (5 ſh.) The arts of preſerving health, by *John Armſtrong*, M. Dr. to which is prefixed a critical eſſay on the poem. 1795. 8. (6 ſh. 6 d.) The ſpleen and other poems by *Matthew Green*, with a prefatory eſſay. 1796. 8. (5 ſh.) The chace, a poem, by *William Sommerville*, Esq. a new edition, to which is prefixed a critical eſſay. 1796. 8. (6 ſh.) A deſcription of the country from thirty to forty miles round Mancheſter; the materials arranged and the work compoſed; Embelliſhed with 73 plates. 1795. 4. (3 L. 3 ſh.). An eſſay on man by *Alex. Pope*; a new edition; to which is prefixed a critical eſſay. 1796. 8. (6 ſh.) Sermons on practical ſubjects by the late *W. Enfield*, LL. D. prepared for the preſs by himſelf. To which are prefixed memoirs of the Author. Vol. 1. 2. 3. 1798. 8. (1 L. 1 ſh.) General biography; or lives, critical and hiſtorical of the moſt eminent perſons of all ages, countries, conditions and profeſſions, arranged according to alphabetical order; chiefly compoſed by *John Aikin* and the late *William Enfield*, L. L. D. Vol. 1–3. 1799–1802. 4. (4 L. 10 ſh. 6 d.) Vol. 4. 1803. (1 L. 1 ſh.) Select eulogies of member of the French academy with notes, by the late *d'Alembert*; translated from the French with a prefacee and additional notes. Vol. 1. 2. 1799. 8. (10 ſh.), On the impreſſion of reality attending dramatic repreſentations. (Mem. of M. Vol. 4. P. 1. p. 96) Explanation of *Howard's* plan for penitentiary houſes. (Monthly Magaz. Y. 1799. Apr. p. 178.) On the humour of *Addi-*

Addiſon and the character of Sir *Roger* de *Coverley*. (Monthly Magaz. Y. 1800. p. 1.) A tribute to the memory of *Gilbert Wakefield*. (Ibid. Y. 1801. Oct. p. 225.) (See *Gilbert White*.) The firſt ſix volumes of a new edition of the poets of Great-Britain, compriſing the works of *Edmund Spencer*, with *Johnſon's* prefaces &c. re-edited with new biographical and critical matter, with embelliſhments. 1802. 8. The works of *Abraham Cowley*, with Dr. *Johnſon's* preface and remarks Vol. 1-3. 1803. (1 L. 1 ſh.) Remarks on the different ſucceſs, with reſpect to health, of ſome attempts to paſs the winter in high Northern latitudes. (American Muſeum Y. 1789. Jan. p. 115. April p. 346.) Biographical account of the late Dr. *Pulteney*. (*Tilloch's* Philoſ. Magaz. Vol. 12. p. 289.)

*AIKIN, [Lucy] *Miſſ.*

Selection of poetry for children, conſiſting of ſuch pieces as may be committed to memory at an early age. 1801. 12. (2 ſh. 6 d.) The inconſtancy of our deſires (Maſſachuſetts Magaz. Y. 1792. June p. 352.)

*AILWAY, [John]

Letter on preſerving hay-ricks. (Tr. of the Soc. for the E. of A. Vol. 4. p. 243.) Letter on deſtroying the red ſpider, and ants in hothouſes and pinerys. (Ib. Vol. 5. p. 59.)

AITON, [William] *Principal-Gardener to his Majeſty at Kew.*

born 1731 in a ſmall village near Hamilton, in Scotland; died the 17 Febr. 1793.

See Gentleman's Magaz. Y. 1793. May. p. 389. June p. 519. *Hutchinſon's* Biographia Med. Vol. 2. p. 522. Monthly Rev. Y. 1793. Febr. p. 187. May. p. 119.

See *Will. Smith*.

*AITON, [William Townſend] *Gardener to his Majeſty at Kew.*

Delineations of exotick plants cultivated in the Royal garden at Kew; drawn and coloured and the botanical characters diſplayed according to the

the Linneen fyftem by *Francis Bauer*; Nrb. 1–4. 1796. fol.

***ALBERT, [......]**
Sonnets from *Shakspeare*. 1791. 8. (2 fh. 6 d.)

***ALBIN, [J....]** *Bookfeller at Newport in the Isle of Wight.*
A new, correct and much improved hiftory of the isle of Wight, from the earlieft times of authentic information, to the prefent period; comprehending whatever is curious or worthy of attention in natural hiftory, with its civil, ecclefiaftical and military ftate, in the various ages, both ancient and modern. 1795. 8.

***ALCOCK, [Thomas]** *A. M. Vicar at Raucorn, Chefhire.*
born 1718. died 1793. Aug. 23.
S. Allg. Litt. Zeitung ItBl. J. 1800. S. 652.
Obfervations on the defects of the poor laws and of the caufes and confequences of the great increafe and burden of the poor. 1752. 8. Remarks on two bills for the better maintenance of the poor 1752. 8. Obfervations on that part of a late act of parliament, which lays on additional duty on cyder and perry. 1763. 8. Curfory remarks on Dr. *Baker's* effay on the endemial colic of Devonfhire with the obfervation of *Francis Geach*. 1768. 8. The endemial colic of Devon not caufed by a folution of lead in the cyder, in reply to Dr. *Saunders* —; 1769. 8. *Nathaniel Alcock* (his brother; died 1779), the rife of Mahomet accounted for an natural and civil principles. 1796. 8. (Several fingle fermons.)

***ALDEN, [Timothy]** Jun.
Memorabilia of Yarmouth. (Coll. of Maffachufetts H. S. Y. 1798. p. 54.)

ALDERSON, [John] *M. Dr.*
Effay on the rhus toxicodendron, pubefcent poifon, oak or fumach, with cafes fhewing its efficacy in the cure of paralyfis and other difeafes of extreme debility. 1794. 8. (1 fh 6 d.) überf. in Samml. fur praktifche Aerzte. B. 17 S. 224. überf. von *Ludw. Fried. Froriep.* Jena, 1799. 8. On the improvement of poor foils —; 1802. 8. (2 fh.)

(2 ſh.) Geological obſervations on the vicinity of Hull and Beverly. (*Nicholſon's* Journal Vol. 3. p. 285.)

ALEXANDER, [Caleb]
A grammatical ſyſtem of the Engliſh language. (Maſſachuſetts Magaz. Y. 1793. May. p. 304.)

*ALEXANDER, [David] *Surgeon at Montroſe.*
Caſes of chorea St. Viti, terminating ſucceſsfully under the uſe of zinc. (*Duncan's* A. of Med. Y. 1801. p. 303.)

*ALEXANDER, [Disney] *Member of the R. Med. Soc. of Edinburgh.*
On the nature and cure of the cynanche trachealis, commonly called the croup. 1794. 8. (2 ſh.)

*ALEXANDER, [Edward] *Surgeon; Halifax, Yorkſhire.*
Hiſtory of a caſe of angina pectoris; cured by the ſolutio arſenici. (*Duncan's* M. C. Y. 1790. Dec. 2. Vol. 5. p. 373.)

*ALEXANDER, [L....]
Anſwer to Mr. *Joſhua Van Oven's* letters on the preſent ſtate of the jewiſh poor in London. 1802. 8. (1 ſh. 6 d.)

*ALEXANDER, [William] *Draftsman to Earl Macartney in his Lordſhip's Chineſe Embaſſy.*
Coſtume of China; Nrb. 1. 2. 1798. 4.

ALISON, [Archibald] *LL. B. F. R. S.*
On the nature and principles of taſte. 1790. 4. (16 ſh.) überſ. mit Anmerk. von *R. H. Heidenreich.* Th. 1. 2. Leipzig. 1792. 8.

*ALLAN, [George] *Esq.*
born . , . . . died 1800. Jul. at the Grange, Darlington, Co. Durham.
See Gentleman's Magaz. Y. 1800. Aug. p. 802.
The recommendatory letter of Oliver Cromwell to *Will. Lenthall* Esq. — for erecting a college and Univerſity at Durham and his letters patent for founding the ſame; — 17.. 4to. The life of St. Cuthbert. 1777. A Sketch of the life and character of Biſhop Trevor. 1776. Collections relating to Sherburn hoſpital. 1773.

*ALLARDYCE, [Alexander] *Esq. M. P. One of the Proprietors of the Bank of England*
An addreſs to the proprietors of the bank of England. Suum cuique. 1797. 8. (1 ſh.). Ed. 3. with addi-

additions. 1798. 4. (9 sh.) A second address to the proprietors of the bank of England Stock. 1801. 4. (4 sh. 6 d.)

*ALLCHIN, [Richard] *Pastor of the Dissenting charity school Maidstone.*

A familiar address to young persons, on the truth and importance of christianity. 1803.

*ALLDRIDGE, [W.... J....]

The goldsmith's repository: containing a concise elementary treatise on the art of assaying metals, rules, directions and correct extensive tables, applied to all the possible occasions of mixing, alloying or finding the value of bullion, under all its various denominations of gold, silver and parting. Also an appendix, in which are contained abstracts of all the acts of parliament now in force, relating to gold and silver, and a view of all the changes in their respective standards. 1791. 8. (10 sh. 6 d.)

*ALLEN, [C....] *School-master.*

New orthographical exercises, for the use of English seminaries; interspersed with pieces on the art of reading and speaking with propriety. 1800. (1 sh. 6 d.)

*ALLEN, [Charles]

born 1729 died 18. Febr. 1792.

Female preceptor; 17.. Polite Lady; 17..

*ALLEN, [Charles] *A. M.*

A new and improved history of England from the invasion of Julius Caesar to the end of the 37 year of George 3. —. 1798. 12. (4 sh.) A new and improved roman history, from the foundation of the city of Rome, to its final dissolution as the seat of empire in the year of Christ 476 —. 1798. 12. (4 sh.)

*ALLEN, [John] *Esq.*

On gypsum. (*Young's* A. of Agr. Vol. 16. p. 300.)

*ALLEN, [John] *Surgeon. Fellow of the Roy. College of Surgeons, Edinburgh.*

An introduction to the study of the animal economy; translated from the French of **Cuvier.** 1801. 8. (2 sh.)

*ALLEN,

*ALLEN, [John] *Esq.*

On gypsum. (*Young's* A. of Agr. Vol. 16. p. 303.)

*ALLEN, [John Wilson] *Esq. of Whepstead.*

Observations in a farming tour. (*Young's* A. of Agr. Vol. 20. p. 397.) Experiment on burner. (Ib Vol. 21. p. 171.) Farmer's cart. (Ibid. Vol. 23. p 404.)

*ALLEN, [Ira] *Esq. Major-General of the Militia in the state of Vermont, America.*

born in the town of Cornwall, in the County of Litchfield and state of Connecticut about the Year 1752.

See Public Characters, of 1802-1803. p. 225.

The natural and political history of the state of Vermont, one of the United states of America: To which is added, an appendix, containing answers to sundry queries, addressed to the author, 1798. 8. (6 sh.)

*ALLEN, [Israel] *M. D.*

A treatise on the scarlatina anginosa and dysentery and sketches on febrile spasm as produced by phlogiston. Leominster, Massachusetts. 1796. 8.

*ALLEN, [Paul] *Jun. A. B.*

A poem, delivered in the Baptist meeting-house in Providence Sept. 4. 1793. being the anniversary commencement of Rhode-Island College. (Massachusetts Magaz. Y. 1793. Oct. p. 594.)

*ALLEN, [William] *Adjutant of the Herefordshire Gentlemen and Yeomanry.*

A few minutes and observations for the use of the gentlemen and yeomanry. 1798. 8. (1 sh.)

*ALLEY, [Jerom] *LL. B: M. R. J. A. Chaplain to Lord Sheffield.*

The widowed queen — a poem. 1778. 4. (1 sh. 6 d.) Historical essays on the lives of William and Henry IV. 17... Observations on the government and constitution of Great-Britain, including a vindication of both from the aspersions of some late writers, particularly Dr. *Price*; *Priestley*; and Mr. *Paine*. 1792. 8. (2 sh. 6 d.) Review of the political principles of the modern whigs. 1792. (2 sh. 6 d.)

*ALLEY, [Peter] *Esq.*

The tears of the muse, an elegiac poem; sacred

to the memory of the Right Hon. Sarah Countess of Westmorland. 1794. 4. (2 ſh. 6 d.)

*ALLINGHAM, [John Till] *Esq.*

Fortune's frolic: a farce, in two acts. 1799. 8. (1 ſh.) The marriage promiſed, a comedy, in 5 acts. 1803. 8. (2 ſh. 6 d.) Mrs. Wiggins, a dramatic piece; 1803. (1 ſh. 6 d.)

*ALLISON, [Burgiſs] *A. M.*

A deſcription of a newly invented globe time-piece. (Tr. of A. S. Vol. 5. p. 82.) A deſcription of the pendent planetarium. (Ib. Vol. 5. p. 87.)

*ALLMAN, [William] *A. B. Trinity-College, Dublin.*

On the application of a converging ſeries to the conſtruction of logarithms. (Tr. of I. A. Vol. 6. p. 391.)

*ALLNATT, [A.... Charles]

Poverty, a poem, with ſeveral others on various ſubjects, chiefly religious and moral. 1801. (2 ſh.)

*ALLSTON, [William] *of George-town.*

Eſſay on dropſy or the hydropic ſtate of fever; Philadelphia 1797. 8.

*ALLWOOD, [Philipp] *A. M. Fellow of Magdalen-College, Cambridge.*

Literary antiquities of Greece; — to which are added, obſervations concerning the origin of ſeveral of the literal characters in uſe among the greeks. 1799. 4. (1 L. 7 ſh.) Remarks upon ſome obſervations edited in the Britiſh Critic, relative to a work lately publiſhed under the title of Literary antiquities of Greece — intended to obviate ſome objections propoſed by the critic and to illuſtrate ſtill further the hiſtory of ancient Egypt and of the earlieſt ages after the flood. 1801. 4. (8 ſh.)

*ALMON, [John] *Formerly a bookſeller in Piccadilly.*

Trial of *J. Almon* upon an information filed ex officio, by his Maj. Attorney general, for ſelling Junius's letter to the King. 1770. 8. (1 ſh.) *Anecdotes of the R. H. *William Pitt*, Earl of Chatham, and of the principal events of his time; with his ſpeeches in parliament from the Y. 1736 to 1778. Vol. 1. 2. 1792. 4. *Biographical, literary and political anecdotes of ſeveral of the moſt eminent perſons of the preſent age; never before

before printed: with an appendix, confifting of original, explanatory and fcarce papers. Vol. 1-3. 1797. 8.

*ALVES, [James]
The banks of Efk; or, a faunter from Roslin to Smeaton; a poem: — 1801. (3 fh. 6 d.)

ALVES, [Robert] *A. M.*
born .... died at Edinburgh 1 Jan. 1794.
Sketches of a hiftory of literature; containing lives and characters of the moft eminent writers in different languages, antient and modern, and critical remarks on their works: Together with feveral litterary effays. — to which is prefixed a fhort biographical account of the author. 1795. 8. (5 fh.)

*AMBLER, [Charles] *Esq. One of his Maj. Counfel at law and Attorney-General to the Queen.*
born .... died 1794. Febr. at his feat at Maidenhead-thicket.
See Gentlemans Magaz. Y. 1794. March p. 281.
Report of cafes argued and determined in the high court of chaucery. 1790. fol. (1 L. 16 fh.)

*AMBROSE, [John] *of Copford, near Colchefter.*
South down rams. (*Young's* A. of Agr. Vol. 20. p. 542.)

*AMES, [Fifher]
Speech in the houfe of reprefentatives of the United ftates when in committee of the whole on 28 April 1796. Bofton. 8. An oration on the fublime virtues of General *George Wafhington* —. Bofton. 1800. 8. (25 Cent.)

AMNER, [Richard] *A Diffenting-Minifter at Cosley in the County of Stafford.*
born 1735. died 1803. June 8. at Hinckley, co. Leicefter.
See Gentleman's Magaz. Y. 1803. July. p. 693.
Confiderations on the doctrines of a future ftate and the refurrection, as revealed or fuppofed to be fo, in the fcriptures; on the infpiration and authority of the fcripture itfelf; on fome peculiarities in St. Paul's epiftles; on the prophecies of Daniel and St. John. To which are added, fome ftrictures on the prophecies of Ifaiah. 1798. 8. (5 fh.)

*AMOS, [William] *at Brothertoft, Boston, Lincolnshire.*

The theory and practice of the drill-husbandry, founded upon philosophical principles and confirmed by experience; with 8 copper plates. 1795. 4. (15 sh.) On the culture of potatoes. (*Young's* A. of Agr. Vol. 30. p. 319.) Description of a bean-drill. (Ib. Vol. 35. p. 22.)

*AMPHLETT, [W....]

The triumphs of war and other poems. 1796. 8. (4 sh.)

ANBUREY [Thomas] *Esq.*

* Travels through the interior parts of America — Vol. 1. 2. 1789. 8 (14 sh.) übers. von *Georg Forster.* Berlin. 1792. 8.

ANCELL, [Samuel] *Clerk to the 58 Regt.*

born in England .... died in Dublin 1802. Oct. 19.

See Gentleman's Magaz. Y. 1802. Dec. p. 1161.

Journal of the — blockage and siege of Gibraltar — 1786. 8 Ed. 5. 1802. (14 sh.) Proposals for a periodical work, The Monthly military companion. Nrb. 1–12. 1801. 1802.

*ANDERDON, [Proctor] *Rev.*

Account of a crop of turnips raised on poor clay soil, between rows of beans, hand-hoed and horse-hoed; with observations on drilling and horse-hoeing turnips. (Mem. of the Bath Agric. Soc. Vol. 3. p. 117.) Observations on a tour into Suffolk and Surry. (Ibid. Vol. 6. p 318.)

*ANDERDON, [Robert Proctor] *Esq. of Henlade, Somersetshire.*

Observations on various interesting subjects in Agriculture. (*Young's* A. of Agr. Vol. 2. p. 1.) On the quarter evil, a disease in cattle. (Ib. Vol. 14. p. 314.) On weighing sheep alive. (Ib. Vol. 16. p. 80.) Experiments on gypsum. (Ib. Vol. 17. p. 295. 513.) Devonshire sheep. (Ib. Vol. 17. p. 299.) On drilling. (Ib. Vol. 23. p. 312.)

*ANDERSON, [Aeneas] *Lieutenant in the Manx-fencibles; before in the service of Lord Macartney in the late Embassy to China.*

A narrative of the British embassy to China in 1792–1794, containing the various circumstances of of the embaſſy with accounts of cuſtoms and manners of the Chineſe and a deſcription of the country, towns, cities. 1795. 4. (1 L. 1 ſh.) überſ. Hamburg. 1795. überſ. mit Anmerk. Erlangen. 1795. 8. An accurate account of Lord Macartney's embaſſy to China carefully abridged from the original work with alterations and corrections by the editor. 1795. 8. (2 ſh. 6 d.) A journal of the forces which ſailed from the downs in April. 1802 under Gen. Pigot — until the complete evacuation of Egypt by the french, with a particular account of Malta —; 1803. 4. (2 L. 2 ſh.)

ANDERSON, [Alexander] *Superintendent of his Maj. Garden in the Island of St. Vincent.*

State of ſome of the moſt valuable plants in the Royal botanical gardens in the Island of St. Vincent. (Tr. of the Soc. for the E. of A. Vol. 16. p. 328.)

ANDERSON, [George] *A. M. Accountant to the commiſſioners for the affairs of India.*

born at Weſton Turvile, in Buckinghamſhire, Nov. 1760. died 30 Apr. 1796.

See Gentleman's Magaz. Y. 1796. May. p. 442. Monthly Magaz. Y. 1796. May. p. 332. The Annual Necrology for 1797. & 1798. p. 245. Allg. Litt. Zeit. ItBl. J. 1800. S. 627.

*The Arenarius of *Archimedes* tranſlated — 1784. 8. (2 ſh. 6 d.) A general view of the variations, which have been made in the affairs of the Eaſt-India company, from the concluſion of the war in India in 1784 to the commencement of the preſent hoſtilities. 1792. 8. (4 ſh.)

ANDERSON, [James] *LL. D. F. R. S. F. A. S. Scot. Farmer at Monkſhill, Aberdeenſhire.*

See Public Characters of 1800-1801. p. 529.

(He furniſh following articles for the Encyclopaedia Britannica: Dictionary; Winds; Smoaky chimneys; He tranſmitted to the Editor of the Weekly Magazine eſſays under the ſignatures, Agricola; Timoleon; Germanicus; Cimon; Scoto Britannicus; E. Aberdeen; Henry Plain; Impartial; A Scot; A Hater of Impudence, Pedentry, and affectation, &c.) A proposal for establishing the Northern British fisheries: 1783. Essays relating to agriculture and rural affairs — Vol. 3. 1796. 8. (8 sh.) Essay on quicklime as a cement and as a manure. Edinb. 1789. 8. Miscellaneous experiments and observations on the culture of potatoes and some other plants. (Bath Agricult. Soc. Vol. 4. p. 1.) On the cultivation of broad clover. (Ibid. Vol. 4. p. 223.) Prefatory remarks; hints respecting potatoes, a machine for bruising furze and a plan for improving the wool of this country. (Ibid. Vol. 5. p. 64.) On the management of the dairy, particularly with respect to the making and curing of butter; (Ibid. Vol. 5. p. 67.) uebers. in der Samml. Oekonomische Winke — 1. Berlin 1792. 8. Of the scotch fir as a food for cattle. (Ibid. Vol. 5. p. 133.) Of raising potatoes from the seed; (Ibid. Vol. 5. p. 127.) Of furze or whins, ulex Europaeus, Linn: as a food for horses and cattle; Description of a machine for bruising them and hints for rearing that plant oeconomically as a crop: (Ibid. Vol. 5. p. 134.) Of the root of scarcity; (Ibid. Vol. 5. p. 146.) On the utility of the leith cart; (Ibid. Vol. 5. p. 460.) Disquisitions concerning the different varieties of woolbearing animals and other particulars connected with that subject. (Ibid. Vol. 8. p. 1.) Answer to queries from the committee of the Bath and West of England Society. (Ibid. Vol. 8. p. 31.) On canal-locks, bridges, peat-moss &c. (Ibid. Vol. 8. p. 35.) Remarks on the county surveys, with a letter on draining. (Ibid. Vol. 8. p. 308.) Account of the manner in which the Lammas's festival used to be celebrated in Mid-Lothian, about the middle of the XVIII century. (Transact. of the S. of A. of Scotland. (Vol. 1. p. 192.) Observations on the effect of the coal duty upon the remote and thinly-peopled coasts of Britain, tending to shew, that if it were there removed, the industry of the people would be excited, the prosperity of the country promoted and the amount of the revenue augmented to an astonish degree. Edinb. 1792. 8. (6 d.) A practical treatise on peat-moss; 1794. 8. (4 sh.) Ed. 2. 1797.

1797. 8. (3 sh. 6 d.) The bee, a periodical work: 1790. An account of the different kinds of sheep found in the Russian dominions and among the Tartar hords of Asia; by Dr. *Pallas.* To which is added five appendices tending to illustrate the natural and economical history of sheep and other domestic animals. 1794. 8. (5 sh.) A practical treatise on draining bogs and swampy grounds, illustrated by figures, with cursory remarks upon the originalty of Mr. *Elkington's* mode of draining; 1797. 8. (6 sh.) Ed. 2. 1799. 8. (5 sh.) Selections from the correspondence of Gen. *Washington* and *James Anderson*, in which the causes of the present scarcity are fully investigated. 1800. 8. (2 sh. 6 d.) A calm investigation of the circumstances that have led to the present scarcity of grain in Britain: suggesting the means of alleviating that evil and of preventing the recurrence of such a calamity in future. 1801. 8. (2 sh. 6 d.) Recreations in agriculture, natural history, arts and miscellaneous literature. Vol. 1-6, 1800-1802. 8. (3 L. 7 sh. or 6 L. 14 sh. royal paper.) A description on wool-bearing animals (Tr. of A. S. Vol. 4. p. 149. 155) On an universal character. (Mem. of M. Vol. 5. P. 1. p. 89.) An approved receipt to preserve butter. (Massachusetts Magaz. Y. 1796. April p. 231.)

ANDERSON, [James] *M. Dr. Physician General to the Hospital board at Fort St. George Madras.* Correspondence for the introduction of cochineal insects from America, the varnish and tallow trees from China, the discovery and culture of white lac, the culture of red lac and also for the introduction, culture and establishment of mulberry trees and silk worms; with a description and drawing of an improved Piemontese reel for the manufacture of raw silk; together with the culture of the finest cinnamon trees of Ceylon, Indigo and some other valuable articles. Madras, 1791. 8. The correspondence on the agricultural improvements of Bengal. (*Young's* A. of Agr. Vol. 31. p. 428. 449. Vol. 32. p. 445.)

*ANDERSON, [James] *Sen, Surgeon at Edinburgh.*

 Exam-

Examples of the good effects from the use of the hydrargyrus muriatus mitis, in cases of the cynanche trachealis, or croup. (*Duncan's* A. of Med. Y. 1799. p. 459.) On the use of the mild muriat of quickfilver in the cure of croups. (Ibid. Y. 1801. p. 388.)

ANDERSON, [James] *Surgeon*.

Account of Morne Garou &c. (Massachusetts Magaz. Y. 1794. Dec. p. 735.) übers. im Hist. Portef. J. 1786. S. XII. nachgedruckt in der Auswahl kleinen Reisen. B. 10. A few facts and observations on the yellow fever of the West-Indies, by which it is shewn, that there have existed two species of fever in the West-India Islands for several years past, indiscriminately called yellow fever, but which have proceeded from very different causes; with the success attending the method of cure. 1798. 8. (1 sh. 6 d.)

ANDERSON, [John] *M. Dr. F. A. S. C. M. S. Physician to and a Director of, the general sea-bathing infirmary at Margate.*

A preliminary introduction to the act of sea-bathing; wherein is shewn its nature, power, and importance; with some necessary hints for the attention of visiters, at the watering places, previous to and during a course of bathing. 1795. 8. (1 sh.) A practical essay on the good and bad effects of sea-water and sea-bathing. 1795. 8. (2 sh.)

*ANDERSON, [John] *F. R. SS. London and Edinburgh; Professor of Natural Philosophy in the University of Glasgow.*

born 1726. died the 13 Jan. 1796.

See Public characters of 1799-1800. p. 423. Gentleman's Magaz. Y. 1796. Jan. p. 85. Allgem. Litterat. Zeit. J. 1796. ItBl. Jul. S. 812. J. 1800. ItBl. S. 626.

Institutes of natural philosophy. 17... Anecdotes of *Cromwell*. (Monthly Magaz. Y. 1798. May. p. 359.)

*ANDERSON, [J...., W....] *A. M.*

The manner pointed out in which the common prayer was read in private by the late Mr. *Garrick*,

rick, for the instruction of a young clergyman. 1797. 8. (2 sh.)

*ANDERSON, [R....] *of Carlisle.*

Poems on various subjects. 1798. 8. (3 sh. 6 d.)

*ANDERSON, [Ralph]

Letter — on the necessity of an immediate change of ministry and an immediate peace. 1797.

*ANDERSON, [Robert] *M. Dr. of Heriot's - Green, Edinburgh.*

The life of *Sam. Johnson*, LL. Dr. with critical observations on his works. 1795. 8. (5 sh.) The works of the British poets, with prefaces biographical and critical. Vol. 1–13. 1794–1796. 8. (8 L. 18 sh. 6 d.) The miscellaneous works of Dr. *Tobias Smollet*, with his life. Vol. 1–6. 1796. 8.

ANDERSON, [Thomas] *Surgeon at Leith; F. R. S. Edinb.*

Pathological observations on the brain: (Tr. of E. S. Vol. 2. p. 17.) Observations on the vaccine inoculation. (*Duncan's* A. of Med. Y. 1799. p. 496. Y. 1800. p. 452.)

ANDERSON, [Walter] *D. D. Minister of Chirnside.* born in Scotland; died Jul. 1800.

See Gentlem. Magaz. Y. 1800. Aug. p. 802. Oct. p. 999. Allgem. Litterat. Zeit. J. 1801. ItBl. S. 839.

Life of Croesus; 17... The philosophy of ancient Greece investigated in its origin and progress, to the aeras of its greatest celebrity, in the Jonian, Italic and Athenian schools, with remarks on the delineated systems of their founders; and some account of their lives and characters and those of their most eminent disciples. 1791. 4.

ANDREE, [John] *M. Dr. at Hertford, before Surgeon to the Magdalen Hospital and Teacher of Anatomy, London.*

Some few cases and observations on the treatment of fistula in ano, haemorrhage, mortification, the venereal disease and strictures of the urethra. 1799. 8. (1 sh. 6 d.) A case of chorea St. Viti, with observations on the locked jaw, and on the hydrophobia. (Mem. of M. S. of L. Vol. 4. p. 428.)

*ANDREWS, [Abraham] *of Higham Ferrers, in Northamptonshire.*
Description of his crane, whereby the body suspended is weighed, during the time of raising. (Tr. of the Soc. for the E. of A. Vol. 10. p. 221)

*ANDREWS, [David]
Letter to *G. Wakefield*, B. A. on his spirit of christianity, compared with the spirit of the times in Great Britain. 1794. 8. (1 sh.)

*ANDREWS, [Eliza]
The manuscripts of Virtudeo, published for the amusement and improvement of young persons: which are subjoined, thoughts on education —; 1801. 8. (3 sh.)

*ANDREWS, [Henry] *of Knightsbridge: Botanical Painter and Engraver.*
Engravings of ericas or heaths, with botanical descriptions, in latin and english, taken from living specimens. Nrb. 1-10. 1796. fol. (2 L. 8 sh.) Botanist's repository comprising colour'd engravings of new and rare plants only with botanical descriptions —, in latin and english, after the Linnean system. Nrb. 1-49. Vol. 1. 2. 1799. 4. (7 L. 5 sh.) A review of the plants hitherto figured in the botanist's repository —; 1801. 4. (4 sh.)

ANDREWS, [James Petit] *F. A. S. One of the magistrates of the police-office in Queen-Square, Westminster.*
born 1737. died the 6 Aug. 1797.
See Gentlem. Magaz. Y. 1797. Sept. p. 796.
Allg. Litterat. Zeit. ItBl. J. 1800. S. 646.
Addenda to anecdotes — ancient and modern, with observations. 1790. 8. (2 sh.) The history of Great-Britain, connected with the chronology of Europe, with notes. Vol. 1. Part. 1. 2. 1794. 1795. 4. (2 L. 2 sh.) History of Great-Britain from the death of Henry VIII. to the accession of James VI of Scotland to the crown of England being a continuation of Dr. *Henry's* history of Great-Britain and written on the same plan. Vol. 1. 1796. 4. (1 L. 1 sh.) Account of Saxon coins found in Kintbury churchyard, Berk. (Archaeol. Vol.

Vol. 7. p. 430.) Description of the rock near Roche in Cornwall. (Gentleman's Magaz. Vol. 57. p. 222.). Views in Freshwater bay, isle of Wight described. (Ibid. Vol. 57. p. 377.) The account of Shaw; (In Mr. *Mores'* Berkshire collections; p. 75.) The savages of Europe, translated from French; 17... The inquisitor, a tragedy, in 5 acts; altered from the german by the late *J. P. Andrews* and *Henry James Pye*. 1798. 8. (2 sh.)

*ANDREWS, [John] *Surgeon in London.*

Case of injury of the brain, without a fracture, relieved by application of the trephine. (*Simmons* Medical Facts and Observat. Vol. 3. p. 12.) übers. Repertor. Chirurg. und Mediz. Abhandl. B. 2. S. 9.

ANDREWS, [John] *LL. Dr.*

Editor of the Historical register. 1796. An historical enquiry into what forms of government are most desirable. (Columbian Magaz. Y. 1788. Aug. p. 437.)

ANDREWS, [Miles Peter] *Esq. M. P. Dealer in Gunpowder.*

Belphegor, or the wishes; a comic opera in two acts. 1778. Better late than never, a comedy. 1791. 8. (1 sh. 6 d.) The mysteries of the castle; a dramatic tale, in three acts; 1795. 8. (2 sh.)

*ANDREWS, [Robert] *Esq. of Auberies, near Sudbury.*

On the advantages of mixing lime with dung. *Young's* A. of Agr. Vol. 4. p. 47.) Account of grazing twelve steers. (Ibid. Vol. 4. p. 114.) On the profit of farming. (Ibid. Vol. 4. p. 252.) On the smut in wheat. (Ib. Vol. 6. p. 173.)

*ANDREWS, [T.....]

Vindication of the church of England, intended as a refutation of the arguments advanced by Mr. *Towgood* in support of the principles on which he grounds his dissents. 1799. 8. (1 sh. 6 d.) Youth's scripture recorder and moral instructor; being passages selected from sacred and moral writings; designed for the use of schools. 1798. (2 sh. 6 d.)

*ANNAN,

*ANNAN, [Robert] *Rev.*

Account of a ſkeleton of a large animal found near Hudſon's river. (Mem. of B. A. Vol. 2. P. 1 p. 160.)

*ANNESLEY, [Alexander]

Obſervations on the danger of a premature peace. 1800. 8. (1 ſh.) Strictures on the true cauſe of the preſent alarming ſcarcity of grain and other proviſions; and a plan for permanent relief. — with an hiſtorical deduction of the prices of proviſions. Interſperſed with various matters connected with the commerce and navigation of Great-Britain. Together with a chronological account of the ſeveral ſtatutes, proclamations and parliamentary regulations, for controuling the markets, and preventing monopoly, engroſſing &c. from the Norman conqueſt to the preſent aera. 1800. 8. (2 ſh.)

ANSPACH, *Marggravine of*, — See *Elizabeth Berkeley*

*ANSTEY, [Arthur] *Esq. of Lincoln's-Inn; Barriſter at law.*

The pleader's guide, a didactic poem in two books; containing the conduct of a ſuit at law, with the arguments of counſellor Bother'um and counſellor Bore'um, in an action betwixt John a Gull and John a-Gudgeon, for aſſault and battery at a late conteſted election; by the late *John Surrebutter*, Esq. Special-pleader and barriſter at law. 1796. 8.

ANSTEY, [Chriſtopher] *Esq.*

See Public Characters of 1802-1803. p. 294. *The new Bath guide; or, memoirs of the Blunderhead family, in a ſeries of poetical epiſtles. 1766. 4. (5 ſh.) Ed. 3. 1766. 8. (3 ſh. 6 d.) On the much lamented death of the Marquis of Taviſtock; a poetical pamphlet. 1767. 4. *The prieſt diſſected; a poem, 1774. 4. (2 ſh. 6 d.) *An election ball, in poetical letters from Mr. Inkle at Bath, to his wife at Glouceſter. 1776. 4. (2 ſh. 6 d.) Ad *C. W. Bampfylde*, Arm. epiſtola poetica familiaris in qua continentur tabulae quinque ab eo excogitatae, quae perſonas repraeſentant poematis cujusdam Anglicani cui titulus,

An

An election Ball. 1776. 4. (5 sh.) Familiar epistle to C. *W. Bampfylde* —— translated 1777. 4. (1 sh.) A paraphrase or poetical exposition of the 13 chapter of the 1 book of St. Paul epistles to the Corinthians. 1779 fol. *Speculation, or a defence of mankind, a poem. 1780. 4. (2 sh. 6 d.) *Liberality, or memoirs of a decayed macaroni; a poetical narrative. 1788. 4. The farmer's daughter, a poetical tale. 1795. 4. (1 sh. 6 d.) Fabulae selectae, auctore *John Gay*, latine redditae. 1798. 8. (2 sh. 6 d.)

*ANSTEY, [L....] *Mrs. at Madras.*
On her introduction of the cinnamon-tree into the British settlement at Madras. (Tr. of the Soc. for the E. of A. Vol. 11. p. 212.)

*ANSTICE. [John] *Chairman of the general wool-meeting in the Year* 1788.
Observations on the nature and necessity of introducing improved machinery into the woolen manufactury —; 1802. 8. (2 sh 6 d.)

ANSTICE, [Robert] *of Bridgewater.*
An enquiry into the laws of falling bodies. 1794. 8. (3 sh)

ANSTIE, [John] *Esq.*
Account of the good effects of friendly societies among hand-craftsmen and labourers, at Devizes. (Bath Agricult. Soc. Vol 3. p. 349.)

*ANSTRUTHER, [Alexander] *Esq. of Lincoln's-Inn; Barrister at Law.*
Reports of cases argued and determined in the court of exchequer from easter term 23 Geo. 3. to trinity term 33 Geo. 3. both inclusive. Vol 1. 2. 3. 1796. 1797. 8. (1 L. 8 sh.) An essay on the nature and connection of heat, electricity and light. 1800. 8. (2 sh.)

*ANSTRUTHER, [Sir John] *Bart.*
Speech — for defence of Mr. *Hastings*. 1788. 8. (1 sh.) Account of a drill-plough of his own construction for sowing different kinds of grain. (Bath Agricult. Soc. Vol. 2. p. 280.) Account of various experiments made during a course of three years, to ascertain the increase of wheat and barley. (Ibid. Vol. 3. p. 354.) Comparative view of two crops of barley, one drilled and the other sown

12. Sermons for the principal feftivals of the year. 17... 12. Sermons. Vol. 1-5. 1794. 12.

*ARCHER, [John] *of Harford County, Maryland.*
On the ufe of the radix fenека (polygala feneka *Linn.*) in the cure of croup (cynanche trachealis *Cullen*) with additional remarks on the treatment of this difeafe. (Medical Repofitory, Vol. 2. p. 27.) On the internal ufe of faccharum faturni (acetate of lead) in diarrhoea. (Ibid. Vol. 3. p. 237.) On the ufe of the polygala feneca in croup. (*Duncan's* A. of Med. Y. 1799. p. 511.)

*ARCHER, [John] *Jun.*
A differtation on cynanche trachealis, commonly called croup or hives. Philadelphia. 1798. 8.

*ARCHER, [Jofeph] *Lieutenant.*
Statiftical furvey of the county of Dublin, with obfervations on the means of improvement; 1803. 8. (8 fh.) (Comm. and Agr. Soc. Vol. 7. p. 293.)

*ARCHER, [Thomas] *Dr. of Harford-town, Maryland.*
A fingular cafe of difficult parturition fuccefsfully treated. (Medical Repofitory. Vol. 1. p. 333.)

*ARKWRIGHT, [T.....] *of Kendal, Weftmoreland.*
Defcription of a machine for raifing ore from mines. (*Nicholfon's* Journal Y. 1802. April. p. 313. Tr. of the Soc. for the E. of A. Vol. 19. p. 276.)

*ARKWRIGHT, [Thomas] *of Chorley, in the County Palatine of Lancafter.*
Defcription of his invented double-bolted lock. (Tr. of the Soc. for the E. of A. Vol. 18. p. 239.)

*ARLEVILLE, [Bridel] *M. A.*
Practical accidence of the french tongue; or introduction to the french fyntax; —. 1798. 12. (3 fh.) The genders of the french fubftantives alphabetically arranged according to their terminations. 1798. (1 fh. 6 d.)

ARMSTRONG, [George] *M. Dr. Phyfician to the Difpenfary in the Infant-poor.* (Brother to *John Armftrong*, M. Dr.)
born .... died. 178 . (?)

ARMSTRONG, [John] *Student in the Univerfity of Edinburgh.*

born

born 1771. died the 21 Jul. 1797. at Leith near Edinburgh.

See Gentleman's Magaz. Y. 1797. July. p. 624. Sept. p. 731. Monthly Magaz. Y. 1797. Aug. p. 153. Allgem. Litterat.Zeit. J. 1797. IrBl. S. 1409.

Sonnets from *Shakespeare*. 1791.

*ARMSTRONG, [Moftyn John] *Geographer and Land-surveyor; Member of the Soc. of Arts — in London.*

Effay on the contour of the coaft of Norfolk — 1792. 4. (1 fh.)

*ARMSTRONG, [Robert] *Rev.*

The elements of the latin tongue, with all the rules in Englifh, for the more ready improvement of youth. 1798. 8. (2 fh.)

*ARMSTRONG, [Simon] *M. Dr. of St. Vincent's.*

Obfervations on the ufe of the muriat of barytes in fcrofulous affections of the WeftIndies, and in a fingularly painful difeafe arifing from the bite of a negro. (*Duncan's* A. of Med. Y. 1801. p. 370.)

*ARMSTRONG, [William] *Rev.*

Catechetical lectures, or, the church catechifm explained. 1796. 8. (3 fh.)

*ARNO, [......] (?)

The fruits of faction; a feries of pictures taken from regenerated France. 1791. 4. (2 fh. 6 d.) (Author of feveral little poems publifhed under that fignature in the Oracle. Critical Review. Y. 1791. Oct. p. 232.)

*ARNOLD, [R.....] *Writing-Mafter and Mathematician; of the Manor-Houfe, Chiswick.*

The arithmetical preceptor, or, practical affiftant; 1792. 12. (2 fh.)

*ARNOLD, [Richard]

Account of *Benj. Young's* new invented harrow and roller. (*Young's* A. of Agr. Vol. 32. p. 637.)

*ARNOLD, [Samuel James]

The creole; or the haunted island, a novel; Vol. 1-3. 1796. 8. (10 fh. 6 d.) Auld Robin Gray, a mufical entertainment; 17... The Irifh legacy. 1797. The fhipwreck, a comic opera, in two acts. 1797. 8. (1 sh.) The veteran tar, a comic opera. 1801.

ARNOLD, [Thomas] *M. Dr. Physician in the borough of Leicester; Fellow of the Roy. Med. Soc. of Edinburgh.*

A case of hydrophobia, commonly called canine madness from the bite of a mad dog, successfully treated. 1793. 8. (4 sh.) übers. Leipzig. 1794. 8. übers. Repertor. Chir. u. Medic. Abhandl. B. 2. S. 303.

ARNOT, [Hugo] *Esq. Advocate.*

born .... died .... (?)

History of Edinburgh, from the earliest accounts to the present time; Ed. 2. 1789. 4. (1 L. 5 sh.)

*ARROT, [James] *Member of the College.*

Remarks on the present mode of chirurgical attendance in the Royal infirmary of Edinburgh, submitted to the consideration of the Roy. College of Surgeon there. 1800. 4.

*ARTHY, [Elliot] *Esq. Surgeon in the African and West-India Merchant's service.*

The seaman's medical advocate; or, an attempt to shew, that 5000 seamen are, annually, during war, lost to the British nation, in the West-India merchant's service and on board ships of war on the West-India station, through the yellow fever, and other diseases and means, from causes which, it is conceived, are chiefly to be obviated and unconnected with the misfortunes of war or dangers of the sea's; illustrated by cases and facts. 1798. 8. (5 sh.) Observations on the griggirrys of the mandingos. (Arch. Vol. 13. p. 227.)

St. ASAPH, *Bishop of,* — See *Lewis Bagot.*

ASH, [Edward] *M. Dr.*

Einige Bemerkungen über den Basalt von Schottland. (*Crell's* Chem. Annalen J. 1792. Th. 1. S. 115.) Ueber die Verbindung der Kohlen-Flötze mit Basalten, in Schottland. (Ibid. J. 1792. Th. 1. S. 248.)

ASH, [John] *M. Dr: F. R. and A. SS. Fellow of the Roy. College of Physicians: Formerly Physician to the general Hospital at Birmingham.*

born .... died in Brompton-row, Knightsbridge the 18 June 1798.

See

See Gentlem. Magaz. Y. 1798. June. p. 544. Aug. p. 720. *Duncan's* Annals of Medec. Y. 1798. p. 474. Allgem. Litterat. Zeit. ItBl. J. 1800. S. 651.

Oratio anniversaria Harvejana. 1790. 4. (1 sh.)

*ASHBURNHAM, [William] *Jun. Esq.*

The restoration of the jews, a poem. 1794. 4. (2 sh.) Elegiac sonnets and other poems. 1795. 4. (5 sh.)

°ASHBY, [George] *Rev. of Barrow, Suffolk.*

Invention of wheel-barrows (*Young's* A. of Agr. Vol. 20. p. 535.) Remarks on Mr *Young's* general view of Suffolk agriculture. (Ib. Vol. 32. p. 252.)

ASHDOWNE, [William]

An attempt to shew, that the opinion concerning the devil or satan, as a fallen angel and that he tempts men to sin, hath no real foundation in scripture. 1791. 8. (1 sh. 6 d.) New and decisive proofs, from scripture and reason, that adults only are included in the design of the new covenant or the gospel dispensation and were members of the church of Christ in the apostolic age. Offered as a reply to Mr. *Williams'* Attempt, in a late treatise, to prove that by baptism infants were initiated into the church of Christ and Members of it, at that time. 1792. 8. (1 sh.) Two letters addresed to the Lord Bishop of Landaff (*Rich. Watson*), occasioned by the distinction his Lordship hath made between the operation of the holy spirit in the primitive ministers of Christ and its operation in men at this day, contained in a address to young persons after confirmation; which distinction is shewn not to have any foundation in the new testament. Also that the promises of the spirit to Christ's disciples extend to the days of the apostles only. 1798. 8. (1 sh.)

*ASHE, [Robert Hoadly] *D. D.*

Letter to *John Milner*, M. A. F. S. A. Author of the civil and ecclesiastical history of Winchester, occasioned by his false and illiberal aspersions on the memory and writings of Dr. *Benj. Hoadley*, formerly Bishop of Winchester. 1799. 8. (2 sh. 6 d.)

*ASHHURST, [Juftice]

Charge to the grand jury for the county of Middlefex. 1792. fol. (1 d.)

*ASHLEY, [. . . . . .]

* The art of painting on and annealing in glafs, with the true receipts of the colours, the ordering of the furnace and the fecrets thereunto belonging, as practifed about the Year 1500 fuppofed to be then in its perfection. 1801. 4.

*ASHLEY, [J . . . .] *Secretary.*

The moral and political magazine of the London correfponding fociety. Nrb. 1. 1796. (6 d.)

*ASHMAN, [John] *of Abbey-Milton, Dorfet.*

Defcription of a comb-pot, to be ufed with pitcoal. (Bath's Agric. Soc. Vol. 4. p. 256.)

*ASHTON, [W . . . . .]

Calculation of the antients. (Monthly Magaz. Y. 1799. June. p. 348.) On the jews. (Ibid. Y. 1800. Jan. p. 945)

*ASHWORTH, [John] *Secretary to the Manchefter Agricultural Society.*

Account of his draining-bricks. (Comm. and Agric. Magaz. Vol. 7. p. 5.)

ASTLE, [Thomas] *Esq. F. R. S. and A. S. One of the Curates of the Britifh Mufeum and Keeper of the Records in the tower of London.*

a native of Staffordfhire.

Account of the feals of the kings, royal burghs and magnates of Scotland. 1792. fol. .. Obfervations on a charter in Mr. *Aftle's* library, which is indorfed, with a hand co-eval with it, Haec eft carta regis Eadgari, de inftitutione Abbatie Elienfis et duplicatus; (Arch: Vol. 10. p. 226.) Obfervations on a charter of King Eadgar. (Ibid. Vol. 10. p 232.) On the tenures, cuftoms &c. of his manor of Great Tey. (Ibid Vol. 12. p. 25.) Obfervations on ftone pillars, croffes and crucifixes. (Arch. Vol. 13. p 208.) Copy of a curious record of pardon in the tower of London. (Ibid. Vol. 13. p. 313.) The origin and progrefs of writing, hierogliphic and elementary — Ed. 2. with additions. 1803. 4. (2 L. 10 fh.)

*ASTLEY, [. . . . .] *Sen. Profeffor of the art of Riding.*

A

A general ſyſtem of equeſtrian education, with engravings. 1801. (10 ſh. 6 d.)

*ASTLEY, [Joſeph]

On the doctrine of heat; particularly with regard to the ſtates of denſe and elaſtic fluidity in bodies. (*Nickolſon's* Journal, Vol. 5. p. 23.)

*ASTLEY, [Philip] *Esq. formerly a Soldier and at preſent, Proprietor of the Royal grove, Hercules-hall, Lambeth, London.*

A deſcription and hiſtorical account of the places now the theatre of war in the low countries —. 1794. 8. (6 ſh.) Remarks on the profeſſion and duty of a ſoldier; with other obſervations relative to the army at this time in actual ſervice on the continent. 1794. 8. (2 ſh.)

*ATCHESON, [Nathaniel] *F. A. S. Solicitor.*

Report of a caſe recently argued and determined in his Maj. Court of King's Bench on the validity of a ſentence of condemnation by an enemy's conſul in a neutral port, and the right of the owner of the ſhip to call upon the underwriters to reimburſe him the money for the purchaſe of the ſhip at a ſale by auction under ſuch ſentence; with an appendix containing the french laws now in force relative to maritime prizes &c. and the Daniſh ordinance of the 20 of April 1796 impoſing a duty on foreign ſhips. 1800. 8. (6 ſh.) A letter on the preſent ſtate of the carrying part of the coal trade. — 1802. 8. (2 ſh. 6 d.)

*ATKINS, [......] *Mathematical Inſtrument-maker.*

An eſſay on the relation between the ſpecific gravities and the ſtrengths and values of ſpirituous liquors — 1803. 4. (5 ſh.)

ATKINS, [James] *M. A. Rector of St. Michael's, in Long Stanton, Cambridgeſhire.*

The aſcenſion, a poem. 1780. 4. A treatiſe on the horizontal ſun and moon, wherein is ſhewn, according to the principles of refraction, how it happens that thoſe bodies ſeem bigger in the horizont than in the zenith; — — 1793. 8. (1 ſh. 6 d.)

*ATKINSON, [James]

Rodolpho; a poetical romance. 1801. 4. (2 ſh.)

*ATKINSON, [Joseph] *Esq.*
Killarney, a poem. 1798. 4. (2 sh. 6 d.)

*ATKINSON, [Thomas]
Hibernian eclogues and miscellaneous poems; Dublin. 17... A poetical epistle from Marie Antoinette, Queen of France to Leopold 2, Emperor of Germany. 1791. 8. (1 sh.) *An oblique view of the grand conspiracy against social order. 1799. 8. (1 sh.)

*ATLAY, [Joseph]
The distiller's vade mecum; being a complete set of tables, exhibiting at one view the exact weight of spirituous liquors; from the lowest quality to alcohol, for any number of gallons, from 50 to 252, or one ton. Together with some useful rules for calculating the different strengths of spirits, adapted to *Clarke's* hydrometer. 1794. 12. (5 sh.)

ATWOOD, [George] *Esq. M. A. F. R. S. Of Sloane-street, Chelsea.*
Investigations, founded on the theory of motion, for determining the times of vibration of watch balances. (Phil. Transact. Y. 1794. p. 119.) The construction and analysis of geometrical propositions, determining the positions assumed by homogeneal bodies, which float freely and at rest, on a fluid surface; also determining the stability of ships and other floating bodies. (Phil. Transact. Y. 1796. p. 46.) A disquisition on the stability of ships. (Ibid. Y. 1798. p. 201.) On the construction and properties of arches. 1801. 4. (7 sh. 6 d.) Review of the statutes and ordinances of assize, which have been established in England from the 4 year of king John 1202 to the 37 of his present majesty. 1801. 4. (5 sh.)

ATWOOD, [Thomas]
History of the island of Dominica; containing a description of its situation, extent, climate, mountains, rivers, natural productions. 1791. 8. (4 sh.) übers. mit Anmerk. von *G. F. Benecke*, Göttingen. 1795. 8.

*AUBREY, [John] *F. R. S.*
The Oxford cabinet; consisting of engravings from original pictures in the Ashmolean museum and other

other public and private collections; with biographical anecdotes. 1797.

*AUCHINCLOSS, [J....] *D. D.*

The sophistry of the first part of Mr. *Paine's* age of reason; or, a rational vindication of the holy scripture as a positive revelation from God: with the causes of deism; in three sermons. 1796. 12. (1 sh.)

*AUCKLAND, [William] *Lord.* See *William Eden.*

*AUDLEY, [John]

A companion to the almanack —; 1802. 12. (1 sh. 6 d.)

AUFRERE, [Anthony] *Esq.*

Travels through various provinces of the kingdom of Naples in 1789. by *Charles Ulysses Salis* of Marschlins: translated from the German. 1795. 8. (8 sh.) A warning to Britons, against french perfidy and cruelty: or, a short account of the treacherous and inhuman conduct of the French officers and soldiers toward the peasants of Swabia, during the invasion of Germany in 1796. Selected from a well authenticated german publication. 1798. 8. (1 sh.)

*AUSTIN, [Gilbert] *M. A. Chaplain to the Magdalen Asylum, Leeson-street, Dublin. M. R. I. A.*

Sermon preached on Sunday April 3. 1791. 4. (2 sh.) Description of a portable barometer. (Tr. of J. A. Vol. 4. p. 99.) A method of cutting very fine screws, and screws of two or more threads &c. (Ibid. Vol. 4. p. 145.) Description of an apratus for impregnating water and other substances strongly with carbonic acid gas. (Ib. Vol. 8. p. 131.)

AUSTIN, [William] *M. Dr. Fellow of the College of Physicians; One of the Physicians of St. Bartholomew's Hospital.*

born at Wotton-Underedge in Gloucestershire, 28 Dec. 1754. died Jan. 21. 1793.

See Gentleman's Magaz. Y. 1793. Jan. p. 94. See *James Earle's* practical observations on the operation for the stone. London 1793. 8. Preface p. VII-XXIV.

On the origin and component parts of the stone in the urinary bladder; 1791. 8. (2 sh. 6 d.) übers. in Samml. für prakt. Aerzte. B. 16. S. 209.

*AUSTIN, [William] *A. B.*

An oration pronounced at Charleston — on the 17 of June, being the anniversary of the battle of Bunker's hill and of that company. Charleston near Boston in New-England. 1802. 8. (1 sh. 6 d.)

*AXFORD, [Benjamin]

On the extirpation of plants; noxious to cattle on dairy and grazing farms; and the cultivation of such as are wholesome and nutritive recommended: with some hints on the breeding and rearing milch cows. (Bath Agricult. Soc. Vol. I. p. 206.)

AYSCOUGH, [Samuel] *F. A. S. Assistant Librarian in the department of British books in the British Museum.* born 1745.

*A general index to the Monthly review — Vol. 3. 1796. 8. *Shakspeare's* dramatic works; with explanatory notes; with a copious index to the remarkable passages and words. Vol. 1-3. 1790. 8. (1 L. 11 sh. 6 d.) Copies of two Manuscripts on the most proper method of defence against invasion by *Waad.* (Arch. Vol. 13. p. 169.) Copy of a Manuscript in the British museum, entitled, an expedient or meanes in want of money: to pay the sea and landforces, or as many of them as shall be thought expedient without money in this year of an almost universal poverty of the english nation by *Fabian Philipps.* (Ibid. Vol. 13. p. 185.)

BABINGTON, [William] *Esq. M. Dr. Assistant Physician and Lecturer in Chemistry at Guy's-hospital. Formerly Apothecary to Guy's-Hospital.*

A systematic arrangement of minerals, founded on the joint consideration of their chemical physical and external characters; reduced to the form of tables and exhibiting the analysis of such species as have hitherto been made the subject of experiment. 1795. 4. (3 sh. 6 d.) A new system of mineralogy, in the form of a catalogue after the manner of *Born's* systematic catalogue of the collection of fossils of *Eleonore de Raab.* 1799. 4. Two cases of rabies canina, in which opium was given, without succes, in unusally large quantities; the one by *Will. Babington*, the other by *Will. Wavell.* (M. Rec. and Ref. p. 117.)

*BACHE,

*BACHE, [William] *Grandson the late Dr. Franklin. M. A. of Philadelphia.*
born . . . . died 1797.
Allg. Litter.Zeit. ItBl. J. 1800. S. 649.
Oration on the history, culture and qualities of the potatoe. (Columbian Magazine Y. 1790. Oct. p. 243.) An dissertation, being an endeavour to ascertain the morbid effects of carbonic acid gas or fixed air, on healthy animals and the manner in which they are produced. Philadelphia. 1796.

*BACKHOUSE, [Thomas] *Late master of H. M. S. Thisbe.*
A new and accurate collection of surveys of the principal harbours on the coast of Nova Scotia between Halifax and Cape Sable, and between Halifax and Cape C nso; forming together with a large chart, a complete Nova Scotia and Cape Breton Pilot, with an entire new book of sailing directions. 1798. (1 L. 11 sh. 6 d.)

*BACKUS, [Azel]
Some account of the epidemics which have occurred in the town of Bethlem, Connecticut, from its settlement to the present time. (Medical Repository. Vol. 1. p. 523.)

*BACKUS, [Isaac] *Pastor of the first Baptist church in Midlebourgh.*
A history of New-England, with particular reference to the denomination of christians called baptist. Vol. 1. Boston 1777. 8. Vol. 2. a church history of New-England extending from 1690 to 1784. Providence. 1784. 8. Vol. 3. — from 1783 to 1796. — Boston 1796. 8. (4 Dollar 50 Cents). Account of Middleborough, in the county of Plymouth, (Coll. of Massachusetts H. S. Y. 1794. p. 148.) Letter on the subject of iron ore at Middleborough. (Ibid. Y. 1794. p. 175.)

*BACON, [James]
The libertine, a novel, in a series of letters. 1791. 12. (3 sh.) The American Indian; or, virtues of nature, a play in 3 acts, with notes; founded on an Indian tale. 1795. 8. (2 sh.)

*BACON, [John] *Esq. F. A. S. Senior Clerk and Receiver at the first-fruits office.*
Liber regis, vel thesaurus rerum ecclesiasticarum;

with an appendix, containing proper directions and precedents relating to presentations, institutions, inductions, dispensations — 1786. 4.

*BACON, [Matthew] *Of the Middle Temple; Esq.*
On leases and terms for years. 1798. 8. (9 sh.)
A new abridgment of the law. Ed. 5. corrected with considerable additions, including the latest authorities; by *Henry Gwillim*, of the Middle Temple, Esq. Barrister at Law. Vol. 1–7. 1798. 8. (5 L. 5 sh.)

*BADELEY, [. . . . .] *Mr. Dr. of Chelmsford.*
Account of a case of uncommon sympathy between the skin and stomach, nearly amounting to disease. (*Duncan's* M. C. Dec. 2. Vol. 8. p. 446.)

*BADGER, [Charlotte]
Friendly admonitions to parents and the female sex in general; — 1803. 8. (6 sh.)

*BADGER, [Stephen] *of Natick.*
Historical and characteristic traits of the American Indians in general, and those of Natick in particular. (Coll. of Massachusetts H. S. Y. 1798. p. 32.)

*BAGE, [Robert]
born at Darley, a hamlet of Derby, Febr. 29. 1728. died at Tamworth Sept. 1. 1801.
See *Hutton's* History of Derby. 1791. Gentleman's Magaz. Y. 1801. Sept. p. 862. Supplem. p. 1206. *William Hutton's* memoirs of *Rob. Bage.* 1802.
Mount Heneth, a novel. 1781. Barham Downs: 17... The fair Syrian. 17... James Wallace; 17...

*BAGGS, [Jeff.] *LL. Dr: F. R. and A. S.*
Essays on amplification, with notes, critical and explanatory and exemplified by quotations from various authors, both ancient and modern. Vol. 1. 2 1802. 8.

*BAGGS, [John] *An illiterate Christian.*
A scriptural view of the millennium, or, an attempt to display the harmony of the bible on the latter day glory. 1798. 8. (1 sh.)

*BAGNAL, [Gibbon] *A. M: Vicar of Home-Lacy, Herefordshire.*
A new translation of Telemachus, in English verse.

verſe. Nrb. 1. 1756. 8. Ed. 2. Vol. 1. 2. 1791. 8. (12 ſh.) A ſermon — 1762. 8. Education, an eſſay (in verſe) 1765. 4.

BAGOT, [Lewis] *LL. D. Lordbiſhop of St. Aſaph, Archdeacon of St. Aſaph.*

born . . . . died 1802. June 4.

See Gentleman's Magaz. Y. 1802. June. p. 591. Nov. p. 1003.

Sermon — 1779. 4. Twelve diſcourſes on the prophecies, concerning the firſt eſtabliſhment and ſubſequent hiſtory of chriſtianity. 1780. 8. Letter to — *William Bell*, D. D. — on the ſubject of his late publications upon the authority, nature and deſign of the Lord's-ſupper. 1781. 8. Sermon — 1783. 4.

*BAILEY, [George] *of Sunderland.*

On ſome courſes of crops. (*Young's* A. of Agr. Vol. 5. p. 361.)

*BAILEY, [Jacob] *Rev. of Annapolis, in Nova Scotia.*

Obſervations and conjectures on the antiquities of America. (Coll. of Maſſachuſetts H. S. Y. 1795. p. 100.)

*BAILEY, [John]

—— and *G. Culley*; a general view of the agriculture of the county of Northumberland with obſervations on the means of its improvement, drawn up for the conſideration of the board of agriculture. 1800. 8. (8 ſh.) Remarks on waſte lands in Northumberland. (Bath Agric. Soc. Vol. 8. p. 114.) — — and *G. Culley* threſhing machines in Northumberland. (*Young's* A. of Agr. Vol. 22. p. 426.)

*BAILEY, [T.... B....]

On prevention the ſcarcity of proviſions at Pariſh Mill &c. (*Young's* A. of Agr. Vol. 35. p. 283.)

*BAILLIE, [Joanna] *Miſſ.*

A ſeries of plays; in which it is attempted to delineate the ſtronger paſſions of the mind. Vol. 1. 2. 1802. 8. (16 ſh.)

BAILLIE, [Matthew] *M. Dr. F. R. S.; Phyſician to St. George's-Hoſpital; Fellow of the Roy. College of Phyſicians.*

Account of a remarkable tranſpoſition of the viſcera. (Phil. Tranſact. Y. 1788. p. 350. London M. J.

M. J. Vol. X. P. 2.) überf. Samml. der neueften Beobacht. Englifcher Aerzte: S. 142. Account of a particular change of ftructure in the human ovarium. (Phil. Transact. Y. 1789. p. 71. London M. J. Vol. X. P. 2. p. 271.) überf. Samml. f. A. Th. 13. S. 354. überf. Samml. der neueften Beobacht. englifcher Aerzte. S. 260.) On the want of a pericardium in the human body. (Transact. of Med. and Chir. Soc. Y. 1793. p. 91.) Of uncommon appearances of difeafe in blood-veffels. (Ibid. Y. 1793. p. 119.) Of a remarkable deviation from the natural ftructure in the urinary bladder and organs of generation of a male. (Ibid. Y. 1793 p. 189.) A cafe of emphyfema, not proceeding from local injury. (Ibid. Y. 1793. p. 202.) An account of a cafe of diabetes, with an examination of the appearances after death. (Ibid. Vol. 2. p. 70.) An account of a fingular difeafe in the great inteftines. (Ibid. Vol. 2. p. 144.) An account of the cafe of a man who had no evacuation from the bowels for nearly fifteen weeks before his death. (Ibid. Vol 2. p. 174.) The morbid human anatomy of fome of the moft important parts of the human body. 1793. 8. (6 fh.) überf. mit Zufätzen von *Sömmering*. Berlin. 1794. 8. Appendix to the 1 Edit. 1798. 8. Ed. 2. corrected and confiderably enlarged. 1797. 8. (7 fh.) A feries of engravings, to illuftrate the morbid anatomy of the human body. Fafc. 1–10. 1799–1802. 4. *William Hunter's* anatomical defcription of the human gravid uterus and its contents, 1794. 4. (5 fh.) überf. mit Anmerk. und Zuf. von *L. F. Froriep*. Weimar. 1802. 8.

*BAILLIE, [Thomas] *Esq. Clerk of the deliveries in the civil branch of the office of ordnance at the tower of London.*

A folemn appeal to the public, from an injured officer, Captain *Thomas Baillie*, late lieutenant-governor of the royal hofpital for feamen, at Greenwich; arifing out of a feries of authenticated proceedings in the court of King's-bench, on fix libels, (as it was alledged), in a printed book, entitled, the cafe and memorial of Greenwich-hofpital, addreffed to the general-gover-nors

nors in behalf of difabled feamen, widows, and children; and the evidence given on the fubfequent enquiry at the bar of the houfe of lords, in confequence of the feveral profecutions difcharged with cofts. 1779. fol.

*BAILY, [Francis] *of the Stock Exchange.*
Tables for the purchaifing and renewing of leafes; —; 1803.

*BAIRD, [Thomas]
New invented tables of intereft, upon one fmall card, that will lay in pocket-book; fhewing the intereft of any fum for any number of days of five per cent. — 1801. 8. Cow-keepers of Middlefex. (*Young's* A. of Agr. Vol. 21. p. 112.) London Frick Fields. (Ibid. Vol. 21. p. 150.) Houfe and grafslambs. (Ib. Vol. 21. p. 151.)

*BAKER, [....] *Apothecary: F. M. S.*
Various cafes of fatality from the natural fmall pox, in families, where inoculation, when practifed, had been uniformly fuccefsfull. (Mem. of M. S. of L. Vol 3. p. 538)

*BAKER, [Gardiner] *of New-York.*
born .... died .... (?)
Meteorological obfervations for the Y. 1797 and 1798 made in the cupola of the exchange in the city of New-York. (Medical Repofitory. Vol. 1. p. 99. 245. 373. 557. Vol. 2. p. 101. 205 319.) Natural hiftory of the wolf. (New-York Magaz. Y. 1797 May. p. 243.)

*BAKER, [George] *A. M. Of the Kingdom of Ireland.*
The hiftory of Rome by *T. Livius*, translated from the original with notes and illuftrations. Vol. 1–6. 1797. 8. (2 L. 16 fh.)

BAKER, [James]
A picturesque guide through Wales and the marches; interfperfed with the moft interefting fubjects of antiquities in that principality. Vol. 1. 1795.

*BAKER, [Richard]
On the black-ruft in wheat. (Bath Agric. Soc. Vol. 4. p. 282.)

*BAKER, [S.....]
Musleiman Adeti, or, a defcription of the man-ners

ners and customs of the Turks, with a sketch of their litterature. 1796. 8. (1 sh. 6 d.)

*BAKEWELL, [Robert] *A Yeoman of considerable property.*

born 1726, at Dishley in Leicestershire, died 1795 Oct. 1.

See Gentleman's Magaz. Y. 1795. Nov. p. 969.

Sheep controversy between *Charles Chaplin* and *Rob. Bakewell.* (*Young's* A. of Agr. Vol. 10. p. 560.)

*BALDPATE, [Grizzle] *Esq.* (??)

The pole tax, an ode. 1795. 4. (1 sh. 6 d.)

*BALDWIN, [Christopher] *Esq. Clapham Common.*

On oil used as manure. (*Young's* A. of Agr. Vol. 13. p. 499.) On gypsum as a manure. (Ib. Vol. 14. p. 86. 89. et seq.) On oil composts and on drilling. (Ibid. Vol. 15. p. 350.) On the state of British agriculture. (Ibid. Vol. 17. p. 290.) Machine for drawing up trees by the roots. (Ib. Vol. 18. p. 164.)

BALDWYN, [Edward] *Rev.*

Farther remarks on two of the most singular characters of the age. 1789. Letter to the author of remarks on two of the most singular characters of the age by *John Crosse*, Vicar of Bradford in the county of York: with a reply by the former 1790. 8. *Remarks on the oaths, declarations and conduct of *Johnson Atkinson Busfield*, Esq. one of his Majesty's justices for the West-riding of the county of York. To which is added an Olla potrida. 1791. 8. *A congratulatory address to the Rev. *John Cross*, on the prospect of his recovery from a dangerous disease, to a state of spiritual health and salvation — 1791. (2 sh. 6 d.)

*BALDWIN, [George] *Esq. Late his Majesty's Consul-General in Egypt and attached to the Commander in Chief during the above glorious campaign.*

Political recollections relative to Egypt; containing observations on its government under the mamaluks; — its geographical position; — its intrinsic and extrinsic resources; — its relative importance to England and France; and its dangers

gers to England in the poſſeſſion of France; with a narrative of the ever-memorable Britiſh campaign in the ſpring of 1801. 1801. 8. (6 ſh.) Bemerk. über die von ihm entdeckte ſpecifiſche Wirkung der Einreibung des Olivenöhls gegen die Peſt; — aus dem Italieniſchen überſ. mit Anmerk. und Zuſ. von Dr. *Paul Scheel.* Kopenhagen. 1801. 8.

BALDWIN, [Loammi] *Esq. F. A. A.*

Directions for raiſing hemp. (American Muſeum Y. 1787. Sept. p. 293.)

BALFOUR, [Francis] *M. Dr: Soc. Reg. Med. Ed. S. H. Of the city of Edinburgh: formerly a Phyſician at Calcutta.*

On the influence of the moon in fevers — überſ. von *A. T. W. Lauth.* Straſsb. 1786. 8. On putrid inteſtinal remitting fevers, in which the laws of the febrile ſtate and ſol lunar influence being inveſtigated and defined, are applied to explain the nature of the various forms criſes and other phaenomena of theſe fevers — Ed. 2. 1790. 8. (6 ſh.) überſ. Breslau u. Hirſchberg. 1792. 8. The forms of Herkern — Calcutta. 1785. 4. On ſol lunar influence in fevers. Vol. 1. Ed. 2. 1795. 8. On the diurnal variations of the barometer. (Tr. of E. S. Vol. 4. H. p. 23.) On the barometer. (Aſiat. Reſ. Vol. 4. p. 195.)

BALGUY, [Thomas] *D. D. Arch-Deacon and Prebendary of Winchester.*

A native of Yorkſhire; died Jan. 12. 1795.

See Gentleman's Magazine Y. 1795. Febr. p. 169. March. p. 252. May. p. 368.

Divine benevolence aſſerted and vindicated from the objections of antient and modern ſcepticks. 1781. 8. (2 ſh. 6 d.) überſ. mit Anmerk. von *Eberhard.* Leipzig. 1782. 8. Preface to an eſſay on redemption by his father *(John Balguy)* 1785. 8.

(Several ſingle ſermons.)

*BALL, [John] *Surgeon, in Williton, in the pariſh of St. Decumans, and county of Somerſet.*

On the growth and cure of rhubarb (Tr. of the Soc. for the E. of A. Vol. 12. p. 229. Vol. 13. p. 178.) On opium, mode of preparing in Eng-

laud

land &c. (Ibid. Vol. 14. p. 254.) On the culture of opium. (Medical Repository. Vol. 1. p. 424.)

*BALLARD, [E....]

The stock brocker's vademecum and ready assistant to all persons concerned in the funds, in calculating the amount of any sum, capital stock, from one penny to one hundred pounds at any rate, from 50 to 100 per cent. — 1799. 8. (3 sh. 6 d.)

BALMAIN, [W....] *Chief Surgeon to the territory of New South Wales.*

On the effects of ipecacoanha in the cure of dysentery, at Norfolk island. (Mem. of M. S. of L. Vol. 5. p. 210.)

*BALMANNO, [John] *Esq. of Lincolns-Inn; Barrister at law.*

born ..... died at Vienna. 1800. Nov. 7.

See Gentlem. Magaz. Y. 1800. Suppl. p. 1290. Allg. Litterat. Zeit. J. 1801. ItBl. S. 839.

An essay on the law of bailments by Sir *Will. Jones;* Ed. 2. with introductory remarks and notes, comprising the most modern authorities. 1797. 8. (5 sh.) (Some criticisms in the Critical Review.)

BANCROFT, [Edward] *M. D: F. R. S.; at London.* (He resided many years ago in America.)

Experimental researches concerning the philosophy of permanent colours and the best means of procuring them by dyeing, callico-printing —. Vol. 1. 1794. 8. (6 sh.) Aus diesem übers. Ueber den Gebrauch der Quer Citron-Rinde. London. 1795. 8. übers. mit Anmerk. von *Dan. Jäger.* Th. 1. Leipz. 1797. 8. Accounts of experiments on lake from stick-lack. (Tr. of the Soc. for the E. of A. Vol. 19. p. 355.)

*BANEN, [Francis]

Delineation of exotic plants cultivated in the Royal garden at Kew. 1796. (5 L. 5 sh.)

*BANGOR, *Bishop of.* — See *Warren*

*BANKS, [John] *Lecturer in natural philosophy.*

Remarks on the floating of cork balls in water. (Mem. of M. Vol. 3. p. 178.) Experiments on the velocity of air issuing out of a vessel in different circumstances; with the description of an an instrument to measure the force of the blast in bellows, etc. (Mem. of M Vol. 5. P 2 p 398. *Nicholson's* Journal Y. 1802. Aug. p. 269.) A treatise on mills in four parts 1) on circular motion; 2) on the maximum of moving bodies, machines, engines &c. 3) On the velocity of effluent water. 4) Experiments on circular motion, water-wheels —. 1795. übers. von *C. G. Zimmermann*. Berlin. 1799. 8.

*BANKS, [Sir Joseph] *President of the R. S.*

See Public Characters of 1800–1801. p. 370. Epistle to Oborea, Queen of Otaheite. 1773. 4. (1 sh.) A speech delivered to the Royal Society on Nov. 30. 1780 being their anniversary. (Phil. Transact. Y. 1781. P. 1. p. 1.) Account of a roman sepulture lately found in Lincolnshire. (Arch. Vol. 12. p. 96.) Copy of an original Manuscript, entitled, a breviate touching the order and governmente of a nobleman's house. (Ibid. Vol. 13. p. 315.) *A project for extending the breed of fine-wooled Spanish sheep, now in the possession of his Maj. into all parts of Great-Britain where the growth of fine clothing wools is found to be profitable (*Nicholson's* Journal. Vol. 4. p. 289.) Instruction given to the council against the wool bill. (*Young's* A. of Agr. Vol. 9. p. 479.) On the late season; 1790. (Ibid. Vol. 15. p. 76.) On the Hasting's turnip. (Ib. Vol. 15. p. 77.) Account of twelve Lincoln-sheep. (Ibid. Vol. 15. p. 357.) On the musca pumilionis. (Ibid. Vol. 16. p. 176. Reply to queries relating to labour in Lincolnshire (Ibid Vol. 19. p. 187.) An effectual method of curing the scab in sheep. (Tr. of the Soc. for the E. of A. Vol. 7. p. 90.) Effects of the equisetum palustre upon drains. (Comm. to the B. of Agr. Vol. 2. p. 349.) American antiquities. (Massachusetts Magaz. Y. 1795. Oct. p. 423.)

*BANKS, [J..... C.....]

An accurate account of the present state of the French republic. (Monthly Magaz. Y. 1801. Febr. p. 1. March. p. 105.)

***BANNANTINE**, [James] *Secretary when King's Superintendant at Honduras.*

Memoirs of Colonel *Edward Marcus Despard*, now under confinement. 1799. 8. (1 ſh.) Opinions of his Majeſty's miniſters reſpecting the french revolution, the war — from 1790 to 1801 chronologically arranged. Selected from the ſpeeches in parliament; with extracts from the ſpeeches of the oppoſition. 1800. 8. (4 ſh.) *New Joe Miller; or, the tickler, containing near two thouſand good things, many of which are original and the others ſelected from the beſt authors. Vol. I. 2. 1801. 12. (3 ſh) A liſt of Scotticiſms; (Monthly Magaz. Y. 1798. Dec. p 434.) Account of the ſettlement of Honduras. (Ibid. Y. 1799. May. p 286) Proofs of the wisdom and capacity of his Majeſty's miniſters, ſelected from their opinions delivered in parliament from 1790 to 1801. with extraits from the ſpeeches of the oppoſition. 1801. (3 ſh. 6 d.)

***BANNERMAN**, [Anne]

Poems. 1800. 12. (5 ſh.)

BANNISTER, [James] *Rever.*

On architecture, (Maſſachuſetts Magaz. Y. 1789. June. p 365. July. p. 401. A translation of all the Pythian, Nemean and Iſthmian odes of *Pindar*, except the 4 and 5 pythian odes and thoſe odes which have been tranſlated by the late *Gilbert Weſte.* Esq. 1791. 8. (5 ſh.) Directions for the ſtudy of divinity —. 1802.

***BANNISTER**, [John] *Gent. of Horton Kirby, in Kent.*

A ſynopſis of husbandry; being curſory obſervations on the ſeveral branches of rural economy —. 1799. 8. (7 ſh.)

***BANTER**, [Benjamin] *Esq.*

An epiſtle of condolence and exhortation, addreſſed to general gunning; To which is added, an elegy written before the ruins of the pantheon, ſhortly after the burning of that ſtately edifice. 1792. 4. (2 ſh.)

BARBAULD, [Anna Laetitia] *Mrs. (Daughter of the late Dr. Aikin of Warrington; Sister to Dr. Aikin of London.)*

A political sermon on a national fast. 17... The hill of science. 17... Epistle to *Will. Wilberforce*, on the rejection of the bill for abolishing the slave trade. 1791. 4. (1 sh.) Remarks on *Gilb. Wakefield's* enquiry into the expediency and propriety of public or social worship. 1792. 8. (2 sh.) *Sins of government, sins of the nation, or a discourse for the fast — by a Volunteer. 1793. 8. (1 sh.) Evenings at home, or the juvenile budget opened: consisting of a variety of miscellaneous pieces for the instruction and amusement of young persons. Vol. 1-6. 1793-1796. 12. (9 sh.) übers. Haelfte 1.2. Leipz. 1795. 1796. 8. The pleasures of imagination by Dr. *Mark Akenside*, which is prefixed a critical essay on the poem. 1795. 8. (6 sh. 6 d.) The poetical works of *William Collins*, with a prefatory essay. 1797. 8. (5 sh.) Sir Bertrand, a fragment. (Columbian Magaz. Y. 1787. Nov. p. 743.)

*BARBER, [J.... T....] *F. S. A.*

A tour through South-Wales and Monmouthshire —; with maps and views; 1803. (1 L. 5 sh.)

*BARBOR, [William]

On feeding cattle with potatoes. (Tr. of the Soc. for the E. of A. Vol. 11. p. 88. 94.)

BARBUT, [James] *late of the Bank.*

born .... died May 25. 1791.

See Gentleman's Magaz. Y. 1791. June p. 587.

*BARCLAY, [David]

An account of the emancipation of the slaves in Unity Valley Pen, in Jamaica. 1801. 8. (6 d.) Directions for dibbling wheat, as performed in the county of Norfolk in 1795. (Bath Agric. Soc. Vol. 8. p. 356.) On hay making. (*Young's A. of Agr.* Vol. 28. p. 530.)

*BARCLAY, [George] *D. D. One of the ministers of Middleton*

Account of the parish of Haddington. (Transact.

 of

of the Soc. of Antiq. of Scotland. Vol. I. p. 40.) Letter to Mr. *Cummyng*. (Ibid. Vol. I. p. 553.)

*BARCLAY, [John] *M. Dr.*

A new anatomical nomenclature, relating to the terms which are expressive of position and aspect. 1803. 8. (5 sh.)

*BARCLAY, [Robert]

On *Agricola's* engagement with the Caledonians under their leader Golgecus. (Transact. of the Soc. of Antiq. of Scotland. Vol I. p. 565.) On gypsum. (*Young's* A. of Agr. Vol. 24. p. 358.)

*BARCLAY, [Robert] *Esq. of Urie, M. P.*

On labourers in husbandry renting land. (Comm. to the B. of Agr. Vol. I. p. 91.)

*BARD, [John] *New-York.*

On the danger of introducing epidemical disorders, through want of proper precautions. (American Museum Y. 1788. May p. 453.)

*BARDSLEY, [Samuel Argent.] *M. Dr. M. R. M. S.*

Miscellaneous observations on canine and spontaneous hydrophobia; to which is prefixed, the history of a case of hydrophobia, occurring twelve years after the bite of a supposed mad dog. (Mem. of M. Vol. 4. P. 2. p. 431. New-York Magaz. Y. 1797. March. p. 115.) Cursory remarks, moral and political, on party prejudice. (Mem. of M. Vol. 5. P. I. p. I.) Critical remarks on Pizarro, a tragedy from the German drama of *Kotzebue* and adapted to the English stage by *Rick. Brinsley Sheridan.* With incidental observations on the subject of the drama. 1800. 8. (1 sh. 6 d.)

*BARFORD, [William] *Rector of Kimpton, Herts; Fellow of Eton College, Prebendary of Canterbury.*

born .... died Nov. 30. 1792.

See Gentlem Magaz. Y. 1792. Dec. p. 1155. Y 1793. May. p. 418.

Dissertatio in *Pindari* primum Pythium. 1751. 4. A latin oration at the funeral of Dr. *George*, Provost of Kings. 1756. 4. Concio ad Synod. from Col. IV, 5. — 1784.

*BARHAM, [Henry] *Dr.*

died .... (?)

Hortus

Hortus Americanus, containing an account of the trees, shrubs and other vegetable productions of South-America and the West-India islands and particularly of the Island of Jamaica, interspersed with many curious and useful observations respecting their uses in medicine, diet and mechanicks; to which are added a *Linnean* Index etc. printed and published by *Alexander Aikman*, Printer to the King's Maj. Kingston, Jamaica. 1794.

*BARING, [Charles] *Esq.*

Peace in our power, upon terms not unreasonable. 1798. 8. (1 sh.)

BARING, [Sir Francis] *Bart. Merchant of the city of London and a Director to the East-India Company.*

Observations on the establishment of the bank of England on the paper circulation of the country. 1797. 8. (1 sh. 6 d.) Observations on the publication of *Walter Boyd* on the influence of the stoppage of issues in specie at the bank of England; on the prices of provisions and other commodities. 1801. 8. (1 sh.)

*BARKER, [J....] *Lieutenant Colonel of the 56 Regt.*

Particulars concerning husbandry in the isle of Wight. (*Young's* A. of Agr. Vol. 9. p. 40.)

*BARKER, [Jeremiah] *of Portland (Maine).*

On the febrifuge virtues of lime, magnesia and alkaline salts in dysentery, yellow-fever and scarlatina angina. (Medical Repository. Vol 2. p. 147.) An account of febrile diseases as they have appeared in the county of Cumberland, district of Maine from July 1798 to March. 1800. (Ibid. Vol. 3. p. 364.) Abstinate eruption over the whole surface of the body cured by chalk (alkaline earth, or carbonate of lime); (Ibid. Vol. 3. p. 412.)

BARKER, [John]

Epidemics or general observations on the air and diseases from the Y. 1740 to 1777 inclusive, and particular ones from that time to the beginning of 1795. — &c. 1796. 8. (5 sh.)

*BARKER, [Robert].

Practical observations on the gonorrhoea virulenta and a new mode of treating that disease. Oxford, 1801. 8. (2 sh. 6 d.)

BARKER, [Thomas] *Esq. of Lyndon-hall, in Rutlandshire.*

born . . . . . died 1803. May.

See Gentleman's Magaz. Y. 1803. July p. 692. An account of the discoveries concerning comets, with the way to find their orbits and some improvements in constructing and calculating their places (with tables). 1757. 4. The messiah: being the prophecies concerning him, methodized, with their accomplishments; P. 1. 1780. 8. (2 sh. 6 d.) P. 2. 1798. 8. (3 sh.) Abstract of a register of the barometer, thermometer and rain at Lyndon in Rutland. With the rain in Surrey and Hampshire, for the Y. 1789 et 1790. (Phil. Transact. Y. 1791. p. 89. 278.) — for the Y. 1791. (Ibid. Y. 1792. p. 362.) — for the Y. 1792. (Ibid. Y. 1793. p. 220.) — for the Y. 1793. (Ibid. Y. 1794. p. 174.) — for the Y. 1794. (Ibid. Y. 1795. p. 410.) — for the Y. 1795. (Ibid. Y. 1796. p. 483.) — for the Y. 1796. (Ibid. Y. 1798. p. 130.) — for the Y. 1797. with some remarks on the recovery of injured trees. (Ibid. Y. 1799. p. 24.) — for the Y. 1798. (Ibid. Y. 1800. p. 46.) The rates of wages of servants, labourers and artificers, set down and assessed at Okeham, within the county of Rutland, by the justices of the peace there the 28 Day of April A. 1610. (Arch. Vol. XI. p. 200.) Abstract of a register of the barometer, thermometer and rain at Lyndon in Rutland, 1793. (Phil. Transact. Y. 1794. p. 174.

*BARLOW, [James] *Surgeon at Blackburn, Lancashire.*

A case of the caesarian operation performed and the life of the woman preserved. (M. Rec. and Ref. p. 154.)

BARLOW, [Joel] *American Consul at Algiers.*

born in Connecticut about the Y. 1758-9.

The vision of Columbus, a poem in 9 books; Ed. 1. 1781. Ed. 5. corrected, to which is added the conspiracy of the kings, by the same Author. Paris.

Paris. 1793. 8. Advice to the privileged orders in the ſeveral ſtates of Europe, reſulting from the neceſſity and propriety of a general revolution in the principle of government. Part 1. 1792. 8. (3 ſh.) Part 2. 1795. 8. (2 ſh.) uberſ. London, 1792. 8. The conſpiracy of kings; a poem, addreſſed to the inhabitants of Europe, from another quarter of the world. 1792. 4. (1 ſh. 6 d.) A letter to the national convention of France on the defects in the conſtitution of 1791. and the extent of the amendments which ought to be applied. 1792. 8. (1 ſh. 6 d.) A letter addreſſed to the people of Piedmont, on the advantages of the french revolution and the neceſſity of adopting its principles in Italy; translated from the French. 1795. 8. (1 ſh. 6 d.) The haſty-pudding, a poem. New-York. 1796. 12. Letters from Paris, to the citizens of the United ſtates of America on the ſyſtem of policy hitherto purſued by their government, relative to their commercial intercourſe with England and France. 1800. 8. (3 ſh.) Oration delivered Jul. 4. 1787. in commemoration of the independence of the United ſtates. (American Muſeum Y. 1787. Aug. p. 13.)

*BARLOW, [John] *Surgeon at Bolton in Lancaſhire.* An account of a mode of practice which has been ſucceſsfully adopted, in caſes of diſtortion of the pelvis, in pregnant women. (*Simmons's* Med. Facts and Obſervat. Vol. 8. p. 185.)

*BARNARD, [Thomas] *Barriſter at Law.* Obſervations on the proceeding of the friends of the liberty of the preſs; and an anſwer to Mr. *Erskin's* ſpeech of Jan. 19. 1793. 1793. 8. (1 ſh.)

*BARNARD, [Thomas] *of Mitchelmarſh, near Romſey.* River weeds for manure &c. (*Young's* A. of Agr. Vol. 6. p. 92.)

*BARNBY, [......] *Mrs.* Kerwald caſtle; or, the memoirs of the Marquis de Solanges; translated from the French. 1803. Vol. 1. 2. (8 ſh.)

*BARNES, [George] *near Mells, Sommerset.*
Account of a new drill-machine, invented by a Sommersetshire farmer and of a crop sown by it. (Bath Agr. Soc. Vol. 4. p. 331.)

BARNES, [Thomas] *D. D. Dissenting Minister at Manchester; Member of the Lit. and Philos. Soc. of Manchester.*
On the voluntary power which the mind is able to exercise over bodily sensation. (Mem. of M. Vol. 2. p. 451.) übers. im Auszug in *Mich. Wagner's* Beytr. zur Philosoph. Anthropologie. B. 1. Wien. 1794. Nro. 5. On the nature and essential characters of poetry. (Massachusetts Magaz. Y. 1791. July p. 410.)

*BARNES, [Thomas] *of Leeds.*
On the culture of turnips. (*Young's* A. of Agr. Vol. 12. p. 336.)

*BARNES, [William]
Epigrams. 1803. 12. (3 sh.)

*BARNETT, [Thomas] *of Aspr, near Warwick.*
On Warwickshire sheep. (*Young's* A. of Agr. Vol. 13. p. 342.)

*BARRETT, [Francis] *F. R. C. Professor of Chemistry, natural and occult philosophy, the cabala &c.*
The magus, or celestial intelligencer, being a complete system of occult philosophy; in 3 books. 1801. 4. (1 L. 7 sh.)

*BARRETT, [Henry]
The alps, a moral and descriptive poem of the great *Haller*, translated from the German. 1796. 8. (1 sh.)

BARRET, [John] *D. D. senior fellow of Trinity College, Dublin.*
An enquiry into the origin of the constellations, that compose the zodiac and the uses they were intended to promote. 1800. 8. (6 sh.)

*BARRETT, [Stephen] *Rector at Hothfield in Kent.* born 1718 at Bent in the parish of Kildwich, in Craven, co. York, died 1801. Nov. 26.
See Gentleman's Magaz. Y. 1801. Dec. p. 1152.
Author of a translation of the epistles of *Ovid* into english

englifh verfe; Of a translation of the paftorals of *Pope* into latin hexameters; Of war, an epic fatire; and Of feveral fmaller publications.

BARRINGTON, [Daines] *F. R. and A. SS. A King's Counfel, and a Bencher of the Society of the Inner temple.*

brother to *Shute Barrington*. born . . . . died March 14. 1800.

See Gentlem. Magaz. Y. 1800. March. p. 291. Allg. Litterat. Zeit. IntBl. J. 1800. S. 1804. J. 1801. S. 329. *Millin* Magazin encyclopedique. An 7. T. 2. p. 402.

Obfervations on the ftatutes, chiefly the more antient, from magna charta to 21 James 1. Chap. 27. with an appendix, being a propofal for new modelling the ftatutes. 1766. 4. Ed. 2. 1776. Ed. 3. Ed. 4. The naturalift's calendar. 1767. * The Anglo-Saxon verfion, from the hiftorian *Orofius*, by Alfred the great; together with an englifh translation from the Anglo-Saxon. 1773. 8. Silver roman denarii found in Lancafhire; (Arch. Vol. 7. p. 414.) A celt found near Segontium, in Wales; (Ibid. Vol. 7. p. 417.) A feal found at Dunftar caftle; (Ibid. Vol. 9. p. 369.) On the language of birds (See *Pennant's* Britifh Zoology. Vol. 3.) Hiftorical account of propagating the filk worms and making filk in England. (Tr. of the Soc. for the E. of A: Vol. 2. p. 172.)

*BARRINGTON, [George] *Superintendent of the convicts at Paramatta.*

A voyage to New South Wales, with a defcription of the country, the manners, cuftoms, religion &c. of the natives in the vicinity of Botany-bay. 1795. 8. (2 fh. 6 d.) Ed. 2. 17... Ed. 3. 17... Sequel to *Barrington's* voyage to New South Wales, comprehending an interefting narrative of the transactions and behaviour of the convicts; the progrefs of the colony; — 1800. 8. (2 fh. 6 d.)

*BARRINGTON, [George]

Live and dead weight of a fix year old cow. (*Young's* A. of Agr. Vol. 24. p. 1.)

*BARRINGTON, [Shute] *LL. D. Lordbifhop of Durham. Formerly of Sarum.*

born about the Y. 1732.

D 5 See

See Public Characters of 1798 – 1799. p. 214.
Miscellanea sacra; — by Lord Barrington (died 1734.) a new edition, with large additions and corrections. Vol. 1. 2. 3. 1772. 8. (15 sh.) Some notes in *Bowyer's* conjectures on the new testament. 17... Letter to the clergy of the diocese of Sarum with directions relating to orders, institutions and licences. 1789. 8. (1 sh.) On the state of the poor. (*Young's* A. of Agr. Vol. 34. p. 225.) Rice applied in the present scarcity. (Ibid. Vol. 34. p. 344.)
(Several single sermons.)

*BARRIT, [Thomas]
Essay on some supposed druidical remains near Halifax in Yorkshire. (Mem. of M. Vol. 3. p. 292.) An attempt to explain the nature and origin of the ancient carved pillars and obelisks, now extant in Great-Britain. (Ibid. Vol. 4. P. 2. p. 506.) Account of some antiques lately found in the river Ribble. (Ibid. Vol. 5. P. 2. p. 527.) Explanation of a roman inscription, found in Castle-field, Manchester, with a note on the same subject by Dr. *Holme*. (Ibid. Vol 5. P. 2. p. 675.)

*BARROW, [Charles]
Letter on oil from sun flower seed. (Tr. of the Soc. for the E. of A. Vol. 2. p. 116.)

*BARROW, [J....] *Private Teacher of the Mathematics.*
A description of pocket and magazine cases of mathematical drawing instruments; — 1794. 8. (3 sh. 6 d.)

*BARROW, [James]
A poem on the peace between the united kingdoms of Great-Britain and Ireland and the French Republic, Spain and Holland. 1802. 4. (1 sh.)

*BARROW, [John] *late Secretary of the Earl of Macartney.*
An account of travels into the interior of Southern Africa, in the Y. 1797 and 1798. — 1801. 4. (1 L. 10 sh.) übers. mit Anmerk. Leipzig. 1801. 8. Description of the table and the paarlberg mountains in Southern Africa. (*Tilloch's* Philos. Magaz. Vol. 10. p. 222.) Account of the discovery

discovery of coal at the Cape of Good Hope. (*Tilloch's* Philos. Magaz. Vol. 11. p. 261.)

*BARROW, [William] *LL. D. F. A S.*

Eight sermons, containing answers to some popular objections against the necessity or the credibility of the Christian revelation. 1799. 8. (7 sh.) An essay on education; in which are particularly considered the merits and the defects of the discipline and instruction in our academies. Vol. 1. 2. 1802. 12. (8 sh.)

*BARRY, [Edward] *L. L. D.*

The present practice of a justice of the peace, and a complete library of parish law. Containing the substance of all the statutes and adjudged cases down to the Year 1790 inclusive, which point out the duty and present practice of justices of the peace, sheriffs, under-sheriffs, clergymen, church-wardens, overseers, high constables, surveyors of the highway, constables, head-boroughs and other county, ward and parish officers. Vol. 1-4. 1791. 8. (1 L. 6 sh.)

BARRY, [Edward] *M. Dr. Chaplain to the Lord Bishop of Kildare.* (Dr. *Jackson.*)

A native of Bristol.

A letter to Mr. *Richard Cumberland*, occasioned by his letter to *Richard* Lord Bishop of Landaff. 1783. 8. Coalitions and compromises! an appeal to the electors of Great-Britain on the subject of coalitions and compromised elections; but principally to the freemen of Bristol; explaining the principles of a society formed to oppose a compromised representation of that city in parliament; with an apology for accepting *David Lewis*, Esq. as candidate. 1790. 8. (1 sh.) Theological, philosophical and moral essays. 1791. 8. A dispassionate address to the subjects of Great-Britain. 1793. 8. (2 sh.) Familiar letters on a variety of subjects; 1794. 8. (5 sh.) On the necessity of adopting some measures to reduce the present number of dogs; with a short account of hydrophobia and the most approved remedies against it. 1795. 8. (1 sh.) Sermons. Ed. 2. with great additions. 1798. The friendly call of truth and reason to a new species of dissenters.

senters. 1799. 8. (2 sh.) A few observations on the expedience of parliamentary interpretation, duly to explain the act of William and Mary, commonly called „the tolerating act„, 1799. 8. (1 sh.)

(Several single sermons.)

BARRY, [James] *R. A. Professor of painting to the Royal Academy.*

born at Corck, in Ireland.

See Public Characters of 1800–1801. p. 303.

A letter to the — President, Vice Presidents and the rest of the noblemen and gentlemen of the society for the encouragement of arts — 1793. 8. (1 sh. 6 d.) A letter to the dilettanti society, respecting the obtention of certain matters essentially necessary for the improvement of public taste and for accomplishing the original views of the Roy. Acad. of Great-Britain. 1798. 4. (2 sh. 6 d.) See *Pilkington*.

*BARRY, [John Melven] *M. Dr. at Cork.*

Letter respecting the cow-pock in Ireland. (*Duncan's* A. of Med. Y. 1800. p. 460.) An account of the nature and effects of cow-pox. Cork. 1800 8.

*BARRY, [Thomas]

Narrative of the singular adventures and captivity of *Thomas Barry* among the Monsisri Indians in the unexplored regions of North-America, during the Years 1797–1799 including the manners, customs &c. of that tribe; also a particular account of his escape, accompanied by an American female; the extraordinary handships they encountered, and their safe arrival in Loudon; written by himself. 1800. 8. (1 sh.)

*BARTELL, [Edmund] *Jun.*

Observations upon the town of Cromer, considered as a watering place and the picturesque scenery in its neighbonrhood. 1800. 8. (3 sh. 6 d.)

*BARTER, [William Brudenell]

Answers to queries respecting draining lands, destroying moss and planting coppices. (Bath Agric. Soc. Vol 8. p. 332.)

*BARTLAM, [J....]

Statement of a plan carried into execution by a Com-

Committee of the principal inhabitants of Alcester, in Warwickshire, for the relief of the poor, in that place and neighbourhood. (*Young's* A. of Agr. Vol. 26. p. 59.)

*BARTLETT, [Josiah]
See *Jedidiah Morse.*

BARTLEY, [Nehemiah] *Esq. Secretary to the Bath Agricultural society.*

On the culture of buck-wheat; wheat and potatoes, alternately, and the uses of buck-wheat. (Bath Agricult. Soc. Vol. 3. p. 288.) Account of an experiment in the cultivation of buck-wheat (fagopyrum) made at Brislington. (Ib. Vol. 3. p. 312.) Account of a series of experiments made on his farm near Bristol. (Ibid. Vol. 4. p. 267.) On the culture and value of potatoes. (Bath Agr. Soc. Vol. 8. p. 343.) On potatoe culture from seed. (Ib. Vol. 8. p. 330.) Observations on the conversion of pasture lands into tillage and after a certain course of crops relaying the same into pasture. Also hints on the utility of applying the potatoe as food for sheep —. To which is added, a copy of a letter to the chancellor of the exchequer on the late proposed measure of permitting starch, manufactured from potatoes, to be exempted from the revenue duties. 1802. 8. (1 sh 6 d.) On crossing the breed of sheep. (Comm. and Agric. Magaz. Y. 1803. Apr. p. 250.)

*BARTON, [Andrew]

The disappointement, or the force of credulity, a new comic opera in 3 acts. Ed. 2. Philadelphia. 1796. 8. (The first comedy, written in America.)

BARTON, [Benjamin Smith] *M. Dr. Professor of Natural philosophy and botany in the University of Pennsylvania. Member of the Roy. Soc. of Edinburgh.*

Account of the most effectual means of preventing the deleterious consequences of the bite of crotalus horridus or rattle-snake. (Tr. of A. S. Vol. 3. p. 100.) Inquiry into the question, whether the apis mellifica or true honey-bee is a native of America. (Ibid. Vol. 3. p. 241.) Botanical description of the podophyllum diphyllum of *Linnaeus.* (Ibid. Vol. 3. p. 334.) Memoir concerning the fascinating faculty which has been ascribed to the

the rattle-ſnake and other American ſerpents. (Ibid. Vol. 4. p. 74. *Tilloch's* Philoſ. Magaz. Vol. 15. p. 193.) überſ. von *E. A. W. v. Zimmermann.* Leipzig. 1798. 8. Some account of an American ſpecies of Dipus or Jerboa. (Tr. of A. S. Vol. 4. p. 114.) Obſervations and conjectures concerning certain articles which were taken out of an ancient tumulus, or grave, at Cincinnati, in the county of Hamilton and territory of the united ſtates, North-Weſt of the river Ohio. (Ibid. Vol. 4. p. 181.) Hints relative to the ſtimulant effects of camphor upon vegetables. (Ibid. Vol. 4. p. 232.) Some account of the poiſonous and injurius honey of North-America. (Ibid. Vol. 5. p. 51. *Tilloch's* Philoſ. Magaz. Vol. 12. p. 121.) On Indian dogs. (*Tilloch's* Philoſ. Magaz. Vol. 15. p. 1. 136.) A memoir concerning the faſcinating faculty which has been aſcribed to the rattleſnake and other American ſerpents. Philad. 1796. Suppl. 1800. 8. überſ. in *Bieſter's* Berliniſchen Blättern. J. 1797. Nov. S. 201. in *Hegewiſch* und *Ebeling's* Americaniſchen Magazin. B. 1. St. 4. S. 1. überſ. mit Anmerk. von *A. W. v. Zimmermann.* 1798. 8. Collections for an eſſay towards a materia medica of the United ſtates. Philad. 1798. 8. New views of the origin of the tribes and nations of America. Philad. 1798. 8. Ed. 2. 1799. Fragments of the natural hiſtory of Pennſylvania. Part. 1. Philad. 1799. fol. (4 ſh.) Papers relative to certain American antiquities. Philad. 1796. 4. A memoir concerning the diſeaſe of goitre as it prevails in different parts of North-America. 1800. 8. überſ. von *Wilh. Liebſch.* Göttingen. 1802. 8.

•BARTON, [Charles] *Esq. of the Inner-temple; Barriſter at law.*

An hiſtorical treatiſe of a ſuit in equity: in which is attempted a ſcientific deduction of the proceedings uſed on the equity ſides of the courts of chancery and exchequer, from the commencement of the ſuit to the decree and appeal; with occaſional remarks on their purport and efficacy; and an introductory diſcourſe on the riſe and progreſs of the equitable juriſdiction of thoſe courts. 1796. 8.

8. (5 sh.) Original precedents in conveyancing, selected from the manuscript collection of the late *Joseph Powell*. Esq. revised and corrected, with notes and remarks. Vol. 1-6. 1802. (3 sh.)

*BARTON, [J....] *Rev.*

On a new method of propagating potatoes. (Bath Agric. Soc. Vol. 8. p. 366.)

*BARTON, [Philip] *B. D. Sub-Dean and Canon of the cathedral church of St. Peter, Exeter.*

born .... died June 24. 1796.

See Gentleman's Magaz. Y. 1796. July. p. 616. Allg. Litt Zeit. ItBl. J. 1800. S. 627.

Plutarch's Parallel lives 17....; Sermon on the consecration of Bishop Lowth. 17...

*BARTON, [Samuel] *of Salem, in New-England.*

— — and *Joseph Blaney*, letter on the culture of hemp. (American Museum Y. 1787. May. p. 425.)

*BARTON, [W....] *Rev. of Bowness, on the lake of Windermere, Westmoreland.*

Fleets restorative for the rot in sheep. (*Young's* A. of Agr. Vol. 29. p. 318.)

*BARTON, [William] *Esq.*

Observations on the probabilities of the duration of human life and the progress of population in the United states of America. (Tr. of A. S. Vol. 3. p. 25.) On the propriety of investing congress with power to regulate the trade of the United states. (American Museum Y. 1787. p. 13.) Remarks on the state of American manufactures and commerce. (American Museum Y. 1790. June. p. 284.)

*BARTRAM, [John] *Esq. F R. S. a Quacker.*

Observations in his travels from Pennsylvania to Onondago. 1751. 8.

BARTRAM, [Isaac]

Memoir on the destillation of persimons. (American Museum Y. 1788. Febr. p. 135.)

BARTRAM, [Moses] *M. Dr. of St. Paul's Parish. South-Carolina.*

born .... died .... (?)

Medical facts and observations; (Tr. of Phys. of Philad. Vol 1. P. 1. p. 195.) Account of one of the causes of the trismus nascentium. (Ibid. Vol. 1. P. 1. p. 227.) Observations on the cicada, or locust

locust of America, which appears periodically once in 16 or 17 years. (American Museum Y. 1788. Dec. p. 502.)

*BARTRAM, [William] (Son of *John Bartram;*)
Travels through North and South - Carolina, Georgia, East and West - Florida, the Cherokee country, the extensive territories of the muscogulges, or creek confederacy and the country of the chactaws; containing an account of the soil and natural productions of these regions, together with observations on the manners of the Indians. Embellished with copperplates. Philad. 1791. (2 Dollars) Reprinted London. 1792. (7 sh. 6 d.) American natural history. (Massachusetts Magaz. Y. 1793. Febr. p. 103.)

*BARWIS, [Jackson] *Esq.*
Three dialogues concerning liberty. 1776. 8. (2 sh.) A fourth dialogue concerning liberty; containing an exposition of the falsity of the first and leading principles of the present revolutionists in Europe. 1793. 8. (1 sh.)

*BASELEY, [T . . . . .] *A. M: Chaplain to the Bishop of Lincoln.*
Sermons on various subjects. 1801. 8. (6 sh.)

*BASIRE, [James]
Some account of the abbey church of Bath, illustrative of ten engravings. 1799. 8. (2 L. 2 sh.)

*BASKERVILLE, [John] *Printer.*
born at Wolverley, in the county of Worcester 1706, died 1775.
William Hutton's account of *John Baskerville.* See Massachusetts's Magaz. Vol. 3. 1791. p. 673.

*BASQUIN, [Anthony]
Authentic memoirs of *Warren Hastings*, Esq. late Governor-General of Bengal, with strictures on the management of his impeachment. To which is added an examination into the causes of allarm in the empire. 1793. 8.

*BASS, [G . . . .] *Captain.*
Account of the island Alamagan, one of the Northern Mariannes. (Monthly Magaz. Y. 1801. March. p. 113.)

*BASSE,

BASSE, [J.... H....]
Catechism of health; for the use of schools and for domestic instruction, by B. C. Faust, M. Dr. Translated from the German. 1794. 12. (2 sh.)

BASSET, [Sir Francis] Bart. M. P.
Experiments in agriculture. (Young's A. of Agr. Vol. 22. p. 145.)

BASSET, [Richard]
On the new inclosure of Glentworth, on Lincoln heath. (Young's A. of Agr. Vol. 33. p. 535.)

BATES, [Ely] Esq.
Observations on some important points of divinity; chiefly those in controversy between the Arminians and Calvinists; with three dialogues in which the said points are further illustrated. The whole intended as an antidote against the pernicious tenets of Antinomians and Necessitarians. Extracted from an author of the last century. 1793. 12. (2 sh. 6 d.) A cursory view of civil government chiefly in relation to virtue and happiness. 1797. 8. (3 sh.) Rural philosophy: or, reflections on knowledge, virtue and happiness; — 1803. 8. (7 sh.)

BATES, [Joah] Esq. One of the Commissioners of his Maj. customs and a Director of Greenwich Hospital.
born ... died in London, July 1799.
See Gentleman's Magaz. Y. 1799. June. p. 534. Monthly Magaz. Y. 1799. July. p. 495. Allg. Litter. Zeitung. IntBl. J. 1800. S. 660.
On harmonics. 17...

BATH and WELLS, Bishop of,
See Charles Moss.

BATH, [Robert] Surgeon.
On the medical character. Ed. 3. 1789. übers. von C. F. Michaelis. Leipzig. 1791. 8.

BATHURST, [Henry] Earl.
born 1708. died 1794. at his seat at Oakley-grove, Aug. 6.
See Gentleman's Magaz. Y. 1794. Aug. p. 770.
The case of Miss Swordfeger; 17.. 4. Theory of evidence. 1761. 8.

BATSON, [Robert] Esq. of Limehouse.
On the dry-rot in timber. (Tr. of the Soc. for the E. of A. Vol. 12. p. 263.)

*BATTY, [R....] *M. Dr.*

— *T.... Bradley*, M. Dr. and *A. A. Noehden*, The medical and physical journal on subjects of medicine, pharmacy, surgery, chemistry and natural history — Vol. 1–9. (Nrb. 1–52.) 1802. 8. (each 15 sh. 6 d.) übers. von *Kühn*, Leipzig.

*BATTY, [William] *M. Dr. Physician in Genoa.*

On the use of the cuprum ammoniacale, in the cure of epilepsy. (*Duncan's* A. of Med. V. 1801. p. 377.)

*BATTYE, [Thomas]

A disclosure of parochial abuse, artifice and peculation in the town of Manchester; which have been the means of burthening the inhabitants with the present enormous parish rates: with other existing impositions of office in a variety of facts, exhibiting the cruel and inhuman conduct of the hireling officers of the town, towards the poor. —; 1796. 8. (2 sh.) The red Basil book, or parish register of arrears for the maintenance of the unfortunate offspring of illicit amours; with a further developpement of most shameful and unprecedented acts of abuse in the town of Manchester. Part 1. 1797. 8. (2 sh. 6 d.)

BAXTER, [Alexander] *Esq. of Odiham, Hants.*

On honesty in agriculture. (*Young's* A. of Agr. Vol. 3. p. 314.) Experiment on fattening hogs. (Ibid. Vol. 3. p. 482.) On the smut in wheat. (Ibid. Vol. 4. p. 201.) On tillage. (Ibid. Vol. 4. p. 330.) Experiments in fatting hogs. (Ibid. Vol. 6. p. 97.) On the North-America wild oats. (Ib. Vol. 6. p. 396.)

*BAY, [William] *Citizen of the state of New-York.*

An inaugural dissertation on the operation of pestilential fluids upon the large intestines, termed by nosologist's dysentery. New-York. 1797. 8.

BAYLEY, [Anselm] *LL. D. Sub-Dean of his Majesty's Chapels Royal.*

born .... died Sept. 1794.

A collection of anthems for the use of the chapels; 17...

BAYLEY, [C....] *Rev.*

The Swedenborgian doctrine of a trinity considered. 1785. 12.

*BAYLEY, [James]

Description of his proportional scale. (Tr. of the Soc. for the E. of A. Vol. 9. p. 153.)

*BAYLEY, [John]

The forester, or the royal seat; a drama, in 5 acts. 1798. 8. (1 sh. 6 d.)

BAYLEY, [John] *Esq. Barrister at Law.*

Reports of cases argued and adjudged in the courts of King's bench and common pleas, in the reigns of K. William, Q. Anne, K. George 1. and K. George 2. by *Robert* Lord *Raymond*. Ed. 4. corrected with additional references to former and later reports. Vol. 1-3. 1790. 8. (1 L. 16 sh.) A summary of the law of bills of exchange cash bills and promissory notes. Ed. 2. 1797. 8. (5 sh.)

*BAYLEY, [Peter] *Jun.*

Poems. 1803. 8.

BAYLEY, [Richard] *A Surgeon of the state of New-York.*

A account of the epidemic fever which prevailed in New-York in 1795, with the method of cure. 1796. (5 sh.) Letters from the health-office, submitted to the common-council of the city of New-York. 1798. 8.

BAYLEY, [Thomas Butterworth] *Esq. F. R. S. Of Hope near Manchester.*

born 1744. died Jun. 24. 1802.

See Gentleman's Magaz. Y. 1802. July. p. 689. Aug. p. 777. Monthly Magaz. Y. 1802. Aug. p. 39. Allg. Litterat.Zeit. IcBl. J. 1803. N. 48. S. 401.

Thoughts on the nature and advantages of cure and oeconomy in collecting and preserving different substances for manure. Ed 2. 1796. 8. (6 d.) (Tr. of Dublin Soc. Vol. 1. P. 2. p. 141.) On turnipe roads. (*Young's* A. of Agr. Vol. 27. p. 1.) Observations in favour of a bill to empower courts of justice to award costs in cases of misdemeanour. (Ibid. Vol. 28. p. 195.) Observations on a bill which is said to be under consideration, to oblige the owners of tenements and houses, under ten

E 2 pounds

pounds a year, to pay the taxes for the same. (Ib. Vol. 28. p. 393.) Charge delivered to the grand jury, at the quarter-sessions at Salford, April 25. 1798. (Ibid. Vol. 31. p. 182.) Observations on the striking advantages resulting from sentencing convicts to hard labour and solitude. (American Museum Y. 1788. June. p. 514.)

*BAYLIES, [William] *A. M. A. A. S. Fellow of the Massachusett's Medical Soc. Physician at Dighton.*
Account of the ulcerated sore throat, as it appeared in the town of Dighton (County of Bristol) in the Years 1785 and 1786. (M. P. of M. S. Nrb. 1. p. 41.) Case of a calculus in the ureters, together with another of the sudden growth of the stone, consequent upon the introduction of a foreign body into the bladder. (Ibid Nrb. 1. p. 90.) Description of gay head. (Mem. of B. A. Vol. 2. P. 1. p. 150.)

BAYNHAM, [William] *Surgeon in Essex County in Virginia.*
Account of an extra-uterine conception. (*Simmons's* Med. Facts. Vol. 1. p. 73.) übers. Repertor. chirurg. u. Medic. Abhandl. Th. 1. S. 156.

*BAYNTON, [George]
Oration in praise of Rum held in the University of Pennsylvania on the 30 July 1789. (Columbian Magaz. Y. 1790. Apr. p. 215.)

*BAYNTON, [Thomas] *Surgeon of Bristol.*
Descriptive account of a new method of treating old ulcers in the legs. 1797. 8. (2 sh. 6 d.) übers. in *Schreger's* und *Harless* Annalen der neuesten Engl. und Franz. Chir. u. Geburtshh. B. 1. S. 294. On nitrous acid in siphilis. (Medical Repository. Vol. 1. p. 278.) See *Rich. Nayler.*

*BAZELEY, [T....]
Sermons on various subjects. 1802. 8. (6 sh.)

*BEAN, [James] *Vicar of Olney, in Buckinghamshire and Curate of Carshalton, in Surry.*
The country minister's affectionate advice to a new married couple 17... Prayers for families; 17... Family worship; a course of morning and evening prayers for every day in the month. 1796. 8. (4 sh. 6 d.)
(Several single sermons.)

*BLANE,

*BEANE, [. . . . .] *Surgeon in the army.*
On the fever of Demerary. (Mem. of M. S. of L. Vol. 5. p. 333.)

*BEARD, [Henry] *of the Inner-Temple.*
Curfory remarks on the laws with refpect to the imprifonment of debtors. 1801. 8. (1 fh.)

BEARDSLEY, [Ebenezer] *M. Dr.*
Hiftory of a dyfentery, in the 22 Regt. of the late continental army, occafioned by the barrack's being over crowded and not properly ventilated. (American Mufeum Y. 1789. March. p. 249.)

*BEATON, [Angus] *Canongate, Edinburgh.*
On the art of making kelp and of increafing the growth of the marine plants from which it is made. (Tr. of Highland Soc. Vol. 1. p. 32.)

*BEATSON, [Alexander] *Lieutenant-Colonel.*
View of the origin and conduct of the war with Tippo Sultan, comprifing a narrative of the operations of the army under the command of Lieut. Gen. *George Harris* and of the fiege of Seringapatam. 1800. 4. (1 L. 11 fh. 6 d.)

BEATSON, [Robert] *Esq. F. R. S. E.* (late of his Maj. Corps Royal Engineers.)
born 1742 at Dyfart, in the county of Fife. Naval and military memoirs of Great-Britain from the Y. 1727 to the prefent time. Vol. 1–3. 1790. 8. (18 fh.) A new and diftinct view of the memorable action of the 27 of July 1778, in which the whole of the afperfions caft on the characters of the flag officers are fhewn to be totally unfounded and the mifcarriage traced to its true caufe. 1791. 8. (1 fh.) An effay on the comparative advantages of vertical and horizontal wind-mills: Containing a defcription of an horizontal wind-mill and water-mill, upon a new conftruction and explaining the manner of applying the fame principle to pumps, fluices, methods for moving boats or veffels — 1798. 8. (2 fh. 6 d.) On farm buildings in general. (Comm. to the B. of Agr. Vol. 1. p. 1.) On cottages. (Ibid. Vol. 1. p. 103.) Obfervations on making and repairing roads, wherein are fuggefted feveral improvements on their conftruction and on wheel

carriages. (Ibid. Vol. 1. p. 119.) Obfervations on embankments, explaining the nature and conftruction of thofe calculated for reclaiming lands from the fea, from rivers and from lakes, or for preventing encroachments and guarding againft inundations; with remarks on fome embankments already executed. (Ibid. Vol. 2. p. 281.)

BEATTIE, [James] *LL. Dr. F. R. S. Edin. Profeffor of Moral Philofophy — Aberdeen.*
born in the county of Kincardine, in Scotland 1735. died 1803. Aug. 18.
See Public Characters of 1801-1802. p. 449. Gentlem. Magaz. Y. 1803. Sept. p. 885.
Elements of moral fcience. Vol. 2. 1793. 8. (7 fh.) Effays; 1777. 4. überf. von C. *Meiners.* B. 1. 2. Leipzig. 1779. 8. Remarks on fome paffages of the 6 book of the Eneid. (Tr. of E. S. Vol. 2. p. 33.) The minftrel: in two books; with fome other poems; to which are added Mifcellanies by *James Hay Beattie**; With an account of his life and character. Vol. 1. 2. 1799. 8. (6 fh.)

*BEAVER, [George] *B. D. Rector of Trent, in the county of Somerfet and Weft-Stafford, cum Frome Billet, Dorfetfhire.*
Several fingle fermons.

BEAUFORD, [William] *A. M.*
A memoir refpecting the antiquities of the church of Killoffy in the county of Kildare; with fome conjectures on the origin of the ancient Irifh churches. (Tr. of J. A. 1789. p. 75. *c.*) A differtation on the reflection and refraction of light from vapours, fogs, mifts &c. with an account of fome curious phaenomena proceeding from thofe caufes, feen in Ireland in the Y. 1796. 1797. and 1801. (*Tilloch's* Philof. Magaz. Vol. 13. p. 336.) Some conjectures refpecting the origin of ftones which have been obferved to fall from the clouds. (Ib. Vol. 14. p. 148.) Caoinan: or fome account of the ancient Irifh lamentations. (Tr. of J. A. Vol. 4. p. 41. *a.*)

*BEAU-

* Affiftant Profeffor of Moral Philofophy and Logic in the Marifchal-college, Aberdeen. died 1790. Nov. 19.

*BEAUFORT, [Daniel Auguftus] *LL. D. Rector of Navan in the county of Meath and Vicar of Collon, in the county of Louth; M. R. I. A.*
Memoir of a map of Ireland, illuftrating the topography of that kingdom and containing a fhort account of its prefent ftate, civil and ecclefiaftical; with a complete index to the map. 1792. 4. (10 fh. 6 d.) The map 16 fh.

*BEAUFORT, [John] *LL. D.*
The daughter of adoption, a tale of modern times. Vol. 1-4. 1800. 12. (16 fh.)

BEAUFOY, [Henry] *Esq. M. P. for Great Yarmouth and Secretary to the board of Controul.*
born .... died 1795. May 17. at Clifton near Briftol.
See Gentleman's Magaz. Y. 1795. May. p. 445.

*BECK, [Edward]
Weight of a South-down fheep. (*Young's* A. of Agr. Vol. 26. p. 184.)

*BECK, [Thomas] *A diffenting minifter at London.*
The paffions taught by truth; an allegorical poem. 1795. 8. (1 fh.) *The miffionary, a poem; to which are fubjoined hints on the propagation of the gofpel at home and abroad. 1795. 12. (1 fh.)

*BECKE, [H ....] *Rev.*
Obfervations on the produce of the income tax, including important facts refpecting the wealth and population of this kingdom. 1799. (2 fh.)

BECKFORD, [Peter] *Esq. Of Steepleton, near Blandford, in the county of Dorfet.*
Thoughts upon hare and foxhunting, — alfo an account of the moft celebrated dog *Kennels* in the kingdom; illuftrated with 20 beautiful engravings; a new edition 1796. 8. (9 fh.)

BECKFORD, [William] *Esq. at Hertford, in Jamaica.*
Defcription of Jamaica. Vol. 1. 2. 1790. 8 (14 fh.) überf. Berlin. 1791. 8. The hiftory of France, from the moft early records, to the death of Louis XVI. The ancient part by *Will. Beckford*, Esq. — The modern part by an Englifh Gentleman, wo has been fome time refident in Paris. Vol. 1-4. 1794. 8. (1 L. 4 fh.) überf. B. 1-4. Leipzig. 1798. 8.

*BECKFORD, [William] *Esq. F. A. S. Of the seat at Fonthill, in Wiltshire.*

*Biographical memoirs of extraordinary painters. 1780. 12. *The history of the Caliph Vatheck. 17.., 8.

*BECKWITH, [John] *F. L. S.*

The history and descriptions of four new species of phalaena. (Transact. of L. S. Vol. 2. p. 1.)

BEDDOES, [Thomas] *M. Dr. Physician at Bristol. A native of Scotland.*

Observations on the nature and cure of calculus, sea-scurvy, consumption, catarrh and fever; together with conjectures upon several other subjects of physiology and pathology. 1793. (4 sh.) übers. B. 1. 2. Leipzig. 1794. 1796. 8. A letter to *Erasmus Darwin*, M. Dr. on a new method of treating pulmonary consumption and some other diseases hitherto found incurable. 1793. 8. (1 sh.) übers. Leipzig. 1794. 8. Observations on the nature of demonstrative evidence; with an explanation of certain difficulties occurring in the elements of geometry and reflections on language. 1793. 8. (3 sh. 6 d.) A guide for self-preservation and parental affection. 1793. 12. (3 d.) Letters from Dr. *Withering*, of Birmingham; Dr. *Ewart* of Bath; Dr. *Thornton* of London and Dr. *Biggs*, late of the isle of Santa Cruz; together with some other papers, supplementary to two publications on asthma, consumption, fever and other diseases. 1793. 8. (1 sh.) Considerations on the medicinal use of factitious airs and on the manner of obtaining them in large quantities, (published in association with *James Watt*, Engineer of Birmingham) P. 1. 2. 3. 4. 5. 1794-1796. (11 sh. 6 d.) übers. nach der 2. Ausg. von *C. Zollikofer* von Altenklingen. Halle. 1796. 8. The elements of medicine of *John Brown*, M. D. Translated from the latin, with comments and illustrations by the author: A new edition, revised and corrected. With a biographical preface and a head of the author. Vol. 1. 2. 1795. 8. (12 sh.) übers. von *T. Christie*. Kopenhagen. 1797.

1797. 8. *Where would be the harm of a speedy peace? 1795. 8. (3 d.) A word in defence of the bill of rights, against the gagging bills. 1795. 8. (3 d.) A new method of operating for the femoral hernia: Translated from the Spanish of Don *Antonio* De *Gimbernat*, Surgeon to the King of Spain; To which are added, with plates by the translator, queries respecting a safe method of performing inoculation and the treatment of certain fevers. 1795. 8. (2 sh. 6 d.). Case of phlegmonic inflammation, with reflections on certain effects of heat and cold on the living system. (*Simmons's* Medical facts and observations. Vol. 4. p. 148.) übers. Repert. chirurg. und Mediz. Abhandl. B. 2. S. 16. An account of the good effects of opium in the case of a person poisoned by digitalis. (Ibid. Vol. 5. p. 17.) Facts relative to the origin of intermittent fevers. (Ibid. Vol. 7. p. 26.) A letter to *William Pitt*, on the means of relieving the present scarcity and preventing the diseases that arise from meagre food. 1796. 8. (1 sh.) Essay on the public merits of Mr. *Pitt*. 1796. 8. (3 sh. 6 d.) Circular letter, respecting the use of the nitrous acid in the venereal disease. (*Duncan's* A. of Med. Y. 1797. p. 384.) Reports principally concerning the effects of the nitrous acid in the venereal disease by the surgeons of the Roy. hospital at Plymouth and by other practitioners. 1797. 8. (2 sh. 6 d.) übers. von Dr. *Fried. Goth. Friese*. Breslau. 1799. 8. Alternations compared; or, what shall the rich do to be safe? to which are prefixed, remarks on the management of the navy and on several recent occurrences. 1797. 8. (1 sh. 6 d.) A lecture introductory to a course of popular instruction on the constitution and management of human body. 1797. 8. (1 sh. 6 d.) Contributions to physical and medical knowledge, principally from the West of England. 1799. 8. (8 sh.) Notice of some observations made at the medical pneumatic institution. 1799. 8. (1 sh. 6 d.) Essay on the causes, early signs and prevention of pulmonary consumption; Ed. 2. much enlarged. 1799. 8. übers. von *L. S. Kramer*, Halberstadt. 1802. 8. A collection of testimonies respecting the treatment of the veneral disease by nitrous acid. 1799. 8. (5 sh.) übers. von *F. G. Friese*. Breslau. 1799. 8. Communications respecting the external and internal use of nitrous acid; demonstrating its efficacy in every form of venereal disease and extending its use to other complaints: with original facts and a preliminary discourse. 1800. 8. (4 sh.) Observations on the medical and domestic management of the consumptive; on the powers of digitalis purpurea and on the cure of scrophula. 1801. 8. (7 sh.) A collection of testimonies respecting the treatment of the venereal disease by nitrous acid. 1801. 8. (4 sh.) Hygëia; or, essays, moral and medical, on the causes affecting the personal state of our middling and affluent classes. Vol. 1–3. 1802. 8. (1 L. 4 sh.) Blue colours obtained from a substance found in smelting furnaces. (Mem. of M. Vol. 4. P. 2. p. 302) Some observations on the flints of chalk-beds; (Ibid. Vol. 4. P. 2. p. 303.) On *Kant's* philosophy. (Monthly Magazine Y. 1796. May. p. 265.) Etymological observations. (Ibid. Y. 1796. July. p. 441. Y. 1800. April. p. 210.) Account of a new insect (curculio anti-odontalgicus) said to be endowed with a remarkable property. (Ibid. Y. 1796. Nov. p. 792 Y. 1797. p. 4.) Letter on the pneumatic institution. (Ibid. Y. 1798. Oct. p. 238.) On teaching arithmetic and mathematics. (Ibid. Y. 1799. Oct. p. 678. cf Dec. p. 851.) Method to prevent the low fever. (Ibid. Y. 1802. Apr. p. 233.) *Th. Beddoes* and *Bradley*, an account of the discovery and operation of a new medicine for gout. 1803. 8. (4 sh.) Observations on the affinity between basaltes and granite. (Phil. Transact. Y. 1791. p. 48.) An account of some appearances attending the conversion of cast into malleable iron. (Ibid. Y. 1791. p. 173) Further observations on the process for converting cast, into malleable iron. (Ibid. Y. 1792. p. 257.) On the discovery of sulphate of Strontian, near Sodbury in Gloucestershire. (*Nicholson's* Journal. Vol. 3. p. 41. 94.) Letter respecting *Fourcroy's* account of the discoveries of *Mayow*. (Ibid. Vol.

3.

3. p. 108.) Account of the strange effects produced, by respiration of the gaseous oxide of azote. (Ibid. Vol. 3. p. 446.) On the experiments made at the Roy. Institut. with the nitrous acide. (Ibid. Vol. 4. p. 75.) On the means of foretelling the character of the summer season and the benefits to be expected from the cultivation of grasses which vegetate at low temperatures. (Ibid. Vol. 5. p. 131.) On prognostics of the weather, the effects of the nitrous oxide, and other objects. (Ibid. Y. 1802. Febr. p. 98.)

*BEDFORD, [.....] *Duke.*
The speech on the motion for an address to his Majesty, for the dismissal of his present ministry, with a copy of the address. 1798. 8. (6 d.)

*BEDFORD, [J....] *of Birch-Manor-Essex.*
On malt-dust as a manure. (Bath Agric. Soc. Vol. 3. p. 366.)

*BEE, [Thomas] *Esq.*
Method of making soap from myrtle wax. (American Museum Y. 1788. Nov. p. 436.)

*BEEKE, [Henry] *B. D.*
*Letter on the means of securing a safe and honourable peace. 1798. 8. Observations on the produce of the income-tax and on its proportion to the whole income of Great-Britain; including important facts respecting the extent, wealth and population of this kingdom. Part 1. 1799. 8. (2 sh.) A new and corrected edition with considerable additions respecting the extent, commerce, population, division of income and capital of this kingdom. 1800. 8. (3 sh. 6 d.)

*BEERE, [Richard] *Rector of Sudbrooke in Lincolnshire.*
An epistle to the chief priests and elders of the jews; containing an answer to Mr. *David Levi's* challenge — 1789. 8. (3 sh.) Dissertation on the 13 and 14 verses of the 8 Chapter of *Daniel*; containing — arguments to prove that the commencement of the final restoration of the jews to the holy land is to take place in the ensuing year A. D. 1791. To which is added an astronomical demonstration of the truth of the computations contained in this work — as also, a second

cond epiftle to the chief priefts and elders of the jews. 1790. 8. (2 fh.)

*BEEVOR, [Miles]

An account of the parifh of Hethel, in Norfolk. (*Young's* A. of Agr. Vol. 8. p. 187.) An experiment of feeding fheep with fpring-fown wheat. (Ibid. Vol. 8. p. 191.) Account of the parifh of Ketteringham, from 1700 to 1786. (Ib. Vol. 8. p. 345.)

*BEEVOR, [Sir Thomas] *Bart.*

On the culture of turnip-rooted cabbage. (Bath Agricult. Soc. Vol. 3. p. 110. Columbian Magaz. Y. 1790. Jan. p. 37.) Of the duration of the wood of different kinds of trees, in their different applications, when expofed to the weather. (Ibid. Vol. 3. p. 155.) Account of the origin, progrefs and regulations with a defcription of the newly eftablifhed Bridewell, or penitentiary houfe at Wymondham, in Norfolk. (Ibid. Vol. 3. p. 227. American Mufeum Y. 1789. Sept. p. 223. Dec. p. 456.) On fetting wheat. (Ibid. Vol. 3. p. 241. 369.) On the Suffolk breed of cows; raifing potatoes. (Ibid. Vol. 3. p. 280.) Value of turnip-rooted cabbage, as a fpring crop. (Ibid. Vol. 3. p. 380.) On the ufe and value of turnip-rooted cabbage. (Ibid. Vol. 4. p. 290.) On the mangel-wurzel, or fcarcity root. (Ibid. Vol. 4. p. 293.) Experiments on various forts of potatoes. (Ibid. Vol. 4. p. 297.) On the mangel-wurzel and a new drill roller. (Ibid. Vol. 5. p. 417.) On the turnip-rooted cabbage, roota-baga and potatoes. (Ibid. Vol. 5. p. 421.) On the roota-baga, the great value of potatoes to the poor and on turnip-rooted cabbage. (Ibid. Vol. 5. p. 457.) Queries of Mr. *Le Blanc*, refpecting the culture of turnip-rooted cabbages, with anfwers to the fame. (Bath Agricult Soc. Vol. 6. p. 87.) Letter on various fubjects. (Ibid. Vol. 6. p. 89.) On moving cabbage. (Ibid. Vol. 6. p. 101.) On accuracy in the characteriftick diftinctions of plants. (Ibid. Vol. 6. p. 103.) Value of land, with the rife and fall of the different publick funds. (Ibid. Vol. 7. p. 381.)

*BEHN

BEHN, [A....] Mrs.

A week's converſation on the plurality of worlds, by de *Fontenelle*. The 7 edit. with conſiderable improvements. Translated by Mr. *A. Behn*; Mr. *J. Glānvil; John Hughes* and *Will. Gardner*. 1801. 12. (3 ſh.)

***BELCHER, [William]** *Bookſeller in London.*

The galaxy; conſiſting of a variety of ſacred and other poetry. 1790. 4. (10 ſh. 6 d.) A ſong, entitled lamentations for the pope, the devil and the pretender. 1797.

BELCHER, [William] *Esq. of Ulcombe, near Maidſtone, Kent.*

Obſervations on the culture of lucerne. (*Young's* A of Agr. Vol. 1. p. 298.) General remarks on the hoſe-hoeing husbandry. (Ibid. Vol. 2. p. 187.) Miſcellaneous obſervations. (Ibid. Vol. 2. p. 343.) Draining and manure. (Ibid. Vol. 2. p. 399.) On the South down husbandry. (Ibid. Vol. 3. p. 133.) Summer fallowing defended. (Ibid. Vol. 3. p. 326. 450.) Obſervations on lucerne. (Ibid. Vol. 3. p. 435.) Reply to queries relative to mud as a manure for lucerne. (Ibid. Vol. 4. p. 34.) Miſcellaneous agricultural remarks. (Ibid. Vol. 4. p. 470.) On fallowing. (Ibid. Vol. 6. p. 18. Vol. 8. p. 121.) On hops. (Ibid. Vol. 7. p. 97.) Experiments in fallowing. (Ib. Vol. 7. p. 336. Vol. 8. p. 184.) On the evaporation of dung and earth., (Vol. 7. p. 466.) Speeding ſainfoine. (Ib. Vol. 7. p. 468.) Agricultural experiments. (Ib. Vol. 8. p. 118.)

BELKNAP, [Jeremy] *D. D. Miniſter of the church in federal-ſtreet, Boſton. Member of the Philoſ. Soc. in Philadelphia and of the Acad. of Arts and Sc. in Maſſachuſetts.*

born in Boſton, June 4. 1744. died 1798. July.

See the Weekly Magazine. Philadelphia. Vol. 2. Y. 1798. Nro. 23.

The hiſtory of new Hampſhire. Vol. 2. Boſton. 1791. 8. (9 ſh.) Vol. 3. 1792. (12 ſh.) überſ. in Hiſtor. Portefeuille. B. 6. 1786. Advantages of preſerving parsnips by drying. (Maſſachuſetts Magaz. Y. 1791. Oct. p. 597. Columbian Magaz. Y. 1791. p. 40.) American biography or an hiſtorical

ſtorical account of thoſe perſons who have been diſtinguiſhed in America as adventurers, ſtatesmen, philoſophers, divines, warriors, authors and other remarkable characters comprehending a recital of the events connected with their lives and actions. Vol. 1. 1793. (9 ſh.) Vol. 2. 1800. 8. Diſſertations on the character, death and reſurrection of Jeſus Chriſt and the evidence of his goſpel; with remarks on ſome ſentiments advanced in a book intitled "the age of reaſon." Boſton. 1795. 8. (3 ſh.) American antiquities. (Maſſachuſetts Magaz. Y. 1795. July. p. 195.) Sacred poetry; conſiſting of pſalms and hymns, adapted to chriſtian devotion in public and private: ſelected from the beſt authors, with variations and additions. Boſton. 1795. 8. ° The foreſters, an american tale; being a ſequel to the hiſtory of John Bull the clothier in a ſeries of letters to a friend. Ed. 2. reviſed and conſiderably enlarged. Boſton. 1796. Account of the mountain Agamenticus, ſix miles from Baldhead and eight from York harbour. (Coll. of Maſſachuſetts H. S. Y. 1794. p. 11.) Letter to Dr. *Kippis*, relative to an errour in his life of Capt. *Cook*, with ſeveral teſtimonies in evidence. (Ib. Y. 1795. p. 79. 98.) Letter containing ſome particulars relative to fire-engines, fires and buildings, at different periods, in Boſton. (Ibid. Y. 1795. p. 188.) Anſwers to the queries, propoſed by *Tucker* of Virginia, reſpecting the ſlavery and emancipation of negroes in Maſſachuſetts. (Ibid. Y. 1795. p. 191.) ° The diſcovery and deſcription of the islands called the Marqueſas, in the South pacific Ocean, with a farther account of the ſeven adjacent islands —; (Ibid. Y. 1795. p. 238.) *Obſervations on the islands of Juan Fernandez, Maſſafuero and St. Ambroſe, in the South pacific ocean and the coaſt of Chili in South-America. Extracted from the journal of Mr. *Bernard Magee*. (Ib. Y. 1795. p. 247.) An account of the diſcovery of a group of islands in the North pacific ocean by Capt. *James Magée* — (Ibid. Y. 1795. p. 261. 298.) *An account of the great fire in Boſton in the Y. 1711. (Ibid. Y. 1798. p. 52.)

52.). Advantages of preserving parsnips by drying. (American Museum Y. 1787. p. 455. Massachusette Magaz. Y. 1791. Oct. p. 596.) Observations on the aurora borealis March 1783. (American Museum Y. 1788. p. 29.) Description of the white mountains in New-Hampshire. (Ibid. Y. 1788. p. 128.) A discourse intended to commemorate the discovery of America by *Christopher Columbus* — —; Boston 1792. 8. (3 sh.)

BELL, [Andrew] *F. S. A. S. Engraver to his R. Highness' the Prince of Wales.*

See *Andrew Fyfe.*

***BELL**, [Andrew] *Rev.*

An experiment in education, made at the male asylum of Madras. 1798. 8. (1 sh.)

BELL, [Benjamin] *F. R. S. Ed. Member of the College of Surgeons of Ireland and Edinburgh.*

On the theory and management of ulcers — Ed 4. Edinb. 1787. übers. Neue Ausg. Leipz. 1792. 8. Zusätze von *E. G. Hebenstreit.* Leipz. 1793. 8. System of Surgery —; übers. Ausg. 2. Th. 1–5. Leipzig. 1792–1798. On gonorrhoea virulenta and lues venera. Vol. 1. 2. 1793. 8 (12 sh.) übers. B. 1. 2. Leipzig. 1794. 8. On the hydrocele, on sarcocele or cancer and other diseases of the testes. 1794. 8. (4 sh.) übers. von *E. G. B. Hebenstreit.* Leipzig. 1795. 8.

***BELL**, [Benjamin] *Member of the Royal Soc. of Edinburgh.*

Essays on agriculture; with a plan for the speedy and general improvement of land in Great-Britain. 1802. 8. (9 sh.) Information respecting the profits of husbandry and the means of preventing scarcity, in the answers of 25 gentlemen to queries. (Comm. and Agric. Magaz. Y. 1802. May. p. 348.)

***BELL**, [Charles] *Fellow of the R. College of Surgeons at Edinburgh.*

A system of dissections, explaining the anatomy of the human body, the manner of displaying the

the parts and their varieties in disease. With plates. Vol. 1. Part 1-5. Append. P. 1. 1799-1800. fol. (1 L. 11 sh. 6 d.) übers. Leipzig. 1800. 8. A series of engravings, explaining the course of nerves. 1803. 4. (1 L. 1 sh.)

BELL, [George] *Surgeon, Edinburgh.*
A treatise on the cow-pox —; 1802. 12. (3 sh.)

*BELL, [George] *M. Dr.*
Some remarks on the opinion that the animal body possesses the power of generating cold. (Columbian Magaz. Y. 1791. Aug. p. 110.)

*BELL, [George Joseph] *Advocate.*
On the law of bankrupcy in Scotland. Vol. 1. 1801. 8. (19 sh.)

*BELL, [James] *M. Dr: one of the Physicians of the Kelso dispensary; and formerly President of the Med. and Nat. histor. Societies of Edinburgh.*
born.... died at Bluecastle, in the parish of Westmoreland, in Jamaica. Jan. 15. 1801.
See Gentlem. Magaz. Y. 1801. Apr. p. 372.
Case of retroversion of the uterus, terminating in abortion and death. (Simmons's) Medical facts and observations. Vol. 8. p. 32.)

*BELL, [James] *D. D. Minister of Coldstream.*
Sermons, preached before the University of Glasgow. 1790. 8. (6 sh.)

*BELL, [John] *M. Dr: Physician in London: (Formerly Surgeon to the late 49. and to the 50 regiment of foot.)*
An inquiry into the causes which produce and the means of preventing diseases among British officers, soldiers and others in the West Indies. Containing observations on the mode of action of spirituous liquors on the human body. 1791. 8. (3 sh. 6 d.) Account of the cure of an obstinate head-ach by cold spring-water. (*Duncan's* M. C. Dec. 2. Vol. 6. p. 386.)

*BELL, [John] *Surgeon in Edinburgh.*
The anatomy of the human body Vol. 1. containing the bones, muscles and joints. Vol. 2. containing the heart and arteries. 1793. 1797. 8. (1 L. 10 sh.) Vol. 3. Part 1. containing the anatomy of the brain and description of the course of the nerves;

ves; Part 2. the anatomy of the eye and ear &c. with plates, published by *Charles Bell*. 1802. 8. (15 sh.) Engravings, explaining the anatomy of the bones, muscles and joints. (28 plates). 1794. (1 L. 1 sh.) Engravings of the arteries illustrating the second volume of the anatomy of the human body by *John Bell* and serving as an introduction to the surgery of the arteries. 1801. 8. (1 L. 1 sh.) The anatomy of the brain explained in a series of engravings. 1802. 4. (2 L. 2 sh.) Discourses on the nature and cure of wounds. 1795. 8. (7 sh. 6 d.) übers. von Dr. *J. C. F. Leune*. Th. 1. 2. Leipzig. 1798. 8. Answer for the junior members of the Roy. College of surgeons of Edinburgh to the memorial of Dr. *James Gregory's* memorial to the managers of the Royal Infirmary (of Edinburgh) 1800. 8. (4 sh.) The principles of surgery, as they relate to wounds, ulcers and fistulas, anevrisms and fractures of the limbs, and the duties of the military and hospital surgeon. Vol. 1. 2. 1801. 4. (4 L. 4 sh.)

*BELL, [John] *Esq. of Maryland.*

Sketches of the President of the United states Gen. *Washington*. (Massachusetts Magaz. Y. 1791. March. p. 139)

*BELL, [John] *at Woolwich.*

Observations on throwing a gun-harpoon. (Tr. of the Soc. for the E. of A. Vol. 11. p. 185.)

*BELL, [Joseph] *Esq. Advocate.*

A treatise on the law of bankruptcy in Scotland. Vol. 1. 1802. 8. (19 sh.)

*BELL, [Robert] *of Huntshill, near Jedburgh, North-Britain.*

born . . . . died . . . . (?)

An account of the improvements upon an extensive farm, containing a large portion of land lying waste and uncultivated. (Tr. of the Soc. for the E. of A. Vol. 17. p. 166.)

BELL, [Sir Thomas] *Knight. M. Dr. in Dublin.*

born . . . . died Nov. 1789.

*BELL, [William] *Surgeon in the service of the East-India Company at Bencoolen.*

Description of the double horned rhinoceros of Sumatra. (Phil. Transact. Y. 1793. p. 3.) De-

 scription

scription of a species of chaetodon, called, by the Malays, ecanbonna. (Ibid. Y. 1793. p. 7.)

BELL, [William] *D. D. Prebendary of St. Peter's Westminster and Vicar of Christ-church, London.*

Arguments in proof of the authenticity of the narratives of the extraordinary conception and birth of John the baptist and the miraculous conception and birth of Jesus Christ; contained in the two first chapters of the gospels of St. Matthew and St. Luke, 1795. 8. (2 sh.) An enquiry into the divine missions of John the baptist and Jesus Christ. Ed. 2. 1796. 8. (6 sh.)

***BELLAMY,** [Elizabeth]

The young lady's assistant, or, an easy introduction to english grammar. 1802. 12. (1 sh.)

***BELLAMY,** [J.....]

Jesus Christ the only god: being a defence of that fundamental doctrine of the christian religion against Arianism and Socinism. 1792. 8. (2 sh.)

***BELLAMY,** [Joseph] *D. D. Pastor at Bethlem, Connecticut.*

born at New-Cheshire, in the County of New-Haven 1719. died 1790. March 6.

See Evangelical Magaz. Y. 1799. Febr. p. 45.

Early piety recommended, a sermon from Eccl. XII, 1. 17... True religion delineated; 1750. Sermons on the divinity of Christ — the millennium — and the wisdom of God, in the permission of sin; 17... Dialogues on Theron and Aspasio; by Paulinus; 17... Essay on the gospel; 17... The great evil of sin; a sermon: 17... The law a school-master; a sermon; 17...

BELLAMY, [Thomas] *Bookseller in King-street, Covent-Garden, London.*

(Editor and publisher of the monthly mirror, a magazine). The benevolent planter; a dramatic piece; Ed. 2. 1792. (1 sh.) Miscellanies, in prose and verse. Vol. 1. 2. 1795. 8. (10 sh.) The school for libertines. (New-York Magaz. Y. 1795. Nov. p. 688.) Sadaski; or the wandering penitent; a novel. Vol. 1. 2. 1798. 8. (7 sh.)

*BELLEN-

*BELLENGER, [W.... A....] (?)
The french and english idioms compared —. 1801. 12. (2 sh. 6 d.)

BELOÉ, [William] *B. D: F. A. S: Rector of Allhallows, London-Wall.*
(a native of Norwich)
The history of *Herodotus*, translated from the greek, with notes. Vol. 1-4. 1791. 8. (1 L. 1 sh.) **Alciphron's* epistles: in which are described the domestic manners, the courtisans and parasites of Greece; now first translated from the greek. 1791. (5 sh.) The Attic nights of *Aulus Gellius*, translated into English. Vol. 1-3. 1795. Miscellanies, consisting of poems, classical extracts and oriental apologues. Vol. 1. 2 3. 1795. 12. (In association with *Nares*, *W. Tooke* and the late *Morrison*, edited the new edition of the *biographical dictionary* in 15 Voll. 8. In association with *Nares*, a principal conductor of the *British critic*, a review: An english translation of the *Arabian nights entertainments* and for *Joseph*, translated from the french of *Bitaubé*.)

*BELSHAM, [James]
*Essays philosophical, historical and literary. Vol. 1. 2. 1789. 1791. 8. (14 sh.) übers. Berlin u. Stralsund. 1798. 8.

*BELSHAM, [Thomas] *A socinian Minister at Hackney.*
The importance of truth and the duty of making an open profession of it; a sermon. 1790. Dishonest shame the primary source of the corruptions of the christian doctrine, a sermon. 1794. 8. Knowledge the foundation of virtue, a sermon. 1795. 8. (6 d.) Review of *Wilberforce's* treatise, entitled, a practical view of the prevailing religious system of professed christians. 1798. 8. (4 sh.) Elements of the philosophy of the mind and of moral philosophy. To which is prefixed a compendium of logic. 1801. 8. (9 sh.)

*BELSHAM, [William] *Esq. Resident at Bedford.*
*Observations on the test laws in reply to a review of the case of the protestant dissenters, 1791.

1791. 8. (1 sh.) Historical memoir on the french revolution, to which are annexed, strictures on the reflections of *Edm. Burke*. 1791. 8. (2 sh.) Examination of an appeal from the new to the old whigs, with an introduction, containing remarks on *Burke's* letter to a member of the national assembly. 1792. 8. (2 sh. 6 d.) Remarks on the nature and necessity of a parliamentary reform. 1793. 8. (1 sh. 6 d.) Memoirs of the Kings of Great-Britain of the house of Brunswic-Luneburg. Vol. 1. 2. 1793. 8. (1 L.) übers. (von *Canzler*) B. 1. 2. Hannover. 1795. 1798. 8. Memoirs of the reign of George III. to the session of Parliament ending A. D. 1793. Vol. 1. 2. 3. 4. 1795. 8. (1 L.) Vol. 5. 6. from the Y. 1796. to the commencement of the Y. 1799. 1801. 8. (18 sh.) History of Great-Britain from the revolution to the accession of the house of Hannover; Vol. 1. 2. 1798. 4. Vol. 3. 4. 5. — to the commencement of the Y. 1799. 4. (5 L. 5 sh.) Remarks on the observations of Major Scott, relative to the administration of *Warren Hastings*, Esq. in India. 1797. 8. Remarks on the bill for the better support and maintenance of the poor, now depending in the house of commons. 1797. 4. (1 sh.) Two historical dissertations; 1) on the causes of the ministerial secession A. D. 1717. 2) on the treaty of Hanover, concluded A. D. 1725. with some prefatory remarks, in reply to the animadversions of the Rev. *Will. Coxe* in his memoirs of Sir *Robert Walpole*. 1798. 8. (3 sh.) Vindication of two passages in his history of the house of Brunswick. (Monthly Magaz. Y. 1799. April. p. 182.) Remarks on a late publication, styled the history of the politics of Great-Britain and France. 1800. 8. (3 sh. 6 d.) Reply to *Herbert Marsh's* vindication of a late work, styled, a history of the politics of Great-Britain and France. 1801. 8. (2 sh. 6 d.) Remarks on the late definitive treaty of peace, signed at Amiens, March 25, 1802. 8. (2 sh.) Two historical dissertations on the Silesian war, and on the character and conduct of Louis XVI. 1800. 4 and 8.

* BELSHES,

*BELSHES, [R....] *Esq. of Greenyards.*
Inclosures in the county of Stirling. (*Young's* A. of Agr. Vol. 29. p. 137.) Carts. (Ibid. Vol. 29. p. 142.) Sheep. (Ib. Vol. 29. p. 144.) The Carron manufactory of iron. (Ibid. Vol. 29. p. 146.)

*BEND, [Joseph] *A. M: Assistant-Minister of Christ-church and St. Peter's.*
Discourse — on occasion of the death of Mrs. *Lucia Magaw* wife of the Rev. *Samuel Magaw*, D. D. Philad. (11 d.)

*BENEZET, [Anthony]
born . . . . died 1795.
See American Museum Y. 1788. Aug. p. 161. Y. 1791. Apr. p. 192. New-York Magaz. Y. 1795. Nov. p. 679. Y. 1797. March p. 142.
The plainness and innocent simplicity of the christian religion with is salutary effects, compared to the corrupting nature and dreadful effects of war. With some account of the blessings which attend on a spirit influenced by divine love, producing peace and good will to men. 1800. 12. (6 d.) The paradise of negro-slaves, a dream. (Columbian Magaz. Y. 1787. Jan. p. 235.) Letter on the slave trade. (American Museum Y. 1787. Febr. p. 128.)

*BENGER, [Elizabeth Ogiluy]
The female geniad, a poem; written at the age of thirteen. 1791. 4. (2 sh.)

*BENJOIN, [George] *of Jesus'-College, Cambridge.*
Jonah, a faithful translation from the original; with philosophical and explanatory notes: To which is prefixed, a preliminary dissertation, proving the genuiness, the authenticity and the integrity of the present text. 1796. 4. (10 sh. 6 d.) The integrity and excellence of scripture; a vindication of the so much controverted passages Deut. VII, 2–5 and XX., 16. 17., whereby the justness of the commands they enjoin are incontrovertibly proved, and consequently the objections of *Thom. Paine* and Dr. *Geddes* completely refuted. 1797. 8. (2 sh.)

BENNET, [Anna Maria] *Mrs.*
Anna or memoirs of a welsh heiress. Vol. 1–4. 1784. 12. Juvenile indiscretions, a novel. Vol. 1–5.

1-5. 1785. 8. Ellen, countess of Castle Howel; a novel. Vol. 1-4. 1794. 8. (14 sh.) The beggar girl and her benefactors. Vol. 1-7. 1797. 8. (1 L. 11 sh.)

BENNET, [Abraham] *M. A. Curate of Worksworth, in Derbyshire. F. R. S.*

born 1750. died May 1799.

See Gentlem. Magaz. Y. 1799. May. p. 442. Allg. Litterat. Zeit. ItBl. J. 1800. S. 663.

Letter on attraction and repulsion. (Mem. of M. Vol. 3. p. 116.) New experiments on electricity, wherein the cause of thunder and lightning as well as the constant state of positive or negative electricity in the air or clouds are explained; 1789. 8. (4 sh.) A new suspension of the magnetic needle, intended for the discovery of minute quantities of magnetic attraction; also an air vane of great sensibility with new experiments on the magnetism of iron-filings and brass. (Philos. Transact. Y. 1792. p. 81.)

***BENNET**, [Andrew] *of Tobago.*

Letters on various species of cotton. (Tr. of the Soc. for the E. of A. Vol. 1. p. 254.)

***BENNET**, [Edmund] *Esq. of Trimaton, near Saltash, Cornwall.*

Note concerning the use of sea sand as a manure in Cornwall. (*Young's* A. of Agr. Vol. 12. p. 34.)

***BENNET**, [George] *Minister of the Gospel in Carlisle.*

A display of the spirit and designs of those who, under pretext of a reform, aim at the subversion of the constitution and government of this kingdom. With a defence of ecclesiastical establishments. 1796. 8. (3 sh.) Olam Haneskamoth; or, a view of the intermediate state, as it appears in the records of old and new testament, the apocryphal books in heathen authors and the greek and latin fathers; with notes. 1801. (7 sh.)

BENNET, [John] *Curate of St. Mary's, Manchester.*

Strictures on the female education; 1787. Ed. 2. 1796. 8. (3 sh.) Letters to a young lady on a variety of useful and interesting subjects, calculated to improve the heart, to form the manners, and enlighten the understanding. Vol. 1. 2. Ed. 2. 1796.

1796. 8. (7 ſh.) (See American Muſeum Y. 1791. Aug. p. 72. Sept. p. 145. Oct. p. 200. Nov. p. 227. Y. 1792. Jan. p. 9. Febr. p. 70. March p. 91. Apr. p. 139. May. p. 193. June. p. 261.)
(Several ſingle ſermons.)

*BENNET, [Nehemiah]
Deſcription of the town of Middleborough, in the county of Plymouth: with remarks. (Coll. of Maſſachuſetts H. S. Y. 1794. p. 1.)

*BENNET, [William] *Formerly a Diſſenting Teacher.*
A conciſe view of religious worſhip and of the nature and order of new teſtament churches. 1784. 12.
(Several ſingle ſermons.)

*BENSELL, [George] *Dr. of Germantown.*
Caſe of hydrophobia. (Tr. of Phyſ. of Philadelphia. Vol. 1. P. 1. p. 238.)

*BENSON, [. . . .]
Inſurance againſt bankruptcy. (Comm. and Agric. Mag. Y. 1799. Nov. p. 224.)

*BENSON, [John]
An apology for the people called methodiſts, containing a conciſe account of their origin and progreſs, doctrine, diſcipline and deſigns. 1801.

BENSON, [Joſeph] *Preacher among the methodiſts.*
A defence of the methodiſts in five letters —; 1793. 12. (1 ſh.) A farther defence of the methodiſts, in 5 letters. Ed. 2. 1794. 12. (8 d.) A vindication of the people called methodiſts, in anſwer to a report from the clergy of a diſtrict in the dioceſe of Lincoln. 1800. 8. (6 d.) An apology for the people called methodiſts. —; 1801. 12. (4 ſh.)

BENSON, [Martin] *M. A. Miniſter in Tunbridge-Wells Chapel, Rector of Merſtham, Surrey.*
Sermons on various ſubjects, moral and theological. 1794. 8. (6 ſh.)

BENSON, [William] *M. A. of St. Mary-Hall, Oxon.*
Obſervations and reflections on the impropriety of interfering with the internal policy of other ſtates. 1802. (1 ſh.)

BENT, [William] *Bookſeller in London.*

A meteorological journal of the year 1789. kept in Pater Noſter row. London. 1790. 4.
A meteorological journal of the Y. 1793. 1794. 8. (1 ſh. 6 d.)
—— —— —— 1794. 1794. 8. (1 ſh. 6 d.)
—— —— —— 1795. 1795. 8. (2 ſh.)
—— —— —— 1796. 1797. 8. (2 ſh.)
—— —— —— 1797. — — (2 ſh.)
—— —— —— 1798. 1799. 8. (2 ſh.)
—— —— —— 1799. 1800. 8. (2 ſh.)
Eight meteorological journals of the Y. 1793 to 1800. kept in London; to which are added obſervations on the diſeaſes in the city aud its vicinity. Alſo an introduction, including tables from 8 preceding journals of the greateſt, leaſt and mean height of the barometer and thermometer in every month of the years 1785 to 1792. 1801. 8. (15 ſh.) A meteorological journal for the Y. 1802. 8. (2 ſh.)

BENTHAM, [James] *M. A. F. A. S. Prebendary of Ely, Rector of Bow-brick-hill in the county of Bucks and Domeſtic Chaplain.*

born 1708. died at Ely Nov. 17. 1794.
See Gentleman's Magaz. Y. 1794. Nov. p. 1062. Dec. p. 1151. Litterariſcher Anzeiger. Leipzig. J. 1801. N. 147. S. 1415. (cf. Gentleman's Magaz. Y. 1792. June. p. 579. Jul. p. 671.)

Queries offered to the conſideration of the principal inhabitants of the city of Ely and towns adjacent and of all the gentlemen elſewhere, who have any eſtates, or intereſt in, or regard for, the ſouth part of isle of Ely. Cambr. 1757. 8. A catalogue of the principal members of his church (Ely), viz. Abbeſſes, Abbots, Biſhops, Priors, Deans, Prebendaries, and Arch-Deacons, from the foundation of the church, A. D. 673 to the preſent Y. 1756. 1756. 4. Conſiderations and reflections upon the preſent ſtate of the fens near Ely. Cambr. 1778. 8.

BENTHAM, [Jeremy] *Esq. of Lincoln's Inn, Barriſter at Law.*

Supply without burthen, or eſcheat vice taxation — to which is prefixed a proteſt againſt law taxes ſhewing

shewing the peculiar mischievousness of all such impositions as add to the expense of an appeal to justice. 1795. 8. (3 sh.) Traités de legislation civile et penale; publiés en françois d'apres les Manuscrits, par *Et. Dumont.* T. 1. 2. 3. à Paris, 1802. 8. *Panopticon, .. 17 .. Situation and relief of the poor. (*Young's* A. of Agr. Vol. 29. p. 393.) Outline of a work entitled pauper management improved. (Ib. Vol 30. p. 89. 241. 393. 457. Vol. 31. p. 33. 169. 273.) 1 and 2 letter to Lord *Pelham*, — giving a comparative view of the system of penal colonization in New South Wales and the home-penitentiary system, prescribed by two acts of parliament of the Y. 1794 and 1799. 1802. 8. A plea for the constitution —, 1803. 8.

*BENTHAM, [Samuel] *Esq. London.*

On preserving fresh water sweet during long voyages. (Tr. of the Soc. for the E. of A. Vol. 19. p. 191; *Tilloch's* Philos. Magaz. Vol. 12. p. 12.)

*BENTLEY, [....]

(Author of some prologues and epilogues:) The prophet, a comic opera. 17..

*BENTLEY, [Elizabeth] *Of the city of Norwich; Daughter of a journeyman cordwainer.*

born at Norwich 1767.

Genuine poetical compositions, on various subjects. 1791. 8. (2 sh.)

*BENTLEY, [John]

The divine logos; or, Jehovah Elohim the only proper object of christian worship. 1803. (3 sh. 6 d.) Remarks on the principal aeras and dates of the ancient Hindus. (Asiat. Res. Vol. 5. p. 315.) On the antiquity of the Surya Siddhanta, and the formation of the astronomical cycles therein contained. (Ibid. Vol. 6. p. 540.)

*BENTLEY, [Richard] *A grandson of the celebrated critic Dr. Richard Bentley.*

Considerations on the state of public affairs, at the beginning of the Year 1796. 1796. 8. Considerations upon the state of public affairs, at the beginning of the Y. 1798. Part 1–3. 1798. 8.

BENTLEY, [Samuel] *of Uttoxeter.*
born 1720. died 1803. Febr. 28.
See Gentleman's Magaz. Y. 1803. April. p. 382. (An able supporter of the poetical department of "the lady's diary") An ode, on completing his 78 year. (Gentleman's Magaz. Y. 1803. April. p. 359.)

*BENTLEY, [Thomas]
Reason and revelation; or a brief answer to *Thomas Paine's* late work entitled, "the age of reason." 1794. 8.

*BENTLEY, [William] *Rev.*
Letter concerning the Abbé de *Mably.* (Coll. of Massachusetts H. S. Y. 1795. p. 157.) A description and history of Salem. (Coll. of Massachusetts H. S. Y. 1799. p. 212.) An address, delivered in the Essex lodge upon the festival of St. John the evangelist. Salem, 1799. 8.

*BENWELL, [Henry] *of Caversham, near Reading, Berkshire.*
On beans as a preparation for wheat. (*Young's* A of Agr. Vol. 4. p. 482.) Bean husbandry. (Ibid. Vol. 5. p. 47.)

*BENWELL, [William] *Rev.*
born, ... 1765. died at Milton in Wiltshire Sept. 6. 1796.
See Gentleman's Magaz. Y. 1796. Sept. p. 797. Y. 1797. Jan. p. 3.
The siege and pillage of Rome by Alaric. 1785. The superiority of the moderns over the antients in art and science. 1787.

*BERDMORE, [Samuel] *D. D. late Master of the Charter-house School.*
born 1739. died 20 Jan. 1802.
See Gentleman's Magaz. Y. 1802. Jan. p. 94.
Specimens of literary resemblance, in the works of *Pope, Gray* and other celebrated writers; with critical observations in a series of letters. 1801. 8. (4 sh.)

BERDMORE, [Thomas] *Surgeon-Dentist to the King.*
born . . . . died 178. (?)

*BERE,

*BERE, [Thomas] *M. A. Rector of Bubcombe near Bristol.*

The controversy between Mrs. *Hannah More* and the Curate of Blagden (in Somersetshire) relative to the conduct of her teacher of the sunday school in that parish; 1801. 8. (3 sh.) An appeal to the public on the controversy betwen H. *More*, the Curate of Blagden and — *A. Elton.* 1801. 8. (2 sh.) An address to *H. More*, on the conclusion of the Blagden controversy; with observations on anonymous tract entitled "a statement of facts." 1801. 8. (2 sh.)

*BERESFORD, [James] *Fellow of Merton-College; Professor at the University of Dorpat*

(He contributed the *Tour of Sentiment*; The imitations of modern history-writing, novel-writing and biography; The *Taylor's triumph* and the subsequent mock criticism; The caricature of Harvey in Covent-garden market; and The parody of *Milton's* Allegro; To the *Looker-on*; The caricature of the late Mr. *James Boswell*, as a biographer.) The Aeneid of *Virgil*, translated into blank verse. 1794. 4. (1 L. 5 sh.) The knights of the swan; or the court of Charlemagne; an historical and moral tale; translated from the french of Mad. *De Genlis*. Vol. 1. 2. 3. 1796. 8. (9 sh.) * The German Erato, or a collection of favourite songs translated into English, with their original music. Berlin. 1797. 4. * The German songster, or a collection of favourite airs with their original music, done into English by the translator of German Erato. Berlin. 1798. 4. A collection of german ballads and songs. Berlin & Leipzig. 1799. 4. Twelve favourite songs with their original music, done into English by the translator of the german Erato. Berlin. 1800. 8. *Elegant extracts in verse, selected from the best poets for the use of the learners of the english language; Berlin. 1801. 8. The most remarkable year in the life of *Augustus v. Kotzebue.* Vol. 1-3. 1802. 8. (15 sh.)

*BERESFORD, [John] *Right Hon.*

See Public Characters of 1798-1799. p. 372. Speech in the house of commons of Ireland, on his

his moving the 6 article of the union, relative to the future commercial arrangement between Britain and Ireland. 1800, 8. (1 sh.)

BERINGTON, [Joseph] *Rever.*

History of the lives of Abeillard and Heloisa — übers. von Dr. *Sam. Hahnemann*. Leipzig, 1789. 8. The state and behaviour of English catholics. 1780. übers. Tubingen. 1783. The memoirs of *Greg. Pancani*; giving an account of his agency in England in the Years 1634–1636. translated from the Italian original and now first published. 1793. 8. (6 sh.) An examination of events, termed miraculous, as reported in letters from Italy. 1796. 8. (1 sh.)

***BERKELEY**, [Elizabeth] *Mrs.*

(Daughter of Augustus late Earl of *Berkeley*; she was married May 10. 1767. to *William* Lord *Craven*, who died Sept. 26. 1791. and she married secondly Oct. 30. 1791. the Margrave of Brandenbourgh Anspach and Bayreuth.)

born 1734. died at Kensington Nov. 4. 1800.

See Gentlem. Magaz. Y. 1798. p. 773. Y. 1800. Nov. p. 1114. Allgem. Litterat. Zeit. ItBl. J. 1801. S. 839.

Heroic epistles; '17.. 8. Letters a son fils, traduites de l'anglois. a Paris. 1788, 12. Modern Anecdote —; 1787. 8. Le philosophe moderne; comedie en 3 actes. 1790. 8. Poems by the late *George-Monk Berkeley*, Esq. LL. B. F. S. S. A. with a preface by the editor, consisting of some anecdotes of Mr. *Monk Berkeley* and several of his friends. 1797. 4. (2 L. 12 sh. 6 d.) Dr. *George Berkeley's* sermons. 1799. 8. (5 sh.)

***BERKELEY**, [George] *LL. Dr. Prebendary of Canterbury, Chancellor of Brecknock, Rector of St. Clement Danes and Vicar of Coockham in the Diocese of Sarum.*

born Sept. 28. 1733. died Jan. 6. 1795.

See Gentlem. Magaz. Y. 1795. Jan. p. 85. Febr. p. 92. May p. 436. Sept. p. 739.

Sermons. 1799. 8. (5 sh.)

(Several single sermons.)

BERKE-

BERKELEY, [George Monk] *Esq. of the Inner Temple; LL. B: F. S. S. A.*

born, ... died Jan. 26. 1793.

See Gentlem. Magaz. Y. 1793. Febr. p. 185.

Poems — with a preface by the editor, consisting of some anecdotes of *G. M. Berkeley* and several of his friends. 1797. published by *Eliza Berkeley.*

*BERKELEY, [Robert] *of Virginia.*

An inaugural dissertation on sedatives. 1800.

BERKENHOUT, [John] *M. Dr. at Islewortk in Middlesex.*

born 1730. at Leeds in Yorkshire. died at Besselsleigh, near Oxford, April 3. 1791.

See Gentlem. Magaz. Y. 1791. April. p. 388. May. p. 485. *Duncan's* Med. Comment. Dec. 2. Vol. 6. p. 418. *Hutchinson's* Biographia Medica. Vol. 2. p. 543.

Dissertatio inauguralis de podagra. Edinb. 1765. Proposals for an history of Middlesex. Vol. 1–4. fol. 17.. Dr. *Campbell's* lives of the admirals; (were continued down to 1779. under the inspection of Dr. *Berkenhout* in a new edition). Vol. 1–4. 1779. 8. Pharmacopoea medica. Ed. 3. 1782. Letters on education to his son at Oxford. Vol. 1. 2. 1791. 12. (5 sh.)

BERNARD, [Sir Francis] *Baronet. Governor at Boston.*

born . . . . died 16 June 1779.

Letters on the trade and government of America and the principles of law and polity applied to the American colonies. 1774. 8. (2 sh.)

*BERNARD, [James] *Esq. of Crowcombe-Court near Taunton, Somersetshire.*

On the damage of fir-plantations; in reply to the enquiry instituted by this society, as before alluded to by Mr. *Davis* of Longleat. (Bath Agricult. Soc. Vol. 6. p. 259.) Account of an experiment made in the Y. 1788. in raising of the mangel-wurzel or root of scarcity. (Ibid. Vol. 5. p. 316.) On the cheapest mode of planting. (*Young's* A. of Agr. Vol. 4. p. 243.) Account of a lusus naturae. (Ibid. Vol. 17. p. 54.) On the parish of Crowcombe. (Ibid. Vol. 32. p. 623.)

*BERNARD,

*BETHAM, [William] *Rev. of Stonham Aspel Suffolk.*

Genealogical tables of the sovereigns of the world from the earliest to the present period. 1795. fol. (3 L. 13 sh. 6 d. common paper; 4 L. 14 sh. 6 d. fine paper; 6 L. 6 sh. best paper.) The history of English baronets, and such baronets of Scotland as are of English families. Vol. 1. 2. 1803.

*BEVAN, [B . . . .]

Meteorological journal for Leighton, Jan. – Dec. 1800. (Monthly Magaz. Y. 1800. Sept. Y. 1801. Febr. p. 25.) Meteorolog. journ. for Leighton, Y. 1801. Jan. – Dec. for the Y. 1802. (Ibid. Y. 1801. Sept. p. 91. Y. 1802. Febr. p. 3. Y. 1803. Aug. p. 14. Febr. p. 8.)

*BEVAN, [Joseph Gurney]

A refutation of some of the more modern misrepresentations of the society of friends, commonly called quakers; with a life of *James Nayler*; 1800. 8. (2 sh.)

*BEVAN, [Silvanus] *Esq. of Riddlesworth.*

South Down sheep in Norfolk. (*Young's* A. of Agr. Vol. 21. p. 218.) Live and dead weight of fourteen Scots. (Ibid. Vol. 23. p. 386.) Plan for regulating the wages of labourers. (Ibid. Vol. 26. p. 33.) Sheep and improvements. (Ibid. Vol. 32. p. 441.)

BEVER, [Thomas] *Esq. LL. D. Advocate of the Admiralty, Judge of the cinqueports, Chancellor of Lincoln and Bangor, and F. of All-souls College, Oxford.*

born . . . . died 1791. Nov. 8.

See Gentleman's Magaz. Y. 1791. Nov. p. 1068. Y. 1798. Sept. p. 753.

*BEVERLEY, [Charlotta] *Mrs.*

Poems on miscellaneous subjects, composed and selected. 1792. 8. (4 sh. 6 d.)

BEVERLEY, [John] *M. A. and Proctor of the Vice-Chancellour's court.*

The trial of *William Frend*, M. A. Fellow of Jesus College, Cambridge — for writing and publishing a pamphlet entitled "Peace and union recommended to the associated bodies of republicans and antirepublicans." 1793. 8. (2 sh.)

*BEVERLY,

*BEVERLY, [W.... M....]
On planting. (*Young's* A. of Agr. Vol. 6. p. 354.)

*BEVILL, [Robert] *Esq. of the Inner-temple; Barrister at law.*
A treatise on the law of homicide and of larceny at common law. 1798. 8. (6 sh.)

BEW, [George] *M. Dr. Physician at Manchester.*
Account of Dr. *Henry Moyes*, the blind philosopher. (Columbian Magaz. Y. 1791. March p. 173. Massachusetts Magaz. Y. 1791. Febr p. 99. New York Magaz. Y. 1794. April. p. 199.) Observations on blindness and on the employment of the other senses to supply the loss of sight. (American Museum Y. 1792. Jan. p. 27. Febr. p 58. March. p. 103. Massachusetts Magaz. Y. 1794. Aug. p. 484. Sept. p. 521.)

*BEWICKE, [Robert] *Merchant.*
Tables of the several European exchanges, shewing the value of any sum of money in all the principal places of Europe; to which is prefixed an account of the usances at which bills are drawn from the several places. Vol. 1. 2. 1802. 4. (4 L. 4 sh.)

*BEWIK, [John] *Engraver in wood.*
born; .... died at Ovingham, near Newcastle. Dec. 5. 1795.
See Gentleman's Magaz. Y. 1795. Suppl. p. 1113. Allg. Litter. Zeitung. ItBl. J. 1796. S. 267.
General history of quadrupeds. 1790. 8. (8 sh.) History of British birds with figures engraved on wood. Vol. 1. 1797. (10 sh. 6 d. Royal hot pressed, 13 sh. Super-royal, 18 sh. Imperial 1 L. 1 sh.) See *Josiah Relph.*

*BEWLEY, [Richard] *M. Dr.*
A treatise on air, containing new experiments and thoughts on combustion; being an full investigation of *Lavoisier's* system; and proving by some stricking experiments, its erroneous principles, with strictures upon the chemical opinions of some eminent men. 1791. 8. (3 sh. 6 d.)

*BICHENO, [James] *M. A: A baptist minister of Newbury in Berkshire.*
A friendly address to the Jews. 1787. 8. The signs of the times; or, the overthrow of the papal

pal tyranney in france, the prelude of destruction to popery and despotism. Part 1. 1792 8. (1 sh. 6 d.) P. 2. 1794. (1 sh. 6 d.) A word in season; or, a call to the inhabitants of Great-Britain to stand prepared for the consequences of the present war. 1795. 8. (1 sh 6 d.) The probable progress and issue of the commotions which have agitated Europe since the french revolution; acquired from the aspect of things and the writings of the prophets. 1797. 8. (2 sh.) A glance at the history of christianity and of English non conformity; Ed. 3 with additional notes and a postscript on the present movement in the East. 1798. 8. (1 sh.) The restoration of the jews, the crisis of all nations — 1800. 8. (2 sh. 6 d) The destiny of the german empire, or, an attempt to ascertain the apocalyptic dragon and to shew that the binding of the dragon, that old serpent the devil and satan and the millenary state are likely to be altogether different from what christian writers have taught us to expect. 1801.

*BICKERSTAFF, [. . . .] *at Newport.*

On the use of bustlers. (American Museum T. 1787. Nov. p. 482.)

BICKNELL, [Alexander]

born . . . . died . . . . (?)

History of England and the British empire; designed for the instruction of youth, with an essay on the english constitution. 1791. 8. (3 sh. 6 d.) Painting personified, or, the caricature and sentimental pictures of the principal artists of the present times, fancifully explained. Vol. 1. 2. 1792. (6 sh.) Instances of the mutability of fortune, selected from ancient and modern history and arranged according to their chronological order. 1792 8. (6 sh.)

*BIDDLE, [Clement] *Marshal for the district of Pennsylvania.*

The Philadelphia directory, 1791. (4 sh.)

*BIDDULPH, [Thomas T . . . .] *A. M.*

An elegy, occasioned on the death of *Will. Bromley Cadogan* A. M. who died Jan. 18. 1797. — 1797. 4. (6 d.) Essays on some select parts of the liturgy of the church of England; being the sub-

substance of a course of lectures delivered in the parish church of St. Werburgh's, Bristol. 1798. 12. (5 sh., 6 d.) Letter to *John Hey*, occasioned by his late publication, entitled „The important question at issue &c. 1801. 8. (9 d.) An appeal to public impartiality, or the manner in which the dispute concerning „the important question at issue" has been conducted. 1801. 8. (9 d.)

'**BIDLAKE**, [John] *B. A. Chaplain to the Duke of Clarence and Master of the Grammar school, Plymouth.*

See Public Characters of 1800 & 1801. p. 248.

Free-mason sermon. 1787. 4. (1 sh.) Sermon on the slave trade. 1789 4. (1 sh.) Sermon, sunday schools recommended, 1787. 4. (1 sh.) Elegy, supposed to be written on revisiting the place of a former residence. 1788. 4. Ed. 2. 1790. 4. (1 sh.) Poems. 1794. 4. (8 sh. 6 d.) Poems. Nrb. 1. 2. 3. 1802. (3 sh.) Sermons on various subjects. Vol. 1. 1795. Vol. 2. 1799. (11 sh.) The sea, a poem in 2 books. 1796. 8. (4 sh. 6 d.) The country parson, a poem. 1797. 8. (1 sh.) Eugenio, or the precepts of Prudentius, a moral tale. 1799. 12. (2 sh. 6 d.) The summer's Eve; a poem 1800. 8. (4 sh.) Virginia, or the fall of the decemvirs, a tragedy. 1800. 8. (1 sh. 6 d.) Youth, a poem. 1802. 8. (1 sh. 6 d.) (In periodical publications have appeared, „An ode to the snow-drop; „the natural child, an elegy, and an ode to the evening star;)

(Several single sermons.)

BIGGE, [Thomas] *A. M.*

Considerations on the state of parties and the means of effecting a reconciliation between them, 1794. 8. (1 sh.) An address to the inhabitants of Northumberland and Newcastle upon Tyne, who petitioned against the two bills lately depending in parliament. 1795. 8. (2 d.)

'**BIGGIN**, [George] *Esq.*

Experiments to determine the quantity of tanning principle and gallic acid contained in the bark of various trees. (Phil. Transact. Y. 1799. p. 259. *Nicholson's* Journal. Vol. 3. p. 392. *Tilloch's* Philos. Magaz. Vol. 5. p. 321.)

G 2 *BIG-

*BIGLAND, [John]

Reflections on the resurrection and ascension of Christ; and on the probable consequences of a public exhibition of his ascension, which some think necessary to the credibility of the fact. 1803. 8. (2 sh. 6 d.)

*BIGLAND, [Richard] *Esq.* (Son of *Ralph Bigland.*)

Historical, monumental and genealogical collections, relative to the county of Gloucester; printed from the original papers of the late *Ralph Bigland*, Esq. Garter principal king of arms. 1791. fol. (3 L. 3 sh.)

*BIGLAND, [William]

The mechanic's guide; or, a treatise on the laws of mechanics as they relate to wheel machines. 1797. 8. (1 sh. 6 d.)

*BILLINGSLEY, [John] *Esq. of Ashwick-grove near Shepton-Mallet, Somersetshire.*

Account of the culture of carrots, and thoughts on burn baiting on mendip-hills. (Bath Agricult. Soc. Vol. 1. p. 214.) On the profit of carrots and cabbages. (Ib. Vol. 2. p. 225.) Remarks on the superior advantage of dairy to arable farms, by *Thomas Davis.* (Ibid. Vol. 3. p. 77.) Account of the culture and produce of six acres of potatoes, on land of the value of 20 s. an acre. (Ibid. Vol. 3. p. 102.) Culture, expences and produce of 6 acres of potatoes, being a fair part of near 70 acres. (Ibid. Vol. 3. p. 114.) On the backwardness of the west-country farmers to use the Norfolk plough. (Ibid. Vol. 3. p. 368.) On the culture of potatoes and feeding hogs with them, during seven years. (Ibid. Vol. 6. p. 339.) A particular return of an experiment made in sheep-feeding. (Ibid. Vol. 7. p. 352.) General view of the agriculture of the county of Somerset, with observations on the means of its improvement. 1797. 8. (6 sh.) Culture, expence, and produce of six acres of potatoes, being a fair part of near 70 acres of that root raised in the Y. 1783. 1784. (*Young's* A. of Agr. Vol. 2. p. 439.) Culture, expences and produce of 20 acres inclosed and burthened with an entire circular fence, in which experi-

experiment a complete ſummer fallow is allowed. (Ibid. Vol. 5. p. 288.) On the culture of potatoes. (Ib. Vol. 21. p. 1.) On drilling. (Ib. Vol. 23. p. 508.) Appendix to the third report from the ſelect committee appointed to take into conſideration the preſent high price of corn. (Ib. Vol. 26. p. 335. 364.) Dairy farm in Somerſetſhire. (Ib. Vol. 30. p. 392.) Riſe of rents in Somerſetſhire. (Ib. Vol. 30. p. 436.) Uſeleſsneſs of commons to the poor. (Ibid. Vol. 30. p. 27.) Mode and expence of improving land lying waſte. (Tr. of the Soc. for the E. of A. Vol. 15. p. 172.)

BINGFIELD, [William]

The voyages, ſhipwreck, travels —. 1799. 8. (1 ſh.)

BINGHAM, [George] *B. D. Fellow of All-ſouls College, Oxford, and Rector of Pimperne and of More Critchell in the county of Dorſet.*

born; .... died Oct. 11. 1800. at Pimperne. See Gentleman's Magaz. Y. 1800. Oct. p. 1012. Allgem. Litterat. Zeit. IntBl. J. 1801. S. 838.

BINGHAM, [Thomas]

The triumph of truth; or proofs of the authenticity of the bible, interſperſed with thoughts on modern infidelity and on the moral, political and religious revolutions of the preſent age. 1800. (3 ſh. 6 d.)

BINGLEY, [Robert] *Esq. King's Aſſaymaſter, Mint, London.*

On the ſtrength of acids, as indicated by the ſpecific gravity and by the areometer of M. *Baumé.* (*Tilloch's* Philoſ. Magaz. Vol. 12. p. 35.)

BINGLEY, [William] *B. A. Fellow of the Linn. Soc. and late of St. Peter's College, Cambridge.*

A tour round North-Wales, performed during the ſummer of 1798, containing not only the deſcription and local hiſtory of the country but alſo a ſketch of the hiſtory of the welſh bards; an eſſay on the language; obſervations on the manner and cuſtoms and the habitudes of above 400 of the more native plants, forming the compleateſt account of that romantic country. Illuſtrated with views in aqua-tinta, by *Alken.* Vol. 1. 2. 1800. 8. (1 L. 1 ſh.) Animal biography; or, anecdotes of the lives manners and economy of the animal creation, arranged according to the system of *Linnaeus*. Vol. 1–3. 1802. 8. (27 sh.)

BINGLEY, [William] *Warehouseman to Mr. John Nichols; formerly a printer and publisher.* born 1738. died Oct. 23. 1799.

See Gentleman's Magaz. Y. 1799. p. 995. Allg. Litt. Zeit ItBl. J. 1800. S. 663.

Publisher of North Briton. 1768–1771. *Velly's* history of France, translated from french. Vol. 1. 1769. *Bingley's* Journal. 1770. Essay on the Baultine fires in Ireland. (Gentlem. Magaz. Y. 1795 March. p. 201.) *Smithfield market; an essay against carcase butchers, monopolisers, forestallers and regraters; including heads of a bill for regulating the sale of cattle and other live stock in the London market. To which are added, remarks on the report of the committee of carcase butchers published by *Henry King* and *J. Edmunds*. 1796. A letter on stones falling from the air, a natural phaenomenon. (Gentleman's Magaz. Y. 1796. Sept. p. 726.) An examination into the discontents in Ireland, with remarks on the writings and interference, ex officio of *Arthur Young*, Esq. 1799. 4. (2 sh. 6 d.) An examination into the origin and continuance of the discontents in Ireland: the true cause of the rebellion; being a faithfull narrative of the particular sufferings of the Irish peasantry; with a plan which, if adopted, cannot fail to bring back the roman catholic insurgents to their allegiance; without injury to the protestant interest; without emancipation, which they never asked; a union, or the aid of an extra military force. To which is annexed a specimen of Irish anecdotes. 1799. 4. (2 sh. 6 d.)

*BINNS, [Abraham]

Remarks on a publication intitled, a serious admonition to the disciples of *Thomas Paine* and other infidels. 1796. 8. (6 d.)

*BINNS, [Jonathan] *F. M. S. Physician to the Liverpool Dispensary.*

History of the treatment of haemorrhages; with a successfull case of amaurosis by *James Gerard*. (Mem. of M. S. of L. Vol. 4. p. 348.)

BIRCH,

BIRCH, [John] *Surgeon to St. Thomas Hospital, London; before Army-Surgeon.*
On electricity, explaining fully the principles of that science and the most approved instruments and apparatus, both to illustrate the theory and render the practice useful and entertaining. With a letter on medical electricity. Ed. 4. with 6 plates, 1798. Letter to Mr. *George Adams* on the subject of medical electricity. 1792. 8. übers. Repertor. Chir. u. Mediz. Abhandl. B. 2. S. 439. An essay on the medical application of electricity. 1803. 8. (2 sh. 6 d.)

'BIRCH, [John]
On drill husbandry. (*Young's* A. of Agr. Vol. 14. p. 319.)

'BIRCH, [J.... E.... R....]
Discovery of septic acid in the alimentary faeces of a person desperately sick of yellow fever. (Medical Repository. Vol. 3. p. 307.)

'BIRCH, [Samuel] *Deputy of Cornhill-ward.*
The mariners, a musical entertainment, in 2 acts, 1793. The adopted child, a musical drama, in 2 acts. 1795. 8. (1 sh.) The smugglers, a musical drama, in 2 acts. 1796. 8. (1 sh.) Fast asleep, a farce. 1797.

'BIRCHALL, [Samuel] *of Leeds.*
A descriptive list of the provincial copper coins or tokens issued between the Years 1786 and 1796, arranged alphabetically. 1797.

'BIRD, [.....]
*The laws respecting landlords, tenants and lodgers, laid down in a plain, easy and familiar manner; and free from the technical terms of the law; — 1794. 8. (2 sh. 6 d.) Ed. 2. enlarged and improved. 1795. 8. (2 sh.) *The laws respecting masters and servants, articled clerks, apprentices, journeymen and manufacturers; — 1795. 8. (2 sh.) *The laws respecting wills, testaments, and codicils and executors and administrators; — 1795. 8. (2 sh.) Ed. 3. corrected and much enlarged. 1799. 8. (2 sh. 6 d.) The laws respecting parish matters, containing the several offices and duties of church-wardens, overseers of the poor, constables, watchmen, and

G 4 other

other parish officers —. Ed. 2. improved and much enlarged. 1799. 8. (2 sh. 6 d.)

*BIRD, [Henry Mertons] *Esq.*

Proposals for paying of the whole of the present national debt and for reducing taxes immediately. 1799. 8. (1 sh. 6 d.)

*BIRD, [James Barry] *Esq. of New-inn, Conveyancer.*

The new pocket conveyancer, or attorney's complete pocket-book —. Vol. 1. 2. 1796. 8. (9 sh.) An assistant to the practice of conveyancing; containing indexes or references of the several deeds, agreements and other assurances — from the time of Sir Orlando Bridgman to the present period, with short remarks —. 1796. 12. (3 sh.) Original precedents of settlements drawn by the most distinguished conveyancers of the present day and now first published. 1800. 8. (9 sh.)

*BIRD, [John]

The castle of Hardayne, a romance. Vol. 1. 2. 1795. (6 sh.)

BIRD, [William] *Surgeon at Chelmsford, Essex.*

A chemosis, or tumour of the tunica conjunctiva cured by excision. (Mem. of M. S. of L. Vol. 4. p. 105.) Case of an anevrism upon the tunica vaginalis propria testis, successfully treated. (Ibid. Vol. 4. p. 406.)

*BIRRELL, [Andrew]

Henry and Almeria, a tragedy. 1802. (2 sh. 6 d.)

*BIRT, [Isaiah] *Minister of the Baptist church at Plymouth Dock.*

A vindication of the baptists, in 3 letters. Bristol. 1795.

*BISHOP, [Samuel] *M. A. Head-master of Merchant Taylor's school, Rector of St. Martin, Outwich, London and of Ditton in the County of Kent and Chaplain to the Bishop of Bangor.*

born 1732. died Nov. 17. 1795.

See Gentleman's Magaz. Y. 1795. Nov. p. 972. Dec. p. 994.

Feriae poeticae s. carmina Anglicana — latino reddita. 1766. 4. (10 sh. 6 d.) Sermon. 1783. 8. (6 d.) Poetical works — to wich are prefixed memoirs of the life of the author, published by *Thomas*

Thomas Clare. Vol. 1. 2. 1796. 4. (2 L. 2 ſh.) Sermons, chiefly upon practical ſubjects; publiſhed by *Thomas Clare.* 1798. 8. (6 ſh.)

*BISHOP, [Sir William] *Knight. Surgeon at Maidſtone in Kent.*

A caſe of dropſy, in wich the water has been twice drawn off by tapping the vagina. (M. C. Vol. 2. p. 360.) An account of the good effects of a decoction of peach leaves, in ſome affections of the urinary paſſages. (*Simmons's* Med. facts and obſervat. Vol. 8. p. 122.)

*BISHOPRIC, [Robert] *Surgeon at York.*

Caſe of aſcites of ſix months continuance, cured in a month by the exhibition of an infuſion of tobacco. (*Duncan's* M. C. Dec. 2. Vol. 8. p. 382.) Caſe of a general lympho-cruſtaceous eruption of the body, of many years continuance, cured in 5 months by a courſe of alterative pills, compoſed of calomel and golden ſulphur of antimony. (Ibid. Dec. 2. Vol. 8. p. 387.) A cancer-like caſe of the uterus cured by a courſe of mercurial antimonial pills. (Ibid. Dec. 2. Vol. 9. p. 257.) A caſe of obſtinate conſtipation of the bowels, ariſing from an accumulation of faeces in the rectum, cured chiefly by manual operation. (Ibid. Dec. 2. Vol. 10. p. 340.) Account of a medicine which he has found highly efficacious in caſes of uterine haemorrhagy. (Ibid. Dec. 2. Vol. 10. p. 359.)

BISSET, [Charles] *M. Dr: Phyſician at Knayton Yorkſhire.*

born 1717, at Glenalbert, near Dunkeld, in Perthſhire, died at Kneyton near Thirſk June 14. 1791.

See Gentleman's Magaz. Y. 1791. June. p. 588. Oct. p. 965. *Duncan's* Med. Comment. Dec. 2. Vol. 6. p. 427.

An eſſay on the theory and conſtruction of fortifications. 1751. 8. A caſe of an extraordinary irritable ſympathetic tumor; (Mem. of M. S. of L. Vol. 3. p. 58.)

*BISSET, [J....]

A poetic ſurvey round Birmingham; with a brief deſcription of the different curioſities and manufactories of the place, intended as a guide to ſtran-

G 5

occasioned by an attempt to abolish subscription to the 39. Art. 1772. 4.

BLACKBURNE, [Francis] *M. A. Archdeacon of Cleveland.*
born .... died 178. (?)
See Gentleman's Magaz. Y. 1789. Febr. p. 128. Monthly Magaz. Y. 1796. Dec. p. 887. Y. 1797. May p. 355. Y. 1799. July p. 461. Y. 1800. Febr. p. 19.

BLACKBURNE, [William] *M. Dr. F. A. S.*
On caloric, light and colours. (*Tilloch's* Philos. Magaz. Vol. 6. p. 334.)

BLACKLOCK, [Thomas] *LL. Dr. at Edinburgh.*
born at Annan in Scotland 1721. died Jul. 14. 1791. (He was totally deprived of his eyesight by the small pox.)
See Gentleman's Magaz. Y. 1791. July p. 685. Sept. p. 867.
Remarks on the nature and extent of liberty, as compatible with the genius of civil societies; on the principles of government, and the proper limits of its powers in free states; and on the justice and policy of the American war; occasioned by perusing the observations of Dr. *Price* on these subjects. Edinb. 1776. 8.
See *Elizabeth Scot* and *Henry Mackenzie.*

***BLACKMAN**, [George]
Method of making oil colour cakes. (Tr. of the Soc. for the E. of A. Vol. 12. p. 271.)

BLACKSTONE, [Henry] *Esq. of the Middle Temple.*
Reports of cases argued and determined in the court of common pleas, (from Easter term, 1788, to Hilary term 1796) Vol. 1. 2. 1788-1796. fol. (4 L. 4 sh.) Ed. 3. corrected with additional notes and improved indexes, Vol. 1. 2. 1801. 8. (2 L. 2 sh.)

***BLACKWALL**, [Jonathan] *at Goory near Londonderry.*
Divine and interesting extracts; or the selected beauties of *Joseph Hall*, D. D. Bishop of Exeter and Norwich, selected and arranged. 1796. 8. (7 sh.)

BLAGDEN,

BLAGDEN, [Sir Charles] *Knight: M. Dr. F. R. S. F. A. S.*

born 1748. April 17.

Report on the best method of proportioning the excise upon spirituous liquors. (Phil. Transact. Y. 1790. p. 321.) Supplementary report — (Ibid. Y. 1792. p. 425.) Account of the tides at Naples. (Ibid. Y. 1793. p. 168.)

***BLAGDEN**, [Francis] *Esq. Professor of the French, Italian, Spanish and German languages.*

Travels in Egypt — by *Vivant Denon*, translated without abridgment: ornamented with engravings and two correct maps of upper and lower Egypt. Vol. 1. 2. 1803. 18. (large paper, 14 sh. Small paper, 10 sh.) — and *F. Prevost*, Mooriana, or, select extracts from the moral, philosophical and miscellaneous works of the late Dr. *John Moore*; —; Vol. 1. 2. 1802. 8. (10 sh.) — and *F. Prevost*, Flowers of literature for 1801–1802. or, characteristic sketches of human nature, and modern manners. To which is added, a general view of literature during that period: with notes, historical, critical and explanatory. Vol. 1. (to be continued annually) 1803. 12. (5 sh.) Modern discoveries; or, a collection of facts and observations principally relative to the various branches of natural history — —. Vol. 1. 2. 1802. 12. (10 sh.) The grand contest deliberately considered; or, a view of the causes and probable consequences of the threatened invasion of Great-Britain. With a sketch of the life and actions of the first Consul; particularly since the peace of 1802. 1803. 8. (1 sh.)

***BLAGDEN**, [R . . . . . B . . . . .] *Surgeon at Petworth, Sussex.*

Tracts relative to pemphigus; (*Simmons's* Medical facts and observ. Vol. 1. p. 105.) übers. *Koch's* Samml. Auserles. Abhandl. B. 14. S. 673. Case of emphysema, brought on by severe labour pains. (Ibid. Vol. 2. p. 45.) übers. Repertor. Medic. u. Chirurg. Abhandl. B. 1. S. 234. Account of the spontaneous cure of an aneurism. (Ibid. Vol 2. p. 48.)

p. 48.) übers. Repert. M. u. Chir. Abh. B. 1. S. 307. An account of the good effects of a mercurial snuff in a case of gutta serena. (Ibid. Vol. 4. p. 126.) übers. Repertor. M. u. Chir. Abh. B. 2. S. 187.

*BLAINE, [Delahere] *Professor of animal medicine.*
A concise description of the distemper in dogs; with an account of the discovery of an efficacious remedy for it. 1800. 18. (6 d.) The outlines of the veterinary art; Vol. 1. 2. 1802. 8. A domestic treatise on the diseases of horses and dogs — 1803. 12. (3 sh. 6 d.)

BLAIR, [Hugh] *D. D. F. R. S. E. Emeritus Professor of Rhetorik in the University of Edinburgh.*
born at Edinburgh April 1718. died Dec. 27. 1800.
See Public Characters of 1800 & 1801. p. 288. Gentleman's Magaz. Y 1801. Jan. p. 84. Monthly Magaz. Y. 1801. March. p. 182. *Wieland's* N. Teutscher Mercur. J. 1801. Febr. S. 150. Allgem. Litter. Zeit. J. 1801. ItBl. S. 739. Der Biograph. Halle. 1802. B. 1. St. 3. S. 303. *Hüttner's* Englische Miscellen. 1801. B. 2. St. 1. S. 26.
Sermons; Vol. 4. 1794. 8. (6 sh.) Vol. 5. to which is annexed a short account of the life and character of the author by *James Finlayson* D. D. 1801. 8. (7 sh.) übers. Th. 3. 4. von *Sack* u. *Schleiermacher*. Leipzig. 1791. 1795. 8. Sermons on practical subjects by *Robert Walker* — (died 1783) to which is prefixed, a character of the author by *Hugh Blair*. Vol. 1-3. new edition 1791. 8. (15 sh.) The compassion and benevolence of the deity, a sermon. 1796. 8. (1 sh.)

*BLAIR, [Robert] *M. Dr.*
Experiments and observations on the unequal refrangibility of light. (Tr. of E. S. Vol. 3. p. 3. *Nicholson's* Journal. Vol. 1. p. 1.)

*BLAIR, [William] *A. M. Surgeon to the Lock-Hospital and the old Finsbury Dispensary.*
The soldiers friend; or, the means of preserving the health of military men; 1798. 8. (2 sh. 6 d.) Essays on the venereal disease and its concomitants affections

affections illustrated by a variety of cases. Essay I. Part 1. 1798. 8. (4 sh.) Part 2. 1800. 8. (6 sh.) übers. von Dr. C. *A. Struve*, Th. 1. Glogau. 1799. Th. 2. 1801. 8. An account of the extraction of an extraneous substance from the rectum; (*Simmons's* Med. Facts; Vol. 6. p. 111.) A short memoir on the antivenereal effects of several acids and other remedies, which have been lately proposed as substitutes for mercury in the cure of siphilis. (Mem. of M. S. of L. Vol. 5. p. 282.) An obstruction of the oesophagus removed by a tobacco glyster, on the third day after the accident. (Ibid. Vol. 5. p. 328.) On nitrous acid in venereal disease. (Monthly Magaz. Y. 1798. Jan. p. 2. Febr. p. 85.)

*BLAIRDINN, [J....]

Powers of genius. Newyork. 1800. 8.

*BLAIREC, [.....] *M. Dr.*

The anatomy of the horse; with plates. 1798. fol.

BLAKE, [Sir Francis] *Bart.*

born .... died 1780. March 29.

On the best proportion for steam engine cylinders of a given content. (Phil. Transact. Y. 1752. p. 379.) Spherical trigonometry reduced to plain. (Ibid. Y. 1752. p. 441.) On the greatest effects of engines, with uniformly accelerated motions. (Ibid. Y. 1752. p. 1.)

BLAKE, [Sir Francis] *Bart: Of Twisel-castle, Durham.*

The efficacy of a sinking fund of one million per annum considered. 1785. 8. (1 sh.) The propriety of an actual payment of the public debt considered. 1786. 8. (1 sh.) The true policy of great Britain considered. 1787. 8. (1 sh.) Political tracts. 1790. 8. (5 sh.) Ed. 2. 1795. 8. (5 sh.)

*BLAKE, [George] *Superintendant to his Maj. breweries in the late war.*

Strictures on a new mode of brewing, lately introduced into his Maj. brewhouse, London, by *Long*, Esq. of Dublin. 1791. 8. (3 sh.)

*BLAKE

*BLAKE, [Mark]
Letter to the clergy of the church of Scotland. 1794. 8. (6 d.)

*BLAKE, [Sir Patrick] *Bart.*
Culture of fugar in the Weft-Indies. (*Young's* A. of Agr. Vol. 31. p. 359-388.)

*BLAKE, [Robert] *M. Dr.*
An effay on the ftructure and formation of the teeth in man and various animals; the domeftic as well as chirurgical treatment of the teeth and gums, from infancy to the adult ftate, particularly explained. 1801. 8. (15 fh.)

*BLAKELEY, [Jofiah] *Baltimore.*
On the retreat of fwallows. (American Mufeum Y. 1788. May. p. 451.)

*BLAKEY, [.....]
A fhort hiftorical account of the invention, theory and practice of fire machinery; or, introduction to the art of making machines, vulgarly called fteam-engines —. 1793. 8. (1 fh.)

BLAND, [Robert] *M. D. F. A. S. Phyfician man-midwife to the Weftminfter general difpenfary.*
Account of two cafes of haematuria. (London M. J. Vol. 4. p. 282.) überf. Samml. F. A. Th. 15. S. 31. Some account of the invention and ufe of the lever of *Roonhuyfen.* (M. C. Vol. 2. p. 397.) Obfervations on human and on comparative parturition. 1794. 8. (4 fh. 6 d.)

*BLAND, [William] *Esq. of Sittinghourn in Kent.*
Experiment on the converfion of a hop-ground to corn land, with obfervations on the culture of beans. (*Young's* A. of Agr. Vol. 9. p. 23.) On a courfe of crops. (Ibid. Vol. 10. p. 539.)

BLANE, [Gilbert] *M. Dr. F. R. S. Phyfician extraordinary to the Prince of Wales, Phyfician to his Roy. Highnefs Houfehold and one of the Commiffioners of the fick and wounded Office.*
Account of the nardus Indica or fpike-nard. (Philof. Transact. Y. 1790. p. 284. *Simmons's* Medical facts and obfervat. Vol. 1. p. 153.) überf. Repertor. Chir. u. Medic. Abhandl. Th. 1. S. 336. A lecture on mufcular motion; 1791. 4. (2 fh.) Obfervations on the difeafes of feamen. Ed. 3. with

with corrections and additions. 1799. 8. (8 sh.) Account of a case in which death was brought on by a haemorrhage from the liver. (Transact. of Med. and Chir. Soc. Vol. 2. p. 18.) On the effect of the pure fixed alkalis and of lime-water, in several complaints. (Ibid. Vol 2. p. 132.) History of some cases of disease in the brain, with an account of the appearances upon examination after death, and some general observations on complaints of the head. (Ibid. Vol. 2. p. 192.) Letters on the present scarcity. (*Young's* A. of Agr. Vol. 36. p. 28.)

*BLAQUIERE, [. , . . .] *Captain of the Roy. Irish Artillery.*

The history of the 30 years war in Germany; translated from the original german of *Fred. Schiller.* Vol. 1. 2. 1799. 8. (12 sh.)

*BLAQUIERE, [W. . . . C. . . .]

The rudhiradhyaya, or sanguinary chapter; translated from the calica puran. (Asiat. Ref. Vol. 5. p. 371.)

BLAYNEY, [Benjamin] *D. D: Regius Professor of Hebrew and Canon of Christchurch, Oxford; Rector of Polshot.*

born 1728. died at Polshot, Wilts. Sept. 20. 1801.

See Gentleman's Magaz. Y. 1801. Nov. p. 1054. Pentateuchus Hebraeo - Samaritanus, charactere hebraeo chaldaico. Oxon. 1790. 8. Zachariah, a new translation, with notes, critical, philosophical and explanatory; and an appendix in reply to Dr. *Eurleigh's* sermon on Zach. 2, 8-11. to which is added (a new edition, with alterations) a dissertation on Daniel 9, 20. to the end, 1797. 4. (10 sh. 6 d.)

(Several single sermons.)

*BLANEY, [Joseph] *Esq.*

— — and *Samuel Barton's* letters on the culture of hemp. (American Museum. Y. 1787. May. p. 425.)

*BLEAMIRE, [William] *Esq. Barrister at Law and one of the police magistrates.*

Remarks on the poor laws and the maintenance of the poor. 1800. (2 sh.)

*BLEGBOROUGH, [Ralph] *M. Dr.*

Facts and observations respecting the air-pump, vapour-bath, in gout, rheumatism, palsy and other diseases. 1803. 8. (3 sh. 6 d.)

*BLEWERT, [William]

Tables for buying and selling stock; 17.. Perpetual and determinable annuities reduced to a level; or, a comparative view of long and short annuities. 1792. 12. (5 sh. 3 d.)

*BLICK, [Francis] *M. A: Vicar of Tamworth in Warwickshire.*

Sermon on John VII, 17. delivered in the parish-church of Sutton-Coldfield, Jan. 30. 1791. with the letters that have passed between him and the Rev. *John Riland*, A. M. Rector, respecting it. 1791. 8.

BLIGH, [William] *Post-Captain in his Maj. Navy.*

A voyage to the South-Sea, undertaken by command of his Maj. for the purpose of conveying the bread-fruit tree to the West-Indies in his Maj. Ship the Bounty. 1792. 4. (12 sh.) Answer to certain assertions, contained in the appendix to a pamphlet, entitled, „minutes of proceedings on the court-martial held at Portsmouth, August 12. 1792. on ten persons charged with mutiny on board his Maj. ship the bounty. 1794. 4. (2 sh.) A list of plants delivered by him at the botanical garden St. Vincent's. (Tr. of the Soc. for the E. of A. Vol. 12. p. 309.) Account of plants landed at Jamaica. (Ib. Vol. 12. p. 313.) Account of the result of his voyage to procure plants in the South-Sea. (Ib. Vol. 12. p. 316.)

*BLISS, [John] *Surgeon.*

Experiments and observations on the medicinal waters of Hampstead and Kilburn. 1802. 8. (2 sh.)

BLIZARD, [William] *F. R. S: F. A. S. Correspondent of the R. S. of Gottingen; Surgeon to the London Hospital,* —

Observations on some epidemical effects (*Simmons's* Med. facts and observ. T. 2. p. 105.) Suggestions for the improvement of hospitals and other charitable institutions. 1796. 8. (3 sh. 6 d.) übers. mit Zus. von *J. A. Albers*, Jena. 1799. 8. A lecture on on the situation of the large blood-vessels of the extremities, and the method of making effectual pressure on the arteries, in cases of dangerous effusions of blood from wounds. Ed. 3. to which is now added, a brief explanation of the nature of wounds, more particularly those received from fire-arms. 1798. 12. (3 sh.)

*BLOMEFIELD, [Francis] *Rector of Fersfield, Norfolk.*
born 1706; died Jan. 5. 1796.
S. Allg. Litt. Zeit. IrBl. J. 1800 S. 625.
History of Norfolk, Fersfield. Vol. 1. 2. 3. 1739.

*BLOOMFIELD, [Nathaniel]
An essay on war, in blanck verse; Honington green, a ballad; the culprit, an elegy; and other poems, on various subjects. 1803. 12. (4 sh.)

*BLOOMFIELD, [Robert] *a Schoemaker.*
born at Honington, Suffolkshire, Dec. 3. 1766.
See *Hüttner's* Englische Miscellen. J. 1800. St. 3. S. 143.
The farmers boy; a rural poem, in four books; with ornaments, engraved in wood by *Anderson.* 1800. 8. (5 sh.) Leipzig. 1801. (12 gr.) Rural tales, ballads and songs. 1802. 8. (4 sh.)

*BLORE, [Thomas] *Esq. F. A. S. Of the Soc. of the Middle Temple.*
History of the manor and manor-house of South Winfield, in Derbyshire: (Published in Nro III. of the miscellaneous antiquities; in continuation of the bibliotheca Brittannica.)

*BLOUNT, [Delabene]
A treatise on the diseases of horses and dogs. 1803. 12. (3 sh. 6 d.)

*BLOUNT, [J....] *Surgeon of Birmingham.*
Case of fractured skull. (Mem. of M. S. of L. Vol. 3. p. 605.)

*BLOWER, [Anne] *Miss.*
The maid of Switzerland. (American Museum Y. 1790. April. p. 216. June. p. 328. New-York Magaz. Y. 1796. Sept. p. 490.)

BLOWER, [Eliza] *Miss.*
born at Worcester 1763.
The parsonage-house; Vol. 1. 2. 3. 1780. 12.

*BLUNDEL, [James] *of Delaware.*
On the dysentery. 1791.

*BLUNT, [Gregory] *Esq.*
Six more letters to *Granv. Sharp*, on his remarks upon the uses of the article in the greek testament. 1803. 8.

BLUNT, [J....]
Man-midwifery dissected; or, the obstetric family instructor — in XV letters. 1790. 12. (3 sh. 6 d.)

*BLUNT, [James T.....] *Ensign.*
A description of the cuttub minar. (Asiat. Res. Vol. 4. p. 313.)

BLUNT, [Robert] *Surgeon at Odiham, in Hampshire.*
born .... died 178. (?)

*BOADEN, [James] *of the Soc. of the Middle Temple.*
The prisoner, a musical romance in 3 acts. 1792. 8. Fontainville forest, a play, in 5 acts 1794. 8. (1 sh. 6 d.) The secret tribunal, a play, in 5 acts. 1795. 8. (2 sh.) A letter to *George Steevens*, Esq. containing a critical examination of the papers of *Shakespeare*, published by *Sam. Ireland.* To which is added extracts from Vortigern. 1796. 8. (2 sh. 6 d.) The Italian monk, a play, in 3 acts. 1797. 8. (2 sh.) Cambro-Britons, an historical play in 3 acts. 1798. 8. Aurelio and Miranda; a drama, in 5 acts, with music. 1799. 8. (2 sh.) A rainy day, or poetical impressions during a stay at Brighthelmstone in the month of July. 1801. 4. (2 sh.) The voice of nature; a play. 1803. 8. (2 sh.) The maid of Bristol, a comedy; with an address to the patriotism of the British people, as an epilogue written by *George Colman*, jun. 1803. (2 sh.)

*BOAG, [William] *Surgeon in the service of the East-India Company at Bombay.*
Observations on the fevers and dysentery of hot climates; and on the use of mercury in those diseases. (*Simmons's* Med. facts and observat. Vol. 4. p. 1.) übers. Repert. Chir. u. Medic. Abh. B. 2. S. 153. Observation on the poison of serpents. (Asiat. Res. Vol. 6. p. 103.)

*BOAK,

*BOAK, [John] *Rector of Brockley.*
Letter to the Rev. *T. Bere*, Rector of Butcombe. 1801. 8. (4 d.) Elucidations of character, occasioned by a letter from the Rev. *R. Lewis*, published in the Rev. *T. Bere's* address to Mrs. *H. More* —. 1802. 8. (6 d.)

*BOARDMAN, [James]
Linguet's critical analysis and review of all Mr. *Voltaire's* works, with occasional disquisitions on epic poetry, the drama, romance —. 1790. 8. (3 sh. 6 d.)

*BOARDMAN, [Thomas] *Veterinary surgeon to the 3d Regt. of Dragoons.*
A dictionary of the veterinary art. Part 1. 1802. 4.

*BOARDMAN, [William]
On harrows. (Comm. and Agric. Mag. Y. 1801. p. 41.) A system of book keeping, on a plan entirely new. 1802. 4. (5 sh.)

*BOBBIN, [Paul] *a fictitious name.*
A dish of hodge podge, or, a collection of poems. 1800. 8. (1 sh.)

S. BOGART, [David]
An oration on the importance and utility of history. (American Museum Y. 1792. Febr. p. 43.) On the duty and propriety of contentment in every condition of life. (New-York Magaz. Y. 1791. July. p. 382.)

*BOGLE, [Robert] *Esq.*
On transplanting and dividing the roots of wheat and of harrowing and rolling the crop. (Bath Agricult. Soc. Vol. 3. p. 338.) On the very great advantages which may be derived from setting out plants of wheat and other kinds of corn, in the autumn, winter and spring. (Ibid. Vol 3. p. 383.) On the hastings turnip. (*Young's* A. of Agr. Vol. 6. p. 424.) Roota Baga. (Ibid. Vol. 11. p. 342.)

*BOGUE, [David]
An essay on the divine authority of the new testament. 1801. (3 sh. 6 d.)

*BOLINGBROKE, [. . . . . .]
Six letters, addressed to *Fitzwilliam*, Earl, and

Lord Lieut. of Ireland. Dublin. 1795. 8. Letters, addressed to *Will. Pitt.* 1796. 8. Letter addressed to a noble Lord, by way of reply to that of *Edmund Burke*. 1796. 8.

*BOLLAND, [William] *M. A. of Trinity College, Cambridge.*

Miracles, a Seatonian prize poem. 1799. 4. (1 fh.) The epiphany, a Seatonian prize poem. 1799. 4. (1 fh.) St. Paul at Athens, a Seatonian prize poem. 1800. 4. (1 fh.)

*BOLTON, [George] *Esq. Teacher of Geography, the use of the globes.*

Remarks on the prefent defective ftate of fire-arms — with an explanation of a newly invented patent gun lock —. 1795. 8. (1 fh.)

BOLTON, [James] *Of Halifax. Natural hiftory painter and Member of the natural Soc. at Edinburgh.*

An hiftory of funguffes —, Vol. 3. 1789. Vol. 4. Appendix or Supplement: 1791. (coloured 2 L. 2 fh. plain 18 fh.) überf. von Dr. C. L. *Willdenow.* Th. 1-3. Berlin. 1795. 1799. 8. Filices Britannicae; — Appendix 1790. (18 fh.) Natural hiftory of Britifh fong-birds; Vol. 1. 2. 1794. 4.

*BOLTON, [William] *of the navy.*

Defcription of his machine for drawing bolts in and out of fhips. (Tr. of the Soc. for the E. of A. Vol. 16. p. 318. *Tilloch's* Phil. Magaz. Vol. 3. p. 189.)

*BOND, [Thomas] *M. Dr.*

On the ufe of the bark in fcrophulous cafes. (American Mufeum. Y. 1787. Nov. p. 464.) Account of a worm bred in the liver. (Ib. Y. 1787. Dec. p. 570.)

BONHOTE, [Elizabeth] *Mrs.*

Olivia; Vol. 1. 2. 3. 1787. 12. The parental monitor; Vol. 1-4. 1797. Bungay caftle, a novel; Vol. 1. 2. 1796. 8. (7 fh.) Rambles of Mr. Frankly; Vol. 1-4. 17 . . 12. On the choice of a husband. (Maffachufetts Magaz. Y. 1795. May. p. 92.)

BONNER,

*BONNER, [J....]
On the nature and uses of honey. (Comm. and Agric. Mag. Y. 1802. p. 189.)

*BONNER, [J....] *Engraver.*
The copper plate perspective itinerary; or pocket port. Numb. 1. 2. 1799. fol. (15 sh.)

*BONNOR, [Charles] *Resident Surveyor and Deputy Comptroller General of the Post-Office.* —
Mr. *Palmer's* case explained. 1797. (1 sh.) To *Benj. Hobhouse*, Esq. M. P. on the subject of Mr. *Palmer's* claim. 1800. Vindication against certain calumnies — on the subject of Mr. *Palmer's* claim. 1800. 4. (2 sh. 6 d.)

BOOKER, [Luke] *LL. Dr: Minister of St. Edmund's, Dudley.*
Sermons on various subjects, intended to promote christian knowledge and human happiness. 1792. 8. (6 sh.) Miscellaneous poems. 1793. 8. (3 sh. 6 d.) Malvern a descriptive and historical poem. 1798. 4. (3 sh. 6 d.) The Hop-garden, a didactic poem. 1799. 8. (3 sh.) A discourse, chiefly addressed to parents on the duty and advantages of inoculating children — with the cow-pox. 1802. Poems, inscribed to — Lord Viscount *Dudley* and *Ward*, having a reference to his Lordship's beautiful seat of Himley. 1802. 4. (2 sh.) Calista; or, a picture of modern life; a poem in three parts. 1803. (2 sh. 6 d.)
(Several single sermons.)

*BOOTE, [John] *of Atherstone upon Stower.*
Letters on drill husbandry. (Tr. of the Soc. for the E. of A. Vol. 5. p. 80.) His reason for failure of some crops. (Ib. Vol. 5. p. 89.) Experiments to determine the comparative advantage of the drill and broad-cast husbandry. (Ib. Vol. 6. p. 74. Vol. 7. p. 16.)

BOOTH, [Abraham] *A Dissenting Minister: (He was formerly a journeyman-weaver.)*
On the reign of grace. 17..12. The christian triumph on the death of Mrs. *Ann Williams*, a sermon. 1772. 8. (6 d.) The death of legal hope, the life of evangelical obedience. 1770. 8.

H 4 (1 sh.

(1 ſh. 6 d.) An eſſay on the kingdom of Chriſt. 1788. 12. (1 ſh.) Commerce in the human ſpecies and the enſlaving of innocent perſons, inimical to the laws of Moſes and the goſpel of Chriſt, a ſermon. 1792. 12. (3 d.) A defence of paedobaptiſm examined; or, animadverſions on Dr. *Williams's* antipaedobaptiſm examined. 1792. 8. (4 ſh.) Glad tidings to periſhing ſinners —; 1795. 8. (2 ſh. 6 d.) Ed. 2. 1800. 8. (3 ſh.)

*BOOTH, [John] *Rev.*

Medullae ſeu radices inſigniores linguae graecae, ordine grammatico; 1801. 4.

*BOOTHBY, [Sir Brooke] *Bart. of Aſhbourne-Hall, in Derbyſhire.*

A letter to — *Edmund Burke.* 1791. 8. (2 ſh. 6 d.) Obſervations on the appeal from the new to the old whigs, and on Mr. *Paine's* rights of man; Part 1. 2. 1792. 8. (5 ſh.) Sorrows; ſacred to the memory of Penelope and miſcellaneous poems. 1796. fol. (1 L. 1 ſh.)

*BORDLEY, [John Beale] *Esq. of Maryland.*

Account of his own and Mr. *Singleton's* experiments, deſigned to aſcertain, with what quantity of ſeed ſown and at what diſtance wheat grows beſt. (Columbian Magaz. Y. 1786. Nov. p. 128.) Account of his experiments in ſowing wheat and clover; (Ibid. Y. 1787. Jan. p. 222.) A new method of reaping wheat. (Ib. Y. 1788. Sept. p. 510.) Some account of treading - out wheat. (American Muſeum Y. 1790. Febr. p. 64. March. p. 121.) Obſervations on raiſing ſheep. (Ib. Y. 1791. p. 112.) Eſſays and notes on husbandry and rural affairs. Philad. 1799. 8. (10 ſh. 6 d.) The courſes of crops of England and Maryland compared. (*Young's* A. of Agr. Vol. 9. p. 511.)

*BORROWE, [.....] *M. Dr.*

Caſe of lumbar abſceſs, remarkable for the circumſtances attending the diſcharge of pus. (Medical Repoſitory. Vol. 1. p. 371.)

BORTHWICK, [George] *M. Dr. Phyſician, Kilkenny.*

The hiſtory of a caſe terminating fatally from ſwallowing a plumbſtone. (*Duncan's* A. of Med. Y. 1796. p. 349.) The hiſtory of three caſes, with

with circumſtances ſomewhat ſingular: terminating favourably; 1) a caſe of wounded kidney, 2) a caſe of inguinal hernia; 3) a caſe of cataract, cured by extraction of the cryſtalline lens. (Ibid. Y. 1799. p. 466.)

BOSANQUET, [John Bernard] *Esq. of Lincoln's-Inn. Barriſter at Law.*
— — and *Chriſtopher Puller*, Reports of caſes argued and determined in the courts of common pleas and exchequer chamber from eaſter term 1796 to ——. Vol. 1. 1800. fol. Vol. 2. 1802. (4 L. 2 ſh.) Vol. 3. Part 1. 2. 3. 1803.

BOSCAWEN, [William] *Esq. Barriſter at Law.*
On convictions on penal ſtatutes. 1792. 8. (4 ſh.) The works of *Horace*, tranſlated into engliſh verſe. Vol. 1. 2. 1793. 1797. 8. (16 ſh.) The progreſs of ſatire, an eſſay in verſe: with notes, containing remarks on the purſuits of litterature. 1798. 8. Supplement. 1799. 8. Poems. 1801. 12. (3 ſh.)

BOSTOCK, [John] *M. Dr.*
Outline of the hiſtory of galvaniſm: with a theory of the action of the galvanic apparatus. (*Nicholſon's* Joutnal Y. 1802. Aug. p. 296. Sept. p. 3.) On the theory of galvaniſm. (Ibid. Y. 1802. Oct. p. 69.)

BOSWELL, [Edward]
A digeſt of the acts of parliament for raiſing a proviſional force of cavalry for the defence of theſe kingdoms, to the end of the laſt ſeſſion 37. Geo. 3. with notes and obſervations. Part 1. 1798. 12. (1 ſh.)

BOSWELL, [George]
A treatiſe on watering meadows — Ed. 3. with conſiderable additions. 1792. (3 ſh. 6 d.) Deſcription of a newly-invented machine for raking ſummer-corn ſtubbles. (Bath Agricult. Soc. Vol. 1. p. 44.) On watering meadows; and the kinds of water found moſt efficacious for that purpoſe. (Ibid. Vol. 2. p. 85.) Deſcription of the model of a Norfolk plough. (Ibid. Vol. 2. p. 351.)

BOSWELL, [J....] *Esq.*
Some particulars concerning the eſcape of the

grandson of King James 2. (New-York Magaz. Y. 1792. May. p. 265.)

BOSWELL, [James] *Esq.*

born in Edinburgh Oct. 29. 1740. died May 19. 1795.

See Gentleman's Magaz. Y. 1795. May. p. 445. June p. 469. 471. 487. 525.

Account of Corsica — and memoirs of *Pascal Paoli* — (letztere übers. im Hannöverschen Magaz. J. 1769) The life of *Sam. Johnson*, L. L. D. Vol. 1. 2. 1791. 4. (2 L. 2 sh.) Ed. 2: revised and corrected. Vol. 1-4. 1799. 8. (1 L. 8 sh.) The principal corrections and additions to the first edition of the life of Dr. *Johnson*. 1793. 4. (2 sh. 6 d.)

*BOSWELL, [John Whitley]

A description of a new instrument called the blast ventilator. (*Nicholson's* Journal. Vol. 4. p. 4.) übers. von *J. C. Hofmann.* Leipzig. 1801. 4. Apparatus for making the hydraulic engine at Schemnitz work itself without attendance. (Ibid. Vol. 4. p. 117.) Improvements in the hydraulic engine of Schemnitz and that of Mr. *Goodwyn*; with comparative remarks on the most useful applications of each and some facts relative to the invention of the pressure engine. (*Nicholson's* Journal Y. 1802. May. p. 1.) Description of his machine for netting. (Tr. of the Soc. for the E. of A. Vol. 14. p. 273.)

*BOSWELL, [T...]

Answer to *Ford's* questions relative to the management of bees. (Comm. and Agric. Magaz. Y. 1801. p. 270.)

*BOUCHER, [Jonathan] *M. A: F. A. S. Vicar of Epsom in Surrey.*

A view of the causes and consequences of the American revolution; in 13 discourses, preached in North-America between the years 1763 and 1775 with an historical preface. 1797. 8. (9 sh.) Two assize sermons, preached at Guilford and Carlisle. 1798. 4.

*BOUGHTON, [Sir C.... W.... Rous] *Bart.; M. P: Chairman of the Meeting.*

Substance of an address to a parochial meeting held at Chiswick in the county of Middlesex, Febr. 20. 1798. to consider the propriety of a voluntary

tary contribution for the defence of the country. 1798. 8. (1 sh.)

*BOURNE, [Robert] *Mr. Dr: Chemical Reader in the University of Oxford.*

An introductory lecture to a course of chemistry — 1797. 8. (2 sh.) Oratio in theatro Coll. Reg. Med. Lond. ex Harveji instituto habita die Oct. 18. An 1797. 1797. 4. (3 sh. 6 d.)

*BOURNE, [Samuel] *Minister of a dissenting chapel at Norwich.*

born 1713. died Oct. 1796.

See Gentleman's Magaz. Y. 1796. Oct. p. 881. Monthly Magaz. Y. 1796. Dec. p. 917. Allg. Litt. Zeit. IBl. J. 1800. S. 629.

Sermons. Vol. 1-3. 1758. 1777. Reply to Dr. *Sam. Chandler* in defence of the eternity of hell torments. 1759.

*BOUSFIELD, [Benjamin] *Esq.*

Observations on *Edm. Burke's* pamphlet on the subject of the french revolution. 1791. 8. (1 sh. 6 d.)

*BOUSSELL, [John] *Leather-cutter at Norwich.*

(who for upwards of 20 years, lived an abstenious life, refraining from animal food and fermented liquors.)

born 1725. died April 30. 1801.

See Gentleman's Magaz. Y. 1801. May. p. 482. June p. 569.

The ram's horn sounded seven times upon lifeless hills and mountains — also remarks upon *Th. Paine's* second part of the age of reason, with an appendix being a journal of seven days. 1799. (6 d.)

*BOWDEN, [John] *A stone-mason of the city of Chester.*

The epitaph writer; consisting of upwards of 600 original epitaphs, moral, admonitory, humourous and satirical, with an essay on epitaph writing. P. 1. 2. 1791. 8. (2 sh. 6 d.)

*BOWDLER, [.....] *Miss.*

Curio — a character. (American Museum Y. 1791. Jan. p. 31.)

*BOWDLER, [John] *Esq. M. Dr.*

Reform or ruin; Take your choice! in which the conduct of the King, the parliament, the ministry, the

the oppofition, the nobility and gentry, the bifhops and clergy etc. is confidered and that reform pointed out which alone can fave the country. 1797. 8.

BOWDOIN, [James] *Esq. LL. D: Governour of the Commonwealth: Prefident of the American Academy at Bofton.*
born in Bofton Aug. 7. 1727. died Nov. 6. 1790.
See Gentleman's Magaz. Y. 1790. Nov. p. 1147. Biographical fketches of him; See the Columbian Magaz. Y. 1791. Jan. p. 73. Maffachufetts Mag. Y. 1791. Jan. p. 5. See *John Lowell*.
Obfervations upon an hypothefis for folving the phenomena of light —; (American Mufeum Y. 1788. March. p. 203.) Obfervations on light, and the wafte of matter in the fun and fixed ftars, occafioned by the conftant efflux of light from them —; (American Mufeum Y. 1788. March. p. 206.) Obfervations tending to prove by phenomena and fcripture, the exiftence of an orb, which furrounds the whole vifible material fyftem —; (Ib Y. 1788. March. p. 213.)

***BOWEN**, [.....] *Captain.*
A ftatement of facts, in anfwer to Mrs. *Gunning's* letter — to the Duke of Argyll. 1791. 8. (2 fh.)

BOWEN, [Thomas] *M. A: Chaplain of Bridewell Hofpital and Minifter of Bridewell-precinct, Chaplain to the Temple-bar and St. Paul's diftrict military affociation.*
born, ... died Jan. 15. 1800.
See Gentleman's Magaz. Y. 1800. Jan. p. 92. Allg. Litt. Zeit. ItBl. J. 1800. S. 1803.
Hiftorical account of the origin, progrefs and prefent ftate of Betlehem Hofpital —; 1783. 4. Thoughts on the neceffity of moral difcipline in prifons, as preliminary to the religious inftruction of offenders. 1798. 8. (1 fh.) A companion for the prifoner. 1798. 8
(Several fingle fermons.)

***BOWES**, [Richard] *Conway, North-Wales.*
born .... died .... (?)
On millftones. (Tr. of the Soc. for the E. of A. Vol. 18. p. 197.)

*BOWLER,

*BOWLER, [William]
Explanation of his improved churn. (Tr. of the Soc. for the E. of A. Vol. 13. p. 251.)

*BOWLES, [John] *Esq. Barrister at Law.*
Considerations on the respective rights of judge and jury, particularly upon trials for libel, occasioned by an expected motion of *Charles James Fox.* 1791. 8. (2 sh.) Letter to — *Ch. James Fox,* occasioned by his late motion in the house of commons, respecting libels. 1791. 8. (1 sh. 6 d.) A second letter — upon the matter of libel —. 1792. 8. (2 sh.) Brief deductions from first principles. applying to the matter of libel: being an appendix to a second letter to *C. J. Fox* on that subject. 1792. 8. (6 d.) The real grounds of the present war with France; with a postscript. 1793. 8. (2 sh. 6 d.) A short answer to the declaration of the persons calling themselves the friends of the liberty of the press. 1793. 8. (6 d.) *Dialogues on the rights of Britons, between a farmer, a sailor and a manufacturer. Part 1. 2. 3. 1793. 8. (8 d.) Reflections submitted to the consideration of the combined powers. 1794. 8. (1 sh.) Further reflections —. 1795. 8. (1 sh. 6 d.) The dangers of premature peace; with cursory strictures on the declaration of the King of Prussia. 1795. 8. (1 sh. 6 d.) Thoughts on the origin and formation of political institutions, suggested by the recent attempt to frame another new constitution for France. 1795. 8. (1 sh.) A protest against *Th. Paine's* rights of man. 1795. Two letters, addressed to a British merchant, a short time before the meeting of the new parliament in 1796. 1796. 8. (2 sh.) A third letter to a British merchant, containing some general remarks in the late negotiation with France, considered in relation to antient and established principles. 1797. 8. (2 sh.) French aggression, proved from Mr. *Erskine's* view of the causes of war; with reflections on the original character of the french revolution and on the supposed durability of the french republic. 1797. 8. (3 sh.) The retrospect, or a collection of tracts, published at various periods of the war. 1799. 8. (6 sh.) Reflections on

on the political and moral ſtate of ſociety at the cloſe of the XVIII. century. 1800. 8. (3 ſh.) Supplement. 1801. 8. (1 ſh.). Reflections on the political ſtate of ſociety at the commencement of the XVIII century. 1800. (3 ſh. 6 d.) Reflexions at the concluſion of the war, being a ſequel to reflexions on the political and moral ſtate of ſociety at the cloſe of the XVIII century. 1800. 8. (2 ſh. 6 d.) Ed. 2. with additions, 1801. 8. (2 ſh. 6 d.) Reflexions on modern female manners as diſtinguiſhed by indifference to character and indecency of dreſs; extracted from reflexions political and moral at the concluſion of the war. 1802. Thoughts on the late general election as demonſtrative of the progreſs of Jacobiniſm. 1802. 8. (2 ſh.)

BOWLES, [William Lisle] *of Donhead, near Shafteſbury: M. A: late of Trinity College, Oxford, Rector of Dumbleton, Glouceſterſhire.*

Sonnets and other poems. Ed. 3. 1794. 8. (3 ſh.) — Ed. 22. 1798. Monody written at Matlock Oct. 1791. 4. (1 ſh. 6 d.) Elegiac ſtanzas; written during ſickneſs at Bath, December 1795. 1796. 4. (1 ſh.) Hope, an allegorical ſketch, on recovering ſlowly from ſickneſs. 1796. 4. (2 ſh.) Song of the battle of the nile. 1799. 4. (1 ſh. 6 d.) Coombe Ellen, a poem, written in Radnorſhire Sept. 1798. 1798. 4. (2 ſh.) Saint Michael's mount, a poem. 1798. 4. (2 ſh. 6 d.) Poems. Vol. 1. 1798. 8. Vol. 2. 1801. 8. (6 ſh.) The ſorrows of Switzerland; a poem. 1801. 4. (3 ſh.) The picture; verſes ſuggeſted by a magnificent landſcape of *Rubens*. 1803. 8. (2 ſh.)

*BOWMAN, [Thomas] *M. A. Vicar of Martham.*

Cauſtoniana; or XII diſcourſes addreſſed to the inhabitants of the pariſh of Cawſton in Norfolk. 1791. 8. (2 ſh. 6 d.)

*BOY, [John]

Remarks on waſte lands in Kent. (Bath Agric. Soc. Vol. 8. p. 135.)

BOYCE, [Thomas] *M. A. Rector of Worlingham Magna cum Parva, co. Suffolk, and Chaplain to the Earl of Suffolk.*

born .... died 1793. Febr. 4.

See Gentleman's Magaz. Y. 1793. Febr. p. 187.

BOYD,

BOYD, [Henry] *M. A. of the Kingdom of Ireland.*
Poems, chiefly dramatic and lyric. Dublin. 1796. 8. The divina commedia of *Dante Alighieri*, consisting of the inferno, purgatorio and paradiso, translated into english verse with preliminary notes and illustrations. Vol. 1. 2. 3. 1802. 8. (1 L. 7 sh.)

***BOYD**, [Hugh] *Esq.*
born in Ireland 1746. died Oct. 19. 1794.
See Allg. Litt. Zeit. J. 1801. ItBl. S. 876.
The Indian observer, being a series of essays and litterature, with the life of the author and some miscellaneous poems by *Lawr. Dundas Campbell.* 1798. 8. (10 sh. 6 d.) übers. Gesandtschafts-reise nach Ceylon — u. dem Leben des Verfassers. Hamburg. 1802. 8. The miscellaneous works of *H. Boyd*, the author of the letter of Junius; with an account of his life and writings by *L. D. Campbell.* Vol. 1. 2. 1800. 8. (16 sh.)

BOYD, [Robert] *LL. D.*
born, ... died 1793. Apr. 20. at Edinburgh.
See Gentleman's Magaz. Y. 1793. May p. 480.
The judicial proceedings before the high court of admiralty and supreme consistorial or commissary court of Scotland; 17..

***BOYD**, [Walter] *Esq. M. P.*
Letter, on the influence of the stoppage of issues in specie at the bank of England, on the prices of provisions and other commodities. 1801. 8. (3 sh. 6 d.)

***BOYNE**, [J....]
Letter to R. B. *Sheridan*, Esq. M. P. on his late proceedings as a member of the society for the freedom of the press. 1792. 8. (6 d.)

***BOYS**, [Henry] *Esq. F. L. S.*
Account of the flustra arenosa and some other marine productions. (Transact. of L. S. Vol. 5. p. 230.)

***BOYS**, [John] *of Betshanger; Farmer.*
A general view of the agriculture of the county of Kent, with observations on the means of its improvement. 1796. 8. (4 sh.) Excellence of the paring and burning husbandry, with observat. by *A. Young.* (*Young's* A. of Agr. Vol. 5. p. 112.)
On

On feeding hogs with potatoes. (Ibid. Vol. 8. p. 97.) Hints concerning sheep, with observat. by *A. Young*. (Ib. Vol. 11. p. 116.) On sheep. (Ib. Vol. 12. p. 94.) Threshing mill. (Ib. Vol. 18. p. 472.) Agricultural minutes, taken during a ride through the counties of Kent, Essex, Suffolk, Norfolk, Cambridge, Rutland, Leicester, Northampton, Buckingham, Bedford, Hertford, Middlesex, Berks and Surry, in 1792. (Ib. Vol. 19. p. 72.) Agricultural notes, taken in a ride from Betshanger to Bradfield and back by the hundreds of Essex. 1793. (Ibid. Vol. 21. p. 69.) Account of Romney marsh. (Ib. Vol. 22. p. 388.) Experiments on fatting hogs. (Ib. Vol. 24. p. 403.) Paring and burning. (Ib. Vol. 24. p. 521.) Political arithmetic of the county of Kent. (Ib. Vol. 28. p. 156.) Notes taken from Betshanger in the counties of Kent, Midlesex and Hertfordshire. (Ib. Vol. 28. p. 661.) Experiments on fattening hogs. (Ib. Vol. 29. p. 150.) Price of provisions and crops in Kent. (Ib. Vol. 34. p. 113.) Brown and white bread compared. (Ib. Vol. 35. p. 58.) Experiments on the culture of different kinds of wheat. (Tr. of the Soc. for the E. of A. Vol. 3. p. 19.) Essay on the best means of converting grass lands on the various soils into tillage, without exhausting the soil; and of returning the same to grass, after a certain period, in an improved state, or at least without injury. (Comm. to the B. of Agr. Vol. 3. P. 1. p. 247.)

BOYS, [William] *F. A. S: Surgeon at Sandwich, Kent.* born at Deal, in Kent, Sept. 7. 1735. died at Sandwich in Kent 1803. March 15.

See Gentleman's Magaz. Y. 1803. March. p. 293. May. p. 421.

Collection of minute and rare shells discovered on the sand of the sea shore near Sandwich; 1784. Observations on Kits Coity house, in Kents. (Arch. Vol. 11. p. 38.) An account of the loss of the Luxborough Galley by fire, on her voyage from Jamaica to London, with the sufferings of her crew in the Year 1727. published by *Will. Boys* second Mate. 1787. 4. * The case of the inhabitants and corporation of the town and

and port of Sandwich — etc. 1775. Collections for an history of Sandwich, Vol. 1. 1788. 4. Vol. 2. Canterbury. 1792. 4.

*BRACKENBURG, [Edward] *Rev.*
The prophecy of Isaiah, concerning the messiah, paraphrased —. 1802.

*BRACKENRIDGE, [H.... H....]
Modern chivalry, containing the adventures of Capt. *John Farrego* and *Teague Oregan*, his servant. Vol. 1. Philadelphia. 1792. (¼ Dollar.) On the mistaken notions of certain philosophers respecting the Indian character, (Columbian Magaz. Y. 1792, Febr. p. 110.)

BRADBERRY, [David]
Tetelestai; the final close, a poem in 6 parts. 1794. 8. (2 sh.)

*BRADFORD, [Alden] *Minister at Wiscasset, S. H. S.*
A topographial description of Duxborough, in the county of Plymouth. (Coll. of Massachusetts H. S. Y. 1793. p. 3.) A description of Wiscasset and of the river Sheepscot. (Ib. Y. 1800. p. 163.)

*BRADFORD, [J....] *A. B.*
Difference between true and false holiness: the substance of two sermons. 1797. (1 sh.)

*BRADFORD, [William] *Esq. Attorney General of the United states in America.*
born, ... died 1795. Aug. 23. at his seat near Philadelphia.
See Gentleman's Magaz. Y. 1795. Oct. p. 879. New-York Magaz. Y. 1795. Sept. p. 540. *Ebeling* und *Hegewisch* Amerikanisches Archiv, B. 1. St. 3. S. 164.
Enquiry how the punishment of death is necessary in Pennsylvania with notes and illustrations — to which is added an account of the gaol and penitentiary house of Philadelphia and of the interior management thereof by *Caleb Lowner*. Philadelphia. 1793. 8. reprinted London. 1795. 8. (2 sh.)

*BRADFUTE, [......] *Minister of Dunsyre, presbytery of Biggar.*
On the fisheries. (Tr. of Highland Soc. Vol. 1. p. 299.)

*BRADICK, [Walter] *Pensioner in the Charterhouse.* born 1706. died 1794. Dec.
See Gentleman's Magazine. Y. 1795. Jan. p. 83. (Author of several detached publications.) Coheleth, or the royal preacher, a poem. 1765.

*BRADLEY, [Thomas] *M. Dr.*
See *R. Batty*, M. Dr. and *Th. Beddoes.* A new medical dictionary, compiled by *Joseph Fox*, M D. revised and augmented. 1803. (7 sh.) Observations on the external use of tartarized antimony. (Mem. of M. S. of L. Vol. 4. p. 247.)

*BRADNEY, [Joseph] *Esq.*
Murepsologia, or the art of the apothecary traced up to its original source in history — etc. 1796. 8. (1 sh.)

*BRAINES, [W....]
Account of the culture, expences and produce of potatoes, per acre, about Ilford and the adjacent parishes, six miles east of London. (Bath Agricult. Soc. Vol. 4. p. 249.)

*BRAMAH, [Joseph] *Engineer.*
Dissertation on the construction of locks. 1787. 8. (1 sh.) Letter — on the subject of the cause *Boulton* and *Watt* v. *Hornblower* and *Maberly*, for infringement of Mr. *Watt's* patent for an improvement of the steam engine. 1797. 8. (2 sh.)

*BRAMLEY, [Richard Ramsden] *Esq. of Leeds.*
On the culture of lands in the neighbourhood of great towns. (Tr. of the Soc. for the E. of A. Vol. 13. p. 201.) On a method of constructing banks to guard against the inundation of the sea. (Ib. Vol. 14. p 238.)

*BRANCH, [J....] *M. A.*
— — and *W. Holloway*, The British museum of natural history. Vol. 1. 1803. (7 sh.)

*BRAND, [Hannah] *Miss.*
Plays and poems. 1798. 8. (7 sh.)

*BRAND, [James] *Esq.*
On the alteration of the constitution of the house of commons and the inequality of the land tax 1793.

BRAND

BRAND, [John] *M. A. Fellow and Secretary of the Soc. of Antiquaries at London.*

(a native of Newcaſtle upon Tyne.)

Conſcience an ethical eſſay. 1772. 4. (2 ſh.) Obſervations on Mr. *Gilbert's* bill, with remarks deduced from Dr. *Price's* account of the national debt. 1776. 8. (2 ſh.) Explanation of the inſcriptions on a roman altar and tablet, found at Tinmouth-caſtle in Northumberland 1783. (Arch. Vol. 8. p. 326.) Account of inſcriptions diſcovered on the walls of an apartment in the tower of London. (Arch. Vol. 13. p. 68.) Explanation of a ſeal of Netley Abbey. (Ibid. Vol. 13. p. 193.) Explanation of a ſeal of the abbey of Lundores, in Scotland. (Ibid. Vol. 13. p. 196.) On the latin terms uſed in natural hiſtory. (Transact. of L. S. Vol. 3. p. 70.) The alteration of the conſtitution of the houſe of commons and the inequality of the landtax, conſidered conjointly. 1793. 8. (4 ſh.) A ſermon on Luke 19, 41. 42. 1794. 4. An hiſtorical eſſay on the principles of political aſſociations in a ſtate: chiefly deduced from the french, engliſh and jewiſch hiſtories; with an application of thoſe principles, in a comparative view of the aſſociations of the Y. 1792. and that recently inſtituted by the Whig-club. 1796. 8. (2 ſh. 6 d.) A defence of the pamphlet aſcribed to *John Reeves*, Esq. and entitled, „thoughts on the engliſh government.„ 1796. 8. (2 ſh. 6 d.) Conſiderations on the depreſſion of the funds and the preſent embarraſſements of circulation: with propoſitions for ſome remedies to each. 1797 8. (2 ſh.) A determination of the average depreſſion of the price of wheat in war below that of the preceding peace; and of its re-advance in the following; according to its yearly rates from the revolution to the end of the laſt peace: with remarks on their greater variations in that entire period. 1800. 8. (2 ſh.) Letter on *Buonaparte's* propoſals for opening a negociation for peace, in which the Britiſh guarantee of the crown of France to the houſe of Bourbon, contained in the triple and quadruple alliances; and renewed by the treaty

I 2 of

of the Y. 1783 is confidered; together with the conduct of our national parties relating to it. 1801. 8. (2 fh.)

*BRANDRETH, [. . . .] *M. Dr. of Liverpool.*
Account of the benefit of wafhing with cold water and vinegar in typhus fever. (*Duncan's* M. C. Dec. 2. Vol. 6. p. 382.)

*BRANSBY, [John]
The ufe of the globes, containing an introduction to aftronomy and geography. 1791. 8. (2 fh. 6 d.)

*BRANSON, [John] *Esq. Surgeon.*
Letter on the vaccine inoculation. (*Tilloch's* Philof. Magaz. Vol. 8. p. 308.)

*BRANTHWAYT, [M . . . S . . . .]
Galloway Scotch heifer. (*Young's* A. of Agr. Vol. 32. p. 344.)

*BRAY, [Edward Atkyns]
Poems. 1799. 8. (5 fh.) Idyls, in two parts. 1800. 8. (4 fh. 6 d.)

BRAY, [William] *Esq. F. A. S.*
Extract from the wardrobe account of Prince Henry, eldeft fon of King James I. (Arch. Vol. 11. p. 88.) Copy of a furvey made of what remained in the armoury of the tower of London in confequence of a commiffion iffued Auguft 2. 1660. 12. Charles II. (Ibid. Vol. 11. p. 97.)

*BRAYLEY, [E . . . . W . . . .]
The grand alphabet of alphabets; being an engraved feries of running hand, every line of which contains all the letters of the englifh language. 1800. (6 d.)

*BREE, [John] *M. A. Rector of Marks Tey, County Effex and of Rysholme in the county of Lincoln.*
born, ... died 1796. Dec. 14.
See Gentleman's Magaz. Y. 1796. Suppl. p. 1115.
A curfory fketch of the ftate of the naval, military and civil eftablifhment, legislature, judicial and domeftic oeconomy of this kingdom during the XIV century; with a particular account of the campaign of king Edward 3 in Normandy and France, in the Y. 1345 and 1346 to the taking of

of Calais, collected merely from the antient MS. in the British museum and elsewhere. Vol. I. 1791. 4. (1 L. 1 sh.)

*BREE, [Martin] *M. Dr.*

Observations upon the venereal disease with some remarks on the cure of barrenness, impotence and certain disorders incident to either sex, from the pernicious habits of youth. 1797. 8. (2 sh.)

*BREE, [Richard]

A practical inquiry on disordered respiration. Birmingham. 1797. 8.

*BREE, [Robert] *M. D. of Birmingham. Licentiate in Midwifery of the Royal College of Physicians.*

A practical inquiry on disordered respiration, distinguishing convulsive asthma, its specific causes and proper indications of cure. 1797. 8. übers. von *K. F. A. S.* Leipzig. 1800. 8. Ed. 2. corrected, with an appendix. 1800. 8. (5 sh.)

See *George Lipscomb.*

BRERETON, [Owen Salisbury] *Esq. Many years Recorder of Liverpool; F. R. and A. SS. Vice-President of the Soc of Antiquaries.*

born 1716. died 1798. Sept. 9.

See Gentleman's Magaz. Y. 1798. Sept. p. 816. Memoir of *O. S. Brereton* by *John Holliday*. See Tr. of the Soc. for the E. of A. Vol. 19. p. IV.

Account of a painted window in Brereton church, Cheshire. (Arch. Vol. 9. p. 368.) A non descript silver coin of Philip King of France; (Ibid. Vol. 10. p. 463.)

*BRERETON, [W.... B....]

Mode in which the inhabitants of Cochin-China, purify sugar. (Comm. and Agric. Mag. Y. 1800. p. 180.)

BREWER, [George] *Esq. Attorney.*

The history of Tom Weston, a novel, after the manner of Tom Jones. Vol. 1. 2. 1791. 8. (6 sh.) The motto; or history of Bill Woodcock. Vol. 1. 2. 1795. 12. (6 sh.) How to be happy; a comedy. 1794. Bannian day; a musical entertainment, in two acts. 1796. 8. (1 sh.) The Country burial. (New-York Magaz. Y. 1796. Jan. p. 21.)

*BREWER, [George]

The rights of poor considered with the causes and effects of monopoly and a plan of remedy, by means of a popular progressive excise. 1800. 8. (2 sh. 6 d.)

*BREWER, [Richard]

The process for dying nankeen colour. (Tr. of Dublin Soc. Vol. 1. P. 1. p. 287.)

BREWSTER, [John] *M. A: Vicar of Greatham, Lecturer of Stockton-upon-Tees.*

On the prevention of crimes and on the advantages of solitary imprisonment. 1792. 8. (1 sh.) The parochial history and antiquities of Stockton-upon-Tees, including an account of the trade of the town, the navigation of the river and of such parts in the neighbourhood as have been connected with that place. 1796. 4. (12 sh.) A secular essay; containing a view of events connected with the ecclesiastical history of England during the XVIII century. With the state of practical religion in that period. 1802. 8. (7 sh.) Meditations of a recluse, chiefly on religious subjects. 1800. 12. (5 sh.)

*BREYLEY, [Edward Wedlake]

See *John Britton.*

*BRICE, [J....]

Scriptural facts and annotations on the divinity of the messiah. 1800. 8. (5 sh.)

*BRICKELL, [John] *Dr. of Savannah.*

Description of the Jeffersonia. (Medical Repository. Vol. 1. p. 573.) Theory of puerperal fever. (Ibid. Vol. 2. p. 15.) Letter on the climate of Georgia. (American Museum. Y. 1789. March. p. 244.)

BRICKNELL, [A....] is a mistake for *A. Bicknell.* See *Alexander Bicknell.*

*BRIDEL, [E.... P....] *Master of an Academy at Stocke Newington.*

*Introduction to english grammar; intended also to assist young persons in the study of other languages and to remove many of the difficulties which impede their progress in learning. 1799. 4. (2 sh. 6 d.)

*BRIDGE-

*BRIDGEMAN, [G.....] *Mariner, of Rotherhithe.*
A full and circumstantial account of the victory obtained over the Dutch fleet, by Adm. *Duncan* on Oct. 11. 1797. including several important circumstances relative to that glorious event. 1797. 8. (6 d.)

*BRIDGMAN, [Richard Whalley] *Esq.*
Thesaurus Juridicus; containing the decisions of the several courts of equity, upon the suits therein adjudged and of the high court of parliament upon petitions and appeals: to which are added, the resolutions of the barons of the exchequer in matters touching the revenues of the crown: from the period of the revolution to the end of easter term 1798; systematically digested. Vol. 1. 1799. (15 sh.)

BRIGHT, [Henry] *A. M. Vicar of Chedlehampton, in Devonshire and formerly Master of the free-school in Abingdon and of New College school, in the University of Oxford.*
born 1723. died 1803. Febr.
See Gentleman's Magaz. Y. 1803. p. 196. May. p. 475. Monthly Magaz. Y. 1803. p. 194.

*BRINKLEY, [John] *A. M. Professor of Astronomy in the University of Dublin. M. R. J. A.*
General demonstrations of the theorems for the sines and cosines of multiple circular arcs, and also of the theorems for expressing the powers of sines and cosines by the sines and cosines of multiple arcs; to which is added a theorem by help whereof the same method may be applied to demonstrate the properties of multiple hyperbolic areas. (Tr. of J. A. Vol. 7. p. 27.) A general demonstration of the property of the circle discovered by Mr. *Cotes*, deduced from the circle only. (Ibid. Vol. 7. p. 151.) A method of expressing when possible, the value of one variable quantity in integral powers of another and constant quantities, having given equations expressing the relation of those variable quantities —; (Ibid. Vol. 7. p. 321.) Tables to improve and render more general the method of finding the latitude, by observing two altitudes of the sun and the interval of time between. (N. A. Y. 1798. Append.

Ibid. Y. 1799. Append. Ibid. Y. 1800. Append.) On determining innumerable portions of a sphere the solidities and spherical superficies of which portions are at the same time algebraically assignable. (Tr. of J. A. Vol. 8. Sc. p. 513.) On the orbits in which bodies revolve, being acted upon by a centripetal force varying as any function of the distance, when those orbit have two apsides. (Ibid. Vol. 8. Sc. p. 215.)

BRISBANE (not BRISBAINE), [John] *M. Dr. Physician to the Middlesex Hospital at London,* born . . . . died 17 . . (?)

BRISTOL, *Bishop of.* — See **Cornwall.**

*__BRISTOW__, [James]

A narrative of his sufferings, belonging to the Bengal artillery, during ten years captivity with Hyder Ally and Tippo Saheb. Ed. 2. 1794. Ed. 3. 1796. 8. (3 sh.) übers. Hamburg. 1794. 8.

*__BRITT__, [Daniel]

— — and *G. Turner*, Thermometrical observations made at Fort Washington, commencing June 1790 and ending April 1791. to which are added, for some time, the rise and fall of the Ohio. (Tr. of A. S. Vol. 4. p. 329.)

*__BRITTON__, [John]

* *Sheridan* and *Kotzebue*, The enterprising adventures of Pizarro, preceded by a brief sketch of the voyages and discoveries of Columbus and Cortez. 1799. 8. (5 sh.) * The beauties of Wiltshire, displayed in statistical, historical and descriptive sketches, illustrated by views of the principal seats etc. with anecdotes of the arts. Vol. 1. 2. 1801. 8. (1 L. 4 sh.) — and *Edward Wedlake Brayley*, The beauties of England and Wales; or, delineations topographical, historical and descriptive of each county. Embellished with engravings. Vol. 1. 2. 1801. 8. (1 L. 10 sh. 6 d. large paper 2 L. 8 sh.) Vol. 3. 1802. (1 L. large paper 1 L. 12 sh.) On druidical remains. (Monthly Magaz. Y. 1802. Oct. p. 200.)

* BROAD-

*BROADLEY, [John] *Merchant.*

Pandora's box and the evils of Britain; with effectual, just and equitable means for their annihilation; and for the preservation of the peace, happiness and prosperity of the country. 1800. 8. (1 sh. 6 d.)

BROCKLESBY, [Richard] *M. Dr. Fellow of the College of Physicians: F. R. S.*

born, ... died Dec. 12. 1797.
See Gentleman's Magaz. Y. 1797. Suppl. p. 1132.
Duncan's Annals of Medic: Y. 1798. p. 471.

Case of an encysted tumour in the orbit of the eye, cured by Messrs. *Bromfield* and *Ingram.* (Med. Observat. Vol. 4.) A dissertation on the music of the ancients; 17..

LE BROCQ, [Philip] *A. M. Domestic Chaplain to his Roy. Highness the Duke of Gloucester.*

Outlines of a plan for making the tract of land called the new forest, a real forest and for various other purposes of the first national importance — 1793. 8. (1 sh. 6 d.)

*BRODBELT, [George Campbell] *Rector of Aston-Sandford and perpetual Curate of Loudwater, Bucks.*

born 1760 in the Island of Nevis, in West-India; died 1801. June 13.
See Evangelical Magaz. Y. 1801. Oct. p. 377.

Doctrines of the reformation and of the church of England: Sermons — 1793. 8. Original essays on miscellaneous subjects in religion; 1795. 8. (2 sh.)

*BRODBELT, [Francis Rigby] *M. Dr. of Jamaica.*

Account of some observations and experiments made on the gas contained in the air-bladder of the sword-fish. (*Duncan's* A. of Med. Y. 1796. p. 393. *Nicholson's* Journal. Vol. 1. p. 264.) Case of deposition of mercury upon the bones. (Mem. of M. S. of L. Vol. 5. p. 112.)

*BRODIE, [Joseph] *Shipmaster, Leith.*

An easy and effectual method for mending shrouds, or other ropes, accidentally cut in time of an engagegagement at sea, or otherwise. (New-York Magaz. Y. 1791. Nov. p. 633.)

*BRODIE, [Patrick] *Tenant in Garvald near Haddington.*

On green crops. (Tr. of Highland Soc. Vol. 1. p. 96.)

*BRODUM, [William] *M. Dr.*

The guide to old age. Vol. 1. 2. 17..

BROMFEILD, [William] *Surgeon to the Queen's Housheld, late Surgeon to St. George's and the Lock Hospitals.*

born 1712. died Nov. 24. 1792.

See Gentleman's Magaz. Y. 1792. Nov. p. 1062.

*BROMLEY, [Henry] *Engraver.*

A catalogue of engraved British portraits, from Egbert the great to the present time; [illegible] 1793. 4. (1 L. 1 sh.)

BROMLEY, [Robert Anthony] *B. D. Rector of St. Mildreds in the Poultry.*

(born in America.)

A philosophical and critical history of the fine arts, painting, sculpture and architecture; with occasional observations on the progress of engraving deduced from the earliest periods through every country in which those arts have been cherished, to their present establishment in Great-Britain. Vol. 1. 1793. 4. (1 L. 10 sh.) Vol. 2. 1795. 4. (1 L. 1 sh.)

*BROMLEY, [Robert]

Description of the pocket memorandum book, invented by him, for the use of persons deprived of their eye-sight. (Tr. of the Soc. for the E. of A. Vol. 7. p. 106.)

BROMWICH, [Bryan Janson] *A. M.*

On mangelwurzel. (Bath Agricult. Soc. Vol. 5. p. 308. 314.) Arthur and Emina, or the first navigator, a poem in IV books. 1796. The doctrines of the church of Rome examined. 1797. 8. (2 sh.)

BROOK, [Abraham] *Of the city of Norwich. An Mechanick.*

Miscell. exper. and remarks on electricity, the air

air pump. &c. 1789. 4. (1 sh.) übers. von *K. G. Kühn*. Leipzig. 1790. 8.

*BROOKE, [....] *Miss.*

Dialogue between a lady and her pupils, describing a journey through England and Wales; in which a detail of the different arts and manufactures of each city and town is accurately given; interspersed with observations and descriptions in natural history. 1796. 8. (3 sh. 6 d.) Emma, or the foundling of the wood; 1803. 8. (3 sh. 6 d.)

*BROOKE, [.....] *M. Dr. Of the city of Bath.*

Observations on the manners and customs of Italy, with remarks on the vast importance of British commerce on that continent, also particulars of the wonderful explosion of mount vesuvius, taken on the spot, at midnight in June 1794. — likewise an account of many very extraordinary cures produced by a preparation of opium, in a variety of obstinate cases according to the practice in Asia, with many physical remarks collected in Italy — by a Gentleman authorized to investigate the commerce of that country with Great-Britain. 1798. 8. (6 sh.)

BROOKE, [John Charles] *Esq. Somerset-Herald; and one of the Lieutenants in the militia of the West-Riding, Yorkshire.* F. A. S.

born 1749. suffocated in attempting to get into the pit at the little theatre in the Haymarket, Febr. 10. 1794.

See Gentleman's Magaz. Y. 1794. Febr. p. 187. March. p. 275.

A deed of the manor of Nether Sitlington, co. York. (Arch. Vol. 7. p. 416.)

*BROOKE, [William] *F. R. A.*

The true causes of the present distress for provisions; with a natural easy and effectual plan for the future prevention of so great a calamity. With some hints respecting the absolute necessity of an encreased population. 1800. 8. (2 sh.)

*BROOM, [Thomas] *Teacher of the classics, geography and other branches of polite litterature at Wokingham, Bucks.*

Sketches of female education, partly original and partly selected from the most approved authors, for

For the instruction and amusement of young ladies both in public seminaries and private families. 1791. 12. (3 sh.)

BROOME, [Ralph] *Esq. Captain in the service of the East-India Company on the Bengal Establishment and Persian translator to the army on the frontier station; during part of the late war in India.*

Elucidation of the articles of impeachment, preferred by the last parliament against *Warren Hasting's*. 1790. 8. (5 sh.) Examination of the expediency of continuing the present impeachment. 1791. 8. (2 sh. 6 d.) The letters of Simkin the second, poetic recorder of all the proceedings upon the trial of *Warren Hasting's* Esq. in Westminster-hall. 1791. 8. A comparative review of the administration of *Hastings* and Mr. *Dundas*, in war and in peace. 1791. 8. (1 sh.) Observations on *Paine's* pamphlet, entitled the decline and fall of the English system of finance, in a letter to a friend. 1796. 8. (1 sh. 6 d.)

BROTHERS, [Richard] *Formerly a Lieutenant in Navy.*

(A native of Placentia in Newfoundland.)

See *Joseph Moser*. Gentleman's Magaz. Y. 1795. March. p. 250. 251. May. p. 434.

A revealed knowledge of the prophecies and times. Book 1. — containing — the restoration of the hebrews to Jerusalem by the Y. 1798. under his revealed prince and prophet; Book 2. containing the sudden and perpetual fall of the Turkish, German and Russian empires. 1794. 8. On exposition of the trinity, with a further elucidation of the XI. Chapt. of Daniel; one letter to the king and two to Mr. *Pitt*. 1795. 8. (1 sh.) Letter to Miss. *Cott*, the recorded daughter of King David and future queen of the hebrews; with an address to the members of his Britannic Majesty's Council. etc. 1798. 8. (3 sh.) A description of Jerusalem with the garden of Eden in the center; also the first chapter of Genesis verified as strictly divine and the solar system and plurality of inhabited worlds, positively proved to be false. 1802. (4 sh.) A letter to his Maj. and to her Maj. also,

also, a poem, with a dissertation on the fall of Eve; and an address to five eminent counsellors. 1802. 8. (2 sh.)

*BROUGHAM, [Henry] *Jun. Esq.*
Experiments and observations on the inflection, reflection and colours of light. (Philosoph. Transact. Y. 1796. p. 227. Y. 1797. p. 352. *Nicholson's* Journal. Vol. 1. p. 551. 585. Vol. 2. p. 147. 193.) General theorems, chiefly porisms, in the higher geometry. (Ibid Y. 1798. p. 378.) An inquiry into the colonial policy of the European powers. Vol. 1. 2. 1803. 8. (18 sh.)

BROUGHTON, [Arthur] *M. Dr. before Physician to the Hospital at Bristol, now in West-India.*
Hortus Eastensis: or, a catalogue of exotic plants in the garden of *Hinton East*, Esq. in the mountains of Liguanea, in the island of Jamaica; — Kingston. 1792. (this Catalogue was begun by the late Dr. *Thomas Clarke*;) Hortus Eastensis. St. Jago de la Vega. 1794. 4.

*BROUGHTON, [Brian] *M. A: Fellow of New College, Oxford.*
Six picturesque views in North-Wales, engraved in aqua tinta, by *Alken*, from drawings made on the spot; with poetical reflections on leaving that country. 1801. 4. (12 sh.)

*BROUGHTON, [Thomas] *Tiverton.*
On the turnip cabbage. (Bath Agricult. Soc. Vol. 5. p. 453 454.) Observations on turnip cabbage. (Ibid. Vol. 7. p. 335. 341. 344.) On the culture of potatoes. (Ibid. Vol. 8. p. LI.) On the culture of the turnip-cabbage. (Ibid. Vol. 9. p. 90.)

BROWELL, [James] *of the Royal Navy.*
An account of the navies of foreign powers, particularly those of France, Spain and Batavia, now at war with Great Britain, including a list of frigates, corvettes and sloops, also the navies of Russia, Sweden, Denmark and Naples; with a comparative state of the line of battle ships in the last war and the present state of the British navy. 1799. 4. (1 sh.)

BROWN, [.....]
Masonic relics; elucidating what is said of his life

life and character by *Beddoes*. (Med. Repos. Vol. 3. p. 85. 89. 340.)

*BROWN, [.....]

— and *Rennie's* remarks on waste lands in Yorkshire. (Bath Agric. Soc. Vol. 8. p. 127.) — *Rennie's* and *Shirreff*, size of farms in Yorkshire. (*Young's* A. of Agr. Vol. 22. p. 409.) On reaping high and low. (Ibid. Vol. 22. p. 413)

*BROWN, [Alexander Campbell]

Colony commerce; or, reflections on the commercial system, as it respects the West-India Islands, our continental colonies and the United states of America: with some remarks on the present high price of sugar and the means of reducing it. 1792. 8. (2 sh.)

*BROWN, [Charles] *Surgeon*.

born 1778. shot himself July 10. 1800.

See Gentleman's Mag. Y. 1800. Jul. p. 701. Aug. p. 793. Allgem. Litterat. Zeit. J. 1801. ItBl. S. 837.

On scrophulous diseases, showing the goods effects of factitious air; illustrated with cases and observations. 1798. 8. (3 sh. 6 d.) On the use of vomits in suspended animation. (Monthly Magaz. Y. 1798. Oct. p. 240.) Controversy on the nitrous acid. (Ibid. Y. 1799. Jan. p. 23.) Inkle and Yarico, a poem. 1799. 4. (1 sh. 6 d.) Description of an improved german key for extracting teeth. (*Tilloch's* Philos. Magaz. Vol. 2. p. 73.)

*BROWN, [C.... B....]

Edgar Huntly, or the memoirs of a sleep-walker. Vol. 1-3. 1802. 8. Arthur Mervyn a tale. Vol. 1-3. 1802. 8. (12 sh.)

*BROWN, [G.... G....] *of Bath*.

Account of the good effects of cold in madness. (*Duncan's* A. of Med. Y. 1799. p. 488.)

*BROWN, [James]

The importance of preserving unviolated the system of civil government in every state; with the dreadful consequences of the violation of it. To which is added an appendix, containing some strictures on the writings of Mr. *Paine*. 1792. 8. (2 sh.) An alarm to the public and a bounty promi-

promifed to every loyal fubject who fhall come forward to repel the enemy. 1798. 8. (2 d.)

BROWN, [Jofiah] *Esq. Barrifter at Law.*

A new abridgment of cafes in equity and of fuch cafes at law as relate to equitable fubjects from 1735 to the prefent time. Vol. 1. 1793. 4. (1 L. 5 fh.)

*BROWN, [Mofes] *Esq. of Providence.*

Brief remarks on the origin of the yellow fever in fome parts of the ftate of Rhode-Ifland. (Medical Repofitory. Vol. 3. p. 267.)

*BROWN, [Robert] *Farmer at Markle, near Haddington, Scotland.*

A general view of the agriculture of the county of the Weftriding of Yorkfhire. 1799. 8. (6 fh.)

*BROWN, [Robert] *Corporal in the Goldftream Guards.*

An impartial journal of a detachment from the brigade of foot guards, commencing 25 Febr. 1793 and ending 9 May 1795. with a map of the feat of war. 1796. 8. (5 fh. 6 d.) The campaign, a poetical effay. 1797. 8. (2 fh. 6 d.)

*BROWN, [Samuel] *M. Dr.*

On the bilious malignant fever. Bofton. 1797. An account of the peftilential difeafe which prevailed at Bofton (Maffachufetts) in the fummer and autumn of 1798. (Medical Repofit. Vol. 2. p. 390.) On the nature, origin and progrefs of the yellow fever, with obfervations on its treatment; comprifing an account of the difeafe in feveral of the capitals of the United ftates but more particularly as it has prevailed in Bofton. 1800.

*BROWN, [Thomas] *Esq. Of the Univerfity of Edinburgh.*

Obfervations on the zoonomia of *Erafmus Darwin*, M. Dr. 1798. 8. (8 fh.)

*BROWN, [Thomas] *Surgeon at Muffelburgh.*

Hiftory of a remarkable inflammatory difeafe, terminating in a fatal affection of the bowels. (*Duncan's* M. C. Dec. 2. Vol. 8. p. 348.) Hiftory of a cafe, in which a recovery took place after a remarkable injury to the brain. (Ibid. Dec. 2. Vol. 8. p. 342.) Hiftory of a cafe of cyftircyſtirrhoea, cured by the uſe of aſtringent injections thrown into the bladder. (Ibid. Dec 2. Vol. 10. p. 223.) The hiſtory of a caſe, in which, after a complete inverſion of the uterus, a favourable termination took place. (*Duncan's* A. of Med. Y. 1797. p. 277.) Caſe of inverted uterus, with retention of the placenta after parturition. (Mem. of M. S. of L. Vol. 5. p. 202.)

*BROWN, [Thomas]

Remarks on waſt lands in Derbyſhire. (Bath Agric. Soc. Vol. 8. p. 152.)

*BROWN, [William] *M. Dr.*

Hints on the eſtabliſhment of an univerſal written character. (Mem. of M. Vol. 5. P. 1. p. 275.)

BROWN, [William] *Esq. F. R. S. Deputy County-clerk of Middleſex.*

born, ... died Apr. 26. 1794.

See Gentleman's Magaz. Y. 1704. June. p 576.

Reports of caſes argued and determined in the high court of chancery. Vol. 2. 1789. fol. (12 ſh.) Vol. 3. 1792. fol. (1 L. 15 ſh.) Vol. 4. 17 . .

*BROWN, [William] *M. Dr.*

A letter to the clergy of the church of Scotland, on domeſtic inoculation. Edinb. 1794. 8.

*BROWN, [William Cullen]

The inſtitutions of the practice of medicine; delivered in a courſe of lectures by *J. Bapt. Burſerius de Kanifeld.* Tranſlated from the latin; in five volumes. Vol. 1 - 3. 1800. 1801. 8. (1 L. 4 ſh.)

BROWN, [William Laurence] *D. D. Principal of Mariſchal College, Aberdeen.*

Oratio habita die 14 Febr. 1788. quum ordinariam in academia Trajectina, hiſtoriae eccleſiaſticae et philoſophiae moralis profeſſionem publice — ſuſciperet. Ultraj. 1788. 4. Oratio habita die 25 Mart. 1790. cum magiſtratu ſe academico abdicaret. Ultrajecti. 1790. 4. Eſſay on the natural equality of mankind, on the rights that reſult from it and the duties which it impoſes. 1793. 8. (3 ſh. 6 d.) überſ. von *Weber*, Frankf. u. Leipzig. 1797. 8. The ſpirits of the times conſidered, a ſermon. 1793. 8. (1 ſh.) The influence of the divine judgements on the reformation of the world; a ſermon. 1794. 8. The influence of religion

ligion on national prosperity; a sermon. 1796 8. Sermon on occasion of the death of Dr. *George Campbell*, late principal and Professor of divinity in Marischall-College, Aberdeen. 1796. 8. The proper method of defending religious truth in times of prevailing infidelity, a sermon. 1796. 8. An essay on the folly of scepticism — Ed. 2. 1796. 8. (3 sh.)

BROWNE, [Arthur] *LL. Dr. Senior Fellow of Trinity College, Dublin; Professor of Civil Law in that University and one of the Representatives of the University in the Irish Parliament.*

Miscellaneous sketches or hints for essays. Vol. 1. 2. 1798. 8. (7 sh.) A compendious view of civil and ecclesiastical law, being the substance of a course of lectures read in the University of Dublin. Vol. 1. 2. 1798. 1800. 8. (1 L. 2 sh.) A compendious view of the civil law and of the law of admiralty. Vol. 1. 1799. 8. (8 sh.) Ed. 2. with great additions. Vol. 1. 2. 1802. 8. (1 L. 1 sh.) Brief strictures on certain observations of Lord *Monboddo* respecting the greek tenses. (Tr. of J. A. 1789. 11. b.) The comparative authenticity of *Tacitus* and *Suetonius* illustrated by the question, whether Nero was the author of the memorable conflagration at Rome? (Ibid. Vol. 5. p. 3. b.) Some observations upon the greek accents. (Ibid. Vol. 7. p. 359.) Some account of the Vicars Cairn, in the county of Armagh. (Ib. Vol. 8. Antiq. p. 3.) An account of some ancient trumpets, dug up in a bog near Armagh. (Ibid. Vol. 8. Antiq. p. 11.)

BROWNE, [Henry] *Chemist at Derby.*

Description of his evaporator. (Tr. of the Soc. for the E. of A. Vol. 12. p. 257.) Quick and easy method of converting weeds and other vegetable matter into manure. (Tr. of the Soc. for the E. of A. Vol. 16. p. 268. *Tilloch's* Philos. Magaz. Vol. 3. p. 32.)

BROWNE, [J....] *P. M. of six lodges, and M. A.*

Masonic master key through the three degrees; by way of polyglot. Under the sanction of the craft in general. And an explanation of all the hieroglyphics. The whole interspersed with illustrations on theology, aftronomy, architecture, sciences. 1803. (5 fh. 6 d.)

*BROWNE, [John] *M. A: late of Sidney Su College, Cambridge.*

An effay on univerfal redemtion, tending to pro that the general fenfe of fcripture favours opinion of the final falvation of all mank 1798. 8. (1 fh.)

*BROWNE, [Jofeph] *M. Dr.*

On the yellow fever, fhewing its origin, cure prevention New-York. 1797. 8.

*BROWNE, [M.... C....]

A leaf out of *Burk's* book, being an epiftle that R. H. Gentleman on his letter to a no Lord &c. 1796. 8. (2 fh.)

*BROWNE, [Patrick] *M. Dr.*

born at Woodftock, in the Parifh of Crofsbo and County of Mayo, about the Y. 17 died at Rufhbrook, County of Mayo Aug. 1790.

Civil and natural hiftory of Jamaica. 1756. Ed. 2. 1789. Map of Jamaica. 1755. Catalo of the birds of Ireland, whether natives, ca vifitors, or birds of paffage, taken from obfe tion; claffed and difpofed according to Linnae (publifhed in Exfhaw's Magazine Y. 1774. Ju Catalogue of fifhes, obferved on our coafts in our lakes and rivers, claffed and difpofed cording to Linnaeus; (publifhed in Exfhaw's gaz. Y. 1774. Auguft.) (His Mff. are: A cat gue of the plants growing in the fugar isla &c. claffed and defcribed according to the neau fyftem. Fafciculus plantarum Hibern or a catalogue of fuch Irifh plants as have b obferved by the author chiefly thofe of the co ties of Mayo and Galway.)

*BROWNE, [Samuel] *Rev.*

A new hiftorical, chronological and geograph dictionary of the holy bible. Vol. 1-3. 179 (17 fh.) The Britifh proteftant youth's inf ctor, or the deliverance god hath wrought preferving us from popery. 1798. (1 fh.)

*BROWNE, [Thomas] *A. M.*

A new claffical dictionary for the ufe of fcho 17

1797. 12. (5 ſh.) Viridarium poeticum ſeu delectus epithetorum in celeberrimis latinis ſcriptoribus ſparſorum — 1799. 8. (8 ſh.)

*BROWNE, [Thomas Gunter] *Esq.*

Hermes unmaſked, or the art of ſpeech founded on the aſſociation of words and ideas; with an anſwer to Dr. *Vincent's* hypotheſis of the greek verb. 1795. 8. (2 ſh. 6 d.) Letters 3 and 4 containing the myſteries of metaphyſics, with an anſwer to le *Broſſe's* ſyſtem of imitation found. 1796. 8. (1 ſh. 6 d.)

*BROWNE, [W.... G....]

Travels in Africa, Egypt and Syria from the Y. 1792 to 1798. 1799. 4. (1 L. 11 ſh. 6 d.) überſ. von *Sprengel.* Weimar. 1800. 8.

*BROWNLOW, [.....] *Lord.*

Queries concerning cottages, with the anſwers. (Comm. to the B. of Agr. Vol. 1. p. 85.)

BROWNRIGG, [William] *M. Dr. F. R. S. Phyſician of Keſwick in Cumberland.*

born, 1711. died at his ſeat at Ormathwaite near Keſwick.

See Gentleman's Magaz. Y. 1800. April p. 386. Monthly Magaz. Y. 1800. June. p. 498. Allg. Litt. Zeit. IıBl. J. 1800. S. 1802. See *Joſhua Dixon.*

*BRUCE, [A....]

On an atmospherical phaenomenon at Edinburgh. (Monthly Magaz. Y. 1798. March. p. 194.)

*BRUCE, [Arthur] *Esq. Secretary to the natural hiſtor. Society of Edinburgh.*

A curious fact in the natural hiſtory of the common mole, talpa Europaea Linn. (Transact. of L. Soc. Vol. 3. p. 5. *Tilloch's* Philoſoph. Magaz. Vol. 2. p. 36.)

*BRUCE, [Baſil]

An exhortation to all people to forſake the ſin of ſwearing oaths &c. 1798. 8. (6 d.)

BRUCE, [James] *of Kinnaird, Esq. F. R. S.*

born about the Y. 1733. died Apr. 1794.

See Gentleman's Magaz. Y. 1794. May. p. 483. Allg. Litterat. Zeit. J. 1794. IıBl. N. 72. S. 569.

Gens Neue Deutsche Monathsschrift, J. 1795 May. S. 241. The Annual Necrology for 1797-1798. p. 127.

BRUCE, [John] *M. A: F. R. S. of London and Edinb. Correspond. of the R. S. of Gottingen; now Historiographer to the East India Company.*

*Historical view of plans for the government of British India and regulation of trade of the East-Indies; and outlines of a plan of foreign government of commercial oeconomy, and of domestic administration for the Asiatic interests of Great-Britain. 1793. 4.

BRUCE, [Robert] *M. Dr,*

An account of the sensitive quality of the tree averrhoa carambola. (Columbian Magaz. Y. 1788. July p. 381.)

***BRUCKNER**, [J....] *Esq,*

Thoughts on public worship; Part 1. containing a full review of Mr *Wakefield's* objections to this practice; with suitable answers. 1792. 8. (1 sh. 6 d.)

***BRUÉE**, [William Urban] *Esq.*

Narrative of the successfull manner of cultivating the clove tree, in the Island of Dominica, one of the windward Charibbee-islands. 1797. 4.

***BRUYN**, [Severyn J....]

Letter on the retreat of swallows and the torpid state of certain animals in winter. (Mem. of B. A. Vol. 2. P. 1. p. 96.)

***BRYAN**, [Margaret] *Mistress of a boarding-school at Margate.*

A compendious system of astronomy, in a course of familiar lectures. 1797. 4. (1 L. 7 sh. 6 d.)

***BRYAN**, [William]

A testimony of the spirit of truth, concerning *Richard Brothers*, the man appointed of God to govern the hebrews, the Elijah promised by the Lord in these last days, to come and restore all things. 1795. 8. (6 d)

BRYANT, [Charles] *Of the city of Norwich.*

A dictionary of the ornamental trees, shrubs and plants

plants, most commonly cultivated in the plantations, gardens and stoves of Great-Britain, 1790. 8 (9 sh. 6 d.)

RYANT, [Henry] *M. A. Rector of Colby and Vicar of Langham, Regis, Norfolk.*

born 1721. died June 4. 1799.

See Gentleman's Magaz. Y. 1799. June. p. 532. Allg. Litt. Zeit. J. 1800. ItBl. S. 664.

Letter on oil from the seeds of the great annual sun flower. (Tr. of the Soc. for the E. of A. Vol. 2. p. 113.)

RYANT, [James] *Esq.*

See *Küttner's* Beyträge zur Kenntniss von England. 1794. St. 8. S. 107.

Vindiciae Flavianae —. Ed. 1. 1777. Ed. 2. 1780. (1 sh. 6 d.) Gemmarum antiquarum delectus ex praestantioribus desumtus in dactyliotheca Ducis Marlburiensis. Vol. 2. 1791. fol. A farther illustration of the analysis of ancient mythology, in answer to some foreign observations. 1778. * A treatise upon the authenticity of the scripture and the truth of the christian religion. 1791. 8. (5 sh.) Ed. 2. 1793. 8. (5 sh.) * Observations on a controverted passage in *Justin* Martyr and upon the worship of angels. London. 1793. 4. Observations upon the plagues inflicted upon the Egyptians, in which is shewn the peculiarity of those judgments and their correspondence with the rites and idolatry of that people. To these is prefixed a prefatory discourse concerning the Grecian colonies from Egypt. 1794. 8. (8 sh.) Observations upon a treatise, entitled a description of the plain of Troy by Mr. *Le Chevalier.* Eaton. 1796. 4. (3 sh.) A dissertation concerning the war of Troy and the expedition of the Grecians as described by *Homer*, shewing that no such expedition was ever undertaken and that no such city as Phrygia existed. 1796. 4. (8 sh.) übers. von *G. H. Nöhden.* Braunschw. 1797. 8. The sentiments of *Philo* Judaeus, concerning the λογος or word of God —. 1797. 8. (3 sh. 6 d.) Some observations upon the vindication of *Homer* and of the ancient poets and historians, who have recorded the siege and fall of Troy, written by *J. B. S. Morritt,*

Morritt, Esq. 1799. 4. (4 sh.) An expostulation addressed to the British critick. 1799. Observations upon some passages in scripture, which the enemies to religion have thought most obnoxious, and attended with difficulties not to be surmounted. 1803. 4. (12 sh.)

*BRYCE, [James] *Of the Kingdom of Scotland; Surgeon.*

An account of the yellow fever, with a successful method of cure. 1796. 8. (2 sh. 6 d.) Practical observations on the inoculation of cowpox, pointing out a test of a constitutional affection in those cases in which the local inflammation is slight and in which no fever is perceptible; illustrated by cases and plates. 1802. 8. (6 sh. 6 d.) Übers. mit Anmerk. von *F. G. Friese.* Breslau. 1803. 8.

BRYDGES, [Samuel Egerton] *Esq. F. A. S. Of Denton-Court, in the county of Kent.*

Sonnets and other poems; a new edition. 1795. 12. (3 sh. 6 d.) Mary de Clifford; a novel. 1792. 12. Verses on the late unanimous resolution to support the constitution; to which are added some other poems. 1794. 4. (1 sh.) Arthur Fitz-Albini, a novel; Vol. 1. 2. 1798. 8. * Theatrum poetarum anglicanorum. Containing the names and characters of all the English poets from the reign of Henry III. to the close of the reign of Queen Elizabeth by *Edward Philipps* the nephew of *Milton*: First published in 1675 and now enlarged by additions to every article. 1800. 8. (8 sh.)

*BRYDSON, [Thomas] *F. A. S. Edinb.*

A summary view of heraldry, in reference to the usages of chivalry and the general economy of the feudal system; with an appendix respecting such distinctions of rank as have place in the British constitution. 1795. 8. (6 sh.)

*BRYSON, [Thomas] *Rev.*

born at Dalkeith in Scotland 1759. died 1799. Apr. 24.

See Gentleman's Magaz. Y. 1799. May. p. 437. Evangelical Magaz. Y. 1800. March. p. 89.

An address to youth; 1792. A comprehensive view of the real christian's character, privileges and

and obligations: being the substance of a course of sermons on the 8 Chapter of St. Paul's Epistle to the Romans. 1794. 12. (3 sh. 6 d.)

BUCHAN, *Earl of*. — See *David Stewart Erskine*.

*BUCHAN, [A.... P.....] *M. Dr.*

Enchiridion syphiliticum; or directions for the conduct of venereal complaints. 1797. 12. (2 sh. 6 d.)

BUCHAN, [William] *M. Dr.*

Letter to the patentee, concerning the medical properties of the fleecy hosiery. Ed. 3. with notes and observations. 1790. 8. (1 sh.) Observations concerning the prevention and cure of the venereal disease —. 1796. 8. (3 sh. 6 d.) Ed. 2. 1797. übers. mit Anmerk. und Zus. von Dr. *J. C. F. Leune*. B 1. Leipz. 1800. 8. B 2. 1801. 8. Observations concerning the diet of the common people, recommending a method of living less expensive and more conducive to health than the present. 1797. 8. (1 sh. 6 d.) Advice to mothers on the subject of their own health and on the means of promoting the health, strenght and beauty of their offspring. 1803. 8. (6 sh.)

*BUCHANAN, [Francis] *Esq. M. Dr. A. L. S.*

Description of the tree called by the Burmas, Launzan. (Asiat. Res. Vol. 5. p. 123.) A comparative vocabulary of some of the languages spoken in the Burma empire. (Ibid. Vol. 5. p. 219.) On the religion and literature of the Burmas. (Ib. Vol. 6. p. 163.) Description of the vespertilio plicatus. (Transact. of L. S. Vol. 5. p. 261. *Tilloch's* Philos. Mag. Vol. 7. p. 145.) An account of the onchidium, a new genus of the class of vermes, found in Bengal. (Transact. of L. S. Vol. 5. p. 132.)

UCHANAN, [George] *M. Dr.*

Diss. de causis respirationis ejusdemque affectibus. Philad. 1789. 8.

BUCHANAN, [John Lane] *A. M. A native of the Highland part of Menteith in the shire of Perth, North Britain.*

See *Henke's* Archiv für die neueste Kirchengesch. B. 5. St. 2. S. 364.

Travels in the western Hebrides from 1782 to

1790. 1793. 8. (3 sh. 6 d.) Übers. von *F. L.* [illegible] *Meyer*. Berlin. 1795. 8. A defence of the Sc[illegible] Highlanders in general and some learned ch[illegible] racters, in particular; with a new and sat[illegible] factory account of the Picts, Scots, Fingal, Ossi[illegible] and his poems; as also of the maes, clans, boc[illegible] tria and several other particulars respecting [illegible] high antiquities of Scotland. 1794. 8. (6 sh[illegible] A general view of the fishery of Great-Brita[illegible] drawn up for the consideration of the undertak[illegible] of the North British fishing, lately begun [illegible] promoting the general utility of the inhabita[illegible] and empire at large. 1794. 8. (5 sh.)

*BUCHANAN, [Robertson] *Engineer. Glasgow.*
Description of the improved pump invented [illegible] him. (*Tilloch's* Philos. Magaz. Vol. 10. p. 19[illegible]) On the velocity of water wheels. (Ibid. Vol. [illegible] p. 278.) Account of some improvements on w[illegible] ter wheels. (Ibid. Vol. 11. p. 79.)

*BUCK, [Charles]
Anecdotes religious, moral and entertaining; [illegible] phabetically arranged and interspersed with a [illegible] riety of useful observations. 1799. 12. (3 sh. 6[illegible]

*BUCKE, [Thomas] *Merchant at Worlington, Suff[illegible]*
On the culture of potatoes. (*Young's* A. of A[illegible] Vol. 5. p. 250.)

*BUCKNAL, [Thomas Skip Dyot] *Esq. M. P. Hampton-Court.*
The orchardist; or a system of close pruning [illegible] medication, for establishing the science of orch[illegible] ding as patronized by the society for the encoura[illegible] ment of arts, manufactures and commerce. [illegible] tracted from the 11. 12. 13. 14 Vols of the So[illegible] ty's transactions with additions, 1797. 8. (3 [illegible] Observations relative to the pruning of orcha[illegible] (Tr. of the Soc. for the E. of A. Vol. 11, p. [illegible] Vol. 13. p. 160.) Letter on pruning orchar[illegible] (Ibid. Vol. 12. p. 206. Vol. 14. p. 207. 229. Vol. [illegible] p. 144. Vol. 18. p. 325.) On the cause of bli[illegible] on fruit-trees. (Ibid. Vol. 17. p. 263. Vol. 18. [illegible] 299.) On the peculiar deficiency in the ap[illegible] crop. (Comm. and Agric. Magaz. Y. 1802. N[illegible] p. 324.) An attempt at improving the fruit g[illegible] den. (Ib. Y. 1802. Dec. p. 406.)

BU[illegible]

*BUCKNELL, [James] *of Knowstone, near Tiverton, Devon.*

On the potatoes for feeding cattle and sheep. (Tr. of the Soc. for the E. of A. Vol. 9. p. 45. Vol. 11. p. 98.)

*BUDD, [J....] *Dr.*

Short account of the climate &c. of South-Carolina. (American Museum Y. 1790. Febr. p. 105.) On porter. (Ib. Y. 1792. Febr. p. 64.)

*BUDD, [John] *A. M.*

Essays and sermons on select subjects. 1803. 8. (3 sh. 6 d.)

*BUDD, [William]

Method of raising calves without milk. (American Museum Y. 1787. Aug. p. 177. Massachusetts Magaz. Y. 1791. Febr. p. 86.)

*BUDWORTH, [Joseph] *Esq. F. A. S. Captain,*

A fortnight's ramble to the lakes in Westmoreland, Lancashire and Cumberland; 1792. 8. (5 sh.) Ed. 2. 1795. 8. (5 sh.) The siege of Gibraltar, a poem. 1795. 4. (2 sh.) Windermare, a poem. 1798. 8. (1 sh.)

*BUEL, [William] *Physician.*

An account of the bilious fever and dysentery, which prevailed in Sheffield, Massachusetts, in the Y. 1796. (Medical Repository. Vol. 1. p. 453.)

BULKELEY, [Charles] *Dissenting-Minister.*

born 1718. Oct. 18. died Apr. 15. 1797.

See Gentleman's Magaz. Y. 1797. May. p. 439. July p. 587. Monthly Rev. Y. 1797. Sept. p. 117. Allg. Litt. Zeit. ItBl, J. 1800. S. 643. See *John Evans.*

Fifteen discourses on public occasions. 1752. 8. An answer to his, „Plea for mixt communion by Grantham Killingworth.„ 1756. The christian minister. 1758. 12. Sermons on public occasions Vol. 1. 2. 1761. 8. Preface to notes on the bible. 1791. An apology for human nature; with a prefatory address to *Will. Wilberforce*, by *John Evans.* 1797. 12. (2 sh. 6 d.) Notes on the bible — published from the author's manuscript, with memoirs of the author and his works by *Joshua Toulmin.* Vol. 1-3. 1803. 8.

(Several single sermons.)

K 5 *BULL,

*BULL, [.....] *of Newport-Pagnel.*
See *William Cowper.*

*BULL, [.....] *Colonel.*
Note concerning a vegetable under ground; (Tr. of A. S. Vol. 5. p. 160.)

*BULLEN, [Henry St. John] *M. A. of Trinity College, Cambridge.*
Elements of geography, exprefsly defigned for the ufe of fchools. 1799. 8. (3 fh. 6 d.)

BULLER, [Sir Francis] *Bart. One of the judges of Common-pleas.*
born 1745. died 1800. June 5.
See Gentleman's Magaz. Y. 1800. June. p. 594.
Public characters of 1798 et 1799. p. 201.
An introduction to the law relative to trials at nifi prius; Ed. 2. corrected with additions. 1790. 8. (9 fh.)

*BULLMAN, [E....]
An eafy guide, or, an introduction to the hebrew language, adapted for the ufe of fchools, and to render perfons capable of teaching themfelves in an expeditious manner. 1795. 8. (1 fh.)

*BULLOCK, [Richard] *D. D. Preacher at the church of St. Paul, Covent-Garden.*
Two fermons, preached at St. Paul's Covent-Garden. 1793.

*BULLOCK, [William]
Account of his drawback lock. (Comm. and Agr. Mag. Y. 1802. April. p. 251. Tr. of the Soc. for E. of A. Vol. 18. p. 243.) Defcription of an improved drawback lock for houfe doors. (*Nicholfon's* Journal. Y. 1802. July. p. 204. Tr. of the Soc. for E. of A. Vol. 19. p. 290.)

*BULT, [John] *of Kingston, near Taunton.*
Account of a crop of beans and turnips in alternate rows. (Bath Agricult. Soc. Vol. 3. p. 259.)

*BUNBURY, [Henry] *Esq. an Artift.*
Hints to bad horfemen, by Geoffry Gambado. 1787.

*BUNBURY, [H.... W.....]
Tales of the devil, with a portrait of the author and

and other engravings from ſketches. 1801. 4. (4 ſh. 6 d.)

*BUNING, [Charles] *Esq.*

Peace in our power, upon terms not unreaſonable. 1798. 8. (1 ſh.).

*BUNTING, [Edmund]

Deſcription of his new conſtructed calender mill. (Tr. of the Soc. for the E. of A. Vol. 15. p. 268.)

*BURBON, [William] *A. M.*

Unanimity recommended; containing an appropriate ſtatement of the arguments made uſe of by the Engliſh and French governments, and a complete vindication of our pacific conduct from the aſperſions of Buonaparte. 1803. 8. (9 d.)

*BURCHELL, [Joſeph] *One of the joint Clerks to the commiſſioners of taxes for Holborn diviſion, Middleſex.*

Obſervations on the income tax, with regulations ſuggeſted for the ſecurity of the revenue and preventing the waſte of public money: Together with a propoſed plan of an auxiliary to the ſinking fund. 1801. 8. (1 ſh.)

*BURD, [William] *Surgeon in the royal navy.*

Hiſtory of a caſe terminating ſucceſsfully, after amputation was performed at the ſhoulder-joint. (*Duncan's* A. of Med. Y. 1797. p. 282.)

BURDER, [George] *of Coventry.*

The weaver's pocket-book, or weaving ſpiritualized; written by the Rev. Dr. *Collins*, Vicar of St. Stephen's, Norwich, in the Y. 1675. and now abridged and reviſed. 1794. 24. (6 d.) An abridgment of Dr. *Owen's* treatiſe on juſtification by faith. 1797. 8. (2 ſh. 6 d.)

°BURDER, [George]

The welch Indians; or, a collection of papers reſpecting a people, whoſe anceſtors emigrated from Wales to America in the Year 1170 with Prince Madoc (300 years before the firſt voyage of Columbus) and who are ſaid now to inhabit a beautiful country on the Weſtſide of the Miſiſſipi. 1797.

1797. 8. (1 sh.) The life of the Rev. *John Machin**, A. M. — formerly Minister of the Parish church of Astbury, near Congleton in Cheshire, with a recommendatory preface by the late Sir *Charles Wolseley*, Bart. revised and republished. 1799. 12. (8 d.) Village sermons — Vol. 1-4. 1800. 12. (4 sh. 6 d.) See *Joseph Whitehouse*.

*BURDER, [Samuel]

The moral law considered as a rule of life to believers. Designed as an antidote to Antinomianism. 1795. 12. (1 sh.) A concise directory for the profitable employment of the christian's sabbath. 1800. 12. (3 d.) Oriental customs, or an illustration of the sacred scriptures, by an explanatory application of the customs and manners of the eastern nation and especially the jews, therein alluded to; together with observations on many difficult and obscure texts, collected from the most celebrated travellers and the most eminent critiks. 1802. 8. (9 sh.)

*BURDETT, [Sir Francis]

See Public Characters of 1802-1803. p. 481. Speech in the House of Commons, 12 Apr. 1802. for an inquiry into the conduct of the administration at home and abroad during the war. 1802. 8. (1 sh.)

*BURDON, [William] *M. A. Fellow of Emmanuel-College, Cambridge.*

Three letters, addressed to the bishop of Landaff. 1795. 8. (1 sh.) An examination of the merits and tendency of the pursuits of literature. Part. 1. 1799. Part 2. 1800. 8. (5 sh.) Various thoughts on politics, morality end literature. 1801. 8. (3 sh.) Materials for thinking. Nrb. 1. (1 sh.) Unanimity recommended. 1803. 8. (1 sh.) Advice addressed to the lower ranks of society, useful at all times, more especially in the present. 1803. (6 d.)

*BURDY, [Samuel] *A. B. Of the kingdom of Ireland.*

The life of the late Rev. *Phil. Skelton*; with some curious

* The original life of *J. Machin* was published in the Y. 1571.

curious anecdotes. Dublin. 1792. 8. (3 sh. 6 d.) See New-York Magaz. Y. 1795. Nov. p. 672.

BUREAU, [James] *F. M. S. Surgeon in London.*
Case of violent pains in the penis and neighbouring parts. (Mem. of M. S. of L. Vol. 3. p. 65.)

*BURGES, [Bartholomew]
A series of Indostan letters, containing a striking account of the manners and customs of the Gentoo nations and of the Moguls and other Mahomedan tribes in Indostan, with other polemical East-India tracts, both amusing, interesting and perfectly original. New-York. 1790. (½ Dollar.)

*BURGES, [George] *A. B. Curate of Whittlesea.*
Remarks on Mr. *Wakefield's* enquiry into the expediency and propriety of public or social worship. 1792. 8. (1 sh. 6 d.) A letter to *Th. Paine*, author of the age of reason. 1794. 8. (1 sh.) A letter to the Lord Bishop of Ely on the subject of a new and authoritative translation of the holy scripture. 1796. 8. (1 sh.) Desultory hints on violence of opinion and intemperance of language. 1796. 8. (6 d.) An address to the people of Great-Britain. 1798. 8. (1 sh.)
Several single sermons.

BURGES, [Sir James Bland] *Bart. LL. Dr. Knight-Marschal of his Maj. houshold and one of the under-Secretaries of state. (of Weston in Cambridgeshire.)*
The birth and triumph of love, a poem with many fine plates. 1796. 4. (2 L. 10 sh.) Richard the first, commonly called coeur de Lion, an epic poem, in XVIII. books. Vol. 1. 2. 1801. 8. (1 L. 5 sh.)

BURGESS, [Thomas] *Prebendary of Durham and domestic Chaplain to the Bishop of Durham.*
Observationes in quasdam *Sophoclis*, *Euripidis* et *Aeschyli* tragoedias. 1778 *Evidence that the relation of *Josephus*, concerning Herod's having new built the temple at Jerusalem is either false or misinterpreted. Ed. 2. 1789. 8. (1 sh. 6 d.) The divinity of Christ proved from his own declarations, attested and interpreted by his living witnesses the jews; a sermon. 1790. 4. (1 sh.) *Remarks on the scriptural account of the dimensions

1796. 8. (2 sh.) übers. mit Anmerk. von *Fried. Gentz.* Berlin. 1796. 8. Original thoughts on the prospect of a regicide peace in a series of letters. 1796. 8. (2 sh. 6 d.) Two letters — on the proposals for peace with the regicide directory of France. 1798. 8. (3 sh. 6 d.) übers. von *Albr. Wittenberg.* Frankf. u. Leipz. 1797. 8. A third letter — 1797. 8. (3 sh.) A general reply to the several answerers — of a letter written to a noble Lord. 1796. 8. (2 sh.) Letter — on the conduct of the minority in parliament: containing 54 articles of impeachment against *C. J. Fox.* 1797. 8. (2 sh. 6 d.) Three memorials on french affairs; written in the Y. 1791. 1792 and 1793. 1797. 8. (3 sh. 6 d.) übers. von Dr. *J. G. Tralles.* Hirschberg. 1798. 8. übers. Hamburg. 1798. 8. Two letters on the conduct of our domestic parties, with regard to french politicks; including observations on the conduct of the minority, in the session of 1793. Ed. 4. 1797. 8. (3 sh.) Thoughts and details on scarcity, originally presented to — *William Pitt* in Nov. 1799. 1800. (1 sh. 6 d.) Original letters between the late *Thomas Mercer* Esq. of Dublin, and — *Edm. Burke.* (Monthly Magaz. Y. 1802. May. p. 317.) Works, a new edition. Vol. 1–8. 1802. 8. (2 L. 16 sh.)

*BURKE, [Richard] *Esq. Recorder of Bristol.*
A charge delivered to the grand jury, at a session of oyer and terminer, and general gaol delivery for the city — of Bristol, held at the Guildhall there April 6. 1793. 8. (6 d.)

BURN, [Edward] *M. A. Minister of St. Mary's chapel, Birmingham.*
Letters to Dr. *Priestley* in vindication of the former letter. 1790. 8. A reply to Dr. *Priestley* appeal to the public on the subject of the late riots at Birmingham, in vindication of the clergy and other respectable inhabitants of the town. 1792. 8. (2 sh.) Pastoral hints; or the importance of religious education; with a familiar plan of instruction designed for the assistance of families. 1801. (1 sh.)

*BURN,

*BURN, [John] *Esq. One of his Maj. Justices of the Peace for the Counties of Westmoreland and Cumberland.*

A new law dictionary, intended for general use as well as for Gentlemen of the profession by *Richard Burn* LL. D. — and continued to the present time by his son. Vol. 1. 2. 1792. 8. (16 sh.) An appendix to the 17 edition of Dr. *Rich. Burn's* justice of the peace and parish officer, containing all the acts of parliament and adjudged cases which relate to the office of a justice of the peace from 32 Geo. III. to the present time. 1795. 8. (3 sh. 6 d.) The justice of the peace and parish officer — by *Rich. Burn.* Ed. XVIII corrected and considerably enlarged. Vol. 1-4. 1797-1800. 8. (2 L. 8 sh.)

*BURN, [John Ilderton] *of the Inner-Temple.*

A practical treatise or compendium of the law of marine insurances. 1801. 12. (5 sh.) A treatise, or summary of the law relative to stock-jobbing. 1803. 8. (2 sh. 6 d.)

BURNABY, [Andrew] *D. D. Archdeacon of Leicester and Vicar of Greenwich.*

Travels through the middle settlements of North-America in 1759 and 1760. New edition corrected and enlarged. 1799. 4. (12 sh.)

(Several single sermons.)

BURNET, [George] *M. A. Minister at Elland, Yorkshire.*

born in Scotland 1733. died July 8. 1793.

See Gentleman's Magaz. Y. 1793. July. p. 676. The Evangelical Magazine for 1793. p. 83.

BURNET, [James] Lord *Monboddo. One of the Lord of Session for the kingdom of Scotland.*

born 1714. died at Edinburgh May 26. 1799.

See Public Characters of 1798-1799. p. 514. Gentleman's Mag. Y. 1799. June p. 529. Dec. p. 1031. Monthly Mag. Y. 1799. Aug. p. 576. *Küttner's* Beytr. zur Kenntniss — von England. St. 8. 1794. S. 70. Allg. Litterat. Zeit. ItBl. J. 1800. S. 998.

*On the origin and progress of language. Vol. 5. 1789. 8. (6 sh.) Vol. 6. 1792. 8. (6 sh.) *Antient metaphysics: Vol. 4. Containing the history of man

man; with an apppendix, relating to the fill sauvage whom the author saw in france. 1795. 4 (1 L. 1 sh.) Vol. 5. containing the history of man in the civilized state. 1797. 4. (15 sh.) Vol. 6 1799. (15 sh.)

BURNEY, [Charles] *Mus. Dr: F. R. S: Organist of Chelsea-Hospital.*

born at Shrewsbury 1726.

See Public Characters of 1798-1799. p. 379.

The cunning man; 17.. An essay towards the history of comets; 17.. Plan of a public music school; 17.. Memoirs of the life and writings of the Abate *Metastasio*; in which are incorporated translations of his principal letters. Vol. 1-3. 1796. 8. (1 L. 1 sh.) Striking views of Lamia, the celebrated Athenian flute player. (Massachusetts Magaz. Y. 1789. Nov. p. 684.)

*BURNEY, [....] *Miss.*

Clarentine. Vol. 1-3. 1796. 12.

BURNEY, [Frances] *now Mrs. D'Arblay.*

* Brief reflections relative to the emigrant french clergy; earnestly submitted to the humane consideration of the ladies of Great-Britain, 1793. 8. * Camilla. Vol. 1-5. 1797. 8. (1 L. 1 sh.) übers. Th. 1-4. Berlin u. Stettin 1798. 8.

*BURNEY, [James] *Esq. Captain in the Royal Navy.*

Plan of defence against invasion. 1796. Ed. 2. 1797. 4. (6 d.) Measures, recommended for the support of public credit. 1797. 4. ((1 sh.) Chronological history of the discoveries in the South-Sea, or pacific Ocean. Part. 1. 1803. 4. (1 L. 4 sh.)

*BURNS, [John] *Surgeon in Glasgow.*

The anatomy of the gravid uterus; with practical inferences relative to pregnancy and labour. 1799. 8. (7 sh.) On inflammation. Vol. 1. 2. 1800. 8. (14 sh.)

BURNS, [Robert] *A Ploughman in the county of Ayr in Scotland.*

born 1758. died Jul. 21. 1796. at Dumfries.

See Gentleman's Magaz. Y. 1796. Aug. p. 703. Monthly Magaz. Y. 1797. March. p. 213. Suppl. p. 552. Critical Review Y. 1800. Sept. p. 44. New-York Magaz. Y. 1797. March. p. 118. Allgem. Litter. Zeit. J. 1797. ItBl. N. 51. S. 429.

S. 429. *Wieland's* Teutscher Merkur. J. 1796. St. 12. S. 391. *Hüttner's* Englische Miscellen, J. 1800. St. 2. S. 70.

Poems, chiefly in the Scottish dialect. Vol. 1. 2. 1798. 8. (7 sh.) Works; with an account of his life and a criticism on his writings (by Dr. *Curry*, of Liverpool) To which are prefixed some observations on the character and condition of the Scottish peasantry. Vol. 1–4. 1800. 8. (1 L. 11 sh. 6 d.) See *Elizabeth Scot*.

BURREL, [Sophia] *Lady; Wife of William Clay.*
born, ... died Jun. 20. 1802. at West Cowes, in the isle of Wight.

See Gentleman's Magaz. Y. 1802. July p. 688.

Poems. Vol. 1. 2. 1793. 8. (12 sh.) The tymbriad (from *Xenophon's* cyropaedia). 1794. 8. (6 sh.) Telemachus. 1794. 8. (4 sh.) Theodora; or, the spanish daughter, a tragedy. 1800. 8. (3 sh. 6 d.) Maximian, a tragedy, taken from Corneille. 1800. 8. (3 sh. 6 d.)

URROW, [Reuben] *Esq.*
born, ... died at Buxar, in the East Indies Jun. 7. 1792.

See Gentleman's Magaz. Y. 1793. Aug. p. 767.

A synopsis of the different cases that may happen in deducing the longitude of one place from another by means of *Arnold's* chronometer and of finding the rates when the difference of longitude is given. (Asiat. Researches. Vol. 2. p. 473.) Memorandums concerning an old building in the Hadjipore district, near the Gunduck river. (Ibid. Vol. 2. p. 477.) Observations of some of the eclipses of jupiter's satellites. (Ibid. Vol. 2. p. 483.) A proof that the Hindoos had the binomial theorem. (Ibid. Vol. 2. p. 487.) A specimen of a method of reducing practical tables and calculations into more general and compendious forms. (Ibid. Vol. 3. p. 141.) A demonstration of one of the Hindoo rules of Arithmetic. (Ibid. Vol. 3. p. 145.)

BURROWES, [George] *M. Dr. M. R. J. A.*
Account of a fistulous opening in the stomach; (Tr. of J. A. Vol. 4. p. 177. *Simmons's* Med. Facts and Observat. Vol. 5. p. 185.) Case of an enlarged spleen; (Tr. of J. A. Vol. 4. p. 183.

Simmons's Med. Facts and Observat. Vol. 7. p. 219.)

BURROWES, [Robert] *D. D. F. T. C. D. M. R. I. A.*
Essay on style in writing, considered with respect to thoughts and sentiments as well as words and indicating the writer's peculiar and characteristic disposition, habits and powers of mind. (T. of I. A. Vol. 5. p. 39. b.) On the poetical character of Dr. *Goldsmith* (Ibid. Vol. 6. p. 71. b.)

BURT, [Adam] *Surgeon at Gya. In the service of East-India Company.*
On the dissection of the Pangolin —. (Asiat. Researches. Vol. 2. p. 353.) Account of a case, in which a fistula in perinaeo was healed by the introduction of a seton. (*Duncan's* A. of Med. Y. 1798. p. 354.)

*BURTELL, [Edmund] *Junior.*
Observations upon the town of Cromer, considered as a watering place, and the picturesque scenery in its Neighbourhood. 1801.

*BURTIS, [Peter]
Letter relative to the Hessian fly. (American Museum Y. 1787. Nov. p. 459.)

*BURTON, [.....] *Mrs.*
The fugitive, an artless tale. Vol. 1. 2. 17.. 12. Laura, or the orphan, a novel. Vol. 1. 2. 1798. 12. (6 sh.)

BURTON, [Edmund] *M. A.*
*Suicide, a dissertation. 1790. 4. (1 sh. 6 d.)

*BURTON, [John] *Esq. Clerk of the rope-yard in his Majesty's dock-yard at Chatham.*
Lectures on female education and manners. Vol. 1. 2. 1793. 12. (6 sh.) übers. B. 1. 2. Leipz. 1794. 1795. 8. Aufl. 2. B. 1. 2. Leipz. 1798. 1799. 8.

BURTON, [Philip] *Esq. First Attorney in the Court of Exchequer.*
born 1710. died at Eltham, Kent, Nov. 17. 1792.
See Gentleman's Magaz. Y. 1792. Nov. p. 1062. The practice in the office of the court of exchequer, epitomized. 1777. 8. Practice of the office of pleas in the court of exchequer, both ancient and modern, compiled from authentic materials. Vol. 1. 2. 1791. 8. (13 sh.) Annihilation no punishment

ment but contempt to the wicked, after the day of judgment, or, the curse of god on Adam's eating the forbidden fruit, as proved from scripture. 1792. 8. (6 sh.)

IURY, [Thomas]

Particulars and description of the Duke of Bridgewater's drain plough. (Comm. and Agric. Mag. Y. 1802. Febr. p. 81. Tr. of the Soc. for the E. of A. Vol. 19. p. 117.)

ISBY, [Thomas] *Mus. Dr: LL. Dr. Of Lambeth.* born in London 1755. Dec...

See Public Characters of 1802–1803. p. 371.

Musical dictionary, by Dr. *Arnold* and *Thom. Busby*. Nr. 1–197. 1786. Divine harmonist. Nr. 1–12. 1788. Melodia Britannica or the beauties of British song. 17.. Monthly Musical journal; 17.. A complete dictionary of music. To which is prefixed a familiar introduction to the first principles of that science. 1801. 8. (6 sh.) Life of *Mozart*, the celebrated german musician. (Monthly Magaz. Y. 1798 Dec. p. 445.) On modern music. (Ibid. Y. 1799. Jan. p. 35.) On vocal music. (Ibid. Y. 1801. Nov. p. 281.) Original memoirs of the late *Jonathan Battishill*; (born in London May 1738. died Dec. 10. 1801.) (Ibid. Y. 1802. Febr. p. 36.)

USFIELD, [J..... A.....] *A. B: Curate of Skipton in Craven.*

The christian's guide in six progressive lectures. 1800. 8. (3 sh. 6 d.)

USHE, [Gervase Parker] *Esq. M. R. J. A.*

An essay towards ascertaining the population of Ireland. (Tr. of J. A. 1789. p. 145.) An account of the population of Ireland. (*Young's* A. of Agr. Vol. 14. p. 81.)

USHNELL, [.....] *Dr. of Connecticut.*

General principles and construction of a submarine vessel. (Tr. of A. S. Vol. 4. p. 303. *Nicholson's* Journal. Vol. 4. p. 229.)

UTCHER, [Edmund] *Rev.*

Sermons; to which are subjoined suitable hymns. 1798. 8. (7 sh. 6 d.) Moral tales; — To which is added by a Lady, the unhappy family or the dreadful effects of vice, a tale. 1801. 12. (2 sh.)

The ſubſtance of the holy ſcriptures methodized and arranged upon an entirely new plan, in ſuch a manner as to form a bible with hymns, notes &c. Nrh. 1. 1801. (1 ſh.) (to be completed in 20 numbers).

*BUTCHER, [George] *late Clerk of the dry ſtores at his Maj. victualling office, Deptford.*

Facts explanatory of the inſtrumental cauſe of the preſent high prices of proviſions; formerly communicated in a letter to *George Cherry* Esq. then one of the commiſſioners for victualling the navy; with obſervations thereon. 1801. 8. (1 ſh. 6 d.)

*BUTLER, [C....]

The age of chivalry; or, friendſhip of other times; a moral and hiſtorical tale; abridged and ſelected from the knights of the ſwan of Mad. *Genlis*; deſigned for youth. 1799. 8. (2 ſh. 6 d.)

*BUTLER, [Charles]

*Horae biblicae, being a connected ſeries of miſcellaneous notes on the original text, early verſions and principal editions of the old and new teſtament. 1799. 8. (5 ſh.)

BUTLER, [Charles] *Esq. of Lincoln's-Inn-new-ſquare; Barriſter at Law.*

The inſtitutes of the laws of England, or a commentary upon *Littleton* — authore *Edward Coke* — the 15 edition reviſed and corrected, with further additions of notes, references and proper tables by *Francis Hargrave* and *Charles Butler*, including alſo the notes of Lord chief juſtice Hale and Lord-chancellor Nottingham and an analyſis of Littleton, written by an unknown hand in 1658. 1659. Vol. 1-3. 1794. 8. (1 L. 18 ſh.) A letter to a nobleman, on the propoſed repeal of the penal laws which now remain in force againſt the Iriſh roman catholics. 1801. 8. (1 ſh.) Hiſtorical account of the laws againſt the roman catholiks. 1801. A letter to a Roman catholic Gentleman of Ireland, on the chief Conſul Bonaparte's projected invaſion. 1803. 8. (3 d.)

*BUTLER, [Charles] *Teacher of the mathematicks at Cheam ſchool.*

An eaſy introduction to algebra, with notes — to which

which is prefixed an essay on the uses of the mathematicks. 1800.

*BUTLER, [George] *Esq.*

Description of his invented bucket, for drawing water out of deep wells. (Tr. of the Soc. for the E. of A. Vol. 12. p. 286.)

*BUTLER, [John] *Hackney.*

Description of a life-boat. (Monthly Magaz. Y. 1801. June. p. 386.)

*BUTLER, [John] *Canterbury.*

Brief reflections upon the liberty of the british subject in address to — *Edm. Burke*, occasioned by his late publication on the french revolution. 1791. 8. (2 sh.)

*BUTLER, [John] *D. D. Lord-Bishop of Hereford.* born 1717. died 1802. Dec. 10.

See Gentleman's Magaz. Y. 1802. p. 1170. Biograph. Litter. and Polit. Anecdotes — Vol. I. p. 70. Monthly Magaz. Y. 1803. Jan. p. 562.

An address to the cocoa-tree from a Whig. (1762) (See scarce tracts Vol. I.) A consultation on the subject of a standing army, held at the King's arms tavern, on the 28 Febr. 1763. serious considerations on the measures of the present administration. 1763. Account of the character of the late R. H. *Henry Bilson Legge.* (See scarce tracts. Vol. I. printed for J. Debrett.) Select sermons —; 1802.

(Several single sermons.)

BUTLER, [Samuel] *A School-master at Shrewsbury.*

M. Musuri carmen in *Platonem*; *Is. Casauboni* in *Josephum Scaligerum* ode; accedunt poemata et exercitationes utriusque linguae; appendicis loco subjiciuntur hymnus Cleanthis Stoici; Clementis Alexandrini hymni duo; *Henr. Stephani* adhortatio ad lectionem novi foederis. Cantabrigiae et Londini. 1797. 8. (3 sh. 6 d.)

*BUTLER, [Weeden] *M. A: Morning-Preacher of Charlotte-street Chapel, Pimlico; and Chaplain to the R. H. Lady dowager Onslow.*

An account of the life and writings of the Rev. Dr. *George Stanhope,* Dean of Canterbury (author of the paraphrase on the epistles and gospels). 17.. 8. Memoirs of *Mark Hildesley,* D. D. Lord-

L 4 Bishop

Bishop of Sodor and Man and Master of Sherburn Hospital* under whose auspices the holy scriptures were translated into the Manks language. 1798. 8. (8 sh.)

(Several single sermons.)

*BUTLER, [Weeden] *Jun. M. A. of Sidney-Sussex-College, Cambridge.*

Prospect of the political relations which subsist between the french republic and the helvetic body; by Colonel *Weiss* — translated from the French. 1794. 8. (1 sh. 6 d.) Bagatelles or miscellaneous productions; consisting of original poetry and translations, principally by the editor. 1795. 8. (3 sh.) The wrongs of Unterwalden; translated. 1799. 8. (2 sh.) Zimao, the African, translated. 1800. 8. (2 sh.)

BUTLER, [William] *Teacher of writing, accounts and geography in Ladies schools and in private families.*

Arithmetical questions on a new plan, designed as a supplement to the author's engraved introduction to arithmetic — —. 1795. 8. Ed. 2. enlarged 1796. 8. (4 sh.) Ed. 3. 1801. (5 sh. 6 d.) A chronological table on a new plan: comprising articles of an historical, biographical and miscellaneous nature, for daily use —. Ed. 2. enlarged 1799. 12. (5 sh.) Geographical and biographical exercises, designed for the use of young ladies. 1798. (3 sh. 6 d.) Exercises on the globes, interspersed with some historical, biographical, mythological and miscellaneous information on a new plan; designed for the use of young ladies. 1798. (4 sh. 6 d.) Arithmetical tables, designed for the use of young ladies. 1802. 32.

*BUTLIN, [Thomas]

Accommodation at Madeira: (Monthly Magaz. Y. 1800. Dec. p. 411.)

BUTT, [George] *D. D. Chaplain in Ordinary to his Majesty,*

* born Dec. 9. 1698. died Nov. 30. 1771. See Gentleman's Magaz. Y. 1798. Dec. p. 1054. Monthly Review Y. 1800. Aug. p. 360.

Majesty, Rector of Stanford and Vicar of Kidderminster.
born, ... 1739. died at Stanford, co. Worcester, Sept. 30. 1795.
See Gentleman's Magaz. Y. 1795. Nov. p. 969.
Sermons; Vol. 1. 2. 17.. Poems; Vol. 1. 2. 17..

BUTTER, [William] *M. Dr. Physician in London, before in Derby; Fellow of the Roy. College of Physicians, Edinburgh.*
On the disease commonly called angina pectoris. 1791. 8. (2 sh.) On the venereal rose. 1799. 8.

BUTTERWORTH, [Laurence]
Thoughts on moral government and agency, and the origin of moral evil; in opposition to the doctrine of absolute, moral, christian and philosophical necessity. 1792. 8. (5 sh.)

*BUTTS, [William] *Rev. of Glemsford, near Sudbury, Suffolk.*
Culture, expense, and produce of one acre of lucerne. (*Young's* A. of Agr. Vol. 4. p. 507. Vol. 5. p. 256.) Rise of poor rates with observat. of *A. Young*. (Ibid. Vol. 17. p. 496.) Remarkable crop of wheat. (Ibid. Vol. 18. p. 168.) Danger of Jacobin principles in England. (Ib. Vol. 21. p. 212.) On poor-rates. (Ib. Vol. 22. p. 45.) On dry sowing wheat. (Ib. Vol. 23. p. 317.)

*BYLAND, [William]
The mechanics guide, or a treatise on the laws of mechanics, as they relate to wheel machines. 1797. 8. (1 sh. 6 d.)

*BYRNE, [William]
Antiquities of Great-Britain with historical descriptions. Vol. 1. 2. Nrb. 1–4. 1799. 4. (each numb. 15 sh.)

BYROM, [John] *M. D. F. R. S.*
born .... died about 1763.
Remarks on Mr. *Jeake's* plan for short hand. (Phil. Transact. Y. 1748. p. 388.) Remarks on Mr. *Lodwick's* alphabet. (Ib. Y. 1748. p. 401.)

*BYWELL, [John] *of Aglethorp, Yorkshire.*
Use of potatoes in feeding cattle. (*Young's* A. of Agr. Vol. 1. p. 402.)

*CADDICK, [Richard] *Rev. of Christ-church, Oxford.*

Hebrew made easy, or, a short and plain introduction to the sacred hebrew language, compiled in a new method, with extracts from the best hebrew grammars. 1799. 8. (1 sh.)

CADE, [John] *Esq. of Durham.*

Further observations on Cataractonium and the parts adjacent. (Arch. Vol. 10. p. 54.)

CADOGAN, [William] *M. Dr. Physician to the army* born; . . . . . died Febr. 26. 1797.

See Gentleman's Mag. Y. 1797. April. p. 352. *Duncan's* Annals of Medec. Y. 1797. p. 433.

On the nursing and management of children. 1750. Dissertat. on the gout and all chronic diseases — übers. von Dr. *W. H. S. Buchholz.* Frankf. und Leipzig. Aug. 2. 1790. 8. Oratio anniversaria Harvejana habita die 18. Oct. 1792. 1793. 4. (2 sh.)

*CADOGAN, [William Bromley] *M. A. Rector of Chelsea and Vicar of St. Giles, Reading.* born 1751. at Caversham Park, Oxfordshire; died at Reading, co. Berks. Jan. 18. 1797.

See Gentleman's Magaz. Y. 1797. Febr. p. 166. Sept. p. 796. Y. 1798. Apr. p. 288. June. p. 470. Evangelical Magaz. Y. 1798. Jan. p. 3.

Liberty and equality; two sermons. 1793. Sermon on the death of Mr. *Romaine.* 1795. The life of the Rev. *Will. Romaine,* M. A. late Rector of the united parishes of St. Andrew — 1796. 8. (1 sh. 6 d.) See *Richard Cecil.* and *J. Cooke.*

*CAINES, [Clement] *Esq.*

Letters on the cultivation of the Otaheite cane; the manufacture of sugar and rum; the saving of melasses; the care and preservation of stock; with the attention and anxiety which is done to negroes; and a speech on the slave trade. 1801. 8. (6 sh.)

CALDECOTT, [Thomas] *Esq. of the Middle-Temple; Barrister at Law.*

Published Sir *James Burrow* Reports of cases, relative to the duty and office of a justice of the peace from the time of the death of Lord Raymond

mond in the Year 1732 to Michaelmas term 1785. incl. Part 1. 2. 3. 1800. 4.

*CALDECOTT, [Thomas] See *Thomas Reid.*

*CALDER, [John] *D. D.*

A new edition of Tattler with notes by Mr. *John Nichols.* Vol. 1–6. 1786. 8. Spectator, Guardian and Tattler with notes chiefly by *Calder*, Bishop *Percy* and Mr. *Nichols.* 1787. *Pierre François le Courayer* last sentiments on religion, translated from the french. 1787. 12.

*CALDWALL, [Thomas] *Apothecary to the city-dispensary.*

A select collection of ancient and modern epitaphs and inscriptions. 1796. 12.

*CALDWELL, [Charles] *A. M: M. Dr. Senior Vice-President of the Academy.*

Elements of physiology; by *J. Fr. Blumenbach*, translated from the original latin and interspersed with occasional notes. To which is subjoined by the translator, an appendix on animal electricity. Vol. 1. 2. Philadelphia. 1798 An attempt to establish the sameness of the phaenomena of fever. 17.. Medical and physical memoirs containing among other subjects, a particular enquiry into the origin and nature of the late pestilential epidemies of the United states. 1801. 8. (8 sh.) A semi-annual oration on the origin of pestilential diseases, Philadelphia. 1799. 8. (25 Cents.) An oration on the causes of the difference in point of frequency and force between the endemic diseases of the United states of America and those of the countries of Europe. Philad. 1802.

CALDWELL, [Sir James] *Bart. F. R. S.*

born .... died 1784.

See Biogr. Liter. and Polit. Anecdotes —; Vol. 1. p. 120.

Debates of the house of Commons of Ireland in the first session after the treaty of peace in 1763. 17..

CALEY, [John] *Esq. F. A. S.*

A survey of the manor of Wymbledon, alias Wimbleton, with the rights, members and appartenance thereof, lying and being in the county of Surrey; (Arch. Vol. 10. p. 399.)

CALL,

CALL, [Sir John] *Bart. M. P. F. R. S.*

On population: (Bath Agric. Soc. Vol. 9. p. 245.) An abstract of the houses inhabitants, produce, consumption, surplu. and deficiency of grain, in several parishes in Cornwall and Devonshire collected Oct. 1790. (*Young's* A. of Agr. Vol. 25. p. 511.) Crops and harvest in Devon and Cornwall. (Ibid. Vol. 34. p. 183.) On the smut in wheat, blights and the manner in which plants are nourished. (Comm to the B. of Agr. Vol. 2. p. 428.) Abstract of baptisms and burials in four parishes of 50 counties in England during a course of ten successive years, Y. 1788-1797. (Ibid. Vol. 2. p 479.)

*CALLANDER, [James Thomson] *An exile; in America He was formerly a Clerk to a senator of the College of justice in Scotland*

born .... drowned himself in James river, Virginia 1803. July 7.

(Editor of an American paper „The Recorder.„)

* The political progress of Britain: or, an impartial history of abuses in the government of the British empire in Europe, Asia and America, from the revolution in 1688 to the present time. Part. 1. 1792. 8. (1 sh) Ed. 2. 1795. (3 sh.) übers. Edinb. Philad. u. London. (Cölln) 1797. 8. The political register: or proceedings in the session of congress, commencing Nov. 3. 1794. and ending March 3. 1795 with an appendix containing a selection of papers laid before congress during that period. Vol. 1. 2. Philad. 1795. 8. (11 sh.) Sketches of the history of America. Philad. 1798. 8. (1 Dollar 50 Cents.)

*CALVERT, [William]

On the agriculture of the county of Nottingham. (*Young's* A. of Agr. Vol. 23. p. 149.)

*CAMBON, [J.... J....]

Letters and conversations ... 17.. Clementina Bedford, a novel, in letters and narrative. 1796. 12. (3 sh)

CAMBRIDGE, [Richard Owen] *Esq.*

born 1716. died 1802. Sept. 17.

See Gentleman's Magaz. Y. 1802. Oct. p. 977.

Works, including pieces never before published; with

with an account of his life and character, by his Son *George* —. 1803. 4. (2 L. 12 ſh. 6 d.)

*CAMERON, [William] *Rev. at Kirknewton.*

A review of the french revolution; – 1802. 8. (6ſh. 6d.)

*CAMILLUS; See *Alexander Hamilton.*

*CAMPBELL, [. . . . .] *Dr. of Lancaſter.*

An eſſay on the beſt means of converting certain portions of graſs land into tillage, without exhauſting the ſoil; and of returning the ſame to graſs, after a certain period, in an improved ſtate. (Comm. to the B. of Agr. Vol. 3. P. 1. p. 206.)

CAMPBELL, [Alexander]

Odes and miſcellaneous poems; 17.. An introduction to the hiſtory of poetry in Scotland, from the beginning of the 13 century down to the preſent time, together with a converſation on Scotiſh ſong To which is ſubjoined, ſongs of the lowlands of Scotland — embelliſhed with characteriſtic deſigns, compoſed and engraved by the late *David Allan*, hiſtorical painter. Vol. 1. 2. 1798. 4. (2 L. 2 ſh.) überſ. von *L. Theob Koſegarten*; (bey ſeiner Ueberſ von *Garnett's* Reiſen durch die Schottiſchen Hochländer. B. 1. Lübeck u. Leipz. 1802. 8.) A journey from Edinburgh through parts of North-Britain — with biographical ſketches relating chiefly to public affairs from the 12 century to the preſent time; embelliſhed with 44 engravings. Vol. 1. 2. 1802. 4. (4 L. 4 ſh.)

*CAMPBELL, [Alexander] *at Kilcalmonell.*

A ſeries of experiments in the culture of potatoes, with remarks on the ſame, and on the general culture of this valuable root. (Bath Agric. Soc. Vol. 9. p. 1.)

*CAMPBELL, [Donald] *of Barbreck, Esq. (He formerly commanded a regiment of Cavalry in the ſervice of the Nabob of the Carnatic.)*

A journey over land to India, partly by a route never gone before by any European —. comprehending his ſhipwreck and impriſonnement with Hyder Alli and his ſubſequent negociations and transactions in the eaſt. 1795. 4. (1 L. 1 ſh.) überſ. Altona. 1796. 8. Abridged 1796. (3 ſh. 6 d.) Letter to the Marquis of Lorn, on the preſent

present times. 1798. 8. (1 ſh. 6 d.) Letter, with an account of various ſeeds ſent by him, by the Queen Indiaman. (Comm. to the B. of Agr. Vol. 2. p. 193.)

CAMPBELL, [George] *D. D. F. R. S. Principal and Profeſſor of Divinity in the Mariſhall College and Univerſity of Aberdeen, and one of the Miniſters of that city.*

born at Aberdeen 1719. died 1796. Apr. 6. See Gentlem. Magaz. Y. 1796. April. p. 357. Monthly Magaz. Y. 1796. April p. 262. May p. 343. Aug. p. 699. Allg. Litter. Zeit. J. 1797. ItBl. N. 51. S. 427. *Millin* Magaz. Encycloped. T. 4. 1797. An 3. p. 533. — See *George Skene Keith.*

The ſpirit of the goſpel neither a ſpirit of ſuperſtition nor of enthuſiaſm, a ſermon. 1771. 8. The philoſophy of rhetorik — überſ. mit Anmerk. von *D. Jeniſch.* Berlin. 1791. 8. The nature extent and importance of the duty of allegiance, a ſermon. 1777. 8. The ſucceſs of the firſt publiſhers of the goſpel a proof of its truth, a ſermon. 1777. 8.

(Several ſingle ſermons)

*CAMPBELL, [H. . . . .] *M. Dr.*

Remarks on the preſent ſtate of paper-making in England and France. (*Nicholſon's* Journal. Y. 1802. May. p. 6.) Account of ſome experiments performed upon a ſcale of conſiderable magnitude and principally by the agency of froſt, to produce ſulphate of ſoda, carbonate of magneſia, and muriate of ammonia, from ſulphate of magneſia, carbonate of ammonia, and muriate of ſoda. (Ib. Y. 1802. June. p. 117.)

*CAMPBELL, [James] *Esq.*

On modern faulconry —, Edinb. 1773. 8.

CAMPBELL, [Ivie]

Letter in anſwer to inquiry reſpecting the vaccina as a diſeaſe of cows in Scotland. (*Duncan's* A. of Med. Y. 1800. p. 459.)

*CAMPBELL, [J. . . . . H. . . . .] *Esq. of Charlton in Kent.*

born. . . . . died (?)

On ſtall-feeding bullocks, on potatoes &c. and on

on the Herefordshire breed of cattle. (*Young's* A. of Agr. Vol. 11. p. 97.) On cattle and sheep. (Ibid. Vol. 12. p. 6.) On the breeds of cattle and sheep. (Ibid. Vol. 13. p. 217.) Flourishing manufactures do not secure a good agriculture. (Ib. Vol. 15. p. 562.) Reflections in Lancashire. (Ib. Vol. 16. p. 138. On the different points of cattle, with a plate. (Ib. Vol. 17. p. 446.) Answers to queries relating to the agriculture of Lancashire. (Ib. Vol 20. p. 109.) On improvements in sheep. (Ibid. Vol. 21. p. 287.) Letters to the Earl of Egremont. (Ib. Vol. 26. p. 437.) Relative to standing folds. (Ib. Vol. 26. p. 539.)

*CAMPBELL, [Lawrence Dundas]

The Indian observer by the late *Hugh Boyd*, Esq. with the life of the author and some miscellaneous poems. 1798. 8. (10 sh. 6 d.) The miscellaneous works of *H. Boyd*, the author of the letter of Junius; with an account of his life and writings. Vol. 1. 2. 1800. 8. (16 sh.) Aus diesem übers. Gesandtschafts-reise nach Ceylon. Hamb. 1802. 8.

CAMPBELL, [Thomas] *LL. Dr. Chancellor of St. Macartin's, Clogher.*

born in Ireland.

A survey of the south of Ireland. 1777. 8. Strictures on the ecclesiastical and literary history of Ireland —. 1789. 8. (6 sh.)

*CAMPBELL, [Thomas] *Esq.*

The pleasures of hope, with other poems. 1799. 8. (6 sh.) Ed. 2. with engravings. 1803. 4. (1 L. 1 sh.)

*CANNING, [T.....]

Substance of his speech in the house of Commons Dec. 11. 1798. on Mr. *Tierney's* motion respecting continental alliances. 1798. 8. (1 sh. 6 d.) The wedding and bedding, or John Bull and his bride fast asleep, a satirical poem. 1801. (2 sh.)

*CANT, [William]

Original letter of Archbishop *Lowth*. (Monthly Magaz. Y. 1799. May. p. 305.)

*CAPELLE, [Joseph] *of Wilmington.*

Account of the taenia discovered in the liver of a number of rats. (Tr. of Phys. of Philad. Vol. 1. P. 1. p. 60.)

*CAPPE,

*CAPPE, [. . . . .] *Med. Dr. of York.*

Account of his experience of the effects of the nitrate of silver. (*Duncan's* A. of Med. Y. 1798 p. 455.)

*CAPPE, [Catherine] *Mrs.*

An account of two charity schools for the education of girls, and of a female friendly society in York: interspersed with reflexions on charity schools and friendly societies in general. 1800. 8. (3 sh.) Account of a female benefit club. (Monthly Magaz. Y. 1797. Dec. p. 415.) On charity schools for girls. (Ibid. Y. 1798. May. p. 320.) On female benefit societies. (Ibid Y. 1798. April p. 239.) On Grey-coat school at York. (Ibid. Y. 1798. July. p. 6.) On the spinning school at York. (Ibid. Y. 1798. Nov. p. 333.) See *Newcome Cappe.*

*CAPPE, [Newcome] *Minister of the dissenting Chapel in St. Saviour gate York.*

born 1732. Febr. 21. died 1800. Dec. 24.

See Gentleman's Magaz. Y. 1800. Suppl. p. 1299. Monthly Mag. Y. 1801. Febr. p. 81. Allgem. Litt. Zeit. J. 1801. ItBl. S. 839.

A series of discourses on the providence and government of God. 1795. 8. (4 sh.) Critical remarks on many important passages of scripture — to which are prefixed memoirs of his life by the editor *Catherine Cappe.* Vol. 1. 2. 1802. 8. (16 sh.)

(Several single sermons.)

*CAPPER, [Benjamin Pitts]

A statistical account of the population and cultivation, produce and consumption of England and Wales; with observations and hints for the prevention of a future scarcity. 1801. 8. (4 sh.)

CAPPER, [James] *formerly Colonel and Comptroller-general of the Army and fortification accompts on the coast of Coromandel.*

Observations on the winds and monsoons. 1801. 8. (15 sh.) General observations on the causes which influence the weather in England and the popular methods of judging of the weather. (*Nicholson's* Journal. Y. 1802. April. p. 275.)

*CARD,

CARD, [Henry] *A. B.*

The hiftory of the revolutions of Ruffia to the acceffion of Catherine I. including a review of the manners and cuftoms of the 16 and 17 centuries. 1803. 8.

CARD, [W.....] *Schoolmafter and Mathematical Profeffor at Hythe.*

The youth's infallible inftructor; for the ufe of fchools. Vol. 1-4. 1798. 8 (6 fh. 6 d.)

CARDONNEL, [Adam de] *Memb. of the Antiq Soc. of Edinb.*

Picturesque antiquities of Scotland. Part 1. 2. 1788. 8. Part 3. 1793. 8. (The fame in 4to.)

CARDIN, [. . . . .] *Capt.*

Letter to Dr. *Lettfom* on dyfentery. (Mem. of M. S. of L Vol. 3. p. 517.)

CARENDEFFEZ, [. . . . .]

Farrago of ingredients in the nitrous and nitric acids whereby they differ from the feptic acid. (Medical Repofitory. Vol. 3. p. 413.)

CAREY, [George Savile] *Printer.*

The balnea; or, an impartial defcription of all the popular watering places in England. 1798. 12. (3 fh.) Ed. 2. confiderably enlarged. 1799. (3 fh. 6 d.) A choice collection of favourite fongs, on ferious moral and lively fubjects. 1800. (1 fh.) On the origin of the celebrated ballad of „Sally in our alley„ and on the author, God fave the king. (Monthly Magaz. Y. 1801. June, p 385)

CAREY, [John] *LL. D.*

Latin profody made eafy, or rules and authorities for the quantity of final fyllables in general and of the increments of noms and verbs, interfperfed with occafional obfervations and conjectures on the pronunciation of the antient greeks and romans. 1800. 8. (5 fh.) On the greek pronunciation. (Monthly Magaz. Y. 1800. Nov. p. 299. Y. 1801. May. p. 313.) Reply on *Dyer's* objections to my conjecture on greek pronunciation. (Ibid. Y. 1801. Febr. p 23.) On the paragogic nu. (Ibid. Y. 1801. July. p. 482) The works of *Virgil*, translated into Englifh verfe by Mr. *Dryden*; a new edition, revifed and corrected.

rected. Vol. 1-3. 1803. 8. (1 L. 7 ſh.) Skeleton of the latin accidence. 1803. (1 ſh. 6 d.)

*CAREY, [John] *Philadelphia.*

Peter penny leſs — a fragment. (American Muſeum. Y. 1790. Nov. p. 207.)

*CAREY, [Matthew]

Sketch of the life of the late *Nathaniel Greene*, Major Gen. of the forces of the United ſtates of America. (American Muſeum Y. 1790. Jan. p. 39. Febr. p. 107. April p. 210.) A ſhort account of the malignant fevers, lately prevalent in Philadelphia; with a ſtatement of the proceedings that tooke place on the ſubject in different parts of the United ſtates. 1793. 8. (1 ſh.) Ed. 2. Philad. 1793. (3 ſh. 4 d.) Ed 3. improved. Philad. 1793. Ed. 4. Philad. 1794. überſ. von *Carl Erdmann*. Lancaſter. 1794. 8. überſ. von *J. W. H. Ziegenbein*, im Braunſchw. Magaz. J. 1794. St. 12. 13.

*CAREY, [William]

Enquiry into the obligations of chriſtians, to uſe means for the converſion of the heathens. In which the religious ſtate of the different nations of the world, the ſucceſs of former undertakings and the practicability of further undertakings are conſidered. 1792. 8. (1 ſh. 6 d.)

*CARLETON, [Osgood]

The United ſtates of America. Boſton. (16 ſh.)

*CARLISLE, [Anthony] *F. L. S: Surgeon to the Weſtminſter Hoſpital.*

A caſe of unuſual formation in a part of the brain. (Tranſact. of Med. and Chirurg. Soc. 1793. p. 212.) Obſervations upon the ſtructure and economy of thoſe inteſtinal worms called taeniae. (Tranſact. of L. S. Vol. 2. p. 247.) Obſervations on the nature of corns and the means of removing them; (*Simmons's* Med. facts and obſervat. Vol. 7. p. 29.) Account of a peculiarity in the diſtribution of the arteries ſent to the limbs of ſlow moving animals; together with ſome other ſimilar facts. (Phil. Tranſact. Y. 1799. p. 98.) Account of a monſtrous lamb. (Ib. Y. 1801. p. 139.)

*CARLIS-

*CARLISLE, [.....] *Rev. D. of Carlisle.*
Account of some roman antiquities lately discovered in Cumberland. (Arch. Vol. 11. p. 63.)

*CARLISLE, [.....]
Experiments in galvanic electricity. (*Tilloch's* Philos. Magaz. Vol. 7. p. 337.)

CARLISLE, [Frederic] Earl of See *Fred. Howard.*

*CARLISLE, [John Housman]
A topographical description of Cumberland, Westmoreland, Lancashire and a part of the West-Riding of Yorkshire — 1800. 8 (12 sh.)

CARLYLE, [Joseph Dacre] *B. D. F. R. S. E. Chancellor of Carlisle and Professor of Arabic in the University of Cambridge.* born 1759
See Public Characters of 1802 - 1803. p. 338.
Mauret Allatafet Jemaleddini filii Togri - Bardii. seu rerum Aegyptiacarum annales, ab A. C 971 usque ad annum 1453. E codice Mss. Bibliothecae Acad. Cantabrigiensis textum arabicum primus edidit, latine vertit, notisque illustravit. 1792. 4. (12 sh.) Specimens of Arabian poetry, from the earliest time to the extinction of the khalifat with some account of the authors. 1796. 4. (17 sh.)

CARMICHAEL, [James]
(Published various tracts concerning the peerage of Scotland;) Collected from the public records; Original instruments and authentic manuscrits. Edinburgh. 1791. 4. (7 sh. 6 d.)

CARNIE, [John]
Letter on culture of cochineal. (*Young's* A. of Agr. Vol 28. p. 304.)

ARPENTER, [Benjamin] *Pastor of the Soc. belonging to the new dissenting chapel in Stourbridge.*
Letter to the Rev. *Robert Foley*, M. A. Rector of Old Swinford, in answer to the charges brought against the dissenters of Stourbridge; with a concise view of the dissenters of Stourbridge, and a concise view of the principles of dissenters; to which is added, an account of the proceedings at the Lyewaste, by *J. Scott.* 1792. 8. (1 sh.) A liturgy, containing forms of devotion for each sunday in the month, with an office for baptism. 1794. 12. (2 sh.)
(Several single sermons.)

*CARPENTER, [Thomas]
Essay on the reigning vices and follies of mankind and the causes of national danger and calamity, deduced from historical evidence. To which are added succinct observations on the happiness and tranquillity that would ultimately result from a due regard to the principles of virtue and religion. 1795. 8. (1 sh.)

*CARPENTER, [Thomas] *Master of the Acad. at Barking, Essex.*
The scholar's spelling assistant. 1798. 8. (1 sh.)
The scholar's orthographical and orthoepical assistant; or, english exercise book, on an improved plan. 1803. 12. (3 sh. 6 d.)

*CARPUE, [Joseph Constantine] *Surgeon to his Maj. Forces and Teacher of Anatomy.*
A description of the muscles of the humane body, as they appear on dissection — with the synonyma of *Cowper*, *Winslow*, *Douglas*, *Albinus*, *Innes* and the new nomenclature of *Dumas*; with coloured prints. 1802. 4. (12 sh.) An introduction to electricity and galvanism, with cases shewing their effects in the cure of diseases. To which is added, a description of Mr. *Cuthberson's* plate electrical machine. 1803. 8. (4 sh.)

CARR, [John] *D. D.*
Extract of a private letter to a critic. 1764. fol.
Dialogues of *Lucian*, from the greek. Vol. 4. 5. 1798. 8. (10 sh.)

*CARR, [John] *Esq.*
The stranger in France; or, a tour from Devonshire to Paris, illustrated by 12 engravings — 1803. 4. (1 L. 1 sh.)

*CARR, [Samuel] *D. D. Prebendary of St. Paul's etc.*
Sermons on practical subjects. Vol. 1-4. 1795-1801. 8. (1 L. 9 sh.)

*CARR, [Thomas] *Esq. Bedingham, near Lewes, Sussex.*
Account of a farm. (*Young's* A. of Agr. Vol. 12. p. 30.)

*CARR, [William Windle]
Poems on various subjects. 1791. 8. (5 sh.)

*CARRICK, [A....] *M. Dr.*
Dissertation on the chemical and medical proper-
tie

ties of the Briftol hot-well water. To which are added, practical obfervations on the prevention and treatment of pulmonary confumption. 1797. 8. (2 fh. 6 d.)

*CARRIE, [William] *F. C. Phyf.*

A fketch of the rife and progrefs of the yellow fever in Philadelphia in 1799. Philadelphia. 1800.

*CARRINGTON, [. . . . .] *Lord.*

His fpeech delivered at the Board of Agriculture, 1803. 4.

*CARTE, [Samuel]

Three letters concerning fonts. (Arch. Vol. 10, p. 208)

*CARTER, [Elizabeth] *Mrs.*

Epictetus, translated from the original greek; with an introduction and notes by the translator. 1758. 4. reprinted Vol. 1. 2. in 8. Poems on feveral occafions. 1762. 8. reprinted in 12. (Contributor of two papers to the Rambler: No. 44 and No. 100.)

*CARTER, [George] *Hiftorical Portrait Painter.*

A narrative of the lofs of the Grosvenor Eaft India man, which was wrecked on the coaft of Caffraria Aug 4 1782. Compiled from the examination of *John Higgins*, one of the unfortunate furvivors. 1791. 8. (3 fh. 6 d.)

*CARTER, [Henry Yates] *Surgeon at Ketsley, near Wellington, Shropfhire.*

Cafe of a compound fracture of the leg, with remarks: (*Simmons's* Med. Facts and Obfervat. Vol. 2. p. 1.) überf. Repert. Chir. u. Medic. Abhandl. B. 2. S. 37. Cafe of a boy, whofe head was preffed between certain parts of an engine employed for draining a coal mine. (Ibid. Vol. 2. p. 11.) überf. Repert. Chir. u. Medic. Abhandl. B. 2. S. 32. Cafe of a boy whofe left leg and thigh, together with part of the fcrotum, were torn of by a flitting mill. (Ibid. Vol. 2. p. 17.) überf. Repertor. Chir. u. Medic. Abhandl. B. 2. S. 25. An account of the good effects of a folution of fal ammoniac, in vinegar, employed, as a topical application, in cafes of lacerated wounds; (Ibid. Vol. 6. p. 66.) Cafe of a difeafed kidney;

M 3 (Ibid.

(Ibid. Vol. 6. p. 85.) Case of a gun-shot wound of the head; (Ibid. Vol. 6 p. 91.)

***CARTER, [J....]** *Rev. of Flempton, Suffolk.*

Experiments on carrots. (*Young's* A. of Agr. Vol. 1. p. 194.) Experiment on weld. (Ibid. Vol. 1. p. 251.) On the culture of carrots, with observations by *A. Young*. (Ibid. Vol. 2. p. 387.) On a new mode of planting wheat. (Ibid. Vol. 4. p. 235.) Annual expence of feeding an horse in constant work upon a farm. (Ib. Vol. 26. p. 533.)

CARTER, [John]

An essay on the use and abuse of reason in matters of religion; translated from the latin of *Herm. Witsius*. 1795. 8. Unwelcome thoughts to the religious world in the 19 century. 1801. 8. (6 sh.)

***CARTER, [John]**

Specimens of ancient sculpture and painting in England. Vol. 1. 2. 17.. fol. Antient architecture in England. Nrb. 1-9. 17.. Account of sepulchral monuments discovered at Lincoln. (Arch. Vol. 12. p. 107.)

CARTER, [William] *M. Dr. Physician at Canterbury; formerly fellow of Orial-College, Oxford.*

born 1711. died Febr. 1799.

See Gentleman's Magaz. Y. 1799. p. 258. Allg. Litt. Zeit. ItBl. J. 1800. S. 659.

***CARTWRIGHT, [Edmund]** *M. A. Rector of Goadby-Merwood, in Leicestershire.*

born at Murnham in the County of Nottingham. April 1743.

See Public Characters of 1800-1801. p. 404.

Constantia, an elegy, to the memory of a lady (Mrs. *Langhorne*) lately deceased; 1768. 4. Armine and Elvira, a legendary tale. 1771. 4. (2 sh.) The prince of peace and other poems. 1779. 4. (2 sh. 6 d.) Sonnets to eminent men; and an ode to the Earl of Effingham. 1783. 4. A memorial read to the Soc. for the Encourag. of Arts, Manuf. and Commerce Dec. 18. 1799. and a speech delivered for the same society Jan. 29. 1800 with an appendix, containing letters from the late Sir *Will. Jones*, Dr. *Thurlow*, late Bishop of Durham and other distinguished characters. 1800. 8. (2 sh.) An essay on the means of of extending the cultivation of corn on strong lands, without diminishing their value or lessening the production of animal food. (Comm. to the B. of Agr. Vol. 3. P. 1. p. 174.)

*CARTWRIGHT, [Edmund] *Rev. of Mary-le-Bone.*

On the production of opium from lettuces. (Tr. of the Soc. for the E. of A. Vol. 19. p. 197.)

*CARTWRIGHT, [George] *Esq.*

born 1739 Febr. 12. at Marnham in the county of Nottingham.

Journal of transactions and events, during a residence of nearly XVI years on the coast of Labrador; containing many particulars, both of the country and its inhabitants, not hitherto known. Vol. 1. 2. 3. 1792. 4. (2 L. 12 sh. 6 d.)

CARTWRIGHT, [John] *Esq. late Major* —.

See Public Characters of 1799-1800. p. 276.

Letter to *Edm. Burke*, controverting the principles of American government, laid down in his speech of April 19, 1774: Declaration of rights, without which no Englishman can be a free man, nor the English nation a free people. 1782. A Nottinghamshire farmer to his brother-freeholders; or, a call to the country-meeting to be holden at Newark, to consider the propriety of petitioning the house of Commons to reform the present unconstitutional representation of the people in that house and to shorten the duration of parliaments; 1785. Letter to the Duke of Newcastle — respecting his grace's conduct in the disposal of commissions in the militia; together with some remarks touching the french revolution; a reform of parliament in Great-Britain and the royal proclamation of the 21 May; with an appendix, containing an effectual plan for providing navy timber; opposed to the dangerous and unprofitable system of cultivating the public forests under the management of officers of the crown. 1792. 8. (2 sh. 6 d.) Letter to a friend at Boston, in the county of Lincoln; and to all other commoners, who have associated in support of the constitution. 1793. 8. (2 sh.) The commonwealth in danger; with an introduction, containing remarks on some late writings of *Arthur Young*. 1795. 8. (5 sh.) A letter to the high sheriff of the county of Lincoln, respecting the bills of Lord *Grenville* and Mr. *Pitt*, for altering the criminal law of England, respecting treason and sedition. 1795. 8. (1 sh.) The constitutional defence of England, internal and external. 1796. 8. (3 sh.) An appeal, civil and military, on the subject of the English constitution. 1797. 8. (6 d.) Ed. 2. to which are added parts the 2 and 3, containing strictures on a gross violation of the constitution; a constitutional system of military defence; reflections on the utter incompatibility of a standing army with national freedom &c. 1799. 8. (5 sh.) *A letter to the electors of Nottingham. 1803. 8. On sheep and wool. (*Young's* A. of Agr. Vol. 20. p 35.) Weekly account of a farm. (Ibid. Vol. 20. p. 40.) Comparison of merit of the new Leicestershire and Lincolnshire sheep. (*Young's* A. of Agr. Vol. 21. p. 355.) Machine for reaping corn &c. (Ibid. Vol. 21. p. 506.)

CARY, [Henry Francis] *A. M.*
born in the Year 1772.
Ode to General *Kosciusko*. 1797. 4. (1 sh.)

*__CARY__, [John] *Surveyor of the roads to the general post-office; Engraver and Map-seller in the Strand.*

Actual surveys of Middlesex, the country fifteen miles round London and ten miles round Hampton-court and Richmond; (each in Octavo, 1786.) New map of England and Wales with part of Scotland; on which are carefully laid down all the direct and principal cross-roads, the course of the rivers and navigable canals cities, market and borough towns, parishes and most considerable hamlets, parks, forests, 1794. 4. (2 L. 7 sh.) New itinerary; or, an accurate delineation of the great roads, both direct and cross, throughout England and Wales; with many of the principal roads in Scotland — 1798. 8. (8 sh.) Ed. 2. with improvements. 1802. 8. (10 sh. 6 d.) New guide for ascertaining Hackney coach fares, and porterage rates; being an actual and minute admeasurefurement of every ftreet which is a carriage way throughout the metropolis —. 1801. 8. (3 fh. 6 d.)

*CASE, [W....] *Jun. of Lynn.*

The minftrel youth; a lyrical romance in 3 parts with other poems. 1801. 8. (1 fh.) Pictures of Britifh female poefy. 1803. 12. (1 fh. 6 d.)

*CASTLEREAGH, [.....] *Lord. In the Irifh Houfe of Commons.*

Speech, Febr. 5. 1800. on offering to the houfe certain refolutions propofing and recommanding a complete et entire union between Great-Britain and Ireland. 1800. 8. (1 fh. 6 d.)

*CASTLES, [John] *Esq.*

Obfervations on the fugar ants. (Philof. Transact. Y. 1790. p. 346.)

*CATCOTT, [George Symes] *Sub-Librarian of the Briftol library.*

born 1728. died 1803. Jan.

See Monthly Magaz. Y. 1803. Jan. p. 567.

The aged chriftian's final farewell to the world and its vanities; a pious meditation — compofed by — *John Whitfon*,* Esq. Alderman of the city Briftol and Member in feveral parliaments. Collected from the author's manufcripts, with an account of the author, collected from authentic records. 1792. 8. (1 fh. 6 d.) A defcriptive account of a defcent made into Pempark-Hole, in the parifh of Weftbury-upon Trim, in the county of Gloucefter in the Y. 1775. now firft publifhed. To which is added, a copper plate engraving of that remarkable cavern. Alfo, the narratives of Capt. *Sturmey*** and *Collins*, containing their defcriptions of the fame in the Years 1669 and 1682. 1792. 8. (1 fh. 6 d.) (New-York Magaz. Y. 1794. July. p. 404.)

*CATHRALL, [Ifaac] *M. Dr. Phyfician at Philadelphia.*

Hiftory of a fingular cafe in midwifery where delivery was accomplifhed in confequence of an incifion

* a diftinguifhed Merchant of Briftol in the reign of James I. See Monthly Rev. Y. 1792. May. p. 112.

** publifhed in Philof. Transact. N. 143. (Y. 1683.) p. 2.

cision by the vagina: (*Duncan's* A. of Med. Y 1798. p. 331.) A medical sketch of the synochu maligna, or malignant contagious fever, as it appeared in the city of Philadelphia. To which is added, some account of the morbid appearances observed on dissections; with a short chemical analysis of the black matter ejected from the stomach in the last stage of the yellow fever: with is dissimilarity to putrid bile and its effects when applied to the healthy system. Philadelphia, 1796. 8. Memoir on the analysis of black vomit (Tr. of A. S. Vol. 5. p. 117.) Memoir on the analysis of the black vomit, ejected in the last stage of the yellow fever. 1800. 8. A case of ruptured uterus, with the appearances on dissection. (*Simmons's* Med. Facts and Observat. Vol 8. p. 146.)

CATLOW, [Samuel] *A Protestant Dissenting Minister of Mansfield; Conductor of a litterary and commercial Seminary at Mansfield, Nottinghamshire.*

Observations on a course of instruction for young persons in the middle classes of life. 1793. 8. (2 sh.) Outlines of a plan of instruction, adapted to the varied purposes of active life —. 1798. fol. (5 sh.)

(Several single sermons.)

*CAULFIELD, [.....] *Roman Catholic Bishop.*

The reply of him and of the roman catholic clergy of Wexford to the misrepresentations of Sir *Richard Musgrave*, Bart: with a preface and appendix. 1801. 8. (1 sh. 6 d.)

CAULFIELD, [James] Earl of *Charlemont.*

See *Charlemont.*

*CAULEFIELD, [James]

Portraits, memoirs and characters of remarkable persons from the reign of Edward III. to the revolution, collected from the most authentic accounts extant. Vol. 1. 1794. Vol. 2. 1795. with plates. 8. (3 L.) The history of the gunpowder plot, with several historical circumstances prior to that event, relative to the plots of the roman catholics to re-establish popery in these kingdoms.

Digested

Digested and arranged from authentic materials. 1796.

CAVENDISH, [Sir Henry] *Bart. of Doveridge, in Derbyshire.*

born 1731. Oct.

Statement of the public accounts of Ireland, 1791. 8. (10 sh. 6 d.)

CAVENDISH, [Henry] *Esq. F. R. S. and A. S.*

On the civil year of the Hindoos and its divisions, with an account of three Hindoo almanacs belonging to *Charles Wilkins*, Esq. (Philos. Transact. Y. 1792. p. 383.) Experiments to determine the density of the earth. (Ibid. Y. 1798. p. 469. *Nicholson's* Journal. Vol. 2. p. 446.)

*CAUSTIC, [Christopher] *M. Dr.* (?)

Terrible tractoration!! a poetical petition against galvanizing trumpery and the Perkinistic institution: in 4 Cantons. Ed. 2. with great additions. 1803. 8. (4 sh. 6 d.)

*CECIL, [Richard] *M. A. Minister of St. John's Bedford Row.*

Discourses of — *William Bromley Cadogan*, A. M. late Rector of St. Luke's Chelsea &c. To which are now added, short observations on the Lord's prayer and letters to several of his friends; the whole collected into one volume, with memoirs of his life. 1798. 8. (7 sh.) Memoirs of *John Bacon* [*], Esq. Royal Artist and Sculptor, with reflections drawn from a review of his moral and religious character. 1801. 8. (2 sh. 6 d.)

(Several single sermons.)

*CHALMERS, [.....] *Lieutenant-Colonel of Chelsea, late Inspector General of the Colonial Troops in St. Domingo.*

*Letters to a nobleman on the conduct of the American war; 17.. °Cool thoughts on the consequences to Great-Britain of American independance; on the expence of Great-Britain in the settlement and defence of the American colonies; and on the value and importance of the American colonies and the West-Indies to the British empire. 1780. 8. (1 sh.) °Plain truth; or, a letter to the

* born in London Nov. 24. 1740. died Aug. 7. 1799. See Gentleman's Magaz. Y. 1799. Aug. p. 724. Sept. p. 808.

the Author of „Dispassionate thoughts on the American war.„ In which the principles and arguments of that author are refuted and the necessity of carrying on that war clearly demonstrated. 1780. 8. (1 sh. 6 d.) Strictures on a pamphlet written by *Thomas Paine* on the English system of finance: To which are added, some remarks on the war and other national concerns. 1796. 8. (1 sh. 6 d.) Remarks on the late war in St Domingo; with observations on the relative situations of Jamaica, and other interesting subjects. 1803. (2 sh. 6 d.)

*CHALMERS, [Alexander] *M. A.*

Shakespeare's plays, printed from the text of the corrected edition, left by the late Mr. *Steevens.* (to be completed in 40 numbres) No. 1. 1803. (2 sh.) The British essayists, containing the Spectator, Tatler and Guardian, the Rambler, Adventurer, World, Connoisseur, Idler, Mirror, Lounger and Observer, with prefaces historical and biographical. Vol. 1 - 45 with portraits. 1803. 8. (9 L.)

CHALMERS, [George] *Esq. F. R. and A. S: Chief Clerk of the committee of Council for trade and foreign plantations.*

Estimate of the comparative strength of Britain —. a new edition. 1794 8. (5 sh) übers. von *V. A. Heinze.* Berlin. 1786. 8. Opinions on interesting subjects of public law —. Ed. 2. with additions. 1792. (3 sh.) Historical tracts by Sir *John Davies,* Attorney - General and Speaker of the house of Commons in Ireland, with a new life of the author from authentic documents; 1786. 8. A collection of treaties between Great - Britain and other powers. Vol. 1. 2. 1790. 8. (14 sh.) The life of *Thomas Ruddiman,* A. M. the keeper for almost 50 years of the library belonging to the faculty of Advocates at Edinburgh. To which are subjoined new anecdotes of *Buchanan.* 1794. 8. (7 sh) Apology for the believers in the *Shakspeare* papers, which were exhibited in Norfolk-street. 1796. 8. (6 sh.) A supplemental apology for the believers — being a reply to Mr. *Malone's* answer, which was early announced but never published; with a dedication to *George Steevens* anc and a poſtſcript to *T. J. Mathias*, the Author of the purſuits of litterature. 1799. 8. (7 ſh.) Appendix to his ſupplemental apology; being the documents for the opinion that *Hugh Boyd* wrote Junius's letters. 1800. 8 (3 ſh.) — On illicit hopes; On the equalization of follies and diſeaſes: (See *Looker-on.*) — The poems of *Allan Ramſay* *; a new edition, corrected and enlarged with a gloſſary; to wich are prefixed, a life of the author from authentic documents and remarks on his poems from a large view of their merits. Vol. 1. 2 1800. 8. (1 L. 1 ſh.) Chalmeriana; or a collection of papers literary and political, intitled letters, verſes &c. on reading a late heavy ſupplemental apology for the believers in the *Shakeſpeare* papers. Arranged and publiſhed by Mr. *Owen* — aſſiſted by his friend and clerk, *Jaſper Hargrave*. Collection I. 1800. 8. (2 ſh. 6 d.) Obſervations on the late continuance of the uſe of torture in Great-Britain (Arch. Vol 10. p. 143.)

HALMERS, [Lionel] *M. Dr. of Charleſtown, South-Carolina.*

born . . . . . died 17.. (?)

A ſketch of the climate, water and ſoil in South-Carolina. (American Muſeum Y. 1788 April p. 316.) On the weather and diſeaſes of South-Carolina —; überſ. Th. 2. Stendal. 1792. 8.

CHAMBERLAIN, [Maſon]

Equanimity, a poem. 1800. 8. (1 ſh. 6 d.) Harveſt, a poem. 1800. 8. (6 d.) Ocean, a poem, in two parts. 1801. 8. (1 ſh. 6 d.)

CHAMBERLAINE, [John] *Keeper of his Maj. drawings and medals.*

Imitations of original drawings by *Hans Holbein*, in the collection of his Maj for the portraits of illuſtrious perſons of the court of Henry VIII with biographical tracts. Numb. 1-13. 1792-1800. fol. (each Numb. to ſubſcribers 2 L. 2 ſh. — to non ſubſcribers 2 L. 12 ſh. 6 d.) Imitations of original deſigns by *Leonardo da Vinci*: conſiſting of various drawings of ſingle figures, heads, compoſitions, horſes and other animals; optics, perſpective,

* died at Edinburgh on the 7 Jan. 1758. aged upwards of 72.

with english translation by *Henry Gladwin*, illustrated with plates, containing exact imitation of Persian and Arabic manuscript. 1801. 4. (3 L. 3 sh.)

*CHAMPION, [Anthony] *Esq. Of the Middle temple.*

born at Croydon in Surrey 1724. Febr. 5. died 1801. Febr. 22.

See Critical Rev. Y. 1802. June. p. 230.

Miscellanies, in verse and prose, english and latin published from the original manuscripts by *Will. Henry* Lord *Lyttelton*. 1801. 8. (10 sh. 6 d.)

CHAMPION, [Joseph] *Esq.*

New and complete alphabets in all the various hands of Great-Britain. fol. (9 sh. 4 d.)

CHAMPION, [Richard] *Esq.*

An enquiry into the situations best adapted to those who are desirous of emigrating to America, and of forming settlements. (Columbian Magaz. Y. 1787. Oct. p. 685.) The situation of the first and present settlers in America, contrasted. (Ib. Y. 1787. Nov. p. 753.)

*CHAMPNEY, [T....] *Esq. Member of the corporation of Surgeons.*

Medical and chirurgical reform proposed, from a review of the healing art throughout Europe, particularly Great-Britain; with considerations on hospitals, dispensaries, poorhouses and prisons &c. 1797. 8. (3 sh 6 d.)

CHANDLER, [Benjamin Bernhard] *M. Dr. Surgeon at Canterbury.*

born . . . . . died 178. (?)

Case of a stone in the bladder. (London M. J. Vol. 5. p. 387.) On the present successfull and most general method of inoculation. 1767. 8. (1 sh.) On the various theories and methods of cure in apoplexies and palsies. 1785. 8. (3 sh.) übers. Leipzig. 1787. 8. übers. Stendal. 1787. 8.

*CHANDLER, [John Westbrooke]

Sir Hubert, an heroic ballad. 1800. 8. (7 sh 6 d.)

CHANDLER, [Richard] *D. D. Fellow of Magdalen College, Oxford. F. A. S.*

*The history of Ilium or Troy; including the adjacent country and the opposite coast of the Cherso-

Cherfonefus or Thrace, by the author of „Travels in Afia minor and Greece. 1802. 4. (10 fh. 6 d.)

CHANNING, [Henry] *Rev.*

Account of the peftilential difeafe which prevailed at New-London (Connecticut) in the fummer and autumn of 1798. (Medical Repofit. Vol. 2. p. 402. 405.)

CHANTRELL, [Mary Ann] *of Newington Butts.*

Poems on various fubjects. 1798. 8. (2 fh. 6 d.)

CHAPLIN, [Charles] *at Tathwell, near Louth, Lincolnfhire.*

Sheep controverfy between *Ch. Chaplin* and *Rob. Bakewell* with obfervat. by *A. Young.* (*Young's* A. of Agr. Vol. 10. p. 560,)

CHAPMAN, [George] *LL. D. Formerly mafter of the grammar-fchool at Dumfries.*

A treatife on education. Ed. 5. 1792. 8. (5 fh.) Rudiments of the latin tongue; or an eafy introduction to latin grammar; to which is prefixed a fhort vocabulary, englifh and latin. Ed. 2. improved. 1793. 12. (1 fh.) An abridgment of Mr. *Ruddiman's* rudiments and grammar of the latin tongue. 1799. 8. (1 fh. 3 d.) Hints on the education of the lower ranks of the people and the appointment of parochial fchoolmafters. 1801. 8. (6 d.)

CHAPMAN, [John] *Surgeon, at Ampthill, Bedfordfhire.*

Cafe of uterine hemorrhage, where the placenta was expelled four hours before the birth of the child. (*Duncan's* A. of Med. Y. 1799. p. 308.) Obfervations on the cowpox. (Ibid. Y. 1799. p. 314.)

CHAPMAN, [Ifaac] *Phyfician.*

An account of a fpecies of cantharis, found in Buck's county, Pennfylvania; including obfervations on its medical qualities: (Med. Repofit. Vol. 2. p. 174.

CHAPMAN, [Samuel] *M. Dr. of Sudbury in Suffolk,* born 1718. died at his houfe in Holywell, Oxford. 1790. Sept. 5.

See Gentleman's Magaz. Y. 1790. Sept. p. 862.

*CHAPMAN, [William] *Member of the Soc. of Civil Engineers in London and M. R. J. A.*

Obfervations on the various fyftems of canal navigation, with inferences practical and mathematical; in which Mr. *Fulton's* plan of wheel-boats and the utility of fubterraneous and of fmall canals are particularly inveftigated, including an account of the canals and inclined planes of China. 1798. 4. (6 fh.) Facts and remarks relative to the Witham and the Welland; or, a feries of obfervations on their paft and prefent ftate; on the means of improving the channel of the Witham and the port of Bofton. P. 1. 2. 1800. 8. Obfervations on the prevention of a future fcarcity of grain, by means contributive to the benefit of the landed, commercial and manufacturing interefts. 1803. 8.

CHAPONE, [H....] *Mrs. Maiden-name Mulfo; Sifter of the late Thomas Mulfo.*

born 1726. died at Hadley 1801. Dec. 25.

See Gentleman's Magaz. Y. 1801. p. 1216. Monthly Magaz. Y. 1802. Febr. p. 39.

*CHAPPLE, [James]

On fteeping feed barley in a dry feafon. (Bath Agricult. Soc. Vol. 3. p. 304. American Mufeum Y. 1790. July. p. 46.) A method of potatoe management for preventing the curl. (Ibid. Vol. 7. p. 350.)

CHARLEMONT, Earl of, [James Caulfield] *Prefident of the R. J. A: F. R. S.*

born 1728 Aug. 18. died 1799. Aug. 4.

See Gentleman's Magaz. Y. 1799. Sept. p. 812. Oct. p. 899. Allgem. Litter. Zeit. J. 1801. IcBl. S. 817.

Under his family name *Caulfield* he publifhed: The manners of paphos; or triumph of love. 1777. 4. (3 fh.) Account of a fingular cuftom at Metelin, with fome conjectures on the antiquity of its origin. (Tr. of J. A. Y. 1789. p. 3. c. New York Magazin. Y. 1792. Oct. p. 613. Maffachufetts Magaz. Y. 1792. June. p. 368.) Some confiderations on a controverted paffage of *Herodotus*. (Tr. of J. A. Vol. 5. p. 3. c.) Some hints concerning the ftate of fcience at the revival of letters grounded on on a paſſage of *Dante* in his inferno Canto IV. v. 130. (Ibid. Vol. 6. p. 3. b.)

HARLESWORTH, [John] *M. A. of Offington in Nottinghamſhire.*

Practical ſermons, ſelected and abridged from various authors. Vol. 3. 1793. 8. (3 ſh.) Two ſhort diſcourſes on the Lord's ſupper and the example of Chriſt, with an exhortation on the proper uſe of the Lord's day. 1792. 8. (6 d.) Two practical ſermons on private prayer and public worſhip, to which is added a ſhort addreſs on the proper manner of employing the Lord's day. 1792. 12. (6 d.) Five practical diſcourſes on the Lord's ſupper, the example of Chriſt, mutual equity &c. 1795. 8. (1 ſh.)

(Several ſingle ſermons.)

HARLTON, [Mary]

Andronica, or the fugitive bride, a novel. Vol. 1. 2. 1797. 12. (6 ſh.) Pariſian, or anecdotes of diſtinguiſhed characters; Vol. 1. 2. 1797. 12. The pirate of Naples, a novel. Vol. 1-3 1801. (13 ſh. 6 d.) The wife and the miſtreſs. Vol. 1-4. 1802. 12. Phedora, or the foreſt of Minſki. Vol. 1-4. 1798. 12. (18 ſh.)

HARNOCK, [John] *Esq.*

Proſpectus and ſpecimen of an hiſtory of marine architecture; drawn from the beſt authorities and chronologically deduced from the earlieſt period to the preſent time — 1796. (6 ſh.) Biographia navalis or impartial memoirs of the lives and characters of officers of the navy of Great-Britain, from the Y. 1660 to the preſent time, drawn from the moſt authentic ſources and diſpoſed in a chronological arrangement; with portraits and other engravings by *Bartolozzi.* Vol. 1-5 1794-1797. (1 L. 17 ſh. 6 d.) Hiſtory of marine architecture. Vol. 1-3. 1801. 4. (9 L. 9 ſh.)

HARNOCK, [John] *Jun.*

A letter on finance, and on national defence &c. 1798. 8. (1 ſh. 6 d.)

HATER, [Thomas]

A poetical tribute to the memory of *William Cowper,* Esq. 1800, 8. (1 ſh.)

N 2 CHAUNCY,

CHAUNCY, [Charles] *D. D. Minister of the first church in Boston, New-England.*
born Jan. 1. 1705. in Boston. died 1787. Febr. 10.
See American Museum Y. 1790. Febr. p. 76.
* The salvation of all men. 1785.

***CHAVERNAC**, [T.....] *Surgeon.*
New progress of surgery in France, or phaenomena in the animal kingdom — translated from the french of *Imbert Delonnes*, M. Dr. embellished with very curious plates by *W. Nutter.* 1801. 4. (4 sh.)

***CHEESE**, [Griffith James].
Description of his machine for teaching music. (Tr. of the Soc. for the E. of A. Vol. 5. p. 122.)

***CHEETHAM**, [Robert Farren] *of Brasen-nose College, Oxford.*
born 1777. died 1801. Jan. 13.
See Gentleman's Magaz. Y. 1801. Jan. p. 92.
Odes and miscellanies. 1796. 8. (6 sh.) Poems. 1798. 4. (2 sh. 6 d.)

CHELSUM, [James] *D. D. Rector of Droxford Hants and Chaplain to the Lord Bishop of Winchester.*
born 1740. died 1801.
See Gentleman's Magaz. Y. 1801. Suppl. p. 1175. Y. 1802. Febr. p. 101. Apr. p. 293. Monthly Magaz. Y. 1802. Apr. p. 290.
Essay on the history of Mezzotinto; 179. The duty of relieving the french refugee clergy stated and recommended, a sermon. 1793. 4. (1 sh.)
(Several single sermons.)

***CHENEVIX**, [Richard] *Esq. F. R. S. M. J. A.*
Remarks upon chemical nomenclature, according to the principles of the french neologists. 1802. 12. Analysis of a new variety of lead ore. (*Nicholson's* Journal. Vol. 4. p. 219.) Analysis of manachanite from Botany Bay. (*Nicholson's* Journal. Vol. 5. p. 132.) Observations on the supposed magnetic property of nickel. (Ibid. Vol. 5. p. 287.) Observations and experiments upon Dr. *James's* powder —; (Phil. Transact. Y. 1801. p. 375. *Tilloch's* Philos. Magaz. Vol. 11. p. 108. *Nicholson's* Journ. Y. 1802. Jan. p. 22.) Note on

on a peculiar vegetable principle contained in coffee. (*Nicholson's* Journaal Y. 1802. Jun. p. 114. *Tilloch's* Philos. Mag. Vol. 12. p. 350.) Analysis of the natural and artificial unhydrous sulphate of lime. (Ibid. Y. 1802. July. p. 196.) Observations and experiments upon oxygenized and hyperoxigenized muriatic acid; and upon some combinations of the muriatic acid in its three states. (Philos. Tr. Y. 1802. p. 126. *Nicholson's* Journal. Y. 1802. Nov. p. 171.) Analysis of the arseniates of copper and of iron, from the county of Cornwall; likewise an analysis of the red octaedral copper ore of Cornwall; with remarks on some particular modes of analysis. (Philos. Transact. Y. 1801. p. 193. *Tilloch's* Philos. Magaz. Vol. 12. p. 141. 212. 302.) Analysis of corundum, and of some of the substances which accompany it; with observations on the affinities which the earths have been supposed to have for each other, in the humid way. (Ibid. Y. 1802. p. 327.) Observations and experiments undertaken with a view to determine the quantity of sulphur contained in sulphuric acid; and of this latter contained in sulphates in general. (Tr. of J. A. Vol. 8. Sc. p. 233. *Tilloch's* Philos. Magaz. Vol. 11. p. 112.)

HESTER, Lord-Bishop of. — See *William Cleaver.*

HESTON, [Richard Browne] *M. D: F. R. S: Physician to the Gloucester Infirmary.*

A case of retroverted uterus, in which the paracentesis vesicae was successfully performed. (M. C. Vol. 2. p. 6.) A singular case in lithotomy. (M. Rec. and Ref. p. 163.)

CHEVALIER, [J.... C....] *of Aspal, near Debenham, Suffolk.*

Account of a plantation. (*Young's* A. of Agr. Vol. 5. p. 145.)

CHEVALIER, [Mary] *Mrs.*

On the management of Suffolk Dairies. (*Young's* A. of Agr. Vol. 5. p. 509.)

CHEVALIER, [Thomas] *M. A. Member of the corporation of Surgeons.*

Observations in defence of a bill lately brought

 into

into parliament for erecting the corporation of surgeons of London into a college and for granting and confirming in such college certain rights and privileges; including a sketch of the history of surgery in England. 1797. 8. (2 sh. 6 d.) An introduction to a course of lectures on the operations of surgery. 1801. 8. (2 sh.)

*CHEYNE, [John] *M. Dr.*

Essays on the diseases of children with cases and dissections; Essay 1. of cynanche trachealis, or croup. 1801. 8. (16 sh.)

*CHIFNEY, [Samuel] *Rider to his Roy. Highness.*

A full disclosure of every circumstance relative to the running of escape, a horse the property of his Roy. Highn. the Prince of Wales, at Newmarket on the 20 and 21 of Oct. 1791. with an affidavit of the facts therein stated. 1800. (2 sh.)

*CHILD, [S.....]

The whole art and mystery of brewing porter, its management in bottels and other vessels — also, the best method of brewing ale, two penny and table beer. 1797. (2 sh.)

*CHIP, [William] *a Country Carpenter.*

Village politics; addressed to all the mechanics, journeyman and day labourers in Great-Britain. 1793. 12. (2 d.)

*CHIPMAN, [Nathaniel]

Sketches of the principles of government. Rutland. 1793. 8. (6 sh.)

CHISHOLM, [C....] *Esq. M. Dr: Surgeon in St. George's in Grenada.*

Observations on the influenza, as it lately appeared in the West-Indies: *(Duncan's* M. C. Y. 1790. Dec. 2. Vol. 5. p. 325.) Essay on the malignant pestilential fever introduced into the West-Indian islands from Boullam, on the coast of Guinea, as it appeared in 1793 and 1794. 1795. 8. (5 sh.) Ed. 2. much enlarged. Vol. 1. 2. 1801. 8. (16 sh.) On the malignant pestilential fever of Grenada as it appeared in 1793 and 1794. (Medical. Reposit. Vol. 2. p. 285.) History of an uncommon epidemic fever observed in the island of Grenada. *(Duncan's* M. C. Dec. 2. Vol. 8. p. 267.) Account of a specific for ophthalmia, employed

ployed by the Arrowawck Indians. (Ib. Dec. 2. Vol. 9. p. 365.) Cafes of yaws and leprofy treated with nitrous acid and oxygenated muriate of potafh. (*Duncan's* A. of Med. Y 1800. p 395.) A curious cafe of fpasmodic affection of the face, cured by the oxygenated muriate of potafh. (Ibid. Y. 1800. p. 402.) A fhort account of the epidemic polypus at Grenada in 1790. (Ib. Y. 1800. p. 407.)

'CHISLETT, [John] *Surgeon to the public difpenfary at Horncaftle Lincolnfhire.*

A cafe of hernia fituated between the recti mus- cles. (New London M. J. Vol. 1. p. 337.)

CHITTY, [Jofeph] *Esq. of the Middle Temple.*

On the laws of bills of exchange, checks on bankers, promiffory notes, banker's cafh notes and bank notes. 1799. 8. (6 fh.)

CHRISP, [J . . . .] *F. R. S.*

Obfervations on the nature and theory of vifion. 1796. 8. (3 fh. 6 d.)

CHRISTALL, [Ann Batten]

Poetical fketches. 1795. 8.

HRISTIAN, [. . . . .] *Lieutenant.*

The revolution, an hiftorical play. 1791. 8. (2 fh.)

CHRISTIAN, [Edward] *Esq. M. A. Barrifter and Profeffor of the laws of England in the Univerfity of Cambridge.*

Examination of precedents and principles: from which it appears that an impeachment is determined by a diffolution of parliament: with an appendix, in which all the precedents are collected. Ed. 1. 1790. 8. (2 fh. 6 d.) Ed. 2. 1791. 8. (2 fh. 6 d.) Differtation that the houfe of Lords in cafes of judicature are bound by precifely the fame rules of evidence as are obferved by all other courts; with an appendix, containing farther obfervations on the effect of a diffolution of parliament on an unfinifhed impeachment. 1792. 8. (2 fh. 6 d.) Commentaries on the laws of England in four books by Sir *Will. Blackftone* —. Ed XII. with the late corrections of the author and with notes and additions. Vol. 1-4. 1795. 8. (1 L. 12 fh.) A fyllabus, or heads of lectures publicly delivered in the University of Cambridge. 1797. 8. (2 sh. 6 d) *Blackstone's* commentaries on the laws of England; Ed. 14. with notes and additions. Vol. 1-4. 1803. 4. (2 L. 2 sh.)

CHRISTIE, [Thomas] *(He quitted medical pursuits and was a merchant in London.)*

born; ..... died at Surinam Oct. 1796.

See Gentleman's Magaz. Y. 1797. March, p. 252. April p. 345. Allgem. Litter. Zeit. J. 1797. ItBl. Dec. S. 1406.

Observations on pemphigus. (London M. J. Vol. 10. P. 4.) übers. in den Samml. der neuesten Beobachr. Engl. Aerzte. S. 291. Miscellanies, philosophical, medical and moral: Vol. I. containing 1) observations on the litterature of the primitive christian writers. 2) reflections suggested by the character of Pamphilus of Caesarea; 3) Hints respecting the state and education of the people; 4) Thoughts on the origin of human knowledge and on the antiquity of the world. 5) Remarks on Prof. *Meiners* history of antient opinions respecting the deity. 6) Account of Dr. *Ellis's* work on the origin of sacred knowledge. 1789. 8. (4 sh.) Sketch of the new constitution of France —. 1790. fol. Letters on the revolution of France and on the new constitution established by the national assembly, occasioned by the publications of — *Burke* and *Alex. de Calonne* — Part. 1. 1791. 8. (6 sh.) The french constitution; — translated — being the first part of Vol. 2. of letters on the revolution —. 1791. 8.

*CHRISTIE, [William]

*Essay on ecclesiastical establishments in religion — with two discourses — by a protestant dissenter 1791. 8. (1 sh. 6 d.)

*CHURCH, [John] *M. A.*

A dissertation on camphor. Philadelphia. 1797. 8

CHURCH, [John] *M. A. Surgeon.*

Extract from a history of sphacelated scrotum (Mem. of M. S. of L. Vol. 3. p. 529.) A cabinet of quadrupeds; consisting of highly finished engravings by *James Tookey* and *Paton Thompson* from elegant drawings, by *Julius Ibbetson*, R. A man;

many of them ſketched from the animals in their native climes; with hiſtoric and ſcientific deſcriptions. P. 1. Nrb. 1–6. 1795. 4. P. 2. 1797. Nrb. 7–12. P. 3. Nrb. 13–26. (2 L. 16 ſh.)

CHURCHEY, [W....]

Poems and imitations of the britiſh poets, with odes miſcellanies and notes. 1789. 4. (1 L. 1 ſh.)

CHURCHILL, [......]

A compleat dictionary of the engliſh language, by *Thomas Sheridan*, A. M. Ed. 4. (publiſhed by him) Vol. 1. 2. 1797. 8. (14 ſh.)

CHURCHILL, [Junius] *Esq.*

Liverpool odes; or affectionate epiſtles for the Y. 1793. Part 1. 1793. 4. (1 ſh. 6 d.)

CHURCHILL, [T....]

Outlines of a philoſophy of the hiſtory of man, translated from the german of *J. G. Herder*. 1800. 4. (1 L. 11 ſh. 6 d.)

CHURCHMAN, [John] *Land-Surveyor* —

The magnetic atlas, or variation charts of the whole terraqueous globe, compriſing a ſyſtem of the variation and dip of the needle, by which, the obſervations being truly made, the longitude may be aſcertained. Philadelphia. 1790. 8. Ed. 2. 1794. 4. (1 L. 1 ſh.) Ed. 3. with additions. New-York. 1800. 4. On the northern and ſouthern lights; On the attraction towards the magnetic points. (American Muſeum Y. 1788. Oct. p. 351. 354. 356.) Addreſs to the members of the different learned ſocieties in America and Europe, in ſupport of the principles of the magnetic variation and their application in determining the longitude at ſea; ſhewing wherein what Dr. *Euler* publiſhed on this ſubject at Berlin, was deficient. (Ibid. Y. 1789. May. p. 496.)

CHURTON, [Ralph] *M. A. Fellow of Brazen-noſe College, Oxford and Rector of Middleton Cheney, Northamptonſhire.*

The lives of *William Smyth*, Biſhop of Lincoln, and Sir *Richard Sutton*, Knight, Founders of Brazen-noſe College — with an appendix of letters and papers never before printed. 1800. *A poſtſcript to an anſwer to *Francis Eyre* — occaſioned by his late publication, intitled a reply to — *Ralph*

Churton, by the author of the anſwer. 1801. 8. (2 ſh. 6 d.)

*CLAP, [Noah] *Town Clerk of Dorcheſter.*
Letter to the Secretary of the Maſſachuſetts Hiſtor. Soc. *(John Elliot)* (Coll. of Maſſachuſetts H. S. Y. 1792. p. 98.)

*CLAPHAM, [Samuel] *M. A. Vicar of Bingley, Yorkſhire and Chaplain to Lord Viſcount Ranelagh.*
An abridgment of the Lord Biſh. of Lincoln's elements of chriſtian theology for the uſe of families. 1802. (6 ſh. 6 d.) Sermons — ſelected from minor ond ſcarce authors —; 1803. 8. (8 ſh.)
(Several ſingle ſermons.)

*CLARE, Earl of [John] *Lord High Chancellor of Ireland.*
See Public Characters of 1798 and 1799. p. 400. Speech on a motion made by the Earl of *Moira*, Febr. 19. 1798. recommending conciliatory meaſures to allay diſcontent in that country. 1798. (1 ſh. 6 d.) Speech on a motion made by him Febr. 10. 1800, that in order to promote and ſecure the eſſential intereſts of Great-Britain and Ireland, to conſolidare the ſtrength, power and reſources of the Britiſh Empire, it will be adviſable to concur in ſuch meaſures as may beſt tend to unite the two kingdoms in fuch manner and in ſuch terms and conditions, as may be eſtabliſhed by acts of the reſpective parliaments of Great-Britain and Ireland. 1800. 8. (2 ſh. 6 d.)

*CLARE, [M....] *A. M.*
On the motion of fluids, natural and artificial, in which that of air and water is particularly conſidered and demonſtrated — — reviſed and corrected with conſiderable additions. 1802. 8. (10 ſh. 6 d.)

CLARE, [Peter] *Surgeon.*
born ..... died ..... (?)

*CLARE, [Richard Auguſtus] *Surgeon at Jamaica.*
Deſcription of a mercurial air pump; and of a double-barreled air pump. (*Nicholſon's* Journal. Vol. 4. p. 264.)

CLARE [Thomas] *M. A.*
See *Samuel Biſhop.*

*CLA-

LARENCE, *Duke of* [William Henry].

Subftance of his fpeech in the houfe of Lords, on the motion for the recommitment of the flave trade limitation bill on the 5 day of July. 1799. 8. (2 fh.) Subftance of his fpeeches in the houfe of Lords against the divorce bill. 1800. 8. (1 fh. 6 d.)

LARENDON, Earl of [Edward]

See *William Gisborne*.

LARENDON, [R..., V...,] *Esq.*

Sketch of the revenue and finances of Ireland and of the appropriated funds, loans and debt of the nation from their commencement: with abftracts of the principal heads of receipt and expediture for 60 years and the various fupplies fince the revolution. 1791. 4. (15 fh.)

LARIDGE, [John] *of Craig's-Court, London.*

Extract from a general view of agriculture, in the county of Dorfet. (Bath Agric. Soc. Vol. 7. p. 66.)

LARK, [A....]

A differtation on the ufe and abufe of tobacco. 1797. 8. A fhort hiftory of the ancient Ifraelites; — written originally in french by the Abbé *Fleury*, much enlarged from the apparatus biblicus of Pere *Lamy*, and corrected and improved throughout. 1802. 8. (4 fh.)

LARK, [Bracy] *Veterinary Surgeon and F. L. S.*

Obfervations on the genus oeftrius. (Transact. of L. S. Vol. 3. p. 289.)

LARK, [Emily] *Grand-daughter of the late Colonel Frederik, fon of Theodore, King of Corfica.*

Janthé, or the flower of Caernarvon; a novel. Vol. 1. 2. 1798. 8. (8 fh.) Ermine Montrofe; or, the cottage of the vale; with characters from life. Vol. 1. 2. 3. 1800. 12. (12 fh.)

LARK, [George]

An addrefs to both houfes of parliament: containing reafons for a tax upon dogs and the outlines of a plan for that purpofe; and for effectually

ctually suppressing the oppressive practice of impressing seamen and more expeditiously manning the royal navy. 1791. 8. (1 sh.) An address to the people of Ireland who are unfriendly to the British government. 1803. 8. (3 d.)

CLARK, [George] *Esq. Attorney at Law.*
Memoranda legalia, or, an alphabetical digest of the laws of England adapted to the use of the lawyer, the merchant and the trader. 1800. 8. (10 sh. 6 d.)

CLARK, [James] *M. Dr. Surgeon in Dominica; F. R. S. Edin. F. R. C. of Phys. of Edinb.*

Account of the good effects derived from the terra ponderosa muriata, in a peculiar species of scrophula, occurring among Negroes in the West-Indies. (*Duncan's* M. C. Dec. 2. Vol. 6. p. 267.) A treatise on the yellow fever, as it appeared in the island of Dominica in the Years 1793–1796. to which are added; observations on the bilious remittent fever, on intermittents, dysentery and some other West-India diseases; also, the chemical analysis and medical properties of the hot mineral waters in the same island. 1797. 8. (3 sh. 6 d.) An account of the poisonous quality of the juice of the root of iatropha manihot, or bitter cassada; and of the use of Cayenne pepper in counteracting the effects of this and some other poisonous substances; with remarks on the efficacy of the spigelia anthelmia in worm-cases; (*Simmons's* Med. Facts and Observ. Vol. 7. p. 289.) An account of some experiments made with a view to ascertain the comparative quantities of amylaceous matter, yielded by the different vegetables most commonly in use in the West-India Islands; (Ibid. Vol. 7. p. 300.)

CLARK, [John] *M Dr. Physician at Newcastle.*
Observations on the diseases in long voyages —, übers. Ausg 2. Kopenh. u. Leipz. 1798. 8. A collection of papers, intended to promote an institution for the cure and prevention of infectious fevers in Newcastle and other populous towns, Part 1. 2. 1802. 12. (6 sh.)

CLARK,

*CLARK, [John]

On commons in Breeknock. (*Young's* A. of Agr. Vol. 22. p. 632.) On watering meadows in Brecknockshire. (Ibid. Vol. 23. p. 192.)

*CLARK, [Thomas] *Surgeon.*

Observations on the nature and cure of fevers and of diseases of the West and East Indies, and of America; with an account of dissections performed in those climates, and general remarks on diseases of the army. Edinb. 1801. 8.

*CLARKE, [.....] *Mrs. of Lawrence farm, near Hedingham, Essex.*

On setting wheat. (*Young's* A. of Agr. Vol. 2. p. 289.)

*CLARKE, [.....]

* Testimonies of different authors, respecting the colossal statue of Ceres, placed in the vestibule of the public library at Cambridge, July 1. 1803. with a short account of its removal from Eleusis Nov. 22. 1801. 1803. 8. (1 sh.)

*CLARKE, [Charles] *F. S. A.*

Observations on the intended tunnel beneath the river Thames; shewing the many defects in the present state of that projection. 1799. 4. (4 sh.) Observations on episcopal chairs and stone seats; as also on piscinas and other appendages to altars still remaining in chancels; with a description of Chalk church, in the diocese of Rochester. (Arch. Vol. XI. p. 317.)

*CLARKE, [Charles] *of Milbank-row, Westminster, London.*

Treatise on the earth called gypsum. 1792. 8. (1 sh. 6 d.)

*CLARKE, [Charles Marshall] *Physician at Lowth.*

The history of a case terminating fatally from a concretion formed in the bowels, in consequence of swallowing the stones of fruit. (*Duncan's* A. of Med. Y. 1798. p. 357.)

*CLARKE, [Edward Goodman] *M. Dr.*

Medicinae praxeos compendium, symptomata, causas, diagnosin, prognosin et medendi rationem exhibens. 1800. 12. (5 sh.)

*CLARKE,

CLARKE, [Joseph] *M. Dr. Master of the Lying-In Hospital at Dublin; M. R. J. A.*

Observations on puerperal fever, more especially as it has of late occurred in the lying-in Hospital of Dublin. (*Duncan's* M. C. Dec. 2. Vol. 5 1790. p. 299.) Account of a disease which, until lately proved fatal to a great number of infants in the lying-in hospital of Dublin, with observations on its causes and prevention. (*Simmons'* Med. Facts and Observat. Vol. 3. p. 78. Transact. of J. A. Vol. 3. 1789. p. 89.) übers. Repert. Chir u. Mediz. Abhandl. B. 2. S. 231.) Remarks on the causes and cure of some diseases of infancy (Transact. of the J. A. Vol. 6. p. 3. *Simmons'* Med. Facts and Observat. Vol. 8. p. 215.)

*CLARKE, [Richard] *Minister of St. Philips Charleston, South Carolina and Lecturer of Stoke-Newington and St. James's Aldgate.*

A series of letters, essays, dissertations and discourses on various subjects. Vol. I. 1795. 8. (5 sh.)

*CLARKE, [Richard] *M. Dr. Surgeon in the Royal Navy.*

Plan for increasing the naval force of Great-Britain by rendering the service a more desirable object to officers and seamen —. 1795. 8. (1 sh. 6 d.) Medical strictures, an effectual method of treating most diseases, in which the prevention, palliation and cure are pointed out. 1799. 8. (1 sh.)

*CLARKE, [Robert] *Surgeon at Sunderland, in the county of Durham.*

An account of a key instrument of a new construction, with observations on the principles on which it acts, in the extraction of teeth, and on the mode of applying it. (*Simmon's* Med. Facts and Observ. Vol. 6. p. 120.)

*CLARKE, [R.... H....] *Esq. of Bridwell, near Cullompton, Devon.*

On draining and rearing calves. (*Young's* A. of Agr. Vol. 3. p. 377.)

*CLARKE,

CLARKE, [Thomas Brooke] *A. M. Secretary for the Library and Chaplain to his R. H. the Prince of Wales. LL. Dr.*

Statiſtical view of Germany in reſpect to the imperial and territorial conſtitutions, forms of government, legiſlation, adminiſtration of juſtice and ecclefiaſtical ſtate. 1790. 8. (4 ſh.) The doctrine of an appeal to the people and the right of reſiſtance, as laid down by Mr. *Saurin* in the Iriſh houſe of Commons, conſidered and confuted. 1799. 8. (1 ſh.) A letter to the Rt. H. Earl *Cholmondeley* on the civil policy of the ancients. To which is prefixed an enumeration of the confiſcations &c. of the french nation, extracted from official documents: tranſlated from the german. 1799. 8. (1 ſh. 6 d.) Union or ſeparation, written ſome years ſince by Dr. *Tucker*, Dean of Glouceſter and now firſt publiſhed in this tract, upon the ſame ſubject: With an appendix on the political, commercial and civil ſtate of Ireland. Ed. 3. 1799. 8. (2 ſh.) The political, commercial and civil ſtate of Ireland. 1799. 8. (1 ſh. 6 d.) Miſconceptions of facts and mis-ſtatements of the public accounts — by the Rt. H. *John Foſter*, Speaker of the Iriſh houſe of Commons, reviſed and corrected according to official documents. 1799. 8. (2 ſh.) A ſurvey of the ſtrength and opulence of Great-Britain; wherein is ſhewn the progreſs of the commerce, agriculture, population — before and ſince the acceſſion of the houſe of Hannover, with obſervations by Dean *Tucker* and *David Hume* in a correſpondance with Lord *Kaimes*, now firſt publiſhed. 1801. 8. (5 ſh.) Hiſtorical and political view of the diſorganization of Europe; wherein the laws and characters of nations and the maritime and commercial ſyſtem of Great-Britain and other ſtates are vindicated againſt the imputations and revolutionary propoſals of M. *Talleyrand* and *Hauterive*. 1803. 8. (5 ſh.)

CLARKE, [William] *late Profeſſor of the Engliſh language and belles lettres in the College of Alais, Languedoc.*

Intereſting letters on the french revolution, extracted

hacted from the celebrated works of Mr. *Malouet* — translated from the french. 1795. 8. (3 sh.)

CLARKSON, [T....] *Rev.*

Letters on the slave trade and the state of the nations in those parts of Africa, which are contiguous to Fort St. Louis and Goree. 1791. 4. (5 sh.) Some account of the new colony at Sierra Leona, on the coast of Africa. (American Museum Y. 1792. April p. 160. May p. 229.)

*CLARKSON, [William] *M. B: F. of the C. of Physic. of Philad.*

Case of tetanus. (Tr. of Phys. of Philad. Vol 1. P. 1. p. 66.)

*CLAXTON, [John] *F. A. S.*

Description of a saxon arch with an inscription in Dinton church, Buckinghamshire and of sundry antiquities found in that parish. (Arch. Vol. 10. p. 167.)

*CLAY, [J.....]

Elegy, supposed to be written in the place de la revolution, after the murder of Louis XVI. 1793. 4. (1 sh.)

*CLAY, [Joseph] *M. A. P. S.*

Observations on the figure of the earth. (Tr. of A. S. Vol. 5. p. 312.)

*CLAYFIELD, [William]

An account of several veins of sulphate of strontian or strontites, found in the neighbourhood of Bristol, with an analysis of the different varieties. (*Nicholson's* Journal. Vol. 3. p. 36.) Description of a mercurial air-holder, suggested by an inspection of Mr. *Watt's* machine for containing factitious air. (*Tilloch's* Philos. Magaz. Vol. 7. p. 148.)

*CLAYTON, [Sir Richard] *Baronet.*

On the cretins of the Vallais. (Mem. of M. Vol. 3. p. 261. Columbian Magaz. Y. 1791. Vol. 2. p. 23. New-York Mag. Y. 1792. Febr. p. 96.) Connubia florum, a poem in latin verses from *de la Croix*, M. Dr. with notes and observations by him. 1791. 8. (3 sh.) A critical inquiry into the life of Alexander the great by the ancients historians, from the french of the Baron de St. *Croix*, with notes and observations; illustrated with a map of the marches of Alexander the great. 1793. 4. (18 sh.)

(18 ſh.) Memoirs of the houſe of Medici, from its origin to the death of Franceſco, the ſecond grand duke of Tuſcany and of the great men who flouriſhed in Tuſcany within that period; from the french of Mr. *Tenhove*, with notes and obſervations. Vol. 1. 2. 1797. 4. (2 L. 2 ſh.) A ſhort journey in the Weſt-Indies, in which are interſperſed curious anecdotes and characters. (New-York Magaz. Y. 1792. Febr. p. 97.)

*CLEAVER, [William] *Lord-Biſhop of Cheſter, Prebendary of Weſtminſter, Principal of Brazenoſe College.*

*De rhythmo graecorum liber, — in uſum juventutis Coll. Aen. Naſ. olim conſcriptus et nunc demum in lucem editus. Oxonii. 1789. 8. Pardon and ſanctification proved to be the privileges annexed to the due uſe of the Lord's ſupper as a feaſt on a ſacrifice, a ſermon. 1791. 8. (1 ſh.)

*CLEEVE, [Alexander] *A. B. Vicar of Wooler in Northumberland.*

A ſelection of pſalms; from tate and brady's verſion. Ed. 2 1793. 12. (1 ſh. 6 d.) *Robert Fleming's* chriſtology, or, a diſcourſe concerning chriſt; in himſelf, his government, his offices &c. abridged in two parts. 1797. 8. (7 ſh.) Devotional exerciſes and contemplations, extracted altogether from the book of pſalms and ſuited to all claſſes and circumſtances of mankind; in 4 parts. 1800. 8. (2 ſh. 6 d.)

CLEGG, [James] *at Mancheſter, Dobefields.*

Account of a ſubſtitute for verdigris, in dying black. (Tr. of the Soc. for the E. of A. Vol. 1. p. 181.)

CLEGHORN, [David] *Brewer in Edinburgh.*

Account of a method of curing burns and ſcalds. (*Simmons's* Med. Facts and Obſervat. Vol. 2. p. 120.)

CLEGHORN, [Robert] *M. Dr. Profeſſor of Materia medica in the Univerſity of Glasgow.*

A caſe of inverſion of the uterus. (M. C. Vol. 2. p. 226.)

CLEMENCE, [M.....]

The true lover of his country; or, a treatiſe on ſovereignty, with reſpect to its origin, its object, its functions, and its several modifications; with a concise description of the revolutions of the roman republic, of the kingdom of England and more particularly that of France. 1801. 12. (4 sh.)

*CLEMENT, [Thomas] *Curate of Brendon, Devon.* The key of natural philosophy, or an introduction into the knowledge of nature, being a plain philosophical treatise —. 1790. 8. (2 sh. 6 d.) Ed. 3. improved. 1794. 8. (2 sh. 6 d.)

*CLEMENTS, [William] *M. A. of Magdalen-College, Oxford.*
born 1711. died 1799. Apr. 8.
See Gentleman's Magaz. Y. 1799. Apr. p. 356. Jun. p. 474. Allg. Litterat. Zeit. ItBl. J. 1800. S. 659.
Eight sermons, preached — in the Year 1757. To which is added a latin oration, spoken July 22. 1733. 179 8. (5 sh.)

*CLENNEL, [John] *at Newcastle-upon-Tyne.*
On the poor laws. (Comm. and Agric. Mag. Y. 1801. Febr. p. 98.) On Tyne keels. (Ibid. Y. 1801. Apr. p. 251.) Reply to a country magistrate on houses of industry. (Ibid. Y. 1801. Apr. p. 252.) On a general canal bill and parliamentary rewards for inland navigation. (Ibid. Y. 1801. May. p. 341.) The Newcastle mode of measuring coals and grindstones. (Ib. Y. 1801. June p. 406.) On the advantages of disclosing the process of manufactories. (Ib. Y. 1801. Jul. p. 15.) On the necessity and importance of topographical information. (Ib. Y. 1801. July. p. 24.) An account of the art of making glue. (*Nicholson's* Journal. Y. 1802. Aug. p. 235.) On the manufacture of glue. (Comm. and Agric. Mag. Vol. 7. p. 34.) On the preservation of butter in Abyssinia. (Ib. Vol. 7. p. 126.) Names given to each kind of wool, by wool throwers. (Ib. Vol. 7. p. 131.) Ointment for sore eyes and reflections on withholding useful recipes. (Ib. Vol. 7. p. 132.)

*CLERK, [John] *Esq. of Edinburgh; F. of A. and R. S. Edinb.*
See Public Characters of 1800 and 1801. p. 456.
Essay on naval tactics, systematical and historical, with

with explanatory plates. Part 1-4. 1790-1798. 4. (1 L 12 sh.)

*CLIFFORD, [Henry] *Esq. of Lincoln's-Inn, Barrister at Law.*

Reflections on the appointment of a catholic bishop to the London district, in a letter to the catholic laity of the said district. 1791. 8. (2 sh.) Account of the two cases of controverted elections of the borough of Southwerk in the county of Surry; which where tried and determined by select committees of the house of commons — with notes and illustrations: To which are added, an account of the two subsequent cases of the city of Canterbury, and an appendix on the right of the returning officer to administer the oath of supremacy to catholics. 1797. 8 (6 sh.) The proceedings of the house of Lords in the case of *Benjamin Flower*, printer of the Cambridge intelligencer, for a supposed libel on the bishop of Llandaff, with prefatory remarks by Mr. *Flower*, to which are added the arguments in the court of king's bench, on a motion for an habeas corpus, and a postscript, containing remarks on the judgment of that court 1800. (4 sh.)

CLIFFORD, [M.... M....] *Esq. Of the 12 or Prince of Wales's light dragoons.*

Egypt, a poem, descriptive of that country and its inhabitants; written during the late campaign. 1802. 8. (4 sh. 6 d.)

CLIFFORD, [Robert] *F. R. S.*

Memoirs, illustrating the history of Jacobinism by the Abbé *Barruel*, translated. Vol. 1-4. 1798. 8.

CLIFFORD, [Thomas]

An approved method of making cider. (Columbian Magaz. Y. 1790. Oct. p. 250.) On the maple sugar of America. (Bath Agric. Soc. Vol. 6. p. 311.)

CLINE, [.....]

On the use of the tinctura ferri muriati in those suppressions of urine which arise from a spasmodic affection of the urethra. (M. Rec. and Ref. p. 83.)

O 3 CLINTON,

CLINTON, [Sir Henry] *Knight of the Bat[h] Lieut. Gener.*
born, ... died 1795. Dec. 23.
See Gentleman's Magaz. Y. 1795. Dec. p. 1060
Obſervations on Mr. *Stedman's* hiſtory of t[he] American war. 1794. 4. (2 ſh.)

*CLOBERY, [Robert Glynn] See *Glynn.*

*CLODMAN, [John]
The progreſs of a countryman. (Columbian M[a]gaz. Y. 1787. March. p. 314.)

*CLOSE, [H. . . . J. . . .] *Rector of Hitcham, Suffo[lk]*
On the half husbandry. (Bath Agricult. S[oc.] Vol. 3. p. 63.). On the culture of potatoes. (Ibi[d.] Vol. 3. p. 104.) Remarks on *Joſeph Wimpe[y's]* practical enquiry concerning the moſt certain a[nd] effectual means of promoting vegetation. (Ibi[d.] Vol. 3. p. 203.) Experiment on horſe-hoed whe[at.] (Ibid. Vol. 3. p. 210.) A table for manuring la[nd.] (Ibid. Vol. 3. p. 321.) Elements of the frenc[h,] latin and engliſh language. 1795. 8. (1 ſh. 6 d.) (fatting with potatoes and on the advantages of dr[il]ling. (Bath Agric. Soc. Vol. 7. p. 319.) On t[he] comparative advantages of the drill husbandry. (I[bid.] Vol. 9. p. 40.) On drilled turnips. (Ibid. Vol. p. 46.) On the half-husbandry. (Ibid. Vol. 9. 50.) On the culture of the Mazagan bean. (Ib. V[ol.] 9. p. 53.) On the value of the ruta-baga, co[m]pared with other turnips. (Ibid. Vol. 9. p. 307 On obtaining a knowledge of practical agricultu[re] (Comm. and Agric. Magaz. Y. 1800. Sept. p. 20[.] Experiments on potatoes. (*Young's* A. of Ag[r.] Vol. 1. p. 397.) On a new culture of whe[at] (Ibid. Vol. 2. p. 450.) Letter on dibbling whe[at] (Tr. of the Soc. for the E. of A. Vol. 4. p. [.] Eſſay on the converſion of graſs lands into tillag[e] (Comm. to the B. of Agr. Vol. 3. P. 1. p. 3 *Tilloch's* Philoſ. Mag. Vol. 15. p. 167. 268.) (tythes as one of the moſt obvious impediments agriculture and on means propoſed for their abo[li]tion, equally advantageous to the clergy and la[nd]holders. (Comm. and Agric. Mag. Y. 1803. Fe[b.] p. 109.)

*CLOSE, [William] *at Dalton.*
Conſtruction of a lamp for burning tallow. (N[i]*cholſo[n]*

cholson's Journal. Vol. 3. p. 363.) On the lamp for tallow and the combuſtion of that material. (Ibid. Vol. 3. p. 547.) Deſcription of an engine for raiſing water by the lateral motion of a ſtream of water through a conical tube. (Ibid. Vol. 4. p. 293. 492.) New application of the ſyphon to raiſe water above the ſurface of the reſervoir. (Ibid. Vol. 4. p. 547. Vol. 5. p. 22.) Experiments and obſervations on the properties of wind inſtruments, conſiſting of a ſingle pipe or channel; with improvement in their conſtruction. (Ibid. Vol. 5. p. 213.) Conſtruction of an hydraulic apparatus, which by means of the ſyphon raiſes water above its level and performs its alternations without attendance. (Ibid. Y. 1802. Jan. p. 27.) Compoſition of writing ink, poſſeſſing the permanent colour and other eſſential properties, of the ink uſed for printing. (Ibid. Y. 1802. July. p. 146.)

CLOTHIER, [Wiltſhire] *F. A. S.*

Wool encouraged without exportation, or practical obſervations on wool and the woollen manufacture, in two parts. 1791. 8. (2 ſh.)

CLOUGH, [Henry Gore] *M. Dr.*

Caſe of the humerus of a child torn from the ſcapula by a mill. (Mem. of M. S. of L. Vol. 3. p. 519.)

CLOUGH, [James] *Surgeon.*

Obſervations on pregnancy and the diſeaſes incident to that period; together with their remedies and ſome uſeful cautions, particularly neceſſary for women during a firſt pregnancy. To which are added obſervations on the diſeaſes of children. 1796. 8. (1 ſh.)

CLOWES, [James] *M. A. Rector of the Pariſh church of St. John Mancheſter and late fellow of Trinity College, Cambridge.*

Swedenborg's celeſtia arcana, tranſlated into engliſh; 17.. Sermons. Vol. 1. 2. 1796. 8. (5 ſh.) Letters to a member of parliament, on the writings of *Swedenborg*, containing a full and complete refutation of all the Abbé *Barruel's* calumnies againſt the honourable author. 1799. 8. (4 ſh.)

rd Biſhop of CLOYNE, ſee *Richard Woodward.*

*CLUBBE, [William] *LL. B. Vicar of Brandeston, Suffolk.*

Six satires of *Horace*, in a style between free imitation and literal version. 1795. 4. (5 sh.) The epistle of *Horace* to the Piso's, on the art of poetry, translated into English verse. 1797. 4. (2 sh. 6 d.) Omnium, containing the journal of a late three days tour into France, curious and extraordinary anecdotes, critical remarks and other miscellaneous pieces in prose and verse. 1798. 8. (6 sh.)

*CLULOW, [Thomas]

Invention of a loom to weave figured ribbands. (Tr. of the Soc. for the E. of A. Vol. 18. p. 259.

*CLUTTERBUCK, [Henry] *Esq. Member of the corporation of Surgeons, and Surgeon to the Roy. universal dispensary.*

An account of a new and successful method of treating those affections, which arise from the poison of lead: To which is added, general observations on the internal use of lead as a medicine. 1794. 8. (2 sh.) (*Tilloch's* Philos. Magaz. Vol. 6. p. 119.) Observations on the small pox. (New London M. J. Vol. 2. p. 28.) Remarks on some of the opinions of the late Mr. *John Hunter* respecting the venereal disease. 1799. 8. (1 sh. 6 d.) Letter containing some objections to the Mitchillian theory of pestilential fluid. (*Tilloch's* Philos. Magaz. Vol. 5. p. 188.)

*COATES, [Charles] *LL. B.*

The history and antiquities of reading. 1802. 4.

COBB, [James] *Esq. Secretary at the India house.* born 1756.

The haunted tower; 17.. The siege of Belgrade; 17.. Ramah droog; or, wine does wonders, a comic opera, in 3 acts. 1800. 8. (2 sh.) A house to be sold, a musical piece; 1802. 8. (2 sh.)

*COBBETT, [William] (*Fictitious name, Peter Porcupine or James Quicksilver.*)

S. *Woltmann's* Gesch. und Politik J. 1800. St. 2. S. 193.

*Observations on Dr. *Priestley's* emigration to America; 17.. Ed. 4. 1798. 8. (1 sh. 6 d.

*A bone to gnaw for the democrats; 17.. Summary of the law of nations founded on the treaties and customs of the modern nations of Europe by Mr. *Martens*, translated from the french. Philad. 1795. 8. *Moreau de St. Mery*, topographical and political description of the spanish part of Saint-Domingo — translated from the french. Vol. 1. 2. Philad. 1796. 8. *James Quickfilver*, the blue shop or impartial and humorous observations on the life and advantures of *Peter Porcupine*. Philad. 1796. 8. A little plan english addressed to the people of the United states on the treaty negotiated with his Britannic Maj. and on the conduct of the President relative thereto; in answer to „the letters of *Franklin*„. With a supplement containing an account of the turbulent and factious proceedings of the late opposers of that treaty. London reprinted 1796. Observations on the debates of the American congress on the addresses to Gen. *Washington* on his resignation. 1796. 8. (1 sh.) A rick for a bite or review upon review; with a critical essay on the works of Mrs. *S. Rowson*. Philad. 1796. 8. The bloody buoy, thrown out as a warning to the political pilots of all nations, or, a faithfull relation of a multitude of acts of horrid barbarity — until the commencement of the French revolution; to which is added, an instructive essay, tracing these dreadful effects to their real causes — 1796. 12. (3 sh.) The life and adventures of *Peter Porcupine*, with a full and fair account of his authoring transactions —. Philad. 1797. 8. (1 sh.) Letter to the infamous *Tom Paine*, in answer to his letter to Gen. *Washington*. 1797. 8. (1 sh.) Democratic principles illustrated by example. Part 1. 2. 1798. (7 d.) The republican judge; or, the American liberty of the press, as exhibited, explained and exposed in the base and partial prosecution of *Will. Cobbett* for a pretended libel against the king of Spain and his Embassador, before the supreme court of Pennsylvania; with an address to the people of England. 1798. 8. (2 sh.) Detection of a conspiracy formed by the united Irishmen; with the evident intention of aiding the tyrants of France in subverting the government of the United states of America. 1799. 8. (1 sh.) Remarks on an explanation lately published by Dr. *Priestley*, respecting the intercepted letters of his friend and disciple *John H. Stone*; to which is added a certificate of civism for *John Priestley*, Jun. 1799. 8. (1 sh.) Observations on the debates of the American congress and on the address presented to Gen. *Washington* on his resignation, with remarks on the timidity of the language held towards France — to which are prefixed *Washington's* address to congress and the answers of the senate and house of representatives. 1799. The American rushlight by the help of which wayward and disaffected persons may see a complete specimen of the baseness, dishonesty, ingratitude and perfidy of republicans and of the profligacy, injustice and tyranny of republican government. 1800. The trial of republicanism; or, a series of political papers, proving the injurious and debasing consequences of republican government and written constitutions; with an introductory address to *Thomas Erskine*. 1801. 8. (2 sh.) Letters — on the peace with *Bonaparte*, to which is added an appendix, containing a collection of all the conventions, treaties, speeches and other documents connected with the subject. 1802. 8. (7 sh.) Letters on the fatal effects of the peace with *Bonaparte;* particularly with respect to the colonies, the commerce, the manufactures and the constitution of the united kingdom. 1802. 8. (3 sh.) Letter 1. 2. to the Hon. *James Fox* on the circumstance, the motive and the consequence of his visit to *Bonaparte*. 1802. Weekly political register. Vol. 1. 2. 1802. Letters to the Chancellor of the exchequer, exposing the deception of the financial statements and shewing the fatal tendency of the peace of Amiens with respect to public credit. 1803. 8. (2 sh. 6 d.)

*COBBOLD, [John Spencer] *M. A. Fellow of Gonville and Cajus College, Ipswich.*

Essay, tending to prove in what sense Jesus Christ hath brought life and immortality to light through the gospel, published in pursuance of the will of the

the late Mr. *Norris*, as having gained the annual prize instituted by him in the university of Cambridge. 1793. 8. (1 sh.) An essay, tending to shew the advantages which result to revelation from its being conveyed to us in the form of history. 1800.

COCHRAN, [Archibald] Earl of *Dundonald*.
See *Archib. Dundonald*.

COCHRANE, [James] *Vicar of Mansfield in the county of York, and formerly Chaplain to the 82 Regt. of foot.*
Plan for recruiting the British army. 1779. 4. (1 sh.) Thoughts concerning the proper constitutional principles of manning and recruiting the british navy and army. 1791. 4. (2 sh.)

COCHRANE, [John]
The seaman's guide; shewing how to live comfortably at sea. 1797. 8. (1 sh. 6 d.) Manufacture of wheat flour in Bengale. (*Young's* A. of Agr. Vol. 28. p. 268.)

COCKBURN, [William] *M. A.*
Saint Peter's denial of christ: a Seatonian prize poem. 1802. 4. (2 sh.)

COCKIN, [W....]
born 1736. died at Kendall, in Westmoreland: 1801. May 30.
See Gentleman's Magaz. Y. 1801. June. p. 575.
Monthly Magaz. Y. 1801. Aug. p. 69.
On arithmetic; 17.. Poems; 17..

COCKRELL, [Richard] *Teacher of the free school at Lartington.*
Introduction to plane trigonometry, with is application to heights and distances. 179. 8. (2 sh.)

COCKS, [John Somers] *M. P.*
Patriotism and the love of liberty defended; in two dialogues. 1791. 8. (1 sh. 6 d.) Short treatise on the dreadful tendency of levelling principles. 1793. 8. (1 sh.)

DE COETLOGON, [Charles Edward de] *M. A. A methodist clergyman.*
Sermons; now first printed from the original manuscripts of *John Wallis*, D. D. to which are prefixed memoirs of the author with some original anecdotes and a recommendary introduction. 1791.

1791. 8. (6 sh.) A seasonable caution against the abominations of the church of Rome. 1800. 8 (2 d.) The fall of antichrist, the triumph of the christian church. 1800. 8. (1 sh.) (Editor of „The theological miscellany.„)

(Several single sermons.)

*COFFIN, [Charles] *M. Dr.*

An account of the pestilential fever which prevailed at Newbury-port, state of Massachusetts in 1796. (Medical Repository. Vol. 1. p. 504.)

*COFFIN, [Peleg]

*Progress of the whale fishery at Nantucket. (Coll. of Massachusetts H. S. Y. 1794. p. 161.)

COGAN, [E....]

Moschi idyllia tria, graece, cum notis in usum studiosae juventutis. 1795. Reflections on the evidence of christianity. 1796. 12. (1 sh.) A passage in *Virgil*, „nihil iste nec ausus nec potuit„ explained. (Monthly Magaz. Y. 1800. Apr. p. 210.) On greek articles; (Ibid. Y. 1800. Aug. p. 33.) Classical remarks. (Ibid. Y. 1800. Sept. p. 137.) On prosody. (Ibid. Y. 1801. June. p 389. July. p. 485.) On a passage of *Virgil* (Aen. libr. 2 — Eripe, nate, fugam). (Ibid. Y. 1801. Dec. p. 384.) Conjectural emendations. (Ibid. Y. 1802. Febr. p. 6.) Correction proposed in *Homer* (Il. I. v. 133.) (Ibid. Y. 1802. Febr. p. 27. Dec. p. 411.) Conjectural emendations. (Ibid. Y. 1802. Febr. p. 6.) Remark in preface to the 2 edit. of the Hecuba by *Porson*. (Ibid. Y. 1802. Sept. p. 104.) An account of the numbers in *Homer* Il. 16. v. 207. (Ibid. Y. 1802. March. p. 107.) On a passage in the 19 book of *Homer* and on a passage in *Euripides*. (Ibid. Y. 1803. Jan. p. 477.)

COGAN, [Thomas] *M. Dr.*

The rhine or a journey from Utrecht to Frankfort, chiefly by the borders of the rhine and the passage down that river from Menz to Bonn; described in a series of letters; written from Holland to a friend in England in the Years 1791 and 1792. embellished with 24 views in aqua tinta and a map of the rhine from Metz to Bonn. Vol. 1. 2. 1795. 8. (1 L. 1 sh.) Memoirs of the society at Amsterdam in favour of drowned persons; 1773.

1773. The works of the late Prof. *Camper* on the connexion between the ſcience of anatomy and the arts of drawing, painting, ſtatuary &c. in two books —. 1794. 4. (1 L. 1 ſh.) A philoſophical treatiſe of the paſſions. 1800. 8. (8 ſh. 6 d.)

COGGAN, [G....] *Merchant of Hull.*
A teſtimony of *Richard Brothers*, in an epiſtolary addreſs to the people of England, on the impending judgments of God; with original letters lately ſent to the Queen, Duke of Glouceſter, Earl Fitzwilliam, Mr. Pitt. 1795. 8. (1 ſh.)

COGGAN, [Samuel] *Secretary of the Devon and Exeter Hoſpital.*
A journal of the weather during the ſevere froſt 1788. 1789. (*Young's* A. of Agr. Vol. 12. p. 507.)

COGSWELL, [Maſon F....] *M. Dr.*
Sketch of the hiſtory of the weather and diſeaſes of Hartford in Connecticut, during the winter and ſpring of 1798. (Medical Repoſitory. Vol. 2. p. 299.)

COIT, [Thomas]
Account of the peſtilential fever which prevailed at New-London (Connecticut). (Medical Repoſit. Vol. 2. p. 407.)

COKE, [.....] *Dr.*
— and Mr. *Moore;* the life of the Rev. *John Wesley*, A. M. including an account of the great revival of religion in Europe and America, of which he was the firſt and chief inſtrument. 1792. 8. (5 ſh.)

COKE, [Sir Edward] *Lord chief Juſtice of England.* born 1549. died 1634. Sept. 3.

COKE, [Thomas William] *Esq. M. P.*
The addreſſes to the freeholders of the county of Norfolk. 1802. (3 d.) Compariſon of South Down, New Leiceſter and Norfolk ſheep. (*Young's* A. of Agr. Vol. 33. p. 109.) See *Edmund Wright.*

COLBURNE, [Benjamin] *of Bath.*
An ineſtimable diſſolvent for the human calculi. (American Muſeum Y. 1788. Jan. p. 60.)

*COLBY,

*COLBY, [Thomas] *Surgeon at Sorrington in Devon shire.*

Account of a cafe in which the tendon of th biceps mufcle was punctured in beeding. (M. C Vol. 2. p. 18.)

*COLDEN, [Alexander]

An examination of the new doctrines in philofc phy and theology propagated by Dr. *Priestley* with fome strictures on the power of the civ magiftrate, as the ordinance of God. 1793. 1 (2 fh. 6 d.)

*COLDEN, [Cadwallader] *Esq.*

Extract of his letter concerning the throat diftem per. (American Mufeum Y. 1788. Jan. p. 53.)

*COLE, [Peter]

On the difappearance of fwallows in autumn. (Me dical Repofit. Vol. 2. p. 178. *Tillock's* Philof Magaz. Vol. 4. p. 414.)

*COLE, [Thomas] *LL. B. Vicar of Dulverton in the county of Somerfet.*

born 1726. died 1796 June 14.

See Gentleman's Magaz. Y. 1796. June. p. 532. Allg. Litt. Zeit. ItBl. J. 1800. S. 627.

*Difcourfe on luxury, infidelity and enthufiafm. 1760. 12. The life of Hubert; a narrative, de-fcriptive and didactic poem. Book 1. to which are added, fome original and translated poems. 1795. 8. Book 2. 3. 1797. 8. (6 fh. 6 d.) The arbor, or the rural philofopher. 1756. 4. (reprinted in *Dodsley's* collection of poems.)

*COLE, [William] *Rev. at Maidftone.*

The contradiction. 1796. 8. (5 fh.) A loyal poetical gratulation prefented to his Majefty at a review of the Kentifh yeomanry volunteers. Aug. 1. 1799. 1799. 4. (1 fh. 6 d.) A tear of regret to the memory of Lieut. Colon. *Shadwell* of the 25 Regt. of light dragoons, fhot through the heart by a deferter the 1 day of june 1799. 1799. 4. (1 fh. 6 d.)

*COLEBROOKE, [Henry T....] *Lieut. in the fer-vice of the H. Eaft-India Company, who atten-ded the army in capacity of furveyor.*

Twelve views of places in the kingdom of My-fore, the country of Tippoo-Sultan, from dra-wings

wings taken on the ſpot; to which are annexed, conciſe deſcriptions of the places drawn, with a brief detail of part of the operations of the army under the Marq. *Cornwallis* during the late war and a few other particulars. 1793. 4. (12 L. 12 ſh.) On the islands Nancowry and Comarty. (Aſiat. Reſ. Vol. 4. p. 129.) Aſtronomical obſervations made on a voyage to the Andaman and Nicobar Islands. (Ibid. Vol. 4. p. 317.) Aſtronomical obſervations made on a ſurvey through the Carnatic and Myſore country. (Ibid. Vol. 4. p. 321.) Table of latitudes and longitudes of ſome principal places in India, determined from aſtronomical obſervations. (Ibid. Vol. 4. p. 325.) On the Andaman islands. (Ibid. Vol. 4. p. 385.) On Barren island and its volcano. (Ibid. Vol. 4. p. 397.) A digeſt of Hindu law, on contracts and ſucceſſions with a commentary by Jagannatha Tercapanchanana. Translated from the original Sanſcrit. Vol. 1–3. 1801. 8. (2 L. 2 ſh.) Enumeration of Indian claſſes. (Aſiat. Reſ. Vol. 5. p. 53.) On Indian weights and meaſures. (Ibid. Vol. 5. p. 91.) On the religious ceremonies of the Hindus and of the Brahmens eſpecially. (Ibid. Vol. 5. p. 345.) On the duties of a faithful Hindu widow. (Ibid. Vol. 4. p. 209.)

COLEMAN, [.....]

Caſes of practice adjudged in the ſupreme court of New-York. 1800.

COLEMAN, [Edward] *Surgeon.*

Diſſertation on ſuſpended reſpiration from drowning, hanging and ſuffocation. In which is recommended a different mode of treatment to any hitherto pointed out. 1791. 8. (5 ſh.) überſ. Leipzig. 1793. 8.

COLEMAN, [Edward] *Profeſſor of the veterinary College, principal veterinary Surgeon to the Britiſh Cavalry and to his Maj. Board of Agriculture.*

Obſervations on the ſtructure, oeconomy and diſeaſes of the foot of the horſe and on the principles and practice of ſhoeing; illuſtrated with 8 engraved copper-plates. Vol. 1. 1798. 4. Vol. 2. 1802.

1802. 4. (3 L. 13 ſh. 6 d.) Obſervations on the formation and uſes of the natural frog of the horſe with a deſcription of a patent artificial frog, to prevent and cure contracted hoofs, thruſhes, cankers and ſandcracks. 1800. 8. (1 ſh 6 d.) * Veterinary transactions; containing obſervations on the effects and treatment of wounds of joints and other circumſcribed cavities; — Numb. 1. 1801. 8 (3 ſh. 6 d.)

*COLEMAN, [Jacob] *of Montgomery county, Pennſylvania.*

A mode to preſerve the peach tree from being injured by a ſpecies of worm, which for ſeveral years paſt has deſtroyed many of them in theſe ſtates. (American Muſeum Y. 1787. Aug. p. 177.)

*COLEMAN, [R....] *of the Royal mills, Waltham Abbey.*

On the manufacture and conſtituent parts of gunpowder. (*Tilloch's* Philoſ. Magaz. Vol. 9. p. 355.)

COLEMAN, [William] *Surgeon at Sandwich in Kent.* born . . . . died . . . . (?)

*COLEPEPER, [J.... Spencer] *Esq.*

Important facts, ſubmitted to the conſideration of the people of England with ſome thoughts on the preſent ſituation of public affairs. 1793. 8. (1 ſh.)

*COLERIDGE, [.....] *S. T. late of Jeſus College, Cambridge.*

a native of Briſtol.

The fall of *Robespierre*, an hiſtoric drama. 1794. 8. (1 ſh.) Conciones ad populum, or addreſſes to the people. 1795. 8. (1 ſh. 6 d.) A proteſt againſt certain bills; or the plot diſcovered. An addreſs to the people againſt miniſterial treaſon. 1795. 12. (1 ſh.) Poems on various ſubjects. 1796. 8. (5 ſh.) Ed. 2. To which are now added poems by *Charles Lamb* and *Charles Lloyd.* 1797. 8. (6 ſh.) The watchman, a weekly miſcellany. Nrb. 1. 1796. (4 d.) A proſpect of peace; 1796. Ode to the departed year. 1797. 4. (1 ſh.) Fears in ſolitude, written in 1798 during the alarm of an invaſion; to which are added, France, an ode; and Froſt at midnight. 1798. 4. (1 ſh. 6 d.) The Picco-

Piccolomini, or the first part of Wallenstein a drama in 5 acts; translated from the german of *Fred. Schiller*. 1800. 8. (4 sh.) The death of Wallenstein, a tragedy; translated from the german of *Fred. Schiller*. 1800. 8. (4 sh.)

OLET, [John Annesley]

An impartial review of the life and writings, public and private character of the late *John Wesley*. Part I. 1791. 8. (1 sh.) *Letter to the Rev. *Thomas Coke*, LL. D. and *Henry More;* occasioned by their proposals for publishing the life of the Rev. *John Wesley*, A. M. in opposition to that advertised to be written by *John Whitehead*, M. D. — by an old member of the society. 1792 8. (2 sh.)

OLINTON, [Sir James FOULIS of] *Baronet*.

Inquiry into the origin of the name of the Scottish nation. (Transact. of the Soc. of Antiq. of Scotland. Vol. I: p. I.) Inquiry into the beverage of the ancient Caledonians and other Norther nations, at their feasts, and of their drinking vessels. (Ibid, Vol. I. p. 12.) Of the league said to have been formed between the emperor Charlemagne and the King of Scotland. (Ibid. Vol. I. p. 26.) Observations on the origin of the Duni pacis. (Ibid. Vol. I. p. 121.) Inquiry into the original inhabitants of Britain. (Ibid. Vol. I. p. 155.) Account of a combat between the Macphersons and the Davidsons. (Ibid. Vol. I. p. 188.) Sketch of three luminaries of the Romans. (Massachusetts Magaz. Y. 1795. Oct. p. 431.)

OLLAND, [John]

The essentiels of logic, being a second edition of *Dralloc's* epitome, improved: comprising an universal system of practical reasoning, illustrated by familiar examples, from approved authors. 1796. 8. (5 sh.) A praxis of logic, for the use of schools. 1799. 8. (5 sh.)

OLLEY, [Thomas] *of Gregynog, near Newtown, Montgomeryshire.*

Contrivance for locking carts in descending steep-hills. (Tr. of the Soc. for the E. of A. Vol. II. p. 193.)

LLIER, [Sir George] *Vice Admiral of the Blue.* born, ... died 1795. April 6.

See Gentlem. Magaz. Y. 1795. p. 358. May. p. 437.

*COLLIER, [John]

Familiar essays on the jewish history and on th new testament. Vol. 1. 2. 1797. 8. (14 sh.) Historical and familiar essays, on the scriptures of the new testament. Vol. 1. 2. 1797. 8. (14 sh. Essays on animation and intellect. 1800. (7 sh.)

*COLLIER, [John Dyer]

Account of Thoydon Garnon, in the county of Essex; (Monthly Magaz. Y. 1800. Febr. p. 28.) An essay on patents — 1803. 8.

*COLLIER, [Joseph]

Observations on iron and steel. (Mem. of M. Vol. 5. P. 1. p 109. *Tilloch's* Philos. Magaz. Vol. 1. p. 46.) Experiments and observations on fermentation and the distillation of ardent spirit. (Mem. of M. Vol. 5. P. 1. p. 243.) Description of the furnace for converting bar-iron into steel. (*Nicholson's* Journal. Vol. 3. p. 88.) Description of his improved apparatus for filtering and sweetening water and other fluids. (*Tilloch's* Philos. Magaz. Vol. 6. p. 240.)

*COLLIER, [Joshua]

A defence of double entry, with a new arrangement of the journal and objections to Mr. *Jones's* plan of book keeping. 1796. 4. (7 sh. 6 d.)

*COLLIER, [William] *Senior Fellow of Trinity College, Cambridge.*

born 1742. died 1803. Aug. 7. at Newington, Surrey.

See Gentleman's Magaz. Y. 1803. Aug. p. 794. Poems on various occasions, with translations from authors in different languages. Vol. 1. 2. 1800. 8. (12 sh.)

*COLLIN, [Nicholas] D. D. *Rector of the Swedish churches in Pennsylvania.*

Essay on those inquiries in natural philosophy, which at present are most beneficial to the United states of North-America. (Tr. of A. S. Vol. 3. p. 111.) Description of a machine for saving persons from the upper stories of a house on fire. (Ibid. Vol. 4. p. 143.) Philological view of some very ancient words in several languages. (Ibid. Vol. 4. p. 476.) Description of a speedy elevator; with two drawings from a model, representing

ting it folded and wound up. (Ibid. Vol. 4. p. 519.) Remarks on the amendments to the federal constitution. (American Museum Y. 1789. Jan. p. 72. March. p. 277. Apr. p. 383. June. p. 600. Sept. p. 234. Oct. p. 303.)

COLLINGWOOD, [Thomas] *M. Dr. Physician at Sunderland.*

History of a case of syphilis, cured by a very simple mercurial preparation. (*Duncan's* M. C. Dec. 2. Vol. 6. p. 274.) Observations on the use of elm bark, in several obstinate diseases. (Ibid. Dec. 2. Vol. 6. p. 281.) History of a case in which singular nervous affections were cured by an incision in the finger. (Ibid. Dec. 2. Vol. 8. p. 390.) On the season Y. 1792. and on crops. (*Young's* A. of Agr. Vol. 19. p. 217.) On rice bread — potatoes — commons. (Ibid. Vol. 35. p. 293.)

*COLLINS, [David] *Lieutenant Colonel, of the Royal Marines; late Judge-Advocate and Secretary of the colony.*

Account of the english colony in new South-Wales — with remarks on the dispositions, customs, manners &c. of the native inhabitants of that country. To which are added, some particulars of New-Zealand; — illustrated by 24 engravings. Vol. 1. 1798. 4. (2 L. 2 sh.) übers. von *M. C. Sprengel.* Halle. 1799. 8. Vol. 2. 1802. 4. (1 L. 1 sh.)

*COLLINS, [J....]

On the different kinds and properties of wool. (Bath Agric. Soc. Vol. 8. p. 69. Comm. and Agric. Magaz. Y. 1803. p. 170.) On the nature of sheep and wool. (Ibid. Vol. 9. p. 113.)

*COLLINS, [John] *Esq. of the Island of St. Vincent.*

Two letters on the subject of a species of angina maligna and the use of capsicum in that and several other diseases. (M. C. Vol. 2. p. 363.)

*COLLINS, [Joshua] *M. A. Rector of Newport.*

An address to instructors and parents on the choice and use of books in every branch of education, pointing out their respective merits and the order in which they should be successively adopted. 1802. 8. (1 sh.) A practical guide to parents and guardians, in the right choice and

ufe of books in every branch of education. 180;
12. (1 fh.)

*COLLINS, [Thomas]
The complete ready reckoner, in miniature 1801. 8. (1 fh. 3 d.)

*COLLIS, [Edward] *F. A. S.*
On gonorrhoea and fome other effects of the venereal virus. 1791. 8 (1 fh.)

COLLINSON, [John] *F. A. S: Vicar of long Afhton and Curate of Whitchurch, co. Somerfet, Vicar of Clanfield, co. Oxford.*
born, ... died at the hotwells Bath, 1793 Aug. 27.
See Gentleman's Magaz. Y. 1793. Sept. p. 865.
The hiftory and antiquities of the county of Somerfet, collected from authentic records and an actual furvey made by the late *Edmund Rack* (died 1787. Febr. 25.) Adorned with a map of the county and engravings of roman and other reliques, townfeals, baths, churches and gentleman's feats. Vol. 1-3. 1791. (4 L. 14 fh. 6 d.)

*COLLS, [John Henry]
A poetical epiftle, addreffed to Mifs. *Wollftonecraft*, occafioned by reading her celebrated effay on the right of woman and her hiftorical and moral view of the french revolution. 1795. 4. (1 fh. 6 d.) Ode to peace; to which is added, the negro's appeal. 1801. 4. (1 fh.)

*COLLYER, [J....] *at Worcefter.*
On the advantages of horfe races. (Comm. and Agric. Magaz. Y. 1799. Aug. p. 17.)

COLMAN, [George] *Esq fenior; Proprietor of the theatre Royal, Haymarket.*
born about 1733. died 1794. Aug. 14. at Paddington.
See Gentleman's Magaz. Y. 1794. Aug. p. 772.
* *G. Colman* and *Thornton*, The connoiffeur. 1754-1756. Ed. 2. Vol. 1-4. 1757. 12. * Polley Honeycomb; 1760. A mid fummer nights dream, altered. 1763. The fpanifh barber; 1777. The female chevalier, altered. 1778. The fuicide. 1778. The feparate maintenance. 1779. Some particulars of the late *G. Colman* written by himfelf and delivered by him to *Richard Jackfon* Esq. (one of his execu-

executors) for publication after his decease. 1795. 8. (2 sh.)

COLMAN, [George] *Junior Esq. Proprietor of the little theatre in the Haymarket.*

born Oct. 21. 1762. in London.

See Public Characters of 1800 and 1801. p. 506. Battle of Hexham, a play, in 3 acts; 17.. The surrender of Calais; 17.. New hay at the old market; or Sylvester Daggewood, an occasional drama, in one act. 1795. 8. (1 sh.) The mountaineers, a play in 3 acts. 1795. 8. (2 sh.) The iron chest, a play, in 3 acts. 1796. 8. (2 sh.) My night-gown and slippers, or tales in verse, written in an elbow-chair. 1797. 4. (2 sh. 6 d.) The heir at law, a comedy. 1798. Blue devils, one act drama; from the french; 17.. Blue beard, or female curiosity, a dramatic romance. 1798 8. (1 sh. 6 d.) Feudal times, or the banquet-gallery, a drama in 2 acts. 1799. 8. (1 sh. 6 d.) Broad-grins, comprising with new additional tales in verse, those formerly published under the title of my night-gown and slippers. 1802. The poor gentleman, a comedy, in 5 acts. 1802. 8. (2 sh. 6 d.) Broad grins; comprising, with new additional tales in verse, those formerly published under the title of „My night-gown and slippers. 1802. 8. (5 sh.) Epilogue to the new play of the maid of Bristol, being an addrefs to the patriotism of the English 1803. (1 d.)

'COLNETT, [James] *Captain in the ship Rattler;*

A voyage to the South Atlantic and round Cape Horn into the pacific ocean for the purpose of extending the sperma ceti, whale-fisheries and other objects of commerce —. 1798. 4. (1 L. 5 sh.)

'COLPITTS, [T....]

A letter addressed to the citizens of London and Westminster: suggesting improvements in the police: congenial with the principles of freedom and the constitution. 1803. 8. (1 sh.)

'COLQUHOUN, [Patrick] *LL. Dr. One of the magistrates of the Police of London.*

* A treatise on the police of the metropolis; explaining the various crimes and misdemeanours

P 3 which

which at present are felt upon the community and suggesting remedies for their prevention by. magistrate. 1796. 8. (5 sh.) Ed. 4. 1797. Ed. 5 1798. Ed. 6. 1800. 8. (10 sh. 6 d.) übers. mit Erläut. von *J. W. Volkmann.* Leipz. 1800. 8. State of indigence in the metropolis explained; with suggestions for the relief of the casual poor, by means of a pauper police establishment. 1799 On the commerce and police of the river Thames containing an historical view of the trade of the port of London and suggesting the means for preventing the depredation thereon by a legislative system of river police. 1800. 8. (10 sh. 6 d.) übers. mit Erläuter. von *J. W. Volkmann.* Leipz. 1800. Observations on the office of constable, with a view to its improvement. 1799. (1 sh.) A treatise on the functions and duties of a constable; — 1803. 8. (3 sh. 6 d.)

*COLSON, [Edward]

On the Hindoo manufacture of sugar. (Comm. and Agric. Mag. Y. 1799. Nov. p. 178.)

*COLVIL, [Samuel]

The whig's supplication; or, the Scots hudibras a mock poem; in two parts. 1797. 12. (3 sh. 6 d.)

*COMBE, [Charles] *of Exeter College, Oxford.*

Account of an elephant's tusk, in which the iron head of a spear was found imbedded. (Phil. Trans. act. Y. 1801. p. 165.)

COMBE, [Charles] *M. Dr. F. R. A. S. Of Bloomsbury square, London.*

born 1743. Sept. 23.

A statement of facts relative to the behaviour of Dr. *Sam. Parr* to the late Mr. *H. Homer* and Dr. *Combe.* 17.. *Q. Horatii* opera cum variis lectionibus, notis variorum et indice locupletissimo. Vol. 1. 2. 1793. 4. (2 L. 12 sh. 6 d.)

*COMBE, [Taylor] *Esq. F. A. S.*

Observations on a greek sepulchral monument in the possession of *Maxwell Garshore* M. Dr. (Arch. Vol. 13. p. 280.)

*COMBER, [Thomas] *A. B. late of Jesus College Cambridge.*

Memoirs of the life and writings of *Thomas Comber* D. D. sometime dean of Durham, in which intro introduced a candid view of the fcope and execution of the feveral works of Dr. *Comber*, as well printed as Mf. alfo, a fair account of his literary correfpondance; compiled from the original Mfc. 1799. 8. (7 fh.)

*COMBER, [William]

On arch-deacon *Francis Blackburn*. (Monthly Magaz. Y. 1800. Febr. p. 19.)

*COMINGS, [Fowler] *Rector of Swords, in Ireland, Prebendary of St. Patrick's, Dublin, Chaplain to the Duke of Cumberland.*

Sermons on various fubjects and occafions. Vol. 1. 2. 1790. 8. (12 fh.)

*COMMINS, [John]

The englifh fcholar's firft book. 1801. (3 d.)

*CONCANEN, [Matthew] *Jun.*

— and *A. Morgan*, the hiftory and antiquities of St. Saviour's, Southwark. 1795. 8. (6 fh.) Letter to *Will. Garrow*, Esq. on the fubject of his illiberal behaviour to the author, on the trial of a caufe (*Ford* againft *Pedder*, and others) at the Lent affizes 1796; held at Kingfton, in the county of Surrey —. 1796. 8. (6 d.) A plan for the effectual diftribution of bankrupt eftates, with remarks on the loffes to which the public are fubject, by the failure and mifconduct of affignees. 1800. 8. (6 d.)

*CONCANEN, [Thomas] *M. Dr. Phyfician at Dundalk.*

The hiftory of an anevrifm of the aorta defcendens, appearing under the form of a tumour at the fcrobiculus cordis. (*Duncan's* M. C. Y. 1790. Dec. 2. Vol. 5. p. 386.)

*CONDER, [James]

An arrangement of provincial coins, tokens and medalets, iffued in Great-Britain, Ireland and the colonies within the laft 20 years, from the farthing to the penny fize. 1799. 8. (7 fh. 6 d.)

*CONDIE, [Thomas]

— and *Richard Follwell*, hiftory of the peftilence, commonly called yellow fever, which almoft defolated Philadelphia in the months of Aug. Sept. and Oct. 1798. Philad. 1799. 8.

P 4 *CONO-

*CONOVER, [Samuel Forman] *of New-Jersey.*
On sleep and dreams. Philadelphia. 1791.

*CONST, [Francis] *Esq. of the Middle Temple; Barrister at Law.*
Decisions of the court of King's bench, upon the laws relating to the poor, originally published by *Edmund Bott*, Esq. of the Inner temple —. Ed. 3. Vol. 1. 2. 1793. (1 L. 5 sh.) Ed. 4. Vol. 1-3. 1800. 8. (1 L. 11 sh. 6 d.)

*CONSTANT, [Silas] *Rev.*
A description of a cement for preserving wood and brick from decay and for stopping leaks and fissures in any body to which it shall be applied and of the manner of using and of the process of compounding the same. (Medical Repository Vol. 3. p. 306.)

CONWAY, [Henry Seymour] *Governour of the Island of Jersey.*
born 1720. died 1795. July 9. at his seat at Park-place, near Henley, co. Oxford.
See Gentleman's Magaz. Y. 1795. July. p. 620.

*CONYERS, [Matilda] *at Biggleswade.*
On domestic economy. (Comm. and Agric. Mag. Y. 1800. p. 192.)

*CONYNGHAM, [Cornelius] *of Virginia.*
Account of a case of tetanus, successfully treated by the use of calomel, bark and wine. (Mem. of M. S. of L. Vol. 2. p. 114.)

*CONYNGHAM, [William Burton] *One of his Ma[jesty's] privy Council, Teller of the exchequer, one of the Commissioners for executing the office of high treasurer in Ireland; Treasurer of the [Royal] Irish Acad. F. A. S. Lond.*
born 1732. died Dublin 1796. May 31.
See Gentleman's Magaz. Y. 1796. June p. 52[?] July p. 611. Allgem. Litterat. Zeit. J. 179[6] ItBl. N. 51. S. 428.
The history of Jack Connor; 17.. (cf. Gentleman's Magaz. Y. 1796. Oct. p. 823. That book was the composition of the late *Will. Chaigneau.*
Observations on the description of the theatre of Saguntum, as given by *Emanuel Marti.* (Tr. of J. A. Y. 1789. p. 21. c. p. 47.)

*COO[K]

*COOK, [J.....]

An addreſs to the public on a ſubject new and intereſting. 1793. 8. (1 ſh.)

*COOK, [Thomas]

Induſtry and idleneſs, part of a new edition of the works of *Hogarth.* 1796. (7 ſh. 6 d.)

*COOK, [Thomas]

Method of preparing and turning a true round or ſpherical figure between two centres. (Tr. of the Soc. for the E. of A. Vol. 17. p. 335.)

*COOK, [William] *of Wilnethan.*

A courſe of crops. (*Young's* A. of Agr. Vol. 29. p. 375.)

*COOKE, [Alexander] *LL. D. Advocate.*

Remarks on Mr. *Schlegel's* work upon the viſitation of neutral veſſels under convoy. 1801. (4 ſh.)

*COOKE, [Charles] *Esq. of Thorngrove, near Worceſter.*

Preventive of the fly in turnips. (*Young's* A. of Agr. Vol. 6. p. 90.)

*COOKE, [Edward]

*Arguments for and againſt an union between Great-Britain and Ireland. Dublin. 1798.

*COOKE, [J.....] *of Maidenhead.*

Five letters to a friend, occaſioned by the death of the Rev. *W. B. Cadogan*, of Reading. 1797. 8. (6 d.)

COOKE, [James] *M. A.*

Deſcription and uſe of *J. Cooke* patent drill machine and ſimple hand-hoe: with a plate. (Bath Agricult. Soc. Vol. 3. p. 244.) Aſcertainments of crops reaped from ſeed ſown by M. *Cooke's* patent drill machine. (Ibid. Vol. 4. p. 320. Vol. 5. p. 467.) On a new drill plough. (*Young's* A. of Agr. Vol. 5. p. 265. Columbian Magaz. Y. 1789. June p. 352.) Deſcription of a patent drill machine, with a ſix ſhare horſe-hoe. (Ib. Vol. 14. p. 20.)

COOKE, [John] *M. A. Chaplain of Greenwich Hoſpital.*

A voyage performed by the late Earl of *Sandwich* round the mediterraneum in the Y. 1738 and 1739 written by himſelf — embelliſhed with a portrait of his Lordſhip and illuſtrated with ſeveral engravings of antient buildings and inſcriptions, with

P 5 a

ftory of phyfiognomy; (Mem. of M. Vol. 3. p. 408.) Propofitions refpecting the foundation of civil government; (Ibid. Vol. 3. p. 481.) Obfervations on the art of painting among the ancients (Ibid. Vol. 3. p. 510.) Reply to Mr. *Burke's* invective againft him and Mr. *Watt* in the houfe of commons, on the 30 April. 1792. 1792. 8. (2 fh.) Some information refpecting America. 1794. 8. (4 fh.)

*COOPER, [William]

On the mapple-fugar. (Columbian Magaz. T. 1790. Aug. p. 133.)

*COOTE, [Charles] *LL. D. Member of Pembroke College, Oxford.*

The hiftory of England from the earlieft dawn of record to the peace of 1783. T. 1-9. 1791-1798. 8. (3 L. 3 fh.) überf. von Dr. *Gottfr. Chrift. Reich.* B. 1. 2. Leipz. 1793. 1794. 8. *Graji* elegia fepulchralis, cultu graeco donata. 1794. 4. (1 fh. 6 d.) The life of *Caj. Julius Caefar* drawn from the moft authentic fources of information. 1796. 12. (3 fh. 6 d.) Hiftory of the union of the kingdom of Great-Britain and Ireland, with an introductory furvey of Hibernian affairs, traced from the times of Celtic colonifation. 1802. 8. (10 fh. 6 d.)

*COPLAND, [Alexander]

Account of an ancient mode of fepulture in Scotland. (Mem. of M. Vol. 4. P. 1. p. 217.) On the combuftion of dead bodies, as formerly practifed in Scotland. (Ibid. Vol. 4. P. 2. p. 330.)

*COPLAND, [Peter] *Surgeon at Swayfield near Colfterworth in Lincolnfhire.*

Account of the external ufe of camphor, in cafes of bronchocele and glandular indurations. (*Duncan's* M. C. 1790. Dec. 2. Vol. 5. p. 380.) Account of two cafes of amenorrhaea, with fome obfervations on the ufe of the root of madder in that difeafe. (London M. J. Vol. XI. p. 230.) An account of the goods effects of opium, adminiftered in clyfters, in cafes of menorrhagia. (*Simmons's* Med. Facts and Obfervat. Vol. 4. p. 118.)

überf.

überf. Repertor. Chir. u. Medic. Abhandl. B. 2. S. 174. Account of the lithontriptic power observed in the muriatic acid.. (Mem. of M. S. of L. Vol. 5. p. 71.)

*COPLAND, [William]

On the management of feed barley in a dry feason; (Bath Agricult. Soc. Vol. 2. p. 381.)

*CORAM, [Robert]

Political inquiries; to which is added a plan for the general eftablifhment of fchools throughout the United ftates. Wilmington. 1790. (½ Dollar.)

*CORBET, [C....] *at Canterbury.*

On the qualities of potatoes as food for horfes. (Comm. and Agric. Magaz. Y. 1799. Sept. p. 87.)

*CORBET, [Edward] *Esq. of Ynyfy Maengwyn, in the parifh of Towyn, in the county of Merioneth.*

Account of improving land lying wafte and uncultivated. (Tr. of the Soc. for the E. of A. Vol. 12. p. 244.)

*CORBETT, [William]

The empire of Germany, divided into departments under the prefectorfhip of the elector of *** translated from the french —; 1802. (2 fh. 6 d.)

CORDINER, [Charles] *Minifter at Bamff in Scotland.* born ..... died ..... (?)

Remarkable ruins and romantic profpects of North-Britain, with ancient monuments and fingular fubjects of natural hiftory. The engravings by *Peter Mazell.* Vol. 1. 2. 1795. 4. (5 L. 5 fh.)

*COREY, [G..... S.....]

Balnea or a defcription of all the watering places in England. Ed. 2. 1799. 8. (3 fh. 6 d.)

*CORFE, [Jofeph] *Of his Maj. Chapel Roy. and Organift of the Cathedral at Salisbury.*

A treatife on finging. 1799. fol. (10 fh. 6 d.)

*CORMACH, [John] *M. A.*

Lives of the ancient philofophers, comprehending a choice felection of their beft maxims; written for the education of a prince by the author of Telema-

Telemachus. Translated from the french, illustrated with notes and preceded by a life of *Fenelon*. Vol. 1. 2. 1803. 12. (8 fh.)

CORNISH, [Jofeph]

Evangelical motives to holinefs; — 1790. 8. (6d.)

CORP, [William] *M. Dr. at Bath.*

born . . . . . died 1790. Oct. 10.

See Gentleman's Magaz. Y. 1790. Oct. p. 959.

Effay on the changes produced in the body by operations of the mind. 1791. 8. (1 fh.)

*CORRIE, [James] *M. Dr.*

On the vitality of the blood. 1791. 8. (2 fh.)

*CORRIE, [John]

An apology for the diverfity of religious fentiments and for theological enquiries. 1802. 8. (1 fh.)

*CORRY, [John]

Satyrical view of London; 17.. The life of Gen. *George Wafhington*, interfperfed with biographical anecdotes of the moft eminent men, who effected the American revolution. 1800. 8. (3 fh. 6 d.) The detector of Quackery; or, analyfis of medical, philofophical, political, dramatic and literary impofture. 1801. 8. (4 fh.) Memoirs of Alfred Berkley; or the danger of diffipation. 1802. 12. (4 fh. 6 d.) Edwy and Bertha; or the force of connubial love; embellifhed with an engraving fewed; being the firft number of a feries of original tales for the amufement of young perfons. 1802.

*CORSE, [John] *Esq.*

Obfervations on the manners, habits and natural hiftory of the elephant. (Phil. Transact. Y. 1799. p. 31. *Nicholfon's* Journal. Vol. 3. p. 181. 193. 247.) Obfervations on the different fpecies of Afiatic elephants and their mode of dentition. (Phil. Transact. Y. 1799. p. 205.) The cafe of Paunchoo, an inhabitant of the village of Gundaffee, in Pergunnah Humnabad, and province of Tiperah, Bengal. (Transact. of Med. and Chir. Soc. Vol. 2. p. 257.) An account of the method of catching wild elephants at Tipura. (Afiat. Ref. Vol. 3. p. 229. *Tilloch's* Philof. Magaz. Vol. 3. p. 5. Vol. 4. p. 130.)

*CORT,

ORT, [Henry] *of Gosport.*

A state of facts relative to the new method of making bar-iron, with raw pit coal and grooved rollers. (*Young's* A. of Agr. Vol. 12. p. 361.) Process for converting cast iron into malleable iron. (American Museum Y. 1787. Sept. p. 261.)

SENS, [John] *D. D. Minister of Teddington, Middlesex; Chaplain to the Earl of Denbigh.*

born .... died .... (?)

Sermons on useful and important subjects — Vol. 1. 2. 1793. 8. (12 sh.)

TTER, [G.... S....]

A receipt for making excellent bread, with one third of potatoes, to two thirds of flour. (Tr. of Dublin Soc. Vol. 1. P. 2. p. 71.)

OTTLE, [A.... S....] *of Magdalen College, Cambridge.*

Icelandic poetry, or the edda of Saemund, translated into English verse. 1797. 8. (6 sh.) A Norwegian ballad, translated from le Nord Litteraire; (Monthly Magaz. Y. 1800. Jan. p. 968.)

OTTLE, [Joseph]

Poems; 1795. 12. (4 sh.) Ed. 2. with additions 1797. 12. (4 sh.) Malvern hills, a poem. 1798. 4. (2 sh. 6 d.) Alfred, an epic poem in 24 books. 1800. 4. (1 L. 1 sh.) John the baptist; a poem. 1801. 8. (1 sh.) A new version of the psalms of David. 1801. 8. (4 sh.)

OTTON, [Nathaniel] *M. Dr.*

Various pieces in verse and prose by the late *Nath. Cotton.* Vol. 1. 2. 1791. 12. (6 sh.) The advantage and disadvantage of the marriage state; by the late Rev. *J. Macgowan:* To which is added, marriage, a vision. 1801. 8. (1 sh.)

QUARD, [J....]

Deism traced to one of its principal sources, or the corruption of christianity the cause of infidelity. 1796. (6 d.)

OVE, [Morgan] *LL. B. Prebendary of Hereford and Rector of Eaton-Bishop, Herefordshire.*

An essay on the revenues of the church of England. Ed. 2. 1797. 8. (5 sh.) An inquiry into the necessity, justice and policy of a commutation of tithes. 1800. 8. (3 sh.)

*COULTER, [Thomas] *Esq. of Bedford County, Pennsylvania.*

Description of a method of cultivating peach-trees, with a view to prevent their premature decay; confirmed by the experience of 45 years, in Delaware state and the western parts of Pennsylvania. (Tr. of A. S. Vol. 5. p. 327.)

*COUPER, [Robert] *Dr.*

The tourifications of Malachi Meldrum, Esq. of Meldrum-Hall. Vol. 1. 2. 1803. 12. (10 sh. 6 d.)

COURTENAY, [John] *Esq. M. P.*

Poetical and philosophical essay on the french revolution, addressed to Mr. *Burke.* 1793. Present state of the manners, arts and politics of France and Italy, in poetical epistles. 1794. 8. (2 sh. 6 d.)

*COURTIER, [P.... L....]

Poems, consisting of elegies, sonnets, odes, canzonets and the pleasures of solitude. 1795. 8. (4 sh. 6 d.) Revolutions, a poem, in two books. 1796. 8. (2 sh.) Pleasures of solitude, a poem. 1800. 8. (2 sh. 6 d.) Ed. 2. with other poems. 1802. 8. (8 sh.)

*COURTNEY, [.....] *Mrs.*

Isabinda of Bellefield; a sentimental novel in a series of letters. Vol. 1-3. 1796. 8. (10 sh. 6 d.)

*COWAN, [Andrew] *M. Dr.*

Anthropaideia, or, a treatise on general education. Vol. 1. 2. 1803. 12. (8 sh.)

*COWAN, [J.... N....] *Doctor of Physic in the city of New-York.*

Decomposition of soap-suds by the septic or pestilential air of New-York in 1798 and 1799. (Medical Repository. Vol. 3. p. 308.) Utility of the carrot-poultice when applied to ulcerated cancers. (Columbian Magaz. Y. 1791. June. p. 399.)

*COWARD, [J.....]

Deism traced to one of its principal sources; or the corruption of christianity the grand cause of infidelity, containing brief reflections on the subject in a letter to the Bishop of Landaff (*Watson*) on his late work, entitled, „an apology for the bible„ in answer to Mr. *Paine's* second part of the age of reason. 1796. 8. (6 d.)

*COWE,

OWE, [James] *M. A. Vicar of Sunbury, Middlesex.* Religious and philantropic tracts: 1) on the principles, the temper and duties of christians — 2) an essay on the state of the poor and on the means of improving it by friendly societies — 3) rules for forming and managing friendly societies with a view to facilitate their general establishment. 1797. 8. (2 sh. 6 d.) Ed. 2. revised and enlarged. 1800. 8. (6 sh.) On the advantages, which result from christianity and on the influence of christian principles on the mind and conduct. 1799. 8. (2 sh.) An admonition to parents and children, chiefly intended for the lower classes of society. 1802. 8.

OWIE, [George] *Minister of the Gospel at Huntley.* The dissenter's guide in choosing a pastor. 1799. (4 d.)

OWLEY, [H....] *Mrs. (Daughter of the late Mr. Parkhouse, of Tiverton in Devonshire.)*

See Public Characters of 1801 and 1802. p. 437. A day in Turkey; or the Russian slaves, a comedy. 1792. 8. (1 sh. 6 d.) The town before you, a comedy. 1795. 8. (2 sh.) The siege of Acre, an epic poem. 1801. 8. (9 sh.)

OWMEADOW, [John William] *Professor by the Military Academy in Berlin.*

born 1749. May 12. at Bickney, Gloucestershire: died 1795. Apr. 18.

An entertaining and instructing miscellany in prose and verse, for the instruction of those, who learn the English language, compiled from the best English authors. Berlin. 1788. 8. Ed. 2. Altona. 1791. 8. Alexina oder ein Tag in der Türkey; Schausp. in 5 Aufzügen. Berlin. 1792. 8. Hans und Gürgen, ein Gespräch zweier Bauern über den Tod Ludwig 16. Berlin. 1793. Leichtsinn und kindliche Liebe oder der Weg zum Verderben; Schausp in 5 Aufz. nach dem Engl. von *Holcroft.* Berlin. 1794. 8. Alfred, König der Angelsachsen, oder der patriotische König, ein Trauersp. in 5 Aufz. Nach dem Engl. frei bearbeitet. Berlin. 1796. 8.

OWPER, [Henry] *Esq. Barrister at Law, of the Middle-Temple.*

Reports of cases adjudged in the court of King's

 bench

bench from Hilary term 1774. to Trinity term 1778. Ed. 2. Vol. 1. 2. 1800. 8. (19 sh.).

COWPER, [William] *Esq. of the Inner-Temple.* born at Berkhamstead, Herts, 1722. died at East Dereham, Norfolk 1800. Apr. 25.

See Public Characters of 1799 and 1800. p. 539. Gentleman's Magaz. Y. 1800. May. p. 487. June. p. 584. Oct. p. 951. Monthly Magaz. Y. 1800. May. p. 409. June. p 498. Allg. Litter. Zeit. ItBl. J. 1800. S. 1804. See *William Hayley.*

Poems, a new edition with considerable additions. Vol. 1. 2. 1798. 12. (6 sh.) (cf. Gentleman's Magaz. Y. 1800. July. p. 636.) The iliad and odyssey of *Homer*, translated into english blank verse. Ed. 1. Vol. 1. 2 1791. 4. (2 L. 12 sh. 6 d.) Ed. 2. with copious alterations and notes, prepared for the press by the translator and now published with a preface by his kinsman *J. Johnson* LL. Dr. Vol. 1-4. 1802. 8. (1 L. 12 sh.) The power of grace illustrated in 6 letters, from a minister of the reformed church, to *John Newton*, Rector of St Mary Woolnoth, London; translated from the original latin. 1792. 12 (2 sh. 6 d.) Poems, translated from the french of Mad. *De la Mothe Guion.* To which are added some original poems of him not inserted in his work, published by *Bull* of Newport-Pagnel 1801. 8. (2 sh. 6 d.) Adelphi, a sketch of the character and an account of the last illness of the late *J. Cowper*, A. M. (Fellow of Corpus Christi college, Cambridge; died 1770. See Gentlem. Magaz. Vol. 53. p. 152.) and published from the original manuscript by *J. Newton*, Foolscap. 1800 8. (1 sh.) Convivalia et saltatoria, or thoughts on feasting and dancing; to which are added, an epistle in praise of tobacco, and a letter in prose, relative to the poem on tobacco. 1800. 12. (1 sh.) Life and posthumous works — by *William Hayley*. Vol. 1. 2. 1803. 4. (2 L. 12 sh. 6 d.) (See *John Newton.*)

*__COX__, [Hiram] *Captain; Resident at Ranghong.*

An account of the petroleum wells in the Burmha dom-

dominions —; (Afiat. Ref. Vol. 6. p. 127. *Tilloch's* Philof. Magaz. Vol. 9. p. 226.)

COX, [John Henry] *Esq.*
See *A. Dalrymple.*

COXE, [John Redman] *M. Dr. One of the Phyficians to the Pennfylvania Hofpital.*
Effay on inflammation. Philadelphia. 1794 Practical obfervations on vaccination or inoculation for the cow-pock. —; 1802. 8. (4 fh.) An inquiry into the comparative effects of the opium officinarum, extracted from the papaver fomniferum or white poppy of *Linnaeus*, and of that procured from the lactuca fativa or common cultivated lettuce; (Tr. of A. S. Vol. 4. p. 387.)

COXE, [Samuel Compton] *Esq. of Lincoln's-Inn.*
Will. Peere Williams's collection of reports of cafes argued and determined in the high court of chancery — Ed. 5. with additional references to the proceedings — Vol. 1-3. 1793. 8. (1 L. 11 fh 6 d.)

COXE, [Tench] *Esq. of Philadelphia, Commiffioner of the Revenue.*
Brief examination of Lord *Sheffield's* obfervations on the commerce of the United States. Philadelphia. 1792. View of the United States of America, in a feries of papers written at various times, between the Y. 1787 and 1794. Philadelphia. 1794. 8. London. 1795. 8. (7 fh.) überf. im Auszug in *Hegewifch's* und *Ebeling's* Amerik. Magazin B. 1. St. 1. S. 61. Addrefs to an affembly of the friends of American manufactures, convened for the purpofe of eftablifhing a fociety for the encouragement of manufactures and the ufeful arts. (American Mufeum Y. 1787. Sept. p. 248.) Thoughts on the prefent fituation of the United ftates. (Ibid. Y. 1788. Nov. p. 401.) *Notes concerning the United ftates of America, containing facts and obfervations relating to that country, for the information of emigrants. (Ib. Y. 1790. July. p. 35.)

COXE, [William] *Rev.*
A letter on the fecret tribunals of Weftphalia. 1796. 8. (1 fh.) überf. von *Ludw. Griefinger.* Hailbronn. 1803. 8.

COXE, [William] *A. M: F. R. S: F. A. S. Rector of Bemerton and Stourton; Chaplain to the Lord Bishop of Salisbury.*
born in London March 7. 1747.
Travels in Swisserland. Vol. 1-3. 1789. 8. (1 L. 4 sh.) Ed. 4. Vol. 1-3. 1802. 8. (1 L. 7 sh.) übers. B. 1. 2. 3. Zürich. 1791-1792. 8. Travels into Poland, Russia — &c. Vol. 3-5. 1792. (1 L. 16 sh.) Explanation of the catechism of the church of England for the use of sunday schools. 1792. 8. (6 d.) *Familiar explanation of the service of confirmation used by the church of England. 1793. (3 sh.) The fables of *John Gay* illustrated with notes and the life of the author. 1796. 8. (4 sh.) Memoirs of the life and administration of Sir *Robert Walpole*, Earl of Orford, with original correspondence and authentic papers never before published. Vol. 1-3. 1798. 4. (3 L. 15 sh.) On the excellence of British jurisprudence, preached. 1799. 8. (1 sh.) Historical tour in Monmouthshire illustraced with views by Sir *R. C. Hoare*, Bart. a new map of the county and other engravings. Vol. 1. 2. 1801. 4. (4 L. 4 sh.) Memoirs of *Horatio* Lord *Walpole*, selected from his correspondence and papers and connected with the history of the times from 1678 to 1757. 1802. 4. (3 L. 3 sh. large paper 5 L. 5 sh.) Encouragement of agriculture by the Empress of Russia. (*Young's* A. of Agr. Vol. 2. p. 233.)

*COYTE, [.....] *Dr.*
Hortus botanicus Gippovicensis; or, a systematical enumeration of the plants cultivated in his botanic garden at Ipswich in the county of Suffolk; — 1796. 4. (10 sh. 6 d.)

*COZENS, [William R.....] *of New-Jersey.*
On the chemical properties of atmospheric air Philad. 1791.

*COZENS, [Zachariah]
The margate hoy, which was stranded Febr. 7 1802, a poem: to which is added, a sketch of the life and experience of *George Bone*, of Margate one of the passengers who were drowned. 1802.

*CRABB

CRABB, [George]

The order and method of inftructing children, with ftrictures on the modern fyftem of education. 1802. 12. (3 fh. 6 d.)

CRACHERODE, [Clayton Mordaunt] *M. A. one of the Truftees of the British Mufeum. F. R. and A. S.*

born 1729. died 1799. Apr. 6.

See Gentleman's Magaz. Y. 1799. April. p. 354. May. p. 373. 395. 434. Allgem. Litter. Zeit. ItBl. J. 1800. p 659.

Carmina quadrigefimalia. 1748.

CRACKNELL, [Benjamin] *A. M.*

The chriftian's views and reflections during his laft illnefs; with his anticipations of the glorious inheritance and fociety of the heavenly world, to which are annexed two fermons on particular occafions by the late *Simon Reader*, publifhed from the author's manufcript. 1794. 12. (2 fh. 6 d.) A difcourfe on the importance of right fentiments in religion, as to their influence on the moral character of mankind. 1796. 8. (8 d.)

CRAIG, [W.... M....]

Effay on the ftudy of nature in drawing landfcape, with illuftrative prints, engraved by the author. 1793. 4. (10 fh. 6 d.)

CRAKELT, [William] *M. A. Rector of Nurfted and Ifield in Kent.*

Latin dictionary, 17.. Spherical trigonometry. 17..

CRANCH, [John] *of Kingsbridge, in Devonfhire.*

The oeconomy of teftaments, or, reflections on the mifchievous confequences generally arifing from the ufual difpofitions of property by will; publifhed with a preface by *William Langworthy*. 1794. 8. (1 fh.)

CRANWELL, [John] *M. A. Rector of Abbots Ripton, Huntingdonfhire*

born, ... died 1793. Apr. 17.

Translation of *Browne's* poem. 1765. De animi immortalitate. 1765. 4. *Vida's* chriftiad in 6 books. 1768. 8.

Q 4 CRAVEN,

CRAVEN, [Elizabeth] See *Elizabeth Berkeley.*

CRAVEN, [William] *B. D. Professor of Arabic at Cambridge.*

Sermons on the evidence of a future state of rewards and punishments, arising from a view of our nature and condition; in which are considered some objections of *Hume.* 1799.

CRAUFURD, [George] *Esq. Formerly a Commissioner from the Court of London to that of Versailles.*

A second enquiry into the situation of the East India company and a postscript to the Indian budget opened 30 March. 1790. 4. (3 sh.) Enquiry into the situation of the East India company, from papers laid before the house of commons in 1787. 1788. 1789 and 1790, with an appendix of interesting papers. 1792. The doctrine of equivalents, or an explanation of the nature, the value and the power of money; together with their application in organising public finance. Part 1. 1794. (2 sh. 6 d.)

*CRAUFURD, [Quintin]

*Sketches chiefly relating to the history, religion learning and manners of the Hindoos. 1790. 8. (6 sh.) Ed. 2. with a concise account of the present state of the native powers of Hindostan. Vol. 1. 2. 1792. 8. (10 sh.)

CRAWFORD, [Adair] *M. Dr. F. R. S. Physician to St. Thomas's Hospital and Professor of Chemistry at Woolwich, in Kent.*

born 1749. died at a seat of the Marquis of Lansdown, Lymington, Hants. 1795. July 29.

See Gentleman's Magaz. Y. 1795. Aug. p. 706. Sept. p. 789.

Experiments and observations on the matter of cancer and on the aerial fluids extricated from animal substances by destillation and putrefaction together with some remarks on sulphureous hepatic air. (Philos. Transact. Y. 1790. p. 391. *Simmon's* Med. Facts and Observat. Vol. 2. p. 182.) On the medicinal properties of the muriated barytes. (M. C. Vol. 2. p. 301.) übers. in Samml. für prakt. Aerzte. B. 13. S. 691.

*CRAW-

CRAWFORD, [Charles] *Esq.*

Obfervations upon negro-flavery; a new edition. Philadelphia. (½ Dollar.) Effay upon the XI chapter of the revelations of St. John. Philadelphia. 1800.

RAWFORD, [John] *of Demerary, formerly in the fervice of the Eaft-India Company.*

Obfervations on native camphor. (*Duncan's* M. C. Dec. 2. Vol. 8. p. 253.)

CREASE, [J....] *Bath.*

Elegance, amufement and utility: or the whole procefs of verniſhing on paper and wood, with every improvement. To which is added, gilding, working in black and gold, mounting drawings, cleaning, pictures &c. 1800. 8. (2 fh. 6 d.)

CREASE, [J....]

Prophecies fulfilling; or, the dawn of the perfect day; with increafing light breaking forth into all directions. Addreffed to all fcoffing fectarians and others, who, in the plenitude of their folly defpife and reject *Richard Brothers*, as the jews alfo defpifed and rejected Jefus Chrift. 1795. 8. (6 d.)

CREASER, [Thomas] *Member of the R. College of Surgeons.*

Evidences on the utility of vaccine inoculation; intended for the information of parents. Bath. 1801. 12. Obfervations on Dr. *Pearfon's* examination of the report of the vaccine pock committee of the houfe of Commons, concerning Dr. *Jenner's* claim for remuneration. 1803. (3 fh.)

CREECH, [William]

Edinburgh fugitive pieces. 1791. 8. (3 fh. 6 d.)

CREIGHTON, [James] *B. A.*

An enquiry into the origin of true religion. — 1803. (1 fh.)

CRESPEL, [.....]

Travels in North-America; with a narrative of his fhipwreck and extraordinary hardfhips and fufferings on the island of Anticofti and of the fhipwrecks of his Maj. fhip active and others. 1797. 12. (3 fh.)

*CRESPIGNY, [Philip Champion] *Esq. formerly King's Proctor and M. P. for Sudbury.*
born . . . . died at Bath 1803. Jan. 1.
See Gentleman's Magaz. Y. 1803. Jan. p. 89.
(He wrote two numbers in the periodical paper, The World.)

CRESWICK, [. . . . . .] *Teacher of elocution and many years a performer at the York and other theaters.*
born . . . . . died 1791. Jan. 18.
See Gentleman's Magaz. Y. 1791. Jan. p. 94.
The lady's preceptor; or a series of instructive and pleasing exercises in reading; for the particular use of females; consisting of a selection of moral essays, narratives, letters, dialogues and poetical composition, materially interesting to the sex. 1792. 8. (3 sh. 6 d.)

CRIBB, [William] *Surgeon in London.*
A case of hydrocephalus internus. (Mem. of M. S. of L. Vol. 4. p. 400.)

CRICHTON, [Alexander] *M. Dr. Physician to the Westminster Hospital and public Lecturer on the theory and practice of Physic and on Chemistry.*
On the medicinal effects of the lichen islandicus — übers. Samml. der neuesten Beobacht. Englischer Aerzte. S. 173. * *J. F. Blumenbach's* essay on generation, translated from the German. 1793. 12. (2 sh.) Inquiry into the nature and origin of mental derangement; comprehending a concise system of the physiology and pathology of human mind and a history of the passions and their effects. Vol. 1-2. 1798. 8. (14 sh.) übers. im Ausz. Leipz. 1798. 8.

*CRICHTON, [Andrew] *M. Dr. of Westmoreland parish, Jamaica.*
History of a case of cynanche, attended with symptoms of a high degree of putrescency, where a favourable crisis succeeded a paroxysm of furious delirium. (*Duncan's* A. of Med. Y. 1796. p. 318.)

*CRICHTON, [James] *of Glasgow.*
On the freezing point of tin and the boiling point of

of mercury; with a defcription of a felf regiftering thermometer invented by him. (*Tilloch's* Philof. Magaz. Vol. 15. p. 147.)

*CRIRIE, [James] *E. D.*
Scottifh fcenery; or, fketches in verfe, defcriptive of fcenes chiefly in the highlands of Scotland, with notes and illuftrations. 1803. 4. (3 L. 3 fh.)

*CRISP, [John] *F. R. S.*
Obfervations on the nature and theory of vifion, with an inquiry into the caufe of the fingle appearance of objects feen by both eyes. 1796. 8. (5 fh. 6 d.)

*CRISP, [John] *Esq.*
An account of the inhabitants of the Poggy islands, lying off Sumatra. (Afiat. Ref. Vol. 6. p. 77.)

*CRISTALL, [Ann Batten]
Poetical fketches. 1795. 8. (5 fh.)

CROCKER, [Abraham] *Land-Surveyor at Frome.*
Inftruction to the children of funday fchools and other charitable feminaries of learning. 1796. 12. (4 d.) The art of making and managing cyder; deduced from rational principles and actual experience. 1799. 8. (1 fh.) Mifcellaneous obfervations on a variety of plants — confidered in an agricultural and commercial view. (Bath Agricult. Soc. Vol. 3. p. 29.) Recipe for making rennet for cheefe. (Ibid. Vol. 4. p. 284.) Characters of fundry apples known in the weft of England for various ufes; (Ibid. Vol. 8. p. 305.) Practical effay on raifing apple-trees and making cyder. (Mem. of B. A. Vol. 2. P. 1. p. 100. Maffachufetts Magaz. Vol. 2. 1790. p. 451.) An effay on farm houfes, and their various appendant offices, accompanied with plans and elevations. (Comm. to the B. of Agr. Vol. 1. p. 66.) On cottages. (Ibid. Vol. 1. p. 114.)

*CROFT, [. . . . .] *Mrs.*
Ankerwick caftle; a novel. Vol. 1-4. 1800. 12. (14 fh.) überf. von *Fried.* v. *Oertel.* Th. 1. 2. Leipzig u. Sorau. 1801. 8.

CROFT,

CROFT, [George] *D. D. Vicar of Arncliffe in Yorkshire* —

Plans of reform proved to be visionary. 17.. Thoughts concerning the methodists and the established church. 1795. A short commentary, with strictures, on certain parts of the moral writings of Dr. *Paley* and Mr. *Gisborne;* to which are added as a supplement, observations on the duties of trustees and conductors of grammar schools and two sermons on purity of principle and the penal laws. 1797. 8. (5 sh.)

CROFT, [Sir Herbert] *Bart.*
born about the Y. 1752.

A brother's advice to his sisters. 1775. The literary fly. 1780. Fanaticism and treason or a dispassionate history of the rise, progress and suppression of the rebellions, insurrections in june 1780. Life of Dr. *Edward Young;* (See *Johnsons* lives of the English poets.) Some account of an intended publication of the statutes on a plan entirely new: Improvement of Dr. *Johnson's* dictionary which in the Y. 1792 he proposed to publish by subscription: Letter from Germany to the princess Roy. of England on the english and german languages, with a table of the different Northern languages and of different periods of the german; and with an index. Hamburgh. 1797. 4. Hints for history, respecting the attempt on the king's life, May 15. 1800. Chatterton and love and madness. 1800. (1 sh.) On the necessity of regulating lazarettos. (*Young's* A. of Agr. Vol. 12. p. 36.)

CROFT, [John] *F. A. S.*

°Excerpta antiqua, or, a collection of original manuscrits. 1797. 8. (2 sh. 6 d.)

CROFT, [Richard] *late of Tutbury, now Surgeon in London* (Brother to *Herbert Croft.*)

Account of two cases of retroverted uterus. (London M. J. Vol. XI. p. 380.)

°**CROKE,** [Alexander] *Esq. LL. Dr. Advocate in Doctor-Commons.*

A report of the case of *Horner* against *Liddiard* on the question of what consent is necessary to the

the marriage of illegitimate minors; — 1800. 8. (5 sh.) Argument in the high court of admiralty 27. Nov. 1799. in the case of the Hendrick and Maria, Joh. Christ. Baar, Master, upon the question of the validity of a sentence of condemnation whilst a vessel is lying in a neutral port. 1800. 8. (2 sh.) Remarks on Mr. *Schlegel's* work upon the visitation of neutral vessels under convoy. 1801. 8. (4 sh.)

CROKER, [Richard] *Esq. Captain in the late 99 Regt. of Foot.*

Travels through several provinces of Spain and Portugal. 1799. 8. (7 sh.)

CROMBIE, [Alexander] *LL. D.*

An essay on philosophical necessity. 1793. 8. (7 sh.) The etymology and syntax of the english language explained and illustrated. 1802. 8. (5 sh. 6 d.) (See *John Golledge*)

CROMPTON, [George] *Esq. of the Inner-Temple*, born . . . . . died . . . . . (?)

Practice common placed, or the rules and practice of the courts of King's bench — Ed. 3. Vol. 1. 2. 1786. 8. (See *Baker John Sellon.*)

CROOK, [. . . . .]

See *Turnbull.*

CROOK, [Thomas] *at Tytherton.*

On rearing calves without milk. (Bath Agricult. Soc. Vol. 5. p. 465.)

CROSFIELD, [B. . . . . T. . . . .] *M. Dr.*

Account of some experiments on the method of injecting fluids into the bladder, without the use of the catheter. (New London M. J. Vol. 1. p. 125.) Observations on the chronic colic of *Aretaeus*, with a case. (Ibid. Vol. 1. p. 128.) A case of anaphrodisia, arising from an ill treated gonorrhoea. (Ibid. Vol. 1. p. 135.) On the angina maligna of the Y. 1789. (Ibid. Vol. 1. p. 360.)

CROSFIELD, [R. . . . J. . . .] *M. Dr.*

An emphyema carried off by urine. (New London Med. J. Vol. 1. p. 249.) Case of angina pectoris. (Ibid. Vol. 1. p. 251.) Account of the efficacy of the carbonic acid in putrid cases. (Ibid. Vol. 1. p. 341.) Remarks on the scurvy as it appeared among the english prisoners in france in in the Y. 1795, with an account of the effects of opium in that disease and of the methods proper to render its use more extensive and easy. 1797. 8. (1 sh. 6 d.)

*CROSS, [Peter Brady] *Esq. of Lincoln's-Inn.*
An interesting and impartial view of the practical benefits and advantages of the laws and constitution of England. 1797. 8. (4 sh.) Peace or war! which is the best policy? 1800. 8. (1 sh.)

*CROSSE, [John] *Vicar of Bradford in the County of York.*
Letter to the author of remarks on two of the most singular characters of the age. 1790. 8.

*CROSSE, [J..... C.....]
British fortitude; 17.. The purse, or, benevolent tar; a musical drama; 1794. 8. (1 sh.) The apparition; a musical dramatic romance in two acts. 1794. 8. (1 sh.)

*CROSTHWAITE, [John] *Watch and Clock-maker, Dublin.*
Account and description of three pendulums invented and constructed. (Tr. of J. A. Y. 1788. p. 7.)

*CROSWELL, [William] *M. A. Teacher of Navigation.*
Tables for readily computing the longitude by the lunar observations; partly new and partly taken from the requisite tables of Dr. *Maskelyne;* with their application, in a variety of rules and examples. Philadelphia. 1791. Rules for resolving two cases in oblique spherical trigonometry. (Mem. of B. A. Vol. 2. P. 1. p. 18.)

*CROWE, [James] *M. A.*
The advantages which result from christianity and the influence of christian principles on the mind and conduct. 1799. (1 sh. 6 d.)

*CROWE, [James] *Esq.*
Experiments on different breeds of sheep. (*Young's* A. of Agr. Vol. 20. p. 71.) Comparison between a new Leicester and South Down fat wether. (Ibid. Vol. 29. p. 326.)

CROWE, [William] *LL. B. of New-College, Oxford.*
Oratio habita VIII Kal. Jul. 1800 in theatro Sheldoniano Oxon. 1800. 4. (1 sh. 6 d.)

*CROW-

CROWFOOT, [William]

Obfervations on the opinion of Dr. *Langslow*, that extravafation is the general caufe of apoplexy. 1801. 8. (1 fh. 6 d.)

CROWTHER, [Bryan] *Surgeon to Bridewell and Bethlem Hofpital.*

Practical obfervations on the difeafe of the joints, commonly called white-fwelling, with fome remarks on fcrofulous abfceffes. 1797. 8. (3 fh.) Obfervations on the good effects of cauftics in cafes of white fwellings of the joints. (*Simmons's* Med. Facts and Obfervat. Vol. 4. p. 157.) überf. Repertor. Chir. u. Medic. Abhandl. B. 2. S. 46.

CROWTHER, [James] *M. Dr. Phyfician to the general Infirmary at Leeds.*

born . . . . . died 1793. May 1. at York.

See Gentleman's Magazine Y. 1793. May. p. 481.

Diff. De fluoré albo. Edinb. 1764. 8.

RUIKSHANK, [William] *Chemift to the Ordnance and Surgeon of Artillery.*

born at Edinburgh 1745. died in London 1800. Jun. 27.

See Gentleman's Magaz. Y. 1800. July. p. 694. Aug. p. 792. Monthly Magaz. Y. 1800. Aug. p. 82. *Duncan's* Annals of Medecine Y. 1800. p. 497. Allg. Litt. Zeit. ItBl. J. 1800. S. 1804. J. 1801. S. 1683.

Letter to Mr. *Clare* upon abforption and on the rubbing of calomel on the infide of the checks in the cure of fyphilis. 1779. Experiments on the nerves, particularly on their reproduction; and on the fpinal marrow of living animals. (Philof. Transact. Y. 1795. p. 177. *Simmons's* Med. Facts and Obferv. Vol. 7. p. 136.) Experiments in which, on the third day after impregnation, the ova of rabbits were found in the fallopian tubes; and on the fourth day after impregnation in the uterus itfelf; with the firft appearance of the foetus. (Philof. Transact. Y. 1797. p. 197.) Experiments and obfervations on the nature of fugar. (*Nicholfon's* Journal. Vol. 1. p. 337. *Tilloch's* Philof. Magaz. Vol. 2. p. 364.) Experiments and obfervations on the nature of fugar, and of vegetable

getable mucilage. (*Nicholson's* Journ. Vol. 2. p. 406.) Some experiments and observations on galvanic electricity. (*Nicholson's* Journ. Vol. 4. p. 187. 254. *Tilloch's* Philos. Magaz. Vol. 7. p. 537.) Some observations on different hydrocarbonates and combinations of carbone with oxygen &c. in reply to some of *Priestley's* late objections to the new system of chemistry. (*Nicholson's* Journ. Vol. 5. p. 1. 201.) Observations in answer to *Priestley's* memoir in defence of the doctrine of phlogiston. (Ibid. Y. 1802. May. p. 42.) Experiments on and the manner of distinguishing several diseases by the urine. (*Tilloch's* Philos. Magaz. Vol. 2. p. 240.) Communication relative to a mistake in the last edition of Dr. *Smyth's* treatise on the effects of nitrous vapor in preventing and destroying contagion, with an account of the methods now employed at Woolwich for fumigating with the sulphureous acid, and with oxygenated muriatic acid gas. (*Tilloch's* Philos. Magaz. Vol. 3. p. 396.) Experiments on the insensible perspiration of the human body, shewing its affinity to respiration; 1779. republished with additions and corrections. 1795. 8. (3 sh.) übers. von Dr. *C. F. Michaelis.* 1798. 8. An account of two cases of the diabetes mellitus — by *John Rollo*; with the results of the trials of various acids and other substances in the treatment of the lues venerea and some observations on the nature of sugar &c. by *Will. Cruikshank* Vol. 1. 2. 1797. 8. (12 sh.) übers. Versuche und Erfahr. über die Wirksamkeit des Sauerstoffes zur Heilung der Lustseuche; mit einer Einleitung von *J. C. F. Leun.* Leipzig. 1801. 8. übers. von *J. H. Jugler.* Th. 1. 2. Stendal. 1801. 8. The result of the trials of various acids and some other substances in the treatment of lues venerea. 1797. 8.

CRUISE, [William] *Esq. of Lincoln's-Inn, Barrister at Law.*

An essay on the nature and operation of fines and recoveries. Ed. 2. 1786. Ed. 3. Vol. 1. 2. 1794. 8. (12 sh.) An essay on uses. 1796. 8. (3 sh.)

*CRUMPE,

RUMPE, [Samuel] *Physician at Limerick. M. Dr. M. R. J. A.*

born 1766. died at Limerick in Ireland, 1796 Jan. 27.

See Gentleman's Magaz. Y. 1796. March p. 255. *Duncan's* Annals of Medecine Y. 1796. p. 423. Allgem. Litter. Zeit. ItBl. J. 1796. Jul. S. 814. Essay on the best means of providing employment for the people: To which was adjudged the prize proposed by the R. Irish Acad. 1793. Ed. 2. 1795. 8. (6 sh.) übers. nach der 2. Ausgabe von *C. A. Wichmann.* Leipzig. 1796. 8. Inquiry into the nature and properties of opium, wherein its component principles, mode of operation and use or abuse in particular diseases, are experimentally investigated and the opinions of former authors on these points impartially examined. 1793. 8. (5 sh.) übers. von *P. Scheel.* Kopenhagen. 1796. 8. übers. Leipzig. 1797. 8. History of a case in which very uncommon worms were discharged from the stomach; with observations thereon; (Transact. of J. A. Vol. 6. p. 57. *Simmons's* Med. Facts and Observat. Vol. 8. p. 229.)

CRUTCHLEY, [John] *of Burley, in the County of Rutland.*

Remarks on waste lands of Rutlandshire. (Bath Agric. Soc. Vol. 8. p. 119.) Agriculture of Rutland. (*Young's* A. of Agr. Vol. 22. p. 353.) Management of the poor in Rutlandshire. (Ibid. Vol. 22. p. 416.) Answers to the queries respecting cottagers renting land. (Comm. to the B. of Agr. Vol. 1. p. 93.)

RUTTWELL, [Clement] *Rev. (Formerly Surgeon at Bath.)*

Advice to lying in women, on the custom of drawing the breasts. Ed. 2. 1779. 4. (1 sh.) The holy bible — with notes by *Thom. Wilson* — Vol. 1–3. 1785. 4. (4 L. 14 sh. 6 d.) A concordance of parallels, collected from bibles and commentaries. 1790. 4. (1 L. 5 sh.) The new universal gazetteer; or geographical dictionary — with 26 whole sheet maps. Vol. 1–3. 1798. 8. (2 L. 2 sh.) *A gazetteer of France, containing every city, town and village in that country —. Vol. 1–3.

1–3. 1793. 12. (10 sh. 6 d.) A gazetteer of the Netherlands, containing a full account of all the cities, towns and villages in the 17 provinces and the bishoprick of Liege — 1794. 8. (4 sh.) A tour through the whole island of Great-Britain; divided into journeys; interspersed with useful observations; particularly calculated for the use of those who are desirous of travelling over England and Scotland. Vol. 1–6. 1801. 8. (2 L. 8 sh.)

*CULLEN, [.....] *Miss.*
*Home; a novel. Vol. 1–5. 1803. (1 L.)

*CULLEN, [Archibald] *Esq. of the Middle Temple, Barrister at Law; Commissioner of bankrupts.*
Principles of bankrupt laws. 1800. 8. (9 sh.)

*CULLEN, [Stephen]
The haunted priory; 17.. The castle of Inchvally, a tale — alas! too true. Vol. 1–3. 1796. 8 (10 sh. 6 d.)

CULLEY, [George] *Farmer at Fenton, Northumberland.* See *J. Bailey.*
Remarks on waste lands. (Bath Agric. Soc. Vol. 8. p. 131.) On cattle. (*Young's* A. of Agr. Vol. 14. p. 180.) Crop of 1790 at Fenton. (Ibid. Vol. 14. p. 253.) Reply to the questions respecting wool, sheep and corn at Fenton 1790. (Ib. Vol 14. p. 470.) On transplanting cabbages. (Ib. Vol. 15. p. 625.) Account of crops, live stock, and the price of wool. (Ib. Vol. 19. p. 147.) A method of drilling turnips. (Ib. Vol. 20. p. 159.) Account of crops in the Y. 1793. (Ib. Vol. 21. p. 223.) Observations on live stock. (Ib. Vol. 23. p. 519. Vol. 24. p. 438.) Oat meal. (Ib. Vol. 35. p. 555.) Remarks upon sheep shearing at Romney Marsh. (Ib. Vol. 37. p. 280.)

*CULLINGWORTH, [W.... W....]
Smut in wheat. (*Young's* A. of Agr. Vol. 26. p. 501.)

*CULLYER, [J.....] *of Wicklewood, Norfolk.*
The gentleman and farmer's assistant. 1798. 12. (2 sh. 6 d.)

*CUMBER-

CUMBERLAND, [George]

Some anecdotes of the life of *Julio Bonasoni*, a Bolognese, artist, who followed the styles of the best schools in the 16 century — to which is prefixed a plan for the improvement of the arts in England. 1793. 8. (3 sh.) Lewina or the maid of Snowdon; a tale and a poem on the landscapes of Great-Britain. 1793. 4. (2 sh 6 d. with etchings by the author 5 sh.) Thoughts on outline, sculpture and the system, that guided the ancient artists in composing their figures and groupes accompanied with free remarks on the practice of the moderns and liberal hints cordially intended for their advantage; to which are annexed 24 designs of classical subjects invented on the principles recommended in the essay. 1796. 4. (15 sh.) An attempt to describe Hafod — an ancient seat belonging to *Th. Johnes*. 1796. 8. (2 sh.) On *Tischbein's* Homer; on national taste &c. (Monthly Magaz. Y. 1803. March p. 101.)

CUMBERLAND, [Richard] *Solicitor and Clerk* —

See Public Characters of 1798 and 1799. p. 408. The fate of Pandora, or a trip to Newmarket. 1774. The observer: — — übers. Th. 1. 2. Leipzig. 1793. 8. Arundel — übers. Th. 1. 2. Leipzig. 1790. 1791. 8. *Songs and choruffes in the comic opera of the armorer. 1793. 8. (6 d.) The box-lobby challenge, a comedy. 1794. 8. (1 sh. 6 d.) The jew, a comedy. Ed. 2. 1794. 8. (1 sh. 6 d.) Henry. Vol. 1-4. 1795. 12. (12 sh.) übers. B. 1-4. Bremen. 1796. 1797. 8. The wheel of fortune, a comedy. 1795. 8. (2 sh.) First love, a comedy. 1795. 8. (2 sh.) The days of Yore, a drama, in three acts. 1796. 8. (1 sh. 6 d.) The last of the family. 1797. False impressions, a comedy in 5 acts. 1797. 8. (2 sh.) Joanna of Montfaucon, a dramatic romance of the XIV century-formed upon the plan of the german drama of *Kotzebue* and adapted to the english stage. 1800. 8. (2 sh. 6 d.)

CUMBERLAND, [Richard] *Esq.*

Calvary, or the death of Christ, a poem in 8 books. 1792. 4. (10 sh. 6 d.) A few plain reasons,

ſons, why we ſhould believe in Chriſt and adhere to his religion, addreſſed to the patrons and profeſſors of the new philoſophy. 1801. 8. (1 ſh. 6 d.) Poetical verſion of certain pſalms of David. 1801. 8. (2 ſh.) Anecdote of Torrigiano. (Maſſachuſetts Magaz. Y. 1792. May p. 287.) Adeliſa, a tale. (Ibid. Y. 1794. Aug. p. 478.) The obſerver. (Ibid. Y. 1794. Oct. p. 589.)

***CUMING, [W....]** *M. Dr. at Dorcheſter.*
Opinions on the virtue and quality of the engliſh rhubarbs. (Bath Agricult. Soc. Vol. 3. p. 442.)

***CUMMING, [Alexander]** *F. R. S. Edin. A mechanic and formerly a Watch-maker in London.*
The elements of clock and watch work. 17.. 4. überſ. von *J. G. Geiſsler.* Leipzig. 1802. 8. A diſſertation on the influence of gravitation conſidered as a mechanic power; 1803. 4. (6 d.) Obſervations on the effects which carriage wheels, with rims of different ſhapes, have on the roads; (Comm. to the B. of Agr. Vol. 2. p. 353.) Short account of experiments on broad wheeled carriages. (Ibid. Vol. 2. p. 393.)

***CUMMYNG, [James]** *Esq. Keeper of the Lyon Records.*
Disquiſition into the proper arrangement of the ſilver coins, applicable to the firſt four James's King's of Scotland. (Tranſact. of the S. of A. of Scotl. Vol. 1. p. 199.)

***CUMMYNG, [Suſanna]** *Mrs.*
Eſtelle; by Mr. *de Florian* — with an eſſay on paſtoral; tranſlated from the french. Vol. 1. 2. 1798. 12. (5 ſh.) Juvenile biography, or lives of celebrated children, inculcating virtue by eminent examples from real life. To which are added reflections addreſſed to the youth of both ſexes by Mr. *Joſſe*, tranſlated. Vol. 1. 2. 1801. 12. (6 ſh.)

***CUNNINGHAM, [G....]**
The chearful companion in his hours of leiſure, containing upwards of 200 ſongs, catches, glees &c. 1797. (1 ſh.)

*CURR,

CURR, [John] *of Sheffield.*
The practical coal viewer and engine builder's practical companion. Sheffield. 1797. 4. (2 L. 12 ſh. 6 d.)

CURRIE, [James] *M. Dr. Phyſician to the Liverpool Infirmary.*
See Public Characters of 1799 and 1800. p. 521.
A letter commercial and political, — to *Will. Pitt*, in which the real intereſts of Britain in the preſent criſis are conſidered and ſome obſervations are offered on the general ſtate of Europe, by *Jaſper Wilſon* (i. e. *James Currie*). 1793. 8. (1 ſh. 6 d.) An account of the remarkable effects of a ſhipwreck on the mariners, with experiments and obſervations on the influence of immerſion in freſh and ſalt water, hot and cold, on the powers of the living body; (Philoſ. Tranſact. Y. 1792. p. 199. *Simmons's* Med. Facts and Obſerv. Vol. 5. p. 103.) * The works of *Robert Burns;* with an account of his life and a criticiſm on his writings. To which are prefixed ſome obſervations on the character and condition of the Scottiſh peaſantry. Vol. 1-4. 1800. 8. (1 L. 11 ſh. 6 d.) Of tetanus and of convulſive diſorders. (Mem. of M. S. of L. Vol. 3. p. 147.) Medical reports on the effects of water, cold and warm, as a remedy in febrile diſeaſes; whether applied to the ſurface of the body or uſed as a drinck; with obſervations on the nature of fever and on the effects of opium, alcohol and inanition. 1797. 8. (6 ſh.) Ed. 2. 1798. überſ. nach der 2. Ausg. von *C. F. Michaelis.* Leipz. 1801. 8.

CURRIE, [William] *M. Dr. Fellow of the College of Phyſicians of Philadelphia.*
Hiſtorical account of the diſeaſes which occur in the different parts of the United States of America; with an explanation of their natnre and cauſes, and an account of the moſt ſucceſsfull method of treatment. 1792. 8. (2 Dollars.) A ſhort account of the influenza which prevailed in America in the Y. 1789. (Tr. of Phyſ. of Philad. Vol. 1. P. 1. p. 150.) Caſe of hydrocephalus internus, attended with equivocal ſymptoms, with the appearances on diſſection (Ibid. Vol. 1. P. 1. p. 249.)

An enquiry into the causes of the insalubrity of flat and marshy situations; and directions for preventing or correcting the effects thereof. (Tr. of A. S. Vol. 4. p. 127.) Observations on the digitalis purpurea or fox glove. (Mem. of M. S. of L. Vol. 4. p. 10.) A treatise on the synochus icteroides, or yellow fever, as it lately appeared in the city of Philadelphia. Philadelphia. 1794. 8. An historical account of the climates and diseases of the United States of America, and of the remedies and methods of treatment, which have been found most useful and efficacious, particularly in those diseases which depend upon climate and situation — Philadelphia. 1794. 8. On the use of mercurial preparations in the scarlatina anginosa. (American Museum. Y. 1787. Nov. p. 459.) A sketch of the principal causes which impair the constitutions, and shorten the lives of people of fashion. (Ibid. Y. 1789. Febr. p. 172. March. p. 245.) Observations on the causes and cure of remitting on bilious fever. To which is annexed an abstract of the opium and practice of different authors; an appendix exhibiting facts and speculations relative to the synochus icteroides or yellow fever. Philad. 1798. (1 Dollar 50 Cents.) Memoirs of yellow fever; which appeared in Philadelphia and other parts of the United States of America in the summer and autumn of the present year 1798. Philad. 1798. 8. A sketch of the rise and progress of the yellow fever and of the proceedings of the board of health in Philadelphia in the Y. 1799. to which is added a collection of facts and observations respecting the origin of the yellow fever in this country and a review of the different modes of treating it. Philadelphia. 1800. 8. — and *B. L. Oliver*, on the kine pox and a variety of other medical subjects. Philadelphia. 1802.

*CURRY, [James] *M. Dr. Physician to the Northampton Hospital.*

Popular observations on apparent death from drowing, suffocation, with an account of the means to be employed for recovery — 1793. 8. (2 sh.) Ed. 2. 1797. 8. (2 sh. 6 d.)

*CURRY,

CURRY, [William] *of the Inner-Temple.*
The commentaries of Sir *Will. Blackstone*, on the laws and constitution of England; carefully abridged in a new manner and continued down to the present time, with notes corrective and explanatory. 1796. 8. (8 sh.)

CURTIES, [T.... J.... Horsley]
Ethelwina or the house of Fitz-Auburne; 17.. Ancient records or the abbey of St. Oswythe; a romance. Vol. 1-4. 1801. 8. (18 sh.) The Scottish legend, or the isle of St. Clothair, a romance. Vol. 1-4. 1802. 12. (18 sh.)

CURTIS, [James] *Surgeon to the Embassy to Marocco.*
Journal of travels in Barbary in the Y. 1801. with observations on the gum trade of Senegal. 1803. (4 sh.)

CURTIS, [Sir Roger] *Bart. Admiral.*
See Public Characters of 1802 and 1803. p. 202.

CURTIS, [William]
born about 1746. died at Brompton near Knightsbridge 1799. July 7.
See Gentleman's Magaz. Y. 1799. July. p. 628. Aug. p. 635. Commercial and Agricultural Magaz. Y. 1799. Sept. p. 148. Allgem. Litt. Zeit. ItBl. J. 1800. S. 661. 1374.
Instructions for collecting and preserving insects. 1771. The Botanical Magazine; — Nrb. 25-163. (7 L.) 8. Some observations on thistles as injurious in agriculture more particularly the seratula arvensis of *Linnaeus.* (Bath Agricult. Soc. Vol. 1. p. 96.) Observations on the cow-clover and cow-wheat. (Ibid. Vol. 2. p. 221.) Some observations on the natural history of the curculio lapathi and silpha grisea. (Tr. of L. S. Vol. 1. p. 86.) Practical observations on the British grasses best adapted to the laying down or improving of meadows and pastures, to which is added an enumeration of the British grasses. 1790. 8. Ed. 2. with additions. 1791. 8. (2 sh. 6 d.) Ed. 3. 1798. 8. Directions for cultivating the crambe maritima or sea cole for the use of the table. 1799. 8. übers. von *C. F. A. Müller.* Göttingen. 1801. 8. General observations on the advantage

which may refult from the introduction of the feeds of our beft graffes. (*Young's* A. of Agr. Vol. 12. p. 343.) Obfervations on aphides, chiefly intended to fhow that they are the principal caufe of blights in plants and the fole caufe of the honey-dew. (Transact. of L. S. Vol. 6. p. 75.)

*CURVEN, [John]
Expence, culture, and profit of half an acre of hemp. (American Mufeum Y. 1791. Jan. p. 43.)

*CUSHING, [John] *of Afhburnham in the County of Worchefter.*
Mode of deftroying canker-worms. (American Mufeum Y. 1791. Jan. p. 45.)

*CURWEN, [J.... C.....] *Esq. M. P.*
Speech — on the 26. June 1797, convened for the purpofe of petitioning his Maj. to dismifs his prefent minifters. 1797. 12. (6 d.)

CUTHBERSON, [John] *Mathematical Inftrument-maker.*
Defcription of an improved air-pump — Ed. 2. 1795. 8. (1 fh. 6 d.)

CUTLER, [Manaffeh] *F. A. A. and M. S. Member of the Philof. Soc. at Philadelphia.*
Extract from an account of fome of the vegetable productions, naturally growing in America, botanically arranged. (Columbian Magaz. Y. 1787. Apr. p. 379. May. p. 436. June p. 469.) Method of preferving the fkins of birds. (Coll. of Maffachufetts H. S. Y. 1795. p. 9.)

*DALBY, [Ifaac] *Profeffor of Mathematics in the Roy. Military College.*
Remarks on Major-General *Roy's* account of the trigonometrical operation; (Philof. Transact. Y. 1790. p. 593.) The longitudes of Dunkirk and Paris from Greenwich, deduced from the triangular meafurement in 1787. 1788. fuppofing the earth to be an ellipfoid. (Ibid. Y. 1791. p. 236.) A fhort account of the late *Reuben Burrow's* meafurement of a degree of longitude and another of latitude, near the tropic in Bengal, in the Years 1790

1790 and 1791. 1796. 4. (1 ſh.) An account of the trigonometrical ſurvey carried on in the Y. 1791 - 1794. by Lieut. Colon: *Edward Williams*, Capt. *Will. Mudge*, and *Iſaac Dalby*. (Philoſ. Transact. Y. 1795. p. 414.) An account of the trigonometrical ſurvey, carried on in the Y. 1795 and 1796. —; (Ibid. Y. 1797. p. 432.) An account of the operations carried for accompliſhing a trigonometrical ſurvey of England and Wales, from the commencement in the Y. 1784. to the end of the Y. 1796. firſt publiſhed in and now reviſed from the Philoſ. Transact. by *Iſaac Dalby* and Capt. *William Mudge*, F. R. S. Vol. 1. illuſtrated with 22 copper-plates. 1799. 4. (1 L. 8 ſh.) A courſe of mathematics, deſigned for the uſe of the officers and cadets of the royal military College. Vol. 1. 1803. (14 ſh.)

DALDORFF, [. . . . . .] *Lieut. of Tranquebar.*
Natural hiſtory of perca ſcandens. (Transact. of L. S. Vol. 3. p. 62.)

DALGLIESH, [William] *D. D.*
Sermons on the chief doctrines and duties of the chriſtian religion in their natural order. Vol. 1. 2. 1799. 8. (12 ſh.)

DALLAS, [. . . . .] *Surgeon on board his Majeſty's ſhip the Union.*
Hiſtories of different tetanic complaints, in which the moſt powerful remedies were employed in vain. (*Duncan's* A. of Med. Y. 1798. p. 323.)

DALLAS, [Sir George] *Bart. Member for Newport.*
Letter — on the ſubject of the trade between India and Europe. 1802. 4. (5 ſh.)

DALLAS, [George] *Esq.*
Thoughts on our preſent ſituation, with remarks on the policy of a war with France. 1793. 8. (2 ſh.)

DALLAS, [R. . . . . C. . . . .] *Esq.*
Miſcellaneous writings; conſiſting of poems; Lucretia, a tragedy; and moral eſſays; with a vocabulary of the paſſions; in which their ſources are pointed out, their regular currents traced and their deviations delineated. 1797. 4. (1 L. 1. ſh.) *Clery's*

ry's journal of occurrences at the temple during the confinement of Louis XVI. King of France, translated from the french. 1798. (6 ſh.) Annals of the frenth revolution, or, a chronological account of its principal events; with a variety of anecdotes and characters hitherto unpubliſhed by *A. F. Bertrand De Molleville* — Translated from the original Manuſcript of the author. Vol. 1–9. and a ſupplement. 1800–1802. 8. (1 L. 10 ſh. 6 d.) Letter — to the Hon. *Ch. James Fox*, reſpecting an inaccurate quotation of the annals of the french revolution made by him in the debate of the houſe of Commons. 1800. Febr. 3. by *A. F. Bertrand De Molleville;* with a translation. 1800. Correſpondence between *A. F. Bertrand De Molleville* and *Ch. J. Fox* upon his quotation on the annals of the french revolution in the debate in the houſe of commons; with a translation. 1800. 8. (1 ſh. 6 d.) The natural hiſtory of volcanoes, including ſubmarine volcanoes and other analogous phenomena by the Abbé *Ordinaire;* Translated from the original Manuſcript. 1801. 8. (7 ſh.) Percival; or nature vindicated Vol. 1–4. 1801. 12. (18 ſh.) Elements of ſelf-knowledge — 1802. 8. (10 ſh. 6 d.) Hiſtory of the Marroons, from their origin to their eſtabliſhment at Sierra Leona; including the expedition to Cuba and the ſtate of the island of Jamaica for the laſt ten years; with a ſuccinct hiſtory of the island previous to that period. Vol. 1. 2 1803. 8. (1 L. 10 ſh.)

DALLAWAY, [James] *A. M: F. A. S: of Trinity College Oxford.*

Inquiries into the origin and progreſs of heraldry in England, with explanatory obſervations on armorial enſigns. 1793. 4. (coloured plates 3 L. 2 ſh.)

*DALLAWAY, [James] *M. B. late Chaplain and Phyſician of the Britiſh Embaſſy at the Port. Earl Marſhall's Secretary.*

Conſtantinople antient and modern, with excurſions to the ſhores and islands of the Archipelago and of the Troas. 1797. 4. (1 L. 12 ſh. coloured 3 L. 3 ſh.) überſ. Chemnitz. 1800. 8.

Anecdo-

Anecdotes of the arts in England; or comparative remarks on architecture, sculpture and painting, chiefly illustrated by specimens at Oxford. 1800. 8. (18 sh. 6 d.) The letters and other works of the R. H. Lady *Mary Wortley Montagu*, now first published from her original manuscripts — with memoirs of her life — Vol. 1-5. 1803. 8. (2 L.) 12mo (1 L. 4 sh.)

DALRYMPLE, [Alexander] *Esq. F. R. S.* (Brother to Sir *David Dalrymple.*)

born 1737. July 24.

Explanation of the map of the East-India Company's lands on the coast of Coromandel, published —. 1778. 4. Memoir of a map of the lands around the North-pole. 1789. 4. with a map. fol. Oriental repertory, published at the charge of the East-India Company. Vol. 1. Nrb. 1-4. (3 L. 14 sh. 6 d.) Vol. 2. Nrb. 1-4. 1791-1794. (3 L. 6 d.) übers. im Auszuge in *Bruns* u. *Zimmermanns* Repositorium —. Th. 1. S. 271. Historical journal of the expedition by sea and land to the north of California in 1768. 1769 and 1770. when Spanish establishments were first made at San Diego and Monte Rey from a Spanish Ms. translated by *Will. Reveley* and now published. 1790. 4. (7 sh.) übers. in *Zimmermanns* Annalen J. 1791. St. 3. S. 220. *Description* of the island called St. Paulo by the Dutch and by the English Amsterdam — by *John Henry Cox*, published 1790. 4. übers. in *Zimmermann's* Annalen J. 1791. St. 1. S. 14. Nautical charts memoirs and journals published by him. Nrb. 1-24. 4to. (31 L.) *Parliamentary reform as it is called improper in the present state of this country. 1792. 8. (1 sh.)

DALRYMPLE, [Sir David] Lord HAILES; *Bart. one of the Senators of the College of Justice in Scotland.*

born ..... died 1792. Nov. 29.

See Gentleman's Magaz. Y. 1792. Dec. p. 1154. Sacred poems, or a collection of translations and paraphrases from the holy scripture, by various authors. Edinb. 1751. 12. The wisdom of Solomon, wisdom of Jesus the son of Sirach or Eccle-

Ecclesiastes. Edinb. 1755. 12. Select discourses by *John Smith*, late Fellow of Queen's College, Cambridge. Edinb. 1756. 12. The World. Y. 1766. Sept. 4. Nro. 149. Y. 1755. Oct. 23. Nro. 147. Y. 1756. Nov. 25. Nro. 204. A discourse of the unnatural and vile conspiracy attempted by John Earl of Gowry and his brother against his Maj. person at St. Johnstoun upon the 5 Aug. 1600. 1757. 12. Sermon upon the 25 Oct. 1761. on Acts 27. 1. 2. Edinb. 1761. 12. The works of Mr. *John Hales* of Eaton, now first collected together. Vol. 1–3. Glasgow. 1765. A specimen of a book entitled, „one compendious book of godly and spiritual songs, collected out of sundrie parts of the scripture with sundrie of other ballates changed out of prophaine songes, for avoyding of sin et harlotrie with augmentation of sundry gude and godly ballates, not contained in the first edition; with a glossary. Edinb. 1765. 8. An account of the preservation of Charles II. after the battle of Worcester, drawn up by himself; to which are added his letters to several persons. Glasgow. 1766. A catalogue of the Lords of session, from the institution of the collegue of Justice in the Y. 1752 with historical notes. Edinb. 1767. 4. The private correspondence of Dr. *Francis Atterbury*, Bishop of Rochester and his friends in 1725 never before published. 1768. 4. An examination of some of the arguments for the high antiquity of regiam majestatem, and an inquiry into the authenticity of the leges Malcolmi. Edinb, 1769. 4. Canons of the church of Scotland, drawn up in the provincial councils held at Perth A. D. 1242 and 1269. Edinb. 1769. 4. Antient Scottish poems, published from the Ms. of *George Bannatyne* 1568. Edinb. 1770. 12. The additional case of Elizabeth, claiming the title and dignity of Countess of Sutherland by her Guardians. Wherein the facts and arguments in support of her claim are more fully stated and the errors in the additional cases for the other claimants are detected 1772. *Huberti Langueti* epistolae ad *Phil. Sydneium* Equit. Angl. Edinb. 1776. 8. Account of the martyrs of Smyrna and Lyons

Lyons in the second century. Edinb. 1776. 12. (This is the first volume of the Remains of Christian antiquity with explanatory notes.) Vol. 2. 1778. Vol 3. 1780. 12. *L. C. F. Lactantii* Divinarum institutionum liber 5. seu de justitia. 1777. Octavius, a dialogue by *Marcus Minucius Felix.* Edinb. 1781. Of the manner in which the persecutors died, a treatise by *L. C. F. Lactantius.* Edinb. 1782. Disquisitions concerning the antiquities of the christian church. Glasgow. 1783. Sketch of the life of *John Barclay.* 1786. 4. Sketch of the life of *John Hamilton*, a secular priest (how lived about A. D. 1600.) 17.. Sketch of the life of Sir *James Ramsay*, a general officer in the armies of Gustavus Adolphus, King of Sweden, with a head. 17.. Life of *George Leslie* (a Capuchin friar in the early part of the 17 Century). 17.. 4to. Sketch of the life of *Mark Alex. Boyd.* 17.. 4to. * The opinions of *Sarah* Dss. dowager of *Marlborough* published from her original MS. 1788. 12. The address of Q. Sept. *Tertullian* to Scapula Tertullus, Pro-Consul of Africa, translated. Edinb. 1790. 8. (3 sh.) The sketch of the life of Dr. *Liddel* of Aberdeen, Professor of Mathem. and Medec. in the University of Helmstedt. 1790. 4. Annals of Scotland, from the accession of Malcolm 3 to the accession of the house of Stuart. Vol. 1-3. 1797. 8. (1 L. 1 sh.) Remarks on the tatler. (Gentleman's Magaz. Vol. 60. p. 679. 793. 901. 1073. 1163.) Critique on the famous miniature of *Milton*; (Ibid. Vol. 61. p. 399. 603. 886.)

DALRYMPLE, [Sir John] *Bart. of Scotland.*

See Biogr. Liter. and Polit. Anecdotes; Vol. 1. p. 182.

Memoirs of Great-Britain and Ireland from the battle of la Hogue — Ed. 3. .... übers. B. 1-4. Winterthur. 1792-1795. 8. Plan of internal defence, as proposed — to a meeting of the county of Edinburgh on the 12. Nov. 1794. 8. (6 d.) *Consequences of the french invasion. 1798. 8. (1 sh. 6 d.)

DALRYMPLE, [William]

On the culture of wheat. 1800. 8. (2 sh.)

*DALTON,

*DALTON, [John] *Professor of Mathematics and natural Philosophy at the New College, Manchester.*

Meteorological observations and essays. 1793. 8. (4 sh.) Extraordinary facts relating to the vision of colours, with observations. (Mem. of M. Vol. 5. P. 1. p. 28.) Experiments and observations to determine whether the quantity of rain and dew is equal to the quantity of water carried off by the rivers and raised by evaporation; with an enquiry into the origin of springs. (Ibid. Vol. 5. P. 2. p. 346.) Experiments and observations on the power of fluids to conduct heat; with reference to Count *Rumford's* seventh essay on the same subject. (Ibid. Vol. 5. P. 2. p. 373.) Experiments and observations on the heat and cold produced by the mechanical condensation and rarefaction of air. (Ibid. Vol. 5. P. 2. p. 515. *Nicholson's* Journal, Y. 1802. Nov. p. 160. *Tilloch's* Philos. Magaz. Vol. 13. p. 59.) Experimental essays, on the constitution of mixed gases, on the force of steam or vapour from water and other liquids in different temperatures, both in a torricellian vacuum and in air; on evaporation; and on the expansion of gases by heat. (Mem. of M. Vol. 5. P. 2. p. 535. *Nicholson's* Journal. Y. 1802. Oct. p. 130.) Meteorological observations, made at Manchester for 1801. (Mem. of M. Vol. 5. P. 2. p. 666.) New theory of the constitution of mixed aeriform fluids and particularly of the atmosphere. (*Nicholson's* Journal. Vol. 5. p. 241.) New theory of the constitution of mixed gases elucidated. (*Tilloch's* Philos. Magaz. Vol. 14. p. 169.) Observations on the law of the expansion of water at temperature below 42°. (Ibid. Vol, 14. p. 355.)

*DALTON, [John] *Teacher of Mathematics.*

Elements of English grammar or a new system of grammatical institution. 1801. 8. (2 sh. 6 d.)

*DALTON, [John] *Esq. Sleningford, near Ripon.*

Essay on the conversion of grass lands into tillage. (Comm. to the B. of Agr. Vol. 3. p. 20.)

DALTON,

ALTON, [Richard] *Esq Keeper of the pictures and Antiquarian to the King. F. A. S.*
born . . . . . died 1791. Febr. 7.
See Gentleman's Magaz. Y. 1791. Febr. p. 188. (Account of his drawings; See ibid. Y. 1791. March. p. 195. 197. 528.).
Remarks on the pyramids of Egypt. (Gentlem. Magaz. Vol. 57. p. 9.) A short dissertation on the antient musical instruments used in Egypt, with some remarks on *Bruce's* travels. (Ibid. Vol. 60. p. 973.) Explanation of the set of prints relative to the manners, customs &c. of the present inhabitants of Egypt, from discoveries made on the spot 1749. etched and engraved by him. 17.. Antiquities and views in Greece and Egypt, with the manners and customs of the inhabitants. 1791. fol. (2 L. 12 sh. 6 d.)

DALYELL, [John Graham]
Scotish poems of the 16 century, collected. Edinb. 1801. 8. (1 L. 1 sh.)

DALZEL, [Andrew] *M. A: F. R. S. Edinb. Professor of Greek, and Principal Librarian in the University of Edinburgh.*
On certain analogies observed by the greeks in the use of their letters, and particularly of the letter σιγμα. (Tr. of E. S. Vol. 2. p. 110.) Description of the plain of Troy — by *Chevalier*, translated. 1791. 4. (10 sh. 6 d.) übers. (von *Karl Fried. Dornedden*) mit Zus. von *Heyne*. Leipz. 1792. 8. Analecta hellynica s. collectanea graeca ad usum academ. juventutis accommodata. 1787. Ed. 2. 1789. 8. T. 2. 1797. * Analecta ellynika issona s. collectanea graeca minora cum notis philologicis atque lexico . . . . Ed. 2. 1791. 8. ed. *J. G. Grohmann*. Lips. 1797. 8. Sermons by the late *John Drysdale* D. D. F. R. S. Edin. To which is prefixed an account of the author's life and character. Vol. 1. 2. 1793. 8. (12 sh.) übers. Th. 1. 2. Wien. 1796. 8. Account of *John Drysdale*, D. D. (Tr. of E. S. Vol. 3. Hist. p. 37.) *Chevalier's* tableau de la plaine de Troye illustrated and confirmed from the observations of subsequent travellers and others. (Ibid. Vol. 4. L. p. 29.)

* DALZEL,

*DALZEL, [Archibald] *Formerly Governour at Whydah and now at Cap Coast Castle.*
The history of Dahomy, an inland kingdom of Africa, compiled from anthentic memoirs, with an introduction and notes. 1793. 4. (15 sh.) übers. Leipzig. 1799. 8.

*DAMON, [Jude] *Rev. of Truro.*
Indian places in Truro. (Coll. of Massachusetts H. S. Y. 1792. p. 257.) * A bill of mortality in Truro, for seven years, beginning Jan. 1. 1787-1793. (Ibid. Y. 1794. p. 201.)

DANCER, [Thomas] *M. Dr. Physician in Jamaica.*
*Catalogue of plants, exotic and indigenous, in the botanical garden, Jamaica, St. Jago de la Vega. 1792. 4. Account of the cinnamon trees growing in the island of Jamaica. (Tr. of the Soc. for the E. of A. Vol. 8. p. 207. 212. Vol. 9. p. 187. Vol. 10. p. 256. Vol. 11. p. 203.) On the che or Oldenlandia umbellata. (Ibid. Vol. 11. p. 208.) The medical assistant or Jamaica practice of physic, designed chiefly for the use of families and plantations. 1801. 4. (1 L. 1 sh.) Strictures on Dr. *Grant's* essay on yellow fever. 1802. 12. (6 d.)

*DANFORTH, [Thomas] *Esq. formerly Fellow of the corporation of Harvard University at Cambridge in America.*
The theory of chimnies and fire places investigated. 1796. 8. (1 sh.)

*DANIEL, [J.....] *at Bath.*
Reply to our correspondent, a traveller on the peculiar failure of orchards. (Comm. and Agric. Magaz. Y. 1802. Nov. p. 353.)

*DANIEL, [William B.....] *Rev.*
Rural sports, embellished with engravings. Vol. 1. 1801. 4. (2 L. 12 sh. 6 d.) Vol. 2. 1803. (3 L. 3 sh.)

*DANIELL, [Thomas] *R. A. F. S. A.*
Antiquities of India. 12 views from the drawings of *Thomas Daniell*, engraved by himself and *Will. Daniell;* taken in the Years 1790 and 1793. Nro. 1. 2. 3. (54 plates).

*DANN, [William] *at Gillingham, Kent.*
Horn's universal five furrow sowing machine, for broad-

broad-casting or drilling all sorts of grain, pulse and seed. (*Young's* A. of Agr. Vol. 12. p. 480.) Crop of 1790. at Gillingham. (Ibid. Vol. 14. p. 183.) On the blood, a disorder in sheep. (Ib. Vol. 14. p. 207.) Drill and broad-cast culture compared. (Ib. Vol. 14. p. 288.) On a sainfoin course. (Ib. Vol. 15. p. 364.) Account of wheat crops &c. and on fattening oxen. (Ib. Vol. 16. p. 304.) Drill husbandry compared. (Ib. Vol. 17. p. 54.) On feeding oxen. (Ib. Vol. 17. p. 225.) On fattening cattle. (Ib. Vol. 19. p. 53.) Expence and produce of 28½ acres of potatoes 1793. (Ib. Vol. 22. p. 165.) Experiments on sheep and wheat. (Ib. Vol. 23. p. 426.) Account of the culture of turnips. (Tr. of the Soc. for the E. of A. Vol. 9. p. 67.) Account of his farm for 1797. (Comm. to the B. of Agr. Vol. 2. p. 433.)

ANSEY, [William] *Lieutenant-Colonel.*
Description of his machine for draining ponds, without disturbing the mud. (Tr. of the Soc. for the E. of A. Vol. 8. p. 188.)

RBLAY, [Frances] *Mrs.* — See *Frances Burney.*

ARBY, [Samuel] *M. A. Rector of Whatfield and Bredfield, co. Suffolk; formerly Tutor of Jesus-College, Cambridge.*
born 1722. died at Ipswich 1794. March 31. See Gentleman's Magaz. Y. 1794. April. p. 386.
He published two visitation sermons 1784 and 1786 and was supposed to be the author of a letter to Mr. *Warton* on his edition of *Milton.*

rl of DARNLEY, [. . . . .]
Comparative culture of wheat. (*Young's* A. of Agr. Vol. 27. p. 564.) Reply to *A. Young's* pamphlet on scarcity. (Ibid. Vol, 34. p. 622.) On the crop and price of corn. (Ib. Vol. 35. p. 588.) On the present scarcity Y. 1800. (Ib. Vol. 36. p. 92.)

ARWALL, [. . . . .] *Mrs. Formerly Miss Whateley.*
Poems on several occasions. Vol. 1. 2. 1794. 8. (6 sh.)

DARWIN, [Erasmus] *M. Dr. F. R. S.*
born at Elston near Newark, in Nottinghamshire, Dec. 12. 1731. died 1802. Apr. 18.
See Gentleman's Magaz. Y. 1802. May. p. 473. Monthly Magaz. Y. 1802. May. p 395. June. p. 457. Public Characters of 1798 and 1799. p. 117. Allg. Litt. Zeit. ItBl. J. 1802. N. 137. S. 1105. *Millin* Magasin Encycloped. A. 8. T. 6. p. 393. See *Rich. Lovell Edgeworth*.
(He edited the posthumous work of his son *Charles*: died in the 20 year of his age.) Experiments establishing a criterion between mucilaginous and purulent matter, and an account of the retrograde motions of the absorbent vessels of animal bodies in some diseases. 1780. The botanical garden, a poem, in two parts. 1789. 4. (12 sh.) Ed. 2. Vol. 1. 2. 1792. 4. (1 L. 1 sh.) Ed. 3. Vol. 1. 2. 1800. (1 L. 1 sh.) Zoonomia, or the laws of organic life. Vol. 1. 2. 1794. 1796. 4. (2 L. 10 sh.) übers. von *J. D. Brandis*. Th. 1. Abtheil. 1. 2. Th. 2. Abth. 1. 2. Th. 3. Hannover. 1795. 1799. 8. Ed. 3. corrected. Vol. 1–4. 1801. 8. (common paper 1 L. 16 sh. Royal Paper 2 L. 12 sh. 6 d.) The golden age, a poetical epistle to *Thomas Beddoes*. 1794. 4. (1 sh. 6 d.) A plan for the conduct of female education, in boarding-schools. 1797. 4. (5 sh.) Phytologia, or the philosophy of agriculture and gardening with the theory of draining morasses and with an improved construction of the drill plough. 1799. 4. (1 L. 11 sh. 6 d.) übers. von *L. B. G. Hebenstreit*. Th. 1. 1801. 8. The shrine of nature, a poem. 1802. The temple of nature or the origin of society; a poem, with philosophical notes. 1803. 4. (1 L. 5 sh.)

DARWIN, [Robert Waring] *M. Dr. F. R. S. of Shrewsbury.* (Son of *Erasmus Darwin*.)
Account of a rupture of the urethra and of a solution of a catgut bougie in the bladder. (Mem. of M. S of L Vol. 3. p. 507.

°DASHWOOD, [. . . . .] *Lady; Bedchamber to the Princesses and Governess of the royal-nursery, Carlton house.*
born . . . . . died 1796. Oct. 6.

See

See Gentleman's Magaz. Y. 1796. Oct. p. 883.
The birth and triumph of Cupid in her Majesty's collection from papers cut by *Dashwood*, engraved by *P. W. Tomkins*. 1795. 4.

DAVJAN, [Kingsmill] *Esq.*

An essay on the passions, being an attempt to trace them from their source, describe their general influence and explain the peculiar effects of each upon the mind. 1799. 12. (3 sh.)

DAUBENEY, [Charles] *LL. D. Minister of Christ's church, Bath.*

A guide to the church, in several discourses — 1798. 8. (7 sh. 6 d.) Appendix Vol. 1. 2. 1799. 8. (10 sh.) The fall of papal rome recommended to the consideration of England. 1798. 8. (1 sh.) Letter to Mrs. *Hannah More* on some part of her late publication, entitled „Strictures on female education„ to which is subjoined a discourse on Genesis XV, 6. 1799. 8. (2 sh.) A layman's account of his faith and practice; with a letter from *Ch. Daubeney*. 1801. 12. (2 sh. 6 d.) VIII Discourses on the connection between the old and new testament and demonstrative of the great doctrine of atonement; with an address to the younger clergy and remarks on the late Prof. *Campbell's* ecclesiastical history. 1802. 8. (9 sh.) Vindiciae ecclesiae Anglicanae —; 1803.

DAUCER, [Thomas] *M. Dr.*

Catalogue of plants, exotic and indigenous, in the botanical garden, Jamaica. St. Jago de la Vega. 1792. 4.

DAVERS, [Sir Charles] *Bart. M. P. of Rusbrook-Hall, near Bury, Suffolk.*

Account of a flock of Norfolk sheep. (*Young's* A. of Agr. Vol. 34. p. 171.)

DAVID, [Job]

A review of Dr. *Priestley's* letter, to an antipaedobaptist. 1803. 8. (1 sh.)

DAVIDGE, [John B.....] *A. M. M. Dr. at Baltimore.*

A treatise on the autumnal endemial epidemic of tropical climates, vulgarly called the yellow fever; containing its origin, history, nature and cure; together with a few reflections on the proximate cause of diseases. Baltimore. 1798. 8.

S 2 *DAVID-

*DAVIDSON, [Alexander] *Esq.*
On fome roman coins found at Nelore. (Afiat. Ref. Vol. 2. p. 331.)

*DAVIDSON, [David] *at Elkton, Cecil county, Maryland.*
Account of an extraordinary lufus naturae; (American Mufeum Y. 1789. Nov. p. 350.)

DAVIDSON, [George]
Obfervations upon the yellow fever and its proximate caufe; (Medical Repofit. Vol. 1. p. 165.) Experiments with the eudiometer, made at Martinique. (Ibid. Vol. 2. p. 279.) Account of the cachexia Africana, a difeafe incidental to negro flaves lately imported into the Weft-Indies. (Ibid. Vol. 2. p. 282.)

*DAVIDSON, [Samuel] *Surgeon at Rothbury in Northumberland.*
Hiftory of a fingular cafe of an intermittent, affecting the right temple; and of a remarkable tumour in the abdomen, fuccefsfully treated. (*Duncan's* M. C. Y. 1790. Dec. 2. Vol. 5. p. 391.)

*DAVIDSON, [William] *Rev.*
The duty and propriety of fafting to the Lord, explained and recommended; a faft fermon. 1793. 8. (6 d.)

*DAVIDSON, [William] *Apothecary in London.*
Cafe of a fingular cutaneous affection, with fome remarks relative to the poifon of copper. (*Simmons's* Medical Facts and Obfervat. Vol. 3. p. 61.) überf. Repertor. Chir. u. Medic. Abhandl. B. 2. S. 197. Two cafes of pulmonary hemorrhage, fpeedily and fuccefsfully cured by abftinence from liquids. (Ibid. Vol. 3. p. 68.) überf. Ibid. B. 2. S. 203. A cafe of pulmonary haemorrhage, with remarks; (Ibid. Vol. 4. p. 129.) überf. Ibid. B. 2. S. 189. An account of the effects of vitriolic aether in a cafe of fpasmodic affection of the ftomach; and in two cafes of intermittent fever. (Ibid. Vol. 5. p. 68.) Obfervations anatomical, phyfiological and pathological on the pulmonary fyftem; with remarks on fome of the difeafes of the lungs, viz. on haemorrhage, wounds, afthma, catarrh, croup and confumption. 1795. 8. (4 fh.)

(4 fh.) A cafe of pulmonary confumption, attended with haemorrhage, fpeedily cured by a limited ufe of liquids. (*Duncan's* M. C. Dec. 2. Vol. 8. p. 395.)

DAVIES, [David] *Rector of Barkham, Berkfhire.* The cafe of labourers in husbandry ftated and confidered in three parts. 1795. 4. (10 fh. 6 d.)

DAVIES, [E.....]
Twelve dialogues on different fubjects, between Titus, Timothy and Archippus; 1801. 8. (2 fh. 6 d.)

DAVIES, [Hugh] *Rev.* F. *L. S.*
Defcriptions of four new Britifh lichens. (Tranfact. of L. S. Vol. 2. p. 283.)

DAVIES, [John]
Receipt to make cows dry. (*Young's* A. of Agr. Vol. 21. p. 508.)

DAVIES, [Thomas] *Major-General. F. R. S. and L. S.*
An account of the jumping moufe of Canada, Dipus Canadenfis. (Tranfact. of L. S. Vol. 4. p. 155. *Tilloch's* Philof. Magaz. Vol. 1. p. 285.) Account of a new fpecies of mufcicapa, from New South Wales. (Tranfact. of L. S. Vol. 4. p. 240.) Defcription of menura fuperba, a bird of New South Wales. (Ibid. Vol. 6. p. 207.)

DAVIES, [Thomas] *Rev. of Beddingham, near Lewes, Suffex.*
On working oxen in harnefs; on marle; and particulars relating to Glynd. (*Young's* A. of Agr. Vol. 11. p. 137.) Account of the culture of cabbage. (Ibid. Vol. 17. p. 109.)

DAVIS, [.....]
The young algebraift companion; or, a new and eafy guide to algebra by *Dan. Fenning*, a new edition. To which is added, 38 felect problems with their folutions &c. 1802. 12.

DAVIS, [Daniel]
*The proceedings of two conventions, held at Portland, to confider the expediency of a feparate government in the diftrict of Maine. (Coll. of Maffachufetts H. S. Y. 1795. p. 25.)

DAVIS, [George] *of Windfor, Berks.*
Defcription of his machine for loading and unloading goods. (Tr. of the Soc. for the E. of A.

S 3 Vol.

Vol. 15. p. 276.) *Tilloch's* Philof. Magaz. Vol. 5. p. 392. Defcription of his invention for preventing paffengers in carriages being injured when the horfes have taken fright. (Tr. of the Soc. for the E. of A. Vol. 18. p. 247.)

*DAVIS, [John]

Poems. Philadelphia. 1800. Travels of four years and a half in the United States of America, during 1798 — 1802. 1803. 8. (8 fh.)

*DAVIS, [M....]

Thoughts on dancing; occafioned by fome late transactions among the people called methodifts. 1791. 8. (6 d.)

*DAVIS, [P.....]

Various modes of deftroying the cock-chafer. (Comm. and Agric. Magaz. Y. 1802. Sept. p. 172.) Comparifon between foiling and pafturing cattle, horfes. (Ibid. Y. 1802. Nov. p. 351.) On the draining of boggyland. (Ibid. Y. 1803. Jan. p. 37.)

*DAVIS, [Richard]

Remarks on wafte lands in Oxfordfhire. (Bath Agric. Soc. Vol. 8. p. 114.)

*DAVIS, [Samuel] *Esq.*

On the aftronomical computations of the Hindus. (Afiat. Ref. Vol. 2. p. 225.) On the Indian cycle of fixty years. (Ibid. Vol. 3. p. 209.)

*DAVIS, [Thomas] *Esq. of Longleat; Steward to the Marquis of Bath.*

On the fuperior advantage of dairy to arable farms. (Bath Agricult. Soc. Vol. 3. p. 74.) Obfervations on the fubjects propofed in a circular letter, by the Bath and Weft of England Society. (Ibid. Vol. 5. p. 172.) Obfervations on the fuppofed neglect and fcarcity of oak timber. (Ibid. Vol. 5. p. 177.) Obfervations on the management of woods and on the prefent ftate thereof, particularly in the Weftern Counties. (Ibid. Vol. 7. p. 1.) Extract from a general view of the agriculture of the county of Wilts; with obfervations on the means of its improvement; drawn up for the confideration of the board of agriculture and internal improvement. (Ibid. Vol. 7. p. 113.) Addrefs to the landholders of this kingdom; with plans of cottages for the habitation of labourers in the country. (Ibid. Vol. 7. p. 294.) On the most practicable mode of giving an equitable compensation for tithes. (Ibid. Vol. 8. p. 239.) Brief observations on different qualities of wool, as produced by the Spanish mixture in breeding. (Ibid. Vol. 8. p. 298.) On some subjects proper to be encouraged by premiums. (*Young's* A. of Agr. Vol. 2. p. 441.) On Wiltshire sheep. (Ib. Vol. 22. p. 97.) Theory of watered meadows. (Ib. Vol. 22. p. 108.) Fact applicable to folding sheep. (Ib. Vol. 22. p. 131.) Essay on the conversion of grass lands into tillage. (Comm. to the B. of Agr. Vol. 3 P. 1. p. 75.) Remarks on the Wiltshire and South-down sheep. (*Young's* A. of Agr. Vol. 37. p. 378.) Remarks on the disposition of sheep to fatten, on horse-tying and vale of Evesham course of crops. (Ib. Vol. 37. p. 456.).

DAVIS, [Wendel] *Esq.*
Description of Sandwich, in the county of Barnstable. (Coll. of Massachusetts H. S. Y. 1801. p. 119.)

DAVIS, [William]
On the use of the globes. 17.. A complete treatise of land surveying by the chain, cross and off set staffs only, in 3 parts 1798. (7 sh.) The mathematical principles of natural philosophy by Sir *Isaac Newton*, translated into English by *Andrew Motte*, — with an account of his life; the whole revised and carefully corrected. Vol. 1-3. 1802. 8. (1 L. 7 sh.) A key to Bonycastle's algebra. 1803. 12. (4 sh.)

DAVISON, [......]
°A letter to *John Bowles*, on the subjects of his two pamphlets — thoughts on the late general election, as demonstrative of the progress of Jacobinism; and a letter to — *Charles James Fox* — on the character of — *Francis* Duke of *Bedford*. 1803. 8. (4 d.) Ten letters, principally upon the subject of the late contested election at Nottingham. 1803. 8. (1 sh.)

***DAULBY, [Daniel]**
A descriptive catalogue of the works of *Rembrandt* and of his scholars *Bol*, *Livens* and *van Vliet*, compiled from the original etchings and from the catalogues of *De Burgy*, *Gersaint*, *Helle* and *Glomy*, *Marcus* and *Yver*. 1796. 4. (15 sh.) 8vo. (10 sh. 6 d.)

DAVY, [Charles] *M. A. Rector of Onehouse, Suffolk, of Tropcrofs co. Norfolk.*
born ..... died 1797. Apr. 8.
See Gentleman's Magaz. Y. 1797. May. p. 438. Allg. Litt. Zeit. ItBl. J. 1800. S. 645.

***DAVY, [Humphry]** *Superintendant of the medical pneumatic institution.*
Chemical and philosophical researches, chiefly concerning nitrous oxide or dephlogisticated nitrous air and its respiration. 1800. 8. (10 sh. 6 d.) A syllabus of a course of lectures on chemistry, delivered at the Royal institution of Great-Britain. 1802. 8. (3 sh.) A discourse introductory to a course of lectures on chemistry, delivered in the theatre of the Royal institution. 1802. 8. (1 sh. 6 d.) On galvanic piles. (*Duncan's* A. of Med. Y. 1801. p. 478.) Experiments and observations on the silex composing the epidermis, or external bark and contained in other parts of certain vegetables. (*Nicholson's* Journal. Vol. 3. p. 56. 138.) Respirability of the gaseous oxyde of azote. (Ibid. Vol. 3. p. 93.) On the nitrous oxide, or gaseous oxide of azote, on certain facts relating to heat and light and on the discovery of the decomposition of the carbonate and sulphate of ammoniac. (Ibid. Vol. 3. p. 515.) An account of some experiments made with the galvanic apparatus of Sign. *Volta*. (Ibid. Vol. 4. p. 275. 326.) Notice of some observations on the causes of the galvanic phenomena, and on certain modes of increasing the powers of the galvanic pile of *Volta*. (Ibid. Vol. 4. p. 337. 394.) Notices concerning galvanism. (Ibid. Vol. 4. p. 527.) An account of a new eudiometer. (Ibid. Vol 5. p. 175.) Outlines of observations relating to nitrous oxide, or dephlogisticated nitrous air. (Ibid. Vol. 5. p. 281.) An account of a new eudiometer. (Ibid. Y. 1802. Jan.

Jan. p. 41.) Note refpecting the abforption of nitrous gas, by folutions of green fulphate and muriate of iron. (Ibid. Y. 1802. Febr. p. 107.) An account of a method of conftructing fimple and compound galvanic combinations, without the ufe of metallic fubftances by means of charcoal and different fluids. (Ibid. Y. 1802. Febr. p. 144.) Account of fome experiments — relating to the agencies of galvanic electricity, in producing heat, and in effecting changes in different fluid fubftances. (Ibid. Y. 1802. Oct. p. 135.) An account of a method of copying paintings upon glafs, and of making profiles by the agency of light upon nitrate of filver, invented by *T. Wedgwood.* (Ibid. Y. 1802. Nov. p. 167.) An account of fome galvanic combinations, formed by the arrangement of fingle metallic plates and fluids, analogous to the new galvanic apparatus of Mr. *Volta.* (Philof. Transact. Y. 1801. p. 397. *Tilloch's* Philof. Magaz. Vol. 10. p. 202.) Account of a new eudiometer. (*Tilloch's* Philof. Magaz. Vol. 10. p. 56.) Outlines of a view of galvanifm, chiefly extracted from a courfe of lectures on the galvanic phaenomena; (Ibid. Vol. 11. p. 326.) An account of a method of conftructing fimple and compound galvanic combinations, without the ufe of metallic fubftance, by means of charcoal and different fluids. (Ibid. Vol. 11. p. 340.)

DAVY, [William] *A. B. of Baliol College, Oxford.*
System of divinity in a courfe of fermons on the firft inftitutions of religion. Ed. 2. Vol. 1. 1795. 8.

DAWES, [John] *Surgeon.*
Pantometry; or, an attempt to fyftematize every branch of admeafurement. 1797. 12. (1 fh.)

DAWES, [John Nic.]
On paffages in *Euripides.* (Monthly Magaz. Y. 1802. Dec. p. 375.)

DAWES, [Matthew] *Esq. of the Inner-Temple, Barrifter at Law and one of the Affeffors to the returning officer.*
Examination into the particulars of the two laft elections for the borough of Southwark in May and Nov. 1796. — 1797. 8. (1 fh. 6 d.)

S 5 *DAW.

*DAWPLUCKER, [Jonathan] *(a fictitious name.)*
Remarks on Mr. *John Bell's* anatomy of the heart and arteries. 1799. 8. (2 ſh. 6 d.)

DAWSON, [Ambroſe] *M. Dr. Senior Fellow of the College of Phyſicians.*
born 1706. died at Liverpool 1794. Dec. 23.
See Gentleman's Magaz. Y. 1794. Supplem. p. 1207.

DAWSON, [Benjamin]
Prolepſis philologiae anglicanae; or, plan of a philological and ſynonymical dictionary. 1797. 4. (2 ſh. 6 d.)

*DAWSON, [J.....]
On the word rowen. (Comm. and Agric. Mag. Y. 1802. Jan. p. 12.)

*DAWSON, [John] *of Sedbergh, near Kendal, in Weſtmoreland.*
born in Garsdale.
See Public Characters of 1801 and 1802. p. 364.
Gentleman's Magaz. Y. 1802. Jan. p. 39.
Four propoſitions; 17.. On the inverſe method of central forces; (Mem. of M. S. Vol. 4. Part 2. p. 369. Vol. 5. Part. 1. p. 102.) The doctrine of public neceſſity briefly invalidated; 1781. (See in *Hutton's* Miſcellanea Mathematica his letters under the ſignature *Wadſon.*)

*DAWSON, [William] *Esq.*
A ſubſtitute for the aſſeſsment bill &c. 1798. 8.

*DAY, [.....] *of Troſton.*
Account of two acres and a half of potatoes. (*Young's* A. of Agr. Vol. 4. p. 454.)

*DAY, [David]
Account of planting aſh. (Tr. of the Soc. for the E. of A. Vol. 1. p. 109.)

*DAY, [Joſeph]
An addreſs to the attornies at law and ſolicitors upon the proceedings of a committee of the London law club &c. 1796. (3 ſh. 6 d.)

*DAY, [Robert] *Esq.*
Report from the committee of ſecrecy appointed to take into conſideration the treaſonable proceedings preſented to the houſe of commons of Ireland

land on April 29. 1797. reported May 10. 1797. by the R. H. Mr. Secret. *Pelham*. To which is added, a charge to the grand jury of the county of Dublin. 1797.

DAY, [William]

An attempt to arrange the cryftals of oxidated tin ore, according to their fuppofed ftructure. (*Tilloch's* Philof. Magaz. Vol. 4. p. 152.)

DAYE, [Eliza]

Poems on various fubjects. 1798. 8. (7 fh.)

DAYES, [Edward] *Painter.*

Remarks on *Sheldrake's* differtation on painting in oil in the manner of the Venetians. (*Tilloch's* Philof. Magaz. Vol. 4. p. 124.) Thoughts on colouring, and particularly with a retrofpect to the method ufed by the Venetians in the mechanical part of the art and to their method of arranging the tints. (Ibid. Vol. 8. p. 3.) An effay to illuftrate the principles of compofition as connected with landscape painting. (Ibid. Vol. 8. p. 293.) On painting. (Ibid. Vol. 13. p. 122. 211. 348. Vol. 14. p. 31. 97. 218. Vol. 15. p. 12. 115.)

EACON, [H.....]

On the venereal difeafe — 1789. 8. (3 fh. 6 d.) überf. Stendal. 1791. 8.

EACON, [John]

A new and large collection of hymns and pfalms, executed from more than forty different authors; the whole being claffed and arranged according to their refpective fubjects. 1801.

DEACON, [William] *B. A. of Trinity College, Cambridge.*

The chriftian doctrine of juftification by faith not deftructive of the principles of natural virtue. 1794. 4. (1 fh.)

EANE, [Samuel] *F. A. A.*

The new-England farmer, or georgical dictionary, containing a compendious account of the ways and methods in which the moft important art of husbandry — is or may be practifed to the greateft advantage in this country. Worcefter, Maffachufetts. 1790. 8. (9 fh.)

DEAR-

DEARBORN, [Benjamin] *Schoolmaster at Portsmouth.*
Description of a simple machine for drawing in perspective, invented by him. (Columbian Magaz. Y. 1791. Febr. p. 67.)

*DEBDIN, [Waldron]
A compendious history of the english stage from the earliest period to the present time. 1800. (2 sh. 6 d.)

DEBRAW, [John] *Apothecary to Addenbrook's Hospital at Cambridge.*
born ..... died in Russia 178. (?)

DELAP, [John] *D. D.*
Sedition, an ode, occasioned by his Majesty's late proclamation. 1792. 4. (6 d.) The lord of nile, an elegy. 1799. 4. (1 sh.)

*DELOLME, [J..... L.....] *LL. Dr.*
Observations on the power of individuals to prescribe by will the future uses of their property —. 1798. (1 sh.)

*DEMING, [Julius] *Merchant of Lichtfield, Connecticut.*
On the instinct of a wren (motacilla domestica, *Linn.*). (Medical Repository. Vol. 1. p. 367.) On the instinct of a male and female robin (turdus migratorius, *Linn.*); (Ibid. Vol. 1. p. 368.)

DEMPSTER, [George] *Esq. of Dunichen.*
Account of the magnetic mountain of Cannay. (Transact. of the Soc. of Antiq. of Scotl. Vol. 1. p. 183.) Method of preserving salmon in snow and ice; (Massachusetts Magaz. Y. 1791. Dec. p. 732. Columbian Magaz. Y. 1788. June p. 316.) An improved mode of preparing peat-fuel. (Tr. of Highland Soc. Vol. 1. p. 303.)

*DENHOLM, [James]
The history of the city of Glasgow: To which is added a sketch of a tour to Loch Lomond and the falls of the Clyde, forming a complete guide for the use of strangers: Embellished with 13 engravings. 1799. 12. (5 sh.)

*DENMAN, [Joseph] *M. Dr.*
Observations on the effects of Buxton water. 1793. 8. (2 sh. 6 d.)

DENMAN,

ENMAN, [Thomas] *M. Dr. Physician-man-midwife to the Middlesex Hospital and Teacher of Midwifery in London.*

Introduction to the practice in midwifery. Vol. 1. 1787. 8. (6 sh.) Vol. 2. 1795. 8. übers. von *Joh. Jac. Roemer.* Th. 1. Zurich und Leipzig. 1791. 8. Ed. 3. London 1801. 4 (1 L. 11 sh. 6 d.) Collection of engravings tending to illustrate the generation and parturition of animals and of the human species. P. 2. 3. 1791. fol. Account of a fact relative to menstruation, not hitherto described: (*Simmons's* Med. Facts and Observ. Vol. 1. p. 108.) übers. *Koch's* Samml. auserlesf. Abhandl. B. 14. S. 675. Some account of a disease lately observed in infants. (London M. J. Vol. XI. p. 374.) Engraving of two uterine polypi. 1801. fol.

ENNE, [Samuel] *M. A. F. A. S.*

born 1720. died Aug. 3. 1799. at Wilmington, near Dartford, Kent.

See Gentleman's Magaz. Y. 1799. Aug. p. 722. Nov. p. 943. Allg. Litter. Zeit. ItBl. J. 1800. S. 661.

Letter — with an attempt to shew the good effects which may reasonably be expected from the confinement of criminals in separate apartments. 1771. 8. Memorials of the cathedral church of Rochester; (See *Thorpe's* custumale Roffense; p. 153-242.) History of the parish of Darent; (Ibid. p. 90-102.) On the cypher. J. H. S. (See Topographer. Vol. 3. p. 3.) Remarks on a passage in a letter from Bp. Atterbury to Pope, in which he refers to an epistle of Cicero to Atticus, that mentions his country neighbours, Arrius and Sebosus; (See Bp. *Atterbury's* epistolary correspondance. Vol. 5. p. 316.) On Canterbury cathedral. (Archaeol. Vol 10. p. 37.) On the painting in Brereton church-windows. (Ibid. Vol. 10. p. 334.) On stone stalls at Maidstone and elsewhere. (Ibid. Vol. 10. p. 261. 298.) Observations on the burning of the steeple of St. Paul's cathedral London. (Ibid. Vol. 11. p. 72.) On the lavatory at Canterbury cathedral and observations on fonts. (Ibid. Vol. 11. p. 108. 149.) Brief survey of Canterbury cathedral as described by *Eadmer* and *Gervase;* (Ibid.

(Ibid. Vol. 11. p. 375.) Review of Mr. *Clark's* opinion on stone seats. (Ibid. Vol. 11. p. 381.) On the figures carved in stone on the porch of Chalk church, Kent. (Ibid. Vol. 12. p. 10.) Observations on a triple stone seat at Upchurch church in Kent. (Ibid. Vol. 12. p. 101.) Observations on paper-marks; (Ibid. Vol. 12. p. 114.) Extracts from a Ms. intituled „the life of Mr. *Phineas Pette*, one of the master ship-wrights to King James I. drawn up by himself. (Ib. Vol. 12. p. 217.) An examination of an inscription on a barn in Kent; the mantle tree in the parsonage house at Helmdon in Northamptonshire — and queries and remarks on the general use of arabic numerals in England. (Ibid. Vol. 13. p. 107.) Additional remarks on the Helmdon mantle-tree inscription and on the knowledge and use of arabic numerals in the 13. 14. 15 and 16 centuries. (Ibid. Vol. 13. p. 141.) Historical particulars of Lambeth parish and Lambeth palace, in addition to the histories by Mr. *Ducarel* in the bibliotheca topographica Brittannica. 1795. 4. (12 sh. 6 d.) Observations on parish registers. 17.. (Communications to Gentleman's Magazine).

*DENNISON, [Francis] *Esq.*

Letter on larch in Russia. (Tr. of the Soc. for the E. of A. Vol. 6. p. 51.)

*DENNY, [John] *Veterinary-Surgeon to the 10 Regt. of Dragoons.*

On the diseases of horses; 1802. 8. (5 sh.)

DENT, [John]

(Formerly the editor of a news-papers (now extinct) called, The London Courant.) ⁋ The Bastile. 17.. The telegraph; or a new way of knowing things; a comic piece. 1795. 8. (1 sh.)

*DERMODY, [Thomas]

Poems, moral and descriptive. 1800. (3 sh.) Peace, a poem. 1801. 4. (1 sh. 6 d.) Poems on various subjects. 1802. 8. (4 sh. 6 d.)

DEVERELL, [Mary] *Mrs. Gloucestershire.*

Mary, queen of Scots; an historical tragedy or dramatic poem. 1792. 8. (3 sh.)

DEVERELL,

EVERELL, [R.....] *Esq. M. P.*

A guide to the knowledge of the ancients; Book I. 1803. (3 sh.)

EVEREUX, [J..... E.....] *Esq.*

Obſervations on the factions which have ruled Ireland on the calumnies thrown upon the people of that country, and on the juſtice, expediency and neceſſity of reſtoring to the catholics their political right. 1801. 8. (4 ſh. 6 d.)

EVIS, [Arthur William] *Esq.*

On the culture of poppies and the procuring opium in the Eaſt-Indies. (Tr. of the Soc. for the E. of A. Vol. 16. p. 272. *Tilloch's* Philoſ. Magaz. Vol. 2. p. 417.)

EWAR, [Henry] *late Aſſiſtant Surgeon to the* 30 *Regt. of Foot.*

Obſervations on diarrhoea and dyſentery, as thoſe diſeaſes appeared in the Britiſh army, during the campaign in Egypt; To which are prefixed, a deſcription of the climate of Egypt and a ſketch of the medical hiſtory of the campaign. 1803. 8.

DEWEES, [William] *M. Dr. Lecturer on Midwifery in Philadelphia.*

A caſe of difficult parturition, ſucceſsfully terminated by bleeding; (Medical Repoſit. Vol. 2. p. 24.) Obſervations on the uſe of the warm bath in caſes of laborious parturition. (Ibid. Vol. 2. p. 181.)

DEXTER, [Aaron] *M. Dr. F. A. A.*

Obſervations on the manufacture of potaſh. (Mem. of B. A. Vol. 2. P. 1. p. 165.) Account of a locked jaw. (Ibid. Vol. 2. P. 1. p. 191. *Simmons's* Med. Facts and Obſerv. Vol. 7. p. 266.) An account of the methods uſed in ſome of the northern parts of America for the cure of the bite of mad dogs. (Mem. of M. S. of L. Vol. 4. p. 404.) On the making of pot-aſh. (Columbian Magaz. Y. 1789. Jan. p. 32.)

DEXTER, [Samuel] *Esq.*

On the retreat of houſe ſwallows in winter. (American Muſeum Y. 1787. Oct. p. 357. Maſſachuſetts Magaz. Y. 1791. Oct. p. 621.)

DIBDIN,

*DIBDIN, [.....]
A three years' tour through England and Scotland. Part I. 1802. 4. (5 ſh.) Obſervations on a tour through almoſt the whole of England, and a conſiderable part of Scotland —; Vol. I. 2. 1802. 4. (3 L. 13 ſh. 6 d.)

*DIBDIN, [Charles] *Jun.*
The ſong ſmith; or, rigmarole repoſitory. 1804. (2 ſh.)

*DIBDIN, [J..... F.....] *A. B.*
An introductory to the knowledge of rare and valuable editions of the greek and roman claſſics; being in part a tabulated arrangement of Dr. *Harwood's* view &c. with notes from de *Bure*, *Maittaire*, Dictionnaire bibliographique and references to the celebrated catalogues and ſales of *Mead*, *Aſkew*, *Beauclerk*, *Croft* and *Pinelli*; with an account of moſt of the firſt editions of the claſſics. 1802. 8. (3 ſh. 6 d.)

*DIBDIN, [Thomas]
The younger brother, a novel. Vol. 1–3. 1794. 8. (13 ſh. 6 d.) Hannah Hewit, or the female Cruſoe. Vol. 1–3. 1796. (10 ſh. 6 d.) Poems. 1797. 8. (3 ſh. 6 d.) The jew and the Doctor; a farce, in two acts. 1799. 8. (1 ſh.) Mouth of the nile. 1799. 8. Five thouſand a year, a comedy, in 3 acts.. 1799. 8. (2 ſh.) The horſe and the widow, a farce, — altered from the german of *A. von Kotzebue* and adapted to the Engliſh ſtage. 1799. 8. (1 ſh.) The birth-day, a comedy in 3 acts; altered from the german of *Kotzebue* and adapted to the Engliſh ſtage. 1800. 8. (2 ſh.) Il Bondocani, or, the Caliph robber; a comic opera in 3 acts. 1802. 8. (1 ſh. 6 d.) The ſchool for prejudice: a comedy, in 5 acts. 1802. 8. (2 ſh.) St. David's day: or, the honeſt welchman: a ballad farce, in 2 acts. 1802. 8. (1 ſh.)

*DICK, [Sir Alexander]
Opinions on the virtue and quality of the engliſh rhubarbs. (Bath Agricult. Soc. Vol. 3. p. 441.) Report upon *John Williams's* plan for a royal foreſt

forest of oak in the highlands of Scotland. (Transact. of the Soc. of the Antiq. of Scotl. Vol. I. p. 39.)

ICK, [John] *A. M: Minister of the gospel in Slateford.*

An essay on the inspiration of the holy scriptures of the old and new testament. 1800. 12. (3 sh.) (Several single sermons.)

ICKENS, [Charles] *LL. Dr. Rector at Hemingford Abbots, co. Huntingdon.*

born 1720. died Aug. 27. 1793.

See Gentleman's Magaz. Y. 1793. Oct. p. 959. (Several single sermons.)

ICKINSON, [H . . . . .] *Captain to the East-India Volunteers.*

Instructions for forming a regiment of infantry for parade of exercise, together with the 18 manoeuvres as ordered to be practised by his Maj. infantry forces, accompanied by explanations and diagrams. 1798. 8. (5 sh.)

ICKINSON, [John] *Esq.*

Letters from a farmer in Pennsylvania, to the inhabitants of the British colonies. (American Museum Y. 1788. Sept. p. 284. Oct. p. 371. Nov. p. 454. Dec. p. 522.)

ICKINSON, [Timothy]

*Description of Hollifton. (Coll. of Massachusetts H. S. Y. 1794. p. 18.)

ICKINSON, [William] *Esq.*

Antiquities, historical, architectural, chorographical and itinerary in Nottinghamshire and the adjacent counties; comprising the histories of Southwell and of Newark; interspersed with biographical sketches and profusely embellished with engravings in four parts. Part 1. Vol. 1. 1801. 4. (14 sh.) Part 2. 1803. 4. (18 sh.) See *Rastall.*

ICKSON, [. . . . .] *Dr.*

Essay on chemical nomenclature, in which are composed observations on the same subject, by *Rich. Kirwan.* 1796. 8. (5 sh.) List of Scotticisms. (Monthly Magaz. Y. 1800. Apr. p. 236. May. p. 322.)

*DILLON, [Theobald] *Esq.*
The military plans of the late operation on the rhine. 1796 (10 sh. 6 d.)

*DILLWYN, [Lewis Weston] *F. L. S.*
Synopsis of the British confervae. Fasc. 1. 2. 1802. 4. (12 sh.) übers. von *F. Weber* und *M. H. Mohr.* Heft 1. 2. Gött. 1803. 8. Letter respecting the effects of the oxymuriatic acid on the growth of plants. (*Tilloch's* Philos. Magaz. Vol. 11. p. 158.). Catalogue of the most rare plants found in the environs of Dover, with occasional remarks. (Transact. of L. S. Vol. 6. p. 177.)

*DIMOND, [J . . . .] *Esq.*
The hero of the North, an historical play; 1803. 8. (2 sh. 6 d.)

*DIMOND, [William] *Jun.*
Petrarchal sonnets and miscellaneous poems. 1800. 8. (5 sh.)

DIMSDALE, [Thomas] *Baron; M. Dr: F. R. S. Body-Physician and actual Counsellor of State to her Imperial Maj. of all the Russies.*
born 1711. died at Herford 1800. Dec. 30.
See Gentleman's Magaz. Y. 1801.; Jan. p. 88. July. p. 669. Monthly Magaz. Y. 1801. July. p. 511. Allgem. Litterat. Zeit. J. 1801. ItB. S. 839. 1681.
The present method of inoculating for the small pox; 1766. 8. Ed. 6. 1772. Thoughts on general and partial inoculation. 1776. 8. Observations on the introduction to the plan of the dispensary for general inoculation. 1778. 8. Remarks on Dr. *Lettsom's* letter on general inoculation. 1779. 8. A review of Dr. *Lettsom's* observations on Baron *Dimsdale's* remarks. 1779. 8. Tracts on inoculation. 1781. 8.

*DINMORE, [R . . . . .] *Jun.*
An exposition of the principles of the english Jacobins, with strictures on the political conduct of *Charles James Fox, William Pitt* and *Edm. Burke,* including remarks on the resignation of *G. Washington.* 1796. 8. (1 sh.)

*DINMORE, [Richard] *Surgeon at Watton in Norfolk.*
A case of monstrous birth. (London M. J. Part II. p. 339.)

*DINSDALE

INSDALE, [William] *of Hawswell, near Bedale, Yorkshire.*

Letter on improving land. (Tr. of the Soc. for the E. of A. Vol. 2. p. 55)

IROM, [. . . . .] *Lieutenant Colonel; Deputy Quarter-Master-General in North-Britain.*

Narrative of the campaign in India, which terminated the war with Tippoo Sultan in 1792. with maps and plans illustrative of the subject and a view of Seringapatam. 1793. 4. (1 L. 1 sh.) Ed. 2. 1794. 4. Published *Alexander Dirom's* (Esq. of Muiresk in the county of Aberdeen, his son): Inquiry into the corn laws and corn trade of Great-Britain and their influence on the prosperity of the kingdom. To which is added, a supplement by Mr. *William Mackie*, of Armiston in East-Lothian, bringing down the consideration of the subject to the present time; investigating the cause of the present scarcity and suggesting measures for promoting the cultivation of the waste lands and for rendering the produce equal to the increasing consumption of the kingdom. 1796. 4. (12 sh.) Ed. 2. 1802. 4. (12 sh.) Plans for the defence of Great-Britain and Ireland. 1797. 8. (2 sh. 6 d.)

IRRILL, [Charles] *Esq.*

Remarks on *Shakspeare's* tempest; containing an investigation of Mr. *Malone's* attempt to ascertain the date of that play, and various notes and illustrations of abstruse readings and passages. 1797. 8. (2 sh.)

SNEY, [John] *D. D. F. A. S. An unitarian clergyman.*

A defence of public or social worship, answer to *Gilbert Wakefield* and to *Paine's* age of reason; a sermon. 1792. 8. (6 d.) Memoirs of the life and writings of *John Jortin*, D. D. 1792. 8. (5 sh.) The progressive improvement of civil liberty, a sermon. 1792. 8. (6 d.) Letter to *Vicesimus Knox*, D. D. occasioned by his reflections on unitarian christians in his advertisement, prefixed to a volume of his sermons. 1792. 8. (1 sh.) A vindication of the apostle *Paul* from the charge of sedition, a sermon. 1792. 8. (6 d.) Sermons. Vol. 1. 2. 1793. 8. (12 sh.) The reciprocal duty of a christian ftian minifter and a chriftian congregation; a fermon. 1793. 8. (6 d.) A caution to young perfons againft infidelity; a fermon. 1796. 8. (6 d.)

*D'ISRAELI, [J.....] *Esq. A Gentleman of jewifh extraction.*

See Public Characters of 1798 and 1799. p. 488. A poetical epiftle on the abufe of fatire; 17.. A defence of poetry, — with a fpecimen of a new verfion of Telemachus; 1790. 4. (2 fh.) *Curiofities of litterature, confifting of anecdotes, characters, fketches and obfervations, litterary, critical and hiftorical; 1791. 8. (6 fh.) Ed. 3. with large additions and confiderable improvements. Vol. 1. 2. 1793. 8. (14 fh.) *A differtation on anecdotes. 1793. 8. (2 fh.) Effay on the manners and genius of the litterary character. 1795. 8. (4 fh.) Mifcellanies or litterary recreations. 1796. 8. (7 fh.) Ed. 2. enlarged. 1801. 8. (4 fh.) Vaurien, a philofophical novel. Vol. 1. 2. 1797. Romances. 1798. 8. (8 fh.) überf. Th. 1. Leipzig 1802. Ed. 2. corrected: To which is now added a modern romance. 1801. 8. (4 fh.) Narrative poems. 1803. 4. (4 fh. 6 d.)

*DIX, [Thomas] *of Oundle.*

On land-furveying in fix parts. 1799. 8.

*DIX, [William] *A. M.*

Inaugural differtation on the dropfy. Cambridge. 1795.

*DIXMERIE, [.....]

The Pyrenean hermits. (New-York Magaz. Y. 1792. July p. 433. Aug. p. 496.)

DIXON, [George] *Captain; late Commander of the Queen Charlotte, in a voyage round the world.*

Remarks on the voyages of *John Meares*, Esq. 1790. 4. (2 fh. 6 d.) Farther remarks on the voyages of *John Meares*, in which feveral important facts, mifreprefented in the faid voyages, relative to the geography and commerce, are fully fubftantiated, with Capt. *Duncan's* letter, containing a decifive refutation of feveral unfounded affertions of Mr. *Meares;* and a final reply to his anfwer. 1791. 4. (3 fh. 6 d.)

*DIXON, [John]

Letter 1-3, being a plan for the improvement of the

the fisheries in the western coasts of the united kingdom. 1802. 4.

IXON, [Joseph]

Contrivance of a preservative wheel to be fixed to a walking-wheel crane. (Tr. of the Soc. for the E. of A. Vol. 11. p. 199.)

IXON, [Joshua] *M. Dr.*

The litterary life of *William Brownrigg*, M. Dr: F. R. S. Whitehaven. 1801. 8.

BBS, [Francis] *Esq. Member for the borough of Charlemont, in Ireland.*

A concise view, from history and prophecy of the great predictions in the sacred writings that have been fulfilled also of those that are fulfilling and that remain to be accomplished. 1800. 8. (6 sh.)

OBBY, [Henry] *Yorkshire.*

On reasing potatoes from seed. (*Young's* A. of Agr. Vol. 18. p. 445.)

OBSON, [Henry] *Carpenter; of Norwich.*

Description of the model of a barn, for which a premium was granted by the society. (Bath Agricult. Soc. Vol. 3. p. 335.)

BSON, [Mary] *Mrs.*

born . . . . . died 1795. Sept.

See Gentleman's Magaz. Y. 1795. Oct. p. 881.

Petrarch's view of human life. 1791. 8. (6 sh.)

ODD, [R . . . . .] *Civil Engineer.*

A short historical account of the greater part of the principal canals in the known world; with some reflections upon the general utility of canals. 1795. 8. Reports, with plans, sections — of the proposed dry tunnel or passage from Gravesend, in Kent, to Tilbury, in Essex; demonstrating the practicability and great importance to the two counties and to the nation at large, also an canal from Gravesend to Stroud; with some miscellaneous and practical observations. Illustrated with plates. 1798. 4. (5 sh.) Letters to a merchant, on the improvement of the port of London; demonstrating its practicability without wet docks or any additional burthens laid on shipping and at a less expence of time and money than any other place proposed. 1799. Plan of the grand Surry canal. (Comm. and Agric. Magaz. Y. 1800. p. 82.)

T 4 * DODDIE,

*DODDIE, [James]
A defence of the associate synod against the charge of sedition. 1800. (1 sh.)

*DODSLEY, [James] *Esq. Bookseller.*
born 1723. died 1797. Febr. 19.
See Gentleman's Magaz. Y. 1797. March. p. 254. Apr. p. 346. Monthly Magaz. Vol. 3. 1797. p. 160.
The muse in livery. 173. The toy-shop. 1732. The oeconomy of the human life. 17.. In conjunction with his brother *Robert Dodsley*, (died Sept. 24. 1794. See Gentlemans Magaz. Vol. 34. p. 450.) Collection of poems; 17.. The preceptor &c. 17.... and commenced in 1758. the Annual Register &c.

*DODSON, [Michael] *Esq.*
born 1732. Sept. 20. died in London 1799. Nov. 13.
See Gentleman's Magaz. Y. 1799. Nov. p. 1004. Suppl. p. 1186. Monthly Magaz. Y. 1801. Jan. p. 567. Allg. Litt. Zeit. ItBl. J. 1800. S. 663. A short memoir of *Mich. Dodson*. 1801.
A report of some proceedings on the commission for the trial of the rebels in the Y. 1746. in the county of Surrey and of other crown cases; to which are added, discourses upon a few branches of the crown law, by *Justice Forster*. 1762. Ed. 2. 1776. Ed. 3. 1792. *A new translation of Isaiah; with notes supplementary to those of Dr. *Lowth*; by a Layman. 1790. 8. (5 sh.) A letter to Dr. *Sturges*, author of short remarks on a new translation of Isaiah by a Layman. 1791. 8. (1 sh.)

*DODSWORTH, [William] *Verger of the Cathedral church of Salisbury.*
A guide to the cathedral church of Salisbury with a particular account of the late great improvements made therein under the direction of *James Wyatt*, Esq. 1792.

*DODWELL, [William] *D. D. Arch-Deacon of Berks and Rector of Shottesbrooke.*
born 1710. died 1785. Oct. 19.
See Gentleman's Magaz. Y. 1785. Oct. p. 837. Nov. p. 878. Y. 1802. June p. 534. *Kippis* Biographica Britannica Vol. 5. p. 327.

The

The Athanasian creed vindicated and explained in 3 charges. (published by his son *Henry Dodwell*). 1802.

OGHERTY, [Thomas] *Esq. of Clifford's-Inn.*

The crown circuit companion — by *W. Stubbs* and *G. Talmosh;* Ed. 6. with several additions, improvements and modern references. 1790. 8. (10 sh. 6 d.) Ed. 7. 1799. 8. (10 sh. 6 d.) Historia placitorum coronae: The history of the pleas of the crown, by Sir *Matthew Hale,* — published from original MSS. by *Sollom Emlyn* — with additional notes and references to modern cases concerning the pleas of the crown by *George Wilson* — a new edition: and an abridgment of the statutes relating to felonies continued to the present time, with notes and references. Vol. 1. 2. 1800. 8. (1 L. 8 sh.)

)OIG, [David] *LL. Dr. F. S. S. A. Master of the Grammar-school, Stirling.*

Two letters on the savage state, addressed to the late Lord *Kaimes.* 1793. 8. (2 sh. 6 d.) Extract from a poem on the prospect from Stirling-castle. 1796. 4. On the ancient Hellenes. (Tr. of E. S. Vol. 3. L. p. 131.)

)OLBEARE, [Thomas]

Case of curvature of the spine. (Tr. of Phys. of Philad. Vol. 1. P. 1. p. 45.)

DONALDSON, [James]

On the husbandry of the carse of gowrie &c. (*Young's* A. of Agr. Vol. 10. p. 422.) On a new threshing machine. (Ibid. Vol. 10. p. 437.) Natural woods in Elgin, in Scotland. (Ibid. Vol. 23. p. 14.)

ONALDSON, [John] *Miniature-Painter.*

born at Edinburgh, 1737. died 1801. Oct. 11. See Gentleman's Magaz. Y. 1801. Nov. p. 1056.

'ONALDSON, [John] *Esq.*

Miscellaneous proposals for increasing our national wealth, 12 millions a year —. Ed. 2. 1795. 8. (1 sh. 6 d.) Sketch of a plan to prevent crimes. 1792. 8. (6 d.) Sketches of a plan for an effectual and general reformation of life and manners. 1794. 8. (4 sh.) Letter to the magistrates, burgesses &c. of the Roy. burghs of Scotland.

T 5 1795.

1795. 8. (6 d.) Letter to the R. H. *Will. Pitt*, on the use of hair powder. 1795. 8. (6 d.) Letter to the R. H. *Will. Pitt*, shewing how crimes may be prevented and the people made happy. 1796. 8. (1 sh.)

*DONN, [James] *Curator.*

Hortus Cantabrigiensis, or a catalogue of plants indigenous and foreign, cultivated in the Walkerian botanic garden. Cambridge. 1796. 12. Ed. 2. 1800. 8. –

DONNE, [Benjamin] *Master of mechanics to his Maj. and many years Teacher of the Mathematics and Lecturer in Philosophy at Bristol.*

born at Biddeford in the county of Devon. ..... died 1798. June .....

See Gentleman's Magaz. Y. 1798. July p. 632. Monthly Magaz. Y. 1798. July p. 76. Allgem. Litterat. Zeit. ItBl. J. 1800. S. 655.

Map of Devonshire, in 12 sheets. 1765. A map of the country 11 miles round Bristol, from an actual survey, in 2 sheets and 2½ sheets. 1770. Essays on trigonometry. 1777. 8.

*DONOGHUE, [J.....]

Juvenile essays in poetry. 1797. 8. (1 sh. 6 d.)

*DONOVAN, [E.....] *F. L. S.*

The natural history of British birds and insects, explaining them in their several states, with the periods of their transformations, their food, oeconomy &c. together with the history of such minute insects as require investigation by the microscope. The whole illustrated by coloured figures, designed and executed from living specimens. Nro. 1-26. 1792–1795. 8. Instructions for collecting and preserving various subjects of natural history; as animal, birds, reptiles, shells, corals, plants with a treatise on the management of insects in their several states — 1794. 8. (4 sh. 6 d.) übers. mit Abänderungen u. Zusätzen von Dr. *J. J. Römer*. Zurich. 1797. 8. The natural history of British birds — &c. Vol. 1–5. 1794–1798. 8. (7 L. 10 sh.) The natural history of the insects of China — 1799. 4. (3 L.) An epitome of the natural history of the insects of China, comprising figures and descriptions of upwards of one hundred

hundred new, fingular and beautiful fpecies. Nrb. 1-7. 1800-1802. 4. (4 L. 4 fh.) überf. von *J. G. Gruber.* Heft 1. 2. Leipzig. 1802. 1803. The natural hiftory of Britifh fifhes. Nrb. 1. 1802. (3 fh. 6 d.)

ONOUGHUE, [A.....]
An effay on the paffions; with other poems. 1799. 8. (3 fh.)

OO, [Thomas] *at Bypar-Baldok, Hertfordfhire.*
Crops in Hertfordfhire. (*Young's* A. of Agr. Vol. 35. p. 44.)

ORE, [James] *A baptift Minifter.*
Letters on faith. 1786. 12. (1 fh. 6 d.) Sermon on the African flave trade. 1788. 8. (6 d.) Sermon by the death of Mr. *John Flight* 1791. 8. (6 d.) The principles of antipaedobaptifm and the practice of female communion completely confiftent: In anfwer to the arguments and objections of, Mr. *Peter Edwards* in his candid reafons; with animadverfions on his temper and conduct in that publication. 1795. 12. (1 fh. 6 d.) An effay on the refurrection of Chrift, in which proofs of the fact are adduced, its import is explained and its beneficial influence illuftrated. 1797. 12. (1 fh.)

ORNFORD, [Jofiah] *Esq. of Lincolns-Inn. M. A. of Oxford, LL. D. of the Univerfity of Gottingen. — Barrifter at Law. Commiffary of accounts to the army in the Leeward Islands.*
born 1763. died at Martinique July 1. 1797.
See Gentleman's Magaz. Y. 1797. Sept. p. 800. Allg. Litt. Zeit. ItBl. J. 1800. S. 646.
Aufpiciis Ernefti-Augufti, Augufti-Friederici, Adolphi-Friederici, M. Britan. Regis Aug. fobolis fauftiff. juvent. Princ. Gottingae, 1790. 8. Prolufiones nonnullae Academicae, nomine univerfitatis Georgiae-Auguftae Gottingenfis fcriptae a C. G. *Heyne*, nunc primum uno volumine editae. 1790. * The motives and confequences of the prefent war impartially confidered. 1793. 8.

DORSET, [......] *Esq. Officer in the army.*
Effay on defenfive war: 17.. The philofophic venus and condolence, an elegiac poem: 17..

*DOR-

*DORTHES, [.....] *F. M. L. S.*
Obfervations on the ftructure and oeconomy of fome curious fpecies of aranea. (Transact. of L. S. Vol. 2. p. 86.)

*DOUCE, [Francis] *Esq.*
Some remarks on the European names of chefs-men. (Arch. Vol. XI. p. 397.) Obfervations on a calendar in his poffeffion.. (Ibid. Vol. XII. p. 200.) Illuftration of the reliefs at Thorpe Salvin. (Ibid. Vol. XII. p. 209.) Obfervations on certain ornaments of female drefs. (Ibid. Vol. XII. p. 215.)

*DOVE, [William] *Surgeon at Thorne in Yorkfhire.*
Hiftory of a cafe of anafarca, cured by the infufion of tobacco. (*Duncan's* M. C. Dec. 2. Vol. 8. p. 379.)

*DOUGLAS, [.....] *Surgeon.*
Cafe of enlarged ftomach, attended with peculiar fymptoms. (Mem. of M. S. of L. Vol. 4. p. 395.)

DOUGLAS, [Andrew] *M. Dr. at London.*
Andrew Douglas and *Archibald Douglas*, are the fame perfon: His chriftian name having been erroneously printed *Archibald* in the Med. Obferv. Vol. 6. p. 163.)

DOUGLAS, [Sir Charles] *Baronet, Rear-Admiral of the blue fquadron in the Royal Navy. F. R. S.* born ..... died 1789.

DOUGLAS, [James] *Rev. F. A. S: of St. Peter's College, Cambridge; Chaplain in ordinary to his R. H. the Prince of Wales.*
Nenia Britannica — 1786-1793. fol. (3 L. 13 fh. 6 d.) Difcourfes on the influence of the chriftian religion in civil fociety. 1792. 8. (5 fh.)

*DOUGLAS, [Niel] *Minifter of the gofpel at Cupar in Fife.*
Sermons on important fubjects, with fome effays in poetry. 1791. 8. (3 fh.) Journal of a miffion to the highlands of Scotland in 1797. by appointment of the relief fynod —. 1799. (1 fh.)

DOUGLAS, [Robert] *D. D. Minifter of Galafhiels.*
A general view of Roxburgh and Selkirk. 1802. 8.

DOUGLAS, [Sylvefter] *of Lincolns-Inn.*
Speech in the houfe of commons, Apr. 22. 1799. on feconding the motion — to an union with Ireland. 1799. 8. (3 fh. 6 d.)

*DOWLING,

DOWLING, [Edward]
The elements and theory of the hebrew language. 1797. 8. (7 sh.)

DOWNING, [J.....]
On the disorders incident to horned cattle, to which are added receipts for curing the gripes, staggers and worms in horses and an appendix containing instructions for the extracting of calves. 1797. 8. (10 sh. 6 d.)

DOWNING, [John] *Captain in the Roy. Regt. of Artillery.*
The case of Capt. *Downing*, with the proceedings of a general court martial and copies of letters to and from the Duke of *Richmond* Sir *Charles Morgan*; — with the opinion of counsel concerning the legality of the trial. 1796. 8. (1 sh.)

DOWNMANN, [Hugh] *M.Dr. Physician of Exeter.*
Infancy, or the management of children, a didactic poem in 6 books. Ed. 5. 1790. 8. (4 sh.) Ed. 6. 1803. 8. (10 sh. 6 d.) Poems. Ed. 2. 1790. 8. (4 sh.) Tragedies. 1792. 8. (3 sh. 6 d.)

D'OYLY, [Catherine] *Mrs.*
The history of the life and death of our blessed saviour. 1794. 8. (9 sh.) Ed. 2. 1798. 8. (7 sh. 6 d.)

DRAKE, [Nathan] *M. Dr.*
Poems. 1793. 4. (5 sh.) Literary hours, or sketches critical and narrative. 1798. 8. (10 sh. 6 d.) Ed. 2. Vol. 1. 2. corrected and greatly enlarged. 1800. 8.

DRAKE, [William] *M. A: F. A. S: Rector at Islaworth, Middlesex.*
born 1721. died 1801. May. 13.
See Gentleman's Magaz. Y. 1801. June p. 574.

*DRALET, [.....]
Account of a method of clearing ground from moles, which is succesfully practised in France: translated from the french. (Comm. and Agric. Magaz. Y. 1802. March. p. 172.)

*DRALLOC, [N.....]
The life and extraordinary adventures of *James Molesworth Hobart*, alias *Henry Griffin*, alias Lord

Lord *Massey*, the New-Market Duke of *Ormond* &c. involving a number of well known characters, together with a short sketch of the early part of the life of Doctor Torquid. Vol. 1. 2. 1794. 8. (6 sh.) An epitome of logic, in four parts. 1795. 12. (3 sh. 6 d.)

*DRAPER, [Eliza] *Mrs.*
Elegant letter. (Massachusetts Magaz. Y. 1793. Jan. p. 21.)

*DRAPER, [William] *Lecturer of Allhallows, London-Wall and late Curate of the new church Wolverhampton.*
A probationary sermon. 1791. 8. (1 sh.) Twenty sermons on various subjects. 1796. 8. (6 sh.)

*DRENNAN, [William] *M. Dr. Physician in Dublin.*
Letter to — Earl *Fitzwilliam*, Lord Lieut. — of Ireland. 1795. 8. (1 sh. 6 d.) Letter 1. 2. to the R. H. *Will. Pitt.* 1799. 8. (1 sh.) Strictures on *Edm. Burke.* (Monthly Magaz. Y. 1799. Sept. p. 595.) On the yellow fever. (Ibid. Y. 1799. Dec. p. 849.) Letter on the yellow fever. (*Duncan's* A. of Med. Y. 1800. p. 349.)

*DREW, [S.....]
On the immateriality and immortality of the human soul, founded solely on physical and rational principles. Bristol. Ed. 2. 1803. (7 sh.) Remarks on the first part of *Thomas Paine* age of reason. Ed. 2. 1803.

*DREWITT, [......] *of Chedder.*
*Why are you a churchman? a plain question answered, in a dialogue between Mr. *Fitz-Adam* and *John Oakley.* 1799. 12. (4 d.)

*DREWITT, [Thomas] *Rev.*
Illustrations of falsehoods contained in Mr. *Spencer's* late publication (Truths respecting Mrs. *Hannah More's* meeting houses — — &c.) 1801. 8. (4 d.)

*DRIVER, [A.....]
— — and *W. Driver's* remarks on waste lands in Hampshire. (Bath Agric. Soc. Vol. 8. p. 144.)

*DROUGHT, [Robert] *Rev.*
Select odes of *Anacreon*, with critical annotations. To which are added translations and imitations of other

other ancient authors; by the late Rev. *Hercules Younge* and publiſhed by *Rob. Draught.* 1802. 12. (3 ſh. 6 d.)

***DRUMMOND**, [.....]

— — and *Bromley*, Jobi or the hiſtory of three fingered jack. 1800. (4 ſh.)

***DRUMMOND**, [George]

Letter on larches. (Tr. of the Soc. for the E. of A. Vol. 7. p. 46.)

***DRUMMOND**, [George Hay]

Verſes ſocial and domeſtic. 1802. 12.

***DRUMMOND**, [J.....] *Surgeon in the Service of the Eaſt India Company.*

Obſervations reſpecting the Guinea worm. (*Duncan's* M. C. Dec. 2. Vol. 8. p. 294.)

***DRUMMOND**, [Pet. A.... H....]

A ſubſtitute for red clover. (*Young's* A. of Agr. Vol. 24. p. 533.)

***DRUMMOND**, [William] *Esq. M. P.*

A review of the governments of Sparta and Athen. 1794. 8. (6 ſh.) The ſatires of *Perſius*, translated. 1798. 8. (4 ſh.)

DRURY, [Obrien] *Captain.*

Obſervations on the magnetic fluid. (New-York Magaz. Y. 1796. Jan. p. 27.)

***DRYDEN**, [John] *Jun. Esq.*

Flagellation of the whigs, a poem, in imitation of the firſt ſatire of *Juvenal.* 1792. 4. (2 ſh. 6 d.)

***DRYSDALE**, [John] *D. D. F. R. S. Edinb. One of the Miniſters of Edinb. One of his Maj. Chaplain's and principal Clerk to the church of Scotland.*

born at Kirkaldy in the county of Fife 1718. April 29. died 1788. June 16.

See Gentleman's Magaz. Y. 1788. June p. 565. Monthly Rev. Y. 1793. May. p. 11.

Sermons by the late *John Drysdale* D. D. To which is prefixed an account of the author's life and character, publiſhed by *Andrew Dalzel.* Vol. 1. 2. 1793. 8. (12 ſh.) überſ. Th. 1. 2. Wien. 1796. 8.

***DRYSDALE**, [William]

The ſacred ſcripture theory of the earth. New-Caſtle. 1798. 8.

*DU

*DU BOIS, [Edward]
The wreath, composed of selections from *Sappho, Theocritus, Bion* and *Moschus*; accompanied by a prose translation, with notes. To which are added remarks on *Shakespeare* &c. and a comparison between *Horace* and *Lucian*. 1799. 8. (6 sh.)

DUCHE, [Jacob] *Preacher at Bow church in Cheapside.*
*Observations on a variety of subjects, literary, moral and religious —. Ed. 3. 1791. 8. (3 sh 6 d.)
Sermons. Vol. 1. 2. 17.. 8.
(Several single sermons.)

*DUCKET, [Mark] *Jun.*
Account of his hand-hoe. (Comm. to the B. of Agr. Vol. 2. p. 424.)

*DUDGEON, [Robert] *of Tynningham.*
Account of culture of beans and wheat. (Tr. of the Soc. for the E. of A. Vol. 17. p. 144.)

DUDLEY, [Henry Bate] *Justice of the peace for the County of Essex.*
(Editor of the morning Herald.) The woodman, a comic opera; the music composed by *W. Shield.* 1791. 8. (10 sh. 6 d.) The travellers in Switzerland, a comic opera. 1793. 8. (1 sh. 6 d.) A few observations on the present state of the poor and the defects of the poor laws, with some remarks upon parochial assessments and expenditures. 1802. 8. (1 sh. 6 d.) Letter on gaining land from the sea. (Tr. of the Soc. for the E. of A. Vol. 6. p. 57.)

*DUDLEY, [Thomas] See *Fosbrooke.*

*DUFFIELD, [Benjamin] *M. Dr: Fellow of the College of Physicians of Philadelphia.*
Case of inverted uterus. (Tr. of Phys. of Philad. Vol. 1. P. 1. p. 167.)

*DUFOUR, [.....]
On diseases in the urinary passages — to which are added some new observations on the venereal disease. 1795. 8. (1 sh.)

*DUFOUR, [Alexander] *Architect.*
Letter to the nobility and gentry composing the committee for raising the naval pillar or monument — in answer to the letter of *John Flaxman*, Sculptor. 1799. 4. (1 sh. 6 d.)

DUGUD,

GUD, [Patrick] *Physician at Durham.*
born 1751. died at Lisbon 1783. March. 12.
(He afterward. added to his name that of *Leslie*: See *Patrick Dugud Leslie*; *Reuss* G. E. p. 118 and 239.)

IGENAN, [Patrick] *Esq. LL. Dr. One of the Representatives of the city of Armagh in Parliament.*
See Public Characters of 1799 and 1800. p. 232. Lachrymae academicae; 17... The speeches of him and of Sir *Thomas Osborne*, Bart. on the catholic bill in the Irish house of commons. 1795. 8. (1 sh.) An answer to the address of the R. H. *Henry Grattan* to his fellow-citizens of Dublin. 1797. A fair representation of the present political state of Ireland in a course of strictures on two pamphlets, one entitled „the case of Ireland reconsidered,„ the other, „considerations on the state of public affairs in 1799 — Ireland; particularly on a pamphlet entitled, „ the speech of Lord *Minto* in the house of peers. 1799. 8. (4 sh. 6 d.) Speech on the subject of an incorporating union between Great-Britain and Ireland. 1800. 8. (1 sh. 6 d.) Speech in the Irish house of commons Febr. 5. 1800. on the motion for approving his Maj. conduct in declining the negotiation with the french government. 1800. (1 sh. 6 d.)

UMMER, [Jeremy]
Defence of the new England charters. 17.. 8. (½ Dollar.)

N, [John] *Minister at Auchinleck, Ayrshire.*
born 1722. died 1792. Oct. 11.
See Gentleman's Magaz. Y. 1792. Oct. p. 965.

NBAR, [James] *LL. Dr. Professor of Moral Philosophy in the University of Aberdeen.*
born ..... died 1798. May. 28.
See Gentleman's Magaz. Y. 1798. June. p. 539. Jul. p. 622.

UNCAN, [......]
Letter to Sir *Walter Farquhar*, Bart. on the subject of a particular affection of the bowels very frequent and fatal in the East-Indies. 1802. 8. (2 sh.)

*DUNCAN, [Alexander] *D. D. Vicar of Belam, Northumberland, Chaplain of his Maj. ship Venerable — and now of his Maj. ship Kent of 74 guns, Lord Duncan's flag ship.*
Miscellaneous essays, naval, moral, political and divine. 1799. 8. (3 sh.)

*DUNCAN, [Alexander] *D. D. Minister of Smalholm.*
History of the revolution 1688. giving an account of the manner in which it was accomplished and its happy effects, particularly to the kingdom and church of Scotland. 1790. 8. The devout communicant's assistant, or, the nature and end of the Lord's supper explained and the obligations to partake of it considered. 1792. 12. (1 sh.)

DUNCAN, [Andrew] *Sen. M. Dr. F. R. and A. S. Edin. Professor of the theory of Medicine in the University of Edinburgh.*
Medical commentaries for the year 1790. (6 sh.) 1791. (6 sh.) 1792. (6 sh.) 1793. (6 sh.) 1794. (6 sh.) 1795. (7 sh.) 8. Annals of Medicine for the Y. 1796. 8. (7 sh.) Y. 1797. (6 sh.) Y. 1798. (6 sh.) Y. 1799. (8 sh.) Y. 1800. (8 sh.) Y. 1801. (8 sh.) Y. 1802. (8 sh.) Account of Sir *Alex. Dick*, Bart. of Prestonfield, late President of the Roy. College of Physic. of Edinb. and F. R. S. Edin (Tr. of E. S. Vol. 2. App. p. 58.) Heads of lectures on the institutions of medicine. Ed. 5. 1801. 8.

*DUNCAN, [Andrew] *Jun. M. Dr.*
Tentamen inaugurale de Swietenia Soymida. Edinb. 1794. 8.

DUNCAN, [John] *D. D. Rector of South Warmborough, Hants.*
Two discourses, tending to assuage the animosity of party spirit in religion and to explore the merciful designs of providence, in the permission of the worst offences. 1792. 8. (1 sh. 6 d.) The condemnation pronounced against all mere pretences of religion; a sermon. 1769. Ed. 2. 1791. 8. (1 sh.) The libertine and infidel led to reflection, by calm expostulation. 1799. 8. (6 sh.)
(Several single sermons.)

*DUNCAN,

'DUNCAN, [John] *D. D. A methodist minister at Winton, in Dorsetshire.*

Theatrical amusements. 17..

'DUNCAN, [Jonathan] *Esq.*

Historical remarks on the coast of Malabar with some description of the manners of its inhabitants. (Asiat. Res. Vol. 5. p. 1.) An account of two fakeers, with their portraits. (Ibid. Vol. 5. p. 37.) An account of the discovery of two urns in the vicinity of Benares. (Ibid. Vol. 5. p. 131.)

'DUNDAS, [Henry] *Right Honourable. Secretary of the state for the war Department &c.*

See Public Characters of 1798 and 1799. p. 216. Heads of his speech in the house of Commons Febr. 25. 1793. on stating the affairs of the East-India Company with an appendix of estimates. 1793. 8. (3 sh.) Substance of his speech on the British government and trade in the East-Indies Apr. 23. 1793. 4. Speech — 15 March 1796. on the farther consideration of the report of the committee upon the bill for the abolition of the slave-trade, with a copy of the bill. 1796. 8. (1 sh.) Substance of his speech — in the house of Commons Febr. 7. 1799. on the subject of the legislative union with Ireland. 1799. 8. (1 sh.) Substance of his speeches — on his Maj. message for declining to treat at present with France and his objections to an inquiry into the late expedition to Holland. With a preface, touching briefly on the state of public affairs. 1799. 8. (2 sh.) Substance of his speech — on Mr. *Grey's* motion for an inquiry into the state of the nation — 1801. 8. (1 sh. 6 d.) Letter to the court of Directors of the East-India Company, on the Indian debt. June 30. 1801. with official documents. 1801. (5 sh.)

DUNDONALD, [Archibald] Earl of (His family name is *Cochran.*)

A treatise shewing the intimate connection that subsists between agriculture and chemistry. — 1795. 4. (1 L. 1 sh.) Directions for extracting gum from the lichen, or tree moss &c. (*Nicholson's* Journal. Vol. 5. p. 228.) The principles

U 2 of

of chemistry, applied to the improvement of the practice of agriculture. 1799. 4. (10 sh. 6 d.) On potatoes. (*Young's* A. of Agr. Vol. 24. p. 514.)

***DUNLAP, [J.....] D. D.**

The lord of nile, an elegy. 1799. 4.

***DUNLAP, [William]**

Tell the truth and shame the devil, a comedy in 2 acts. 1797. 8. The archers or mountaineers of Switzerland, an opera in 3 acts. 1797. 8. Pizarro, or the death of Rollo, with notes marking the variations from the original. New-York. 1800. First idyl of *Gesner*, translated from the german. (New-York Magaz. Y. 1796. Jan. p. 49.)

***DUNMORE, [R.....] Jun.**

An exposition of the principles of the english Jacobins. 1796. 8. (1 sh.)

***DUNN, [.....]**

Strictures on peace; The englishman and reformer, a dialogue. 1796. 8. (1 sh.)

***DUNN, [Edward]**

The investigator, or universal criterion of knowledge, explaining the mysterious phaenomena of nature, from the commencement to the conclusion of time. Numb. 1: 1797. 8. (1 sh.) The existence of God, in three persons philosophically proved, with the manner by which they influence each other and also mankind, submitted to the consideration of jews, christians, deists — 1799. 8. (3 d.) The diurnal and annual motions of the world philosophically accounted for; with the causes of the variation of time — necessary for the perusal of astronomers. 1799. 12. (4 d.)

***DUNN, [Samuel] Esq.**

Letter on potatoes. (Tr. of the Soc. for the E. of A. Vol. 9. p. 38.)

***DUNNING, [John] Esq.**

Directions to a student of law. (Columbian Magaz. Y. 1791. Aug. p. 81. New-York Magaz. Y. 1792. April, p. 233.)

*DUN-

DUNNING, [Richard] *Surgeon, at Plymouth-Dock.*
Some obſervations on vaccination or the inoculated cow-pox, with a view to determine the queſtion of puſtules. 1800. 8. (2 ſh. 6 d.)

DUNSCOMBE, [T....]
The tribute of affection to the memory of the late Dr. *Evans*, a diſcourſe — to which is added Dr. *Evans* advice to the ſtudents written and addreſſed to them in the Y. 1770. 1792. 8. (1 ſh.)

DUNSFORD, [Martin] *Merchant.*
Hiſtorical memoirs of the town and pariſh of Tiverton in the county of Devon, collected from the beſt authorities, with notes and obſervations. 1790. 4. (12 ſh. 6 d.)

DE DUNSTANVILLE, [......] *Lord.*
Account of a fat ox. (*Young's* A. of Agr. Vol. 33. p. 636.) Crops and prices. (Ib. Vol. 34. p. 263.) Proviſion for the poor. (Ibid. Vol. 34. p. 264.) Queries on the ſtate of poors, crops and prices, with the anſwers from various countries (Ibid. Vol. 34. p. 266. 594-617. 635-660. Vol. 35. p. 1-22.) Crops in Cornwall. (Ibid. Vol. 36. p. 106.)

DUNSTER, [Charles] *M. A.*
Cider, a poem, in two books by *John Philips*; with notes provincial, hiſtorical and claſſical; 1791. 8. (4 ſh.) Paradiſe regained, a poem in 4 books, by *John Milton*, with notes of various authors. 1795. 4. (18 ſh.) Conſiderations on *Milton's* early reading and the prima ſtamina of his „paradiſe loſt,„ together with extracts from a poet of the XVI century in a letter to *Will. Falconer*, M. D. 1800. 8. (5 ſh.) On apple trees. (*Young's* A. of Agr. Vol. 33. p. 1.)

DUPPA, [Richard]
A journal of the moſt remarkable occurrences that took place in Rome, upon the ſubverſion of the eccleſiaſtical government in 1798. 1799. 8. (4 ſh.) Ed. 2. 1799. 8. (7 ſh.)

DUQUERY, [Henry] *Esq.*
Speech in the houſe of Commons in Ireland the 22 Jan. 1795. on the addreſs to the King, on propoſing

U 2 poſing

on the genuineness and authenticity of the new testament. 1794. The true means of establishing public happiness, a sermon. 1795. The nature and danger of infidel philosophy in two discourses. 1799. (1 sh. 6 d.) The friend. (American Museum Y. 1789. Jan. p. 69. March p. 220. May p. 445. June p. 564. Aug. p. 154. Oct. p. 283.) Reflexions on second marriages of men — ; (Ibid. Y. 1789. Dec. p. 437.) Essay on taste. (Ibid. Y. 1791. July p. 52.)

*DWYER, [P.... W.....]
The shield of the united kingdom of Great-Britain and Ireland, a poem. 1803. 4. (2 sh. 6 d.)

*DYDE, [W.....] *Printer of Tewkesbury.*
The history and antiquities of Tewkesbury from the earliest periods to the present time — with account of the medicinal water near Tewkesbury. 1790. 8. (3 sh.) Ed. 2. with considerable additions and corrections. 1798. 8. (6 sh.)

*DYER, [George] *Esq. A. B. late of Emanuel College, Cambridge; now a Member of Clifford's-Inn.*
See Public Characters of 1798 and 1799. p. 480. Enquiry into the nature of subscription to the 39 articles 1790. Ed. 2. 1792. 8. (6 sh. 6 d.) Poems. 1792. 4. (3 sh.) The complaints of the poor people of England — Part 1-4. Ed. 2. 1793. 8. (2 sh.) Slavery and famine; punishment for sedition; or an account of New South Wales and of the miserable state of the convicts, by *George Thompson*, who sailed in the Roy. Admiral, May 1792. with some preliminary remarks; and a sketch of the character of *Thomas Fysche Palmer* B. D. late senior fellow of Queen's College, Cambridge. 1794. 8. (2 sh.) Dissertation on the theory and practice of benevolence. 1795. 8. (2 sh.) Memoirs of the life and writings of *Robert Robinson*, late Minister of the dissenting congregation in St. Andrew's Parish, Cambridge. 1796. 8. (8 sh.) übers. von *Ludw. Theobul Kosegarten*. Leipzig. 1800. 8. The poet's fate, a poetical dialogue. 1797. 8. (1 sh. 6 d.) An english prologue and epilogue to the latin comedy of ignoramus, written by *George Ruggle*, formerly fellow of Clare-Hall, Cambridge, and performed by members

bers of the University, before King James in 1614 and 1615, with notes — 1797. 8. (1 sh. 6 d.) An address to the people of Great-Britain on the doctrine of libels and the office of jurors. 1799. (2 sh. 6 d.) Poems and critical essays on various branches of poetry. Vol. 1; 2. 1802. 8. (10 sh. 6 d.) On english versification. (Monthly Magazin Y. 1798. Febr. p. 114. April p. 260.) On coins. (Ibid. Supplem. to Vol. 5. p. 542.) On the peculiarities of the quackers. (Ibid. Y. 1798. Nov. p. 341.) On *Robinson's* translation of *Claude*. (Ibid. Y. 1799. Sept. p. 621.) On the word dramatic. (Ibid. Y. 1800. Febr. p. 8.) On *ισοψηφα*, a singular kind of verse in the greek anthologia. (Ibid. Y. 1800. Sept. p. 134. Y. 1801. May. p. 318.) On greek pronunciation. (Ibid. Y. 1801. Jan. p. 496.)

DYSON, [R..... R.....]
See *H. G. Oldfield*.

DYSON, [Theophilus] *Surgeon*.
Extract from a description and dissection of a diseased spermatic vein. (Mem. of M. S. of London. Vol. 3. p. 556.) A case of ulceration of the larynx and superior part of the trachea. (Ibid. Vol. 4. p. 390.)

EADON, [John] *Teacher of the Mathematics in the free writing and grammar schools, Sheffield.*
Arithmetician's guide; 17.. The arithmetical and mathematical repository, being a new improved system of practical arithmetic, in all its branches, designed for the use of schools, academies, counting-houses. — Vol. 1. 1793. 8. (6 sh. 6 d.)

EAGER, [Richard] *of Grafham farm, near Guildford, Surry.*
Explanation of the cut of his instrument for relieving hoven cattle. (Tr. of the Soc. for the E. of A. Vol. 14. p. 242. 249.)

EARLE, [James] *Esq. F. R. S. Surgeon extraordinary to his Majesty's Household and Senior Surgeon to St. Bartholomew's Hospital.*
The chirurgical works of *Percival Pott's*: To which are added, a short account of the life of the author; a method of curing the hydrocele by injection and occasional notes and observations. Vol. 1-3. 1790. 8. (1 L. 1 sh.) On the hydrocele

U 5

cele — with the radical cure. 1791. 8. Appendix. 1793. 8. (6 d.) übers. Leipzig. 1794. 8. Practical observations on the operation for the stone. 1793. 8. (4 sh.) Observations on the cure of the curved spine, in which the effect of mechanical assistance is considered; also an essay on the means of lessening the effects of fire on the human body. 1799. 8. (4 sh.) An account of a new mode of operation for the removal of the opacity in the eye, called cataract. 1801. 8. (3 sh.)

*EARLE, [John] *Rever.*
Remarks on the prefaces prefixed to the 1 and 2 volumes of a work entitled, the holy bible or books accounted sacred by jews and christians, faithfully translated by *Alex. Geddes*, LL. D. in 4 letters addressed to him. 1799. 12. (2 sh.)

*EARLE, [William] *Jun.*
Natural faults, a comedy. 17... The welshman, a romance. Vol. 1-4. 1801. 12. (16 sh.)

*EARNSHAW, [C.....]
The wreath: or, miscellaneous poetical gleanings; including originals from respectable sources. 1801. 8. (4 sh. 6 d.)

EASON, [Alexander] *M. Dr. Physician in Manchester,* born .... died at Manchester 1796 May 2.
See Gentleman's Magaz. Y. 1796. June. p. 527.
Duncan's Annals of Medicine Y. 1796. p. 424.
On the uses of acids in bleaching of linen. (American Museum Y. 1789. March. p. 226.)

EAST, [Edward Hyde] *Esq. of the Inner-Temple: Barrister at Law.*
See *Charles Durnford*.
Reports of cases argued and determined in the court of King's bench with tables of the names of cases and principal matters. Vol. 1. containing the cases in the forty first year of George 3. Y. 1800-1801. 1801. 8. (1 L. 3 sh. 6 d.) Vol. 2. P. 1. 2. 1802. 8. (1 L. 2 sh. 6 d.) Vol. 3. P. 1. 2. 1803. 8. (1 L. 2 sh. 6 d.) A treatise on the pleas of the crown. Vol. 1. 2. 1803. 8. (1 L. 18 sh.)

*EAST,

:AST, [Hinton]

Account of cinnamon. (Tr. of the Soc. for the E. of A. Vol. 9. p. 193.)

'ASTCOTT, [Richard] *Rev. of Exeter.*

Sketches of the origin, progrefs and effects of mufic, with an account of the antient bards and minftrels. 1793. 8. (5 fh.)

ASTON, [James] *Esq. Juftice of the peace and Alderman of Salisbury.*

born 1723. died at Salisbury 1799. Dec. 21. See Gentleman's Magaz. Y. 1800. Jan. p. 84. Allg. Litt. Zeit. ItBl. J. 1800. p. 1802.

Human longevity or the records of 1712 perfons, who attained a century and upwards, from A. D. 1666 to 1799, comprifing a period of upwards 1733 years, with anecdotes of the moft remarkable. 1799.

ATON, [. . . . .] *Formerly Conful at Baffora.*

Account of the Arabian mode of curing fractured limbs. (*Duncan's* M. C. Dec. 2. Vol. 9. p. 292.)

ATON, [David]

Scripture the only guide to religious truth: a narrative of the proceedings of the fociety of baptifts in York, in relinquifhing the popular fyftems of religion, from the ftudy of the fcriptures. 1800. 8. (2 fh.) Letters to *John Graham* in anfwer to his defence of fcripture doctrines as underftood by the church of England and in vindication of a narrative of the proceedings of a fociety of baptifts in York, in relinquifhing popular fyftems of religion. 1801. 8. (3 fh.)

ATON, [Samuel]

On the woollen, cotton and filk manufactures. (*Young's* A. of Agr. Vol. 10. p. 440.)

:CCLESTON, [Thomas] *Esq. of Scaresbrick-Caftle, near Ormfkirk, Lancafhire.*

Improvement of a bog, with obfervat. by *A. Young*. (*Young's* A. of Agr. Vol. 6. p. 1.) Account of Martin meer, formerly a large pool or lake of frefh water. (Tr. of the Soc. for the E. of A. Vol. 7. p. 51-77.) Defcription of his invented augre or peat-borer, for draining boggy land. (*Young's*

(*Young's* A. of Agr. Vol. 19. p. 165.) Remarkable culture of potatoes. (Ibid. Vol. 37. p. 87.)

*EDDIS, [William] *Late Surveyor of the customs &c. at Annapolis in Maryland.*
Letters from America, historical and descriptive, comprising occurrences from 1769 to 1777 inclusive. 1792. 8. (7 sh. 6 d.)

*EDDY, [J.....] *M. S. D.*
Plain and useful instructions for the relief and cure of ruptures. 1800.

EDEN, [William] Lord AUCKLAND. *LL. Dr. F. R. S. Privy-Counsellor in Ireland and Auditor and Director of Greenwich-Hospital.*
See Public Characters of 1802 and 1803. p. 1.
*Some remarks on the apparent circumstances of the war in the 4 week of October 1795. 1795. 8. (1 sh. 6 d.) uberf. Hamburg. 1795. 8. The substance of his speech — the 2 May 1796 on the occasion of a motion made by the Marquis of Lansdown. 1796. 8. (1 sh.) The substance of his speech — the 8 Jan. 1799. in the house of peers on the 3 reading of the bill for granting certain duties upon income. 1799. 8. (1 sh.) The substance of his speach — in the house of peers, April 11. 1799. — on the proposed addrefs to his Maj. respecting the resolutions adopted by the two houses of parliament as the basis of an union between Great-Britain and Ireland. 1799. 8. (1 sh.) Substance of his speeches in the house of Lords May 16 and 23. 1800. in support of the bill for the punishment and more effectual prevention of the crime of adultery. 1800. 8. (1 sh.) Discourse on banishment. (See History of New Holland from its discovery in 1616 to the present time. 1787. 8.) A comparative view of certain public circumstances in the respective periods of 1783. 1784 and 1785. 1796. (*Young's* A. of Agr. Vol. 26. p. 487.)

*EDEN, [Sir Frederik Morton] *Bart. His Majesty's Envoy at the Court of Vienna.*
The state of the poor: or an history of the labouring classes in England from the conquest to the present period —. Vol. 1-3. 1797. 4. (3 L. 3 sh.)

5 sh.) Porto-Bello, or a plan for the improvement of the port and city of London, illustrated by 4 plates. 1798. 8. (2 sh 6 d.) An estimate of the number of inhabitants in Great-Britain and Ireland. 1801. 8. (2 sh. 6 d.) Observations on friendly societies, for the mainteuance of the industrious classes, during sicknets, infirmity, old age and other exigencies. 1801. 8. (1 sh.) Eight letters on the peace and on the commerce and manufactures of Great-Britain. 1802. 8. (3 sh. 6 d.) State of the poor in the town ship of Headingley. (*Young's* A. of Agr. Vol. 28. p. 246.) Of the diet, dress, fuel and habitation of the labouring classes. (Ibid. Vol. 28. p. 449.) Soup for the poor. (Ibid. Vol. 28. p. 581.) State of the poor at different periods. (Ibid. Vol. 29. p. 5.) Parochial guilds. (Ibid. Vol. 29. p. 105.) Employment of the poor at Shrewsbury house of industry. (Ib. Vol. 34. p. 571.)

DGEWORTH, [Henry] *Esq. at Edgeworths town in the County of Longford in Ireland.*

An abstract of observations of the weather of 1798. (Tr. of J. A. Vol. 7. p. 317.)

DGEWORTH, [Marie]

(*Pictet* lettre sur *Marie Edgeworth* et de sa famille; See Decade Philosophique &c. An. X. Trim. 2. p. 489. — *Pictet* Voyage en Angleterre — &c. à Geneve. 1802. p. 184.) Letters for literary ladies; 17.. The parent's assistant; 17.. Practical education. 1798. 4. (1 L. 10 sh.) übers. von *G. W.* Th 1. Göttingen. 1803. 8. Belinda; Vol. 1-3. 1801. 8. (16 sh. 6 d.) übers. Th. 1. Leipzig. 1803. 8. Early lessons. P. 1. 2. Harry and Lucy; P. 3-5. Rosamond P. 6-10. Frank. 1801. 24. (5 sh. 6 d.) Castle Rackrent; 17.. Three stories for young children. 1802. 24. (6 d.) — and *Richard Lovell Edgeworth* essay on Irish bulls. 1803. 8. (5 sh.) Moral tales for young people. Vol. 1-5. 1802. 12. (15 sh. 6 d.)

GEWORTH, [Richard Lovell] *Esq. F. R. S. and M. R. J. A.*

Letter on the telegraph and on the defence of Ireland. 1796. 8. (1 sh.) Poetry explained, for the

*EDWARDS, [Edward] *M. A. Vicar of Llanarmon in Yall and Curate of Wraxham in the Diocese of St. Asaph.*

Browne Willis's (died 1760.) survey of St. Asaph considerably enlarged and brought down to the present time — with the life of the author prefixed. Vol. 1. 2. 1802. 8. (18 sh.)

*EDWARDS, [Edward] *Associate and Teacher of Perspective in the Roy. Acad.*

A practical treatise on perspective, on the principles of Dr. *Brooke Taylor.* 1803. 4. (1 L. 16 sh.)

*EDWARDS, [Enoch]

Introduction to a charge delivered to a grand jury for the county of Philadelphia, March 7. 1791. (Columbian Magaz. Y. 1791. March. p. 158.)

*EDWARDS, [George] *Esq. of Bernard Castle.*

On perfecting the agriculture of this kingdom and on breeding calves. (*Young's* A. of Agr. Vol. 3. p. 194.) On the present scarcity. (Ibid. Vol. 35. p. 209.)

EDWARDS, [George] *Esq. M. Dr.*

The great and important discovery of the 18 century and the means of setting right the national affairs —. 1791. 8. (5 sh.) The descriptions and characters of the different diseases of the human body; to which is added an arrangement of the medicines and preparations in the London pharmacopoeia, according to their respective virtues, being the first volume of the *Franklinian* improvement of medicine — 1791. 4. (10 sh. 6 d.) Effectual means of providing, according to the exigencies of the evil against the distress apprehended from the scarcity and high prices of different articles of food. 1800. 8. (1 sh.) Practical means of counteracting the present scarcity and preventing famine in future; including the proposal of a maximum founded on a new principle: to which is prefixed an address to the legislature, on a plan for melioration the condition of society at large. 1801. 8. (3 sh. 6 d.) The political interests of Great-Britain. — 1801. 8. (7 sh.)

*EDWARDS,

DWARDS, [Gerard Noel] *Esq. M. P.*
Letter to the Secretary of the New-Town society of the friends of the people, in answer to his letter, inclosing, by order of the society, the resolutions agreed upon at their meeting, dated Edinburgh 31 Dec. 1792. — 1793. 8. (6 d.)

DWARDS, [J....] *an Unitarian Minister.*
A vindication of the sentiments contained in a late address to the congregation of baptists, assembling in Byrom-Street, Liverpool. 1791. 8. (1 sh.) Letter to the Rev. Mr. *Medley*, (Preacher among the baptists) occasioned by his late behaviour, while engaged in the performance of divine service, in his new chapel. 1790. 8. Letters to the british nation and to the inhabitants of every other country, who may have heard of the late shameful outrages committed in this part of the kingdom, occasioned by the appearance of a pamphlet intitled, „a reply to the Rev. Dr. *Priestley's* appeal to the public on the subject of the riots in Birmingham — P. 1-4. 1791. 1792. 8. (3 sh.)

DWARDS, [J.....]
On apple trees. (*Young's* A. of Agr. Vol. 33. p. 5.)

DWARDS, [Jonathan] D. D. *Pastor of a church in Newhaven and Member of the Connecticut Soc. of arts and sciences.*
Observations on the languages of the Muhhekaneew Indians; in which the extent of that language, in North-America, is shewn, its genius is grammatically traced; some of its peculiarities, and some instances of analogy between that and hebrew, are pointed out. (American Museum Y. 1789. Jan. p. 21. Febr. p. 141.)

DWARDS, [Peter] *Pastor of a baptist church at Portsea, Hants.*
Candid reasons for renouncing the principles of antipaedobaptism. 1795. 8. (3 sh.)

DWARDS, [T.....] *Law-Stationer.*
New table of all the stamp duties, completed to the 9 of July 1801. Ed. 2. 1801. (1 sh.)

DWARDS, [Timothy] *of Stockbridge. Esq.*
Description of a horn or bone, lately found in

the river Chemung or Tyoga, a western branch of the Susquehanna about 12 miles from Tyoga point. (Mem. of B. A. Vol. 2. P. 1. p. 164.)

*EDWARDS, [Thomas] *LL. D.*

born .... died .... (?)

Plutarchi de educatione liberorum liber; gr. et lat. cum variorum notis et animadversionibus. 1791. 8. (3 sh. 6 d.) Discourse on the limits and importance of free inquiry in matters of religion, with a postscript on greek accents. 1792. 8. (1 sh.) Remarks on Dr. *Kipling's* preface to *Beza*. P. 1. 1793. 8. (1 sh. 6 d.)

*EDWARDS, [Thomas] *Surgeon, of Peckham.*

Case (Mem. of M. S. of London. Vol. 3. p. 555.)

*EDY, [J.....] *M. S. D.*

Plain and useful instructions for the relief and cure of ruptures; — illustrated with engravings of the several instruments invented, made and improved by him, for the various deformities and infirmities of the human body. 1800. 8. (2 sh. 6 d.)

*EGAN, [James]

Information of his improved method of teaching latin. (Tr. of the Soc. for the E. of A. Vol. 5. p. 115.)

*EGERTON, [Francis Henry]

Euripidis Hippolytus, graece cum scholiis, versione latina, variis lectionibus, *Valckenari* notis integris ac selectis aliorum VV. DD quibus suas adjecit. 1796. 4. (1 L. 16 sh.) Description of the underground inclined plane, executed at Walkden Moor in Lancashire by the Duke of Bridgewater. (*Nicholson's* Journal. Vol 4. p. 454. Tr. of the Soc. for the E. of A. Vol. 18. p. 265. *Tilloch's* Philos. Magaz. Vol. 9. p. 31.)

*Earl of EGREMONT, [....]

Experiment on dibbling wheat. (*Young's* A. of Agr. Vol. 28. p. 396.) Cross of new Leicester and Dorset sheep. (Ibid. Vol. 28. p. 534.)

EKINS, [Jeffery] *D. D. Dean of Carlisle and Rector of Sedgefield and Morpeth, co. Durham.*

born .... died 1791. Nov. 20.

See Gentleman's Magaz. Y. 1791. Nov. p. 1070.

*ELDER,

*ELDER, [Dwarf]
Wonderful cure of the dropſy. (Maſſachuſetts's Magaz. Y. 1789. June. p. 364.)

*ELGAN, [T....]
The fallen farm-houſe. 1796. (6 d.)

*ELIOT, [Andrew] *Rev.*
Letter, concerning the burning of Fairfield in July 1779. (Coll. of Maſſachuſetts H. S. Y. 1794. p. 103.)

*ELIOT, [F..... P.....] *Esq. of Shenſtone-Moſs, near Litchfield.*
On the culture of Shenſtone moſs, near Litchfield. (*Young's* A. of Agr. Vol. 4. p. 414.)

*ELIOT, [Jared] *M. A. at Killingworth in Connecticut.*
Account of an animal ſurviving the loſs of all the ſmall guts. (American Muſeum Y. 1788. Dec. p. 504.)

*ELIOT, [John] *Esq.*
Obſervations on the inhabitants of the Garrow Hills, made during a publick deputation in the Years 1788 and 1789. (Aſiat. Reſ. Vol. 3. p. 17.)

*ELIOT, [John] *D. D.*
Topographical deſcription of New-Bedford. (Coll. of Maſſachuſetts H. S. Y. 1795. p. 232.) *A liſt of writers, who were citizens of Boſton, with the time of their deceaſe. (Ibid. Y. 1794. p. 300.) *Hiſtorical ſcraps. (Ibid. Y. 1798. p. 206.) *A narrative of the news papers printed in New-England. (Ibid. Y. 1798. p. 208. Y. 1799. p. 64.)

*ELIZA, [.....]
Poems and fugitive pieces. 1796. 12. (6 ſh.)

*ELKINGTON, [.....] See *John Johnſtone.*

*ELLEN, [.....] *of Exeter.*
The Neapolitan, or the teſt of integrity. Vol. 1-3. 1796. 12. (10 ſh. 6 d.)

*ELLERKER, [James]
On the cultivation of flax and hemp. (Bath Agricult. Soc. Vol. 4. p. 255.)

*ELLIA, [Felix]
Norman banditti or the fortreſs of Coutance; a tale. Vol. 1. 2. 1799. 8. (7 ſh.)

X 2 *ELLI-

*ELLICOTT, [Andrew] *Esq. Commissioner on the part of the United States, for running the line of demarcation between them and the Spanish territory.*

Description of the falls of Niagra. (Massachusetts Magaz. Y. 1790. July. p. 387. Columbian Magaz. Y. 1790. June. p. 331. New-York Magaz. Y. 1794. Febr. p. 97.) Remarkable effect of terrestrial refraction on a distant Headland; Extract of a letter, containing observations on a singular phaenomenon, by seamen termed looming, made at lake-Erie. (Tr. of A. S. Vol. 3. p. 62. *Nicholson's* Journal. Vol. 1. p. 152.) Accurate determination of the right ascension and declination of β bootes and the polar-star. (Tr. of A. S. Vol. 3. p. 116.) Astronomical observations made in the Y. 1784 at Wilmington on the Delaware, by *Rittenhouse, Page, Andrews* and *Lukens, Ewing, Madison, Hutchins* and *Andr. Ellicott*. (Ibid. Vol. 4. p. 32.) Of the aberration of the fixed ... nutation of the earth's axis and semi-annual equation. (Ibid. Vol. 4. p. 51.) A method of calculating the eccentric anomaly of the planets. (Ibid. Vol. 4. p. 67.) Miscellaneous observations relative to the western parts of Pennsylvania, particularly those in the neighbourhood of lake Erie. (Ibid. Vol. 4. p. 224. *Nicholson's* Journal. Vol. 3. p. 539.) Observations on the old french landing at Presqu' isle to determine the latitude of the town of Erie. (Tr. of A. S. Vol. 4. p. 231.) Observations for determining the latitude and longitude of the town of Natchez. (Ibid. Vol. 4. p. 447.) Astronomical and thermometrical observations, made at the confluence of the Missisippi and Ohio rivers (Y. 1796-1799). (Ibid. Vol. 5. p. 162.) Astronomical and thermometrical observations, made on the boundary between the United States and his catholic Majesty (Y. 1798. 1799). (Ibid. Vol. 5. p. 203.)

*ELLIOT, [Charles Harrington] *Esq.*

The republican confuted in a series of biographical, critical and political strictures on *Thom. Paine's* rights of man. 1791. 8. (2 sh. 6 d.)

*ELLIOT,

ELLIOT, [E.....] *of Rotheram.*
A paraphrase on the book of Job, agreeable to the meaning of the sacred text. 1792. 12. (2 sh.)

ELLIOT, [Francis Percival] *Major of the Staffordshire Volunteer Cavalry.*
Letters on the subject of the armed Yeomanry. 1794. 8. (6 d.) Ed. 2. 1796. (2 sh.)

ELLIOT, [James] *Surgeon's mate.*
Account of a remarkable enlargement of the spleen. (*Duncan's* M. C. Dec. 2. Vol. 7. p. 495.)

ELLIOT, [John] *M. Dr. Apothecary at London.* born .... died in Newgate. 1788.
Observations on the affinities of substances in spirit of wine. (Philos. Transact. Y. 1786. p. 155.)
* Experiments and observations on light and colours; and the analogy between heat and motion. 1787. 8. (3 sh.)

ELLIS, [.....]
On washing roads. (Comm. to the B. of Agr. Vol. 1. p. 207.)

ELLIS, [Charles Thomas] *Of the Inner-Temple, Solicitor.*
The solicitor's instructor in parliament — to which is added an appendix of the various forms of proceedings, namely, notices, petitions, orders, breviats, affidavits, letters of attorney, state of property, certificate, table of fees. 1799. 8. (3 sh.)
Practical remarks and precedents of proceedings in parliament; comprizing the standing orders of both houses, relative to applying for and passing bills in general, with practical directions for every case and occasion. 1802. 8. (7 sh. 6 d.)

ELLIS, [George] *Esq.*
* Specimens of the early English poets. 1790. 8. (6 sh.) Specimens of the early English poets, to which is prefixed an historical sketch of the rise and progress of the english poetry and language. Vol. 1. 2. 3. 1801. 8. (1 L. 1 sh.) See *Greg. Lewis Way.*

ELLIS, [Henry] *Fellow of St. John's College, Oxford.*
The history and antiquities of the parish of St. Leonard Shoreditch and liberty of Norton Folgate in the suburbs of London. 1798. 4. (16 sh.)

*ELLIS, [Henry] *Governour.*
Causes of hurricanes explained. ((American Museum Y. 1791. Apr. p. 215.)

*ELLIS, [John] *Deputy of Broad-street ward, London.*
born 1705. died 1791. Dec. 31.
See Gentleman's Magaz. Y. 1791. Suppl. p. 1238. (He wrote some Hudibrastic translations, but never put his name to any thing he published.)

*ELLIS, [John] *of New-Jersey.*
An account of a method of preventing the premature decay of peach trees. (Tr. of A. S. Vol. 5. p. 325)

*ELLIS, [Jonathan] *Rev.*
A topographical description of Topsham, in the county of Lincoln. (Coll. of Massachusetts H. S. Y. 1794. p. 141.)

*ELLIS, [William] *Clerk of the Peace for the county of Sussex.*
Assize of bread. (*Young's* A. of Agr. Vol. 25. p. 27.)

*ELLIS, [William] *Surgeon at Jamaica.*
History of a tetanic affection terminated favourably. (*Duncan's* M. C. Dec. 2. Vol. 9. p. 341.)

*ELLIS, [William] *Engraver.*
The campagna of London or view in the different parishes within the circumference of 25 miles from that metropolis, with some account of the history and topography of each parish and biographical anecdotes of persons who have resided in them. The whole recollected from authentic records and from local and personal information. Numb. 1-4. (each 6 sh.) 1791. 1792. 4.

*ELLISON, [J.....] *at Hexham.*
Answer to Mr. *Ford* on planting potatoes. (Comm. and Agric. Mag. Y. 1801. March. p. 194.)

*ELLMAN, [John] *of Glynd, near Lewes.*
An account of the expence and produce of a flock of 560 Southdown ewes, stating the average for the last seven years, with observat. by *A. Young.* (*Young's* A. of Agr. Vol. 11. p. 345.) Crop of 1790. at Glynd. (Ibid. Vol. 14. p. 183.) On sheep. (Ibid. Vol. 20. p. 172.) Lewes agricultural meeting. (Ibid. Vol. 31. p. 389. 394.) Steeping wheat-seed.

feed. (Ibid. Vol. 32. p. 192.) South-Down wether. (Ibid. Vol. 33. p. 220.) Markets and poor, Suffex. (Ibid. Vol. 34. p. 165.) On folding fheep. (Ibid. Vol. 38. p. 5.)

ELMER, [Jonathan] *M. Dr. and Prefident of the medical fociety of New-Jerfey.*

Differtation on the chemical principles of bodies. (Columbian Magaz. Y. 1788. Sept. p. 493.) On air. (Ibid. Y. 1788. Dec. p. 677.)

ELMORE, [H.... M....] *Many years a Commander in the country in India and late Commander of the Varuna extra Eaft-India man.*

The British mariner's directory and guide to the trade and navigation of the Indian and China feas, with an account of the trade, mercantile, habits, manners and cuftoms of the natives. 1802. 4.

PHINSTON, [James] *Esq.*

Forty year's co-refpondence between geniuffes ov boath fexes and him; in fix pocket volumes: foar ov oridginal letters, two' ov poetry. 1791. 8. (1 L. 1 fh.). Poetae fententiofi latini, Dhe fententious poets; *Pubblius*, dhe Syrrian; *C. D. Laberius*, dhe roman knight; *L. A. Sepneca*, dhe philofopher; *D. Cato*, dhe morralift; alfo, from *Aufonius*, dhe fayings ov dhe fevven greek fages; arranged and tranflated into' correfpondent inglifh mezzure. 1794. 12. (3 fh.) Fifty year's correfpondence, inglifh, french and latin, in proze and verfe, between geniuffes ov boath fexes, and him; including an appendix — — — Vol. 1. 2. 1794. 12. (7 fh.)

ELRINGTON, [Thomas] *D. D. M. R. J. A. Senior Fellow and Profeffor of Mathematics, in Trinity College, Dublin.*

Sermons preached in the chapel of Trinity-College Dublin —. 1796. 8. (6 fh.)

ELSAM, [Richard] *Architect.*

An effay on rural architecture, illuftrated with originals and economical defigns; being an attempt alfo to refute by analogy the principles of Mr. *Malton's* effay on cottage architecture. To which are added, hints for rural retreats, &c. and a defign for the naval pillar. 1803. (2 L. 2 fh.)

*ELSON, [Jane]

Romance of the castle; — 17.. The village romance; Vol. 1. 2. 1802. 12. (7 sh.)

*ELTON, [Sir Abraham]. *Bart.*

Letter to *Thomas Bere*, Rector of Butcombe, occasioned by his late unwarrantable attack on Mrs. *Hannah More*; with an appendix, containing letters and others documents relative to the extraordinary proceedings at Blagdon. 1800. 8. (1 sh. 6 d.)

*EMERSON, [Thomas] *An Attorney of the Court of King's-Bench and one of the 4 Attornies of the Lord Mayor's Court.*

born .... died at Newcastle upon-Tyne 1801. Oct. 1.

See Gentleman's Magaz. Y. 1801. Dec. p. 1149.

A concise treatise on the courts of law of the city of London. 1794. 8. (2 sh. 6 d.)

*EMMONS, [Nathaniel]

Sermons on some of the first principles and doctrines of true religion. 1800. 8.

ENFIELD, [William] *LL. Dr. Pastor of the Congregation of Protestant Dissenters at Norwich; formerly Lecturer in the belles letters at the Academy at Warrington.*

born at Sudbury March 29. 1741. died 1797. Nov. 2.

See Gentleman's Magaz. Y. 1797. Nov. p. 987. Dec. p. 1068. Monthly Magaz. Y. 1797. Nov. p. 400. The new Annual Register. Y. 1798. P. 2. p. 36. Monthly Review Y. 1800. Sept. p. 67. Allgem. Litterat. Zeit. ItBl. J. 1800. S. 1101. See *John Aikin.*

Institutes of natural philosophy, theoretical and experimental, Ed. 2. with corrections and considerable additions. 1799. 4. (1 L. 1 sh.) The history of philosophy from the earliest times to the beginning of the present century; drawn up from *Brucker's* historia critica philosophiae. Vol. 1. 2. 1791. 4. (2 L. 2 sh.) A selection of hymns for social worship. 1795. 12. Sermons on practical subjects, prepared for the press by himself. To which are prefixed memoirs of the author. Vol. 1-3. 1798. 8. (1 L. 1 sh.) The absur-

absurdity of those fanaticks who depreciate morality. (Massachusetts Magaz. Y. 1791. Oct. p. 603.) (Several single sermons.)

ENGLEFIELD, [Sir Henry] *Bart: F. R. S. and F. A. S.*
On the determination of the orbits of comets, according to the methods of father *Boscovich* and *De la Place*, with new and complete tables and examples of the calculation by both methods. 1793. 4. (15 sh.) A walk through Southampton; illustrated with plates of its antiquities. 1801. 8. (5 sh.)

*ENGLEFIELD, [Sir Henry Charles] *F. R. and A. S.*
Account of antiquities discovered at Bath. 1790. (Arch. Vol. 10. p. 325.) On the effect of sound upon the barometer, with a note by Dr. *Young.* (*Nicholson's* Journal. Y. 1802. July. p. 181.) Experiments on the separation of light and heat by refraction. (Ibid. Y. 1802. Oct. p. 125.) Observations on some remarkable strata of flint in a chalk-pit in the isle of Wight. (Transact. of L. S. Vol. 6. p. 103. 303.)

*ENGLISH, [John George] *late Teacher of the Mathematics in the Royal Navy.*
The first principles of arithmetic, vulgar and decimal, with the extraction of roots of different powers. To which is added, a concise compendium of book-keeping by *Single Entry.* 1795. 12. (1 sh. 6 d.) On the principles of equilibrium, and the stability of floating bodies applied to river and canal boats of different forms. (*Tilloch's* Philos. Magaz. Vol. 1. p. 393.)

*ENGLISH, [T....] *at Wooburn, Bucks.*
The dignity and uses of the moral law —; 1795. 8. (1 sh.)

*ENSOR, [George] *Esq.*
The principles of morality. 1801. 8. (6 sh.)

*ERRATT, [Thomas] *Surgeon.*
Case of diseased kidneys and stone in the bladder. (Mem. of M. S. of L. Vol. 5. p. 53.)

ERSKINE, [David Stewart] Earl of BUCHAN, *in the kingdom of Scotland.*
See Public Characters of 1798 and 1799. p. 246. Essay on the lives and writings of *Fletcher* of *Sal-*

son and the poet Thomson; biographical, critical and political: With some pieces of *Thomson*, never before published. 1792. 8. , Memoirs of the life of Sir *James Stewart Denhalm*, Baronet. (Transact. of the Soc. of the Antiq. of Scotl. Vol. I. p. 129.) Account of the parish of Uphall. (Ibid. Vol. I. p. 139.) Account of the island of Ikolumkill; (Ibid. Vol. I. p. 234.) Life of Mr. *James Short*, Optician, (Ibid. Vol. I. p. 251.)

ERSKINE, [John] *D. D. Minister of Edinburgh.* born ..... died 1803. Jan. 12.

See Gentleman's Magaz. Y. 1803. Jan. p. 91. Apr. p. 377.

Sketches and hints of church history and theological controversy, chiefly translated and abridged from modern foreign writers. 1790. 8. (3 sh.) Ed. 2. 1802. Reply to a printed letter directed to him by A. C.; in which the gross and palpable misrepresentations, in the said letter of his late sketches of church history, as promoting the designs of the infamous sect of the illuminati, are considered. 1798. The fatal consequences and the general sources of anarchy, a sermon on Isaiah. 24, 1-5. 1792. 8. (6 d.) Discourses preached on several occasions. 1798. 8. (6 sh) Letters written for comforting those bereaved of children or friends. 1800. (1 sh.) Supplement to Dr. *Gill's* historical collections relative to the success of the gospel. 1800. (1 sh.) Discourses on various subjects by some of the most eminent divines of the United States. 1801. (7 sh.)

(Several single sermons.)

*ERSKINE, [John Francis] *Esq. of Mar.*

Price of corn in Scotland. (*Young's* A. of Agr. Vol. 17. p. 414.) An account of the Mid-Lothian prices of oats — with a progressive account of an average of 25 years, from 1636 to 1790. (Ibid. Vol. 17. p. 572.) Ploughing matches in Scotland. (Ibid. Vol. 35. p. 119.) On iron roads, or waggon-ways. (Comm. to the B. of Agr. Vol. I. p. 203.) On Kilndrying wheat. (*Young's* A. of Agr. Vol. 37. p. 371.)

*ERSKINE,

ERSKINE, [Thomas] *M. P.*

See Public Characters of 1799–1800, p. 63.

The argument on the rights of juries, in the case of the dean of St. Asaph. 1791. 8. (2 sh. 6 d.) Declaration of the friends of the liberty of the press. 1793. 8. (4 d.) His speeches at large, in defence of *Thomas Hardy* and *John Horne Tooke*, Esq. tried by special commission on a charge of high treason; accurately taken in short hand by *Manoah Sibly*. 1795. 8. (3 sh.) A view of the causes and consequences of the present war with France, 1797. 8. Ed. 1. Ed. 22. (2 sh.) übers. *Archenholz* Minerva, J. 1797. May. Junius. His speeches (at length) and *S. Kyd*, Esq. at the court of Kings-Bench, Westminster, June 24. 1797. on the trial of *T. Williams*, for publishing *Paine's* age of reason; with Lord *Kenyon's* charge to the jury. 1797. 8. (6 d.) Substance of his speech — on the motion for an address to the throne approving the refusal of ministers to treat with the french republic. 1800. 8. (1 sh.) Dissertation on the origin of the english house of commons, delivered — Trinity college, Cambridge in June 1777. (Monthly Magaz. Y. 1798. April p. 247.) Parody upon *Gray's* ode of the bard. (Ibid. Y. 1799. Aug. p. 545.) Description of Buxton. (Ibid. Y. 1797. Febr. p. 92.)

ERSKINE, [W....]

On a new method of fencing. (*Young's* A. of Agr. Vol. 13. p. 482.) Police of the poor. (Ib. Vol. 13. p. 490.) An account of the price of wheat at Windsor market from 1595 to 1789 inclus. (Ib. Vol. 14. p. 227.)

ESPINASSE, [Isaac] *Esq. of Gray's-Inn, Barrister at Law.*

A digest of the law of actions and trials at nisi prius. Vol. 1. 2. 1790. 8. (12 sh.) Ed. 2. corrected with considerable additions. Vol. 1. 2. 1793. 8. (18 sh.) Ed. 3. Vol. 1. 2. 1798. 8. (18 sh.) Cases argued at nisi prius, in the courts of King's Bench and common pleas from Eastern term 33 George 3 to Hilary term 34 George 3 with some additional cases of an earlier period. 1794. 8. (5 sh.) Reports of cases argued and ruled at nisi

prius

prius in the courts of King's-Bench and common pleas, from Easter term 1793 to Hilary term 1796. 1796. 8. (16 sh. 6 d.) Vol. 2. from Easter term 1796 to Hilary term 1799. 1799. 8. (10 sh.) Vol. 3. 4. P. 1. from Easter term 1799 to Hilary term 1802. 1803. 8. (15 sh.)

*ESTCOURT, [Thomas] *Esq. M. P.*

Plan for making bread. (*Young's* A. of Agr. Vol. 26. p. 181.) Provisions for the poor. (Ibid. Vol. 34. p. 148.)

ESTE, [Charles] *Rev. One of the Readers at Whitehall-Chapel and Member of the company of Apothecaries in London.*

Tracts on medical subjects. 1776. 4. (1 sh. 6 d.) My own life. 1787. 8. (1 sh. 6 d.) A journey in the Y. 1793. through Flanders, Brabant and Germany to Switzerland. 1794. 8. (6 sh.) (Principal Director of the news-papers, The World; The Morning post; The Telegraph.)

*ESTLIN, [John Prior]

Evidences of revealed religion and particularly christianity, stated with reference to a pamphlet called the age of reason, in a discourse. 1796. 8. (1 sh. 6 d.) The nature and the causes of atheism — to which are added, remarks on a work, entitled origine de tous les cultes ou religion universelle par *Dupuis*. 1797. 8. (2 sh.) *David Jardine's*, of Bath, sermons, published from the original manuscripts. Vol. 1. 2. 1798. 8. (14 sh.) An apology for the sabbath. 1801. 8. (1 sh. 6 d.) Sermons. 1802. 8. (7 sh. 6 d.)

*ETHELSTON, [Charles Wickfted] *M. A. Rector of Worthenbury.*

A Pindaric ode to the genius of Britain. 1803. 4. The suicide; with other poems. 1804. 8. (5 sh.)

*ETON, [William] *Esq. many years Resident in Turkey and in Russia.*

Survey of the Turkish empire. 1798. 8. (8 sh.) On the present state of surgery in Turkey. (*Tilloch's* Philos. Magaz. Vol. 3. p. 127.) Observations on the British trade with Turkey. (Ibid. Vol. 3. p. 262.)

*EVANS,

EVANS, [Cadwallader] *M. Dr.*
Relation of a cure performed by electricity. (American Museum Y. 1787. Nov. p. 465.)

EVANS, [Caleb] D. D. *many years President of the Baptist Academy and Pastor of the Congregation of Protestant Dissenters in Broad-mead at Downend, co. Gloucester, near Bristol.*
born 1737. died 1791. Aug. 9.
See Gentleman's Magaz. Y. 1791. Aug. p. 781. (His publications were principally occasional sermons which are enumerated from 1771 to 1780 in *Cooke's* historical register.) See *T. Dunscombe.*

EVANS, [Field] *Pool-Quay, Montgomeryshire.*
Account of his discovery of a quarry of burr-stone proper for mill stones. (Tr. of the Soc. for the E. of A. Vol. 19. p. 280.)

EVANS, [J.....]
The conjugation of french verbs, regular and irregular simplified on a sheme entirely new. 1795. 8. (6 d.)

EVANS, [John] *M. A. Master of a Seminary for a limited number of pupils, Pullin's-row, Islington.*
An address humbly designed to promote a religious revival amongst the general baptists. 1793. 12. (4 d.) Juvenile pieces: designed for the youth of both sexes. Ed. 2. enlarged and corrected. 1794. 12. (2 sh. 6 d.) Ed. 3. 1798. (2 sh.) A brief sketch of the several denominations into which the christian worlds is divided; accompanied with a persuasive to religious moderation. Ed. 2. with considerable additions. 1795. 12. (1 sh. 6 d.) Ed. 5. with considerable additions and improvements. 1801. 8. (3 sh. 6 d.) A preservative against the infidelity and uncharitableness of the XVIII century or testimonies in behalf of christian candour and unanimity, in 3 parts. Part 1. by Divines of the church of England; P. 2. by Divines of the church of Scotland; P. 3. by Divines among the protestant dissenters. To which is prefixed an essay on the right of private judgment in matters of religion; the whole being a sequel to the sketch of the denominations of the christian world. 1796. 8. (3 sh. 6 d.) Sermon —

to

to the memoirs of the Rev. *Samuel Stennett* D. D. the Rev. *Andrew Kippis*, D. D. F. R. S. A. S. and the Rev. *Rice Harris*, D. D. To which are prefixed, a few particulars of their lives and writings. 1796. Sermon on the decease of *Charles Bulkley* — with a ſketch of his life character and writings. 1797. 8. (1 ſh.) An apology for human nature by the late *Ch. Bulkley*, with a prefatory addreſs to *Will. Wilberforce*, Esq. 1797. 12. (12 ſh. 6 d.) An attempt to account for the infidelity of the late *E. Gibbon*, Esq. founded on his own memoirs, with reflections on the beſt means of checking the preſent alarming progreſs of ſcepticiſm; including an account of the converſion and death of the R. H. *George* Lord *Lyttleton*. 1797. 8. (1 ſh. 6 d.) Moral reflexions ſuggeſted by a view of London from of the monument. 1798. 12. (6 d.) On the education of youth. 1798. 12. (1 ſh.) An epitome of geography, arranged after a new manner, and enlivened by references to hiſtory: in 3 parts. 1801. 8. (1 ſh.) Ed. 2. with conſiderable additions and improvements. 1802. 8. (3 ſh. 6 d.) An addreſs to young people on the neceſſity and importance of religion. 1800. 12. (6 d.) A ſketch of the denominations of the chriſtian world, accompanied with a perſuaſive to religious moderation. To which is prefixed an account of atheiſm, deiſm, theophilanthropiſm, judaiſm, mahometaniſm, and chriſtianity, adapted to the preſent times. 1801. 12. (3 ſh. 6 d.) Sequel to the ſketch of the denominations. Ed. 2. 1801. 8. (2 ſh. 6 d.) Original anecdotes of *Goldſmith*. (Monthly Magaz. Y. 1802. Dec. p. 382.)

*EVANS, [John] *B. A.*

A tour through part of North Wales in the Year 1798 and at other times; principally undertaken with a view to botanical reſearches in that alpine country, interſperſed with obſervations on its ſcenery, agriculture, manufactures, cuſtoms, hiſtory and antiquities. 1800. 8. (8 ſh.) A nine-ſheet map of North-Wales. 1796. (3 ſh.)

*EVANS, [Nathaniel] *of Glouceſter, New-Jerſey.*

Account of *Thomas Godfrey*. (American Muſeum Y. 1789. Dec. p. 471.)

*EVANS,

EVANS, [Oliver]

The young mill-wright and miller's guide. Philadelphia. 1795. 8. (1 sh.)

EVANS, [Robert] *M. A.*

The dream, or noble Cambrians. Vol. 1. 2. 1801. 12. (8 sh.)

EVANS, [Thomas] *Attorney at Law.*

Letter — on the actual state of the master's mates, midshipmen, inferior officers and seamen of his Maj. navy, their wives, children, executors and legal representatives —. 1791. 8. (2 sh. 6 d.)

EVANS, [Thomas]

Cambrian itinerary or welsh tourist; containing an historical and topographical description of the antiquities and beauties of Wales. 1801. 8. (10 sh. 6 d.)

EVANS, [William] *Vicar of Lawhadon, co. Pembroke.*

born . . . . . died 1796. March. . . . .

See Gentleman's Magaz. Y. 1796. March. p. 258. *Rees Prichard's* poems, translated from the welsh into English verse. The welsh'man's candle, or divine exercises. 1766. (He was the author of several poetical pieces and religious tracts.)

EVANS, [William David] *Esq. Barrister at Law.*

Reports of cases adjudged in the court of King's-Bench; with some special cases in the courts of chancery, common pleas and exchequer, alphabetically digested from the first of King William and Queen Mary to the tenth of Queen Anne, by *William Salkeld*, late Serjeant at law. The 6 Edition, including the notes and references of knightley d'*Anvers*, Esq. and Serjeant *Wilson* and large additions of notes and references to modern authorities and determinations. Vol. 1—3. 1795. 8. (1 L. 7 sh.) Essays on the action for money lent and received; on the law of assurances and on the laws of bills of exchange and promissary notes. 1802. 8. (10 sh. 6 d.) A general view of the decisions of Lord Mansfield in civil causes. Vol. 1. 2. 1803. 4. (1 L. 14 sh.)

EVANSON, [Edward] *M. A. Clergyman.*

Letter to the Lord Bish. of Worcester, *Richard Hurd*, wherein the importance of the prophecies of of the new testament and the nature of the grand apostacy predicted in them, are particularly and impartially considered. Ed. 2. 1792. 8. (2 sh.) Arguments against and for the sabbatical observance of sunday, by a cessation from all labour. 1792. 8. (2 sh. 6 d.) The dissonance of the four generally received evangelists and the evidence of their respective authenticity examined. 1792. 8. (5 sh.) Letter to Dr. *Priestley's* young man; with a postscript concerning the Rev. Dr. *Simpson's* essay &c. in answer to *Evanson's* dissonance and *Volney's* ruins. 1794. 8. (2 sh.) Observations on Mr. *Marsh's* dissertat. upon the origin of the three first gospels. (Monthly Magaz. Y. 1802. Dec. p. 377.) Reflections upon the state of religion and christendom, particularly in the countries situated within the limits of the western roman empire, of the commencement of the 19 century of the era — 1803. 8. (2 sh. 6 d.)

*EVANSON, [J.....]
Mode of destroying the gooseberry caterpillar. (Monthly Magaz. Y. 1800. March. p. 105.)

*EVELEIGH, [John] *D. D. Provost of Oriel-College and Prebendary of Rochester.*
Eight sermons preached — at the Bampton's lectures. 1792. 8. (5 sh.) The doctrine of the holy trinity stated from the scriptures of the old and new testament; two sermons. 1791. 8. (1 sh.)

*EVELYN, [Sir George Shuckburgh] *Bart. F. R. S. and A. S.*
An account of some endeavours to ascertain a standard of weight and measure. (Philos. Transact. Y. 1798. p. 133. *Nicholson's* Journal. Vol. 3. p. 97. 147. 200. 243.)

*EVERETT, [.....]
Daranzel, or persian patriot. 1800.

*EVES, [.....] *Mrs. Crescent-school, Birmingham.*
The grammatical play-thing, or winter evening's recreation for young ladies from four to twelve years old. 1800. 8. (6 sh.)

*EUSTACE, [John Chetwood] *Rev.*
An elegy to the memory of the Right Hon. *Edm. Burke.* 1797. 4. (1 sh.)

*EUSTON,

USTON, [. . . . .] *Lord-Lieutenant of Suffolk.*
On the prefent fcarcity. (*Young's* A. of Agr. Vol. 34. p. 342.)

WART, [John] *M. Dr. Phyfician General of his Maj. forces in the Eaft-Indies and formerly one of the Phyficians of the Bath city Infirmary and Difpenfary.*
born . . . . , died at Columbo in the island of Ceylon 1800.
See Gentleman's Magaz. Y. 1803. Apr. p. 381.
The hiftory of two cafes of ulcerated cancer of the mamma; one of which has been cured, the other much relieved by a new method of applying carbonic acid air; illuftrated by a copper-plate; with obfervations. 1794. 8. (1 fh. 6 d.)

WART, [J. . . . S. . . .] *Lieutenant.*
Summary account of the weather at Nagpore, lat. 21° 8′ 28″ N. long. 79° 24′ E. from Greenwich. (*Dalrymple's* Oriental Repofitory. Nrb. 1. p. 45.)

'ING, [Alexander] *Teacher of Mathematics, Edinburgh.*
Practical aftronomy; — 1797. 8. (5 fh.)

WING, [Grenville] *Minifter of the tabernacle, Glasgow.*
Remarks on *Dick's* fermon, concerning the call and qualification of miffionaries. 1801. 8. Elements of the greek language fhortly illuftrated and a compendious lexicon for the ufe of thofe who whifh to make themfelves acquainted with the new teftament in the original. 1802. 8.

ETER, Bifhop of — See *John Rofs.*

XTER, [John] *of Pilton, Devon.*
On drilling corn. (Bath Agric. Soc. Vol. 9. p. 22.) Damage to wheat occafioned by the berbery plant. (*Young's* A. of Agr. Vol. 27. p. 540.) On drilling corn. (Ibid. Vol. 30. p. 20.) On irrigation; and particularly on the different effects of rich water, as a manure, on different foils. (Ibid. Vol. 30. p. 204.) Crops and prices in Devonfhire. (Ibid. Vol. 34. p. 179.) On the comparative culture of turneps. (Tr. of the Soc. for the E. of A. Vol. 16. p. 182.)

*EYRE, [Edmund] *Esq.*
A friend to old England. 1793. 4. (2 sh.) The two bills! a political poem. 1796. 4 (1 sh.)

*EYRE, [Edmund John] *late of Pembroke College, Cambridge, and now of the theatres, Shrewsbury, Worcester, Wolverhampton and Shrewsbury.*
The dreamer awake, or, pugilist matched, a farce in 2 acts. 1791. 8. (1 sh.) The maid of Normandy, or the death of the Queen of France, a tragedy. 1793. 8. (1 sh. 6 d.) Consequences or the school for prejudice, a comedy, in 3 acts. 1794. 8. (1 sh. 6 d.) The fatal sisters or the castle of the forest; a dramatic romance of 5 acts; with a variety of poetic essays. 1797. 8. (4 sh.) The discarded secretary, or, the mysterious chorus, an historical play, in 3 acts. 1799. 8. (2 sh.)

*EYRE, [Edward] *late Captain in the 40 Regt. and Lieut. Colon. in the Army.*
Secret instructions by Frederick 2 King of Prussia — translated from the original german into french by the Prince de *Ligne* and now first translated into English. 1798. 12. (4 sh 6 d.).

*EYRE, [Francis] *Esq. of Warckworth.*
Letter to the Rev. Mr. *Ralph Churton* M. A. — on his addrefs to his parishioners. 1795. 8. (2 sh. 6 d.) *A short essay on the christian religion descriptive of the advantages which have accrued to society by the establishment of it, as contrasted with the manners and customs of mankind before that happy period — by a sincere friend of mankind. 1795. 8. A reply to the Rev. *Ralph Churton.* 1801. 8.

*EYRE, [Sir James] *Lord Chief Justice of the Court of Common pleas and one of the Commissioners in a special commission of Oyer and Terminer.*
Charge — to enquire of certain high treasons and misprisions of treasons, within the county of Middlesex, to the grand jury at the session-house on Clerkenwell-green, Oct. 2. 1794. (1 sh.)

*EYRE, [John] *M. A.*
Rules for the composition of a sermon, chiefly extracted from *Claude.* 1797. 8. (6 d.)

*FABER

FABER, [George Stanley] *M. A. Fellow of Linc. Coll.*
Horae mosaicae, or a view of the mosaical records, with respect to their coincidence with profane antiquity; their internal credibility, and their connection with christianity — Vol. 1. 2. 1801. 8. (14 sh.) A dissertation on the mysteries of the cabiri — with an engraving of a nympheum, or cabiric grotto. Vol. 1. 2. 1803. 8. (16 sh.)

FAIR, [George]
Tables of weights and measures. Nrb. 1–8. 17..

FAIRBAIRN, [John] *F. L. S.*
An account of several plants presented to the Linnean Society. (Transact. of L. S. Vol 1. p. 249.) An account of two genera of plants from New South Wales; Goodenia and Platylobium. (Ibid. Vol. 2. p. 346.) See *Thomas Hoy.*

FAIRFAIX, [Thomas] *of Bury.*
An experiment on samfoin; with observat. by *A. Young.* (*Young's* A. of Agr. Vol. 11. p. 314.)

FAIRFAX, [Ferdinando]
Plan for liberating the negroes within the United States. (American Museum Y. 1790. Dec. p. 285.)

FAIRMAN, [William] *of the Royal exchange assurance.*
The stocks examined and compared, or, a guide to purchasers in the public funds; containing an introduction, in which the origin and nature of the public debts are explained —. 1795. 8. (4 sh.) Ed. 2. considerably improved. 1796. 8. (4 sh.) Appendix. 1797. (1 sh.) Ed. 3. considerably improved 1798. 8. (5 sh.)

FAITHORN, [J.....] *at London.*
Account of the bite of a viper, cured by applying the fat of the same animal. (New London Med. Journ. Vol. 1. p. 345.)

FALCONAR, [Harriet] and
——— [Maria]
Poetic laurels for characters of distinguished merit, interspersed with poems, moral and entertaining; 1791. 4. (5 sh.)

FALCONBRIDGE, [Alexander] *Surgeon in the African trade.*
born .... died at Sierra Leona 1792.

*FALCONBRIDGE, [Anna Maria] *(This lady went to Africa in Company with her husband Alexander Falconbridge.)*
Two voyages to Sierra Leona during the Y. 1791–1793 in a series of letters, to which is added a letter to *Henry Thornton*, Esq. M. P. and Chairman of the court of Directors of the Sierra Leona Company. Ed. 2. 1794. 8. (4 sh.) Ed. 3. 1795. 8. (4 sh.)

*FALCONER, [J.....] *D. D.*
Observation on agriculture. 1800.

FALCONER, [Magnus] *Surgeon and Professor of Anatomy.*
born ...... died ..... (?)

FALCONER, [Thomas] *Esq. of the city of Chester.*
born ..... died (?)
Observations on *Pliny's* account of the temple of Diana at Ephesus. (Arch. Vol. II. p. 1.) Chronological tables; beginning with the reign of Solomon and ending with the death of Alexander the great; with a prefatory discourse. 1796. 4. (15 sh.)

*FALCONER, [Thomas] *Rev.*
The tocsin, or, an appeal to good sense, by *L. Dutens* — translated from the french. 1798. 8. (1 sh. 6 d.)

*FALCONER, [Thomas] *Fellow of C. C. College, Oxford.*
The voyage of *Hanno*, translated and accompanied with the greek text, explained from the accounts of modern travellers; defended against the objections of Mr. *Dodwell* and other writers, and illustrated by maps from *Ptolemy*, *D'Anville* and *Bougainville*. 1797. 8. (4 sh.) Remarks on some passages in Mr. *Bryant's* publications respecting the war of Troy; by the editor of the voyage of *Hanno*. 1799. 8. (2 sh. 6 d.)

*FALCONER, [William] *a Purser of the Navy.*
born ..... died .... (?)
* The Shipwreck, a poem, by a sailor. 1762. 4. (5 sh.) Ed. 2. 1764. 8. (2 sh. 6 d.)

FALCONER, [William] *M. Dr. F. R. S. Physician to the general hospital at Bath.*
On the Bath waters — übers. Leipzig. 1777. 8. Ed. 2.

Ed. 2. 1793. 8. (4 ſh.) Account of the efficacy of the aqua mephitica alkalina, or ſolution of fixed alkaline ſalt ſaturated with fixible air, in calculous disorders and other complaints of the urinary paſſages. Ed. 3. 1789. 8. (2 ſh. 6 d.) Ed. 4. 1792. uberſ. Leipzig. 1794. 8. Obſervations on ſome of the articles of diet and regimen uſually recommended to valetudinarians. 1778. 8. (1 ſh.) überſ. Leipz. 1791. 8. Miſcellaneous tracts and collections relating to natural hiſtory ſelected from the principal writers of antiquity on that ſubject. 1793. 4. (7 ſh. 6 d.) Obſervations reſpecting the pulſe; intended to point out with greater certainty the indications which it ſignifies, eſpecially in feveriſh complaints. 1796. 8. (2 ſh. 6 d.) überſ. mit Anmerk. von *Kauſch.* Leipzig. 1797. 8. Eſſay on the plague — 1801. 8. (2 ſh.) Examination of two parcels of Engliſh rhubarb, with experiments of its comparative effects with the foreign rhubarbs. (Bath Agricult. Soc. Vol. 3. p. 391. 401.) On the preſervation of the health of perſons employed in agriculture and on the cure of the diſeaſes incident to that way of life. (Ibid. Vol. 4. p. 341.) überſ. von *Michaelis.* Leipzig. 1793. 8. überſ. in der Samml. Oekon. Winke, Vorſchläge u. Verſ. für denkende u. prakt. Oekonomen Teutſchlands. Berlin. 1793. 8. Obſervations on the knowledge of the ancients reſpecting electricity. (Mem. of M. Vol. 3. p. 278.) Sketch of the hiſtory of ſugar, in the early times and through the middle ages. (Mem. of M. Vol. 4. P. 2. p. 291. *Nicholſon's* Journal. Vol. 2. p. 136.) Influenzae deſcriptio. (Mem. of M. S. of L. Vol. 3. p. 25.) Of the lepra graecorum. (Ibid. Vol. 3. p. 368.) Caſe of a man, woho took by miſtake two ounces of nitre inſtead of *Glauber's* ſalt. (Ibid. Vol. 3. p. 527.) On the Portland powder. (Monthly Magaz. Y. 1801. Apr. p. 209.) Obſervations on the poiſon of copper and braſs, and the very great danger attending the uſe of utenſils made of theſe metals, and other mixed metals, wherein copper and braſs make a part, eſpecially in the preparing and keeping of food and phyſic. (Columbian Magaz. Y. 1789. May. p. 286.) An account of the epide-

epidemical catarrhal fever, commonly called the influenza, as it appeared at Bath in the winter and spring of the Y. 1803. 8. (1 sh. 6 d.) An examination of Dr. *Heberden's* observations on the increase and decrease of different diseases and particularly the plague. 1802. 8. (6 d.)

*FALKLAND, [.....]

Essay on bigotry, religious innovation and infidelity, as respectively supported by *Burke, Priestley* and *Toulmin*. 1791. 8. (1 sh. 6 d.)

*Lord Viscount FALKLAND, [Charles]

Consideration on the competency of the parliament of Ireland to accede to an union with Great-Britain. 1799. 8. (6 d.)

FALKNER, [Thomas] *Domestic Chaplain to Robert Berkeley, Esq. of Spetchly near Worcester.*

born ..... died about 1801.

See *Colnett's* voyage to the South Atlantic. 1798. 4. p. 25.

*FALLOWFIELD, [J.....] *A. M: Senior fellow of Clare-Hall, Cambridge.*

Account of the recovery of a boy, who swallowed by mistake a large spoonful of strong vitriolic acid. (New London M. J. Vol. 1. p. 149.)

*FARAR, [Samuel] *Surgeon at Deptford.*

Account of a very uncommon blindness in the eyes of newly born children. (M. C. Vol. 2. p. 463.)

*FAREY, [John]

On *Salmon's* claim to the mode of transferring paintings. (Monthly Magaz. Y. 1803. Jan. p. 477.) On top dressings, in the neighbourhood of Dunstable. (*Young's* A. of Agr. Vol. 25. p. 66.)

FARMER, [Richard] *D. D. F. R. and A. SS. Master of Emanuel College, Cambridge; Principal Librarian in the University of Cambridge; One of the Canon's residentiary of St. Paul's, London, Chancellor of the Diocese of Lichfield and Coventry, Prebendary of Worcester.*

born at Leicester 1735. died 1797. Sept. 8.

See Gentleman's Magaz. Y. 1797 Sept. p. 805. Oct. p. 888. Y. 1800. July. p. 649. Monthly Magaz. Y. 1797. Oct. p. 315. The Annual Necrology for 1797. 1798. p. 390. Allg. Litterat. Zeit. ItBl. J. 1801. S. 647.

On

On the learning of *Shakespeare*. Ed. 2. 1767. Ed. 3. 1789. and in Mr. *Steven's* and *Reed's* edition of *Shakespeare* 1793. Cursory remarks on the edition of *Shakespeare*, published by *Edmund Malone*. 1792. 8. (2 sh 6 d.)

*FARMER, [R.....]

The soldiers, an historical poem, in three parts; containing an epitome of the wars entered into by Great-Britain, from the Y. 1739 to the present time. Part I. 1802. 8. (1 sh. 6 d.)

*FARNELL, [.....] *Apothecary at Bath.*

Experiments with the english rhubarbs made in the general hospital at Bath. (Bath Agricult. Soc. Vol. 3. p. 396.)

*Earl of FARNHAM, [Barry Maxwell]

born ....., died at Dublin. 1800. Nov.

See Gentleman's Magaz. Y. 1800. Dec. p. 1220.

An examination into the principles contained in a pamphlet, entitled the speech of Lord *Minto*, with some remarks upon a pamphlet, entitled, observations on that part of the speaker's speech, which relates to trade. 1800. 8. (1 sh. 6 d.)

FARQUHARSON, [William] *M. Dr. Edinburgh.*

Case of an abscess of the breast successfully treated. (Mem. of M. S. of L. Vol. 3. p. 123.)

*FARRAR, [J.....]

The history of Limerick, ecclesiastical and civil, from the earliest record to the Year 1787. Illustrated by 15 engravings. 1792. (7 sh.)

*FARRE, [J..... R.....] *Surgeon.*

Observations on the cure of hydrocele by injection. (M. Rec. and Ref. p. 183.)

*FARRELL, [.....] *Mrs. (Daughter of the late Admiral Fielding.)*

Charlotta, or a sequel to the sorrows of Werter; a struggle between religion and love in an epistle from Abelard to Eloisa; a vision, or evening walk; and other poems. 1792. 4. (6 sh.)

*FARRELL, [R.....]

Union or separation. 1798. (1 sh.)

FARRER, [John] *M. A.*

Sermons on the parables. Vol. 1. 2. 1801. 1802. 8. (14 sh.)

*FEILDE, [Matthew] *M. A. Rector of the united churches of St. Anne Aldersgate and St. John Zachary, Vicar of Uggley, in Essex and Undergrammar to Christ's Hospital.*
born .... died 1796. Aug. 11.
See Gentleman's Magaz. Y. 1796. Aug. p. 708. Sept. p. 787. Allgem. Litt. Zeit. ItBl. J. 1800. p. 628.
(Is said to have been the author of Vertumnus and Pomona, acted Coventgarden theater in 1782.)

FELL, [John] *formerly Pastor of a congregation of Protestant Dissenters at Thaxted in Essex and Tutor of the Dissenting Academy at Homerton.*
born at Cockermouth Aug. 22. 1732. died at Homerton near Hackney 1797. Sept. 6.
See Gentleman's Magaz. Y. 1797. Oct. p. 893. The Annual Necrology for 1797. 1798. p. 503. Allgem. Litter. Zeit. J. 1798. ItBl. N. 32. S. 283.
Essay on the love of our country. 17.. 8. A review of the επεα πτεροεντα, or, diversions of Purley, by Mr. *Horne Tooke*; 17.. A review of *Savary's* letters on Egypt; 17.. 8. The justice and utility of penal laws for the direction of conscience examined in a letter to *Burke.* 1774. 8. Remarks on the appendix of the editor of *Rowley's* poems, printed at the end of observations on the poems attributed to *Rowley* by *Rayner Heckford*, Esq. 1783. 8. An essay towards an english grammar; with a dissertation on the moral and peculiar use of certain hypothetical verbs in the English language. 1784. 12. Letters on the evidences of christianity; four by *John Fell* — and eight by *Henry Hunter*. 1798. 8. (6 sh.)

*FELL, [R.....]
A tour through the Batavian republic during the latter part of the Y. 1800. containing an account of the revolution and recent events in that country. 1801. 8. (8 sh. 6 d.)

*FELLOWES, [Robert] *A. M. of St. Mary Hall, Oxford.*
A picture of christian philosophy; or a theological, philosophical and practical illustration of the character

racter of Jesus; in which the genuine christian temper is contrasted with the benevolent system maintained by *Godwin*, and other philosophers and with the view of christianity by *Will. Wilberforce* &c. 1798. 8. (2 sh. 6 d.) Ed. 2. with corrections and considerable additions. 1799. 8. (5 sh.) A supplement to a picture of christian philosophy —; 1803. 8. (1 sh.) An address to the people, on the present relative situations of England and France, with reflections on the genius of democracy and on parliamentary reform. 1799. 12. (1 sh. 6 d.) Morality united with policy; or reflections on the old and new government of France, and on various important topics of civil and ecclesiastical reform. 1800. 12. (2 sh. 6 d.) The anti-calvinist; or, two plain discourses on redemption and faith. 1800. (1 sh.) Religion without cant: or, a preservative against lukewarmness and intolerance, fanaticism, superstition and impiety. 1801. 8. (9 sh.)

FELTHAM, [John]
A tour through the isle of Man in 1797 and 1798, comprising sketches of its ancient and modern history, constitution, laws, commerce, agriculture, fishery &c. including whatever is remarkable in each parish; its population, inscriptions, registers, embellished with a map of the island and other plates. 1798. 8. (7 sh.) On sundry topics. (Bath Agric. Soc. Vol. 9. p. 105.)

FELTHAM, [John]
The english enchiridion; being a selection of apophthegms, moral maxims &c. 1799. 8. (2 sh. 6 d.)

FELTHAM, [John]
A popular view of the structure and economy of the human body; interspersed with reflections, moral, practical and miscellaneous; including modern discoveries —. 1803. 12. (7 sh.)

FELTON, [William] *Coach-maker.*
A treatise on carriages, comprehending coaches, chariots, phaetons, curricles, whiskeys &c. together with their proper harness: in which the fair prices of every article are accurately stated.
Vol.

Vol. 1. 2. 1795. 8. (1 L. 1 sh.) Supplement. 1796. 8.

FENN, [Sir John] *Knight. M. A. F. A. S. In the commission of the peace and a Deputy-Lieutenant of East Dereham, Norfolk.*

born in Norwich Nov. 26. 1739. died at East Dereham. 1794. Febr. 14.

See Gentleman's Magaz. Y. 1794. Febr. p. 189. On the post and postage of letters and on the privilege and modes of franking letters. (Gentlem. Magaz. Vol. 54. Sept. p. 644.) Three chronological tables of the members of the society of Antiquaries. 1784. 4.

*__FENNA__, [Joseph] *of Baddely, near Namptwich.*

On irrigation, or watering land. (Comm. to the B. of Agr. Vol. 2. p. 334.) Experiments with salt. (Ibid. Vol. 2. p. 342.)

*__FENNELL__, [. . . . .] *Esq.*

Lindor and Clara, or the british officer, a comedy, in 5 acts. 1791. 8. (1 sh. 6 d.) A review of the proceedings at Paris during the last summer, including an exact and particular account of the memorable events, on the 20 June, the 14 July, the 10 Aug. and the 2 Sept. With observations and reflections on the characters, principles and conduct of the most conspicuous persons concerned in promoting the suspension and dethronement of Louis XVI. 1792. 8. (6 sh.) übers. Berlin. 1794. 8.

*__FENNING__, [Daniel]

The young algebraist's companion; or, a new and easy guide to algebra; a new edition. To which is added 38 select problems with their solutions. 1802. 12.

*__FENWICK__, [. . . . .] *Mistress.*

*Secrecy. 17..

*__FENWICK__, [John]

The Indian, a farce. 1800. (1 sh. 6 d.)

*__FENWICK__, [John]

Memoirs of Gen. *Dumourier*, written by himself, translated. P. 1. 2. 1794. 8. (6 sh. 6 d.) Observations on the trial of *James Coigly*, for high treason,

treason, together with an account of his death, including his address to the spectators. — 1798. (3 sh.)

ENWICK, [John Ralph] *M. Dr.*
Reflections on calcareous manure and on the importance of elastic fluids in vegetation and on the preservation and application of fold-yard manure, 1798. Essay on calcareous manures. (*Young's* A. of Agr. Vol. 31. p. 289.) Some reflections on the importance of elastic fluids in vegetation and on the preservation and application of fold-yard manure. (Ibid. Vol. 36. p. 59.)

ENWICK, [Thomas] *Coal-viewer.*
Four essays on practical mechanics; the first on water wheels, the second on the steam engine; the third on mills; and the fourth on the simplification of machinery. 1801. 8. (3 sh.)

:RGUSON, [Adam] *LL. D: F. R. S. E. Emeritus Professor of Moral Philosophy in the University of Edinburgh.*
born 1724. at Logierait in the presbytery of Dunkeld.
See Public Characters of 1799 and 1800. p. 431. Principles of moral and political sciences; being chiefly a retrospect of lectures delivered in the college of Edinburgh. Vol. 1. 2. 1792. 4. (1 L. 16 sh.) übers. mit einer Abhandl. über den Geist der *Fergusonschen* Philosophie, von *K. G. Schreiter.* Th. 1. 1796. 8.

'ERGUSON, [Alexander] *of Aberdeen, M. Dr.*
Medical researches and observations, being a series of essays, on the practice of physic: Essay 1. On the nature, cause and cure of fever: with forms for extemporaneous prescription. Aberdeen, 1801. 8. (6 sh.)

FERGUSON, [William] *Shipmaster at Peterhead.*
On the fisheries. (Tr. of Highland Soc. Vol. 1. p. 294.)

FERGUSSON, [Robert] *Esq. of Lincoln's-Inn.*
The proposed reform of the representation of the counties of Scotland considered. 1792. 8. (1 sh.) Proceedings against the Earl of *Thanet*, *Robert* Fer-

Ferguson, Esq. and others, upon an information plea, ex officio, for a riot. To which are added observations on his own case. 1799. 8. (5 sh.)

*FERMOR, [William] *Esq.*

Reflections on the cow-pox, illustrated by cases to prove it an absolute security against the small-pox. 1800. 8. (1 sh.)

*FERNEL, [John] *Portrait and Miniatur-Painter.*

The christian reconciler; or, religious bigotry reproved. 1801. 12. (1 sh.)

*FERON, [John] *Veterinary Surgeon to the 13 Regt. of Dragoons.*

A new system of farriery — 1803. 4. (1 L. 1 sh.)

FERRAR, [John] *Citizen of Limerick.*

A view of ancient and modern Dublin, with its improvements to the Year 1796. 1796. 8. (6 sh. 6 d.)

*FERRIAR, [John] *M. Dr. Physician to the Infirmary at Manchester, Lunatic-Hospital and Asylum.*

Of popular illusions and particularly of medical demonology. (Mem. of M. Vol 3. p. 31.) Essay on the dramatic writings of *Massinger*. (Ibid. Vol. 3. p. 123.) Observations concerning the vital principle. (Ibid. Vol. 3. p. 216.) Account of an ancient monument in Huln Abbey, Northumberland. (Ibid. Vol. 3. p. 302.) Case of hydrophobia, with the appearances on dissection. (*Simmons's* Medical Facts and Observat. Vol. 1. p. 1.) übers. *Koch's* Samml. auserles. Abhandl. B. 14. S. 651. Medical histories and reflections. Vol. 1. 1792. 8. (4 sh.) übers. Leipzig. 1793. 8. Vol. 2. 1795. 8. (5 sh.) übers. unter dem Titel: Neue Bemerk. über Wassersucht, Wahnsinn, Veränderungen der Krankheiten, Heilkräfte der verschiedenen Luftarten und andere medicinische Gegenstände. Leipzig. 1797. 8. Vol. 3. 1798. 8. (5 sh.) übers. Neue Bemerk. über die Hundswuth, die heutige Bräune, den Keichhusten, die Lust-seuche — übers. von *C. F. Michaelis*. Leipzig. 1801. 8. An argument against the doctrine of materialism. (Mem. of M. Vol. 4. P. 1. p. 20.) Comments on *Sterne*. (Ibid. Vol. 4. P. 1. p. 45. New-York Magaz. Y. 1794. Febr. p. 86.) vergl. *Fried. Nicolai* über die Quellen

Quellen, woraus *Sterne* schöpfte: Berlinische Monaths-schrift J. 1795. Febr. S. 99. Illustrations of *Sterne;* with other essays and verses. 1798. 8. (5 sh.) Conjectures on the use of the ancient terrassed works, in the North of England. (Mem. of M. Vol. 4. P. 2. p. 422.) On the medical properties of the digitalis purpurea or foxglove. 1799. 12. (1 sh. 6 d.) (cf. *Duncan's* A. of Med. Y. 1799. p. 505.) Regulations of the police in the town of Manchester and Salford for the prevention of disease. (*Duncan's* M. C. Dec. 2. Vol. 8. p. 447.)

ERRIER, [W.....]

Two discourses, preached: the first, on occasion of the death of the Rev. Mr. *Alice;* and the second, before the friends of the sabbath evening schools in Paisley: with a short authenticated account of the rise, progress and present state of the sunday schools in Paisley. 1801. 8. (1 sh. 6 d.)

ERRIS, [Samuel] *M. Dr: F. A. S. Physician in London.*

A case of petechiae sine febre. (*Simmons's* Med. Facts and Observat. Vol. 1. p. 79.) A view of the establishment of physic as science in England, by the incorporation of the College of physicians. 1794. (3 sh. 6 d.)

FIELD, [G.....]

Prospectus and catalogue of the British school instituted for the perpetual exhibition and sale of the original work of modern artists. 1802. 8.

FIELD, [Henry] *Apothecary.*

Cases of cynanche trachealis, successfully treated, with observations on that disease. (Mem. of M. S. of L. Vol. 5. p. 165.)

FIELD, [William] *Esq. of the Inner-Temple.*

A letter addressed to the inhabitants of Warwick, in answer to several charges of a very extraordinary kind, advanced against the dissenters, assembling at the chapel in high-street. Ed. 2. 1791. 8. (6 d.) A second letter — in reply to the remarks upon the first letter. 1791. 8. (1 sh.) The practice of the court of King's-Bench in personal actions. Part 1-3. 1798. (3 sh. 6 d.)

*FIFE,

*FIFE, [.....] *Earl of*
On planting. (*Young's* A. of Agr. Vol. 9. p. 105.) Reply to queries on planting. (Ibid. Vol. 10. p. 527.). Account of his plantations. (Tr. of the Soc. for the E. of A. Vol. 6. p. 5.) Trial of the mangel-wurzel or root of scarcity, turneps, carrots and turnep-rooted cabbage, as food for cattle. (Ibid. Vol. 7. p. 29.)

FILSON, [John]
The discovery, settlement and present state of Kentucky, republished with considerable additions. 1793. 8. (2 sh.) *John Filson's* and *George Imlay's* topographical description of the western territory of North-America — Ed. 2. 1793. 8. (6 sh.)

*FINCH, [Robert Pool] *D. D. Prebendary of Westminster and Rector of St. John Evangelist.*
born 1723. died 1803. May 18.
See Gentleman's Magaz. Y. 1803. May. p. 486.
Considerations upon the use and abuse of oaths judicially taken. 1788. 8. (6 d.) The christian sabbath vindicated, in opposition to sceptical indifference and sceptical practice. 1798.
(Several single sermons)

FINCH, [Thomas] *Chaplain of the Caesar and late of St. Mary Hall, Oxon.*
Early wisdom, designed to improve young people in religion and virtue, in the knowledge of themselves and of the world, of the beauties of nature and the ingenuity of art. Vol. 1. 2. 1794. 8. (5 sh.) A discourse to sailors on pardon and allowance for offences. 1797. 8.

*FINCH, [William] *LL. D.*
The objections of infidel historians and other writers against christianity, considered in 8 sermons, preached at the Bampton lecture at Oxford in the Y. 1797. 1797. 8. (5 sh.)

*FINDLATER, [Charles] *Minister of the Parish of Newlands in the County of Peebles.*
General survey of the agriculture of the county of Peebles, with suggestions as to the means both of local and general improvement of agriculture; with a map of the county. 1802. 8. (7 sh.)

FINDLAY,

NDLAY, [Robert] *D. D.*
The divine inspiration of the jewish scriptures and old testament asserted by St. Paul, 3 Timothy, C. 3. v. 16. and Dr. *Gedder's* reasons against the tenor of his words, examined. 1803. 8. (3 sh.)

INDLEY, [William] *Member of the house of Representatives of the United States.*
History of the insurrection in the four western counties of Pennsylvania in the Y. 1794. with a recital of the circumstances specially connected therewith; and an historical review of the previous situation of the country. Philadelphia. 1796. 8.

INIGAN, [J..... T.....]
An attempt to illustrate a few passages in *Shakespeare's* works. 1803. 8. (1 sh. 6 d.)

INLAYSON, [James] *D. D.* See *Hugh Blair.*

IOTT, [John] *Merchant in London.*
An address to the proprietors of East-India stock and to the public: containing a narrative of the cases of the ship Tartar and Hartwell, late in the company's service. 1791. 8. (1 sh 6 d.) Second address. 1792. 8. (2 sh. 6 d.) Letter to the proprietor's of East-India stock. 1793. 8 (6 d.)

IRTH, [John Scholefield] *Esq of Kipping, Yorkshire.*
On the culture of the spanish chesnut tree. (Tr. of the Soc. for the E. of A. Vol. 12. p. 125.)

IRTH, [William] *Esq. Barrister at Law; of Lincoln's-Inn.*
The Lord *Thanet's* case considered as to the question „whether the judgment be specific or arbitrary?„ with the fullest reports of the cases on the subject. 1799. 8. (1 sh.)

ISHER, [Henry]
Discord, an epic poem; occasioned by observing the present troubles in France. 1794. 4. (2 sh.)

ISHER, [James]
John Bull's answer to Bonaparte's declaration, that England was not equal to France; a new song. 1803. (1 sh.)

ISHER, [James] *of Delaware.*
Dissertation on that grade of the intestinal state of fever, known by the name of dysentery. Philad. 1797. 8.

*FISHER, [John] *A. B.*

The valley of Llanherne (on the Northcoaſt of Cornwall) and other pieces in verſe. 1801. 12. (5 ſh.)

*FISHER, [Jonathan] *Artiſt.*

A picturesque tour of Killarney, deſcribing in 20 views, the moſt pleaſing ſcenes in that celebrated lake; accompanied by ſome general obſervations and neceſſary inſtructions — with a map of the lake and its environs; Engraved in aqua tinta. 1791. fol. (2 L. 12 ſh.)

FISHER, [Joſeph] *M. Dr. Member of the Phyſ. Soc. of Edinb.*

Obſervations and enquiries concerning the coal works at Whitehaven in the county of Cumberland made in the Y. 1793. (Tr. of J. A. Vol. 5. p. 266.)

*FISHER, [Miers]

Account of a remarkable change of colour in a negro. (Mem. of M. Vol. 5. P. 1. p. 314.)

*FISHER, [Richard Barnard] *Esq. Steward of Saint Mary Magdalen-College, Oxford.*

A practical treatiſe on copy hold tenure, with the method of holding courts leet, courts baron, and other courts, and an appendix containing forms of entries on court rolls and minute books, ſurveys, ſteward's fees, and a variety of precedents on the mode of conveying copyhold eſtates. 1794. 8. (6 ſh. 6 d.)

*FISHER, [Walter] *Miniſter at Cranſtoun.*

Four theorems for reſolving all the caſes of plane and ſpherical triangles. (Tr. of E. S. Vol. 4. H. p. 4.)

*FISKE, [....] *Rev. of Shimpling, near Bury.*

On beans as a fallow, with obſervations by *A. Young.* (*Young's* A. of Agr. Vol. 3. p. 97.) On ſummer fallowing. (Ibid. Vol. 4. p. 49.) Reply to the advocates for ſummer fallowing. (Ibid. Vol. 5. p. 225.) On fallowing. (Ibid. Vol. 6. p. 369.)

*FISKE, [Nathan] *D. D. Paſtor of the third church at Brookfield*

An hiſtorical account of the ſettlement of Brookfield, in the county of Worceſter, and its diſtreſſes during

during the Indian wars. (Coll. of Massachusetts H. S. Y. 1792. p. 257.)

[T]TLER, [James] *Engraver to his Majesty.*
Scotia depicta, or the antiquities, castles, public buildings, gentleman's seats, towns and picturesque scenery of Scotland, from drawings by *John Claude Natter*, accompanied with descriptions. Nrb. 1. 1801. (10 sh. 6 d.)

[FI]TZGERALD, [Gerald] *D. D. F. T. C. and Professor of Hebrew in the University of Dublin.*
On the originality and permanency of the biblical hebrew: with an application to the leading principle of a modern unbeliever, who denies the existence of any written word of God. 1796. 8. (8 sh.) Poems. 1797. 8. (3 sh. 6 d.) A hebrew grammar, for the use of the students of the university of Dublin. 1799 8.

[FI]TZGERALD, [Keane] *F. R. S.*
born . . . . died . . . . 1782. June 29.

[FI]TZGERALD, [William Thomas] *Esq.*
Prologues and epilogues. 1793. The tribute of an humble muse to an unfortunate captive queen, the widow of a murdered king. 1793. 4. (1 sh.) Lines on the murder of the queen of France, with admonition to the infant Louis XVII. being a sequel to the tribute of an humble muse — 1794. 4. (1 sh.) *Nelson's* triumph; or the battle of the nile: a poem. 1799. 4. (1 sh.) Miscellaneous poems. 1801. 8. (9 sh.) The tears of Hibernia dispelled by the union. 1802. 4. (1 sh.)

[F]ITZ-JOHN, [Matilda]
Joan!!! a novel. Vol. 1-4. 1796. 8. (14 sh.)

[F]ITZPATRICK, [Sir Jeremiah] *M. Dr. Knight. Inspector general of health to his Maj. landforces.*
Suggestions on the slave trade, for the consideration of the legislature of Great-Britain. 1797. 8. (1 sh. 6 d.)

[Lor]d FITZWILLIAM, [.....]
Letter 1. 2. to the Earl of *Carlisle*, explaining the causes of that event. 1794. 8. Ed. 2. 1795. (1 sh.) Ed. 3. 1795. (1 sh.)

[FL]AGG, [Henry Collins] *Esq. of South-Carolina.*
Observations on the numb-fish, or torporific eel. (American Museum, Y. 1787. Nov. p. 490.)

Z 2 *FLAVELL,

*FLAVELL, [John]

A faint indeed: or, the great work of a christian opened and preffed; — 1803. 8. (1 fh. 6 d.)

*FLAXMANN, [John] *Sculptor.*

The Iliad of *Homer* engraved by *Thomas Piroli* from the compofition of *Flaxmann.* London. 1795. 4. engraved by *Riepenhaufen,* Gottingen. 1803. 4. (5 Rthlr.) The Odyffey of *Homer* engraved by *Thomas Piroli* from the compofition of *J. Flaxmann.* Rome. 1793. 4. Gottingen. 1803. 4. Compofitions from the tragedies of *Aefchylus,* defigned by *J. Flaxmann,* engraved by *Th. Piroli.* 179. La divina commedia di *Dante* Alighieri — 1793. 4. Letter to the committee for raifing the naval pillar or monument. 1799. 4. (2 fh. 6 d.)

*FLEET, [Charles] *M. A. Rector of Durweston and Bruanfton, in the County of Dorfet.*

Four fermons on public occafions. 1796. (2 fh.)

*FLEMING, [S.....]

An impartial ftatement of the merits and fervices of oppofition: with a view to the prefervation of the Britifh conftitution and the means of reftoring peace and profperity to thefe countries; 1797. 8. (1 fh.)

*FLETCHER, [Ann]

— — *S.* and *H. F. Dutton,* the ftudy of hiftory rendered eafy, by a plan founded on experience. Vol. 1. England. Vol 2. Rome. 1799. 12. (9 fh.)

FLETCHER, [Charles] *M. Dr.*

The naval guardian Vol. 1. 2. 1800. (14 fh.)

*FLETCHER, [Sir Henry] *Bart.*

Fleets reftorative for the rot in fheep. (*Young's* A. of Agr. Vol. 29. p. 320.)

*FLETCHER, [J....] *Esq.*

Defcription of *Atkins's* hydrometer for afcertaining the fpecific gravities of fpirituous liquors. (*Nicholfon's* Journal. Y. 1802. Aug. p. 276.)

*FLETCHER, [John] *near Northleach, Gloucefterfhire.*

On planting boggy foils with afh and the flopes of fteep hills with foreft trees. (Bath Agricult. Soc. Vol. 1. p. 131.)

*FLETCHER, [Samuel]

A treatife on the art of enamel painting on porcelaine

celains, metals, glass and potter's ware, describing the materials, process and qualities of the several kinds of porcelains and pottery — 1803. 8. (4 sh.)

LEXMAN, [Roger] *D. D. Minister of a Dissenting Congregation at Rotherhite.*

born 1707. died 1795. June. 14.

See Gentleman's Magaz. Y. 1795. June. p. 534. Y. 1796. Apr. p. 308.

(One of the compilers of the Index to the journals of the House of Commons;) Charity sermon. 17.. (6 d.) Sermon on the death of Dr. *T. Amory.* 1774. Account of the life and writings of the Rev. *Samuel Bourne*, prefixed to his posthumous sermons. 1775. Account of the life and writings of Dr. *Chandler*, annexed to his funeral sermon by Dr. *Amory.* 1776. Critical and political miscellany, containing remarks on various authors. 1752–1762.

LINDERS, [Matthew] *Surgeon at Donington, Lincolnshire.*

Case of a child born with variolous pustules. (Mem. of M. S. of L. Vol. 5. p. 330.)

OOD, [Henry] *M. of P.*

born 1732. died at Farmley, his seat in the county of Kilkenny. 1791. Dec. 2.

See Gentleman's Magaz. Y. 1791. Dec. p. 1163. Suppl. p. 1224. Y. 1792. Jan. p. 44.

Verses on the death of Frederick Prince of Wales, published in the Oxford Collection 1751. Ode on fame; 17.. Translation of the first Pythian ode of *Pindar.* 1785. (Several speeches in the English and Irish parliaments.)

LORIAN, [J.... B....] *M. A.*

Essay on analytical course of studies, containing a complete system of human knowledge. 1796. 8. (2 sh. 6 d.)

LOWDEN, [Charles] *Rev.*

Answer to the second blue book, containing a refutation of the principles, charges and arguments of the catholik committee against their bishops; addressed to the Roman catholiks of England. 1791. (2 sh. 6 d.)

*FLOWER, [Benjamin] *Formerly a Grocer in London, now a Printer at Cambridge.*
(He is conductor and printer of the Cambridge Intelligencer, a weekly Newspaper, which commenced in 1793.) The french constitution; with remarks on some of its principal articles, in which their importance in a political, moral and religious point of view is illustrated and the necessity of a reformation in church and state in Great-Britain enforced. 1792. 8. (6 sh.) National sins considered in two letters to — *Thomas Robinson*, Vicar of St. Mary's — on his serious exhortation to the inhabitants of Great-Britain, with reference to the fast. To which are added, a letter from the Rev. *Robert Hall* to the Rev. *Charles Simon*, Vicar of Trinity church — and reflections on war by the late *W. Law* 1796. 8. (2 sh. 6 d.) Reflexions on the preliminaries of peace between Great-Britain and the french Republic. 1800. 12. (4 d.)

*FLOWER, [Richard]
Observations on beer and brewers, in which the inequality, impolicy and injustice of the malt and beer tax are demonstrated. 1802. 8. (1 sh.)

*FOBES, [Peres] *LL. Dr. Minister of the Gospel in Raynham and Prof. of Natural Philosophy in the College of Rhode-Island.*
A topographical description of the town of Raynham in the County of Bristol, Febr. 6. 1793. (Coll. of Massachusetts H. S. Y. 1794. p. 166.)

*FOGG, [Peter Walkden]
Elementa Anglicana, or the principles of english grammar displayed and exemplified, in a method entirely new. Vol. 1. 2. 1797. 8.

*FOLEY, [Richard] *Secondary of the circuit.*
The practice of the court of great sessions for the several counties of Carmarthen, Pembroke and Cardigan; the county of the borough of Carmarthen and the town and county of Haverfordwest. 1792. 8. (5 sh.)

*FOLEY, [Robert] *M. A. of Oriel College, Oxford, and Rector of Old-Swinford, Worcestershire.*
Letter to Dr. *Priestley*, in answer to the appendix (Nro. XIX. p. 197.) of his late publication, entitled, „An appeal to the public, on the subject of the

the riots in Birmingham Part 2.„ to which is added a sermon. 1793. 8. (1 sh. 6 d.) A defence of the church of England; in a series of discourses — on Ephesians v. 27. 1795. 8. (5 sh.)

'OLGER, [Walter] *Jun.*

A topographical description of Nantucket. (Coll. of Massachusetts H. S. Y. 1794. p. 153.)

OLLOWES, [William] *Commander of a ship.*

Narrative of the loss of the pocket lady *Hobart.* 1803.

'ONBLANQUE, [John] *Esq. Barrister at Law.*

A treatise of equity, with the addition of marginal references and notes. Vol. 1. 1793. 8. (8 sh.) Vol. 2. 1794. 8. (9 sh.) Ed. 2. with additions. 1799. 8. (19 sh.)

'OORD, [Humphrey] *Captain of the ship Manchester, of Hull.*

Letter on the use of gun harpoons for taking whales. (Tr. of the Soc. for the E. of A. Vol. 2. p. 197.)

)OT, [Jesse] *Surgeon at London.*

Essay on the bite of a mad dog. Ed. 2. 1791. 8. (2 sh.) A plan for preventing the fatal effects from the bite of a mad dog, with cases. 1793. 8. (6 d.) Complete treatise on the origin, theory and cure of the lues venerea and obstructions in the urethra, illustrated by a great variety of cases. 1792. 4. (1 L. 10 sh.) übers. von Dr. *G. C. Reiche.* Th. 1. 2. Leipzig. 1793. 1794. 8. A defence of the planters in the West-Indies, comprized in four arguments, 1) on comparative humanity; 2) on comparative slavery; 3) on the African slave trade and 4) on the condition of negroes in the West-Indies. 1792. 8. (2 sh.) Facts relative to the prevention of hydrophobia. (*Simmons's* Med. Facts and Observat. Vol. 3. p. 33.) übers. Repertor. Chirurg. und Mediz. Abhandl. B. 2. S. 13.) Life of *John Hunter.* 1794. 8. (6 sh. 6 d.) Dialogues between a pupil of the late *John Hunter* and *Jesse Foot.* 1795. 8. Case of the successfull practice of vesicae lotura in the cure of diseased bladders. 1798. 8. (2 sh.) Ed. 2. Part 1. 2. 1803. 8. (4 sh. 6 d.)

'OOTE, [John] *of Brandon.*

On spaying cows. (*Young's* A. of Agr. Vol. 13. p. 460.)

Z 4

übers. von Dr. C. F. *Michaelis*. Breslau. 1797. 8. On the digestion of food. 1791. 8. (4 sh.) übers. von Dr. C. F. *Michaelis*. Zittau u. Leipzig. 1793. 8. Dissertation 1. 2. on fever. 1794. 1796. 8. (6 sh. 6 d.) übers. von Dr. C. F. *Michaelis*. Th. 1. 2. Zittau u. Leipzig. 1797. 1799. 8. Dissertat. 3. on fever. Part 1. 2. 1798. 1799. (7 sh. 6 d.) Dissert. 4. on fever. 1802. 8. (2 sh. 6 d.) A fifth dissertation on fever. — edited by *Will. Ch. Vells*, M. Dr. 1803. 8. (2 sh.) On the cause of the additional weight which metals acquire on being calcined. (Philos. Transact. Y. 1792. p 374.) Account of a new pendulum. (Ibid. Y. 1794. p. 2.) Observations on the small-pox and the causes of fever. (Transact. of Med. and Chirurg. Soc. Y. 1793. p. 1.) An attempt to improve the evidence of medicine. (Ibid. Y. 1793. p. 243.) Some observations upon the combination of medicines. (Ibid. Y. 1800. p. 314.)

FORDYCE, [James] *D. D: many years Pastor of the Dissenting Congregation at Bath.*

born 1720. died 1796. Oct. 1.

See Gentleman's Magaz. Y. 1796. Oct. p. 883. Dec. p. 1052. Monthly Magaz. Y. 1796. p. 753. Monthly Review. Y. 1797. July. p. 357.

The eloquence of the pulpit, an ordination sermon; to which is added a charge Acts XVIII, 24. An essay on the action proper for the pulpit; both these are printed at the end of Theodorus a dialogue concerning the art of preaching. Ed. 3. 1755. The temple of virtue. Ed. 2. 1796. 8. (2 sh. 6 d.) Sermons to young women. Ed. 2. Vol. 1. 2. 1796. 8. (7 sh.) Address to young men. Ed. 2. Vol. 1. 2. 1796. 8. (8 sh.)

(Several single sermons.)

FORDYCE, [Sir William] *M. Dr. F. R. S. Knight and one of the College of Physicians.*

born 1724. died 1792. Dec. 4.

See Gentleman's Magaz. Y. 1792. Dec. p. 1156. Supplem. p. 1218.

The great importance and proper method of cultivating and curing rhubarb in Britain for medicinal uses. 1792. 8. (1 sh.) On the use of the cluster

cluster potatoe in feeding horses. (*Young's* A. of Agr. Vol. 1. p. 279.) The great importance and proper method of cultivating and curing rhubarb. (Ibid. Vol. 18. p. 24.) Letter on siberian wheat and clustered potatoe. (Tr. of the Soc. for the E. of A. Vol. 1. p. 134.) Letter on the culture of rhubarb. (Tr. of the Soc. for the E. of A. Vol. 2. p. 75.)

*FORREST, [Alexander]

On roads of unvarying level, not the most convenient for draught. (Comm. and Agric. Magaz. Y. 1799. Sept. p. 104.)

*FORREST, [John] *M. Dr. Physician at Stirling.*

Account of a deception with respect to vaccine inoculation. (*Duncan's* A. of Med. Y. 1801. p. 344.)

*FORREST, [Robert] *Esq. of the Middle-Temple; Barrister at Law.*

Report of cases determined in the court of exchequer from Michaelmas to Trinity term the 41 year of George 3. Part 1. Vol. 1. 1802. (5 sh.)

FORREST, [Thomas] *Esq. Captain in the East-India Service.*

A voyage from Calcutta to the Mergui Archipelago lying on the east side of the bay of Bengal —. 1792. 4. (1 L. 1 sh.)

*FORRIS, [Samuel] *M. D. F. S. A.*

A general view of the establishment of physic as a science in England, by the incorporation of the college of Physicians, London —; 1795. 8.

*FORSTER, [B.... M....]

Description of a new hygrometer. (*Tilloch's* Philos. Magaz. Vol. 11. p. 166.) Description of a new invented astronomical instrument, for placing globes in a proper situation, by means of the sun, without the help of a magnetic compass, or other instrument. (Ibid. Vol. 12. p. 83.) Remarks on the clathrus cancellatus (Linn.) and two other species of fungus. (Ibid. Vol. 13. p. 256.)

*FORSTER, [Edward] *Rev. M. A. F. R. S.*

The arabian nights entertainments, translated; embellished by a series of 24 finished engravings from pictures by *Smirke*, done purposely for the work. Vol. 1-5. 1802. 8. (3 L.) Anacreontis odaria, 1802. 8.

*FORSTER,

*FORSTER, [George] *In the civil Service of the East-India Company.*

born . . . . . died 1791. Febr.

A journey from Bengal to England through the northern part of India, Kashmire, Afghanistan and Persia and into Russia by the Caspian sea. Vol. 1. 1790. Vol. 2. 1798. 4. (2 L. 2 sh.) übers. von *C. Meiners*. Th. 1.2. Zürich. 1800. 8.

*FORSTER, [M. . . .] *at Durham.*

Account of a sheep, with observat. by *A. Young*. (*Young's* A. of Agr. Vol. 22. p. 337.)

*FORSTER, [Matthew] *Esq.*

An account of the experiments made on a 21 acre field of light sandy loam, from four to six inches deep on a sandy substratum, to determine the comparative advantage of the drill or broad cast method in the cultivation of turneps. (Tr. of the Soc. for the E. of A. Vol. 17. p. 241.)

*FORSTER, [Thomas Furly] *Esq. F. L. S.*

Description of a new species of viola. (Transact. of L. S. Vol. 6. p. 309.)

*FORSTER, [Thompson] *Surgeon on the Staff of the Army and Surgeon to Guy's Hospital.*

An account of two cases of popliteal anevrism. (*Simmons's* Med. Facts and Observ. Vol. 5. p. 1.) A case of anevrism of the crural artery. (Ibid. Vol. 6. p. 114.)

*FORSYTH, [Alexander John] *Rev.*

On certain usefel properties of the oxygenated muriatic acid. (*Nicholson's* Journal. Vol. 3. p. 158.)

*FORSYTH, [J. . . . .] *at Harworth, Notts.*

On the necessity of an agricultural lexicon. (Comm. and Agric. Mag. Y. 1801. March. p. 171.) On cottage gardens. (Ibid. Y. 1801. Apr. p. 263.)

*FORSYTH, [William] *F. A. S. Gardener to his Majesty at Kensington.*

Observations on the diseases, defects and injuries in all kinds of fruit and forest trees, with an account of a particular method of cure invented and practised — 1791. 8. (2 sh.) übers. von *Georg Forster*. Mainz. 1791. 8. Aufl. 2. mit Anmerk. von *J. L. Christ*. Frankf. a. M. 1801. A treatise on on the culture and management of fruit trees — to which is added an improved edition of obſervations on the diſeaſes, defects and injuries of fruit and foreſt trees. 1802. 4. (1 L. 11 ſh. 6 d.) On trees. (*Young's A.* of Agr. Vol. 26. p. 355.) Method of renovating fruit and foreſt trees. (Maſſachuſetts Magaz. Y. 1792. July. p. 414.)

FORSYTH, [William] *Jun.*

A botanical nomenclator; containing a ſyſtematical arrangement of the claſſes, orders, genera et ſpecies of plants as deſcribed in the new edition of *Linnaeus's* ſyſtema naturae, by *Gmelin* — 1794. 8. (6 ſh.)

FORTUNE, [T.....]

An epitome of the ſtocks and publick funds &c. to which is annexed, a copious equation-table. 1796. 12. (1 ſh. 6 d.)

FOSBROOKE, [Thomas Dudley] *M. A. of Pembroke College, Oxford, Curate of Horsley, Glouceſterſhire.*

The economy of a monaſtic life (as it exiſted in England), a poem; with philoſophical and archaeological illuſtrations, from *Lyndwood*, *Dugdale*, *Selden*, *Wilkins*, *Wills*, *Spelman*, *Warton* &c. with copious extracts from original MSS. 1795 4. (5 ſh.) Britiſh monachiſm; or, manners and cuſtoms of the monks and nuns of England, to which are added, emendations of Biſh. *Gibſon's* verſion of the Saxon chronicle and triumphs of vengeance, or the count of Julian, an ode. Vol. 1. 2. 1802. 8. (14 ſh.)

FOSSAT, [George]

The glory of religion, founded on the doctrine of the ever bleſſed trinity; or, Sabellianiſm refuted: to which is added a refutation of his erroneous work, entitled, an appeal to the chriſtian profeſſing world. Ed. 2. carefully corrected. 1796. 8. (1 ſh. 6 d.).

FOSTER, [.....] *Lieutenant of the firſt or Royal Dragoons.*

Military inſtruction from the late king of Pruſſia to his generals: illuſtrated with plates; To which is added particular inſtruction to the officers of his

his army and especially those of the cavalry: Translated from the french. 1797. 8. (7 fh. 6 d.) Ed. 2. 1800. (7 fh. 6 d.)

*FOSTER, [J.....]

How do we account for the economy of vegetation and can we explain the motion of particular plants, or any other principle than that of irritability? (*Young's* A. of Agr. Vol. 31. p. 474.)

*FOSTER, [John] *A. B. Scholar of Trinity College, Cambridge.*

On the method of illustrating scripture from the relations of modern travellers in Palestine and the neighbouring countries. 1802. 8 (2 fh.)

*FOSTER, [John] *Speaker of the House of Commons of Ireland.*

See Public Characters of 1798–1799. p. 374. An accurate report of his speech on the bill for allowing roman catholics to vote at the elections of members of parliament in that kingdom, to prove that this bill has a direct tendency to subvert the protestant establishment in Ireland, and to separate that kingdom for ever from Great-Britain. 1793. 8. (1 fh. 6 d.) Speech on the union between Great-Britain and Ireland, April 11. 1799. 8. (2 fh. 6 d.)

*FOSTER, [John] *Shoemaker, of Winteringham.*

Poems, chiefly on religious subjects; recommended by *Robert Storey*, Vicar of St. Peter's, Colchester. 1798. 12. (1 fh.)

*FOSTER, [T.....]

Chrestomathia; or, a collection of morality and sentiment; extracted from a variety of authors. 1793. 8. (2 fh. 6 d.)

FOTHERGILL, [Anthony] *M. Dr. F. R. S. at Bath.*

Cautions to the heads of families in three essays, on the poison, of lead, copper. 1791. 8. (1 fh. 6 d.) A new enquiry into the suspension of vital action, in cases of drowning and suffocation — 1795. 8. (2 fh. 6 d.) übers. von Dr. *Christ. Fr. Michaelis*, Leipz. 1796. 8. On the abuse of spirituous liquors; being an attempt to exhibit, in its genuine colours, is pernicious effects upon the property, health and morals, of the people, with rules and admonitions respecting the prevention and

and cure of this great national evil. 1796. 8. (1 sh.) Preservative plan; or, hints for the preservation of persons exposed to those accidents which suddenly suspend or extinguish vital action and by which many valuable lives are prematurely lost to the community. 1798. übers. mit Zus. von Dr. *Christ. Aug. Struve.* Breslau. 1800. 8. An essay on the preservation of shipwrecked mariners, in answer to the prize questions proposed by the royal humane society. 1) what are the best means of preserving mariners, from shipwreck? 2) of keeping the vessels a float? 3) of giving assistance to the crew, when boats dare not venture out to their aid? 1799. (2 sh. 6 d.) On the application of chemistry to agriculture and rural oeconomy. (Bath Agricult. Soc. Vol. 3. p. 54. Columbian Magaz. Y. 1787. Nov. p. 754.) Observations and experiments on certain specimens of english and foreign rhubarb, being an attempt towards estimating their comparative virtues. (Bath Agricult. Soc. Vol. 3. p. 422.) Observations and experiments on the comparative virtues of the roots and seeds of rhubarb; wherein some singular properties of their residua, (after aqueous or spirituous tinctures had been extracted from them) are discovered. (Ibid. Vol. 3. p. 427.) On the culture and management of rhubarb in Tartary, method of using the recent plant; curing the root, nature of its selenitic salt. (Ibid. Vol. 4. p. 174.) Experiments and observations on cyder wine, with remarks on fruit liquors and hints for their improvement. (Ibid. Vol. 5. p. 332.) On the poison of lead, with cautions to the heads of families concerning the various unsuspected means by which that insidious enemy may find admission into the human body. (Ibid. Vol. 5. p. 351.) On the poison of copper. (Ibid. Vol. 5. p. 387.) On the abuse of spirituous liquors; its effects on publick and private property and consequently on national prosperity. (Ibid. Vol. 7. p. 253.) On the nature of the disease occasioned by the bite of a mad dog. (Ibid. Vol. 9. p. 166.) An account of the epidemic catarrh, termed influenza, as it appeared at Northampton and in the adjacent villages in 1775, with a compa-

comparative view of a similar disease as it was observed in London, and is environs in 1782. (Mem. of M. S. of L. Vol. 3. p. 30.) An instance of a fatal pulmonary consumption, without any evident hectic fever. (Ibid. Vol. 4. p. 133.) Effects of arteriotomy in cases of epilepsy. (Ibid. Vol. 5. p. 221.)

*FOTHERGILL, [Charles] *Esq.*
The wanderer, a collection of original tales and essays, founded upon facts, illustrating the virtues and vices of the present age; in which are introduced the oriental travels of a learned Mahometan of the last century; interspersed with original poetry. Vol. 1. 2. 1803. 12. (10 sh.)

*FOUDRAS, [C.....]
Marengo; or the campaign of Italy, by the army of reserve, under the command of the chief - Consul Bonaparte, translated from the french of *Joseph Petit* — with a map of the North-West part of Italy, shewing the route of the army: To which is added, a biographical notice of the life and military actions of General *Desaix*. 1800. 8. (2 sh. 6 d.)

*FOULD, [John] *Engineer to the London — Bridge Water-works.*
Description of his machine for cutting off piles under water. (Tr. of the Soc. for the E. of A. Vol. 13. p. 241.)

*FOULIS, [Sir James] of COLINTON, Baronet.
See *Colinton.*

*FOWLE, [William] *M. Dr. F. R. S. Edinb.*
P. van Woensel's, M. D. new experiments with mercury in the small-pox, by which is demonstrated its specific virtue in that disease; translated from the french. 1793. 8. (1 sh.) A practical treatise on the different fevers of the West-Indies and their diagnostic symptoms. 1800. 8. (2 sh. 6 d.)

*FOWLER, [David Burton] *Esq. One of the six Clerks of the Court of Exchequer.*
The practice of the court of exchequer, on proceedings in equity. Vol. 1. 2. 1795. 8. (13 sh.)

*FOWLER, [R.....]
On sheep and wool. (*Young's* A. of Agr. Vol. 23. p. 545.)

*FOWLER,

)WLER, [Richard]

Experiments and obſervations relative to the influence lately diſcovered by Mr. *Galvani* and commonly called animal electricity. 1793. 8. (3 ſh. 6 d.)

WLER, [Thomas] *M. Dr. at York; formerly Phyſician of the Stafford Infirmary*

born 1736. Jan. 22. died 1801. July 22.

See Gentleman's Magaz. Y. 1801. p. 767. *Duncan's* A. of Med. Y. 1801. p. 489.

Medical reports of the effects of blood-letting, ſudorifics and bliſtering in the cure of the acute and chronic rheumatiſm. 1795. 8. (5 ſh.) überſ. Breslau. 1795. 8. A caſe of an obſtinate quartan ague of five months continuance, cured by electricity; (Mem. of M. S. of L. Vol. 3. p. 114.) Account of the effects of a ſolution of arſenic in the cure of intermittent fever. (*Duncan's* M. C. Dec. 2. Vol. 9. p. 337.)

)X, [Charles]

Tancred, a tale of ancient times. Vol. 1. 2. 1791. 8. (5 ſh.) Ac ſi per tu (the reflected ſun-beam) a ſeries of poems, containing the plaints, conſolations and delights of Achmed Ardebeili; a perſian exile; with notes hiſtorical and explanatory. 1797. 8. (8 ſh.) Santa Maria, or the myſterious pregnancy. Vol. 1-3. 1797. (10 ſh. 6 d.)

X, [Charles James] *Privy Counſellor and Member of Parliament for Weſtminſter, London.*

born 1749. Jan. 13.

See Public Characters of 1798 and 1799. p. 79.

Letter to the worthy and independent electors of the city and liberty of Weſtminſter. 1793. 8. Ed. XI. (1 ſh.) Speech — on Mr. *Whitbread's* motion of the ruſſian armament, March 1. 1792. 8. (2 ſh. 6 d.) Speech containing the declaration of his principles, reſpecting the preſent criſis of public affairs and a reform in the repreſentation of the people. 1792. 8. (2 d.) Speech — at the opening of parliament Dec. 13. 1792. commonly called the King's ſpeech. 1792. 8. (3 d.) Speech on Mr. *Grey's* motion for a reform in parliament May 7. 1793. 8. (2 ſh.) Speech the 24 March

March 1795, on a motion that the houſe do reſolve itſelf into a committee of the whole houſe to conſider of the ſtate of the nation. To which is added a correct liſt of the minority. 1795. 8. (1 ſh.) The propoſals for a general peace, ſubmitted to the french republic through the negotiation of Lord *Malmesbury*, examined and expoſed, in a ſpeech. 1797. 8. (1 ſh.) The ſubſtance of his ſpeech on Mr. *Grey's* motion — 26 May 1797 for leave to bring in a bill to amend and regulate the election of members to ſerve in the common's houſe of parliament, as reported in the Morning chronicle. 1797. 8. (2 d.) Two ſpeeches on the third reading of the aſſeſſed tax bill on the 14 Dec. 1797. and 4 Jan. 1798. 1798. (6 d.) Speech againſt the addreſs to his Maj. approving of the refuſal to enter into a negotiation for peace with the french republic: with a liſt of the minority. 1800. 8. (1 ſh.) Speech at the Shakeſpeare tavern Oct. 10. 1800. being the anniverſary of his firſt election for Weſtminſter. 1800. 8. (1 ſh.) Speech on the motion for an inquiry into the ſtate of the nation. 1801. 8. (2 ſh. 6 d.) Speech on the happy reſtoration of peace with france with the other proceedings at the Shakeſpeare tavern on the 10 Oct. 1801. 8. (1 ſh.) A ſketch of the character of the laſt moſt noble *Francis* Duke of *Bedford*. 1802. 8. (6 d.) An eulogium on the late Duke of *Bedford*, delivered in the houſe of Commons March 16. 1802. Subſtance of the ſpeech on moving a new writ for the borough of Taviſtock March 16. 1802. 8. (6 d.) Speech on the ſtate of the nation, to which is added an illuſtration of ſome paſſages of the ſpeech and contributing to the means of forming a full judgment upon the moſt momentous queſtions which agitate the public mind in the preſent criſis. 1801. (2 ſh. 6 d.) Speech on the renewal of the war with France, May 24. &c. 1803. 8. (3 ſh. 6 d.) (Three fugitive poems, An invocation to poetry; Lines addreſſed to Mrs. *Crewe*; and an epiſtle to the Hon. *John Towſend* in 1780. they are to be found in a collection of fugitive pieces.)

*FOX,

*FOX, [John]
Remarks on wafte lands in Monmouthfhire. (Bath Agric. Soc. Vol. 8. p. 163.)

*FOX, [Jofeph] *Surgeon.*
The natural hiftory of the human teeth, defcribing the proper treatment to prevent irregularities of the teeth. To which is added, an account of the difeafes which affect children during the firft dentition, with engravings. 1803. 4. (1 L. 1 fh.)

*FOX, [William] *Attorney at Law.*
Remarks on various agricultural reports, tranfmitted to the H. Board of Agriculture in the Y. 1794. 1796. 4. (3 fh.)

*FOX, [William]
Addrefs to the people of Great-Britain on the propriety of abftaining from Weft-India fugar and rum. 17.. The intereft of Great-Britain, refpecting the french war. 1793. 8. (3 d.) Thoughts on the death of the king of France. 1793. 8. (3 d.) An examination of Mr. *Paine's* writings. 1793. 8. (3 d.) A difcourfe on national fafts particularly in reference to that of April 19. 1793. on occafion of the prefent war. 1793. 8. (2 d.) The Eaft-India charter, confidered. 1793. 8. (3 d.) On Jacobinifm. 1794. 8. (3 d.) Defence of the war againft France. 1794. 8. (3 d.) On peace. 1794. 8. (3 d.)

*FOX, [William] *Jun.*
La bagatella; or, delineations of home fcenery, a defcriptive poem; in two parts, with notes critical and hiftorical. 1801. 8. (5 fh.)

*FOXCROFT, [Alexander] *Attorney at Law, Nottingham.*
Letter to *Robert Davifon*, worfted fpinner, Arnold. 1803. 8. (6 d.)

FRANCIS, [Anne] *Mrs. (Wife of the Rev. Robert Bransby.)*
born .... died at Edgefield parfonage, near Holt, co. Norfolk. 1800. Nov. 7.
See Gentlemans Magaz. Y. 1800. Supplem. p. 1290.

FRANCIS, [Philip] *Member of Parliament.*
Remarks on defence of Mr. *Hafting's* as far as it concerned the Rohilla war; .... Letter to Lord

North late Earl of Guildford, with an appendix. 1793. 8. (2 ſh.) Heads of his ſpeech in reply to Mr. *Dundas* on the 23 Apr. 1793. in a committee of the whole houſe to conſider of the government and trade of India. 1793. 8. (6 d.) Proceedings in the houſe of commons on the ſlave trade and ſtate of the negroes in the Weſt-India islands, with an appendix. 1796. 8. (2 ſh. 6 d.) Speech in anſwer to S. *Douglas*. 1796. (6 d.) Speech on the affairs of India. Jul. 29. 1803. (1 ſh.)

***FRANCIS, [S.... L....]**

An elegy on the late Colonel *Robert Montgomery*. 1803. 8. (1 ſh. 6 d.)

FRANCKLYN, [.....] *Esq.

*A candid inquiry into the nature of government, and the right of repreſentation. 1792. 8. (3 ſh.) *Club law, or the conſequences of a reform in the repreſentation of the commons of Great-Britain, exemplified in a ſhort deſcription of what has followed a reform in the repreſentation of the tiers-etat or houſe of Commons in France. 1793. 8. (1 ſh.)

FRANCKLYN, [Gilbert] *Esq.

Remarks on a pamphlet entitled, Bengal ſugar; and on the manner in which the trade of the Eaſt India Company is carried on in the Eaſt Indies by foreign ſhipping, in violation of the laws enacted for the ſupport of the commerce and navigation of Great-Britain. 1795. 8. (2 ſh.)

FRANK, [J.....] *Surgeon in his Majeſty's navy.

Obſervations deduced from facts and experiments tending to evince the non exiſtence of typhus contagion, interſperſed with remarks on animal life and on thoſe laws by which it is governed: alſo with ſome remarks on the nature of thoſe diſeaſes, which are epidemic at ſea. 1799. 8.

FRANKLAND, [Sir Thomas] *Bart. F. R. S.

On welding caſt ſteel. (Phil. Transact. Y. 1795. p. 296. *Nicholſon's* Journal. Vol. 1. p. 575.)

FRANKLEN, [J....] *at Lamnihangle.

On mangel-wurzel and other crops for feeding cattle. (Bath Agric. Soc. Vol. 6. p. 139.) On miſcellaneous topics of husbandry. (Ibid. Vol. 6. p. 283.)

* FRANK-

FRANKLIN, [.....] *Dr.*

Wholesome scraps. (Comm. and Agric. Magaz. Y. 1800. July. p. 23.) *An infallible cure for hard times. (Ibid. Y. 1800. July. p. 32.)

FRANKLIN, [Andrew]

The wandering jew or love's masquerade, a comedy in 2 acts. 1797. 8. (1 sh.) A trip to the Nore, an musical entertainment in one act, 1797. 8. (1 sh.) The Egyptian festival, an opera in 3 acts. 1800. 8. (2 sh.)

FRANKLIN, [J.....] *Esq.*

The history of ancient and modern Egypt —. Vol. I. 1800. 12. (5 sh. 6 d.)

RANKLIN, [William] *Captain in the service of the East India Company's Bengal establishment.*

The loves of Camarupa and Camalata an ancient Indian tale, elucidating the customs and manners of the orientals, in a series of adventures of Raja Camarupa and companions; translated from the persian. 1793. 8. (3 sh. 6 d.) The history of the reign of Shah Aulum, the present emperour of Hindoustan, containing the transactions of the court of Delhi and the neighbouring states, during a period of 36 years, interspersed with geographical and topographical observations on several of the principal cities of Hindoustan; with an appendix, containing the following tracts, 1) an account of modern Delhi; 2) a narrative of the late revolution at Rampore in Rohilcund, in 1794. 3) translation of a letter, written in the persian language from the prince Mirza Juwaun Bukht Jehaundar Shah, eldest son of the king of Delhi to his Maj. George III. King of Great-Britain, in the Y. 1785. with a copy of the original. 4) translation in verse of an elegy, written by the king of Delhi after the loss of his sight. 1798. 4. (1 L. 1 sh.) Remarks and observations on the plain of Troy, made during an excursion in June 1799. 1800. 4. (3 sh. 6 d.) An account of the present state of Delhi. (Asiat. Res. Vol. 4. p. 419.)

FRANKS, [James] *A. M. and Curate of Halifax.*

Sermon, on the atonement of Christ. 1790. 8. (6 d.)

(6 d.) The pious mother, or evidences for heaven written in the Y. 1650. by Mrs. *Thomasin Head*, publiſhed from the original MSS. 1794. 12. (2 ſh.)

FRANKS, [John]

On the non-exiſtence of typhus contagion, with remarks on animal life and diſeaſes epidemic at ſea. 1799. 8.

FRASER, [John] *of Chelſea.*

Account of a new graſs. (*Young's* A. of Agr. Vol. 12 p. 106.) Botanical deſcription of the American graſs. (Ibid. Vol. 12. p. 552.) Agroſtis cornucopiae. (Ibid. Vol. 13. p. 306.) Deſcription of a ſtopper for the openings by which the ſewers of cities receive the water of their drains. (Tr. of A. S. Vol. 5. p. 148.)

***FRASER**, [Robert] *Esq.*

Agriculture reports of Devon and Cornwall; 17.. Gleanings in Ireland, particularly reſpecting its agriculture, mines and fiſheries. 1801. (3 ſh.) A general view of the agriculture, mineralogy &c. of the county of Wicklow. 1801. 8. (7 ſh. 6 d.) On potatoes in Cornwall. (*Young's* A. of Agr. Vol. 23. p. 61.) Letter — containing an inquiry into the moſt effectual means of the improvement of the coaſts and weſtern isles of Scotland and the extenſion of the fiſheries. With a letter from Dr. *Anderſon* — on the ſame ſubject. 1803. 8. (3 ſh.)

***FRASER**, [Simon] *Esq. of Lincoln's-Inn; Barriſter at Law.*

Reports of the proceeding's before ſelect committees of the houſe of commons in the following caſes of controverted elections, viz: Hellſton, Oakhampton, Pontefract, Dorcheſter — 1792. 8. (6 ſh. 6 d.) Vol. 2. — viz. Horsham, Sutherland, Honiton, Steyning, Roxburgh, Cirenceſter. 1793. 8. (6 ſh. 6 d.) Eccleſiaſtical law by *Rich. Burn.* Ed. 6. with notes and references. Vol. 1-4. 1797. 8. (1 L. 16 ſh.)

***FRASER**, [William] *Esq. Under-Secretary of State (from the Y. 1765 to 1789.)*

born 1727. died 1802. Dec. 11.

(Writer of the London gazette.)

FREDERICK,

FREDERICK, [....] *Colonel; Son of the late Theodore, King of Corsica.*

The description of Corsica, with an account of its union to the crown of Great-Britain. Including the life of Gen. *Paoli* and the memorial presented to the national assembly of France, upon the forests in that island. With a plan highly beneficial to both states, illustrated with a map of Corsica. 1795. 8. (4 sh.)

FREE, [John] *D. D. Vicar of East Coker, Somerset.* born at Oxford in July 1711. died 1791. Sept. 9.

See Gentleman's Magaz. Y. 1791. Sept. p. 877. Oct. p. 966. Nov. p. 1048.

A sermon on the being and providence of God. 1739. A sermon, when the rebells were advancing to Derby. 1745. Twelve sermons preached before the university of Oxford, with a preface, tending to expose some remarkably bad practices both in church and state. 1750. 8. An antigallican sermon, 1753. A second antigallican sermon. 1756. Two sermons upon the creation, the first, the operations of God and nature —; Ed. 2. the other, the analysis of man; — Ed. 2. 1764. A sermon on the murder of Mr. Allen. 1768. A second on the same occasion. 1769. The monthly reviewers reviewed by an antigallican, 1755. Ode to the King of Prussia; (Gentleman's Magaz. Vol. 27. p. 228.) Ex tempore verses on the choice of a poet laureat. (Ibid. Vol. 27. p. 564.) Will the ferry-man, a water eclogue. (Ibid. Vol. 28. p. 280.) Translation of some french verses on the death of Capt. *Gardner.* (Ibid. Vol. 28. p. 371.) Sermons before the university of Oxford. 1743. Poems and miscellaneous pieces. 1751. Speech on taking his freedom of the city of Oxford. 1753. Seasonable reflections upon the importance of the name of England. 1755. Sentiments of an antigallican; 17.. History of the English tongue —; Part 1-4. 1743. A controversy with the people called methodists. 1758 and 1759. Poems upon several occasions. Ed. 2. 1757. A poetical dialogue, intituled, the voluntary exile. 1765. Stadia physiologica duo — 1762. 4. A genuine petition to the king and likewise a letter to — the Earl of *Bute*; concerning the very hard case of an eminent divine of the church of England. 17.. The petition of *John Free* relative to the conduct of the archbishops of Canterbury and York; 17.. Matrimony made easy &c. a serio-comic satire, tending to expose the tyranny and absurdity of a late act of parliament, intituled, an act for the better prevention of clandestine marriages &c. 17.. A plan for the use of the empress of Russia, in founding a free university for the reception of people of all nations and religions; Ed. 2. 1761. Tyrocinium geographicum Londinense &c. 17..

*FREEMAN, [Harriot Augusta]
(*Mercier's*) Astraea's return; or, the halcyon days of France in the Y. 2440; a dream, translated from the french. 17..

*FREEMAN, [James]
*A short account of *Daniel Gookin*, author of the historical collections of the Indians in New-England, (Coll. of Massachusetts H. S. Y. 1792. p. 228.) *A list of the governours and commanders in chief of Massachusetts and Plymouth (Ib. Y. 1794. p. 194.) *A topographical description of Truro, in the county of Barnstable. (Ib. Y. 1794. p. 195.) **Roger Williams's* key into the language of the Indians of New-England. (Ib. Y. 1794. p. 203.) *Vocabulary of the Narroganset language, (Ib. Y. 1798. p. 80.)

*FREEMAN, [S.....]
Select specimens of British plants. Nrb. 1. 1797. fol. (1 L.)

*FREEMAN, [Samuel] *Esq. Register of Probate for the county of Cumberland.*
The Massachusetts justice, being a collection of the laws of the commonwealth of Massachusetts, relative to the power and duty of justices of the peace. 1795. (10 sh. 6 d.) The probate auxiliary; or, a director and assistant to probate courts, executors administrator and guardians: being the laws of commonwealth of Massachusetts — 1793. 8.

*FREEMAN,

REEMAN, [Strickland] *Esq.*
Obſervations on the mechaniſm of the horſe's foot, its natural ſpring explained and a mode of ſhoeing recommended by which the foot is defended from external injury, with the leaſt impediment to its ſpring, illuſtrated by copper plates. 1796. 4. (1 L. 1 ſh. coloured 2 L. 2 ſh.)

'REEMAN, [Theophilus]
A general epiſtle of brotherly admonition and counſel, to the people called quakers, iſſued at the yearly meeting in London. 1803. (8 d.)

'REER, [Adam] *M. Dr. on the Bengal eſtabliſhment.*
Account of a method employed in Bengal for the cure of the cutaneous diſeaſe, commonly known by the name of ring-worms, the herpes ſerpigo of *Sauvages*, by means of caſſunda vinegar. (*Duncan's* A. of Med. Y. 1800. p. 371.)

'REETH, [John]
The political ſongſter, or a touch on the times on various ſubjects and adapted to common tunes. Ed. 6. with additions. 1790. 8. (3 ſh. 6 d.) The annual political ſongſter. 1793. 12. (1 ſh.)

RENCH, [William] *Surgeon.*
Caſe of a fractured cranium, attended with a loſs of a ſmall portion of the brain. (Mem. of M. S. of L. Vol. 3. p. 604.)

REND, [William] *M. A. formerly Tutor and ſtill Fellow of Jeſus's College, Cambridge.*
Peace and union recommended to the aſſociated bodies of republicans, and anti-republicans. 1793. 8. (1 ſh.) A ſequel to the account of the proceedings in the univerſity of Cambridge, againſt the author of a pamphlet, entitled peace and union; containing the application to the court of King's Bench, a review of ſimilar caſes in the univerſity and reflections on the impolicy of religious perſecution and the importance of free enquiry. 1795. 8. (2 ſh. 6 d.) The principles of algebra for the uſe of ſchools. 1796. 8. (4 ſh.) Part. 2. 1799. 8. (3 ſh.) A letter to the Vice-chancellor of the univerſity of Cambridge. 1798. 8. (6 d.) Principles of taxation. 1799. 8. (1 ſh. 6 d.) Animadverſions on the elements of chriſtian theology by *George Pretyman*, D. D. F. R. S. Lord-Biſhop of Lincoln,

Aa 5 in

in a series of letters. 1800. 8. (3 sh.) The effect of paper-money on the price of provisions, or the point in dispute between Mr. *Boyd* and Sir *F. Baring* examined; the bank paper-money proved to be an adequate cause for the high price of provisions and constitutional remedies recommended. 1801. 8. (1 sh. 6 d.)

*FRERE, [B.....]
The man of fortitude, or, Schedoni in England. Vol. 1-3. 1801. 12. (10 sh. 6 d.)

*FRERE, [John] *Esq. F. R. S. F. A. S.*
Account of flint weapons discovered at Hoxne in Suffolk. (Arch. Vol. 13. p. 204.)

FRESTON, [A....] *M. A.*
Discourse on laws, intended to shew that legal institutions are necessary not only to the happiness but to the very existence of man. 1792. 4. (1 sh.)

FREWEN, [Thomas] *M. Dr. of Lewes in Sussex.*
born .... died 17.. (?)

*FRITH, [W.....] *Esq. of Lincoln's-Inn.*
Lord *Thanet's* case considered, as to the question — whether the judgement be specific or arbitrary? with report of cases. 1799. (1 sh.)

*FROST, [John] *Citizen of London.*
Cheap coals, or, a countermine to the minister and his three city members. 1792. 8. (2 sh.)

*FRY, [Caroline]
The history of England in verse. 1802. 12.

*FRY, [Edmund] *Letter-founder.*
Prospectus of a new work, intitled pantographia —. 1798. Pantographia, containing accurate copies of all the known alphabets in the world — to which are added, specimens of all well authenticated oral languages, forming a comprehensive digest of phonology. 1799. 8. (2 L. 2 sh.)

*FRY, [Thomas]
The guardian of public credit; .... A new system of finance. 1797. 8. (2 sh. 6 d.)

*FRYER, [Henry] *Surgeon at Stamford.*
Cases of pins extracted from the breast of a woman; after remaining there 60 years. (*Simmons's* Med. Facts and Observat. Vol. 7. p. 86.) Two cases of hernia congenita; (Ibid. Vol. 8. p. 131.)

Case

Cafe of imperforate hymen; (Ibid. Vol. 8. p. 133.) Cafe of fungus from a wound in the ear; (Ibid. Vol. 8. p. 135.) Cafe of a wound penetrating the cavity of the abdomen. (Ibid. Vol. 8. p. 137.) Cafe of ftrangulated hernia, where the operation fucceeded after the obftruction had continued eight days. (Transact. of Med. and Chir. Soc. Vol. 2. p. 305.)

'ULHAM, [. . . . .] *Mrs.*
Effay on combuftion, with a view to a new art of dying and painting; wherein the phlogiftic and antiphlogiftic hypothefes are proved erroneous. 1794. 8. (3 fh. 6 d.) überf. von *A. G. L. Lentin.* Göttingen. 1798. 8.

'ULLAGER, [John]
Effay on religion: — 1801. 12. (6 d.)

JLLARTON, [William] *Colonel; M. P: F. R. S.*
On Ayrfhire fheep. (*Young's* A. of Agr. Vol. 22. p. 132.) Effect of manufactures on agriculture. (Ibid. Vol. 22. p. 139.) Letter — to Lord *Carrington.* 1801. 8. (2 fh. 6 d.)

JLLER, [. . . . .] *Miff.*
The convent, or Sophia Nelfon, a novel, in a feries of letters. 17..

'ULLER, [Andrew] *A Baptift Minifter of Kettering in Northamptonfhire.*
The calviniftic and focinian fyftems examined and compared as to their moral tendency. Ed. 2. with additions and corrections. 1793. Ed. 3. 1796. 8. (3 fh. 6 d.) A new edition, with a poftfcript eftablifhing the principles of the work againft the exceptions of Dr. *Toulmin*, Mr. *Belfham* &c. 1802. 8. Socianifm indefenfible on the ground of its moral tendency, containing a reply to two late publications; the one by Dr. *Toulmin*, entitled the practical efficacy of the unitarian doctrine confidered, the other by Mr. *Kentifh*, entitled the moral tendency of the genuine chriftian doctrine. 1797. 8. (1 fh. 6 d.) Expofitory remarks on the difcipline of the primitive churches. 1799. 12. (3 d.) The gofpel its own witnefs, or the holy nature and divine harmony of the chriftian religion,

gion, contrasted with the immorality and absurdity of deism. 1799. 8. (5 sh.) Memoirs of the late Rev. *Samuel Penn*, A. M. Minister of the gospel, Birmingham; with extracts from his most interesting letters. 1800. 8. (3 sh. 6 d.) The blackslider, or, an enquiry into the nature, symptoms and effects of religious declension, with the means of recovery. 1801. 8. (1 sh.) The gospel worthy of all acceptation, or, the duty of sinners to believe in Jesus Christ; Ed. 2. with corrections and additions —; 1801. 12. (2 sh.)
(Several single sermons.)

FULLER, [John] *M. Dr. at Berwick.*
The history of Berwick upon Tweed, including a short account of the villages of Tweedmouth and Spittal. 1799. 8. (7 sh. 6 sh. on fine paper 10 sh. 6 d.)

*FULLER, [Thomas] *Rev. of Heathfield, Sussex.*
Use of potatoes in feeding sheep. (*Young's* A. of Agr. Vol. 12. p. 265.)

*FULLER, [Thomas] *Rev.*
born ..... died ..... (?)
Sermons on various subjects. 1796. (5 sh. 6 d.)

*FULTON, [G....] *Teacher of English.*
— — and *G. Knight*, a general pronouncing and explanatory dictionary of the English language; to which is added a complete vocabulary of scripture proper names. 1802. 12. (4 sh.)

*FULTON, [J.... W....] *Of the Office of the Accountant to the Board of Revenue, Bengal.*
British Indian book-keeping, a new system of double entry and progressive adjustment, by a perspicuous process never before adverted to, saying much trouble and preventing delay. 1800. (6 sh.)

*FULTON, [R....] *Civil-Engineer.*
On the improvement of canal navigation, — illustrated with XVII plates. 1796. 4. (18 sh.)

FURBEN, [Francis] *Bailiff to J. P. Anderson Esq.*
On the long earth worm. (Bath Agric. Soc. Vol. 9. p. 129.)

*FURBES, [Francis] *at Henlade.*
Experiment wether hog sheep. (*Young's* A. of Agr. Vol. 37. p. 138.)

*FURLEY,

FURLEY, [.....] *Lieutenant.*
Maxims and morals for our conduct through life. 1791. 12. (2 sh.)

FURLON, [Lawrence] *Captain.*
The American coast pilot. Newburyport. 1796. 8. Ed. 2. largely improved. 1798. 8.

FYFE, [Andrew] *Professor of Anatomy at Edinburgh.*
Anatomia Britannica; a system of anatomy in six parts; illustrated by upwards of 300 folio copper plates from the most celebrated authors in Europe, by *Andrew Bell*, F. S. A. S. Engraver. Part. 1-3. 1798. fol. A compendium of the anatomy of the human body, illustrated by upwards of 160 tables, containing nearly 700 figures, copied from the most celebrated authors and from nature. Vol. 1-3. 1802. 4. (5 L. 5 sh.)

FYNNEY, [Fielding Best] *Esq. Surgeon.*
The history of hydatids discharged with the urine. (Mem. of M. S. of L. Vol. 2. p. 516.)

GABELL, [Henry] *Rev.*
On the expediency of altering and amending the regulations, recommended by parliament for reducing the high price of corn, and of extending the bounty on the importation of wheat to other articles of provision. 1796. 8. (1 sh.)

GABRIELLI, [.....]
The mysterious wife, a novel. Vol. 1-4. 1797. 12. (12 sh.) Independence, a novel. Vol. 1-4. 1802. 12. (16 sh.)

GAITSKELL, [William] *Surgeon at Rotherhithe.*
Observations on the pathology and mode of treatment of calculi in general, but more particularly of intestinal calculi; with a description and chemical analysis of the intestinal calculi of horses. (*Simmons's* Med. Facts and Observat. Vol. 4. p. 31.) übers. in Samml. für prakt. Aerzte. B. 16. S. 135.) History of a case of pemphigus. (Mem. of M. S. of L. Vol. 4. p. 1.) Observations and experiments on the external absorption of emetic tartar and arsenic. (Ibid. Vol. 4. p. 79.) History of a case of hydrophobia. (Ibid. Vol. 5. p. 1.)

GALE,

GALE, [Benjamin] *F. A. A.* —
Obſervations on the bite of a mad dog. (American Muſeum Y. 1787. Dec. p. 569.) Hiſtorical memoirs, relating to the practice of inoculation for ſmall-pox, in the Britiſh American provinces, particularly in New-England. (Ib. Y. 1789. March p. 242)

*GALLATIN, [Albert]
A ſketch of the finances of the United States. New-York. 1796 8.

GALLOWAY, [Joſeph] *Esq.*
born . . . . , died at Watford. 1802. Aug. 29.
See Gentleman's Magaz. Y. 1803. Sept. p. 887. Letters to a nobleman; 17 . . Brief commentaries, or ſuch parts of revelation and other prophecies as immediately relate to the preſent times; in which the allegorical types and expreſſions are tranſlated into their liberal meanings and applied to their appropriate events. 1802. 8. (9 ſh.) The prophetic or anticipated hiſtory of the church of Rome — 1802.

*GALTON, [S. . . . .]
Experiments on colours. (Monthly Magaz. Y. 1799. Aug. p. 509. cf. Dec. p. 852.)

*GAM, [David] *Esq.*
Memoirs of the adminiſtration of the R. H. *Will. Pitt*, or an inquiry into the cauſes and conſequences of his conduct, in reſpect to different departments, bodies and public individuals of the ſtate. In a letter to — the Earl of *Suffolk*, in conſequence of his Lordſhip's motion in parliament and conferences with his Maj. for the removal of miniſters. 1797. 8. (2 ſh.)

*GAMBLE, [J. . . . .] *A. M. Fellow of Pembroke College, Cambridge; Chaplain to Field-Marſhall his Roy. Highn. the Duke of York and Chaplain-General to his Maj. forces.*
Eſſay on the different modes of communication by ſignals, containing an hiſtory of the progreſſive improvements in this art, from the firſt account of beacons to the moſt approved methods of telegraphic correſpondence. 1797. 4. (12 ſh.)

GANDER.

ANDER, [Gregory] *(a fictitious name.)*
Poetical tales. 1779. 4. (1 sh.)

ANNETT, [Caleb] *Esq. F. A. A.*
Account of a curious and singular appearance of the aurora borealis on the 27 March. 1781. (Mem. of B. A. Vol: 2. P. 1. p. 364)

GAPPER, [Edmund Pitts] *Surgeon at Mere in Wiltshire.*
A case of phthisis pulmonalis, with remarks. (London M. J. Vol. 11. p. 388.)

ARDEN, [Alexander] *M. Dr. Physician in London, before in Charles-town, South-Carolina.*
born 1730. Jan. .... died 1791. Apr. 15.
See Gentleman's Magaz. Y. 1791. Apr. p. 389.

GARDEN, [Charles] *D. D. Minister of the parish of Harwell, in Berkshire and late a Tutor of Eton College.*
An improved version, attempted of the book of Job, a poem, consisting of parallels, constructive, synonymous and triplet; with a preliminary dissertation and notes, critical, historical and explanatory. 1796. 8. (8 sh.)

GARDENSTONE, [Francis] *of Gardenstoun. One of the Senators of the College of Justice.*
born at Edinburg 1721. June 24. died at Morning side near Edinburgh 1793. July 21.
See Gentleman's Magaz. Y. 1793. Aug. p. 769.
Travelling memorandums, made in a tour upon the continent of Europe in the Years 1786-1788. 1791. 8. (3 sh.) Ed. 2. 1792. 8. (3 sh.) Vol. 2. 1792. (3 sh.) Miscellanies in prose and verse. 179 . 12.

GARDINER, [James]
Cowley's history of plants, a poem in 6 books; with *Rapin's* disposition of gardens, a poem in 4 books; translated from the latin; the former by *N. Tate* and others, the latter by *James Gardiner*. 1795. 8. (3 sh. 6 d.)

GARDINER, [John] *D. D.*
Sermons on various subjects, preached at the Octagon chapel, Bath. 1802. 8. (8 sh.)

GARDI-

GARDINER, [John] *M. Dr. Fellow of the Roy. College of Physicians and F. R. S. Edin.*

Pharmacopoea collegii regii medicorum Edinburgensis. 1792. 8. (5 sh.) Inquiry into the nature cause and cure of the gout and of some diseases with which it is connected. Edinb. 1792. 8. (4 sh.) übers. mit Anmerk. von Dr. C. F. *Michaelis.* Leipzig. 1792. 8.

*GARDINER, [John] *Curate at the church of St. Mary Magdalen, Taunton; Rector of Brailsford, in the county of Derby.*

Sermon, preached the 10 Apr. 1793. 4. (1 sh. 6 d.) Brief reflections on the eloquence of the pulpit, occasioned by a pamphlet entitled, remarks on a sermon preached on the fast-day 1795. by *J. Gardiner*, in which, among others are considered the sentiments of Dr. *Gregory*, Dr. *Johnson* and Dr. *Blair.* 1796. 8. (1 sh. 6 d.)

*GARDNER, [Edward]

Observations on the utility of inoculating for the variolae vaccinae or cow-pox. 1801. 8. (1 sh. 6 d.)

*GARDNER, [Edward]

Reflections upon the evil effects of an increasing population upon the present high price of provisions, particularly corn; upon the bounty act and upon the propriety of general inclosures: in which a mode is suggested of relieving of equity. To which is added, an appendix, containing some remarks upon the subject of tythes, further observations upon population and animadversions upon some late publications on the present scarcity. 1800. 8. (2 sh 6 d.)

*GARDNER, [William] *Esq.* See *A... Behn.*

*GARDNOR, [John] *Member of the Roy. Acad. Vicar of Battersea.*

Views taken on or near the river rhine at Aix la Chapelle and on the river Maese, engraved in aqua tinta. Nrb. 1-8. 1788. 4. (12 L. 12 sh.) The history of Monmouthshire by *David Williams;* illustrated and ornamented by views of its principal landscapes, ruins and residences, engraved by *J. Gardnor* and *Hill.* 1796. 4. (2 L. 2 sh.)

GARNET,

RNET, [Thomas] *M. Dr. late Prefident of the Roy. Phyf. and natural biftory Societies, Member of the Roy. Soc. at Edinburgh; Phyficiaa at Harrogate . . Profeffor of Natur. Philof. and Chemiftry in the Roy. Inftitution of Great-Britain.*

born near Kirkby-Lonsdale, Weftmoreland, 1765. died 1802. June 28.

See Public Characters of 1799 and 1800. p. 415. Gentleman's Magaz. Y. 1802. July. p. 690. Aug. p. 777. Nov. p. 990. Monthly Magaz. Y. 1802. Aug. p. 48. *Nicholfon's* Journal. Y. 1802. Sept. p. 62. *Tilloch's* Philof. Magaz. Vol. 13. p. 209. Allgem. Litter. Zeit. J. 1803. ItBl. N. 43. S. 361.

De vifu, an inaugural differtation, Edinb. 1788. Experiments and obfervations on the crefcent water at Harrogate. 1791. 8. (1 fh. 6 d.). Treatife on the mineral waters of Harrogate: containing the hiftory of thefe waters, their chemical analyfis, medical properties and plain directions for their ufe. 1792. 8. (2 fh. 6 d.) Meteorological obfervations made on different parts of the weftern coaft of Great-Britain. (Mem. of M. Vol. 4. P. 1. p. 234. P. 2. p. 517.) A cafe of petechiae unaccompanied with fever, with obfervations on the fame. (Mem. of M. S. of L. Vol 4. p. 233.) Obfervations on the Wigglesworth water. (Ibid. Vol. 5. p. 119.) Obfervations on the nature and virtues of the Harrogate water. (Ibid. Vol. 5. p. 123.) Hiftory of a cafe of dropfy, cured by the ufe of the infufum nicotianae. (*Duncan's* M. C. Dec. 2. Vol. 6. p. 271.) Account of the difcovery of azote, or phlogiftical air, in the mineral waters of Harrogate. (New London M. J. Vol. 1. p. 25.) A cafe of taenia, or tape worm, cured by flowers of fulphur, (Ibid. Vol. 1. p. 32.) Obfervations on the methods ufed for obtaining the different permanently elaftic fluids from mineral waters. (Ibid. Vol. 1. p. 233.) Outlines of a courfe of lectures on chemiftry. 1797. 8. (4 fh.) A lecture on the prefervation of health. 1797. 8. (2 fh.) Obfervations on a tour through the highlands and part of the weftern isles of Scotland, particularly Staffa and Icolmkill; to which are added, a description of the falls of the Clyde, of the country round Moffat and an analysis of its mineral waters: Illustrated by a map and 52 plates engraved in the manner of aqua tinta, from drawings taken on the spot by *W. H. Watts*, miniature and landscape painter. Vol. 1. 2. 1800. 4. (2 L. 12 sh. 6 d.) übers. von *L. Theob. Kosegarten*. B. 1. 2. Lübeck und Leipzig. 1802. 8. Account of the benefit of oxygenated muriate of potash, employed as a medicine. (Medical Repository. Vol. 1. p. 578.) Letter on the use of oxygenated muriat of potash. (*Duncan's* A. of Med. Y. 1798. p. 444.) Annals of philosophy, natural history, chemistry, literature, agriculture and the mechanical and fine arts for the Y. 1800. Vol. 1. 1801. 8. (10 sh. 6 d.) Outlines of a course of lectures on chemistry, delivered at the Roy. Instit. of Great-Britain. 1801. 8. (5 sh.) A lecture on the preservation of health being a popular illustration of the Brunonian doctrine. 1891. 8. (4 sh.) übers. Leipzig. 1802. 8. A short account of Gilsland and its mineral waters. (Monthly Magaz. Y. 1800. Febr. p. 40.) Observations on the irritability of vegetables. (Ibid. Y. 1801. Oct. p. 190.) Observations on rain gages. (Tr of J. A. Vol. 5. p. 357.) Account of the good effects obtained from sulphurated vegetable alkali and powder of charcoal in florid consumptions. (*Duncan's* M. C. Dec. 2. Vol. 10. p. 368.) Letter respecting the benefit derived from the oxygenated muriate of potash employed as a medicine. (*Duncan's* A. of Med. Y. 1797. p. 409.)

*GARNHAM, [Robert Edward] *Rev. of Bury.* born at Bury St. Edmunds 1753. May 1. died 1802. Aug. 24.

See Gentleman's Magaz. Y. 1802. July. p. 689. Suppl. p. 1220. Monthly Mag. Y. 1802. Aug. p. 89. Examination of Mr. *Harrison's* sermon preached — May 1788. 1789. Letter to the — Bishop of Norwich (Dr. *Bagot*) requesting him to name the prelate to whom he referred as „contending strenuously for the general excellence of our present

present authorised translation of the bible,,, 1789. Letter to the Bishop of Chester (Dr. *Cleaver*) on the subject of two sermons addressed by him to the clergy of his diocese, comprehending also a vindication of the late Bishop *Hoadly*, 1796. Review of Dr. *Hay's* sermon, intitled ,,Thoughts on the Athanasian creed.,, 1790. Outline of a commentary on Revelations XI, 1-14. 1794. (Several single sermons.) (Papers in ,,Commentaries and essays,,, signed Synergus. Papers in ,,The theological Repository. Signed Ereunetes and Idiota.)

GARRARD, [Elizabeth] *of Bath.*

Miscellanies in verse and prose. 1800. 8. (4 sh.)

GARTSHORE, [Maxwell] *M. Dr: F. R. S: F. A. S: Physician to the british Lying Inn Hospital, St. Martin's-lane, Westminster, London.*

A remarkable case of numerous births with observations. (Philos. Transact. Y. 1787. p. 344. London M. J. Vol. X. P. 1.) übers. Samml. der neuesten Beobacht. Engl. Aerzte 1789. S. 81. Observations on extra-uterine cases and on ruptures of the uterus. (London M. J. Vol. VIII. P. 4.) übers. Repertor. chirurg. u. Mediz. Wahrnehm. Th. 1. S. 173. An account of the species of erysipelas — as it has appeared in infants at the british Lying-Inn hospital. (M. C. Vol. 2. p. 28.)

GASKIN, [George] *D. D: Rector of St. Benet Gracechurch and of Stoke-Newington, Middlesex.*

Sermons preached to parochial congregations by the late Rev. *Richard Southgate*, B. A. &c. with a biographical preface. Vol. 1. 2. 1798. 8. (12 sh.)

GAST, [John] *Arch-Deacon at Glandelagh.*

The history of Greece. 1782. 4. (1 L. 1 sh.) übers. Leipzig. 1798. 8.

GATES, [R.....]

Letters on fine spinning wool. (Tr. of the Soc. for the E. of A. Vol. 7. p. 151-166.)

GAY, [Nicholas] *Esq. F. R. S.*

born in Ireland .... died 1803. Sept. 20. at Margate.

See Gentleman's Magaz. Y. 1803. Sept. p. 891. Strictures on the proposed union between Great-Britain and Ireland, with occasional remarks. 1799. 8. (1 sh. 6 d.)

GEACH, [Francis] *M. Dr. F. R. S. Principal Physician to the Roy. Hospital at Plymouth.*
born 1724. died 1798. Febr. 17.
See Gentleman's Magaz. Y. 1798. March. p. 259. Apr. p. 305. *Duncan's* Annals of Medic. Y. 1798. p. 474.

*GEARD, [John]
The beauties of *Henry*, a selection of the most stricking passages in the exposition of that celebrated commentator: To which is prefixed a brief account of the life, character, labours and death of the author. Vol. 1. 1797. 8. (4 sh. 6 d.)

GEDDES, [Alexander] *D. D. a Roman catholic Clergyman.*
born at Arradowl in the parish of Ruthven, Bamffshire, Sept. 4. 1737. died 1802. Febr. 26.
See Gentleman's Magaz. Y. 1802. March. p. 279. Apr. p. 312. 371. June. p. 491. Y. 1803. June p. 511. Aug. p. 723. Monthly Magaz. Y. 1802. Apr. p. 255. Allgem. Litt. Zeit. ItBl. J. 1803. N. 41. S. 345.
Letter to a member of parliament on the expediency of a general repeal of all penal statutes that regard religious opinions. 17.. Epistola Macaronica ad fratrem de iis, quae gesta sunt in nupero dissentientium conventu, Londini habita prid. Id. Febr. 1790. adjuncta est versio anglica ad usum dominarum, dominorumque ruricolarum. 1790. 4. (1 sh. 6 d.) * Carmen seculare pro gallica gente tyrannidi aristocraticae erepta. 1790. 4. (1 sh.) translated from the original latin. 1790. 4. (1 sh.) L'Avocat du diable: 17.. *A Norfolk tale, or, a journal from London to Norwich, with a prologue and a epilogue. 1792. 8. *Ververt, or, the Parrot of Nevers, a poem in 4 Cantos, freely translated from the french of *J. B. Gresset*; 1793. 4. Letter to — *John Douglasr*, Bishop of Centurio and Vicar apostolic in the London district. 1794. 4. (2 sh.) * The battle of Bangor, a satirical poem; 17.. * The battle of the bards, an heroic poem in two cantos. The author *Mauritius Moonshine.* 1800. 4. (2 sh.) Three Scottish poems, with a previous dissertation on the

the Scoto-Saxon dialect. (Transact. of the Soc. of the Antiq. of Scotland. Vol. 1. p. 402.) Epiſtle to the Preſident, Vice-preſident and members of the Scottiſh ſociety of Antiquaries, on being choſen a correſpondent member. (Ibid. Vol. 1. p. 441.) The firſt eklog of *Virgil*, translatit into ſkottis vers. (Ibid. Vol. 1. p. 457.) The firſt idillion of *Theocritus*, translatit into ſkottis vers. (Ibid. Vol. 1. p. 462.) The holy bible-faithfully translated from the corrected texts of the originals. With various readings, explanatory notes and critical remarks. Vol. 1. 1792. 4. (1 L. 11 ſh. 6 d.) Vol. 2. 1797. 4. (1 L. 11 ſh. 6 d.) Addreſs to the public on the publication of the firſt volume of his new trauslation of the bible. 1793. 4. (1 ſh.) *A modeſt apology for the roman catholics of Great-Britain, addreſſed to all moderate proteſtants; particularly to the members of the houſe of parliament. 1800. 8. (7 ſh.) überſ. von Dr. *Paulus*. Jena. 1801. 8. Critical remarks on the hebrew ſcriptures; correſponding with a new translation of the Bible; Vol. 1. containing remarks on the pentateuch. 1800. 4. (1 L. 11 ſh. 6 d.) *More wonders! an heroic epiſtle to *M. G. Lewis*, Esq. M. P. with a praeſcript extraordinary and an ode to the union; by *Mauris. Moonſhine*. 1801. 4. (2 ſh.)

EDDES, [John] *Dr.*

Account of the province of Biſcay, in Spain; (Transact. of the Soc. of the Antiq. in Scotl. Vol. 1. p. 205.)

EDDES, [William] *at Proſpect Hill.*

On the benefit of reaping wheat early. (American Muſeum Y. 1787. Aug. p. 176.)

EE, [Joſhua]

The trade and navigation of Great-Britain conſidered —; a new edition. 1792. (3 ſh.)

ELL, [John] *of Lewes.*

Enquiry into the cauſes of inſolvencies in retail buſineſſes, with hints for their preventions and the plan of a fund for the relief of decayed tradesmen, their widows, children or orphans. 1796. 8. (1 ſh. 6 d.)

*GENT, [Thomas] *of Homerton.*

Defcription of his new invented crane, for raifing and delivering heavy bodies. (Tr. of the Soc. for the E. of A. Vol. 19. p. 294.)

*GENTLEMAN, [Robert] *Minifter of the New Meeting-houfe, Kidderminfter.*

born .... died 1795. July 10.

See Gentleman's Magaz. Y. 1795. July. p. 621. *Orton's* expofition of the old teftament. Vol. 5. 6. 1792. 8. (12 fh.) Plain and affectionate addrefs to youth. 1792. 12. (3 fh.)

*GEOGHEGAN; [Edward] *Surgeon at Dublin.*

Practical obfervations on the nature and treatment of fome exafperated fymptoms attending the venereal difeafe. 1801. 3. (3 fh.)

GERARD, [Alexander] *D. D. F. R. S. Profeffor of Divinity in the Univerfity and King's College, Aberdeen, and one of his Maj. Chaplains for Scotland.*

born ..... died 1795. Febr. 22.

See Gentleman's Magaz. Y. 1795. Apr. p. 349. On tafte. 1758. 8. (4 fh.) überf. Breslau u. Leipzig. 1766. 8. Ed. 3. London. 1786. 8. On the genius; 1774. 8. The paftoral care, publifhed by his fon and fucceffor *Gilbert Gerard.* 1799. 8. (7 fh.) überf. von *Mich. Feder.* Wirzburg. 1803. 8.

(Several fingle fermons.)

*GERARD, [Gilbert] *D. D. Profeffor of Divinity in the Univerfity and King's College, Aberdeen, and one of his Maj. Chaplains in ordinary for Scotland.*

On indifference with refpect to religious truths; a fermon. 1797. 8. (1 fh.)

GERARD, [James] *Phyfician to the Liverpool Infirmary.*

A fuccefsful cafe of amaurofis. (Mem. of M. S. of L. Vol. 4. p. 359.)

*GERARD, [William] *Mafter of the Naval and Military Academy, Ormondhoufe, Chelfea.*

The feaman's preceptor; confifting of the fcholaftic rules and examples for the ftudent's progrefs in navigation. 1803. 8. (8 fh.)

*GERATHY,

GERATHY, [James] *Esq. Barrister at Law.*
The present state of Ireland and the only means of preserving her to the empire, considered in a letter to the Marquis *Cornwallis.* 1799. 8. (1 sh.) The consequences of the proposed union — considered in a second letter to — *Cornwallis.* 1799. 8. (1 sh. 6 d.)

GERLIVIN, [William]
Saint-Leon, a tale of the 16 century. Vol. 1-4. 1800. 12. (16 sh.)

GERRALD, [Joseph]
A convention, the only means of saving us from ruin, in a letter addressed to the people of England. 1793. 8. (1 sh.)

GERRARD, [John] *Ecclesiae Anglicanae Presbyter Londinensis.*
Siglarium romanum; sive explicatio notarum ac litterarum, quae hactenus reperiri potuerunt in marmoribus, lapidibus, nummis, auctoribus aliisque romanorum veterum reliquiis, ordine alphabetico distributa. 1792. 4. (1 L. 1 sh.)

GHOGAN, [. . . .] *M. Dr.*
Agricultural experiments on gypsum or plaister of Paris, with some observations on the fertilizing quality and natural history of that fossil. Philad. 1797. 8.

GIBBES, [George Smith] *B. M. late Fellow of Magdalen College, Oxford; One of the Physicians to the Bath city Dispensary. F. L. S.*
On the conversion of animal muscle into a substance much resembling spermaceti. (Philos. Transact. Y. 1794. p. 169. Y. 1795. p. 239. *Simmons's* Medical Facts and Observat. Vol. 7. p. 121.) A few observations on the component parts of animal matters and on their conversion into a substance resembling sperma-ceti. 1796. 8. (1 sh. 6 d.) A treatise on the Bath waters. 1800. 8. (3 sh.) A second treatise - 1803. 8. (8 sh.) Discovery of sulphate of strontian, near Sodbury, in Gloucestershire. (*Nicholson's* Journal. Vol. 2. p. 535. Vol. 3. p. 96. 137.) A chemical examination of the Bath waters. (Ibid. Vol. 3. p. 359. 403. 452.) Account of a cavern discovered on the north west side of the Mendiphills, in Somersetshire. (Transact.

act. of L. S. Vol. 5. p. 143. *Tilloch's* Philos. Magaz. Vol. 7. p. 146.)

GIBBON, [Edward] *F. R. S. F. A. S.*
born 1738. May. 8. at Putney in the county of Surry. died 1794. Jan. 16.

See Gentleman's Magaz. Y. 1794. Jan. p. 94. Febr. p. 178. March. p. 199. April. p. 382. Y. 1797. Nov. p. 915. Allg. Litterat. Zeit. J. 1794. ItBl. April. Nr. 31. S. 241.

Essai sur l'etude de la litterature. 1760. 8. übers. von *J. J. Eschenburg.* Hamb. 1792. 8. (*Gibbon et Deyverdun*) Memoires litteraires de la grande Bretagne. 1767. *A criticism on the 6 book of *Virgil*, in answer to *Warburton.* 1767. (?) A serious call to a devout and holy life, adapted to the state and condition of all orders of christians by *W. Law*, A. M. the 14 Edit: to which is added, some account of the author by *Edw. Gibbon.* 1802. 8. Miscellaneous works. Vol. 1. 2. 1796. 4. (2 L. 10 sh.)

*GIBBONS, [Thomas] *M. Dr. Physician at Hadleigh in Suffolk.*

Medical cases and remarks: Part 1. On the good effects of salivation in jaundice arising from calculi: Part 2. On the free use of nitre in haemorrhagy. 1799. 8. (1 sh.) Some cases of biliary obstructions, from calculi, cured by salivation. (*Duncan's* A. of Medic. Y. 1796. p. 279.)

*GIBBS, [Adam] *late Rev. of Edinb.*
born .... died .... (?)

Tables of the four evangelists. 1800. (6 d.)

*GIBBS, [Jane]

Account of his starch from arum maculatum vulgare. (Tr. of the Soc. for the E. of A. Vol. 15. p. 238.)

*GIBBS, [Robert]

Account of the Earl of upper-Ossory plantations. (Tr. of the Soc. for the E. of A. Vol. 3. p. 4-12.)

*GIBBS, [Vicary] *Esq.*

Speech in defence of *Thomas Hardy*, tried by special commission on a charge of high treason — 1795. 8. (1 sh.) Speech in defence of *John Horne Tooke*, Esq. tried by special commission on a charge of high treason —. 1795. 8. (1 sh.)

*GIBSON,

*GIBSON, [Francis] *Esq.*

Streanshull abbey, or the Danish invasion. A play of 5 acts. 1800. 8. (2 sh. 6 d.)

*GIBSON, [Francis] *Esq. F. A. S.*

Observations on the machine called the Lewis. (Arch. Vol. 10. p. 123.)

GIBSON, [John] *M. Dr. Surgeon in the Royal Navy.*

On bilious diseases and indigestion, with the effects of quassy and natron in these disorders. 1799. 8. (2 sh.)

*GIBSON, [Kennet] *late Curate of Castor.*

A comment upon part of the fifth journey of Antoninus through Britain; in which the situation of Durocobrivae, the seventh station there mentioned, is discussed; and Castor, in Northamptonshire is shewn, from the various remains of roman antiquity, to have an undoubted claim to that situation. To which is added, a dissertation on a image of jupiter found there. Printed from the original MSS. and enlarged with the parochial history of Castor and its dependences to the present time. To which is subjoined, an account of Marham and several other places in its neighbourhood. 1800. 4. (15 sh.)

*GIBSON, [Robert]

History of the old mango tree. (Tr. of the Soc. for the E. of A. Vol. 4. p. 223.)

*GIDDY, [Edward] *Esq.*

On Mr. *Pitt's* poor bill. (*Young's* A. of Agr. Vol. 27. p. 355.)

*GIDLEYKING, [Phillip] *Esq.*

See *Arthur Phillip*, Esq. Governor of New South Wales.

GIFFORD, [John] *Esq.*

The history of France, from the earliest times to the present important era — &c. Vol. 1–4. 1791. 1794. 4. (3 L.) A plain address to the common sense of the people of England, containing an interesting abstract of *Paine's* life and writings. 1792. 8. (6 d.) History of Spain from the establishment of the colony of Gades by the Phoenicians to the death of Ferdinand, surnamed the

Bb 5 sage.

ſage. Vol. 1–3. 1793. überſ. Th. 1. Leipzig. 1794. 8. The reign of Louis XVI. and complete hiſtory of the french revolution, with notes critical and explanatory. 1796. 4. Letter to the Earl of *Lauderdale*, containing ſtrictures on his Lordſhip's letters to the peers of Scotland. 1796. 8. (3 ſh. 6 d.) *Hiſtory of Rome from the foundation of the city by Romulus to the death of Marcus Antoninus, by the author of the hiſtory of France. Vol. 1–3. 179. überſ. von *K. F. C. Wagner*. B. 1. Braunſchweig. 1796. 8. A reſidence in France, during the Years 1792–1795. deſcribed in a ſeries from an Engliſh lady. Vol. 1. 2. 1796. 8. (14 ſh.) The banditi unmaſked, or, hiſtorical memoirs of the preſent times. Tranſlated from the french of General *Danican*, with a preface explanatory of the preſent ſtate of France. 1797. 8. (6 ſh. 6 d.) Letter to the H. *Thomas Erskine*, containing ſome ſtrictures on his view of the cauſes and conſequences of the war; ſome reflections on the ſubject of the preſent negotiation; and obſervations on the voluntary loan; with a word to the critics, ſubjoined. 1797. (3 ſh.) A defence of the French emigrants — by *Trophime Gerald De Lally-Tolendal*, translated from the french. 1797. 8. (7 ſh.) A ſhort addreſs to the numbers of the loyal aſſociations on the preſent ſtate of public affairs. Ed. 5. 1798. 8. (1 ſh.) Addreſs from *Camille Jordan*, member for the department of the Rhone, to his conſtituents, on the revolution of the 4 Sept. 1797. translated from the french, with an original preface and notes. 1798. 8. (3 ſh.) Letter to the Earl of *Lauderdale*, containing ſtrictures on his letter to the peers of Scotland and proving from authentic documents, that the french were the aggreſſors in the preſent war; with an original letter from the late *Edm. Burke*, explaining the much perverted expreſſion of the ſwiniſh multitude, and ſome reflections on Mr. *Sheridan's* attack on the revolution and on the omiſſion of the cuſtomary ſermon at Weſtminſter on the 30 of January 1800. 1800. (4 ſh.)

*GIFFORD,

GIFFORD, [William] *Esq.*
born in April 1757. at Afhburton, in Devonfhire.
See Gentleman's Magaz. Y. 1802. Oct. p. 897. Public Characters of 1802 and 1803. p. 303.
The fatires of *Junius Juvenalis*, translated into Englifh verfe, with notes and illuftrations. 1802. 4. (1 L. 11 fh. 6 d.) An examination of the ftrictures of the critical reviewers on the translation of *Juvenal*. 1803. 4. (3 fh. 6 d.)

GILBERT, [Charles]
Winter barley in Suffex. (*Young's* A. of Agr. Vol. 38. p. 124.)

GILBERT, [Thomas] *Member of Parliament.*
born 1719. died at Cotton, his feat, in the County of Stafford. 1798. Dec. 18.
See Gentleman's Magaz. Y. 1798. Dec. p. 1090. Suppl. p. 1146. Allg. Litt. Zeit. IrBl. J. 1800. S. 654.
The principal caufe of the miferies of the poor. 17..

GILBERT, [William]
The hurricane, a theofophical and weftern eclogue. To which is fubjoined a folitary effufion in a fummer's evening. 1797. 8. (1 fh. 6 d.)

GILBY, [William] *M. Dr. Phyfician to the General Hofpital at Birmingham.*
Account of the fuccefsful application of electricity in a cafe of wry neck. (London M. J. Vol. XI. p. 358.) Account of the good effects of electricity in a cafe of paralytic affection, ferving to prove that in fuch cafes, the electric fparks fhould be taken from the mufcles which are antagonifts to thofe that are contracted. (*Simmons's* Med. Facts and Obfervat. Vol. 2. p. 102.) Repertor. Chirurg. und Mediz. Abhandl. B. 1. S. 311.

GILCHRIST, [John] *Esq.*
A Grammar of the Hinduftanee language. Calcutta. 179. 4. The oriental linguift, or, an eafy and familiar introduction &c. Calcutta. 179. 4. Englifh and Hinduftanee and Hinduftanee and Englifh dictionary. Vol. 1. 2. Calcutta. 179. 4. * The antijargonift, or a fhort introduction to the Hinduftanee

dustanee language, (vulgarly but erroneously called the Moors.) Calcutta. 8. (16 Rupees.) A new theory and prospectus of all the persian verbs with their synonims in England and Hindustanee. 1802. A sheme of Hindustanee orthoepy in roman characters. 1802. Annotations upon *Milton*. (Monthly Magaz. Y. 1802. p. 346.) Account of the Hindustanee horometry. (Asiat. Ref. Vol. 5. p. 81.) A new theory and prospectus of the Persians verbs, with their Hindustanee synonims. 1803. 4. (10 sh. 6 d.)

GILL, [John] *D. D.*
born .... died 1777.
Reasons for separating from the church of England calmly considered; a new edition with some corrections and enlargement. 1800. 8. (4 d.)

*GILLAN, [Hugh] *M. Dr. Physician to the Embassy to China under Lord Macartney and Physician General to the Army at the Cape of Good-Hope.*
born .... died Y. 1798. May 19. at Newhall, near Cromarty, Scotland.
See Gentleman's Magaz. Y. 1798. June. p. 537. Allg. Litt. Zeit. Itbl. J. 1800. S. 650.
De Igne. Edinb. 1786. 8.

*GILLESPIE, [James] *D. D. late Principal of St. Mary's College in the University of St. Andrews, and one of his Maj. Chaplains in Ordinary for Scotland.*
born .... died 1791. June 2.
Sermons, published from the author's MSS. by *George Hill.* 1796. 8. (5 sh. 6 d.)

GILLESPIE, [Leonard] *M. Dr. Surgeon and Agent to the Naval Hospital, Fort Royal, Martinique.*
Advice — on the preservation of the health of seamen. 1799. 8. (1 sh.) Observations on the diseases, which prevailed on board a part of his Maj. squadron on the Leeward Island station between Nov. 1794. and April 1796. 1800. 8. (5 sh.)

*GILLESPY, [E....] *Curate of Blisworth, Northamptonshire.*
A disquisition upon the criminal laws. 1792. 8. (1 sh.)

*GILLET,

GILLET, [R....] *Lecturer in philosophy; F. R. S.*
born .... died ..,. (?)
The pleasures of reason, or the hardened thoughts of a sensible young lady. 1796. 12. (3 sh.) Moral philosophy or logic, adapted to the capacities of youth. 1798. 12. (1 sh. 6 d.)

GILLIAM, [James S....] *M. Dr. of Petersburg, Virginia.*
Reflections on the gout. (American Museum Y. 1789. Sept. p. 211)

ILLIES, [John] *Minister of the College Kirk at Glasgow.*
born 1711. died 1796. March. 29.
See Gentleman's Magaz. Y. 1796. Apr. p. 355. Aug. p. 699. Allgem. Litterat. Zeit. ItBl. J. 1800. S. 627.
Devotional exercises on the new testament. 1769. 8.

ILLIES, [John] *LL. D: F. A. S: Historiographer to his Maj. for Scotland.*
born at Brechin in the Shire of Angus, in Scotland.
See Public Characters of 1800 and 1801. p. 223.
Defence of the study of classical litereture; 17.. übers. Gesch. von Alt-Griechenland. Th. 3. 4. Leipz. 1797. 8. *Aristotle's* ethicks and politicks, comprising his practical philosophy, translated from the greek and illustrated by introductions and notes, the critical history of his life and a new analysis of his speculative works. Vol. 1. 2. 1797. 4. (1 L. 16 sh)

ILLINGWATER, [Edmund]
An historical account of the antient town of Lowestoft in the county of Suffolk, with some cursory remarks on the adjoining parishes and a general account of the island of Lothingland. 1791. 4. On the depravation of apple-trees. (Bath Agric. Soc. Vol. 4. p. 250.) The poll for knights of the shire, to represent the county of Kent, July 1802, by *Thomas Godfrey*, Esq. High Sheriff; arranged from the sheriff's books - with an abstract of this and of the poll in the Y. 1796. (5 sh.)

'GILLUM, [R....] *M. Dr.*
Letter to Dr. Browne Mill, of Marlbro' buildings, Bath. 1803. 8. (1 sh.)

GILLUM,

GILLUM, [William] *Esq. late Clerk in the India House.*

born .... died 1797. Jan. 9.

See Gentleman's Magaz. Y. 1797. Jan. p. 82. Allg. Litt. Zeit. J. 1800. S. 641.

The origin, progress and expediency of continuing the present war with France, impartially considered. 1794. 8. (2 sh.)

*GILPIN, [George] *Clerk to the Royal Society.*

Appendix to *Charles Blagden's* report on the best method of proportioning the excise upon spirituous liquors. (Phil. Transact. Y. 1792. p. 439.) Tables for reducing the quantities by weight, in any mixture of pure spirit and water, to those by measure; and for determining the proportion, by measure of each of the two substances in such mixtures. (Philos. Transact. Y. 1794. p. 275.)

GILPIN, [John]

Observations on the annual passage of herrings. (Columbian Magaz. Y. 1786. Dec. p. 155. New-York Magaz. Y. 1792. Dec. p. 717.)

*GILPIN, [Joshua] *Vicar of Rockwardine in the county of Salop.*

The portrait of St. Paul; or, the true model for christians and pastors, translated from a french MSt of the late Rev. *John William de la Flechere* Vicar of Madeley, (born at Nyon Y. 1729. died 1785. Aug. 14.) with some account of the author. Ed. 2. corrected. Vol. 1. 2. 1791. 8. (10 sh. 6 d.)

*GILPIN, [R.....]

Essay on satan's temptations; new edition. 1800. 8. (6 sh.)

GILPIN, [William] *A. M. Prebendary of Salisbury, Vicar of Boldre in the Newforest, near Lymington.*

On temptation 179. 8. Observations relative to picturesque beauty made in the Y. 1776 on several parts of Great-Britain particularly the highlands of Scotland. Vol. 1. 2. 1789. 8. (1 L. 16 sh.) übers. Th. 1. 2. Leipz. 1792. 1793. 8. Remarks on forest scenery and other woodland views (relative chiefly to picturesque beauty), illustrated by the scenes of new Forest in Hampshire. Vol. 1. 2. 1791.

1791. 8. (1 L. 16 sh.) übers. Th. 1. 2. Leipzig. 1800. 8. Three essays: on picturesque beauty; on picturesque travel; on sketching landscape; with a poem on landscape painting. 1792. 8. (10 sh. 6 d.) Moral contrasts; or, the power of religion exemplified under different characters. 1798. 12. (3 sh.) Observations on the western parts of England, relative chiefly to picturesque beauty; To which are added a few remarks of the picturesque beauty of the isle of Wight, with plates. 1798. 8. (2 L. 5 sh.) Sermons preached to a country congregation: to which are added, a few hints for sermons. Vol. 1. 1799. 8. (6 sh.) Vol. 2. 1800. 8. (7 sh.) Vol. 3. 1803. 8. (7 sh.)

GILSON, [David] *M. A. Curate of St. Saviour's, Southwark, London.*

The story of Abimelech, a lesson to conspirators, a fast sermon. 1793. 4. (1 sh.)

*GIRDLER, [J..... S.....] *Esq.*

Observations on the pernicious consequences of forestalling, regrating and engrossing with a list of the statutes, thoughts on the coal-trade, as also on the sale of cattle at Smithfield with various notes and hints. 1800. 8. (6 sh.) On the causes of the high price of provisions. 1800.

GIRDLESTONE, [Thomas] *M. Dr.*

A case of diabetes, with an historical sketch of that disease. 1799. 8. (3 sh.)

*GIRVIN, [John]

The impolicy of prohibiting the exportation of rock-salt from England to Scotland to be refined there, illustrated. 1799. 8. (1 sh. 6 d.)

*GISBORNE, [J.....] *Esq.*

The vales of Wever, a loco-descriptive poem, inscribed to the Rev. *John Granville*, of Calwich, Staffordshire. 1797. 4. (5 sh.)

GISBORNE, [Thomas] *M. A.*

The principles of moral philosophy. Ed. 3. 1795. 8. Ed. 4. 1798. 8. Remarks on the late decision of the house of Commons respecting the abolition of the slave trade. 1792. 8. (1 sh.) Enquiry into the duties of man, in the higher and middle classes of society

society in Great-Britain resulting from their respective stations, professions and employments. 1794. 4. (1 L. 1 sh.) Ed. 2. Vol. 1. 2. 1795. 8. Ed. 3. Vol. 1. 2. 1785. 8. Ed. 4. 1799. *Walks in a forest, as poem descriptive of scenery — at different seasons; 1794. 4. Ed. 2. 1796. 8. (3 sh.) Leipzig. 1802. 8. Enquiry into the duties of the female sex. 1796. 8. (6 sh.) übers. von *Bonath*. Altona. 1800. On the benefits and duties resulting from the institution of societies for the advancement of literature and philosophy. (Mem. of M. Vol. 5. P. 1. p. 70.) Poems, sacred and moral. 1798. 8. (4 sh.) A familiar survey of the christian religion and of history, as connected with the introduction of christianity and with its progress to the present time; Ed. 2. 1799. 8. (8 sh.) Ode to the memory of *William Cowper*, Esq. 1800. 4. (1 sh.) Sermons. Vol. 1. 2. 1802. 8. (16 sh.)

*GISBORNE, [William] *D. D.*

An inquiry into the principles of national order with reflections on the present state of the christian world, the probable causes of war and the best means of promoting and securing the future peace of Europe: To which are prefixed two tracts, written by *Edward* Earl of *Clarendon* on the subjects of war and peace. 1798. (4 sh.)

GLADWIN, [Francis] *Esq.*

The Ayen Akbery; or the institutes of the emperor Akber, translated from the original Persian. Vol. 1. 2. London. 1800. 4. (2 L. 2 sh.) A persian vocabulary; 17.. Dissertations on the rhetoric, prosody and rhyme of the persians. Calcutta. 17.. 4. The persian Moonshee. 1801. 4. Dictionary of the Mohammedan law and Bengal revenue terms; Calcutta. 1797. 4.

*GLANVIL, [J.....] See *A. Behn*.

GLASSE, [George Henry] *Rector of Hanwell, Middlesex, Chaplain to the Earl of Radnor: formerly of Christ-church College, Oxford* (Son of *Samuel Glasse*, D. D.)

Translation of *Mason's* caractacus into greek verse. 1781.

1781. 8. (5 sh.) *Joh. Miltoni* Samson agonistes, graeco carmine redditus cum versione latina. 1788. 8. (5 sh.) Contemplations on the sacred history, altered from the works of Bishop *Hall*. Vol. 1–4. 1793. 12. (12 sh.) Ed. 3. 1799. Sermons on various subjects, more particularly on christian faith and hope and the consolations of religion. 1798. 8. (7 sh.) Louisa, a narrative of facts, supposed to throw light on the mysterious history of the lady of the Hay-Stack, translated from a french work. 1785. 12. (1 sh. 6 d.) Ed. 2. 1801. 8. (4 sh.) Ed. 3. 1802. (Several single sermons.)

GLASSE, [H . . . . . .] *Mrs.*

The complete confectioner, or house keeper's guide to the art of confectionary, with additions by *Maria Wilson*. 1800. 8. (5 sh.)

GLASSE, [Samuel] *D. D. F. R. S. Rector of Wanstead in Essex and Chaplain in ordinary to his Majesty.*

On the affinity of certain words in the language of the Sandwich and Friendly isles in the pacific ocean with the hebrew. (Arch. Vol. 8. p. 81.) Advice from a lady of quality, to her children, translated from the french. Vol. 1. 2. 1779. 8. (5 sh.) Lectures on the festivals celebrated by the church of England, with practical observations. 1796. 8. A plain and practical exposition of the ten commandements. 1801. 12. (2 sh.) Six lectures on the church-catechism —. Ed 3. 1801. 12. (1 sh.) (Several single sermons.)

GLAZEBROOK, [James] *Vicar of Belton, co. Leicester, Minister of St. James's, Latchford, near Warrington, co. Lancaster.*

born . . . . died 1803. July 1.

See Gentleman's Magaz. Y. 1803. July. p. 695. Defence of infant baptism, in answer to *Gilb. Wakefield* 17 . .

GLEIG, [George] *Esq. LL. Dr: F. R. S. E.*

Sam. Johnson's works; (he published the Vol. XV.) *Lobo's* voyage to Abyssinia 1789. 8. (6 sh.) Supplement to the third edition of the Encyclopaedia Britannica (in 18 Vols) illustrated with 50 copper plates. Vol. 1. 2. 1800. 4. (3 L.) Sermons — 1803. 8. (7 sh.)

GLENIE, [James] *Esq. M. A. F. R. S. late Lieutenant in the corps of Engineers.*

The doctrine of univerſal compariſon, or general proportion. 1789. 4. (5 ſh.) The antecedental calculus, or, a geometrical method of reaſoning, without any conſideration of motion or velocity applicable to every purpoſe to which fluxions have been or can be applied; with the geometrical principles of increments. 1793. 4. (2 ſh. 6 d.) Obſervations on conſtruction. 1793. 8. On the principles of the antecedental calculus. (Tr. of E. S. Vol. 4. P. 2. p. 65.)

*GLENTON, [Frederik] *Surgeon.*

Addreſs to the faculty and the public on the expediency of eſtabliſhing a fund for the benefit of the widows and orphans of medical men, in the counties of Durham and Northumberland and the town of Newcaſtle upon Tyne. 1792. 8. (1 ſh.)

*GLOVER, [Joſeph]

An attempt to prove, that digeſtion in man depends on the united cauſes of ſolution and fermentation. Philad. 1800.

*GLYNN, [Clobery Robert] *Esq. M. Dr. Fellow of the Roy. College of Phyſicians in London: Fellow of King's College.*

born Aug. 5. 1719. at Kelland near Bodmin, in Cornwall. died 1800. Febr. 8.

See Gentleman's Magaz. Y. 1800. March. p. 276. Monthly Magaz. Y. 1800. p. 397. Allg. Litt. Zeit. IttBl. J. 1800. S. 1803.

The day of judgment, a poetical eſſay. 1757. Ed. 2. 1801. 12. (6 d.)

*GODFREY, [C.... B....] *M. Dr.*

An hiſtorical and practical treatiſe on the venereal diſeaſe. 1797. 8. (2 ſh. 6 d.)

*GODFREY, [Samuel] *Attorney at Law,*

The great queſtion of bills of exchange, called fictitious — wherein the origin of that queſtion and its frivolity is ſhewn. 1791. 8. (1 ſh.)

GODSCHALL, [William Man] *F. R. S. F. A. S. of Weſtonhouſe in Surry, F. R. S. one of his Maj. Juſtices of the peace for that country.*

born 1719. died 1802. Dec. 1.

See Gentleman's Magaz. Y. 1802. Dec. p. 1169.

*GODWIN,

GODWIN, [. . . . .]
* Considerations on Lord *Grenville's* and Mr. *Pitt's* bills, concerning treasonable and seditious practices by a lover of order. 1795. 8. (1 sh. 6 d.).

GODWIN, [Mary] *Mrs.* See *Mary Wollstonecraft.*

GODWIN, [William] *Esq. formerly a Dissenting Clergyman.*
See Public Characters of 1799 and 1800. p. 368. Memoirs of the author of a vindication of the rights of woman; (*Mary Wollstonecraft*) 1798. 8. (3 sh. 6 d.) übers. von *Lenz.* Schnepfenthal. 1799. 8. * The herald of literature; or, a review of the most considerable publications which will be made in the ensuing winter, 17.. An enquiry concerning the political justice and its influence on general virtue and happiness. Vol. 1. 2. 1793. 4. (1 L. 16 sh.) Ed. 2. Vol 1. 2. 1795. 8. (14 sh.) Ed. 3. 1797. 8. übers. mit Anmerk. u. Zus. von *G. M. Weber.* B. 1. Frankf. u. Leipzig. 1803. 8. Things as they are, or, the adventures of *Caleb Williams.* Vol. 1-3. 1794. 12. (10 sh. 6 d.) Ed. 2. 17.. übers. von *Aug. Wilhelmi.* Th. 1. 2. Leipzig. 1797. 1798. 8. Cursory strictures on the charge delivered by Lord chief justice *Eyre* to the grand Jury on the 2 Oct. 1794. 1794. The enquirer: reflections on education, manner and litterature in a series of essays. Vol. 1. 1796. (6 sh.) St. Leon, a tale of the 16 century. Vol. 1-4. 1799. 8. (16 sh.) Antonio, a tragedy in 5 acts. 1801. 8. (2 sh. 6 d.) Thoughts occasioned by the perusal of Dr. *Parr's* spital sermon April 15. 1800. being a reply to the attacks of Dr. *Parr;* Mr. *Mackintosh*, the author of an essay on population, and others. 1801. 8 (2 sh. 6 d.) The history of the life and age of *Geoffrey Chaucer*, the early english poet, including memoirs of his kinsman John of Gaunt; — Vol. 1. 2. 1803. 4. (3 L. 13 sh. 6 d.)

GOLDEN, [William]
The triumph of friendship; an historical poem. 1791. 4. (2 sh. 6 d.) The distressed village, a poem; — 1802.

*GOLDHAWK, [Thomas]

Culture of carrots. (*Young's* A. of Agr, Vol. 23. p 534.) Culture of carrots. (Ibid. Vol. 24. p. 4.) On hedge wheat. (Ibid. Vol. 24. p. 408.) Method to prefent mischief by the horns of cattle, (Ibid. Vol. 28 p. 162.)

*GOLDING, [Widdows] *Surgeon at Wallingford, in Berkshire.*

An account of a remarkable affection of the testes; (*Simmons's* Med. Facts and Obferv. Vol. 7. p. 62.) Cafe of a man who caftrated himfelf. (Ibid. Vol. 7. p. 74.)

*GOLDINGHAM, [J.....] *Esq.*

Some account of the fculptures at Mahabalipoorum, ufually called the feven pagodas. (Afiat. Ref. Vol. 5. p. 69.) Some account of the cave in the island of Elephanta. (Ibid. Vol. 4. p. 409.)

*GOLDSMITH, [John] *A. M. Vicar of Dunnington.*

Geography for the ufe of fchools: divided in three parts — to the whole are prefixed an account of the moft fuccefsful and rational mode of teaching geography and directions for projecting and drawing maps. 1802. 8. (10 fh. 6 d.) An eafy grammar of geography —. 1803. 8. (2 fh. 6 d.)

*GOLDSMITH, [Lewis]

The crimes of cabinets — translated from the french of *Hauterive*. 1801. 8. (6 fh.)

*GOLDSON, [William] *Esq.*

Obfervations on the paffage between the atlantic and pacific oceans, in two memoirs on the ftrait of Anian and the difcoveries of *De Fonte*, elucidated by a new and original map. To which is prefixed an hiftorical abridgment of difcoveries in the North of America. 1793. 4. (8 fh.)

GOLLEDGE, [John]

Strictures on a work entitled; an effay on philofophical neceffity by *Alex. Crombie* — to which is added an appendix, fhewing in various particulars the affinity there is between neceffity and predeftination. 1799. 12. (1 fh.)

GOMERSALL, [.....] *Mrs. of Leeds.*

The citizen, a novel. Vol. 1. 2. 1791. 8. (6 fh.)

*GOMER-

GOMERSALL, [A....]
The disappointed heir, or memoirs of the Ormond family. Vol. 1. 2. 1796. 8. (7 sh.)

GOMM, [James] *Esq. late Lieutenant and Commander of the Tickler Gun-vessel.*
Narrative founded on a series of events which took place in the island of St. Marcou. 1801. 8. (1 sh.)

GOOCH, [Benjamin] *Surgeon at Shottisham in Norfolk.* born .... died 177. (?)
Chirurgical works, a new edition with corrections and additions. Vol. 1-3. 1792. 8.

GOOCH, [Elizabeth Sara Villa Real] *Mrs.*
Life written by herself. Vol. 1-3. 1792. 8. (10 sh. 6 d.) The wanderings of the imagination. Vol. 1. 2. 1796. 8. (6 sh.) The contrast, a novel. Vol. 1. 2. 1795. 12. (6 sh.) Truth and fiction, a novel. Vol. 1-4. 1801. 12. (18 sh.) The beggar boy, by the late Mr. *Thomas Bellamy* with a portrait of the author by *Drummond;* to which are prefixed biographical particulars of his life. Vol. 1-3. 1801. 12. (12 sh.)

GOOD, [John Mason] *F. M. S.*
Dissertation on the diseases of prisons and poorhouses — to which is added a singular case of praeternatural foetation, with remarks on the phenomena that occurred. 1795. 8. (2 sh. 6 d.) übers. von *Carl* Graf v. *Harrach.* Wien. 1798. 8. The history of medicine, so far as it relates to the profession of the apothecary from the earliest accounts to the present period. The origin of druggists, their gradual encroachments, on compound pharmacy and the evils to which the public are thence exposed —. 1795. 12. (3 sh. 6 d.) On the best means of maintaining and employing the poor in parish work-houses. 1798. 8. (3 sh. 6 d.) Reply to Mr. *Wood* on the poor. (Monthly Magaz. Y. 1798. Dec. p. 411. Y. 1799. Febr. p. 121.) On the epic poems of Germany: on the Messias of *Klopstock.* (Ibid. Y. 1800. Aug. p. 1.) On oriental poetry. (Ibid. Y. 1801. Jan. p. 519.) On the culture of rice. (Ibid. Y. 1801. Febr. p. 8.) On the origin of the greek alphabet. (Ibid. Y. 1802. Jan. p. 485.) Songs of songs; or, sacred

 idyls.

idyls. Translated from the original Hebrew, with notes —. 1803. 8. (7 sh. 6 d.) The triumph of Britain, an ode. 1803. Memoirs of the life and writings of the Rev. *Alex. Geddes* LL. D. 1803. 8. (10 sh. 6 d.)

*GOOD, [Joseph] *Rev.*
Poems on several occasions. 1792. 8. (3 sh.)

*GOOD, [Thomas] *Esq.*
Speech in the Irish house of commons Febr. 14. 1800. on the subject of the union with Great-Britain. 1800. (1 sh. 6 d.)

*GOODACRE, [Robert] *Master of a seminary at Nottingham.*
Arithmetic adapted to different classes of learners, but more particularly to the use of large schools —. 1803. (6 sh.)

*GOODENOUGH, [Samuel] *LL. D. F. R. S. F. L. S.*
Observations on the british species of carex. (Transact. of L. S. Vol. 2. p. 16. Vol. 3. p. 76.) — — and *Th. J. Woodward's* observations on the british fuci, with particular descriptions of each species. (Ibid. Vol. 3. p. 84.) A description of the porbeagle shark, the squalus cornubicus of *Gmelin*, Var. α. (Ibid. Vol. 3. p. 80.)

*GOODRICH, [Simon]
Description of a new escapement for clocks. (Tr. of the Soc. for the E. of A. Vol. 17. p. 327. *Nicholson's* Journal. Vol. 3. p. 342.)

*GOODSIR, [John] *Surgeon at Largo.*
History of a fracture of the skull, with very considerable injury to the brain, terminating in complete recovery, without any operation. (*Duncan's* A. of Med. Y. 1801. p. 300.)

*GOODWIN, [George]
Rising castle, with other poems. 1798. 8. (3 sh. 6 d.)

*GOODWYN, [H. . . .] *Esq.*
On the unities of weight and measure best adapted to the British empire; on the new measures of France; with a description of an engine for raising water. (*Nicholson's* Journal. Vol 4. p. 163.) On the quotients arising from the division of an unit

unit by prime numbers. (Ibid. Vol. 4. p. 402.) Construction and use of an universal table of interest. (Ibid. Vol. 4. p. 433.)

GORDON, [. . . . .] *Principal of the Scots College in Paris.*

Remarks made in a journey to the Orkney islands. (Transact. of the Soc. of Antiq. of Scotland. Vol. 1. p. 256.)

GORDON, [Sir Adam] *Bart. Rector of Hinxworth, Herts.*

The contrast, or an antidote against the pernicious principles dissiminated in the letters of the late Earl of *Chesterfield*. Vol. 1. 2. 1791. 8. (6 sh.) Affectionate advice from a minister of the established church to his parishioners, upon the most plain and positive duties of religion, with some cautions against the prevailing spirit of innovation. 1791. 8. (1 sh.) The plain duties of wife and christian subjects; two sermons. 1793. 8. (1 sh. 6 d.) A collection of sermons on several subjects and occasions, particularly on the festivals and fasts of the church of England. 1796. 8. (8 sh.) Homilies of the church modernized. Vol. 1. 2. 179. 8. An assistant for the visitation of the sick. 179.. 12.

GORDON, [Alexander] *Esq. M. Dr. Physician to the Dispensary of Aberdeen.*

A treatise on the epidemic puerperal fever of Aberdeen. 1795. 8. (3 sh.) Account of an alarming case of flooding, which happened in the 9 month of pregnancy. (*Duncan's* M. C. Dec. 2. Vol. 8. p. 317.) übers. in Repertor. Chir. u. Medic. Abhandl. B. 2. S. 142. A singular case of extra-uterine conception, assuming the appearance of retroverted uterus. (Ibid. Dec. 2. Vol. 8. p. 323.) übers. in Repertor. Chir. u. Medic. Abhandl. B. 2. S. 148. A curious case of expectoration of bile. (Ibid. Dec. 2. Vol. 8. p. 326.)

GORDON, [Alexander] *Reader on Botany in London.*
See *Colin Milne*, LL. Dr.

Lord GORDON, [George]

born in upper Grosvenor-ſtreet London 1750. Dec. 19. died at his apartements on the maſter's ſide of the gaol of Newgate. 1793. Nov. 1.

See Gentleman's Magaz. Y. 1793. Nov. p. 1056. Life of Lord G. *Gordon* with a philoſophical review of his political conduct, by *Robert Watſon*, M. Dr. 1795. 8. His ſpeeches in parliament motions and trial may be ſeen in Gentleman's Magaz. Vol. 49. (Y. 1779.) p. 6. 42. 266. 615. 626. Vol. 50. (Y. 1780.) p. 7. 159. 200. 293. 248. 265. 269. 308. 312. 353. 440. 442. 454. 500. 504. 539. 540. 553. 599. Vol. 51. (Y. 1781.) p. 44. 60. 63. 90. 108. 110. 158. 250. 255. 267. 310. 311. 391. 401. 459. 467. 630. Vol. 53. (Y. 1783.) p. 249. 340. 869. 870. 871. 872. Vol. 56. (Y. 1786.) p. 437. 993. Vol. 57. (Y. 1787.) p. 87. 440. 450. 451. 531–533. 545. 634. 734. Vol. 58. (Y. 1788.) p. 80. Vol. 59. (Y. 1789.) p. 851. 856. Vol. 60. (Y. 1790.) p. 265. Vol. 61. (Y. 1791.) p. 175. Letter to the Marquis of Carmarthen againſt Mr. *Adams* the American ambaſſador. Vol. 56. (Y. 1786.) p. 436.

*GORDON, [James] *Rector of Killegny in the Dioceſe of Ferns and of Canneway in the Dioceſe of Cork.*

Terraquea, or, a new ſyſtem of geography and modern hiſtory. Vol. 1. 1791. 8. (6 ſh.) Vol. 2. 1793. 8. (5 ſh 3 d.) Hiſtory of the rebellion in Ireland, in the Y. 1798. &c. containing an impartial account of the proceedings of the Iriſh revolutioniſts, from the Y. 1782. till the ſuppreſſion of the rebellion. 1801. 8. (8 ſh.)

*GORDON, [John] *D. D. F. S. A. Precentor and Arch-Deacon of Lincoln, Rector of Henſtead in the county of Suffolk.*

born 1725. at Whitworth in the county of Durham. died at Lincoln 1793. Jan. 5.

See Gentlemans Magaz. Y. 1793. Jan. p. 92. A new eſtimate of manners and principles. 1760. Occaſional thoughts on the ſtudy of claſſical authors. 1762. An addreſs to the members of the

ſenate

senate of the university of Cambridge, on an attention due to worth of character from a religious society, with a view to the ensuing election of high Steward; to which is added a letter from Mr. *Joseph Mede*, formerly of Christ's College (from a Manuscript in the Harleian collection) giving a very particular account of the circumstances attending the Duke of *Buckingham's* election in King Charles I. time, by a master of arts. 1764.

(Several single sermons.)

GORDON, [William] D. D. *a Dissenting Minister, formerly established at Ipswich; but upon the breaking out of the American war, he went to America. He was there Minister of Raxbury: now Pastor of a Dissenting Congregation at St. Neots in Huntingdonshire.*

An abridgment of *Jonathan Edward's* treatise on religious affections. 17..

GORDON, [William] *Master of the mercantile Academy, Edinburgh.*

born ..... died 1793.

*GORDON, [William] *Nursery and Seedsman, of Bow.*

On the cultivation of gallium verum or luteum. (*Young's* A. of Agr. Vol. 18. p. 385.)

*DE GORGY, [.....]

(Author of Blansay, Victorina and St. Alme.) Lidora, an ancient chronicle. Vol. 1. 2. 1791. 8. (6 sh.)

*GORING, [Charles] *of Weston, near Steyning, Esq.*

Essay on the conversion of grass lands into tillage. (Comm. to the B. of Agr. Vol. 3. P. 1. p. 189.)

*GOSLING, [Jane]

Ashdale village: a moral work of fancy. Vol. 1. 2. 1794. 12. (6 sh.)

*GOSLING, [Robert] *Surgeon.*

born .... died 1794. Sept. 7.

See Gentleman's Magaz. Y. 1794. Sept. p. 868.

Desault chirurgical journal, translated from the french. 17..

*GOSNELL, [Thomas Knolles] *Accomptant of London.*

An elucidation of the Italian method of book-keeping, with examples calculated to simplify and perfect that long approved fyftem and to fupply the defects of the prefent practice. Prefaced by free obfervations on. *Jones's* englifh fyftem of book-keeping and concluded by concife ftrictures on *Collier's* defence of double entry. 1796. 4. (5 fh.)

GOUGH, [J.....] *A. B.*
A plain and rational account of man's falvation, by Jefus Chrift; to which are added a caution to men in general, and an exhortation to believers. 1791. 8. (1 fh. 6 d.)

*GOUGH, [John] *of Kendal.*
Reafons for fuppofing that lakes have been more numerous than they are at prefent, with an attempt to affign the caufes, whereby they have been defaced. (Mem. of M. Vol. 4. P. 1. p. 1.) The laws of motion of a cylinder, compelled by the repeated ftrokes of a falling block to penetrate an obftacle, the refiftance of which is an invariable force. (Ibid. Vol. 4. P. 2. p. 273.) Experiments and obfervations on the vegetation of feeds. (Ibid. Vol. 4. P. 2. p. 310.) On the variety of voices. (Ibid. Vol. 5. P. 1. p. 58.) An inveftigation of the method whereby men judge, by the ear, of the pofition of fonorous bodies relative to their own perfons (Ibid. Vol. 5. P. 2. p. 622. *Nicholfon's* Journal Y. 1802. June. p. 122.) On the theory of compound founds. (Ibid. Vol. 5. P. 2. p. 653.) On the fuppofed revival of infects after long immerfion in wine or other intoxicating liquor. (*Nicholfon's* Journal. Vol. 2. p. 353.) A ftatical inquiry into the fource of nutrition in fucculent vegetables. (Ibid. Vol. 3. p. 1.) Inftances of fufpended animation in vegetables. (Ibid. Vol. 4. p. 509.) On the exhibition of a feries of primes, and the refolution of a compound number into all its factors. (Ibid. Y. 1802. Jan. p. 1.) Reply to Dr. *Young's* letter on the theory of compound founds. (Ibid. Y. 1802. Sept. p. 39.)

*GOUGH, [John Parker]
An effay on cantharides. Philad. 1800.

OUGH, [Richard] *F. R. S. Director of the society of Antiquaries.*

Sepulchral monuments in Great-Britain. Vol. 2. 1797. fol. (9 L. 9 sh.) Description of two ancient mansion houses in Northamptonshire and Dorset. (Arch. Vol. 10. p. 67.) Illustration of a roman altar inscribed to Belatucader. (Ibid. Vol. 10. p. 118.) A mosaic pavement in the Prior's chapel at Ely: with a brief deduction of the rise and progress of mosaic works since the introduction of christianity. (Ibid. Vol. 10. p. 151.) Observations on a roman horologium, found in Italy. (Ibid. Vol. 10. p. 172.) Description of an old font in the church of East Meon, Hampshire, 1789, with some observations on fonts. (Ibid. Vol. 10. p. 183.) Collection of a subsidy 1382 by the prior of Barnwell. (Ibid. Vol. 10. p. 386.) A charter of Barnwell priory. (Ibid. Vol. 10. p. 396.) On the analogy between certain antient monuments. (Ibid. Vol. 11. p. 34.) Observations on a greek inscription at London. (Ibid. Vol. 11. p. 48.) *Thomas Martin's* (died 1771. March 7.) history of Thetford. 1779. *Thomas Simon's* medals, coins, great seals — a new and improved edition, with an appendix by *Rich. Gough* and two additional plates finely engraved by *Basire.* 1780. *Perlin's* description des royaulmes d'Angleterre et d'Escosse, with *De la Serre's*, histoire de l'entrée de la reine du mere du roy tres chrestien dans la grande Bretagne. 1772. Dissertation on the coins of Canute. 1777. 4. (He is also concerned in conducting the Gentleman's Magazine.)

GOULD, [William] *D. D. Rector of Stamford-Rivers.*

born .... died 1799. March 16. aged upwards of 80.

See Gentleman's Magaz. Y. 1799. March. p. 262. April. p. 345. Allgem. Litt. Zeit. ItBl. J. 1800. S. 659.

An account of english ants. 1747. 12. Concio ad Clerum habita Cantabrigiae. 1774. 4. (6 d.)

GOURLAY, [Robert]

An inquiry into the state of the cottagers in the counties

counties of Lincoln and Rutland. (*Young's* A. of Agr. Vol. 37. p. 514. 578.)

*GOWER, [Richard Hall] *In the Service of the East-India Company.*

On the theory and practice of seamanship; 1793. 8. (5 sh.) Ed. 2. corrected and enlarged. 1796. 8. (7 sh.) Reply to a critique on his five masted ship. (Comm. and Agric. Mag. Y. 1801. Febr. p. 103.) An attempt to determine the true form and necessary angles of weather that ought to be given to vanes of a vertical windmill as they recede from the centre, left undetermined by *Smeaton*. (*Tilloch's* Philos. Mag. Vol. 4. p. 174.)

*GRAEFER, [John]

A descriptive catalogue of upwards of eleven hundred species and varieties of herbaceous or perennial plants. 1790. 8. (2 sh. 6 d.)

*Duke of GRAFTON, [....]

See Public Characters of 1799 and 1800. p. 258. Hints submitted to the serious attention of the clergy, nobility, and gentry, newly associated. 1789. Account of a flock of sheep, with observations by *A. Young*. (*Young's* A. of Agr. Vol. 7. p. 1.) On the profit of sheep. (Ibid. Vol. 7. p. 282.) Remarks on the value of turnips applied to feeding sheep. (Ibid. Vol. 7. p. 299.) Culture of beans and wheat. (Ibid. Vol. 33. p. 543.) Beans and wheat, explanation. (Ibid. Vol. 34. p. 91.)

*GRAGLIA, [G.... A....]

The castle of Cridan, or, the history of Don Alvarez and Eugenia Dutchess of Savoy. 1801. (4 sh. 6 d.)

GRAHAM, [Catherine Macaulay] *Mrs. (Maiden name Catherine Sawbridge. Her first husband was George Macaulay M. Dr.*

born .... died 1791. June 23. at Binfield, Berks.

See Gentleman's Magaz. Y. 1791. June. p. 589. *Pennant's* History of London. p. 388.

*Observations on the reflections of *Edm. Burke's* on the revolution in France; in a letter to Earl *Stanhope*. 1791. 8.

GRAHAM,

GRAHAM, [Charles]
On the hiſtory of tobacco. (Monthly Magaz. 1800. Febr. p. 38.)

*GRAHAM, [Charles Alexander] *Phyſician in Stirling.*
Account of a caſe in which a fiſtula in perinaeo was ſucceſsfully treated by the introduction of a ſeton. (*Duncan's* Annals of Medic. Y. 1798. p. 354.)

*GRAHAM, [James]
Diſſertatio de ſcrophula. Philad. 1791. 8.

*GRAHAM, [J.... A....] *LL. Dr. late Lieut. Colonel in the Service of the United States of America.*
A deſcriptive ſketch of the preſent ſtate of Vermont one of the United States of America. 1797. 8. (6 ſh.)

*GRAHAM, [John]
A defence of ſcripture doctrines as underſtood by the church of England; in reply to a pamphlet, intitled, „ſcripture the only guide to religious truth„. 1800. 8. (2 ſh. 6 d.)

*GRAHAM, [William] *Rev. of Newcaſtle.*
A review of eccleſiaſtical eſtabliſhments in Europe containing their hiſtory, with a candid examination of their advantages and disadvantages, both civil and religious. 1792. 8. (4 ſh.) An eſſay tending to remove certain ſcruples reſpecting the conſtitution and direction of miſſionary ſocieties eſpecially that of London. 1797. (6 d.)

*GRAND, [William] *Candidate for the Lucaſian Profeſſorſhip.*
Letter to the vice-chancellor of the univerſity of Cambridge. 1798. (6 d.)

*GRANGE, [.....] *Lady.*
Epiſtle to *Edward D....* Esq. written during her confinement in the island of St. Kilda. 1798. 4. (2 ſh.)

*GRANGER, [Joſeph]
Remarks on waſte lands in the county of Durham. (Bath Agric. Soc. Vol. 8. p. 149.)

*GRANT, [.....] *Mrs.*
Poems on various ſubjects; the highlanders. 1803. 8. (10 ſh. 6 d.)

*GRANT.

subjects; To which is added a letter from a father to his son at the university. 1799. 8. (5 sh.) Sermons on the following subjects: On the clerical character; on superstition; on miracles; on submission to the existing powers; on the love of pleasure; on temperance; on the temporal disadvantages of vice; on happiness; on evangelical righteousness, on justice. 1799. 8. (5 sh.) *Senilities; or, solitary amusements: in prose and verse; — 1801. 8. (5 sh.)

*GRAVES, [Robert] *M. Dr. Physician at Sherborne in Dorsetshire and extralicentiate of the college of Physicians, London.*

Instance of a disease, to which *Sauvages* has given the name of meteorismus ventriculi, with remarks. (*Simmons's* Med. Facts and Observat. Vol. 1. p. 90.) Case of a scirrhous affection of the stomach, with an account of the appearances on dissection. (London M. J. P. 4. p. 343.) A fatal instance of the poisonous effects of the oenanthe crocata Linn. or hemlock dropwort. (*Simmon's* Med. Facts and Observat. Vol. 7. p. 308.) An experimental inquiry into the constituent principles of the sulphureous water at Nottington near Weymouth; together with observations relative to its application in the cure of diseases. 1792. 8. (1 sh. 6 d.) A pocket conspectus of the new London and Edinburgh pharmacopoeias. 1796. 8. (3 sh.) Ed. 2. corrected and improved. 1799. 8. (3 sh.)

GRAY, [Edward Whitaker] *M. Dr. F. R. S. Under-librarian of the British Museum in the Department of Natural History.*
born in London 1748. March 21.

Account of the epidemic catarrh of the Year 1782. (M. C. Vol. 1. p. 1.) Account of the earth quake felt in various parts of England Nov. 18. 1795. with some observations thereon. (Phil. Transact. Y. 1796. p. 353.) — — — and *Wyatt*, *The repertory of arts and manufactures. Vol. 1-16. 1794-1803. (Nrb. 1-93. each Nrb. 1 sh. 6 d.)

*GRAY, [John] *LL. Dr.*

Practical observations on the proposed treaty of union between the legislatures of Great-Britain and

and Ireland. 1800. 8. (2 ſh. 6 d.) The income tax ſcrutinized and ſome amendments propoſed to render it more agreeable to the Britiſh conſtitution. 1802. 8. (2 ſh.)

GRAY, [John] *Esq.*

On the watering and management of flax. (Bath Agricult. Soc. Vol. 5. p. 297.)

GRAY, [Robert] *A. M. formerly of Mary-Hall Oxford: Vicar of Farringdon, Berks.*

Diſcourſes on various ſubjects, illuſtrative of the evidence, influence and doctrine of chriſtianity. 1793. 8. (5 ſh.) Letters during the courſe of a tour through Germany, Switzerland and Italy in the Year 1791 and 1792. with reflections on the manners, litterature and religion of thoſe countries. 1794. 8. (6 ſh.) Sermons on the principles upon which the reformation of the church of England was eſtabliſhed. 1796. 8. (6 ſh.)

GRAY, [Robert] *B. D. Prebendary of Chicheſter, Rector of Craike in the county of Durham.*

A dialogue between a churchman and a methodiſt, in which the grounds of the communion and ſeparation are well examined and the principal points of difference fairly diſcuſſed with a reference to ſcripture. Ed. 2. 1802.

GRAYDON, [George] *LL. B: M. R. J. A.*

On the fiſh incloſed in ſtone of Monte Bolca. (Tr. of J. A. Vol. 5. p. 281.)

GREAVES, [Thomas]

Proceſs uſed in making the paper from the bark or peel of withen twigs. (Tr. of the Soc. for the E. of A. Vol. 6. p. 164. Vol. 7. p. 112.)

GREBELL, [Allen]

Account of a fat ox. (*Young's* A. of Agr. Vol. 23. p. 538.) Account of a late planted crop of potatoes. (Ibid. Vol. 30. p. 384.)

GREEN, [. . . . .]

* An examination of the leading principle of the new ſyſtem of morals, as that principle is ſtated and applied in Mr. *Godwin's* enquiry concerning political juſtice. 1798. 8. (1 ſh. 6 d.)

GREEN, [Andrew] *of Trinity-College.*

An eſſay tending to ſhew the ſtate of the jews ſince

the death of Chrift, affording an argument for the truth of chriftianity. 1800.

*GREEN, [Afhbel] Rev.

Character of *George Duffield*, late paftor of the 3 presbyterian congregation in the city of Philadelphia, who died Febr. 2. 1790. (American Mufeum. Y. 1790. Febr. p. 66.) Obfervations on hope, fear and disappointment. (Ibid. Y. 1791. Febr. p. 65.) Obedience to the laws of God, the fure and indifpenfable defence of nations, a difcourfe. Philad. 1798. 8. (25 Cents.)

*GREEN, [B....]

A felection of examples, for the ufe of the drawing fchool, Chrift's hofpital. 1796. (1 L. 1 fh.)

*GREEN, [E....] *at Bowlney.*

Experiments on fatting fheep. (Comm. to the B. of Agr. Vol. 2. p. 192.)

*GREEN, [Edward]

Obfervations on the drama, with a view to its more beneficial effects on the morals and manners of fociety. 1803. (2 fh. 6 d.)

*GREEN, [Francis] *Esq.*

Vix oculis fubjecta, a differtation on the art of imparting fpeech to the naturally deaf and confequently dumb: with a particular account of the academy of Meffrs *Braidwood* of Edinburgh and a propofal to perpetuate and extend the benefits thereof. 1783.

*GREEN, [James] *Lieutenant in his Maj. Marine Force.*

On the principles of the Britifh conftitution. 17..
An hiftorical effay on different governments. 17.. 8. (3 fh. 6 d.)

GREEN, [Valentine] *F. A. S. Mezzotinto Engraver to his Maj. and to the Elector Palatine.*

The hiftory and antiquities of the city and fuburbs of Worcefter. Vol. 1. 2. 1796. 4. (2 L. 12 fh. 6 d.)
An account of the difcovery of the body of king John in the cathedral church of Worcefter 17 Jul. 1797. 1797. 4. (2 fh.)

GREEN, [William] *M. A. Rector of Hadingham, Norfolk.*

born ... died in a very advanced age 1794. Sept.
See Gentleman's Magaz. Y. 1794. Nov. p. 1060.

*GREEN,

*GREEN, [William] *of Sutton Hall, near Bury.*
On the culture of cabbages. (*Young's* A. of Agr. Vol. 3. p. 182.) On burnt wheat, with observat. by *A. Young*. (Ibid. Vol. 3. p. 372.)

*GREENALL, [William] *of Ecclepton, Lancashire.*
An account of the methods of converting grass lands into tillage, and of returning them to grass again after a certain period. (Comm. to the B. of Agr. Vol. 3. P. 1. p. 261. Comm. and Agric. Mag. Y. 1802. April. p. 273. May. p. 353.)

GREENAWAY, [Stephen] *Minister at Dalby on the Woulds, co. Leicester, Rector of Nether Broughton, Vicar of Cropwell Bishop Nottinghamshire and Domestic Chaplain to the late Lord Feversham.*
born at Salisbury 1713. died 1795. Sept. 5.
See Gentleman's Magaz. Y. 1795. Sept. p. 795. Allg. Litt. Zeit. 1796. ItBl. S. 2.
An address to honest English hearts. 1762. Remarks on a pamphlet called memoirs of the contested election. 1775.

*GREENE, [G....]
A relation of circumstances which occurred in lower Normandy, during the revolution and under the government of *Robespierre*; with a detail of the sufferings of the author and an account of the manners and customs of the inhabitants of the country called the Bocage in lower Normandy, with the treatment of their cattle, nature and soil, cultivation &c. 1802. 8.

*GREENE, [James] *Esq. M. P.*
Cross of Dishley and Ryland sheep. (*Young's* A. of Agr. Vol. 29. p. 124.) Crops and prices. (Ibid. Vol. 34. p. 164.)

GREENFIELD, [William] *M. A. F. R. S. Edin.* —
Account of Sir *James Hunter Blair*, Bart. (Tr. of E. S. Vol. 3. Hist. p. 31.)

*GREENLAND, [Emma Jane] *Miss.*
Letter on painting in the ancient greek manner. (Tr. of the Soc. for the E. of A. Vol. 5. p. 105.) Description of her method of uniting wax and mastich

ſtich with water. (Ibid. Vol. 10. p. 167.) On the culture of ſilk in England. (Ibid. Vol. 10. p. 177.)

GREENLEAF, [Joſeph] *Esq. of Boſton.*

Experiment for raiſing Indian corn in poor land. (American-Muſeum. Y. 1787. Jan. p. 39.)

*GREENSTED, [Frances] *a maid ſervant at Maidſtone, in Kent.*

Fugitive pieces. 1797. 8. (2 ſh.)

*GREENWAY, [James] *Dr. at Dinwiddie-County, in Virginia.*

Account of the beneficial effects of the caſſia chamæcriſta, in recruiting worn-out lands and in enriching ſuch as are naturally poor; together with a botanical deſcription of the plant. (Tr. of A. S. Vol. 3. p. 226.)

*GREENWOOD, [Abraham]

An affectionate addreſs to young people, publiſhed with a deſign of engaging their attention to thoſe ſubjects which moſt affect their preſent and future welfare. 1796. 8. (6 d.)

*GREEVES, [R.....] *A. M.*

A new tranſlation of M. *Antoninus's* meditations. 1791. 8.

*GREGG, [John] *Rever.*

The ſolitary frenchman on the banks of the Thames, to a friend in Switzerland, a poem, tranſlated. 1794. 8. (1 ſh. 6 d.)

*GREGG, [John] *Practitioner in Midwifery and Surgeon to the pauper Charity in Bath.*

Advice to the female ſex in general, particularly thoſe in a ſtate of pregnancy and lying-in. 1793. 8.

*GREGG, [John Anthony] *Rev.*

Hierogamy, or, an apology for the marriage of roman catholic prieſts, without a diſpenſation. 1801. 8. (1 ſh. 6 d.)

*GREGORY, [.....] *M. A.*

Diſcourſes on hiſtorical ſubjects. Vol. 1. 1791. 8. (2 ſh. 6 d.)

*GREGORY, [Edward] *M. A. Rector of Langar, Nottinghamſhire.*

Account of the diſcovery of a comet, with obſervation thereon. (Philoſ. Tranſact. Y. 1793. p. 50.)

GREGORY,

GREGORY, [George] *D. D. F. A. S. Domestic Chaplain to the Bishop of Landaff and Joint Evening Preacher at the Foundling Hospital, Curate of St. Giles's Cripp-legate.*

An history of the christian church from the earliest periods to the present time; a new edition, corrected and enlarged. Vol. 1. 2. 1795. 8. (14 sh.) Philosophical and litterary essays. Vol. 1. 2. 1792. 8. (12 sh.) History of England from the revolution to the commencement of the present administration, written in continuation of *Hume's* history, which was left unfinished by *Mrs. Catherine Macaulay Graham*. 1795. 8. The adventures of Telemachus — from the french of *Solignac de la Mothe Fenelon* — by the late *John Hawkesworth* LL. Dr. corrected and revised, with a a life of the author and a complete index, historical and geographical: embellished with XI elegant engravings. Vol. 1. 2. 1795. 4. (1 L. 16 sh. large paper 3 L. 3 sh.) The economy of nature explained and illustrated on the principles of modern philosophy in ten books. Vol. 1.-3. 1796. (1 L. 7 sh.) Ed. 2. with considerable additions. Vol. 1-3. 1798. übers. von Dr. *K. G. Kühn* u. *C. F. Michaelis*. B. 1. 2. Nürnberg. 1798. 1800. 8. On suicide, a sermon. 1797. 8. (1 sh.) The elements of a polite education; carefully selected from the letters of the late *Phil. Dormer Stanhope*, Earl of *Chesterfield*, to his son. 1800. 12. (4 sh. 6 d.) On the uses of classical learning. (Mem. of M. Vol. 4. P. 1. p. 109.)

GREGORY, [G....] *D. D. Chaplain to the philanthropic Society.*

Family prayers for the philantropic reform, with a short catechism and an address to the children. 1792. 8. (6 d.)

GREGORY, [James] *M. Dr. Professor of the practice of Physic in the University of Edinburgh.* born at Aberdeen 1753. Jan.

See Public Characters of 1800 and 1801. p. 135. Memorial to the managers of the royal infirmary of Edinburgh. 1800. 4.

*GREGORY, [Jos.] *M. A.*
Historical discourses. 1792.

*GREGORY, [Olinthus] *A journeyman printer in the office of Mr. Flower, at Cambridge. Teacher of Mathematics.*
Lessons astronomical and philosophical for the amusement and instruction of british youth. — the whole interspersed with moral reflections. 1796. 8. (3 sh.) A treatise on astronomy, in which the elements of the science deduced in a natural order from the appearances of the heavens to an observer on the earth. 1802. 8. (15 sh.) On Dr. *Gall's* cranioscopical lectures and *Blumenbach's* collection of skulls. (Monthly Magaz. Y. 1802. Dec. p. 379.) On Mr. *Pearson's* analogy for deducing the greatest equation from the excentricity. (*Nicholson's* Journal Y. 1802. June. p. 65.)

*GREGORY, [O..... G.....]
On halos. (Monthly Magaz. Y. 1796. Oct. p. 689.)

*GREGORY, [William] *One of the Missionaries.*
A visible display of divine providence, or, the journal of a captured missionary designated to the Southern Pacific Ocean in the second voyage of the ship Duff, Capt. Thomas Robson, captured by le Grand Bonaparte off cape Frio; including every remarkable occurrence which took place on board the Duff, the grand Bonaparte in the province of Paraguay, Spanish South-America and Portugal, on the return home in 1798 and 1799. 1800. 8. (5 sh.)

*GREIG, [John] *Teacher of Writing, Geography &c.*
The young lady's new guide in arithmetic. 1800. 12.

*GRELLIER, [J.... J....]
The terms of all the loans which have been raised for the public service during the last 50 years — with an introductory account of the principal loans prior to that period and observations on the rate of interest paid for the money borrowed. 1799. 8. (1 sh.) On the progress of the national debt. (Monthly Magaz. Y. 1799. Jan. p. 4.) The principles of political arithmetic illustrated in an estimate of the national wealth of Great-Britain. (Ibid.

(Ibid. Y. 1800. Aug. p. 23. Sept. p. 113. Oct. p. 213.) A view of the manufactures in Great-Britain with respect to their extent and the number of individuals employed therein. (Ibid. Y. 1801. Jan. p. 493.) Remarks on the returns of the population of Great-Britain. (Ibid. Y. 1801. Sept. p. 89.)

GRENVILLE, [T....]
Letters on his machine for teaching blind persons arithmetic. (Tr. of the Soc. for the E. of A. Vol. 4. p. 132.)

Lord GRENVILLE, [William Windham] *Secretary of State; formerly Speaker of the House of Commons.*
Speech, on the motion of the Duke of *Bedford* for the dismissal of ministers March 22. 1798. 8. (6 d.) Substance of his speech Nov. 1801. on the motion for an address approving of the convention with Russia, with notes. 1802. 8. (3 sh. 6 d.)

GRESWELL, [W.... Parr] *Curate of Denton in Lancashire.*
Memoirs of *Angelus Politianus*, *Actius Sincerus Sannazarius*, *Petrus Bembus*, *Hieron. Fracastorius*, *Marcus Antonius Flaminius* and the *Amalthei*: translations from their poetical works and notes and observations concerning other literary characters of the 15 and 16 centuries. 1801. 8. (5 sh.)

GREVILLE, [.....] *Esq.*
*British India analyzed. Vol. 1-3. 1793.

GREVILLE, [.....] *Mrs.*
Ode to indifference. 17.. (author of some other pleasing fugitive poetry.)

GREVILLE, [Charles] *Right Hon.* F. R. S.
On the corundum stone from Asia. (Phil. Trans. Y. 1798. p. 403. *Nicholson's* Journal Vol. 2. p. 477. 536. Vol. 3. p. 5.)

GREVILLE, [Fulke] *Esq.*
Reflection, a poem, in four cantos. 1790. 4. (7 sh. 6 sh.) . Letter to the reviewers of the Monthly Review. 1790. 8. (1 sh. 6 d.)

*GREY, [.....] *of the Lottery-office.*

*The essential principles of the wealth of nations illustrated, in opposition to some false doctrines of Dr. *Adam Smith* and others. 1797. 8. (3 sh.)

*GREY, [Charles] *Esq.*

The remonstrance moved in the house of commons Febr. 21. 1793. against a war with France. 1793. 8. (6 d.)

*GREYSON, [T....] *Surgeon.*

Observations on the veneral disease. 1796. 8. (6 d.)

*LE GRICE, [Charles Valentine] *Esq. of Trinity College.*

The tineum, containing essiaonomy or the art of stirring a fire; the icead, a mock heroic poem: an imitation of *Horace* Ep. I. lib. 1. Epigrams, a fragment. &c. 1794. 12. (1 sh.) A prize declamation — on the subject: *Richard Cromwell* if he had possessed his father's abilities, might have retained the protectorate. To which is added a speech delivered Dec. 18. 1794. being the day of public commemoration, to prove that the reign of Anne has been improperly called the Augustan age of English genius. 1795. 8. (1 sh.) Analysis of *Paley's* principles of moral and political philosophy. Ed. 2. 1796. 8. (1 sh. 6 d.)

GRIEVE, [John] *M. Dr. F. R. S. Edin. late Physician to the Russian Army* —

Account of the method of making a wine called by the Tartars, koumiss — (Tr. of E. S. Vol. I. p. 178. London M. J. Vol. 10. P. 2.) übers. Samml. der neuesten Beobacht. für Aerzte. S. 161. A description of the Russian ploughs. (Bath Agricult. Soc. Vol. 3. p. 344.)

*GRIFFIN, [Elizabeth]

The friends, or the contrast between virtue and vice, a tale, designed for the improvement of youth. 1799. 12. (2 sh.) (Author of the Selector; Moral amusements &c.)

GRIFFIN, [Gregory] *Of the College of Eton. (A fictitious name.)*

The microcosm, a periodical work. 1787. 8. (7 sh.)

*GRIFFITH,

GRIFFITH, [Hugh Davies] *Esq.*
On the uſe of lime mixed with gunpowder, in rending rocks and ſtones. (Bath Agric. Soc. Vol. 8. p. 326.)

GRIFFITH, [Moſes] *M. Dr. at Colcheſter.*
born .... died 178. (?)

GRIFFITH, [Richard] *Esq. M. R. J. A.*
Thoughts and facts relating to the increaſe of agriculture, manufactures and commerce, by the extenſion of the inland navigation of Ireland. Wherein is conſidered, the propriety of directing into channels more productive of permanent improvement, the bounties now paid on the inland and coaſt carriage of corn to Dublin. 1795. Dublin. 8. (1 ſh. 1 d.)

GRIFFITH, [Richard]
A ſingular caſe of reproduction of the ſpinctor ani and three other caſes annexed; which illuſtrate the uſe of a freſh porter fomentation and ſeed poultice in the cure of mortification. 1792. 8. (1 ſh. 6 d.)

GRIFFITHS, [Frances] *Mrs.*
born ...., died at Milleſcent, in Ireland. 1793. Jan. 5.
Eſſays addreſſed to young married women. 1782. (2 ſh. 6 d.) überſ. (von *Chriſt. Lang.*) Erlangen. 1792. 8. On temper, as it reſpects the happineſs of the married ſtate. (Maſſachuſetts Magaz. Y. 1794. June. p. 346.)

GRIFFITHS, [J.....] *Esq.*
Muſeum of French monuments — translated from the french of *Alex. Lenoir.* Vol. 1. 1803. 8.

GRIFFITHS, [Ralph] *Esq. LL. D.*
born 1720. died 1803. Sept. 28. at Turnham-green.
See Gentleman's Magaz. Y. 1803. Sept. p. 891. (The original inſtitutor of the Monthly Review.)

GRIFFITTS, [Samuel Powel] *Profeſſor of Materia Medica in the Univerſity of Pennſylvania.*
Publiſhed *Will. Buchan's* domeſtic medicine. Philad. 1795. 8. (18 ſh. 9 d.)

*GRIGBY, [Joshua] *Esq. of Drinkston Link. M. P. for the County of Suffolk.*

On planting and the use of resinous trees. (*Young's* A. of Agr. Vol. 4. p. 301.) Experiments on oats. (Ibid. Vol. 9. p. 97.)

*GRIGG, [. . . . .]

Remarks on waste lands in Essex. (Bath Agric. Soc. Vol. 8. p. 134.)

*GRIGG, [John Anthony] *Rev.*

Hierogamy, or, an apology for the marriage of the roman catholic priests without a dispensation. 1801. (1 sh. 6 d.)

*GRIMSHAW, [Nicholas] *Esq.*

On the quantity of iron in cotton and linen cloth: evil effects, simple means of eradicating and observations on bleaching, the result of long experience. (Tr. of Dublin Soc. Vol. 1. P. 2. p. 11.)

*GRIMWOOD, [Daniel]

On the degeneracy of apples. (Bath Agricult. Soc. Vol. 4. p. 242.)

*GRINDALL, [Richard] *Esq. F. R. S. One of the Surgeons extraordinary to the Prince of Wales; Surgeon to the London Hospital and Warden of the Surgeon's company.*

born 1718. died 1797. Apr. 2.

See Gentleman's Magaz. Y. 1797. Apr. p. 358. *Duncan's* A. of Med. Y. 1797. p. 434.

Case of the efficacy of peruvian bark in a mortification. (Philos. Transact. Y. 1757. p. 379.)

GROSE, [Francis] *F. A. S. of London and Perth, Captain in the Surrey militia.*

born 1739. died at Dublin. 1791. May 12.

See Gentleman's Magaz. Y. 1791. May. p. 492. June. p. 581.

On antient armours and weapons; Supplement. 1789. 4. A guide to health, beauty, honour and riches; being a collection of humourous advertisements, pointing out the means to obtain those blessings, with a suitable introductory preface. 1785. A classical dictionary of the vulgar tongue. 1785. The history of Dover Castle, by the Rev. *William Darrell*, Chaplain to Queen Elizabeth. 1786. (12 sh. 6 d.) *Rules for drawing caricatures — with an essay on comic painting. 1788.

The

The antiquities of Scotland. Vol. 1. 2. 1791. 4. (Super Roy. paper. 8 L. 15 sh. in Imperial 6 L. 6 sh.) The grumbler: containing XVI essays. 1791. 12. (1 sh. 6 d.) The olio, being a collection of essays, dialogues, letters, biographical sketches, anecdotes, pieces of poetry, parodies, bons mots, epigrams, epitaphs — chiefly original. 1791. 8. (5 sh.) The antiquities of Ireland. (published by *Edward Ledwich.*) Vol. 1. 1793. 4. (5 L. 14 sh. In 8. 4 L. 2 sh.) Military antiquities respecting a history of the English armes from the conquest to the present time — a new edition —, by an officer of infantry. Vol. 1. 2. 1801. 4. (4 L. 4 sh. large paper 6 Guin.)

GROSE, [John] *A. M. F. A. S. Curate of the united parishes of St. Margaret Pattens and St. Gabriel Fenchurch, &c.*

Twelve sermons. 1801. 8. (7 sh. 6 d.) Sermons on various subjects. 1803. 8. (8 sh.)

GROSE, [John Henry]

Voyage to the East-Indies. Vol. 1. 2. 1772.

GROSE, [Sir Nash] *Knt.*

See Public Characters of 1798 and 1799. p. 393. Charge to the grand jury of the county of Hereford. 1795.

GROSS, [Daniel] *D. D.*

Natural principles of rectitude for the conduct of man in all states and situations of life. New-York. 1795.

GROVE, [William]

born .... died 178. (?)

GROVES, [Webber]

born 1705. died at New Hampshire in North-America. 1793. Jan.

See Gentleman's Magaz. Y. 1793. March. p. 281. Prior to the American revolution; 17.. On the commercial intercourse between Great-Britain and America. 17..

GUILLAN, [Thomas] *Surgeon in Antigua.*

Account of a singular appearance in the ventricles of the heart discovered on the dissection of a negro girl. (*Duncan's* M. C. Dec. 2. Vol. 6. p. 377.)

GUISE, [Samuel]

A catalogue and detailed account of a very valuable

luable and curious collection of manuscripts, collected in Hindostan. 1800. 4. (2 sh. 6 d.)

*GUISY, [T.....]

A method entirely new of learning french. 1801. 12. (3 sh.)

*GULLET, [Charles] *Esq. of Exeter.*

On lime. (*Young's* A. of Agr. Vol. 4. p. 490.)

GULLET, [Christopher] *Esq. of Exeter.*

A method of sowing turnip-seed to prevent the fly from taking it. (Bath Agricult. Soc. Vol. 2. p. 246.) On the means of preserving apple blossom and orchards from injury. (Ibid. Vol. 4. p. 196. *Young's* A. of Agr. Vol. 7. p. 58. 62.) Success of an experiment of fumigating an orchard. (Bath Agricult. Soc. Vol. 4. p. 199.) Means of insuring full crops of turnips. (Ibid. Vol. 4. p. 201. *Young's* A. of Agr. Vol. 7. p. 101.) On voluntary public granaries. (Ibid. Vol. 14. p. 121.) On the effects of elder in preserving growing plants from insects and flies. (American Museum Y. 1787. Febr. p. 143.)

*GUNDY, [Sir Solomon] *LL. D. F. R. S. F. A. S. R. A. et M. P. !!! (a fictitious name.)*

A member of parliament's review of his first session, in a poetical epistle to his wife in the country. 1792. 4. (1 sh.) For the Year 1792. to the Academicians; bad pictures placed in a good light. 1792. 4. (1 sh. 6 d.)

*GUNN, [John] *Teacher of the German-flute and Violoncello.*

The theory and practice of fingering the violoncello; containing rules and progressive lessons for attaining the knowledge and command of the whole compass of the instrument. 1793. fol. (1 L. 1 sh.) The art of playing the german flute on new principles, calculated to increase its powers and give to it greater variety, expression and effect. 1793. fol. (10 sh. 6 d.)

*GUNNING, [.....] *Mrs. (Widow of Gen. Gunning; maiden name Minifie.)*

born .... died 1800. Aug. 28.

See

See Gentleman's Magaz. Y. 1800. Sept. p. 904. Oct. p. 1000. Allgem. Litter. Zeit. J. 1801. ItBl. S. 763. *Hüttner's* Englische Miscellen. 1801. B. 2. St. 1. S. 17.

Letter to his Grace the Duke of Argyll. 1791. 8. (3 sh.) Anecdotes of the Delborough family. Vol. 1-5. 1792. 12. (15 sh.) Virginius and Virginia, a poem in 6 parts from the Roman history. 1792. 4. (5 sh.) Memoirs of Mary. Vol 1-5. 1794. 8. (15 sh.) Delves; Vol. 1. 2. 1796. 8. (10 sh.) Love at first sight, a novel from the french with alterations and additions. Vol. 1-5. 1797. 8. (15 sh.) Fashionable involvements. Vol. 1-3. 1800. (10 sh. 6 d.) The heir apparent — revised and augmented by her daughter Miss *Gunning*. Vol. 1-3. 1802. 12. (12 sh.)

GUNNING, [.....] *Miss.*

The packet, a novel. Vol. 1-4. 1794. 12. (12 sh.) Lord Fitzhenry, a novel. Vol. 1-3. 1794. 8. (10 sh. 6 d.) Memoirs of Mad. *de Barneveldt*: translated from the french. Vol. 1. 2. 1795. 8. (12 sh.) The foresters, altered from the french. Vol. 1-4. 1796. (12 sh.) The orphans of Snowdon. Vol. 1-3. 1797. (11 sh.) The gipsey countess; Vol. 1-5. 1799. (18 sh.) The farmer's boy. Vol. 1-4. 1802. 12. Family stories, or evenings my grand mother's house, intended for young persons of 8 years old. Vol. 1. 2. 1802. 12. (4 sh.) The village library. 1802. 18. (2 sh.)

GUPPY, [.....] *Mrs.*

Instructive and entertaining dialogues for children. Vol. 1. 2. 1800. (1 sh.)

GURNEY, [.....] *Miss.*

The war office. Vol. 1-3. 1802. (12 sh.)

GURNEY, [Samuel] *Redruth Parsonage, Cornwall.*

Crops and prices. (*Young's* A. of Agr. Vol. 34. p. 266.)

GUTCH, [John] *M. A: Chaplain of All Souls and Corpus Christi Colleges.*

Appendix to the history and antiquities of the colleges and halls in the University of Oxford, containing fasti Oxonienses; or a commentary on the supreme magistrates of the University by *Anth. Wood*,

Wood, now firſt publiſhed in Engliſh from the original MSS. — with a continuation to the preſent time. Oxford. 1790. The hiſtory and antiquities of the Univerſity of Oxford in two books by *Anth. Wood*. Now firſt publiſhed in Engliſh from the original MSS. in the Bodlejan library. Vol. 1. 1792. 4. (1 L. 11 ſh.) Vol. 2. P. 1. 2.

*GUTHRIE, [Maria] *Mrs. formerly acting Directreſs of the Imperial convent for the education of the female nobility of Ruſſia.*
born .... died .... (?)
A tour, performed in the Y. 1795. 1796. through the Tauride or Crimea — and all the other countries of the North ſhore of the Euxine, ceded to Ruſſia by the peace of Kainardge and Jaſſy, edited by *Mathew Guthrie* M. Dr. with a map and other engravings. 1803. 4. (1 L. 11 ſh. 6 d.)

GUTHRIE, [Matthew] *M. Dr. Phyſician to the Imperial Corps of Cadet at St. Petersburg. F. R. S.*
Some account of the Perſian cotton tree. (Mem. of M. Vol. 5. P. 1. p. 214. *Nicholſon's* Journal Vol. 2. p. 457.) Some account of the Dysopia. (Mem. of M. S. of L. Vol. 4. p. 368.) Obſervations on the Kuritſha ſlepota, or hen-blindneſs of Ruſſia. (*Duncan's* M. C. Dec. 2. Vol. 9. p. 284.) Letter — concerning various articles of medical information reſpecting Ruſſia. (*Duncan's* A. of Med. Y. 1798. p. 396.)

*GUY, [J....] *of the Bedforge loge of Free-Maſons.*
Songs, catches &c. 1799. (3 ſh.)

*GUY, [William] *Surgeon at Chicheſter.*
A caſe of violent diſtortion of the foot, occaſioned by a rotation of the aſtragalus, in conſequence of a fall and accompanied with a laceration of the integuments at the outer ancle and expoſure of a portion of the fibula. (*Simmons's* Med. Facts and Obſervat. Vol. 5. p. 54.)

*GUYSE, [.....] *Dr.*
— and Dr. *Watts*, a faithfull narrative of the ſurprizing works of God in the converſion of many hundred ſouls in Northampton and in the neighbouring towns and villages of New-Hampſhire

ſhire in New-England in a letter by *Edwards*, Miniſter of Northampton, on Nov. 6. 1737. publiſhed with a large preface. 1800. 8. (1 ſh.)

GWILLIM, [Henry] *Esq. One of his Maj. Judges of the Supreme Court of Madras.*

A new abridgment of the law, by *Math. Bacon*, of the Middle-temple, Esq. The 5 Edit. corrected, with conſiderable additions, including the lateſt authorities. Vol. 1-7. 1798. 8. (5 L. 5 ſh.)

A charge delivered to the grand jury at the aſſizes holden at Ely 27 March. 1779. 4. (1 ſh. 6 d.)

A collection of acts and records of parliament, with reports of caſes, argued and determined in the courts of law and equity, reſpecting tithes. Vol. 1-4. 1801. 8. (2 L. 12 ſh. 6 d.)

GWILT, [John] *Esq. of Icklingham, Suffolk.*

Plantation for ſheltering ſheep. (*Young's* A. of Agr. Vol. 1. p. 353. Vol. 5. p. 364.) Quantity of water in different ſoils. (Ibid. Vol. 1. p. 354.)

GWILT, [R.....] *Rev.*

Account of the pariſh of Icklingham, in Suffolk. (*Young's* A. of Agr. Vol. 4. p. 51.)

GWYNN, [Albinea]

born . . . . , died at Wrington, co. Somerſet. 1791. March 5.

See Gentleman's Magaz. Y. 1791. March. p. 285.

* The hiſtory of the Hon. *Edward Mortimer.* Vol. 1. 2. 1785. 8.

HACKETT, [Philip]

On the utility on hand-mills for grinding of corn. (Monthly Magaz. Y. 1800. Jan. p. 965. cf. Febr. p. 30.)

'HADDOCK, [Theophilus]

Error detected and fiction rebuked in a letter to *Edward Tatham*, D. D. ſo called and Rector of Lincoln-College, Oxford on his ſermon 1 John 4, 1. publiſhed under the title of a ſermon ſuitable to the times. 1794. 12. (6 d.)

'HADEN, [Thomas] *Surgeon, at Derby.*

A caſe of rupture of the uterus, from which the woman recovered. (Tranſact. of Med. and Chir. Soc. Vol. 2. p. 184.)

HADLEY,

HADLEY, [George] *Esq. formerly an Officer on the Bengal Military establishment.*
born .... died 1798. Sept. 10.
See Gentleman's Magaz. Y. 1798. Sept. p. 816.
On the dialect of the jargon of Hindostan. 17..
A translation of *Tootic Naumeh*, or tales of a parrot. 17..

*HAGGETT, [George] *M. A.*
A familiar treatise on the sacrament: with an appendix on the expediency of a correction of our present translation of the scriptures. 1793. 8. (1 sh. 6 d.)

*HAGGITT, [George] *at Mileham in Norfolk.*
Account of the parish of Mileham, in Norfolk. (*Young's* A. of Agr. Vol. II. p. 305.)

*HAIGH, [Thomas] *A. M. Master of the grammar school, Tottenham.*
Conjugata latina, or, a collection of the purest and most usual latin words, distinguished into classes according to the times of their occurrence and arranged according to their derivations. 1802. 8. (3 sh.)

HAIGHTON, [John] *Surgeon at London. M. Dr. F. M. S.*
Two experiments on the mechanism of vomiting, supplementary to a paper lately read before this society; Vol. 2. p. 250. (Mem. of M. S. of L. Vol. 2. p. 512.) A case of original deafness with the appearances on dissection. (Ibid. Vol. 3. p. 1.) Experiments made on the laryngeal and recurrent branches of the eight pair of nerves, with a view to determine the effects of the division of those nerves on the voice. (Ibid. Vol. 3. p. 422.) An experimental inquiry concerning the reproduction of nerves. (Philos. Transact. Y. 1795. p. 190. *Simmons's* Med. Facts and Observat. Vol. 7. p. 155.) An experimental inquiry concerning animal impregnation. (Philos. Transact. Y. 1797. p. 159.) A case of tic douloureux, or painful affection of the face, successfully treated by a division of the affected nerve. (M. Rec. and Ref. p. 19.) übers. in *Arnemann's* Mag. für die Wundarzneyw. B. 2. S. 303.) An inquiry concerning the true and spurious caesarian operation, in which their distinctions

distinctions are insisted on, principally with a view to form a more accurate estimate of success; to which are annexed some observations on the cause of the great danger. (Ibid. p. 242.)

ord HAILES, See *David Dalrymple.*

HAILS, [William Anthony]
Further particulars relative to Mr. *Greathead's* important invention of life-boats, with observations on their construction. (Monthly Magaz. Y. 1802. Nov. p. 319.)

HAILSTONE, [John] *Woodwardian Professor of Fossils in the University of Cambridge.*
A plan of a course of lectures on mineralogy. To which is prefixed an essay on the different kinds of mineral collections: translated from the german of Prof. *Werner.* 1791. 8. (1 sh. 6 d.)

HALCOTT, [Thomas] *Captain.*
Letter on drilling in Bengal. (*Young's* A. of Agr. Vol. 28. p. 294. 301.) On the drill husbandry of the East. (Comm. to the B. of Agr. Vol. 1. p. 352.)

HALDANE, [Henry] *Lieutenant-Colonel.*
A method of measuring the force of an electrical battery during the time of its being charged. (*Nicholson's* Journal. Vol. 1. p. 156.) Experiments made with a view to ascertain the cause of buildings, which have metallic conductors belonging to them, being struck by lightning. (Ibid. Vol. 1. p. 433.) Experiments and observations made with the newly discovered metallic pile of Sign. Volta, with remarks by W. N. (Ibid. Vol. 4. p. 241. 313.)

HALDANE, [Robert] *Esq.*
Address to the public, concerning political opinions and plans lately adopted to promote religion in Scotland. 1800. 8. (1 sh. 6 d.)

HALE, [.....] *Mrs.*
Poetical attempts. 1800. 8. (1 L. 1 sh.)

HALE, [....] *Lord chief justice.*
The jurisdiction of the Lord's house, or parliament, considered according to antient records. To which is prefixed by the editor, *Francis Hargrave,* Esq. an introductory preface, including a narra-

tive of the same jurisdiction from the accession of James I. 1796. 4. (1 L. 7 sh.)

*HALE, [Samuel] *Esq. of Portsmouth. F. A. A.*
Conjectures of the natural courses of the north west winds, being colder and more frequent in the winter in New-England than in the same degrees of latitude in Europe. (Mem. of B. A. Vol. 2. P. 1. p. 61.)

*HALE, [William] *Esq.*
An account of the produce of two acres of land sown with barley and lucern. (*Young's* A. of Agr. Vol. 33. p. 302.)

HALES, [Charles]
born .... died 177.. (?)

*HALES, [Charles] *Esq.*
The bank mirror, or a guide to the funds. 1796. 8. (1 sh. 6 d.) A correct detail of the finances of this country —. 1797. 8. (1 sh.)

*HALES, S.....] *D. D.*
Method of preserving corn in sacks. (Comm. and Agric. Mag. Y. 1801. April. p. 260.)

HALES, [William] *D. D. Rector at Killesandra, Ulster &c.*
Observations on tithes, shewing the inconveniences of all the schemes that have been proposed for altering that ancient manner of providing for the clergy of the established church of Ireland. To which is annexed a second edition of the moderate reformer (by Baron *Maseres*) or a proposal for abolishing some of the most obvious and gross abuses that have crept into the church of England and are the occasion of frequent complaints against it. 1794. 8. (1 sh. 6 d.) The inspector, or select literary intelligence for the vulgar A. D. 1798. but correct A. D. 1801. the first year of the 19. century. 1799. 8. Analysis fluxionum. 1800. 4. (6 sh.) Methodism inspected; with an appendix on the evidences of a state of salvation. 1803. (2 sh.)

*HALFPENNY, [Joseph] *at York.*
Gothic ornaments in the cathedral church of York, drawn and etched by him. Numb. 1–12. (each 6 sh.) 4.

HALHED,

HALHED, [Nathaniel Braſſey] *M. P.*
(The oriental MSS. of him the Britiſh Muſeum has very laudably purchaſed; See Gentleman's Magaz. Y. 1796. March. p. 252.) The whole of the teſtimonies to the authenticity of the propheeies of *Richard Brother's* and of his miſſion to recall the jews. 1795. 8. (1 ſh.) A word of admonition to the R. H. *Will. Pitt*, in an epiſtle to that gentleman, occaſioned by the propheeies of brothers, — and the notable expoſitions of the ſcripture prophecies. 1795. 8. (1 ſh.) A calculation of the millenium, with obſervations on the pamphlets intitled, „ſecond argument &c. and the age of credulity„ together with a ſpeech delivered in the houſe of commons 31 March 1795. reſpecting the confinement of *Brother's* the prophet. To which is added, an original letter written by *Brothers* in 1790. to *P. Stephens*, Esq. and alſo a paper, painting out thoſe parts of *Brothers* propheeies that have been already fulfilled. 8. (1 ſh. 6 d.) An anſwer to Dr. *Horne's* ſecond pamphlet, intitled „occaſional remarks.„ 1795. 8. (6 d.) Second ſpeech — delivered in the houſe of Commons April 21. 1795. reſpecting the detention of Mr. *Brother's* the prophet. 1795. 8. (4 d.) Two letters to the R. H. Lord *Loughborough*. 1795. 8. (4 d.) *Imitations of the epigrams of Martial. P. 1. 2. 1793. 4. (5 ſh.) P. 3. 4. 1794. 4. (5 ſh.) Speech — 31 March 1795. reſpecting the confinement of Mr. *Brother's*, the prophet. 1795. 8. (6 d.)

*HALL, [Agnes E....]
Diſputes in book ſocieties. (Monthly Magaz. 1800. Dec. p. 402.)

*HALL, [Archibald] *Late Paſtor of the Presbyterian church, Well-ſtreet, Oxford-ſtreet, London.*
An humble attempt to exhibit a ſcriptural view of the conſtitution, order, diſcipline and fellowſhip of the goſpel church. Ed. 2. 1795. 8. (3 ſh.)

*HALL, [Charles Henry] *B. D.*
Sermons — 1799. 8. (5 ſh.)

*HALL, [Eliſha J....]
On the neceſſity of paſſing a law for the regulation of the practice of medicine. (American Muſeum Y. 1789. Jan. p. 25. Febr. p. 171.)

*HALL, [Sir James] *Bart. F. R. et A. S S. Edin.*
Obſervations on the formation of granite. (Tr. of E. S. Vol. 3. H. p. 8.) On the origin and principles of gothic architecture. (Ibid. Vol. 4. L. p. 3.) Experiments on whinſtone and lava. (Ibid. Vol. 5. Part 1. p. 43. *Nicholſon's* Journal Vol. 2. p. 285. Vol. 4. p. 8. 56.)

*HALL, [James] *Dr. Principal of Cokesbury-College in Maryland.*
Account of the effects of electricity in the removal of an obſtruction in the biliary duct. (Tr. of Phyſ. of Philad. Vol. 1. P. 1. p. 192.)

*HALL, [James] *A. M. Jun.*
An account of a ſuppoſed artificial wall, diſcovered under the ſurface of the earth near the Yadkin, in North-Carolina. (Medical Repoſitory. Vol. 2. p. 272.)

*HALL, [John] *Miniſter of the Engliſh Presbyterian church in Rotterdam.*
Martinet's catechiſm of nature, for the uſe of children, translated from the Dutch. 1790. 8. (1 ſh.) Addreſs delivered at the engliſh church at Rotterdam, previous to the thanksgiving ſervice April 10. 1793. for the total retreat of the french, from the dutch territories. 1793. 8. (1 ſh.)

*HALL, [Peter]
Wet ſoil unfit for turnips. (Comm. and Agric. Mag. Y. 1803. Apr. p. 255.)

*HALL, [P.... W....]
Thoughts and inquiry on the principles and nature of the revealed and ſupreme law. 1792. 8. (5 ſh.)

HALL, [Richard] *Esq. Surgeon to the Mancheſter Infirmary.*
born 1751. died at Mancheſter 1801. Jun. 1. See Gentlemans Magaz. Y. 1801. July. p. 673.

*HALL, [Richard] *M Dr. formerly Phyſician at Jedburgh, now Phyſician in London.*
Obſervations on the pemphigus major of Sauvage, with a brief account of two caſes of that diſeaſe. (*Duncan's* A. of Med. Y. 1798. p. 386. Y. 1799. p. 328.) A further ſtatement of the caſe of *Eliſabeth Thompſon* upon whom the caeſarean operation was performed in the Mancheſter lying-in Hoſpital; in

in addition to that publiſhed by Mr. *Wood* in the Memoirs of the Med. Soc. of London Vol. 5. by *Charles White* and *Rich. Hall*, *George Tomlinſon* and *John Thorp*. 1799. 4. Experiments upon the circulation of the blood, throughout the vaſcular ſyſtem; on languid circulation; on the motion of the blood, independent of the action of the heart, and on the pulſations of the arteries; by the Abbé *Spallanzani*; with notes and a ſketch of the literary life of the author, by *J. Tourdes*, translated into Engliſh and illuſtrated with additional notes. 1801. 8. (9 ſh.) A treatiſe on the means of purifying infected air and preventing contagion by *L. B. Guyton Morveau*, translated from the french. 1802. 8. (6 ſh.) Proofs that the late Dr. *James Johnſtone* was the firſt propoſer of acid fumigations. (Monthly Magaz. Y. 1802. Oct. p. 204.) Obſervations on cold applications to the head in caſes of inſanity. (*Duncan's* A. of Med. Y. 1800. p. 364.) Account of a ſingularly fatal epidemic diſeaſe among cats, which prevailed in the neighbourhood of Jedburgh. (Ibid. Y. 1800. p. 481.)

HALL, [Robert] *Phyſician, St. Pancras, London.*
Obſervations on cow pox; (*Duncan's* A. of Med. Y. 1801. p. 316. 323.)

HALL, [Robert] *Jun. at Basford.*
Deſcription of his expanding crane. (Tr. of the Soc. for the E. of A. Vol. 12. p. 284.)

HALL, [Robert] *M. A. A Diſſenting Miniſter at Cheſterton near Cambridge.*
Chriſtianity conſiſtent with a love of freedom, being an anſwer to *John Clayton's* ſermon. 1791. 8. (1 ſh. 6 d.) Apology for the freedom of the preſs and for general liberty; with remarks on Biſh. *Horsley's* ſermon; preached on the 13 Jan. 1793. 8. (2 ſh. 6 d.) Modern infidelity conſidered with reſpect to its influence on ſociety, a ſermon. 1800. 8. (2 ſh.)

HALL, [Thomas] *M. Dr. Phyſician at Eaſt Retford, Nottinghamſhire.*
A ſingular variety of chorea St. Viti conſiderably relieved by the uſe of the argentum nitratum. (*Duncan's* A. of Med. Y. 1799. p. 374.)

*HALL, [Thomas] *Esq. at Preston-Candover near Odiham.*
A plan for the better maintenance and regulation of the parochial poor. (Bath Agricult. Soc. Vol. 6. p. 254.)

*HALL, [Thomas]
Achmet to Selim, or, the dying negro, a poem. 1792. 4. (1 sh.)

*HALL, [William] *Esq. of Whitehall. F. R. S. Edin.*
Account of a variety of the bramble (Rubus); (Tr. of E. S. Vol. 3. Hist. p. 20.) Account of a singular halo of the moon. (Ibid. Vol. 4. Ph. p. 174 *Nicholson's* Journal. Vol. 2. p. 485.)

*HALL, [William] *Esq. of Elmstone-Court, Kent.*
A system of husbandry explained, with observations by *A. Young.* (*Young's* A. of Agr. Vol. 4 p. 221.) Summer fallowing necessary. (Ibid. Vol. 4. p. 499.) Produce of 70 acres of corn and seeds, with observations by *A. Young* 1782. (Ibid. Vol. 4. p. 505.) On summer fallows, with observations by *A. Young.* (Ibid. Vol. 5. p. 99.) On turnips-courses-drilling. (Ibid. Vol. 5. p. 440.) Reply to Mr. *Fiske* on fallowing. (Ibid. Vol. 5. p. 471.) An account of the annual average expence for the last three years to Jan. 1. 1786. (Ibid. Vol. 6. p. 159.)

*HALL, [William Henry]
Royal encyclopedia; 17.. The creation, in 6 books, after the manner and as an introductory companion to the death of Abel and death of Cain. 1801. 8. (2 sh. 6 d.)

*HALLEY, [Thomas] *at Pontefract, Yorkshire.*
On method of cure rhubarb. (Tr. of the Soc. for the E. of A. Vol. 11. p. 126.)

*HALLORAN, [Lawrence] *D. D.*
Lachrymae hibernicae, or the genius of Erin's complaint, a ballad; 1801. 4. (1 sh. 6 d.)

*HALLORAN, [Lawrence Hynes] *Master of Alphiston Academy, near Exeter.*
Collection of odes, poems and translations. 1790. 8. (2 sh.) Poems on various subjects. 1791. 4. (5 sh.)

(5 sh.) An ode to the proposed visit of their majesties to the city of Exeter. 1791. 4. (1 sh.)

[ALLS, [Robert] *M. Dr. Physician at Colchester.*
Account of the good effects obtained from washing the body with cold water and vinegar in cases of typhus fever. *(Duncan's* M. C. Dec. 2. Vol. 10. p. 327.)

IALY, [Aylmer] *Captain of King's (own) Infantry.*
Military observations. 1801. 8. (3 sh. 6 d.)

AMILTON, [Alexander] *M. Dr. F. R. S. Edin. Professor of Midwifery in the University and Fellow of the Roy. College of Physicians of Edinburgh.*
born .... died 1802. Jun. ... at Blandfield, near Edinburgh.
See Gentleman's Magaz. Y. 1802. Aug. p. 787.
On the management of female complaints and of children in early infancy. 1792. 8. (6 sh.) übers. Leipzig. 1793. 8. Letters to Dr. *William Osborne*, on certain doctrines contained in his essays on the practice of midwifery. 1793. 8. (3 sh.) übers. von Dr. *C. F. Michaelis* — Liegnitz. 1794. 8. A case of inverted uterus. *(Duncan's* M. C. Dec. 2. Vol. 6. p. 315.)

IAMILTON, [Alexander] *Esq. Secretary of the United States of America.*
*Report of the secretary of the treasury of the United States on the subject of manufactures, presented Dec. 5. 1791. 1793. 8. (2 sh. 6 d.) American budget, 1794. — to which is added, the report to the congress of the United States of America, on the nature and extent of the privileges and restrictions of the commercial intercourse of the United States with foreign nations by *Thomas Jefferson* Esq. Secretary of State. 1794. 8. (1 sh. 6 d.) The federalist. 17.. Reports, containing 1) a plan for the further support of public credit, 2) for the improvement and better management of the revenues of the United States; to which is annexed an act for making provisions for the support of public credit and the redemption of the debt. 1795. 4. (4 sh.) *Report, read in the house of representations of the United States

Jan. 19. 1795. containing a plan for further support of public credit. Philadelphia. 1795. 8. London. 1795. 4. übers. in *Hegewisch* u. *Ebeling* Amerikanischen Magazin, B. 1. St. 1. S. 159. *Report read — Febr. 2. 1795. fol. übers. in *Hegewisch* u. *Ebeling* Amerik. Magaz. B. 1. St. 2. S. 101. A defence of the treaty of amity, commerce and navigation entered into between the United States of America and Great-Britain by *Camillus*. New-York. 1795. 8. übers. in *Hegewisch* u. *Ebeling* Amerik. Magaz. B. 1. St. 4. S. 56. Observations on certain documents contained in Nro. 5 and 6. of „the history of the United States for the Year 1796, in which the charge of speculation against *Alex. Hamilton*, is fully refuted, written by himself. Philadelphia. 1797. 8. Letter concerning the public conduct and character of *J. Adams*. Ed. 2. New-York. 1800. 8. (25 Cents.)

HAMILTON, [Charles] *Lieutenant in the service of the East India Company.*
born .... died 1792. March. 14.
See Gentleman's Magaz. Y. 1792. March. p. 286.
The Hedaya, or guide; a commentary on the Mussulman laws; translated by order of the Governor General and Council of Bengal. Vol. 1-4. 1791. 4. (5 L. 5 sh.)

HAMILTON, [Charles] *Esq.*
Transactions during the reign of Queen Anne: from the union to the death of that princess. 1790. 8. (6 sh.) *Vaurien, or, sketches of the times, exhibiting views of the philosophies, religious, politics, litterature and manners of the age. Vol. 1. 2. 1797. 8. (8 sh.)

***HAMILTON**, [Eliza] *Sister to the late Lieut. Charles Hamilton.*
Translation of the letters of a Hindoo Rajah, written previous to and during the period of his residence in England. To which is prefixed a preliminary dissertation on the history, religion and manners of the Hindoos. Vol. 1. 2. 1796. 8. (10 sh.)

*HAMIL-

HAMILTON, [Elizabeth] *Miss.*
Memoirs of modern philosophers. Vol. 1–3. 1800. 8. (15 sh.) Letters on the elementary principles of education. Vol. 1. 2. 1802. 8. (15 sh.)

HAMILTON, [G....]
A short description of the island of Carnicobar, with some accounts of its inhabitants. (Asiat. Researches. Vol. 2. p. 337. New-York Magaz. Y. 1795. Nov. p. 660.)

HAMILTON, [George] *late Surgeon of the Pandora.*
Voyage round the world in his Maj. frigate Pandora, performed under the direction of Capt. *Edwards*, in the Y. 1790–1792 with the discoveries made in the South-sea and the many distresses experienced by the crew from shipwreck and famine, in a voyage of eleven hundred miles in open boats, between Endeavour straits and the island of Timor. 1793. 8. (4 sh.) übers. (von *F. L. W. Meyer.*) Berlin. 1794. 8.

HAMILTON, [Hugh] *D. D. Dean of Armagh. F. R. S. and R. J. A.*
Letter to *J. A. Hamilton* on his new kind of portable barometer for measuring heights, with remarks and hints for the further improvement of barometers. (Tr. of J. A. Vol. 5. p. 117.) On the power of fixed caustic alkaline salts to preserve the flesh of animals from putrefaction. (Ibid. Vol. 5. p. 319.)

HAMILTON, [James] *Esq. M. Dr. Fellow of the Royal College of Physicians, Edinburgh. Professor of Midwifery in the University of Edinburgh.*
Observations on the seats and causes of diseases; illustrated by the dissections of the late Prof. *Morgagni* of Padua. Vol. 1. 1795. 8. (6 sh.) Select cases in midwifery. 1795. 8. Observations on the instrument employed in the practice of midwifery commonly called Lowder's lever. (*Duncan's* M. C. Dec. 2. Vol. 8. p. 400.) A collection of engravings, designed to facilitate the study of midwifery, explained and illustrated. 1797. 4. History of a case of convulsions during the latter months of pregnancy, with practical remarks on

convulsions during pregnancy and labour. (*Duncan's* A. of Med. Y. 1800. p. 313.)

HAMILTON, [James Archibald] *D. D. M. R. J. A. Professor of Astronomy at Armagh.*

On a new kind of portable barometer for measuring heights. (Tr. of J. A. Vol. 5. p. 95.) On the method of the determining the longitude, by observations of the meridian passages of the moon and a star made at two places. (Ibid. Vol. 6. p. 193.)

HAMILTON, [James Edward] *Esq.*

Reflections on the revolution in France by *Edm. Burke* considered, also, observations on Mr. *Paine's* pamphlet, the rights of men, with cursory remarks on the prospect of a Russian war and the Canada bill now pending. 1791. 8. (2 sh. 6 d.) Strictures upon primitive christianity by the Rev. Dr. *Knowles*, Prebendary of Ely; as also upon the theological and polemical writings of the Lord Bish. of St. David's, Dr. *Priestley*, Mr. *Gibbes* and the late Rev. Mr. *Badcock*. Vol. 1. 2. 1792. (13 sh.) Letters on christianity. 1792. 8. (4 sh.)

*HAMILTON, [James Ed...] *Esq.*

On the improvement of agriculture in Great-Britain and Ireland. (*Young's* A. of Agr. Vol. 13. p. 74.)

*HAMILTON, [Joseph]

Occasional reflections on the operation of the small pox or the traveller's pocket doctor. Catskill. 1799. 12.

HAMILTON, [Robert] *M. Dr. F. R. S. Edin. Physician at Lynn-Regis, Norfolk.*

born Dec. 6. 1721. died 1793. Nov. 9.

See Gentleman's Magaz. Y. 1793. Nov. p. 1060. Practical hints on opium, considered as a poison. 1790. 8. The duties of a regimental surgeon considered; Ed. 2. Vol. 1. 2. 1795. (12 sh.) Observations on scrophulous affection, with remarks on schirrus, cancer and rachitis. 1792. 8. (3 sh.) übers. Leipzig. 1793. 8. Remarks on hydrophobia, or the disease produced by the bite of the rabid animal. Ed. 2. with additions and corrections. Vol. 1. 2. 1798. 8. (14 sh.) *Rules for recovering

ring perfons recently drowned; 1794. 8. Account of a fuccefsfull method of treating inflammatory difeafes by mercury and opium. (M. P. of M. S. Nrb. 1. p. 125. *Duncan's* Med. C. Vol. 9. p. 191. überf. Samml. F. A. Th. 11. S. 265.) Obfervations on the marfh remittent fever, more particularly in regard to its appearance and return every autumn, after the inundation from the fea — alfo on the water-canker, or cancer aquaticus of van *Swieten*, with fome remarks on the leprofy; With memoirs of the author's life. 1801. 8. (4 fh.)

HAMILTON, [Ronald] *Major of the 14 Regt. of Foot.*

born 1762. died 1797. July 1. at Fort Royal, Martinique.

See Gentleman's Magaz. Y. 1797. Oct. p. 889. Allg. Litt. Zeit. J. 1800. ItBl. S. 646.

Sketch of the prefent ftate of the army. 17..

HAMILTON, [William]

born . . . . . died 1792. Febr. 29.

The election, a poem. 17..

HAMILTON, [Sir William] *Knight of the Bath, Privy Counfellor, Envoy to the Court of Naples. F. R. S.*

born 1729. died 1803. April 5.

See Gentleman's Magaz. Y. 1803. April. p. 390.

A collection of engravings from antique vafes, the greater part of Grecian fabric: found in ancient tombs in two Sicilies in the Y. 1789 and 1790. with the remarks of the proprietor — publifhed by *William Tifchbein.* Vol. 1. Naples. 1791. fol. Vol. 2. 1795. fol. Vol. 3. 4. (489 Paoli.) An account of the late eruption of mount vefuvius. (Phil. Transact. Y. 1795. p. 73.)

HAMILTON, [William] *B. D. M. R. J. A. Rector of Fanet in the county of Donegal.*

born .... murdered at Sharon 1797. March 2.

See Gentleman's Magaz. Y. 1797. March. p. 180. 256. Allgem. Litt. Zeit. J. 1800. ItBl. S. 642.

Letters concerning the northern coaft of the county of Antrim; in Ireland. Ed. 2. Dublin and London. 1790. 8. Letters on the principles of the french democracy and their application and influence on the

the conſtitution and happineſs of Britain and Ireland. 1792. (2 ſh.) Memoir on the climate of Ireland. (Tr. of J. A. Vol. 6. p. 27. *Nicholſon's* Journal. Vol. 2. p. 381. 431.)

*HAMILTON, [William] *M. Dr. Phyſician to the London Hoſpital and Lecturer on Chemiſtry.*
Elements of the art of dying by *Bertholet*, translated from the french. Vol. 1–3. 1791. 8. (12 ſh.)

*HAMLEY, [Edward] *Fellow of New College.*
Poems on various kinds. 1796. 8. (3 ſh. 6 d.)

*HAMMICK, [. . . . .]
Caſes of the antiſyphilitic efficacy of the nitric acid. (Medical Repoſit. Vol. 1. p. 438.)

*HAMMICK, [Stephen] *Jun. One of the Aſſiſtant Surgeons to the Royal Hoſpital at Plymouth.*
Account of the benefit obtained from the external uſe of hops in the cure of large ſordid ulcers. (Med. Repoſit. Vol. 1. p. 576. *Duncan's* A. of Med. Y. 1797. p. 403.)

*HAMPDEN, [. . . . .]
A mirror for princes, in a letter to his Roy. Highneſs the Prince of Wales. 1797. 8. (1 ſh. 6 d.) Miniſters the cauſe of the miſeries and diſaffection of the people. 1797. 8. (1 d.)

HAMPSON, [John] *A. M.*
Memoirs of the late Rev. *John Wesley*, A. M. with a review of his life and writings and a hiſtory of methodiſm, from its commencement in 1729. to the preſent time. Vol. 1–3. 1791. 8. (9 ſh.) überſ. von *A. H. Niemeyer.* Th. 1. 2. Halle. 1793. 8. The poetics of *Marc. Hieron. Vida*, Biſh. of Alba, with tranſlations from the latin of Dr. *Lowth*, Mr. *Gray* and others. 1793. 8. (6 ſh.)

*HAMPSON, [W. . . . .]
Dukinfield lodge, a poem, in two cantos. 1793. 4. (1 ſh.)

*HAMPSON, [William]
An eſſay on the management of cows. 1796. 8. (1 ſh.) On the means of preventing caterpillars on fruit-trees. (Tr. of the Soc. for the E. of A. Vol. 13. p. 172.)

HAMPTON,

HAMPTON, [George] *M. A. Pastor of Protestant Dissenters in Banbury.*
born 1717. died 1796. Sept. 22.
See Gentleman's Magaz. Y. 1796. Sept. p. 798. Allg. Litterat. Zeit. ItBl. J. 1800. S. 629.
Candid remarks upon *Taylor's* discourse entitled, the scripture doctrine of atonement examined. 1752. 8. (1 sh. 6 d.) Answer to *Priestley's* objections to the doctrine of the atonement by the death of Christ in the history of the corruptions of christianity. 1785. 8. (2 sh.)

HANCOCK, [Blith] *of Norwich; Teacher of the Mathematics.*
born 1722. died 1795. May 27.

*HANCOCK, [John]
Reasons for withdrawing from society with the people called Quackers with additional observations on sundry important subjects. —; 1802. 8. (4 sh.) Thoughts on the abuse of figurative language as applied to religious subjects; with observations addressed to the people called Quackers. 1803. 8.

*HANCOCK, [Philipp] *Jun. of Ford, President.*
On the Wiveliscombe agricultural society. (*Young's* A. of Agr. Vol. 33. p. 107.)

*HANCOCK, [William] *of Birmingham.*
Description of his metal rope or chain. (Tr. of the Soc. for the E. of A. Vol. 14. p. 308.)

*HAND, [Edward]
Utility of preparing seed-oats with plaster of Paris. (Columbian Magaz. Y. 1791. May. p. 311. American Museum Y. 1791. Aug. p. 75.)

*HAND, [Richard]
Essay on the method of gilding on glass. (Tr. of Dublin-Soc. Vol. 1. P. 1. p. 294.) Essay on spirit varnish. (Ibid. Vol. 1. P. 1. p. 295.)

*HANDS, [William] *One of the Attornies of the Court.*
A selection of rules occurring in the prosecution and defence of personal actions in the court of King's Bench; with notes on each rule, illustrated of the practice of the court. 1795. 8. (3 sh.) The modern practice of levying fines and suffering recoveries in the court of common pleas at Westminster,

minster, with an appendix of select precedents. 1800. 8. (4 sh. 6 d.) The solicitor's practice on the crown side of the court of King's Bench, with an appendix containing the form of the proceedings &c. 1803. 8. (10 sh. 6 d.)

*HANDY, [Hast] *of Maryland.*
On opium. 1791.

HANGER, [George] *Lieutenant-Colonel.*
Anticipation of the freedom of Brabant. 1792. Military reflections on the attack and defence of the city of London; proved by the author to have been the most vulnerable part of consequence in the whole island, in the situation it was left in the Y. 1794. &c. 1795. 8. (3 sh.) The life, adventures and opinions — written by himself. Vol. 1.2. 1801. 8. (14 sh.) übers. Leipzig. 1802. 8.

*HANMER, [Sir Thomas] *Bart. of Bettesfield Park, near Whitchurch, Shropshire.*
Account of his improvement of waste land, in North Wales. (Tr. of the Soc. for the E. of A. Vol. 9. p. 76.) Account and drawing of a method of laying on water upon water-wheels. (Ib. Vol. 17. p. 349.)

*HANNAM, [T....]
The analytical compendium, or, outlines of sermons, with an essay on the composition of a sermon, extracted from various authors. Vol. 1. 1800. 18. (3 sh.) Vol. 2. and last. 1803. (1 sh. 6 d.)

*HANWAY, [Mary Ann] *Miss.*
Ellinor, or the world as it is, a novel. Vol. 1-4. 1798. 12. (18 sh.) Andrew Stuart, or the northern wanderer, a novel. Vol. 1-4. 1800. 8. (18 sh.)

*HARD, [Josiah] *Esq.*
Imposture exposed, in a few brief remarks on the irreligiousness, profaneness, indelicacy, virulence, and vulgarity of certain persons who style himselves anti-jacobin reviewers. 1801. 8. (6 d.)

*HARDIE, [David]
Taxation of coals, considered in an address to the inhabitants of the cities of London and Westminster and all places supplied with coals from the port of London. 1792. 8. (1 sh. 6 d.)

*HARDIE,

*HARDIE, [James] *A. M.*

The American remembrancer and univerſal tablet of memory, containing a liſt of the moſt eminent men, whether in ancient or modern times. Philad. 1795. 8. An account of the malignant fever lately (1798.) prevalent in the city of New-York. New-York. 1799. 8.

*HARDING, [E.....]

See *Thomas Pennant.*

*HARDING, [Thomas] *M. R. J. A.*

Obſervations on the variation of the needle. (Tr. of J. A. Vol.4. p.107.)

*HARDINGE, [George] *Esq. M. P.*

A ſeries of letters to *Edm. Burke*, in which are contained enquiries into the conſtitutional exiſtence of an impeachment againſt Mr. *Haſting's*, with an appendix, in which are contained obſervations upon Maj. *Scott's* letter, publiſhed in the diary, Apr. 11. 1791. 1791. 8. (2 ſh 6 d.) The eſſence of *Malone*, or the beauties of that faſcinating writer, extracted from his immortal work — entitled, ſome account of the life and writings of *John Dryden*. 1800. 8. (2 ſh. 6 d.)

*HARDWICKE, [Thomas] *Capt.*

Deſcription of a ſpecies of meloe, an inſect of the firſt or coleopterous order in the Linnean ſyſtem; found in all parts of Bengal, Behar and Oude; and poſſeſſing all the properties of the ſpaniſh bliſtering fly, or meloe veſicatorius. (Aſiat. Reſ. Vol. 5. p. 213.) Narrative of a journey to Sirinagur. (Ibid. Vol. 6. p. 309.)

*HARDY, [.....]

The patriot, addreſſed to the people on the preſent ſtate of affairs in Britain and in France: with obſervations on republican government and diſcuſſions of the principles advanced in the writings of *Thomas Paine*. 1793. 8. (1 ſh.)

*HARDY, [Henry]

A viſion from the Lord God almighty, the great and mighty god of the whole earth, a viſion that muſt bring about that great and glorious day of peace, when nation ſhall no more lift up ſword againſt nation or learn war any more. 1792. 8. (6 d.)

*HARDY,

*HARDY, [Robert] *M. A.*
An addreſs to the loyal volunteer corps of Great-Britain, in two parts. 1799. 8. (2 ſh.)

HARDY, [Samuel] *B. A. formerly Fellow of Emanuel College, Cambridge; Rector of Blakenham Parva, co. Suffolk, and late Lecturer and Maſter of the free-ſchool at Enfield.*
born 1720. died at Tottingham-high-croſs 1793. Dec. 14.
See Gentleman's Magaz. Y. 1793. Dec. p. 1156. Y. 1794. p. 275.
An anſwer to Mr. *Chubb's* eſſay concerning redemption. 1744. 8. The indiſpenſable neceſſity of conſtantly celebrating the chriſtian ſacrifice; 1746. 8. The euchariſt, a material ſacrifice, a ſermon. 1748. 8.

*HARE, [J....] *A. M. Rector of Coln St. Denys, Glouceſterſhire.*
An eſſay on the unreaſonableneſs of ſcepticiſm. 1801. 8. (6 ſh.)

*HARE, [Robert]
Memoir on the ſupply and application of the blow-pipe. (*Tilloch's* Philoſ. Mag. Vol. 14. p. 238. 298.)

HARGRAVE, [Francis] *Esq. Barriſter at Law and Recorder of Liverpool.*
See *Charles Butler* and .... *Hale.*
Juridical arguments and collections. Vol. 1. 1797. 4. (1 L. 7 ſh.) Vol. 2. 1799. 4. (1 L. 1 ſh.) An addreſs to the grand jury at the Liverpool ſeſſions Oct. 11. on the preſent criſis of public affairs. 1804. 8. (1 ſh.)

HARGROVE, [E....]
The hiſtory of the caſtle, town and foreſt of Knareshorough with Harrogate and its medicinal waters. York. 1798. 8.

*HARLAND, [C....]
Deſcription of his butter-churns on a new principle. (Comm. and Agric. Mag. Y. 1800. June. p. 384.)

HARLEY, [George Davies] *Of the Theatre Royal, Coventgarden.*
Poems. 1796. 8. (6 ſh.) Ballad ſtories, ſonnets &c. Vol. 1. 1799. 8. (4 ſh.)

HARLSTONE, [T....]

Juſt in time, a comic opera, in 3 acts. 1792. 8. (1 ſh. 6 d.)

HARNESS, [John] *M. Dr. Phyſician to his Maj. fleet in the Mediterraneum.*

On the uſe of the gaſtric juice of graminivorous animals in the cure of ulcers. (*Duncan's* A. of Med. Y. 1797. p. 398. Medical Repoſit. Vol. 3. p. 102.) On the uſe of the application of gaſtric juice to ſores. (Transact. of Med. and Chir. Soc. Vol. 2. p. 164.)

HARPER, [Andrew] *Surgeon to the Garriſon at the Bahama Islands.*

The oeconomy of health &c. überſ. Leipzig. 1792. 8. On the real cauſe and cure of inſanity &c. überſ. von Dr. *G. W. Consbruch.* Aufl. 2. Marburg. 1792. 8.

HARPER, [Henry] *of Bank-Hall, near Liverpool.*

Experiment on the extraordinary quality in butter made after the Lancaſhire manner. (Bath Agric. Soc. Vol. 8. p. 295.) Account of a farm. (*Young's* A. of Agr. Vol. 21. p. 568.) An account of the incloſing and improving 75 acres, of eight yards to the rod, the whole of bootle marſh —; (Tr. of the Soc. for the E. of A. Vol. 13. p. 182.) Obſervations relative to the different modes of cultivating wheat. (Ibid. Vol. 16. p. 147.) On the culture of potatoes and the application of that root to the feeding various kinds of ſtock. (Ibid. Vol. 16. p. 197.)

HARPER, [Robert Goodloe] *Esq. Member of Congreſs for South-Carolina.*

Obſervations on the North-American land-company lately inſtituted in Philadelphia; to which are added remarks on American lands in general more particularly the vine lands of the ſouthern and weſtern ſtates in two letters. 1796. (2 ſh.) Obſervations on the diſpute between the United States and France; 1797. 8. (2 ſh.) überſ. 1798. 8. Speech on the foreign intercourſe bill, delivered — March 2. 1798. 8. (1 ſh. 6 d.) A ſhort account of the principal proceedings of congreſs in the late ſeſſion, and a ſketch of the ſtate of affairs between the United States and France in July 1798. 1798. 8. (1 sh.)

*HARPER, [Walter] *Late Assistant-Lecturer and Joint-Lecturer of St. Andrew, Holborn.*

The christian remembrancer, a farewell sermon. 1791. 4. (1 sh.)

*HARRAL, [T.....]

Leisure moments. 17.. A monody on the death of Mr. *John Palmer*, the Comedian, to which is prefixed a review of his theatrical powers: with observations on the most eminent performers on the London stage. 1798. 8., (1 sh.)

*HARRIES, [Edward] *Esq. of Hanwood, near Shrewsbury.*

Observations on planting and the growth of trees. (*Young's* A. of Agr. Vol. 1. p. 389.) On Colebrook dale and its vicinity. (Ibid. Vol. 4. p. 343.) Observations and experiments on the growth of trees. (Ibid. Vol. 3. p. 425.) A hint to the minister on the crown lands. (Ibid. Vol. 5. p. 410.) Observations on the growth of trees. (Ibid. Vol. 6. p. 84.) On the management of the poor. (Ibid. Vol. 7. p. 179.) Thoughts for the consideration up the legislature on watering of meadows. (Ibid. Vol. 8. p. 101.) Cursory thoughts on the poor. (Ibid. Vol. 10. p. 419.) Farming minutes. (Ibid. Vol. 11. p. 8.) Thoughts on some papers in *Young's* Annals of Agric. (Ibid. Vol. 13. p. 41.) On the growth of trees, and account of a crop of flax. (Ibid. Vol. 13. p. 98.) Thoughts on the employment of agriculture. (Ibid. Vol. 14. p. 127.) Sundry remarks on practical agriculture. (Ibid. Vol. 15. p. 66.) Thoughts on a general inclosure bill. (Ibid. Vol. 15. p. 72.) General observations on the state of oak timber. (Ibid. Vol. 15. p. 553.) American farms recommended. (Ibid. Vol. 19. p. 254.) Agricultural observations and on vineries. (Ibid. Vol. 21. p. 363.) Observations made in a ride from Shrewsbury to Bewdley in Worcestershire, begun the 30 Oct. 1794. (Ibid. Vol. 23. p. 511.) Journal of a tour. (Ibid. Vol. 24. p. 379.) On the larch tree. (Ibid. Vol. 30. p. 57.) On planting. (Ibid. Vol. 35. p. 78.) On planting vetches.

vetches. (Ibid. Vol. 35. p. 554.) On the culture of potatoes. (Ibid. Vol. 37. p. 83.)

HARRIES, [John Charles] *Esq.*

On the ftate of Europe before and after the french revolution by *Fred. Gentz.* Translated from the German. Ed. 2. 1803. 8. (8 fh.)

HARRINGTON, [....] *M. Dr. Chief Magiftrate of Bath. Phyfician to the Duke of York.*
born at Kelfton, Somerfetfhire 1727.

See Public Characters of 1799 and 1800. p. 494.

Hugo Antigues; 1768. Damon and Clora; 17.. Ode to the harmony; 17.. Ode to difcord; 17.. Witch of Wokey, a poem; 17.. Old Thomas day; 17.. Give me the fweet Quacker's wedding; 17.. The ftammering fong; 17.. The Alderman's thumb; 17..

HARRINGTON, [Sir Edward] *Knight.*

*Excurfion from Paris to Fontainebleau; — by a gentleman, late of Bath. 1786. 8. (5 fh.) *A fchizzo on the genius of man; in which, among various fubjects, the merit of Mr. *Thomas Barker,* the celebrated young painter of Bath is particularly confidered and his pictures reviewed. 1793. 8. (6 fh.) Remarks on a letter relative to the late petitions to parliament for the fafety and prefervation of his Maj. perfon and for the more effectually preventing feditious meetings and affemblies: with compleat abftracts of the feveral claufes contained in each bill, for the ufe of the public. 1796. 8. (1 fh. 6 d.) Defultory thoughts on the french nation. 17..

HARRINGTON, [John Herbert] *Esq.*

**Sadi's* works, in perfian with an englifh preface. Vol. 1. 2. Calcutta. 1795. fol. The plan of a common-place book. (Afiat. Ref. Vol. 3. p. 249.)

HARRINGTON, [Robert] *M. Dr.*

Chemical effays; being a continuation of my reflections on fixed air, with obfervations and ftrictures upon Dr. *Prieftley's, Fordyce's, Pearfon's* and *Beddoe's* late papers in the Philofophical Transactions and an anfwer to the reviewers. 1793. 8. (2 fh.) Some new experiments, with obfervations upon heat, clearly fhewing the erroneous principles of the french theory, alſo a letter to *Henry Cavendiſh*, containing ſome pointed animadverſions with ſtrictures upon ſome late chemical papers in the Philoſoph. Transactions and other remarks. 1798. 8. (3 ſh.) Some experiments and obſervations on *Volta's* electrical pile, clearly elucidating all the phaenomena — alſo obſervations on Dr. *Herſchell's* paper on light and heat, with other remarks. 1801. 8. (3 ſh.) A new ſyſtem on fire and planetary life ſhewing that the ſun and planets are inhabited; alſo, an elucidation of the phaenomena of electricity and magnetiſm. To which is now added an appendix. 1800. (2 ſh. 6 d.)

*HARRIOT, [John]

Letters on gaining land from the ſea. (Tr. of the Soc. for the E. of A. Vol. 4. p. 44. 52. 56.) Deſcription of his invented machine called a road-harrow. (Ibid. Vol. 7. p. 197-204.)

*HARRIS, [Catherine]

Edwardina, a novel. Vol. 1. 2. 1800. 12. (6 ſh. 6 d.)

*HARRIS, [George] *Doctor of Common Law.*

born ..... died 1796. April 19.

See Gentleman's Magaz. Y. 1796. Apr. p. 358. May. p. 437. Sept. p. 715. Allgem. Litt. Zeit. IntBl. J. 1800. S. 627.

Juſtinian's inſtitutes translated. 1756. 4. Ed. 2. 1761. Obſervations upon the Engliſh language, in a letter to a friend. 17..

*HARRIS, [James] Lord MALMSBURY. *Formerly Ambaſſador by the Dutch Republic.*

born 1746. Apr. 20.

See Public Characters of 1798 and 1799. p. 229.

*Introduction to the hiſtory of the Dutch Republic for the laſt ten years reckoning from the Year 1777. London. 1788. 8. überſ. (von *Gebhardt*) Leipz. 1792. 8. The works of *James Harris* *), Esq. with an account of his life and character by his ſon — Vol. 1. 2. 1801. 4. (3 L. 13 ſh. 6 d.)

*HARRIS,

*) born 1709. July 20. died 1780. Dec. 22. See Monthly Rev. Y. 1802. Jan. p. 1. Crit. Rev. Y. 1802. Jul. p. 260

*HARRIS, [John] *M. Dr. at Kingston, Jamaica.*
Case of haematocele, with an account of the efficacy of zanthoxylon. (Mem. of M. S. of L. Vol. 5. p. 37.)

*HARRIS, [Thaddeus Mason] *A. M. Librarian of Harvard University Cambridge.*
Description of Lungwort and its properties. (Massachusetts Magaz. Y. 1792. Sept. p. 563.) The natural history of the bible; — Boston. 1793.

*HARRISON, [.....]
The infant vision of Shakespeare, with an apostrophe to the immortal bard and other poems. 1794. 4. (1 sh. 6 d.)

HARRISON, [Edward] *M. Dr. Physician at Horncastle, Lincolnshire: Member of the R. S. of Scottish Antiquaries.*
Case of bony excrescence on the inside of the jaw. (New-London Med. Journal. Vol. 1. p. 11.) Case of nasal haemorrhage, with petechiae. (Ibid. Vol. 1. p. 17.) An obstinate case of diarrhoea linteria. (Ibid. Vol. 2. p. 24.) Experiments performed with a view to ascertain the effect of the nitric acid upon iron deposited in the stomach of an animal. (Mem. of M. S. of L. Vol. 5. p. 132.) Case of scirrhous pylorus. (Ibid. Vol. 5. p. 150.) Case of fistula in ano, from an uncommon cause. (Ibid. Vol. 5. p. 154.)

*HARRISON, [George] *Esq. Barrister at Law.*
An abstract of the act lately passed for consolidating the former acts for the redemption of the land-tax and for removing doubts respecting the rights of persons to vote for members of parliament with occasional notes. Ed. 3. 1802. 8. (3 sh. 6 d.)

*HARRISON, [George]
Some remarks relative to the present state of education, in the society of the people called quackers. 1802. 8. (1 sh.)

*HARRISON, [George] *Vestry Clerk of the parish of Windlesham.*
Proposals for enclosing and cultivating some parts of Bagshot heath, in the parish of Windlesham. 1776. (*Young's A.* of Agr. Vol. 36. p. 371.)

*HARRISON, [John] *Citizen at Cheffield.*
Letter to — *Henry Dundas*, M. P. — or, an appeal to the people of Great-Britain, being an anſwer to ſome reflections caſt upon a citizen, whoſe loyalty (it was ſaid) was only confined to his razor! in a debate in the houſe of commons Febr. 21. 1794. occaſioned by an intercepted letter, ſigned *J. Harriſon*, a ſans culotte, to which is added, an abſtract of a trial for an aſſault committed on the author in the name of church and king for ever. 1794. 8. (6 d.)

*HARRISON, [John] *M. Dr.*
Diſſertatio de pertuſſi. Gottingae. 1793. 4.

*HARRISON, [John] *of Preſton Court, near Wingham.*
Crop of 1790. at Welwyn, Baldock, Eaton, Becking, Alcoubury Hill &c. (*Young's* A. of Agr. Vol. 14. p. 186. 259.)

*HARRISON, [J..... E.....] *of Philadelphia.*
Caſe of ſcirrhous pylorus. (Mem. of M. S. of L. Vol. 5. p. 150.)

HARRISON, [Richard] *late Rector of St. John, Clerkenwell, Miniſter of Brompton Chapel and one of the joint preachers at the Magdalen.*
born .... died 1793. Dec. 23.
See Gentleman's Magaz. Y. 1793. Dec. p. 1157. Y. 1797. Jan. p. 10. Febr. p. 127.

*HARRISON, [Suſanna] *a young woman under heavy afflictions.*
Song in the night. 1788. Ed. 5. 1796. 12. (2 ſh. 6 d.) Ed. 6. 1800. 18. (2 ſh.)

*HARRISON, [William] *M. Dr. of Rippon.*
Hiſtories of three caſes of typhus, ſucceſsfully treated. (Mem. of M. S. of L. Vol. 4. p. 107.)

*HARROP, [Edward Atkins]
Original miſcellaneous poems. 1796. 8. (6 ſh.)

*HARRUP, [R.....] *Surgeon at Crief, North-Britain.*
Account of ſome hairy balls voided by ſtool. (New-London Med. Journ. Vol. 1. p. 254.) Two caſes of white ſwelling in the knee. (Ibid. Vol. 1. p. 343.) Caſe of luxated vertebrae of the neck. (Ibid. Vol. 1. p. 358.)

*HARRUP,

*HARRUP, [R....] *at Cobham, Surrey.*
On the opinion or inference that the chemical actions of light and heat are the same. (*Nicholson's* Journal Vol. 5. p. 245.)

*HARSNET, [Adam] *B. Dr.*
God's summons unto a general repentance, wherein is discovered the folly and danger of putting of and delaying repentance till sickness or old age, and also the necessity of a daily repentance. 1794. 8. (3 sh. 6 d.)

*HART, [Richard] *A. M.*
Dr. *Gill's* reasons for separating from the church of England calmly considered. 1801. 12. (6 d.)

HARTLEY, [David] *Esq. M. P.*
See Biogr. Liter. and Polit. Anecdotes —; Vol. 2. p. 139.
The right of appeal to juries, in causes of excise; 17.. *The budget; inscribed to the man who thinks himself minister; 1764. The state of the nation; with a preliminary defence of the budget. 1765. A caveat on the part of public credit, previous to the opening of the budget for the present year 1768. 1768. Letter, respecting Mr. *Cort's* process for converting cast iron into malleable iron. (Columbian Magaz. Vol. 2. Supplem. p. 868.) Argument on the french revolution and the means of peace. 1794. 8. (1 sh. 6 d.)

*HARTLEY, [Ralph] *Teacher of the Mathematics, Berkhamsted.*
Philosophical questions, selected for the use of the upper classes in Berkhamsted school. 1799. 8. (3 sh.)

HARVEST, [George] *Fellow of Magdalen-College, Cambridge; Curate of Thames-Ditton.*
born .... died Y. 1780.
See *Gilb. Wakefield's* Memoirs. 1792. 8. p. 52. &c.

*HARVEST, [William]
Discourse by Abbé *Fauchet* on the liberty of France, translated from the french. 1790. 8. (1 sh.)

*HARVEY, [J....] *of Elmly Lovet, near Hartlebury, Worcestershire.*
Use of carrots &c. (*Young's* A. of Agr. Vol. 4. p. 98.) On a drill plough. (Ibid. Vol. 6. p. 197.)

*HARVEY, [John] *at Norwich.*
Letter on fine ſpinning of wool. (Tr. of the Soc. for the E. of A. Vol. 7. p. 167.)

*HARVEY, [Samuel]
Obſervations on alphabetical characters and particularly on the engliſh alphabet; with an attempt to ſhew its inſufficiency to expreſs, with due preciſion, the variety of ſounds, which enrich the language. (Mem. of M. Vol. 4. P. 1. p. 135.)

HARWOOD, [Buſick] *M. Dr: F. R. A. S. Profeſſor of Anatomy in the Univerſity of Cambridge.*
A ſyſtem of comparative anatomy and phyſiology. Faſc. 1. Cambridge. 1796. überſ. von *C. R. W. Wiedemann.* Berlin. 1799. 4.

HARWOOD, [Edward] *D. D. A Diſſenting Clergyman in London.*
born 1729. died 1794. Jan. 14.
See Gentleman's Magaz. Y. 1794. Febr. p. 184. March. p. 200.
The great duty and delight of contentment. 1783. 8. The melancholy doctrine of predeſtination expoſed and the delightful truth of univerſal redemption repreſented. 1778. 8. Diſcourſe on St. Paul's deſcription of death. 1790. 8. Sermons. Vol. 1. 2. 1794. 8. (10 ſh.)

HARWOOD, [Thomas] *Maſter of Lickfield ſchool, and late of Univerſity College, Oxford.*
Sermons. Vol. 1. 2. 1794. 4. Alumni Etonenſes, or, a catalogue of the provoſts and fellows of Eton College and King's College, Cambridge, from the foundation in 1443 to the Year 1797, with an account of their lives and preferments collected from original MSS. and authentic biographical works. 1797. 4. (1 L. 1 ſh.) The ſacred hiſtory of the life of Jeſus Chriſt, illuſtrative of the harmony of the 4 evangeliſts; to which is added an index of parallel paſſages. 1798. 12. (3 ſh.) Grecian antiquities, or an account of the public and private life of the greeks. 1801. 8. (9 ſh.)

*HASKINGS, [John]
Some obſervations on the depredations of inſects on fruit-trees. (Bath Agric. Soc. Vol. 9. p. 299.)

*HASLAM,

HASLAM, [John] *Apothecary to Bethlem-Hospital; late of Pembroke-hall, Cambridge.*
Obſervations on inſanity: with practical remarks on the diſeaſe and an account of the morbid appearances on diſſection. 1798. 8. (3 ſh.) überſ. Stendal. 1800. 8.

HASLAM, [Percival] *Esq.*
born 1755. died at Perſhore, in Worceſterſhire 1800. Nov. 24.
See Gentleman's Magaz. Y. 1800. Dec. p. 1216.
A few hints to whiſt players. 17..

HASSALL, [Charles]
Remarks on waſte lands in Carmartenſhire. (Bath Agric. Soc. Vol. 8. p. 103.) Remarks on waſte lands in Pembrokeſhire. (Ibid. Vol. 8. p. 116.) On tithes. (*Young's* A. of Agr. Vol. 22. p. 641.) Paring and burning, in South Wales. (Ibid. Vol. 28. p. 157.)

HASTINGS, [Thomas] *an itinerant bookſeller and pamphleteer; his traveling name was Dr. Green.*
native of the Biſhoprick of Durham: died 1801. Aug. 12. near 60 years of age.
See Gentleman's Magaz. Y. 1801. Sept. p. 859.
The wars of Weſtminſter; 17.. 4to. (For many years he had been in the habit of publiſhing, in different news-papers, on the 12 of Auguſt a voluntary ode on the Prince's of Wales's birth-day;) The devil in London. 17.. 12mo. The regal rambler, or Lucifer's travels. 17.. 8vo.

HASTINGS, [Warren] *Esq. formerly Governour General of Bengal.*
See Public Characters of 1799 and 1800. p. 568. Maſſachuſetts Magaz. Y. 1795. Sept. p. 328.
Speech, in the high court of juſtice in Weſtminſter hall. 1791. 8. (3 ſh.) Correſpondence between *Warren Haſtings*, Esq. and Sir *Stephen Luſhington*, Bart. 1795. 8. (1 ſh.) Trial. P. 1. 2. London. 1788. 8. (9 ſh. 6 d.) Hiſtory of his trial. 1796. 8. (11 ſh. 6 d.) Ceremony of the fiery ordeals. (Maſſachuſetts Magaz. 1792. May. p. 292.)

HASWORTH, [H.... H....]
The lady of the cave. Vol. 1-3. 1802. 12.

***HATCHET**, [Charles] *Esq. F. R. S.*

An analysis of the Carinthian molybdate of lead; with experiments on the molybdic acid. To which are added some experiments and observations on the decomposition of the sulphate of ammoniac. (Phil. Transact. Y. 1796. p. 285.) An analysis of the earthy substance from New South Wales, called Sydneja or Terra australis. (Ibid. Y. 1798. p. 110. *Nicholson's* Journal. Vol. 2. p. 72.) See *Benj. Wisemann.* Experiments and observations on shell and bone. (Phil. Transact. Y. 1799. p. 315. *Nicholson's* Journal. Vol. 3. p. 500. 529. *Tilloch's* Philos. Magaz. Vol. 6. p. 21. 355.) Chemical experiments on zoophytes; with some observations on the component parts of membrane. (Phil. Transact. Y. 1800. p. 327.) Observations on bituminous substances, with a description of the varieties of the elastic bitumen. (Transact. of L. S. Vol. 4. p. 129. *Nicholson's* Journal. Vol. 2. p. 201. 248.) A letter on ores of iron. (Ibid. Vol. 3. p. 454.) An analysis of a mineral substance from North-America containing a metal hitherto unknown. (Phil. Tr. Y. 1802. p. 49. *Nicholson's* Journal. Y. 1802. June. p. 129. July. p. 176.) On the utility of prussiate of copper as a pigment. (*Tilloch's* Philos. Magaz. Vol. 14. p. 359.)

***HATFIELD**, [.....] *Miss; of Manchester.*

The lives in hopes, or Caroline, a narration founded upon facts. Vol. 1. 2. 1801. 8. (9 sh.) Letter on the importance of the female sex; with observations on their manners and on education. 1803.

HATSELL, [John] *Clerk of the House of Commons.*

* Precedents of proceedings in the house of commons under separate titles; with observations. Vol. 4. relating to conference and impeachment. 1796. 4. (14 sh. Vol. 1-4. 2 L. 16 sh.)

HATTON, [Thomas]

Account of an universal standard. (Tr. of the Soc. for the E. of A. Vol. 1. p. 239.)

HAWEIS,

IAWEIS, [Thomas] *LL. B. and M. Dr. A Calvinist: Chaplain to the Countess of Huntingdon; Rector of All-Saints, Aldwinkle in Northamptonshire.* (a native of Cornwall.)

See Public Characters of 1798 and 1799. p. 312. The evangelical expositor; Vol. 1. 2. 17.. fol. The communicant's spiritual companion; 17.. An exposition on the church catechism; 17.. Essays on the evidence, characteristic doctrines and influence of christianity. Ed. 2. 1791. 8. (3 sh.) A translation of the new testament from the original greek —; 1795. 8. (6 sh.) A word in season; designed to encourage my brethren of the missionary society to faithful perseverance in the work —; 1795. 8. (3 d.) A plea for peace and union among the living members of the church of Christ; 1795. 8. (6 d.) Missionary instructions —; 1795. 8. (6 d.) A memoir respecting an African mission, with the observations of Gov. *Macaulay*; 1795. 8. (6 d.) Discourses designed as hints for my brethern's use, who are going to preach the gospel to the heathen —; Nrb. 1. 1795. 12. (1 d.) Sermon the first, with an introductory address to the people of Israel throughout the world. 1797. (6 d.) An impartial and succinct history of the rise, declension and revival of the church of christ from the birth of our Saviour to the present time: with faithful characters of the principal personages ancient and modern. Vol. 1-3. 1800. 8. (1 L. 1 sh.) The life of the Rev. *William Romaine*, M. A. late Rector of St. Ann's blackfriars and lecturer of St. Dunstan's in the West. 1797. A reply to the animadversions of the Dean of Carlisle (*Joseph Milner*) on the succinct and impartial history of the church of Christ. 1801. 8. (6 d.)

*HAWES, [Robert] *Gent. Steward of the manors of Framlingham and Saxted.*

The history of Framlingham in the county of Suffolk; including brief notices of the master and fellows of Pembroke-Hall in Cambridge from the foundation of the college to the present time, with considerable additions and notes by *Robert Loder*. 1798. 8. (1 L. 1 sh.)

*HAWES.

*HAWES, [Samuel]
Miſſionary poems. 1800. (1 ſh.)

HAWES, [William] *M. Dr. formerly Apothecary. Senior Phyſician to the Surry and London diſpenſaries.*
born at Islington about the Y. 1736.
See Public Characters of 1800 and 1801. p. 421.
Reports of the Roy. humane ſociety, with an appendix of miſcellaneous obſervations on the ſubject of ſuſpended animation for the years 1787 and 1788. 1789. 8. The tranſactions of the royal humane ſociety from 1774 to 1784. with an appendix of miſcellaneous obſervations on ſuſpended animation to the Y. 1794. Vol. 1. 1794. 8. (10 ſh. 6 d.) überſ. von Dr. *Chriſt. Aug. Struve* B. 1. Breslau. 1798. 8. Brief ſtate of the royal humane ſociety — laid before the preſident — at their anniverſary feſtival. 1799. 8. Cautions againſt the burial of perſons ſuppoſed dead. (Columbian Magaz. Y. 1789. Dec. p. 740. 742.)

*HAWKE, [M....]
— — and Sir *R. Vincent*, Bart. The ranger, a collection of periodical eſſays. 1794. Ed. 2. Vol. 1. 2. 1795. 12. (10 ſh. 6 d.)

*HAWKER, [Robert] *D. D. Vicar of the pariſh of Charles, Plymouth and formerly of Magdalen-Hall, Oxford.*
Sermons on the divinity of Chriſt. Ed. 2. 1793. 8. (5 ſh.) The evidences of a plenary inſpiration; a letter to Mr. *Thomas Porter*, in reply to his defence of unitarianiſm. 1793. 8. (1 ſh. 6 d.) Sermons on the divinity and operations of the holy ghoſt. 1794. 8. (6 ſh.) Ed. 2. 17.. Ed. 3. 1797. (7 ſh.) Miſericordia; or compaſſion to the ſorrows of the heart. 1795. 12. (1 ſh. 3 d.) 1802. 12. (1 ſh.) Ten minutes recommendation of private prayer, conſidered as to its pleaſures and advantages. 1794. (6 d.) The chriſtian's pocket companion — 1797. Sermons. Vol. 1. 2. 1797. 8. (7 ſh.) Youth's catechiſm, on the order in which the ſeveral books of ſcripture are to be placed —; 1798. 12. (9 d.) Specimens of preaching. 1801. 8. (5 ſh.) A ſhort account of the

work

work of grace in the life of *Will. Coombs*, a youth of Buckfastleigh, in the county of Devon. — 1802. 8. (6 d.)

(Several single sermons.)

HAWKESBURY, [Charles] Lord, See *Charles Jenkinson.*

*HAWKINS, [John] *Esq. of Dorchester.*

Account of a species of bark, the original quimaquina of Peru, sent over by *De la Condamine* — about 1749. (Transact. of L. S. Vol. 3. p. 59.)

HAWKINS, [John Sidney] *Esq. F. A. S.*

A treatise on painting by *Leonardi da Vinci* faithfully translated from the original italian and now first digested under propre heads by *John Francis Rigaud*, Esq. R. A. to which is added a new life of the author drawn up from authentic materials till now inaccessible. 1802. 8. (Royal 8. 13 sh. 6 d. Demy paper 9 sh. 6 d.)

*HAWLEY, [Gideon] *A. M.*

Biographical and topographical anecdotes respecting Sandwich and Marshpee Jan. 1794. (Coll. of Massachusetts H. S. Y. 1794. p. 188.) An account of his services among the Indians of Massachusetts and New-York, and a narrative of his journey to Onohoghgwage. (Ibid. Y. 1795. p. 50.)

*HAWORTH, [Adrian Hardy] *Esq. late of Cottingham, Yorkshire, now of little Chelsea, Middlesex. F. L. S.*

Observations on the genus mesembryanthemum in two parts. 1794. 8. (7 sh. 6 d.) A new arrangement of the genus narcissus. (Transact. of L. S. Vol. 5. p. 242.)

*HAWTAYNE, [William] *Rector of Elstree, Herts.*

Sermons on various and particular occasions. 1792. 8. (7 sh.)

*HAWTREY, [Charles] *M. A: Vicar of Bampton, Oxfordshire.*

born .... died 1796. June 26. at Bath.

See Gentleman's Magaz. Y. 1796. July. p. 617. Aug. p. 699. Sept. p. 716.

Various opinions of the philosophical reformers considered, particularly *Paine's* rights of man. 1792. 8. (3 sh.) *A letter to Lord Stanhope, on the subject of the test. 1790. *Free thoughts on on liberty and the revolution in France. 1790. 8. Θεανθρωπος της καινης διαθηκης or an appeal to the new testament, in proof of the divinity of the son of God. 1794. 8. (3 sh. 6 d.) A sequel to the appeal. 1796. 8. A particular enquiry into the doctrine of an eternal filiation. 1796. 8. (2 sh.)

*HAXBY, [John] *M. Dr. Physician at Pontefract.*
Medical histories; 1) A case of epilepsy, terminating favourably, under the use of musk and opium; 2) a case in which the testicles had not descended into the scrotum, till the patient had attained his fourth year. 3) a case of enlargement of one of the spinal vertebrae, gradually disappearing on an enlargement of the trochanter major of the right thigh, which was succeeded by hydrocephalus, terminating fatally. (*Duncan's* A. of Med. Y. 1799. p. 434.)

*HAYES, [Samuel] *M. R. J. A. and Member of the Committee of Agriculture of the Dublin Society.*
A practical treatise on planting and the management of woods and coppices. 1795. 8. (5 sh.)

HAYES, [Samuel] *A. M. formerly Usher of Westminster-school.*
Sermons on different occasions and on practical duties. 1797. 8. (5 sh.)
(Several single sermons.)

*HAYES, [Samuel] *Apothecary to the New-York Hospital.*
Cure of gonorrhoea virulenta by soap-injection. (Medical Repository. Vol. 3. p. 302.)

HAYES, [Thomas] *Surgeon at London, before Apothecary and Surgeon at Hampstead.*
born .... died 1788. Jun. 16.

HAYGARTH, [John] *M. Dr. F. R. S. Lond. F. R. S. and R. M. S. Edinb. Fellow of the American Acad. of Arts and Sc. Physician at Chester.*
Description of a glory. (Mem. of M. Vol. 3. p. 463.) A sketch of a plan to exterminate the casual small-pox from Great-Britain and to introduce general inoculation — Vol. 1. 2. 1793. 8. (8 sh.) übers. und abgek. von *Joh. Bapt. Bonzel*, mit einem Anhange von *G. C. Reich.* Gotha. 1799. 8. On the imagination, as a cause and as a cure of disorders of the body; exemplified by fictitious tractors

tractors and epidemical convulsions. 1800. 8. (1 sh.) Letter to Dr. *Percival*, on the prevention of infectious fevers; and on the prevention of the American pestilence. Bath. 1801. 8. (5 sh.) Mode of preventing the dreadful consequences of the bite of a mad dog. (American Museum Y. 1789. Aug. p. 111.) Cure for the bite of a mad dog; (Massachusetts Magaz. Y. 1789. Aug. p. 511.)

*HAYLEY, [....] *Mrs. Wife of William Hayley, Esq. of Eartham, Sussex and daughter of the Rev. Thomas Ball, Dean of Chicester.*
born .... died 1797. Nov. 8.

See Gentleman's Magaz. Y. 1797. Nov. p. 989. Dec. p. 1068. Allg. Litt. Zeit. ItBl. J. 1800. S. 648.

The Marchioness *Lambert's* essays on friendship and old age, with an introductory letter to *William Melmoth* Esq. 1780. 8. The triumph of acquaintance over friendship, an essay for the times. 1796. 12.

HAYLEY, [William] *Esq. of Eartham, Sussex.*
born 1745. Oct.

See Public Characters of 1799 and 1800. p. 455.

An epistle to Admiral Keppel. 1779. 4. An elegy on the ancient greek model. 1779. 4. The triumphs of temper; a poem. 1781. 4. (6 sh.) übers. Zürich. 17.. — On old maids — übers. von *Ch. Fel. Weiße*. Leipzig. Th. 1-3. 1786. 8. *Dialogues containing a comparative view of the lives, characters and writings of Lord *Chesterfield* and Dr. *Johnson*. 17.. The poetical works of *John Milton*, with his life. Vol. 1-3. 1794-1797. fol. (15 L. 15 sh.) An elegy on the death of Sir *Will. Jones*, a judge of the supreme court of judicature in Bengal. 1795. 4. (2 sh. 6 d.) The life of *Milton*, in 3 parts: to which are added conjectures on the origin of paradise lost; with an appendix. 1796. 4. (15 sh. large paper 1 L. 1 sh.) Basel. 1799. 8. A poetical essay on sculpture, in a series of epistles to *John Flaxmann*, 1800. 4. (1 L. 7 sh.) A life and some posthumous works of *Will. Cowper*. Vol. 1. 2. 1803. 4. (2 L. 12 sh. 6 d.) abridged, from the Quarto edition. 1803. 12. (3 sh. 6 d.)

*HAYNES,

*HAYNES, [John] *Surgeon at Chipping Norton.*
Case of fatal termination after the bite of a mad dog. (Mem. of M. S. of L. Vol. 5. p. 289.)

*HAYS, [J....]
Hair changed through fright. (Monthly Magaz. Y. 1800. Nov. p. 321.)

*HAYS, [Mary] *Miss.*
Letters and essays, moral and miscellaneous. 1793. 8. (5 sh.) Memoirs of Emma Courtney. Vol. 1. 2. 1796. 8. (6 sh.) The victim of prejudice. Vol. 1. 2. 1799. 12. (6 sh.) Remarks on Dr. *Reid*, on insanity. (Monthly Magaz. Y. 1800. July. p. 523.) Female biography; or, memoirs of illustrious and celebrated women, who have flourished in all countries from the earliest periods to the present time. Vol. 1-6. 1803. 12. (1 L. 11 sh. 6 d.)

HAYSHAM, [John] *M. Dr. Physician at Carlisle in Cumberland.*
(Is more properly written *John Heysham.* See *Reuss* Gel. Engl. p. 186.)

*HAYTER, [John] *A. M. Chaplain to the Earl of Clarendon.*
Essay on a passage in St. Paul 1 Cor. XI, 10. 1791. 8. (1 sh. 6 d.)

HAYTER, [Thomas] *A. M. Senior fellow of King's-College, Cambridge.*
born 1746. died 1799. Dec. 17.
See Gentleman's Magaz. Y. 1799. Dec. p. 1094. 1187. Allg. Litt. Zeit. ItBl. J. 1800. S. 663.
Strictures on the confessional. 1772. On faith and election, a sermon. 1791. 8. (1 sh.)

*HAYWARD, [William] *at Banbury.*
Method of cultivating turkey rhubarb from seed. (Tr. of the Soc. for the E. of A. Vol. 8. p. 79.) On the growth and cure of rhubarb. (Ibid. Vol. 12. p. 225.)

*HAYWOOD, [Samuel] *Serjeant at Law.*
A digest of so much of the law respecting borough elections, as concerns cities and boroughs in general, their representation and returning officers; the carriage and delivery of the writ, the history, form, conveyance and delivery of the precept; the duty of the returning officer, previous to the election;

election; the form and effect of decisions and last determinations; the right of electors for boroughs in general and of burgage tenants, free-holders, lease-holders and copy-holders in particular. 1797. 8. (3. sh. 6 d.)

HAZARD, [Ebenezer]

Historical collections, consisting of state papers and other authentic documents, intended as materials for an history of the United States of America. Vol. 1. 2. Philad. 1792. 1794. 4. (8 Dollar 50 Cents.)

HAZARD, [Josiah] *of Stoney-Littleton, Holt.*

On making butter and cheese. (Bath Agricult. Soc. Vol. 3. p. 136.) Instructions for raising of potatoes. (Ibid. Vol. 3. p. 273.) On the culture of rape or cole seed. (Ibid. Vol. 4. p. 189.) On the culture of parsnips. (Ibid. Vol. 4. p. 244.) On the advantage of hoeing. (Ibid. Vol. 4. p. 278.) The different methods of making cheese in England; (Columbian Magaz. Y. 1787. Nov. p. 745.)

HEAD, [James Roper] *Esq. of Hermitage in the county of Kent.*

An essay on the causes which have produced, the principles which support and the consequences which may follow from, the two bills of Lord *Grenville* and Mr. *Pitt*, intitled, „an act for the safety of his Majesty„ and „an act for preventing sedition meetings. 1796. 8. (1 sh.) A sketch of an act of parliament to permit, under certain regulation, in wet and casual harvests, the appropriation of two sunday's in a year for the purpose of carrying and securing corn; with the reasons, oral and religious, upon which this proposed act is grounded. 1797. 8. (1 sh.)

HEAD, [Thomason] *Mrs.*

The pious mother; or evidences for heaven, for the benefit of her children. 1794. 8. (1 sh. 6 d.)

HEADRICK, [James] *Rev.*

On the practicability and advantages of opening a navigation between the Murray Frith, at Inverness and Loch Eil, at Fort William. (Tr. of Highland Soc. Vol. 1. p. 355.) Effects of manures in the production of plants. (Ibid. Vol. 33. p. 275.) Essay on the various modes of bringing land into a ſtate fit for cultivation and improving its natural productions. (Comm. to the B. of Agr. Vol. 2. p. 250.)

HEALDE, [Thomas] *M. Dr. F. R. S. Lumleyan Lecturer at the College of Phyſicians and Senior Phyſician of the London Hoſpital.*
born .... died 1789.

*HEALY, [Robert] *A. B.*
An account of a new method of ſupplying diving-bells with freſh air. (*Tilloch's* Philoſ. Magaz. Vol. 15. p. 9.)

*HEARN, [Thomas] *M. Dr. late Phyſician to the Britiſh Factory at Cadiz.*
A ſhort view of the riſe and progreſs of freedom in modern Europe, as connected with the cauſes which led to the french revolution. 1793. 8. (2 ſh. 6 d.)

*HEARNE, [Samuel]
born 1745. died Nov. 1792.
See Gentleman's Magaz. Y. 1797. Aug. p. 691.
Journey from Prince of Wales's Fort in Hudſon's-bay to the Northern Ocean, undertaken by order of the Hudſon's-bay company, for the diſcovery of copper-mines a northweſt paſſage — in the Y. 1769-1772. 1795. 4. (1 L. 10 ſh. 6 d.)

*HEART, [Jonathan] *Major.*
Account of ſome remains of ancient works, on the muskingum, with a plan of theſe works. (Columbian Magaz. Y. 1787. May. p. 425.) Obſervations on the ancient works of art, the native inhabitants &c. of the weſtern country. (Tr. of A. S. Vol. 3. p. 214.)

*HEARTWELL, [Henry] *Esq.*
The priſoner; or, the reſemblance (from the french) a comic opera, in one act, adapted to the Engliſh ſtage. 1799. 8. (1 ſh.) The caſtle of Sorrento; a comic opera, in two acts, altered from the french and adapted to the Engliſh ſtage. 1799. 8. (1 ſh.)

*HEATH, [.....] *Major-General.*
Memoirs of Major-Gen. *Heath*, containing anecdotes, details of ſkirmiches and other military events, during the american war, written by himſelf. 1800.

*HEATH,

HEATH, [J....] *at Newcastle.*

The veterinary college method of shoeing horses defended. (Comm. and Agric. Mag. Y. 1800. Aug. p. 103.)

HEATH, [John] *Surgeon in the Royal navy.*

A system of midwifery, translated from the french of *Baudelocque.* Vol. 1-3. 1790. 8. (1 L. 1 sh.)

HEATH, [William] *Esq. F. A. A.*

Letter on the darkness in Canada, in Oct. 1785. (Mem. of B. A. Vol. 2. P. 1. p. 139.)

HEATHCOTE, [Charles]

Observations on the corporation and test acts in a letter to a friend. 1794. 8. (2 sh.)

HEATHCOTE, [Ralph] D. D. *Vicar of Sileby, co. Leicester, Rector of Sawtry all saints, co. Huntingdon, a Prebendary and Vicar-General of the collegiate church of Southwell.*

born at Barrow upon Soar Leicestershire 1721. Dec. 19. died 1795. May. 28.

See Gentleman's Magaz. Y. 1795. June. p. 532. Jul. p. 569. Dec. p. 984.

Historia astronomiae. Cantabrigiae. 17.. Fidei fundamentum ratio, concio ad Clerum habita. 1758. 4. (6 d.) Cursory animadversions upon the Middletonian controversy upon the miraculous powers. 1752. Remarks upon a charge by Dr. *Chapman.* 1752. A letter to the Rev. *Thomas Fothergill* M. A. relating to his sermon preached before the University of Oxford, Jan. 30. 1753. upon the reasonableness and uses of commemorating King Charles's martyrdom. 1753. A sketch of Lord *Bolingbroke's* philosophy. 1755. The use of reason asserted in matters of religion. 1755. (The articles, *Simon Ockley*; Dr. *Robert James*; Queen *Elizabeth*, Madame *de Maintenon*, in the Biographical dictionary; 11 Vols. 8. 1761. belongs to him.) The irenarch, or, justice of peace's manual. 1771. Sylva, or, the wood 1786. Ed. 2. 1788.

(Several single sermons.)

*HEBBES, [Thomas] *A. M. of Trinity-College, Cambridge, Vicar of Hernhill in Kent.*
born .... died .... (?)
Sermons 1802 8.

HEBERDEN, [William] *M. Dr. F. R. S. F. A. S.*
born 1711. Aug. died 1801. May 17.
See Gentleman's Magaz. Y. 1801. May. p. 485.
Antitheriaca, an essay on mithridaticum and theriaca. 1745. 8. Dr. *Conyers Middleton* dissertationes de servili medicorum conditione appendix: published 1761. Account of a very large human calculus. (Philos. Transact. Y. 1750. p. 596.) Account of the effects of lightning at South Weald, in Essex, June 18. 1764. (Ibid. Y. 1764. p. 198.)

*HEBERDEN, [William] *Jun. M. Dr. F. R. S.*
Of the influence of cold upon the health of the inhabitants of London; (Philos. Transact. Y. 1796. p. 279. *Simmons's* Med. Facts and Observat. Vol. 8. p. 208.) Observations on the increase and decrease of different diseases, and particularly of the plague. 1801. 4. (5 sh.) Commentaries on the history and cure of diseases. 1802. 8. Commentarii de morborum historia et curatione. 1802. (7 sh. 6 d.)

HECKFORD, [William] *Esq.*
A succinct account of all the religious and various sects of religion, that have prevailed in the world and in all ages from the earliest account of time to the present period, from the most indisputable traditions. 1792.

*HEDGEHOG, [Humphrey]
A bone to gnaw for the democrats, by Peter Porcupine; to which is prefixed a rod, for the backs of the critics. 1797. 12. (2 sh. 6 d.)

*HEDGES, [Phineas] *Physician at Newburgh.*
Case of an extraordinary disease, in a child apparently scrophulous. (Medical Reposit. Vol. 1. p. 172.)

*HEDLEY, [J....]
On preserving corn in public granaries. (Comm. and Agric. Mag. Y. 1801. Jan. p. 13.)

HEELY, [Joseph] *Esq.*
*A description of Hagley park: by the author of letters on the beauties of Hagley &c. 1777. 8.

HELLINS,

HELLINS, [John] *B. D. F. R. S. Vicar of Potter's Pury, in Northamptonshire.*

Dr. *Halley's* quadrature of circle improved: being a transformation of his series for that purpose to others which converge by the powers of 80. (Phil. Transact. Y. 1794. p. 217.) Mr. *Jones's* computation of the hyperbolic logarithm of 10 improved: being a transformation of the series which he used in that computation to others which converge by the powers of 80. To which is added a postscript, containing an improvement of Mr. *Emerson's* computation of the same logarithm. (Philos. Transact. Y. 1796. p. 135.) A new method of computing the value of a slowly converging series, of which all the terms are affirmative. (Ibid. Y. 1798. p. 183.) An improved solution of a problem in physical astronomy; by which, swiftly converging series are obtained, which are useful in computing the perturbations of the motions of the earth, mars and venus by their natural attraction. To which is added an appendix, containing an easy method of obtaining the sums of many slowly converging series which arise in taking the fluents of binomial surds &c. (Ibid. Y. 1798. p. 527. Y. 1800. p. 86.) Of the rectification of the conic sections. (Ibid. Y. 1802. p. 448.) Analytical institutions, in four books; originally written in Italian, by Donna *Maria Gaetana Agnesi* — translated into English by the late *John Colson*, Prof. of the Mathem. at Cambridge; now first printed from the translator's manuscript. Vol. 1. 2. 1802. 4. (2 L. 2 sh.)

ELME, [Elizabeth] *Mrs.*

Louisa, or the cottage on the moor; Ed. 7. with material additions. Vol. 1. 2. 1801. (8 sh.) Duncan and peggy, a scottish tale. Vol. 1. 2. 1794. 12. (7 sh.) *Plutarch's* lives, abridged; in which the historical parts are carefully preserved and the comparisons of the respective lives accurately delineated. 1794. 8. (8 sh.) The farmer of Inglewood forest, a novel. Vol. 1-4. 1796. 8. (14 sh.) Instructive rambles in London and the adjacent villages, designed to amuse and improve the understanding of youth. Vol. 1. 2.

 1798.

(2 ſh.) On the age and ſignification of the exceedingly curious zodiac lately diſcovered by the french in Egypt, accompanied by two very large copperplates. (Monthly Magaz. Y. 1802. Nov. p. 295. *Tillock's* Philoſ. Mag. Vol. 14. p. 107.)

HENLEY, [William] *F. R. S. (he was a linnendraper.)*
born .... died about 1779.

*HENNIKER, [John] *Major, Esq. F. A. S. and M. P. for New Romney.*
Letter to George Earl of Leiceſter. 1788. 8. *Two letters on the origin, antiquity and hiſtory of Norman tiles, ſtained with armorial bearings. 1794. 8. (4 ſh.)

*HENRY, [David] *Esq.*
born at Fovron, about 16 miles from Aberdeen 1710. Dec. 26. died at Lewisham 1792. June 5.
See Gentlemans Magaz. Y. 1792. June. p. 578. Jul. p. 671. Aug. p. 697.
The tell tale, or anecdotes, ſtories &c. Vol. 1. 2. 17.. Twenty diſcourſes on the moſt important ſubjects, carefully abridged from the works of the late Archbp. *Tilloſon* —. Ed. 2. 1763. Ed. 4. 1779. The complete engliſh farmer, or, a practical ſyſtem of husbandry; 1772. An hiſtorical account of all the voyages round the world performed by Engliſh navigators. Vol. 1–5. 1774. 1775. 8. (For more than half a century he take an active part in the management of the Gentleman's Magazine: He was in 1758 or 1759. the principal writer, editor and proprietor of „The Grand Magazine of Magazines.)

*HENRY, [Peter]
On the action of metallic oxydes and earths upon oils in low degrees of heat. (Mem. of M. Vol. 4. P. 1. p. 209.)

HENRY, [Robert] *D. D. Miniſter of Edinburgh. F. A. S. Edin.*
born Febr. 18. 1718. died 1790. Nov. 24.
See Gentleman's Magaz. Y. 1791. June. p. 583. Oct. p. 907. *Millin* Mag. Encycl. T. 3. p. 194.
The hiſtory of Great-Britain. Vol. 6. with his life. 1793. 4. (1 L. 5 ſh.) Ed. 8. Vol. 1–10. 1788.
Letter

Letter — to *William Tytler* of Woodhouse-Lee, Esq. (Transact. of the Soc. of the Antiq. of Scotland. Vol. 1. p. 538.)

(Several single sermons.)

HENRY, [Thomas] *Apothecary at Manchester. F. R. S.*

Instances of the medicinal effects of magnetism. (London M. J. Vol. 3. p. 303.) übers. Repertor. Chir. u. Medic. Abhandl. B. 1. S. 287. Observations on the bills of mortality for the towns of Manchester and Salford. (Mem. of M. Vol. 3. p. 159.) Case of a person becoming short-sighted in advanced age. (Ibid. Vol. 3. p. 182.) Considerations relative to the nature of wool, silk and cotton, as objects of the art of dying — with some observations on the theory of dying in general and particularly the turkey red. (Mem. of M. Vol. 3. p. 343.)

HENRY, [Thomas] *Jun.*

Conjectures relative to the cause of the increase of weight acquired by some heated bodies, during cooling. (Mem. of M. Vol. 3. p. 174.) On the external use of nitrous acid. (Monthly Magaz. Y. 1798. Febr. p. 88.)

HENRY, [William]

A general view of the nature and objects of chemistry and of its application to arts and manufactures. 1799. 8. (1 sh.) Ed. 2. 1802. übers. mit Anmerk. von *J. B. Trommsdorff*. Erfurt. 1803. 8. An epitome of the chemistry. 1801. 8. Experiments on carbonated hydrogenous gaz; with a view to determine whether carbon be a simple or a compound substance. (Phil. Transact. Y. 1797. p. 401. *Nicholson's* Journal. Vol. 2. p. 241.) Account of a series of experiments, undertaken with the view of decomposing the muriatic acid. (Phil. Transact. Y. 1800. p. 188. *Nicholson's* Journal. Vol. 4. p. 209. 245. *Tilloch's* Phil. Magaz. Vol. 7. p. 211. 332.) A review of some experiments, which have been supposed to disprove the materiality of heat. (Mem. of M. Vol. 5. P. 2. p. 603. cf. p. 679. *Tilloch's* Philos. Magaz. Vol. 15. p. 45. *Nicholson's* Journal Y. 1802. Nov. p. 197.) On the extraction of sugar from carrots, and experiments

*HERIOT, [J....]

*An hiftorical fketch of Gibraltar, with an account of the fiege which that fortrefs ftood againft the combined forces of France and Spain, including a circumftantial detail of the fortie made by the garrifon. 1792. 8.

*HERON, [M.....] at *Newcaftle*.

The conflict, a fentimential tale, in a feries of letters. Vol. 1. 2. 1793. 12. (4 fh.)

HERON, [Robert] *a native of Scotland*. See *Pinkerton*.

*Letters of literature. 1785. 8. (6 fh.) Arabian tales; or, a continuation of the arabian nights entertainments: — translated from the original arabic into french by Dom *Chavis*, a native arab, and *Cazotte* — translated from the french Vol. 1-4. 1792. 8. (10 fh.) *Niebuhr's* travels through Arabia and other countries in the Eaft — translated into Englifh with notes by the tranflator and illuftrated with engravings and maps. Vol. 1. 2. 1792. 8. (12 fh.) Obfervations made in a journey through the weftern counties of Scotland in the autumn 1792. relating to the fcenery, antiquities, cuftoms, manners, population, agriculture, manufactures, commerce, political condition and litterature of thefe parts. Vol. 1. 2. 1793. 8. (12 fh.) The hiftory of Scotland from the earlieft times to the aera of the abolition of the hereditary jurisdictions of fubjects in the Year 1748. Vol. 1-6. 1794-1799. 8. (2 L. 8 fh.) Letters, which paffed between Gen. *Dumourier* and *Pache*, Minifter at the war to the french republic, during the campaign in the Netherland in 1792. translated from the original french. 1794. 12. (2 fh.) Information, concerning the ftrength, views and interefts of the powers prefently at war; intended to affift true friends to themfelves and their country, to judge of the progrefs and effects of the prefent war, and to decide upon the grand queftion of immediate peace? or war for another campaign? 1794. 8 (5 fh.) Memoirs of the revolution, or, an apology for my conduct, in the public employments which i have held by *J. Garat*, late Minifter of Juftice — in the fervice of the French republic: translated from the french. 1797. 8. (5 fh.)

Account

Account of the life of Muley Leizit, late Emperor of Morocco; — translated from the original french: to which is prefixed a short review of the Moorish history, from the earliest times to the accession of Muley Leizit, with a philosophical enquiry into the causes which have hitherto retarded the civilization of the Moors. 1797. 8. (3 sh.) The letters of Junius, with notes and illustrations, historical, political, biographical and critical. Nrb. 1. (1 sh.) (to be completed in 20 numbers.)

*HERON, [Robert]

Elegant extracts of natural history, corrected and revised, from a great variety of the most elegant and authentic writers, with a preface, containing some hints on education. Vol. 1.2. 1793. 8. (12 sh.) Elements of chemistry and natural history to which is prefixed the philosophy of chemistry, by *A. F. Fourcroy*, translated from the 4th and last edition. Vol. 1-4. 1796. 8. (1 L. 4 sh.) Elements of chemistry; comprehending all the most important facts and principles in the works of *Fourcroy* and *Chaptal;* with the addition of the more recent chemical discoveries which have been made known in Britain and on the continent, and with a variety of facts and views, which have never before been communicated to the world —. 1800. 8. (12 sh.) On the general nature of light. (*Tilloch's* Philos. Magaz. Vol. 8. p. 161.) Chariot way-wiser — pedometer — known by the antients. (Ibid. Vol. 11. p. 38.) The same methods of reasoning common to mathematics and to natural history and other branches of physics. (Ibid. Vol. 11. p. 294.)

*HERON, [Robert]

New and complete system of universal geography. 8. (1 L. 8 sh.)

*HERRIES, [.....] *Colonel.*

Instructions for the use of yeomanry and volunteer corps of cavalry. 1804. (5 sh.)

HERRIES, [John] *M. A.*

born . . . . . died 178. (?)

*HERRIES, [John Charles] *Esq.*

*Sketch of financial and commercial affairs, in the autumn

The captive monarch, a tragedy, in 5 acts. 1794. 8. (1 sh. 6 d.) Edington, a novel. Vol. 1. 2. 1796. 12. (6 sh.)

HEY, [William] *F. R. S. Senior Surgeon to the General Infirmary at Leeds.*

A description of the eye of the seal. (Mem. of M. Vol. 3. p. 274.) Practical observations on surgery. 1803. 8. (10 sh. 6 d.)

***HEYRICK**, [John] *Jun. Lieut. in the 15 Regt. of light Dragoons.*

First flights, containing pieces in verse on various occasions. 1797. 4. (3 sh. 6 d.)

***HEYWOOD**, [Samuel] *Esq. of the Inner-Temple.*

A digest of the law respecting county elections — 1790. 8. (7 sh. 6 d.) A digest of the law respecting borough elections. Vol. 1. 2. 1796. 1797. 8. (3 sh. 6 d.)

***HIBB**, [.....] *Jun. Dr.*

On the size of cattle. *(Young's A. of Agr. Vol. 28. p. 604.)*

***HICKEY**, [Thomas]

Storia della pittura e la scultura da i tempi Pittanbohi — the history of painting and sculpture from the earliest accounts. Vol. 1. Calcutta; 1788. 4.

HICKS, [George] *M. Dr. of St. James's Palace, Member of the Roy. College of Physicians and Physician to the Asylum and Westminster Infirmary.*

born .... died at Rochester. 1792. Dec. See Gentleman's Magaz. Y. 1793. Jan. p. 90.

***HICKS**, [Henry]

Observations on a late publication of Dr. *Pearson*, entitled, an examination of the report of the committee of the house of commons, on the claims of remuneration for the vaccine-pock inoculation. 1803. (3 sh.)

HIGGINS, [Bryant] *M. Dr.*

Minutes of the society for philosophical experiments. 1794. 8. (8 sh.) übers. Halle. 1803. 8. Observations and advices for the improvement of the manufacture of muscovado sugar and rum. Part. 1–3. printed at St. Jago de la Vega and sold in London by Cadell. 1801. 8. (9 sh.)

IGGINS, [Jesse] *of Delaware.*
A method of draining ponds in level grounds. (Tr. of A. S. Vol. 3. p. 325.)

GGINS, [William] *M. R. J. A. Professor of Chemistry and Mineralogy at the Repository of the Dublin Society.*
An essay on the theory and practice of bleaching, wherein the sulphuret of lime is recommended as a substitute for potash. 1799. 8. (2 sh.) übers. mit Anmerk. Halle. 1802. 8. On sulphuret of lime, to be used as a substitute for potash in bleaching with the oxygenated muriatic acid. (*Nicholson's* Journal. Vol. 3. p. 253. Tr. of Dublin Soc. Vol. 1. P. 1.) Letter respecting the time of the discovery of the sound produced by a current of hidrogen gas passing through a tube. (Ibid. Y. 1802. Febr. p. 129.)

IGGINS, [William] *Esq.*
The American; a novel. Vol. 1. 2. 1803. 12. (8 sh.)

GHMORE, [Anthony] *Jun. Esq. Solicitor; formerly of Burycourt, St. Mary Axe, London.* born 1718. died 1799. Oct. 3.
See Gentleman's Magaz. Y. 1799. Oct. p. 905. Allg. Litterat. Zeit. ItBl. J. 1800. S. 662.
Reflections on the distinction usually adopted in criminal prosecutions for libel; and on the method lately introduced of pronouncing verdicts in consequence of such distinction. 1791. 8. (2 sh.) Addenda to the law of charitable uses, comprising the cases reported and adjudged since the publication of the history of Mortmain — until Hilary term 1793. 1793. 8. (2 sh.) A practical arrangement of the laws relative to the excise. Vol. 1. 2. 1796. 8. (1 sh.)

IIGSON, [.....] *Vicar of Bath-Easton.*
On the culture of potatoes. (Bath Agric. Soc. Vol. 1. p. 26.)

IILDRETH, [W.....]
The niliad, an epic poem, written in honour of the glorious victory obtained by the British fleet under the command of — Lord *Nelson* over a superior fleet of the french, off the mouth of the nile, on the 1 Aug. 1798. 1799. 4. (2 sh. 6 d.)

*HILL, [Aaron]
On the manufacture of beech oil and other projects of improvement. (*Nicholson's* Journal Vol. 3. p. 229.)

HILL, [Brian] *A. M. late of Queen's College, Oxford and Chaplain to the Earl of Leven and Melvill.*
Henry and Acasto, a moral tale, in 3 parts; a new edition. 1798. 8. (5 sh.) Observations and remarks in a journey through Sicily and Calabria in the Y. 1791. with a postscript containing some account of the ceremonies of the last holy week at Rome and of a short excursion to Tivoli. 1792. 8. (7 sh. 6 d.)
(Several single sermons.)

*HILL, [Daniel] *M. Dr. Fellow of the London Medical Society.*
Practical observations on the use of oxygen or vital air, in the cure of diseases: To which are added a few experiments on the vegetation of plants. Part 1. 1800. 4. (7 sh. 6 d.) übers. von *E. H. W. Münchmeyer.* Th. 1. Göttingen. 1802. 8.

*HILL, [Daniel] *Rev. of East-Malling near Maidstone in Kent.*
Kentish agriculture, (being answers to the society's printed queries). (Bath Agric. Soc. Vol. 3. p. 94.)

*HILL, [George] *D. D: F. R. S. Ed. Principal of St. Mary's College in the University of St. Andrew, one of the Ministers of that city and one of his Maj. Chaplain's in ordinary for Scotland.*
born at St. Andrews.
See Public Characters of 1802 and 1803. p. 180.
Sermons 1795. 8. (6 sh.) Sermons by *James Gillespie,* D. D. published from the author's manuscript. 1796. 8. (5 sh. 3 d.) Theological institutes. 1803. 8. (7 sh. 6 d.)

HILL, [James] *Surgeon at Dumfries in Scotland.*
born .... died 178 (?)

HILL, [John] *LL. Dr. F. R. S. Edin. and Professor of Humanity in the University of Edinburgh.*
An essay upon the utility of defining synonymous terms in all languages: with illustrations by examples from the latin. (Tr. of E. S. Vol. 3. L. p. 93.)

*HILL,

HILL, [John] *at Greathouse, Leigh, near Worcester.*
Enclosing wastes, composition for tithes. (*Young's* A. of Agr. Vol. 38. p. 8.)

HILL, [John]. *Member of the Roy. College of Surgeons, London.*
The means of reforming the morals of the poor, by the prevention of poverty and a plan for meliorating the condition of parish paupers and diminishing the enormous expence of maintaining them. 1801. 8. (4 sh. 6 d.)

HILL, [John] *Philologus.*
Lectures and reflections on various subjects, viz. divinity, law, civil and ecclesiastical, philosophy, characters, atheism and hypocrisy, manliness, godliness and gratitude, coalition, marriage, industry and sloth. 1792. 8. (3 sh.)

HILL, [R....] *Esq.*
Experiment in planting potatoe shoots. (Bath Agric. Soc. Vol. 8. p. 299.)

ILL, [Sir Richard] *Bart. M. P. for the county of Salop. (of Hawkstone in Shropshire; a Methodist.)*
See Public Characters of 1802 and 1803. p. 150.
A detection of gross falshood and a display of black ingratitude, being an answer to a pamphlet lately published by some evil-minded person, under the name of *William Woolley*, styling himself, A. M. and addressed to Sir *Rich. Hill.* 1794. 8. (1 sh. 6 d.) The substance of a speech intended to have been delivered in the house of Commons on Mr. *Grey's* first motion for peace Jan. 26. 1795. 8. (1 sh.) Hard measure, or, a real statement of facts, in a letter to the burgesses and freemen burgesses of the town of Shrewsbury — with a supplement. Ed. 2. 1796. 8. (9 d.) An apology for brotherly love and for the doctrines of the church of England. 1798. 8. (5 sh.) Reformation — truth restored; being a reply to *Charles Daubeny's* appendix to his guide to the church — 1800. 8. (4 sh.) An appendix to the guide to the church; in which the principles advanced in that work, are fully maintained in answer to objections against them. Vol. 1. 2. 1799. 8. (10 sh.) *Daubenism* confuted and *Mart.*

Luther vindicated; with further remarks on the false quotations adduced by *Charles Daubeny* — in his late publications; intended as a supplement to reformation truth restored. 1800. 8. (1 sh.)

HILL, [Rowland] *A. M: a Methodist Preacher:* (Brother to Sir *Rich. Hill.*)

See Public Characters of 1802 and 1803. p. 156.
Aphoristic observations proposed to the consideration of the public, respecting the propriety of admitting theatrical amusements into country manufacturing towns. 1790. 8. (1 sh.) An expostulatory letter to *W. D. Tatterfal*, A. M. in which the bad tendency of the admission of stage amusements, in a religious and moral point of view, is seriously considered. 1795. 8. (6 d.) Journal of a tour through the north of England and parts of Scotland, with remarks on the present state of the established church of Scotland and the different secessions therefrom. 1799. 8. (2 sh. 6 d.) Extract of a journal of a second tour from London through the highlands of Scotland and the north western parts of England: with observations and remarks. 1800. 8. (6 d.) A plea for union and for a free propagation of the gospel, being an answer to Dr. *Jamieson's* remarks on the late tour of *Rowl. Hill* addressed to the Scot's society for the propagation of the gospel at home. 1800. 8. (1 sh.) Village dialogues. 1801. 12. (1 sh.) An apology for sunday schools —; 1801. 8. (1 sh)

HILL, [Thomas Ford] *Esq. F. A. S.*

born . . . . died at Arriano 1795. Jul. 16.
See Gentleman's Magaz. Y. 1795. Aug. p. 704. Sept. p. 789. Y. 1796. Febr. p. 126. Allgem. Litt. Zeit. ItBl. J. 1796. Jul. S. 809.
Observations on the politics of France and their progress since the last summer, made in a journey from Spa to Paris during the autumn of 1791. 1792. 8. (2 sh. 6 d.)

*HILL, [William] *at Butt-Lane, Deptford.*
Description of his invented machine for drawing bolts out of ships bottoms, when under repair. (Tr. of the Soc. for the E. of A. Vol. 10. p. 124.)

*HILLHOUSE,

HILLHOUSE, [William] *Esq. Attorney at Law.*
An oration in commemoration of Major Gen. *Nathaniel Greene*, composed for a late commencement and meeting of the cincinnati, at Newhaven; (American Museum Y. 1787. Oct. p. 337.)

HINCHCLIFFE, [John] *D D. Bishop of Peterborough and Dean of Durham.*
born 1731. at Westminster, died 1794. Jan. 11. See Gentleman's Magaz. Y. 1794. Jan. p. 93. Febr. p. 99. 178.
Sermons. 1796. 8. (5 sh.)
(Several single sermons.)

HINCKES, [.....] *of Cork.*
An account of some manuscript papers — who filled several important offices in the reign of King Edward VI. (Tr. of J. A. Vol. 6. p. 7. e.)

HINCKES, [T....]
Letters in answer to *Paine's* age of reason. 1796. 8. (2 sh. 6 d.)

HINCKLEY, [John] *Esq.*
The people's answer to the Lord-Bishop of Landaff. 1797. 8. (1 sh.) The history of Rinaldo Rinaldini, Captain of banditti. Translated from the german of *Vulpius*. Vol. 1-3. 1800. 12. (10 sh. 6 d.) Travels in Portugal by *H. F. Link*, translated from the german, with notes. 1801. 8. (9 sh.)

HINDERWALL, [Thomas]
The history and antiquities of Scarborough and the vicinity, with views and plans. 1798. 4. (12 sh.)

HINDLEY, [.....]
*Persian lyrics, or scattered poems from *Hafiz*: with paraphrases in verse and prose, a catalogue of the gazels as arranged in a manuscript of the works of *Hafiz* in the Chatham library at Manchester and other illustrations. 1800. 4. (15 sh.)

HINDMAN, [John] *at Newcastle.*
On fat meat. (Comm. and Agric. Mag. Vol. 7. p. 115.)

HINDMARSH, [James]
A new dictionary of correspondencies, representations &c. or the spiritual significations of words, sentences

sentences &c. as used in the sacred scriptures; compiled from the theological writings of *Eman. Swedenborg*. 1794. 12. (3 sh.) Account of Mr. *Rowntree's* trial for patent property. (Comm. and Agric. Magaz. Y. 1801. Jan. p. 22.)

*HINSDALE, [Theodore] *at Windsor, Connecticut.* Account of an extraordinary halo. (American Museum Y. 1790. Apr. p. 204.)

*HINTON, [James] *A Dissenting Minister at Oxford.* Vindication of the dissenters in Oxford, addressed to the inhabitants, in reply to Dr. *Tatham's* sermon, lately published. 1792. 8. (3 d.)

*HINTON, [William] *D. D. of Northwold, Norfolk.* Experiments with Mr. *Cook's* drill plough. (*Young's* A. of Agr. Vol. 5. p. 156.) On Mr. *Ducker's* husbandry. (Ibid. Vol. 7. p. 216.) Of night-rolling turnips, with observat. by *A. Young*. (Ibid. Vol. 10. p. 207.) On land for cottages. (Ibid. Vol. 37. p. 265.) On the culture of the Chinese hemp. (Tr. of the Soc. for the E. of A. Vol. 6. p. 105.)

*HITCHCOCK, [Enos] *D. D. resident at Providence in the state of Rhode-Island.*
Memoirs of the blooms grove family, in a series of letters to a respectable citizen of Philadelphia, containing sentiments on a mode of domestick education, suited to the present state of society, government and manners in the United States of America, and on the dignity and importance of the female character, interspersed with a variety of interesting anecdotes. Boston. 1790. 8. (10 sh.) The farmer's friend, or the history of Mr. *Charles Worthy* —; Boston. 1793. 8.

*HITCHCOCK, [Samuel] *Major.*
Account of frogs found in the earth. (Mem. of B. A. Vol. 2. P. 1. p. 63.)

*HITCHINS, [Malachy] *Rev.*
Account of the discovery of silver in Herland copper mine. (Phil. Transact. Y. 1801. p. 159. *Tilloch's* Philos. Magaz. Vol. 10. p. 77.)

*HOADLY, [....]
Arch-Deacon *Blackburne's* political sentiments explained. (Monthly Magaz. Y. 1800. June. p. 420.)

*HOARE,

*HOARE, [Prince] *Esq. an Artist.* born at Bath.

Such things were, a tragedy. 1788. Ed. 2. 1796. No song no supper, a comic opera. 1790. The cave of Trophonius. 1791. Dido, Queen of Carthage. 1792. The prize, or 2. 5. 3. 8. 1793. My grandmother; 1793. *Love's victim: the hermit's story. 1793. 4. (2 sh. 6 d.) Mahmoud, a musical opera. 1796. The Italian villagers, an opera. 1796. Lock and key; a musical entertainment, in two acts. 1796. 8. (1 sh.) Sighs or the daughter, a comedy, in 5 acts — taken from the german drama of *Kotzebue*, with alterations. 1799. 8. (2 sh. 6 d.) Indiscretion, a comedy, in 5 acts. 1799. 8. (2 sh.) Chains of the heart, or the slave by choice in 3 acts. 1802. 8. (2 sh.) Extracts from an correspondance with the academies of Vienna and St. Petersburg, on the cultivation of the arts of painting, sculpture and architecture, in the Austrian and Russian dominions. To which is prefixed a summary account of the transactions of the royal academy at London from the close of the exhibition 1801 to the exhibition at Somerset-house. 1802. 4. (2 sh. 6 d.)

*HOARE, [Sir R.... C....] *Bart.*

An historical tour in Monmouthshire, illustrated with views; a new map of the county and other engravings by *William Coxe*, in two parts. 1801.

*HOBHOUSE, [Benjamin] *Barrister at Law; A. M. of Brazen-Nose College, Oxford. M. P.*

A reply to *F. Randolph's* letter to Dr. *Priestley;* or, an examination of *Randolph's* scriptural revision of socinian arguments, in a series of letters to the author. 1793. 8. (3 sh.) *A treatise on heresy, as cognizable by the spiritual courts; and an examination of the statute 9 and 10 William 3. C. 32. entitled: An act for the more effectual suppressing of blasphemy and profaneness in denying by writing, printing, teaching or advised speaking the divine original of the scriptures or the doctrine of the holy trinity, by a barrister a law. 1792. 8. (2 sh.) A collection of tracts. 1797. 8. On rendering inclosure bills more simple. (Bath Agric. Soc. Vol. 9. p. 55.)

*HODGES, [Phinehas]
Stricture on the elements medicinae of Dr *Brown*. 1795. 8.

*HODGES, [W....] *Attorney at Law.*
An historical account of Ludlow castle; the ancient palace of the princes of Wales and supreme court of judicature of the president and council of the welsh marches: compiled from original manuscripts — with an appendix. 1794. 8. (2 sh. 6 d.)

*HODGES, [Wickens] *Surgeon.*
Funesta passionis iliacae historia; partiumque morbosarum post mortem anatomia. (Mem. of M. S. of L. Vol. 5. p. 6.)

HODGES, [William] *R. A. of Brixham, Devon.*
born .... died 1797. Febr. 27.
See Gentleman's Magaz. Y. 1797. March. p. 255. Allg. Litt. Zeit. ItBl. J. 1800. S. 641.
Travels in India during the years 1780 – 1783. 1793. 4. (1 L. 1 sh.) übers. (von *F. L. W. Meyer.*) Hamburg. 1793. 8. Ed. 2. London. 1794. 4.

*HODGSON, [.....] *Rev.*
A practical english grammar. 1796. (1 sh. 6 d.)

HODGSON, [Bernard] *LL. Dr. Principal of Hertford College, Oxford.*
Ecclesiastes, a new translation from the original hebrew. 1791. 4. (4 sh.)

*HODGSON, [C....] *LL. B. Rector of Marlholm in Northamptonshire and late of Pembroke-Hall, Cambridge.*
An evangelical summary of corroborating testimonies, concerning the birth, rise, death, resurrection and ascension of Jesus Christ. To which are prefixed, the prophecies relative to the same events; 1797.

*HODGSON, [William]
The commonwealth of reason. 1795. 8. (2 sh. 6 d.)

*HODGSON, [William] *M. Dr.*
The system of nature, or, the laws of the moral and physical world, translated from the french of Mr. *Mirabaud.* Vol. 1. 1795. 8. (5 sh.) The temple

temple of Apollo, being a felection of the beft poems from the moft admired writers, confifting of odes, eclogues, elegies, infcriptions, paftorals, defcriptions, fables, epitaphs, hymns, tales, invocations. 1796. 8. (1 fh. 6 d.)

*HODSKINSON, [Jofeph]

Plain and ufeful inftructions to farmers, or an improved method of management of arable land, with fome hints upon drainage, fences and the improvement of turn-pike and crofs roads. 1794. 8. (1 fh.) überf. mit Anmerk. 1796. 8.

*HODSON, [C....] *LL. B.*

An evangelical fummary of corroborative teftimonies, concerning Jefus Chrift; to which, are prefixed the prophecies relative to the fame events, 1798. (1 fh.)

*HODSON, [Frodfham] *M. A. Fellow of Brafen-Nofe College, Oxford.*

The eternal filiation of the fon of God afferted on the evidence of the facred fcriptures, the confent of the fathers of the three firft centuries and the authority of the Nicene council. 1796. 8. (2 fh.)

HODSON, [James]

A letter to the Rev. *J. Edwards* containing ftrictures on that part of the unitarian creed, which he has explained in his late addrefs to the congregation of the Rev. Mr. *Medley*, of Liverpool. 1791. 8. (1 fh.) The evangelical clergyman, or a vindication of the religious principles and conduct of a minifter of the gofpel. 1801. 8. (1 fh. 6 d.)

*HODSON, [Septimus] *M. B. Rector of Thrapfton in Northamptonfhire, Chaplain to the Afylum for female Orphans, and Chaplain in Ordinary to his R. H. the Prince of Wales.*

Sermons on the prefent ftate of religion in this country and on other fubjects. 1792. 8. (4 fh.) Addrefs to the different claffes of perfons in Great-Britain on the prefent high price of provifions. To which is added an appendix containing a table

Hh 5 of

of the averagenprice of wheat in every year, from the year 1595 to 1790. inclusive. 1795. 8. (1 sh. 6 d.) Two discourses. 1795. 8. (6 d.) The evangelical clergyman, or, a vindication of the religious principles and conduct of a minister of the gospel. 1801. 8. (1 sh.)

(Several single sermons.)

*HODSON, [T....]

The index to the arts, or, a complete system of drawing, etching, engraving, painting, perspective and surveying; containing the whole theory and practice of the fine arts in general; illustrated with engravings and also containing curious and useful miscellaneous articles. Nrb. 1. (to be completed in 30 numbers.) 1803. 4. (1 sh. 6 d.)

*HODSON, [Thomas]

The accomplished tutor, or, complete system of liberal education. Vol. 1. 2. 1802. 8. (18 sh.)

*HODSON, [W....]

The fabulator, or, the hall of Aesop, being a selection of fables in prose and verse. 1801. (1 sh. 6 d.)

HODSON, [William] *M. A. Vice-Master of Trinity-College, Cambridge and Vicar of Hitchin, Hertfordshire.*

born .... died 1793. Oct. 6.

See Gentleman's Magaz. Y. 1793. Oct. p. 961.

*HOGARTH, [Harry] *at Philadelphia.*

On the inconsistency of mankind. (American Museum Y. 1787. p. 559.) On giving and receiving advice. (Ibid. Y. 1787. p. 561.) Remarks on the different ideas of mankind, respecting the acceptation of the term, business. (Ibid. Y. 1788. June, p. 507.)

HOLCROFT, [Thomas] *Actor at Drury - Lane Theater.*

S. *Wieland's* N. Deutscher Merkur. J. 1797. St. 7. S. 283.

Posthumous works of Frederic 2. King of Prussia; translated from the french. Vol. 1-13. 1789. 8. (4 L. 4 sh.) The school for arrogance, a comedy. 1791. 8. (1 sh. 6 d.) The road to ruin, a comedy. Ed. 10. 1792. 8. (1 sh. 6 d.) übers. von

Com-

Cowmeadow mit dem Titel: Leichtſinn und kindliche Liebe oder der Weg zum Verderben —; Berlin. 1794. 8. Anna St. Ives, a novel. Vol. 1–7. 1792. 8. (1 L. 1 ſh.) Love's frailties, a comedy. 1794. 8. (2 ſh.) The adventures of Hugh Trevor. Vol. 1–7. 1794–1797. (1 L. 1 ſh.) A narrative of facts, relating to a proſecution for high treaſon; including the addreſs to the jury, which the court refuſed to hear; with letters to the Attorney-General — and the defence which the author had prepared, if he had been brought to trial. 1794. 8. (3 ſh. 6 d.) Letter to the R. H. *William Windham*, on the intemperance and dangerous tendency of his public conduct. 1795. 8. (1 ſh. 6 d.) The deſerted daughter, a comedy. 1795. 8. (2 ſh.) The man of ten thouſand, a comedy. 1796. 8. (2 ſh.) Travels through Germany, Switzerland, Italy and Sicily; translated from the german of *Fred. Leop.* Count *Stolberg*. Vol. 1. 2. 1797. 4 (3 L. 3 ſh.) A new edition. Vol. 1–4. 1802. Knave or not? a comedy in 5 acts. 1798. 8. (2 ſh.) Herman and Dorothea: a poem, from the German of *Goethe*. 1801. 8. (10 ſh. 6 d.) A tale of myſtery, a melo-drama, as performed at the theatre Roy. Coventgarden. 1802. 8. (2 ſh.) Hear both ſides; a comedy in 5 acts. 1803. 8. (2 ſh. 6 d.)

*HOLDEN, [G.....] *Rev.*

born .... died 1793. May .... at Tatham, near Lanceſter.

See Gentleman's Magaz. Y. 1793. June. p. 578.

Tide table. 17..

*HOLDEN, [H.... E....]

On the cultivation and manufacture of ſugar in the Weſt Indies. (Comm. and Agric. Magaz. Y. 1801. Febr. p. 92.)

*HOLDEN, [Richard]

Deſcription of the reliefs on the font at Thorpe Salvin in Yorkſhire. (Arch. Vol. 12. p. 207.)

*HOLDER, [.....] *Rev.*

The ſecluded man, or, the hiſtory of Mr. *Oliver*. Vol. 1. 2. 1798. 12. (6 ſh.)

HOLDER,

HOLDER, [Henry Evans] *formerly of the Island of Barbadoes and since of the city of Bristol.*

A system of french accidence and syntax — Ed. 4. with notes by *G. Satis.* 1794. 8. (4 sh.) A familiar guide to the hebrew language, in a series of letters addressed to a lady. 1791. 8. (1 sh.) Discourses on various subjects, delivered in the island of Barbadoes. Vol. 1-4. 1791. 1792. (1 L. 2 sh.) The doctrine of the divine trinity in unity briefly asserted and vindicated. 1791. 8. (1 sh.) A brief, but, it is presumed, a sufficient answer to the „philosophy of masons„ 1791. 12. (4 d.) Fragments of a poem, intended to have been written in consequence of reading Major majoribanks's slavery. 1792. 4. (1 sh. 6 d.) Miscellaneous poems. 1792. 8. (1 sh. 6 d.) Observations on the West Indian climate, with some reference to animal health, vegetation, agriculture &c. (Comm. and Agric. Mag. Y. 1801. March. p. 176.)

*HOLE, [John] *Musician.*

A complete dictionary of music —; 1791. 8.

HOLE, [Richard] *LL. B. Rector of Faringdon and Inwardleigh, co. Devon.*

born at Exeter ..... died 1803. May 28.

See Gentleman's Magaz. Y. 1803. June. p. 599. Remarks on the arabian nights entertainments, in which the origin of Sinbad's voyage and other oriental fictions is particularly considered. 1797. 8. (4 sh.)

*HOLFORD, [.....] *Mrs.*

Neither's the man, a comedy, in 5 acts. 179. 8. (2 sh.) Fanny and Selima; 17.. Gresford vale and other poems. 1798. 4. First impressions, or the portrait, a novel. Vol. 1-4. 1801. 8. (18 sh.)

*HOLLAND, [Henry] *Esq. Architect.*

On cottages. (Comm. to the B. of Agr. Vol. 1. p. 97.) Pisé, or the art of building strong and durable walls, to the height of several stories, with nothing but earth, or the most common materials. (Ibid. Vol. 1. p. 387.)

*HOLLAND, [Mary] *a Cook.*

The complete British cook —. 1800. 12. (1 sh.)

*HOLLAND,

HOLLAND, [William] *M. Dr.*
born .... died at Fast-Retford, co. Nottingham 1797. Dec. 18.
Diss. De Cynanche tonsillari. Edinburgi. 1776.

HOLLAR, [C....]
Tournaments reviewd in Sweden. (Comm. and Agric. Mag. Y. 1800. Jan. p. 1.)

HOLLIDAY, [John] *Surgeon.*
A short account of the origin, symptoms and most approved method of treating the putrid bilious fever vulgarly called the black vomit; which appeared in the city of the Havanna — in the months of June, July and part of the August 1794. 1795. 8.

HOLLIDAY, [John] *Esq. of Lincoln's-Inn, Barrister at Law; F. R. S. Governor of the Roy Hospitals of Christ, Bridewell and Bethlem and of the Foundling Hospital: Member of the Soc. of Arts and Manufactures.*
born 1730 died 1801. March. 9.
See Gentleman's Magaz. Y. 1801. March. p. 283.
The life of *William* Earl of *Mansfield.* 1797. 4. (1 L. 1 sh.) On a favourite Norfolk Bantam; (Gentleman's Magaz. Y. 1800. Nov. p. 1081.) * The British oak; (which, in its fallen state, is the cause of England's glory) a poem. 1801. Memoir of *Owen Salisbury Brereton*; (Transact. of the Soc. for the Encourag. of Arts. Vol. 19. p. IV.)

IOLLINGBERY, [Thomas] *D. D. F. R. and A. SS. Chaplain in ordinary to his Majesty, Arch-Deacon of Chichester, Chaplain to Dover-castle and the cinque ports, and Rector of Rostingdean.*
born .... died 1792. Aug. 1.
See Gentleman's Magaz. Y. 1792. Aug. p. 769.
Alex. Cunningham's history of Great-Britain from the revolution in 1688 to the accession of George I: with *Will. Thomson's* account of the author and his writings. Vol. 1 2. 1787. 4. (1 L. 16 sh.) übers. Breslau. Th 1. 2. 1789. 4.

'HOLLINGSHEAD, [J....] *Esq.*
born 1718. died at Chorley Dec. 1802.
See Gentleman's Magaz. Y. 1803. Jan. p. 87.

On

On the national importance of salt as a manure; 17..

*HOLLINGSWORTH, [N....] *A. M. Curate of Sedgfield.*

A few plain practical sermons on important subjects. 1801. 12. (5 sh.)

*HOLLINS, [William] *at Berriew, in Montgomeryshire.*

An account of the disease in the potatoe plant called the curl potatoe. (Tr. of the Soc. for the E. of A. Vol. 8. p. 19. Vol. 9. p. 52. Vol. 11. p. 75.)

*HOLLIS, [John] *Esq.*

Sober and serious reasons for scepticism as it concerns revealed religion, in a letter to a friend, 1796. 8. (1 sh.) An apology for the disbelief of revealed religion, being a sequel to sober and serious reasons for scepticism. 1799. 8.

*HOLLOWAY, [William]

Poems on various occasions, chiefly descriptive, elegiac, didactic and pathetic. 1798. 8. The peasant's fate, a rural poem, with miscellaneous poems 1802. 8. (5 sh.) The baron of Lauderbrooke, a tale. 1800. 12. (2 sh. 6 d.) Scenes of youth, or rural recollections; with other poems; with cuts. 1803. 8. (4 sh.) See *J. Branch.*

*HOLMAN, [Joseph George] *Actor at Coventgarden Theatre.*

Abroad and at home, a comic opera in 3 acts. 1796. 8. (2 sh.) The votary of wealth, a comedy, in 5 acts. 1799. 8. (2 sh.) The red-cross knights, a play, in 5 acts. 1799. 8. (2 sh.) What a blunder! a comic opera in 3 acts. 1800. 8. (2 sh.)

*HOLME, [E.....]

Practical observations on the treatment of strictures in the urethra. 1796. (3 sh. 6 d.)

*HOLME, [Edward] *M. Dr.*

The inverse method of central forces. (Mem. of M. Vol. 4. P. 2. p. 369. Vol. 5. P. 1. p. 102.) See *Thomas Barritt.*

*HOLMES, [Abiel] *A. M. Member of the Massachusetts Hist. Soc.*

Life of *Ezra Stiles*, D. D. LL. Dr. President of Yale

Yale College. 1799. The history of Cambridge. (Coll. of Massachusetts H. S. Y. 1800. p. 1.)

HOLMES, [Edward] *M. A. Master of Scorton school, co. York.*

born .... died 1799. Jul. 31.

See Gentleman's Magaz. Y. 1799. Aug. p. 720. Monthly Magaz. Y 1799. Nov. p. 833. Allg. Litt. Zeit. ItBl. J. 1800. S. 664.

On education. 17.. Queries on lime (Young's A. of Agr. Vol. 3. p. 384.) On the food of plants. (Ibid. Vol. 6. p. 185.) On meteorology, as applicable to husbandry. (Ibid. Vol. 8. p. 1.) Strictures upon *A. Young's* observations on *Mosley's* tares and buck wheat, as a substitute for fallows. (Ibid. Vol. 8. p. 110.) On the smut. (Ibid. Vol. 8. p. 115.)

*HOLMES, [G....]

Sketches of some of the southern counties of Ireland collected during a tour in the autumn 1797. in a series of letters. 1801. 8. (9 sh.)

HOLMES, [Robert] *D. D. Canon of Christ church, Rector of Stanton and formerly Fellow of New College, Professor of Poetry in the University of Oxford.*

Sermon on the resurrection. 1777. Proposal for a collation of all the manuscripts of the 70 version of the old testament. 1788. The 3-13th annual account of the collation of the MSS of the 70 version. 1791-1800. 8. Ode for the encaenia, held at Oxford Jul. 1793. for the reception of his Grace *Will. Henry Cavendish*, Duke of Portland, Chancellor of the University, set by *Phil. Hayes*, D. D. Professor of Musick. 1793. 4 (1 sh.) Epistola complexa Genesin ex codice purpureo argenteo Caesareo Vindobonensi expressum et testamenti veteris graeci versionis LXX, cum variis lectionibus denuo edendi specimen. Oxford. 1795. fol. (6 sh.) Epistolae — *Shute Barrington*, LL. D. Episc. Dunelmensi, nuper datae appendix — Oxfordiae. 1795. (15 sh.) Vetus testamentum Graecum cum variis lectionibus. Genesis. 1798. fol. (15 sh.) Exodus. (1 L. 10 sh.) Leviticus. (10 sh. 6 d.)

*HOLMES, [S....] *a Smith.*

Description of his conducting oven, heated without flues;

flues; (Comm. and Agrib. Magaz. Y. 1801. May. p. 350. Tr. of the Soc. for the E. of A. Vol. 18. p. 224. *Tilloch's* Phil. Magaz. Vol. 9. p. 30.)

*HOLMES, [Samuel] *Serjeant Major of the XI light dragoons.*

Journal during his attendance as one of the guard on Lord *Macartney's* embassy to China and Tartary 1792–1793. 1798. 8.

*HOLROYD, [John Baker] See Lord *Sheffield.*

*HOLSTEN, [Esther]

Ernestina, a novel. Vol. 1. 2. 1801. 8. (7 sh.)

*HOLT, [Charles]

A short account of the yellow fever, as it appeared in New-London in Aug. Sept. and Oct. 1798 with an accurate list of those who died of the disease — New-London. 1798. 8.

*HOLT, [Daniel] *Printer of the Newark Herald.*

A vindication of the conduct and principles of the printer of the Newark Herald. An appeal to the justice of the people of England, on the result of two recent and extraordinary prosecutions for libels. 1794. 8. (3 sh. 6 d.)

HOLT, [John]

born at Mottram in Cheshire. 1742. died at Walton near Liverpool 1801. March 21.

See Gentleman's Magaz. Y. 1801. March p. 285. April. p. 370. Sept. p. 793.

Remarks in a tour taken in the summer of 1793 from Walton to London: (Gentleman's Magaz. Y. 1793. July p. 619. Aug. p. 720.) Essay on the curle in potatoes; 17.. General view of the agriculture of the county of Lancaster, with observations on the means of its improvement — 1795. 8. (5 sh.) On a particular kind of apple. (Bath Agric. Soc. Vol. 6. p. 160.) On transplanting wheat &c. (Ibid. Vol. 6. p. 163.) On the loss of weight in grain &c. (Ibid. Vol. 6. p. 167.) Remarks on waste lands in Lancashire. (Ibid. Vol. 8. p. 128.) Singular crop of wheat. (Ibid. Vol. 30. p. 202.) On the cause and prevention of the curl in potatoes. (Tr. of the Soc. for E. of A. Vol. 8. p. 36.) Hints on the subject of roads. (Comm. to the B. of Agr. Vol. 1. p. 183.)

*HOLT,

OLT, [S....]

An account of a remarkable pig. (*Young's* A. of Agr. Vol. 33. p. 639.)

LWELL, [John Zephaniah] *Esq. F. R. S. formerly Governour of Bengal. (the only survivor of that ever memorable and fatal cataſtrophe the black-hole priſon at Calcutta.)*

born 1700. died 1798. Nov. 5.

See Gentleman's Magaz. Y. 1798. Nov. p. 998. Monthly Magaz. Y. 1798. Nov. p. 390. Aſiatic new regiſter for the Y. 1799. Allgem. Litterat. Zeit. J. 1800. ItBl. S. 653. J. 1801. ItBl. S. 873.

Vindication (of Mr. *Holwell's* character) from the aſperſions thrown out in an anonymous pamphlet entitled: „reflections on the preſent ſtate of our Eaſt India affairs.„ 1764. 4. Addreſs to *Luke Skrafton*, Esq. in reply to his pamphlet entitled obſervations on Mr. *Vanſittart's* narrative. 1767. 8.

LWELL, [William] *B. D. F. R. S. Vicar of Thornbury, co. Glouceſter, Prebendary of Exeter and formerly Chaplain to the King.*

born 1725. died 1798. March 13.

See Gentleman's Magaz. Y. 1798. March. p. 259. Allg. Litt. Zeit. J. 1800. ItBl. S. 650.

Selecti *Dionyſii* Halicarneſs: De priſcis ſcriptoribus tractatus; graece et latine. 1776. A mythological, etymological and hiſtorical dictionary; extracted from the analyſis of ancient mythology (by Mr. *Bryant*) 1793. 8. (6 ſh.)

LYOKE, [Edward Auguſtus] *M. Dr. A A. S. and Fellow of the Maſſachuſett's Med. Soc.*

Account of the weather and of the epidemies at Salem in the county of Eſſex, for the Y. 1786. to which is added a bill of mortality for the ſame year. (M. P. of M. S. Numb. 1. p. 17.) An eſtimate of the exceſs of the heat and cold of the American atmosphere beyond the European, in the ſame parallel of latitude; to which are added ſome thoughts on the cauſes of this exceſs. (Mem. of B. A. Vol. 2. P. 1. p. 65. *Simmons's* Med. Facts and Obſerv. Vol. 7. p. 225.) überſ. in *Hegewiſch* u. *Ebeling* Amerikaniſchen Magazin. B. 1. St. 2. S. 1. A table of reſults, from a courſe of obſervaſervations made on the heat of the atmoſphere by *Fahrenheit's* thermometer in the Years 1786-1792 at Salem in Maſſachuſetts. (Ibid. Vol. 2. P. 1. p. 89.) Account of an uncommon caſe of emphyſema, and of an external abſceſs whoſe contents were discharged by coughing. (Ibid. Vol. 2. p. 186. *Simmon's* Med. Facts and Obſervat. Vol. 7. p. 259.) On the mercurial practice in the vicinity of Boſton, Maſſachuſetts. (Medical Repoſitory. Vol. 1. p. 500.) A caſe of diſeaſed os innominatum ſucceſsfully treated. (Ibid. Vol. 2. p. 1.) An eaſy and cheap method of preparing ſal aeratus (carbonate of potaſh.) (Ibid. Vol. 2. p. 5. *Tilloch's* Philoſ. Magaz. Vol. 5. p. 36.)

*HOME, [. . . . .]

Select views in Myſore, the country of Tippo Sultan; from drawings taken on the ſpot, with hiſtorical deſcriptions. 1795. 4. (6 L. 6 ſh.)

*HOME, [Charles] *Esq.*

A new chronological abridgment of the hiſtory of England from the earlieſt times to the acceſſion of the houſe of Hanuover, — written upon the plan of *Henault's* hiſtory of France. 1791. 8. (6 ſh.)

HOME, [Everard] *Esq. F. R. S. Surgeon to the Army and St. George's Hoſpital.*

Account of Mr. *Hunter's* method of performing the operation for the popliteal anevriſm. (London M. J. Vol. 7. P. 4. Vol. 8. P. 2. Transact. of Med. and Chir. Soc. Y. 1793. p. 138. Vol. 2. p. 235.) überſ. Repertorium Chirurg. u. Mediz. Abhandl. B. 1. S. 31. 44. Account of a child with a double head. (Philoſ. Transact. Y. 1790. p. 296. Y. 1799. p. 28. *Simmons's* Med. Facts and Obſerv. Vol. 1. p. 164.) überſ. Repertor. Chirurg. u. Mediz. Abhandl. B. 1. S. 224. Obſervations on certain horny excreſcences of the human body. (Philoſ. Transact. Y. 1791. p. 95. *Simmons's* Med. Facts and Obſervat. Vol. 3. p. 105.) überſ. Repertor. Chirurg. u. Mediz. Abhandl. B. 2. S. 253. Some obſervations on the looſe cartilages found in joints and moſt commonly met with in that of the knee. (Transact. of Med. and Chir. Soc. Y. 1793. p. 229.)

429.) Some observations on ulcers; (Ibid. Y. 1793. p. 330.) Some facts relative to *John Hunter's* preparation for the Croonian lecture. (Philos. Transact. Y. 1794. p. 21.) On the blood, inflammation and gun-shot wounds. by the late *John Hunter*. To which is prefixed a short account of the Author's life. 1794. 4. (1 L. 11 sh. 6 d.) übers. von Dr. *E. B. G. Hebenstreit*. B. 1. 2. Leipzig. 1796. 8. Practical observations on the treatment of strictures in urethra. 1795. 8. (3 sh. 6 d.) Ed. 2. 1797. übers. mit Anmerk. von Dr. *Sam. Hahnemann*. Leipzig. 1800. 8. Vol. 2. 1804. (7 sh.) Practical observations on the treatment of ulcers on the legs, considered as a branch of military surgery. 1797. 8. (4 sh. 6 d.) übers. von Dr. *L. F. Froriep*. Leipz. 1799. 8. On muscular motion of the structure and actions of the animal called hydatids; (Philos. Transact. Y. 1795. p. 1. 202. Y. 1796. p. 1. *Simmons's* Med. Facts and Observat. Vol. 8. p. 193.) Some observations on the mode of generation of the Kanguroo, with a particular description of the organs themselves. (Ibid. Y. 1795. p. 221.) A description of the anatomy of the sea otter, from a dissection made Nov. 15. 1795. (Ibid. Y. 1796. p. 385.) — and *Archib. Menzie's* observations on the changes which blood undergoes, when extravasated into the urinary bladder, and retained for some time in that viscus, mixed with the urine. (Ibid. Y. 1796. p. 486.) The Croonian lecture, in which some of the morbid actions of the straight muscles and cornea of the eye are explained and their treatment considered. (Ibid. Y. 1797. p. 1.) An account of the orifice in the retina of the human eye, discovered by *Soemmering*. To which are added proofs of this appearance being extended to the eyes of other animals. (Ibid. Y. 1798. p. 332.) Experiments and observations upon the structure of nerves. (Ibid. Y. 1799. p. 1.) An account of the dissection of an hermaphrodite dog. To which are prefixed, some observations on hermaphrodites in general. (Ibid. Y. 1799. p. 157.) Some observations on the structure of the teeth of graminivorous quadrupeds; particularly

larly those of the elephant and sus aethiopicus. (Ibid. Y. 1799. p. 237.) On the structure and uses of the membrana tympani of the ear. (Ibid. Y. 1800. p. 1. *Nicholson's* Journal. Vol. 5. p. 93.) See *Astley Cooper*. Some observations on the head of the ornithorhynchus paradoxus. (Phil. Transact. Y. 1800. p. 432. *Nicholson's* Journal. Vol. 4. p. 506.) Cases and observations on strangulated hernia. (Transact. of Med. and Chir. Soc. Vol. 2. p. 99.) An account of an uncommon tumour, formed in one of the axillary nerves. (Ibid. Vol. 2. p. 152.) The case of a person who was shot through the lungs and survived for thirty-two years; with an account of the appearance of the contents of the thorax after death. (Ibid. Vol. 2. p. 169.) A case of pregnancy in which the ovum had be come diseased and was entirely filled with small hydatids. (Ibid. Vol. 2. p. 300.) The operation of puncturing the bladder above the pubis and through the rectum illustrated by cases. (Ibid. Vol. 2. p. 344.) On the irritability of nerves. (Phil. Transact. Y. 1801. p. 1.) Observations on the structure and mode of growth, of the grinding teeth of the wild boar and animal incognitum. (Ibid. Y. 1801. p. 319.) On the power of the eye to adjust itself to different distances, when deprived of the crystalline lens. (Ibid. Y. 1802. p. 1.) A description of the anatomy of the ornithorhynchus paradoxus. (Ibid. Y. 1802. p. 67.) Description of the anatomy of the ornithorhynchus hystrix. (Ibid. Y. 1802. p. 348.)

*HOME, [John] *Esq.*

The history of the rebellion in the Year 1745. 1802. 4. (1 L. 1 sh.)

HOME, [Robert] *Surgeon to the Savoy. (Father of Everard Home.)*

born .... died 178. (?)

*HOME, [Thomas] *D. D. Vicar of Wilkington, Herefordshire and late Fellow of Trinity College, Oxford.*

Reflections on the sabbath. 1796.

*HOMER, [Harry]

Admonitory epistles to his brother *Peter Pindar.* Epistle 1. 1792.

* HOMER,

HOMER, [Henry] *Rector of Birdingbury, co. Warwick and formerly of Magdalen-College, Oxford.*

born .... died 1791. July 14.

See Gentleman's Magaz. Y. 1791. July. p. 685. Dec. p. 1156.

* *C. Corn. Taciti* opera omnia; sumptibus editoris. Vol. 1-4. 1790. 8. (large paper 3 L. 13 sh. 6 d. Small paper 1 L. 11 sh. 6 d.) * *T. Livii* historiarum libri; sumptibus editoris. Vol. 1-8. 1790. 8. (large paper 6 L. 6 sh.) * *Sallustius*; 1789. 8. (15 sh.) * *C. Julii* Caesaris opera omnia, Vol. 1. 2. 1790. 8. (large paper 1 L. 16 sh. Small paper 14 sh.)

HOMER, [Jonathan] *Rev.*

Description and history of the town of Newtown, or Newton in the county of Middlesex. (Coll. of Massachusetts H. S. Y. 1798. p. 253.)

HONEYWOOD, [.....]

Poems, with some pieces in prose. 1802.

HOOD, [Catherine]

Remonstrance, with other poems. 1801. 12. (2 sh. 6 d.)

HOOD, [Nathaniel] *Lieut. H. P. 40th Regt.*

Elements of war; or, rules and regulations of the army, in miniature: shewing the duty of a regiment in every situation. 1803. 12. (7 sh.)

HOOK, [A....] *Esq.*

A letter-complaining of injustice and pointing out the danger to society from perjury and the facility with which the loose and equivocal testimony of servants may destroy the peace of private families. 1798. 4. (1 sh.)

HOOK, [James] *M. A. F. S. A.*

Anguis in herba: a sketch of the true character of the church of England and her clergy, as a caveat against the misconstruction of artful and the misconception of weak men, on the subject of a bill about to be brought into parliament for the revisal of certain statutes concerning non residence &c. 1802. 8. (2 sh. 6 d.)

HOOK, [Sarah Ann]

The widowed bride; or, Celina: Vol. 1-3. 1802. (12 sh.)

*HOOKE, [.....] *Dr.*
On the invention of the telegraph, with a description. (*Tilloch's* Philos. Magaz. Vol. 1. p. 312.)

*HOOKE, [Robert]
Early developement of the antiphlogistian theory of combustion. (*Nicholson's* Journ. Vol. 3. p. 497.)

HOOLE, [Charles] *Rev.*
The curate, a poem; 17.. Letters, in imitation of the Bath guide; 17.. Sermons; 17..

HOOLE, [John] *Esq. of Tenterden, Kent, formerly Auditor to the East India Company.*
born 1727, died 1803. at Durking, Surrey.
See Gentleman's Magaz. Y. 1803. Aug. p. 793.
S. Neue Biblioth. der Schönen Wissensch. B. 51. S. 141.
The Orlando of *Ariosto*, reduced to 24 books the narrative connected and the stories disposed in a regular series. Vol. 1. 2. 1791. (12 sh.) Rinaldo, a poem, in XI books, translated from the Italian of *Torquato Tasso.* 1792. 8. (6 sh.) Dramas and other poems of the Abate *Pietro Metastasio.* Translated from the Italian. Vol. 1-3. 1800. 8. (1 L. 1 sh.)

*HOOLE, [Richard] *at Sowton, a village by Exeter.*
Translation of hymn to Ceres; 17.. Arthur; 17.. Fingal; 17.. (Author of some poetry in the poems, chiefly by Gentlemens of Devonshire and Cornwall. Vol. 1. 2. 1792. 8.)

HOOLE, [Samuel] *A. M.* (Son of *John Hoole.*)
*Modern manners, in a series of familiar epistles, 1781. *Aurelia or the contest, an heroic comic poem, 1783.

*HOOLE, [Samuel]
The select works of *Ant. v. Leeuwenhoek*, containing his microscopical discoveries in many of the works of nature; translated from the dutch and latin editions published by the author. Part. 1. 1798. 4. Part 2. 3. 1800. 4. (1 L. 11 sh. 6 d.)

*HOOPER, [J....] *M. Dr. F. M. S.*
born ...., died (?)
Discourse on the best means of improving the science of medicine delivered at the anniversary of the medical society in London in 1787. 1792. 8. (3 sh.)

*HOOPER,

IOOPER, [James Hill] *Surgeon.*

A case of an haemorrhage from an ulcer on the penis. (Mem. of M. S. of L. Vol. 2. p. 509.)

IOOPER, [Robert] *of Pembroke College, Oxford. M. D: F. L. M. S: and F. L. S.*

Observations on the structure and economy of plants, to which is added the analogy between the animal and vegetable kingdom. 1797. 8. (3 sh.) The hygrology, or chemico-physiological doctrine of the fluids of the human body, translated from the latin of *J. J. Pleuck.* 1797. 8. (5 sh.) The anatomist vade mecum; containing a concise and accurate description of the structure, situation and use of every part of the human body: to which is added, an explanation of anatomical terms. 1798. 8. Ed. 2. revised and enlarged. 1800. (3 sh. 6 d.) Ed. 4. corrected and enlarged. 1802. 12. (7 sh.) A compendious medical dictionary, containing an explanation of terms in anatomy, physiology, surgery, materia medica, chemistry and practice of physic; collected from the most approved authors. 1798. 8. (5 sh. 6 d.) Ed. 2. 1801. 8. (7 sh.) Anatomical plates of the bones and muscles diminished from *Albinus* for the use of students and artists, accompanied by explanatory maps. 24 plates. 1802. 12. (5 sh.) Observations on the epidemical diseases now prevailing in London —; 1803. 8. (1 sh. 6 d.) Observations on human intestinal worms, being an attempt at their arrangement into classes, genera and species. (Mem. of M. S. of L. Vol. 5. p. 224.) Anatomical engravings of the viscera of the thorax —; 1803. (5 sh.)

IOPE, [.....] *Lieutenant-Colonel.*

Letter to the volunteers. 1804. (1 d.)

IOPE, [Charles] *Rev. of Derby.*

Account of his plantations of mixed timbertrees. (Tr. of the Soc. for the E. of A. Vol. 12. p. 161.)

IOPE, [Thomas Charles] *Professor of Chemistry in the University of Edinburgh.*

Account of a mineral from strontian and of a peculiar species of earth which it contains. (Tr. of E. S. Vol. 4. P. p. 3.)

*HOPKINS, [Lemuel] *M. Dr.*
born in Waterbury, Connecticut, about the Y. 1755 or 1756.
See Monthly Magaz. Y. 1798. Nov. p. 343.
Poems: (inserted in the „American poems,„ Vol. 1.) Speech of Hesper; (inserted ibid.) The anarchiad, a poem on the restoration of chaos and substantial night in 24 books. 17..

*HOPKINS, [Richard] *An Arian Clergyman.*
Appeal to the common sense of all christian people respecting the doctrine of the trinity. 17..

*HOPKINS, [Samuel] *D. D. at Rhode-Island, North-America.*
A treatise on the millenium, shewing from scripture prophecy, that it is yet to come — when it will come — in what it will consist: and the events which are first to take place, introductory to it. 1794. 8. (1 sh. 6 d.)

HOPKINSON, [Francis] *Esq.*
born 1738. died 1791. May 9.
See Massachusetts Magaz. Y. 1791. Dec. p. 750. Columbian Magaz. Y. 1791. May. p. 291.
A pretty story. 1775. What is a salt-box? (American Museum — Vol. 1. 1787. Febr. p. 154.) *F. Hopkinson's* and *Dav. Rittenhouse's* account of the effects of a stroke of lightning in a house furnished with two conductors. (Tr. of A. S. Vol. 3. p. 122.) Description of a machine for measuring a ship's way. (Ibid. Vol. 3. p. 239.) Description of a spring-block, designed to assist a vessel in sailing. (Ibid. Vol. 3. p. 331.) Some account of a horse with a living snake in his eye. (American Museum Y. 1788. June. p. 503.) Speech on the learned languages. (Ibid. Y. 1788. June. p. 538.) Some thoughts on the diseases of the mind; with a scheme for purging the moral faculties of the good people of Pennsylvania — quite new, and very philosophical. (Ibid. Y. 1788. Oct. p. 327.) Miscellaneous essays and occasional writings. Vol. 1-3. Philad. 1792. 8. (1 L. 1 sh.)

*HOPKINSON, [Samuel] *B. D. late Fellow of Clare-Hall.*
Prayers and thanksgivings, principally intended for the use of children —. 1795. 12. (1 sh.)

Causes

Caufes of the fcarcity inveftigated; alfo an account of the moft ftriking variations in the weather from Oct. 1798 to Sept. 1800. To which is prefixed the price of wheat every year from 1660 to the prefent aera. 1801. 8. (2 fh.)

HOPSON, [Charles Rivington] *M. Dr. formerly Phyfician to the Finsbury Difpenfary.*
born .... died 1796. Dec. 23.
See Gentlemans Magaz. Y. 1797. Jan. p. 80.
Duncan's Annals of Medecine Y. 1797. p. 431.
Allg. Litter. Zeit. J. 1800. S. 629.
Forfter's voyages and difcoveries in the North translated. 17.. *Sparrman's* travels translated. 17.. *Thunberg's* travels translated. 17.. *Wolff's* account of Ceylon, translated. 17..

HORACE, [Humphrey] *Esq.*
The rights to life, a fermon preached by *R. Ramsden*, M. A. translated into verfe with notes and illuftrations. 1797. 8. (1 fh.)

HORE, [Charles] *Esq.*
Divine meditations, with a daily directory. 1804. 12. (2 fh. 6 d.)

HORN, [George] *Apothecary.*
An entire new treatife on leeches, where in the nature, properties and ufe of that moft fingular and valuable reptile is moft clearly fet forth. 1798. 8. (1 fh. 6 d.)

HORNBLOWER, [J.... C....]
Defcription of a model of machine for communicating motion at a diftance. (Bath Agric. Soc. Vol. 4. p. 302.) Defcription of an hydraulic bellows for a fmith's forge. (*Nicholfon's* Journ. Y. 1802. March. p. 219.) On the contruction of the beams of fteam-engines. (Ibid. Y. 1802. June. p. 68.)

HORNBY, [Thomas] *of York.*
Brandy from carrots. (*Young's* A. of Agr. Vol. 9. p. 168.) — — and *Hunter*, On the diftillation of ardent fpirit from carrots. (*Tilloch's* Philof. Magaz. Vol. 6. p. 12.)

HORNE, [George] *D. D. Lord-Bifhop of Norwich.*
born in the County of Otham, 1730. died 1792. Jan. 17.
See Gentleman's Magaz. Y. 1792. Jan. p. 19. 93.

Ii 5 Febr.

Febr. p. 135. 181. Monthly Magaz. Y. 1796. March. p. 127. April p. 303. May. p. 399. Y. 1798. Aug. p. 663.

William Jones's Memoirs of Bifh. *Horne*. 1795. 8. His character by *S. Parr*, LL. D. (See Gentlem. Magaz. Y. 1800. Nov. p. 1023.) Confiderations on the life and death of John the Baptift. 1769. Difcourfes on feveral fubjects and occafions. Vol. 3. 4. 1794. 8. (10 fh.) A letter to Dr. *Prieftley*. 1787. 8. Obfervations on the cafe of proteftant diffenters; 1790. 8. XVI. fermons on various fubjects and occafions; now firft collected. 1793. 8. (5 fh.) Character of Dr. *Johnfon*. (Gentleman's Magaz. Y. 1800. Jan. p. 9.)

*HORNE, [George] D. D. *Of the Univerfity of Oxford.*
Sound argument, dictated by common fenfe, in anfwer to *Nath. Braffey Halhed's* teftimony to the authenticity of the prophecies of *Richard Brothers*. 1795. 8. (1 fh.) Occafional remarks, addreffed to *N. B. Halhed*, in anfwer to his late pamphlet entitled „a calculation of the commencement of the millennium &c. with curfory obfervations on that gentleman's fpeech in the houfe of commons, refpecting the pretended prophecies of *Rich. Brothers*. 1795. 8. (1 fh. 6 d.)

HORNE, [John] See *Tooke*.

*HORNE, [John] *of Dover.*
The defcription and ufe of the new invented patent univerfal fowing machine for broad-cafting or drilling every kind of grain, pulfe and feed. (Bath Agricult. Soc. Vol. 3. p. 215.)

*HORNE, [Melvil] *Vicar of Olney, Bucks; formerly a Preacher in Mr. Wesley's connection and afterward Chaplain to the new fettlement at Sierra Leona.*
Letters on miffions addreffed to the proteftant minifters of the britifh churches, 1794. 8. (1 fh. 6 d.) (Several fingle fermons.)

*HORNE, [Melvill] *Curate of Madeley.*
Pofthumous pieces of the late Rev. *John Will. de la Flechere.* 1792. 12. (3 fh. 6 d.)

*HORNE, [T....] *D. D.*
Reflections on the fabbath. 1796. (1 fh.)

*HORNE,

*HORNE, [Thomas Hartwell]

A brief view of the neceſſity and truth of the chriſtian revelation. 1800. 12. (2 ſh. 6 d.) An eſſay on privateers, captures and particularly on recaptures according to the laws, treaties and uſages of the maritime power of Europe by *de Martens*, — tranſlated from the french with the notes. 1801. 8. (6 ſh.) A view of the commerce of Greece from 1787 to 1797. by *Felix Beaujour* — tranſlated from the french. 1800. 8. (9 ſh.) A compendium of the court of admiralty, relative to ſhips of war, privateers, prizes, recaptures, and prize-money; with notes and precedents. 1803. (4 ſh. 6 d.)

*HORNE, [W....] *of Great-Yarmouth.*

The faith of the goſpel vindicated in two ſermons. 1800. (1 ſh. 6 d.)

*HORNE, [W.... W....] *Miniſter at Tibenham, Norfolk.*

The new ſongs of Zion; or ſhort hymns, collected from the ſcriptures of the old teſtament. 1794. 8. (1 ſh. 6 d.)

*HORNSEY, [John] *Schoolmaſter at Scarborough.*

A ſhort grammar of the engliſh language in two parts; ſimplified to the capacities of children. Ed. 2. 1798. 12. (1 ſh. 6 d.)

*HORRIDGE, [John] *of Raikes, near Bolton in the moors, Lancaſhire.*

On the preparation and application of compoſts for manure. (Tr. of the Soc. for the E. of A. Vol. 19. p. 183.)

*HORSEY, [John]

On the diſſolution of the Northampton academy. (Monthly Magaz. Y. 1798. Nov. p. 318.)

*HORSFIELD, [Thomas] *of Lethlem.*

An experimental diſſertation on the rhus venix, rhus radicans and rhus glabrum commonly known in Penuſylvania by the names of poiſon-aſh, poiſon-wine and common ſumach. Philadelphia. 1798. 8.

HORSLEY, [Samuel] *LL. Dr: F. R. S: F. A. S: Lord Biſhop of Rocheſter, Dean of Weſtminſter and Dean*

Dean of the order of the Bath; late Bishop of St. Davids and formerly Arch-Deacon of St. Albans.

born about the Y. 1737.

See Public Characters of 1798 and 1799. p. 188. Gentleman's Magaz. Y. 1789. Oct. p. 884.

*An apology for the liturgy and clergy of the church of England. 1790. Sermon being the anniversary of the martyrdom of King Charles I. with an appendix, concerning the political principles of Calvini. 1793. 4. (1 sh. 6 d.) On the prosodies of the greek and latin languages. 1796. 8. (4 sh.). Critical disquisition on the 18 Chapter of Isaiah in a letter to *Edw. King*. 1799. 4. (4 sh.) Substance of his speech in the house of Peers July 5. 1799. in the debate upon the second reading of the bill to prohibit the trading in slaves on the coast of Africa within certain limits. 1799. 8. (1 sh.). Elementary treatises on the fundamental principles of practical mathematics. 1801. 8. (8 sh. 6 d.) Hosea, translated from the Hebrew with notes explanatory and critical. 1802. 4. (1 L. 1 sh.) (Several single sermons.)

*HOSACK, [Alexander] *Jun. M. Dr. of New-York.* History of the yellow fever, as it appeared in the city of New-York in 1795. Philad. 1797. 8.

*HOSACK, [David] *M. Dr. Professor of Botany and Materia Medica in Columbia-College, New-York.*

Dissertation on cholera morbus. Philadelphia. 1791. Observations on vision. (Philos. Transact. Y. 1794. p. 196.) Syllabus of a course of lectures on botany, delivered in Columbia-College. New-York. 1795. 8. A case of hydrocele, cured by injection. (Medical Reposit. Vol. 1. p. 419.) Singular cases of disease in infancy. (Ibid. Vol. 1. p. 507.) Case of tetanus cured by wine. (Ibid. Vol. 3. p. 21. *Tilloch's* Philos. Magaz. Vol. 7. p. 63. *Duncan's* A. of Med. Y. 1799. p. 389.) Oxydation of silver by the septic acid contained in the abdomen of a person dead of enteritis. (*Tilloch's* Philos. Magaz. Vol. 3. p. 411.) An introductory lecture on medical education. New-York. 1801. 8. A case cafe of hydrocele cured by injection. (*Duncan's* A. of Med. Y. 1796. p. 306,) A cafe of obftinate conftipation of the bowels cured by calomel. (Ibid. Y. 1796. p. 310.) Outline of the courfe of lectures on botany and materia medica, delivered in Columbia-College. May 15. 1797. (New-York Magaz. Y. 1797. May. p. 257.)

IOUGHTON, [J....]

Obfervations on the evidence of Chrift's refurrection; the principal objections anfwered and the divine origin of the chriftian religion clearly proved. 1798. 8. (2 fh.)

IOUGHTON, [Pendlebury]

Sermons. 1790. 8. (5 fh.)

OULSTON, [Thomas] *M. Dr. Phyfician to the Liverpool Infirmary.*

born ..... died 178. (?)

OULSTON, [William] *Surgeon; F. A. S. and F. M. S. London.*

Cafe of injury of the brain — überf. Samml. auserlef. Abh. zum Gebrauch prakt. Aerzte. B. 15. St. 1. S. 13. *J. O. Juftamond's*, Surgeon to the Weftminfter Hofpital, furgical tracts — überf. von *Ch. F. Michaelis*. Leipzig. 1791. 8. Sketches of facts and opinions refpecting the venereal difeafe. 1792. 8. (1 fh. 6 d.) Ed. 2. with amendments, and an additional fection on the formation and cure of ftrictures in the urethra. 1794. 8. (1 fh. 6 d.)

IOULTON, [R....] *M. A.*

Letter interefting to every lottery department, containing a critical examination of the plan — of the new lottery fyftem. 1802. 8. (2 fh.)

IOULTON, [R....] *M. B.*

Wilmore Caftle, a new comic opera, in two acts, the mufic entirely new, by Mr. *Hook*. 1800. 8. (1 fh. 6 d.) A review of the mufical drama of the theatre-royal Drurylane, for the Y. 1797-1799 and 1800, which will tend to develope a fyftem of private influence injurious to mufical emulation and public entertainment and to elucidate feveral interefting points of matter in *Plowden's* late diftinguifhed publication. 1801. 8. (2 fh.)

*HOUS-

*HOUSMAN, [John] *of Corby, near Carlisle.*

A descriptive tour and guide to the lakes, caves, mountains and other natural curiosities in Cumberland, Westmoreland, Lancashire and a part of the Westriding of Yorkshire. 1800. 8. (5 sh.) A topographical description of Cumberland, Westmoreland, Lancashire and part of the Westriding of Yorkshire. 1800. 8. Journal of a tour almost every county in England, part of Wales and Scotland. (Monthly Magaz. Y 1796. Dec. p. 862. Y. 1797. p. 201. 365. 429. Sept. p. 198. Nov. p. 363. Dec. p. 445. Y. 1798. Jan. p. 35. Febr. p. 106. Apr. p. 276. June. p. 428. Jul. p. 22. Sept. p. 193. Oct. p. 274. Nov. p. 349. Dec. p. 423. Y 1799. Jan. p. 32. May. p. 289. June. p. 372. Jul. p. 457. Y. 1800. Jul. p. 540. Oct p. 224. Nov. p. 308. Dec. p. 420. Y. 1801. Febr. p. 31.) Plan for consolidating friendly societies. (Ibid. Y. 1797. Aug. p. 88.) Particulars relating to the agriculture of Cumberland. (*Young's* A. of Agr. Vol. 21. p. 444.)

*HOUSMAN, [R....] *A. B.*

Sermons upon select names and titles ascribed in the world of God to Jesus Christ. Vol. 1. 1793. 8. (3 sh.) (Several single sermons.)

*HOW, [Richard] *of Apsley in Bedfordshire.*

Cases. (Mem. of M. S. of L. Vol. 3. p. 515.)

*HOWARD, [Edward] *Esq. F. R. S.*

On a new fulminating mercury. (Phil. Transact. Y. 1800. p. 204. *Nicholson's* Journal. Vol. 4. p. 173. 200. 249. *Tilloch's* Phil. Magaz. Vol. 7. p. 17. 122.) Experiments and observations on certain stony and metalline substances, which at different times are said to have fallen on the earth, also on various kinds of native iron. (Philos. Tr. Y. 1802. p. 168. *Nicholson's* Journal Y. 1802. July p. 216. Aug p. 254 Oct. p. 88. Nov. p. 153. *Tilloch's* Philos. Magaz. Vol. 13. p. 23. 136. 219. 331. Vol. 14. p. 49.)

HOWARD, [Frederick] Earl of CARLISLE; *Knight of the Garter.*

Letter to the Earl *Fitzwilliam* in reply to his Lordship's two letters. 1794. The step-mother, a tragedy.

tragedy. 1800. 8. (2 ſh.) Tragedies and poems. 1801. 8. (7 ſh. 6 d.)

HOWARD, [Henry] *Esq.*

Enquiries concerning the tomb of King Alfred, at Hyde Abbey, near Winchester. (Arch. Vol. 13. p. 309.)

HOWARD, [John] *Surgeon.*

Practical obſervations on the natural hiſtory and cure of the venereal diſeaſe. Vol. 3. 1794. 8. Supplem. 1801. 8. (2 ſh.). überſ. von Dr. C. F. *Michaelis.* Leipz. 1798. 8. The plan adopted by the governours of the Middleſex hoſpital, for the relief of perſons afflicted with cancer, with notes and obſervations. 1792. 8. (2 ſh.)

HOWARD, [John] *Schoolmaſter.*

born .... died at the Leaſes, near Newcaſtle, May 1799.

See Monthly Magaz. Y. 1799. May. p. 335.

A treatiſe on ſpherical geometry, containing its fundamental properties, the doctrine of its loci, the maxima and minima of ſpherical lines and areas; with an application of theſe elements to a variety of problems. 1798. 8. (6 ſh.)

HOWARD, [Luke]

On a periodical variation of the barometer, apparently due to the influence of the ſun and moon on the atmosphere. (*Tilloch's* Philoſ. Magaz. Vol. 7. p. 355.) Account of a microſcopical inveſtigation of ſeveral ſpecies of pollen, with remarks and queſtions on the ſtructure and uſe of that part of vegetables. (Transact. of L. S. Vol. 6. p. 65.) Conſiderations on Dr. *Hutton's* theory of rain: (*Tilloch's* Philoſ. Magaz. Vol. 14. p. 55.)

HOWARD, [Philip] *Esq.*

Thoughts on the ſtructures of the globe and the ſcriptural hiſtory of the earth and of mankind compared with the cosmogenies, chronologies and original traditions of antient nations; an abſtract and review of ſeveral modern ſyſtems, with an attempt to explain philoſophically, the moſaical account of the creation and deluge and to deduce from this laſt event the cauſes of the actual ſtructure of the earth: with notes and illuſtrations. 1797.

1797. 4. (1 L. 1 sh.) übers. von *J. F. Lehzen*, Hannover. 1799. 8.

*HOWARD, [Robert]

A few words on corn and quakers. 1800. 12. (6 d.)

*HOWARD, [Sylvanus] *Esq. of the Middle-Temple, Barrister at Law.*

Every tradesman his own lawyer, or a digest of the law concerning trade, commerce and manufactures. 1794. 8. (3 sh.)

*HOWE, [Thomas]

Episcopacy, a letter to Mr. *Forster*. 1765. 8. (2 sh.) Five sermons. 1771. 8. (1 sh. 6 d.) The millennium, or, cheerful prospects of the reign of truth, peace and righteousness and serious reflexions on the commencement of the new century. Two discourses. 1801. 8. (1 sh. 6 d.)
(Several single sermons.)

*HOWELL, [.....] *Mrs.*

Georgina, or, the advantages of grand connections, a novel. Vol. 1. 2. 1796. 8. (6 sh.) Anzoletta Zadoski, a novel. Vol. 1. 2. 1796. 8. (6 sh.) The spoiled child. Vol. 1. 2. 1797. 12. (7 sh.)

*HOWELL, [William]

Account of an improved escapement. (Tr. of the Soc. for the E. of A. Vol. 16. p. 216.)

*HOWISON, [James] *Surgeon on the Bengal Establishment of the East-India Company.*

A case of phthisis pulmonalis completely cured from the patient breathing mephitic air. (*Duncan's* A. of Med. Y. 1797. p. 324.) Some account of the elastic gum vine of Prince of Wales's Island, and of experiments made on the milky juice which it produces; with hints respecting the useful purposes to which it may be applied. (Asiat. Ref. Vol 5. p. 157. *Nicholson's* Journal. Vol. 3. p. 53. *Tilloch's* Phil Magaz. Vol. 6. p. 14.) Account of Prince of Wales's Island. (Tr. of E. S. Vol. 3. H. p. 13.)

*HOWISON, [William] *Esq.*

An investigation into the principles and credit of the circulation of paper money or banknotes in Great-Britain. 1803. 8. (1 sh. 6 d.)

*HOWLDY,

HOWLDY, [Thomas]

On an electric property of India rubber. (Monthly Magaz. V. 1797. Nov. p. 368.)

HOWLETT, [John] *Vicar of Great-Dunmow in Essex.*

Appendix to some account of the Shrewsbury house of Industry. 1792. (6 d.) Examination of Mr. *Pitt's* speech in the house of Commons 1796 relative to the condition of the poor. 1796. 8. (1 sh.) Dispersion of the gloomy apprehensions of late repeatedly suggested, from the decline of our corn-trade, and conclusions of a directly opposite tendency established upon well-authenticated facts: to which are added, observations upon the first report from the committee on waste lands &c. 1797. 8. (1 sh. 6 d.) The monthly reviewers reviewed — pointing out their misrepresentations and fallacious reasonings in their account of a pamphlet entitled, „Dispersion of the gloomy apprehensions —„ 1798. 8. (1 sh.) An enquiry concerning the influence of tithes upon agriculture, whether in the hands of the clergy or the laity. 1801. 8. (3 sh.) On the population of Cavenham. (*Young's* A. of Agr. Vol. 9. p. 113.) On the provision for the poor. (Ibid. Vol. 11. p. 1. Vol. 14. p. 174.) On the population of France. (Ibid. Vol. 15. p. 537.) The different quantity, and expence of agricultural labour, in different years. (Ibid. Vol. 18. p. 566.) On the population and situation of the poor in England. (Ibid. Vol. 18. p. 573.) On the number of people in the parish of Great-Welnetham, in Suffolk. (Ibid. Vol. 21. p. 108.) On the parish of Welnetham. (Ibid. Vol. 21 p. 377.) Prosperity of English Agriculture. (Ibid. Vol. 29. p. 521.) Crops and scarcity. (Ibid. Vol. 34. p. 95.) On the state of the poor, crops, bran-water bread &c. (Ibid. Vol. 34. p. 562.) Influence of tithes upon agriculture. (Ibid. Vol. 38. p. 131.)

HOWMAN, [E....] *Rev. of Bracon in Norfolk.*

Account of the cultivation of Siberian barley. (Bath Agricult. Soc. Vol. 1. p. 108.)

*HOWORTH, [.....] *Mrs.*
The poems of Bar. *Haller*, translated into English. 1794. 8. (3 sh.)

*HOY, [Thomas] *of Gordon-Castle. F. L. S.*
Account of a spinning limax or slug. (Transact. of L. S. Vol. 1. p. 183.) An account of two new genera of plants from New-South Wales, presented — by *Thomas Hoy* and *John Fairbairn*. (Ibid. Vol. 2. p. 346.) On China hemp. (Tr. of the Soc. for the E. of A. Vol. 4. p. 35.)

*HOYLE, [John] *Musician.*
Complete dictionary of music. 1790. 8. (3 sh.)

*HOYLE, [Thomas] *Jun.*
Experiments and observations on the preparation and some remarkable properties of the oxygenated muriat of potash. (Mem. of M. Vol. 5. P. 1. p. 221. *Nicholson's* Journal. Vol. 2. p. 290.)

*HOYTE, [Henry] *Land-Valuer.*
An essay on the conversion of soils, with observations and remarks on the breeding of sheep and cattle. 1802. 4. (4 sh. 6 d.) On the advantages of inclosures. (*Young's* A. of Agr. Vol. 32. p. 530.)

*HUBBARD, [George] *at Bury St. Edmunds.*
Account of bees. (Tr. of the Soc. for the E. of A. Vol. 9. p. 91.)

*HUBBARD, [John] *Rev.*
Account of the town of Northfield. (Coll. of Massachusetts H. S. Y. 1793. p. 30.)

*HUBBARD, [J.... C....] *A. M.*
Jacobinism — 17.. The triumph of poesy, a poem. 1803. 4. (2 sh.)

HUBBARD, [Leverett] *M. Dr. of Newhaven in Connecticut.*
Treatment of a person struck by lightning. (Mem. of M. S. of L. Vol. 4. p. 423.)

*HUCKS, [J....] *A. M. Fellow of Catharine-Hall, Cambridge.*
A pedestrian tour through North-Wales, in a series of letters. 1795. 8. (2 sh. 6 d.) Poems. 1798. 12. (3 sh. 6 d.)

HUDDART, [Joseph] *Esq. F. R. S. formerly Captain.*
Account of persons who could not distinguish colours. (Phil. Transact. Y. 1777. p. 260.) Sketch

of

the ſtraits of Gaſpar — 1788. 8. (5 ſh.) Obſervations on horizontal refractions which affect the appearance of terreſtrial objects, and the dip, or depreſſion of the horizon of the ſea. (Phil. Tranſact. Y. 1797. p. 29. *Nicholſon's* Journal Vol. 1. p. 145.)

HUDDESFORD, [George] *M. A. late Fellow of New-College, Oxford.*

Poems — including Salmagundi, Topſy-Turvy, Bubble and Squeak and crambe repetita, with corrections and original additions. Vol. 1. 2. 1801. 8. (12 ſh.)

HUDSON, [.....]

Anſwer to the Rev. *E... Wall's* two letters to Mr. *John Parkinſon* on the ſubject of the Welton incloſure bill. 1796. (6 d.)

HUDSON, [Robert] *of the Office of Examiner of India Correſpondance.*

The New Eaſt-India Kalendar for 1801. — 1801. 8. (4 ſh. 6 d.)

UDSON, [William] *Eſq. F. R. S.*

born in Kendal 1733. died 1793. May 23.

See Gentleman's Magaz. Y. 1793. May. p. 485.

HUGELL, [....] *Mrs.*

Iſidora of Gallicia. Vol. 1. 2. 1797. 8. (6 ſh.)

HUGER, [Francis K....]

An inaugural diſſertation on gangrene and mortification. Philad. 1797. 8.

HUGHES, [Francis] *Surgeon of the General Infirmary at Stafford.*

An account of the effects of mahogany wood in caſes of diarrhoea. (*Simmons's* Med. Facts and Obſervat. Vol. 6. p. 156.) Account of the effects of the external application of aether in a caſe of ſtrangulated hernia. (*Duncan's* M. C. Dec. 2. Vol. 8. p. 443.)

HUGHES, [H....]

Retribution and other poems. 1798. (2 ſh.)

HUGHES, [Hugh]

Deſcription of his machine for twitching wool. (Tr. of the Soc. for the E. of A. Vol. 7. p. 193.)

HUGHES, [J....]

A week's converſation on the plurality of worlds, tranſlated from the french of *Fontenell*, with conſiderable fiderable improvements. To which is added *Addifon's* defence of the Newtonian philofophy. 1801. 8. (3 fh.)

*HUGHES, [John] See *A. Behn.*

*HUGHES, [John] *of the Stamp-Office.*
The new law lift, corrected to the 25th of May 1802. 1802.

*HUGHES, [J.... T....] *Esq. of Lincoln's-Inn.*
Reflexions on the politics of France and England at the clofe of the year 1797. 1797. (2 fh. 6 d.)

*HUGHES, [Lewis] *B. D.*
Hiftorical view of the rife, progrefs and tendency of the principles of jacobinifm. 1798. 8. (1 fh. 6 d.)

*HUGHES, [Rice] *A. M. of Aldenham, Herts: Chaplain to Earl Poulett.*
Sermon: focial union and benevolence. 1790. 4. (1 fh. 6 d.) Letter on the meeting at the crown and anchor tavern on the 4 Jul. 1791. for the purpofe of celebrating the anniverfary of the revolution in France — 1791. 8. (1 fh. 6 d.) A defence of the Lord-Bifhop of Bangor, with remarks on a moft extraordinary trial. 1796. 8. (1 fh. 6 d.)

*HUGHES, [Richard] *Surgeon at Stafford.*
Account of a ftrangulated hernia, fpeedily cured by the application of aether. (*Duncan's* M. C. Dec. 2. Vol. 7. p. 487.)

HUGHES, [T....] *Surgeon* —
Cafe of cancer of the breaft: — überf. Samml. der neueften Beobacht. Engl. Aerzte. J. 1789. S. 35. Cafe of a fungous enlargement of the extremity of the female urethra, with remarks, (*Simmon's* Med. Facts and Obfervat. Vol. 2. p. 26.) Two cafes of fracture, one of the upper, the other of the lower jaw. (Ibid. Vol. 3. p. 36.) überf. Repert. Chir. u. Mediz. Abhandl. B. 2. S. 55.

*HUGHES, [W....] *Rev.*
A tour through feveral of the Midland and Weftern departments of France in 1802, with remarks on the manners, cuftoms and agriculture of the country; with engravings. 1803. 8. (7 fh.)

*HUITSON, [.....]
Cafe of paralyfis cured by the inhalation of vital air.

air. (Med. and Phyf. Journal. . . . . Medical Repofitory Vol. 3. p. 319.)

HULL, [John] *M. Dr. Member of the corporation of Surgeons: Secretary of the literary and philofophical Soc. of Manchefter.*

Elements of botany, illuftrated by 16 engravings. Vol. 1. 2. 1800. 8. (18 fh.) An effay on phlegmatia dolens, including an account of the fymptoms, caufes and cure of peritonitis puerperalis et conjunctiva. 1800. 8. (1 fh. 6 d.) A defence of the caefarean operation, with obfervations on embryulcia and the fection of the fymphifis pubis. 1799. 8. (3 fh. 6 d.) Obfervations on *Simmons's* detection &c. with a defence of the caefarean operation, derived from authorities. Part. 1. 2. 1799. 1800. 8. (11 fh.) The Britifh flora, or a Linnean arrangement of Britifh plants. Part 1. 1799. 8. (8 fh. 6 d.) Two memoirs on the caefarean operation, by Mr. *Baudelocque*, translated from the french, with a preface, notes, an appendix and 6 engravings. 1801. 8. (6 fh. 6 d.) Obfervations on the nervous fyftems of different animals; on original defects in the nervous fyftem of the human fpecies and their influence on fenfation and voluntary motion. (Mem. of M. Vol. 5. Part 2. p. 475.)

ULL, [Thomas] *late of Covent-Garden Theatre.*

Publifhed Sir *William Harrington*, a novel, revifed by Richardfon. 1771. reprinted 1797. The comedy of errors; with alterations from *Shakefpeare*, adapted for theatrical reprefentation. 1793. 8. (1 fh.) Moral tales in verfe, founded on real events. Vol. 1. 2. 1797. 8. (9 fh.) Elifha or the woman of Shunem; a new facred oratorio: fet to mufic by Dr. *Arnold*. 1801. 8. (1 fh.)

HULL, [Thomas] *M. Dr. Phyfician, Retford.*

Obfervations on the ufe of the argentum nitratum in chorea St. Viti. (*Duncan's* A. of Med. Y. 1800. p. 344.)

HULLOCK, [John] *Esq. of Gray's-Inn, Barrifter at Law.*

The law of cofts. 1792. 8. (9 fh.) The law of cofts in civil actions and criminal proceedings: with an appendix, containing the cafes to Hilary term 1796 inclufive. 1797. 8. (9 fh.)

HULME, [Nathaniel] *M. Dr. F. R. S. and A. S.*
Experiments and obſervations on the light which is ſpontaneously emitted, with ſome degree of permanency, from various bodies. (Phil. Transact. Y. 1800. p. 161. Y. 1801. p. 403. *Nicholſon's* Journal. Vol. 4. p. 421. 451. Y. 1802. May. p. 31. June. p. 100.)

*HULME, [Obadiah] *of Charterhouſe-ſquare, London.* born .... died 1791. May 30.
See Gentleman's Magaz. Y. 1791. June. p. 586.
Hiſtorical eſſay on the Engliſh conſtitution; 1770. 8. (Author of ſeveral other tracts.)

HUME, [David] *Esq. Advocate, Profeſſor of the law of Scotland in the Univerſity of Edinburgh.*
Commentaries on the law of Scotland, reſpecting the deſcription and puniſhment of crimes. Vol. 1. 2. 1797. 4. (2 L. 2 ſh.)

*HUME, [Guſtavus] *Sen. State-Surgeon of Dublin.*
Obſervations on the treatment of internal and external diſeaſes and management of children. 1803. 8. (5 ſh.)

*HUME, [J....] *Esq.*
Remarks on certain properties of barytes in its combination with mineral acids; and on two new ſalts never before deſcribed. (*Tilloch's* Philoſ. Mag. Vol. 14. p. 357.)

*HUMFRIES, [Iſaac] *Esq. reſident in India and employed in the company's ſervice.*
Account of a ſpontaneous inflammation. (Philoſ. Transact. Y. 1794. p. 426.)

HUMPAGE, [Benjamin] *Surgeon.*
Phyſiological reſearches into the moſt important parts of the animal oeconomy; — 1795. 8. (5 ſh.)

*HUMPHREY, [George] *A. L. S.*
Account of the gizzard of the ſhell called by Linnaeus bulla lignaria. (Transact. of L. S. Vol. 2. p. 15.)

*HUMPHREYS, [.....] *of Virginia.*
Account of the good effects of the magnolia acuminata in rheumatiſm. (*Duncan's* M. C. Dec. 2. Vol. 8. p. 445.) An account of the life and character of Mr. *John Pierce*, Paymaſter Gen. in the U. St. —; who died at New-York, Aug. 1788. (American Muſeum Y. 1788. Oct. p. 366.)

HUMPHREY,

UMPHREYS, [David] *Colonel in the ſervice of the United States and Miniſter plenipotentiary of the U. St. at Madrid.*

born at Derby, ſtate of Connecticut about the Y. 1752 or 1753.

See Monthly Magaz. Y. 1798. Sept. p. 167. *Hegewiſch* u. *Ebeling's* Amerik. Magaz. B. 1. S. 31.

Addreſs to the armies of the United States of America, a poem. 1785. 4. (2 ſh.) On the happineſs of America, addreſſed to the citizens of the United States. 1786. 4. (2 ſh.) Eſſay on the life of Gen. *Putman.* Hartford. 1788. The widow of Malabar, translated from the french. 1790. Miſcellaneous works. New-York. 1790. 8. (12 ſh.) Poem on induſtry. 1794. Devices and inſcriptions of American medals. (American Muſeum. Y. 1787. p. 494.)

HUNT, [Charles N....] *Conveyancer of Lincoln's-Inn.*

A deed of appointment of truſtees in purſuance of the 66 ſection of an act of parliament, paſſed 38 Geo. 3 Chap. 60. intitled, an act for making perpetual, ſubject to redemption and purchaſe in the manner therein ſtated, the ſeveral ſums of money now charged in Great-Britain as a landtax for one year from the 25 day of March 1798. — 1798. (1 ſh.)

HUNT, [John] *Surgeon.*

Hiſtorical ſurgery, or the progreſs of the ſcience of medicine on inflammation, mortification and gunſhot wounds. 1801. 4. (1 L. 3 ſh.)

HUNT, [Iſaac] *A. M. Of the Colleges of New-York and Philadelphia.*

Sermon preached before the aſſociation of Antigallicans. 1778. 4. (1 ſh. 6 d.) Sermon on taxes. 17.. Rights of Engliſhmen: an antidote to the poiſon now vending by the tranſatlantic republican *Thomas Paine.* In reply to his whimſical attacks againſt the conſtitution and government of Great-Britain. 1791. 8. (2 ſh.)

HUNT, [J.... H.... L....] *late of the grammar ſchool of Chriſt's Hoſpital.*

Juvenilia, or, a collection of poems, written between the ages of 12 and 16. 1801. 8. (6 ſh.)

*HUNT, [J.... N....]
Letter 1. 2. on the bank of England. (Monthly Magaz. Y. 1801. Oct. p. 191. Dec. p. 399.)

*HUNT, [Rowland] *Esq. a Magistrate of the county of Salop.*
A new year's gift, to all workmen and apprentices. 1796. (6 d.) The prosperity of Great-Britain compared with the state of France, her conquests and allies; 1796. 8. (1 sh. 6 d.) Provision for the poor, by the union of houses of industry with country parishes. 1797. 8. (1 sh.) A word on the times, to those who buy: also, five minutes advice before going to market, to those who sell. 1800. 8. (4 d.) Memoir on the distribution of farms, farm-buildings. (Comm. to the B. of Agr. Vol. 1. p. 58.)

*HUNT, [Samuel Reeves]
On feeding horses with potatoes. (Comm. and Agric. Magaz. Y. 1799. Aug. p. 13.)

*HUNT, [Thomas] *D. D. F. R. and A. S. S. Professor of Arabic and Hebrew in the University at Oxford.*
born 1704. died Oct. 31. 1774.
See Gentleman's Magaz. Y. 1788. June. p. 508. Y. 1800. Jan. p. 8. Y. 1801, Febr. p. 101.
De antiquitate, elegantia, utilitate linguae arabicae. 1739. Dissertation on Proverbs VII, 22. 23. 1743. De usu dialectorum orientalium ac praecipue arabicae in hebraico codice interpretando. 1748. Proposals for printing *Abdollatiphi* historiae Aegypti compendium; 1746. (with a full account of the work accompanying them: which however he never published: See Gentleman's Mag. Vol. 51. p. 455. Vol. 72. (Y. 1802.) Dec. p. 1109.) Works of Bishop *Hooper*. 1757. Observations on several passages in the book of proverbs. Oxf. 1775. 4. (5 sh.)

*HUNT, [William] *Esq. A. M. of Lincoln's-Inn; Barrister at Law.*
The law and practice of distresses and replevin by the late Lord chief Bar. *Gilbert* Ed. 3. with considerable additions. 1793. 8. (5 sh.) Collection of cases on the annuity act, with an epitome of the

the practice relative to the enrolment of memorials. 1794. 8. (4 sh.)

*HUNTER, [.....] *Mrs. of Norwich.*

Letitia, or, the castle without a spectre. Vol. 1-4. 1801. 12. (1 L. 1 sh.) The history of the Grubthorpe family, or, the old batchelor and his sister Penelope. Vol. 1-3. 1802. 8. (13 sh. 6 d.) Letters from Mrs. *Palmerstone* to her daughter, inculcating morality, by entertaining narratives. Vol. 1-3. 1803. 12. (15 sh.)

*HUNTER, [.....]

Considerations on the causes and effects of the present war. 1794. (2 sh.)

*HUNTER, [.....] *Dr.*

—— and *Hornby*, of York, on the distillation of ardent spirit from carrots. (*Tilloch's* Philos. Magaz. Vol. 6. p. 12.)

*HUNTER, [A....] *of York.*

A new method of raising wheat for a series of years on the same land. (*Young's* A. of Agr. Vol. 27. p. 242. 440.)

*HUNTER, [Alexander] *Surgeon at Dumbarton,*

History of a case, terminating successfully, in which an inverted uterus was extirpated. (*Duncan's* A. of Med. Y. 1799. p. 366.)

HUNTER, [Alexander] *M. Dr. F. R. S. L. and E. Physician at York.*

Observations on the nature and method of cure of the phthisis pulmonalis, or, consumption of the lungs — by the late *William White* — with the origin, progress and design of the York lunatic asylum. 1792. 8. (2 sh. 6 d.) Outlines of agriculture. 1795. 8. (2 sh.) übers. von *B. v. Salis*. Altona, 1799. 8. A new method of raising wheat for a series of years on the same land. 1796. 4. (2 d.) Ed. 2. 1797. 4. (3 d.) (Monthly Magaz. Y. 1796. Nov. p. 768.) An illustration of the analogy between vegetable and animal parturition. 1797. 8. (1 sh.) General view of a plan of universal and equal taxation. 1797. 8. (6 d.) Reflections on the state of an egg in incubation. (*Young's* A. of Agr. Vol. 3. p. 381.) On *Brogniart's* vegetable powder. (Ibid. Vol. 7. p. 312.) On the nourishment of vegetables. (Comm. and

Agric. Magaz. Y. 1803. April p. 263.) On a rich and cheap compoſt &c. (Ibid. 1803. April. p. 281.) Georgical eſſays. Vol. 1–4. 1803. 8.

*HUNTER, [D....] *M. Dr.*

Outlines of agriculture. 1802. 8. (2 ſh.)

HUNTER, [Henry] *D. D. Miniſter of the Scots-church at London-Wall.*

born in Scotland 1741. died 1802. Oct. 27. at Briſtol.

See Gentleman's Magaz. Y. 1802. Nov. p. 1072. Monthly Magaz. 1802. Dec. p. 456.

Sacred biography — Vol. 5. 1791. 8. Vol. 6. 1792. 8. (12 ſh.) Vol. 7. 1802. (10 ſh. 6 d.) A courſe of lectures delivered at the Scots-church at London-Wall. Vol. 1–6. 1784–1792. 8. Sermon on occaſion of the trial, condemnation and execution of Louis XVI late King of France: with ſome additions and illuſtrations. To which is ſubjoined — a republication of a diſcourſe on the riſe and fall of the papacy, originally publiſhed in the firſt year of the preſent century by *Robert Fleming* V. D. M. then Miniſter of the Scots-church in London. 1793. 8. (3 ſh. 6 d.) Eſſays on phyſiognomy, deſigned to promote the knowledge and the love of mankind by *John Caſpar Lavater*, tranſlated from the french. Vol. 1–5. 1789–1798. 4. (30 L.) Letters of *Euler* to a german princeſs, on different ſubjects in phyſics and philoſophy; tranſlated from the french with original notes and a gloſſary of foreign and ſcientific terms. Vol. 1. 2. 1795. 8. (16 ſh.) Sermons preached at different places and on various occaſions; collected and republiſhed in their reſpective order: to which are ſubjoined, memoirs, anecdotes and illuſtrations relating to the perſons, inſtitutions and events, connected with the ſeveral ſubjects. 1795. 8. (12 ſh.) Studies of nature by *J. H. Bernardin de St. Pierre*, tranſlated. Vol. 1–5. 1796. 8. (1 L. 10 ſh.) Ed. 2. Vol. 1–3. 1799. 8. (1 L. 7 ſh.) Sermons tranſlated from the original french of *James Saurin*, Vol. 6. (in continuation of the 5 tranſlated by Mr. *Robinſon*.) 1796. 8. (6 ſh.) A new edition. Vol. 1–6. 1800. 8. (1 L. 10 ſh.) Travels in upper and lover

lover Egypt by C. S. *Sonnini*, translated from the french. Vol. 1-3. 1799. 8. (1 L. 7 fh.) Letters on the evidences of chriftianity; four by *John Fell* and eight by *Henry Hunter*. 1798. 8. (6 fh.) Life of Catherine 2. Emprefs of Ruffia by *J. Caftera*, translated from the french edition. 1800. 8.
(Several fingle fermons.)

*HUNTER, [James] *Veterinarian.*
A complete dictionary of farriery and horfemanfhip. 1796. 8. (5 fh.)

*HUNTER, [John] *Mrs.*
Poems. 1802. 8. (5 fh.)

HUNTER, [John] *F. R. S. Edint Profeffor of Humanity in the Univerfity of St. Andrews.*
Virgilii Opera. Vol. 1. 2. 1799. 12.

HUNTER, [John] *M. Dr. F. R. S: Surgeon Extraordinary to the King and Surgeon General to the army.* (Brother of the late *Will. Hunter.*)
born 14 July 1725. died 1793. Oct. 16.
See Gentleman's Magaz. Y. 1793. Oct. p. 964. Nov. p. 1049. Allg. Litt. Zeit. J. 1793. ItBl. N. 125. S. 997. *Hutchinfon's* Biographia Medica. Vol. 1. p. 472. *Jeffe Foot*, life of *John Hunter*. 1794. 8. See *Everard Home.*
Obfervations on certain parts of the animal oeconomy. 1787. 4. (16 fh.) Im Auszuge überf. u. mit Anmerk. von *A. F. A. Scheller.* Braunfchweig. 1803. 8. Obfervations on the cafe of mollities offium — überf. Repertor. Chir. u. Mediz. Abhandl. Th. 1. S. 17. On the blood, inflammation and gun fhot wounds, to which is prefixed a fhort account of the Author's life by *Everard Home.* 1794. 4. (1 L. 11 fh. 6 d.) überf. mit Anmerk. von *E. B. G. Hebenftreit.* B. 1. 2. 1797. 1800. 8.

*HUNTER, [John] *M. Dr. Phyfician to the Army, F. R. S.*
Diff. De hominum varietatibus et harum caufis. Edinb. 1775. 8. Account of the fuccefsfull treatment of a fuppofed hydrocephalus internus. (Med. Obferv. Vol. 6. p. 52.) Some experiments made upon rum, in order to afcertain the caufe of the colic, frequent among the foldiers in the island of Jamaica in the Years 1781 and 1782. (Med. Transact.

Transact. Vol. 3. p. 327.) Account of a case of an uncommon disease in the omentum; and of a double kidney on one side of the body with none on the other. (Ibid. p. 250.) Observations on the disease commonly called the jail or hospital fever. (Ibid. p. 345.) Some observations on the heat of wells and springs in the island of Jamaica and on the temperature of the earth below the surface in different climates. (Phil. Transact. Y. 1788. p. 53. übers. *Gren* J. d. Phys. Th. 1. S. 111.) Observations on the diseases of the army in Jamaica and on the best means of preserving the health of Europeans, in that climate. 1788. 8. (5 sh.) übers. Leipzig. 1792. 8. Observations on the inflammation of the internal coats of veins. (Transact. of Med. and Chir. Soc. Y. 1793. p. 18.) Account of a dissection of a man, that died of a suppression of urine, produced by a collection of hydatids, between the neck of the bladder and rectum, with observations on the manner in which hydatids grow and multiply in the human body. (Ibid. Y. 1793. p. 34.) On introsusception. (Ibid. Y. 1793. p. 103.) A case of paralysis of the muscles of deglutition, cured by an artificial mode of conveying food and medicines into the stomach. (Ibid. Y. 1793. p. 182.) Observations and heads of inquire on canine madness drawn from the cases and materials collected by the society, respecting that disease. (Ibid. Y. 1793. p. 294.) Account of the appearances after death. (Ibid. Vol. 2. p. 63.) Experiments and observatious on the growth of bones. (Ibid. Vol. 2. p. 277.) Observations on the fossil bones presented to the R. Soc. by — the Margrave of Anspach. (Phil. Transact. Y. 1794. p. 407.) Observations on bees. (Ibid. Y. 1792. p. 128. New-London Med. Journ. Vol. 1. p. 314.) An account of the free-martin. (American Museum Y. 1788. Dec. p. 521.) Account of the organ of hearing in fish. (Massachusetts Magaz. Y. 1791. March. p. 160.) Curious observations on the spermaceti whale. (Ibid. Y. 1795. July. p. 216.)

*HUNTER, [John] *Esq. Post-Captain in his Majesty's navy.*

Historical journal of the transactions at Port Jackson

ſon and Norfolk Island with the diſcoveries which have been made in New-South Wales and in the Southern Ocean ſince the publication of *Phillip's* voyage, compiled from the official papers — 1793. 4. (1 L. 11 ſh. 6 d.) überſ. von *John Balbach*. Th. 1. 2. Nürnberg. 1794. 8.

*HUNTER, [John] *Esq.*

A tribute to the manes of unfortunate poets in four cantos, with other poems on various ſubjects. 1798. 8. (5 ſh.) Cecco's complaint, translated from il lamento di cecco da Varluugo of *Franceſco Baldovini*. 1800. 8. (2 ſh.)

*HUNTER, [Maria]

Fitzroy, or the impulſe of the moment; a novel. Vol. 1. 2. 1792. 8. (6 ſh.) Ella; or, He's always in the way. Vol. 1. 2. 1798. 8. (7 ſh.)

*HUNTER, [Robert] *in the ſervice of the Eaſt-India Company, Chief-Surgeon at Fort William in Bengal.*

Account of the island of Bourbon, as it was in the year 1763. (European Magaz. Y. 1795. April p. 228.)

*HUNTER, [William] *Esq. of the Inner-Temple.*

Conſiderations on the cauſes and effects of the preſent war and on the neceſſity of continuing it, till a regular government is eſtabliſhed in France. 1794. 8. (2 ſh.) Travels in the year 1792 through France, Turkey and Hungary to Vienna; concluding with an account of that city. 1796. 8. (6 ſh.) Ed. 2. Vol. 1. 2. 1798. 8. (14 ſh.) überſ. von *J. G. Gruber*. Leipzig. 1797. 8. A ſhort view of the political ſituation of the northern powers, founded on obſervations made during a tour through Ruſſia, Sweden and Denmark, in the laſt ſeven months of the Year 1800 with conjectures on the probable iſſue of the approaching conteſt. 1801. 8. (2 ſh. 6 d.) A few reflections on recent events, concluding with a defence of Sir *Hyde Parker's* convention with Denmark. 1801. 8. (1 ſh.) A vindication of the cauſe of Great-Britain; with ſtrictures on the conduct of France ſince the ſignature of the preliminaries of peace. 1803. 8. (2 ſh.)

*HUNTER,

HUNTER, [William] *Esq. Surgeon in the East-Indies.*

Some account of the aſtronomical labours of Jayaſinha, Rajah of Ambhere or Jayanagar. (Aſiat. Reſ. Vol. 5. p. 177.) Report on the meloe, or lytta. (Ibid. Vol. 5. p. 216.) Aſtronomical obſervations made in the upper parts of Hinduſtan (Y. 1791. 1792.) and on a journey thence to Oujein. (Ibid. Vol. 4. p. 141.) Aſtronomical obſervations (Y. 1793. 1794.) (Ibid. Vol. 4. p. 359.) Aſtronomical obſervations made in the upper provinces of Hinduſtan. (Ibid. Vol. 5. p. 413.) Hiſtory of an anevriſm of the aorta. (Mem. of M. S. of L. Vol. 5. p. 349.) On the plant morinda and its uſes. (Ibid. Vol. 4. p. 35.) Narrative of a journey from Agra to Oujein. (Ibid. Vol. 6. p. 7.)

HUNTINGFORD, [George Iſaac] *D. D. Warden of St. Mary's College, near Winchester, formerly Fellow of New-College, Oxford.*

Twelve diſcourſes on different ſubjects. 1795. Vol. 2. 1797. 8. (12 ſh.) A call for union with the eſtabliſhed church. 1800. 8. (4 ſh. 6 d.)
(Several ſingle ſermons.)

HUNGTINFORD, [J....]

Queries relating to agriculture, ſubmitted by the Soc. at Odiham, in Hampſhire for the encouragement of that art —; (*Young's* A. of Agr. Vol. 3. p. 231.)

***HUNTINGTON, [William]** *S. S. Miniſter of the goſpel at Providence Chapel, little Titchfield-ſtreet and at Monkwell-ſtreet meeting; a Methodiſt Preacher.*

(His name is originally *Hunt.* He has tacked S. S. to his aſſumed name, which, as he ſays, ſignifies „Sinner Saved;„ (See Gentleman's Magaz. Y. 1798. Oct. p. 827.)) Forty ſtripes ſave none for ſatan, or, the devil beaten with rods. 1792. 8. (1 ſh. 6 d.) Advocates for devils refuted and their hope of the damned demoliſhed, or, an everlaſting taſk for Wincheſter and all his confederates. 1794. 8. (1 ſh. 6 d.) The lying prophet examined and his falſe predictions diſcovered, being a diſſection of the prophecies of *Richard Brothers.* 1795. 8. (1 ſh.) Arminianiſm ſkeletoniſed. 17..

HURD,

HURD, [Richard] *D. D. Lord-Bishop of Worcester and Clerk of the closet to his Majesty, F. R. S. of Gottingen.*

See Public Characters of 1798 and 1799. p. 242. Horatii ars poetica; Epistola ad Pisones — übers. von *Eschenburg*. Th. 1. 2. Leipzig. 1772. 8. Ode on the peace of Aix-la-Chapelle 17.. Works of *William Warburton*, Lord-Bishop of Gloucester. Vol. 1-7. 1788. 4. (6 L. 6 sh.) An octavo supplemental volume of *W. Warburton* works, or, a collection of all the new pieces contained in the quarto edition. 1788. Discourse by way of general preface to the quarto edition of Bish. *Warburton's* works, containing some account of the life, writings and character of the author. 1794. 4.

HURDIS, [C....]

Extraordinary crop of wheat. (*Young's* A. of Agr. Vol. 29. p. 445.)

HURDIS, [James] *B. D. late Professor of Poetry in the University of Oxford; Fellow of Magdalen College, Oxford.*

born 1763. died 1801. Dec. 23. at Blackburn, co. Lancaster.

See Gentleman's Magaz. Y. 1801. Supplem. p. 1216. Y. 1802. Febr. p. 179.

The village curate. 1788. 4. Poems. 17.. 8. *Mich. Drayton*, Englands heroical epistles, published with notes and illustrations. 1788. 8. Cursory remarks upon the arrangement of the plays of *Shakespeare*, occasioned by reading Mr. *Malone's* essay on the chronological order of those celebrated pieces. 1792. 8. (1 sh.) Reflections upon the commencement of a new year. 1793. 8. (6 d.) Select critical remarks upon the english version of the first ten chapters of Genesis. 1793. 8. (1 sh.) *Sir *Thomas More*, a tragedy, by the author of the village curate and other poems. 1792. 8. (2 sh.) Equality, a sermon. 1794. 8. (2 sh.) Tears of affection, a poem, occasioned by the death of a sister tenderly beloved. 1794. 8. (2 sh. 6 d.) A poem written towards the close of the Y. 1794. on the prospect of the marriage of the Prince of Wales. 1795. 4. (1 sh. 6 d.) Lectures on poetry. Nrb. 1. 1797. 4. (2 sh. 6 d.) On the nature and occa-

occafion of pfalm and prophecy, twelve critical differtations. 1800. 8. (5 fh.) The favourite village, a poem. 1800. 4. (6 fh.)

*HURLSTONE, [Thomas]

Juft in time, a comic opera. 1792. 8. (1 fh .6 d.) Crotchet lodge, a farce, in 2 acts. 1795. 8. (1 fh.)

*HUTCHESON, [Robert Kyrle] *Esq. Barrifter at Law; Briftol.*

On excife and „quitam„ informations, as they relate to fummary proceedings before juftices of the peace; the mode of profecuting and defending fuch informations; and the law, evidence and modern determinations thereon; — 1797. 8. (4 fh.) For maltfters, brewers and hop-planters; all the excife laws and adjudged cafes, as they relate to the above perfons, claffed under each ftage and procefs of manufacture — &c. 1798. 8. (2 fh. 6 d.)

*HUTCHINS, [Henry]

Humorous oration on nofes. (Maffachufetts Magaz. Y. 1791. Oct. p. 622. Columbian Magaz. Y. 1790. July p. 38.)

HUTCHINS, [Thomas] *Esq. Geographer General to the United States of America.*

born in Monmouth county, Newjerfey. died 1788. Apr. 20.

See Maffachufetts Magaz. Y. 1791. July. p. 422. Defcription of the Miffifippi rivers. (Maffachufetts Magaz. Y. 1790. July. p. 415. New-York Magaz. Y. 1794. Jan. p. 9.) Defcription of a remarkable rock and cafcade, near the weftern fide of the Youghiogeny river —. (Tr. of A. S. Vol. 2. p. 50. New-York Magaz. Y. 1794. June. p. 368.)

*HUTCHINSON, [....] *Miff.*

Exhibitions of the heart; a novel. Vol. 1-4. 1799. 12. (1 L. 1 fh.)

*HUTCHINSON, [.....]

*Collection of original papers relative to the hiftory of the colony of Maffachufetts-bay. Bofton. 1769. 8. The remarkable adventures of three of Charles I judges who paffed into New-England after the reftoration of Charles II and there died, having been fequeftered from the world for many years. (Columbian Magaz. Y. 1788. Sept. p. 497.)

*HUTCHIN-

*HUTCHINSON, [Benjamin] *Surgeon at Southwell, Nottinghamshire.*

Account of the epidemic disease, commonly called the influenza, which appeared in Nottinghamshire and most other parts of the kingdom, in the months of Nov. and Dec. 1792. (New-London Med. Journ. Vol. 2. p. 174.) A case of the psora or itch, in which it appears, that mercury is not a specific in that complaint. (Ibid. Vol. 2. p. 176.) Observations on hydrophobia. (Ibid. Vol. 2. p. 179.)

*HUTCHINSON, [Benjamin] *M. M. S. of Lond. Phys. Soc. of Guys Hospital and of the London Company of Surgeons.*

Biographia medica, or, historical and critical memoirs of the lives and writings of the most eminent medical characters that have existed from the earliest account of time to the present period, with a catalogue of their literary productions. Vol. 1. 2. 1799. 8. (16 sh.) Experiments on the external use of tartarised antimony. (Mem. of M. S. of L. Vol. 5. p. 81.)

*HUTCHINSON, [H....]

Curious fact in the growth of oats. (Comm. and Agric. Mag. Y. 1801. p. 310.)

*HUTCHINSON, [J....]

Natural history of the frog fish of Surinam. York. 1797. 4.

HUTCHINSON, [Sir John Hely] *Principal Secretary of state for Ireland; Privy-counsel of that kingdom, M. P. for the city of Cork; Provost of Trinity-College, Dublin and LL. Dr. Commander in Chief of the Army of Egypt.*

born 1715. died 1794. Sept. 5.

See Public Characters of 1801 and 1802. p. 479. Gentleman's Magaz. Y. 1794. Sept. p. 866.

*HUTCHINSON, [Michael] *M. Dr. Physician at Wolverhampton.*

Account of a singular tumour on the arm and the appearances on dissection. (New-London Med. Journ. Vol. 1. p. 121.) Account of a case of spina bifida. (Ibid. Vol. 1. p. 338.) Case of abortion at 7 months, during the small-pox, terminating favourably. (Ibid. Vol. 1. p. 353.)

HUTCHINSON, [Thomas] *Esq. late Governour of Massachusetts.*

The history of Massachusetts, from the first settlement thereof in 1628 until the year 1750. Ed. 3. with additional notes and corrections. Vol. 1. 2. Salem. 1795. 8. (4 Dollar.)

HUTCHINSON, [William] *F. A. S.*

The history and antiquities of the county palatine of Durham. Vol. 3. 17.. The history of the county of Cumberland and some places adjacent, from the earliest account to the present time — Vol. 1. 2. 1795. 1797. 4. (2 L. 2 sh.)

HUTTON, [Charles] *LL. Dr. F. R. S. Lond. and Edinb. Professor of Mathematics in the royal military Academy, Woolwich.*

born at Newcastle-upon-Tyne, in Northumberland 1737.

See Public Characters of 1799 and 1800. p. 97. The principles of bridges — Ed. 2. with corrections and additions. 1801. 8. (5 sh.) Logarithmic tables, with improvements. Ed. 3. 1801. 8. (1 L. 1 sh.) A complete treatise on practical arithmetic and book-keeping, for the use of schools. 1764. A key to the complete treatise on practical arithmetic —. 17.. Elements of conic sections; 1787. 8. A mathematical and philosophical dictionary — Vol. 1. 2. 1795. 1796. 4. (2 L. 14 sh.) A new course of mathematics composed — for the use of the — cadets in the R. military academy at Woolwich. Vol. 1. 2. 1798. 8. (15 sh.) Select amusements in philosophy and mathematics — translated from the french of *M. L. Despiau*, with several corrections and additions, particularly a large table of the chances or odds at play. 1801. 12. (5 sh. 6 d.) Recreations in mathematics and natural philosophy, first composed by *Ozanam*, lately greatly enlarged by *Montucla* and now translated into English and improved with many additions and observations. Vol. 1-4. 1803. 8. (3 L. 3 sh.) — — *George Shaw*, M. Dr. and *Richard Pearson*, M. Dr. An abridgement of the philosophical transactions of the royal society, London. Vol. 1. Part 1. 2. (1 L. 1 sh.) to be continued monthly. 1803. The compendious measurer, being

being a brief yet comprehensive treatise on mensurations — Ed. 5. 1803. 12. (4 sh.)

HUTTON, [George] *B D: Curate of Plumbtree near Nottingham and late Fellow of St. Mary Magdalen College, Oxford.*

An appeal to the nation on the subject of Mr. *Gilbert Wakefield's* letter to *Will. Wilberforce*, Esq. M. P. To which are subjoined four sermons on important subjects, connected with the appeal. 1798. 8. (3 sh.)

HUTTON, [George]

Amantus and Elvira, or, ingratitude exemplified in the character of ingratus. 1794. 12. (3 sh.)

HUTTON, [James] *M. Dr: F. R. S. Edin.*

Investigation of the principles of knowledge and of the progress of reason, from sense to science and philosophy. Vol. 1-3 Edinb. 1794. 4. (3 L. 15 sh.) Dissertations on different subjects in natural philosophy. 1792. 4. (1 L. 1 sh.) Dissertation upon the philosophy of light, heat and fire, in seven parts. 1794. 8. (6 sh.) (Tr. of E. S. Vol. 4. H. p. 7.) Theory of the earth, with proofs and illustrations. Vol. 1. 2. 1795. 8. (14 sh.) Observations on granite. (Tr. of E. S. Vol. 3. P. p. 77.) Of the flexibility of the Brasilian stone. (Ibid. Vol. 3. P. p. 86.) On the sulphurating of metals. (Ibid. Vol. 4. H. p. 27.)

HUTTON, [William] *F. A. S. Edin.*

born at Derby 1723. Sept. 30. and long resident at Birmingham.

See Public Characters of 1802 and 1803. p. 402. History of Derby from the remote ages of antiquity to the year 1791. describing its situation, air, soil, water, streets, buildings and government, with the illustrious families which have inherited its honours. 1791. 8. (7 sh.) The barbers, or the road to riches. 1793. 8. (1 sh.) The history of the roman wall, which crosses the island of Great-Britain from the german ocean to the Irish sea, describing its ancient state and its appearance in the year 1801. 1802. 8. Memoirs of Mr. *Robert Bage* in the parish of St. Alkmond's (born at Darley, Derby, Febr. 29. 1728. died 1801.

Ll 2 Sept.

Sept. 1.) 1802. An account of *John Baskerville*, printer. (New-York Magaz. Y. 1791. April p. 209. Massachusetts Magaz. Y. 1791. Nov. p. 673.) Remarks upon North Wales: being the result of 16 tours through that part of the principality. 1803. 8. (7 sh. 6 d.)

*HYNAM, [Robert] *Surgeon at Ratcliff Highway.*
Case of an ophthalmia cured by the application of oleum terebinthinae. (Mem. of M. S. of L. Vol. 5. p. 325.)

*HYNAM, [Robert] *of St. Petersbourg.*
Description of his instrument for gauging cutters for wheel for the use of clock and watch-makers. (Tr. of the Soc. for the E. of A. Vol. 17. p. 307.)

*JACKSON, [Hall] *Dr. at Portsmouth (N. H.)*
On the efficacy of the digitalis purpurea in dropsies. (American Museum. Y. 1788. Jan. p. 59.)

*JACKSON, [J.....] *Judge Advocate.*
Minutes of the proceedings of the court martial upon Admiral Cornwallis. 1796. (2 sh. 6 d.)

*JACKSON, [John] *Esq.*
Journey from India towards England in the year 1797. by a rout commonly called over land through counties not much frequented and many of them hitherto unknown to Europeans — 1799. 8. (7 sh.) übers. im Auszz. Weimar. 1803. 8.

*JACKSON, [John]
Poems on several occasions, written chiefly in the remote parts of Cumberland and Northumberland. 1797. 12. (2 sh. 6 d.)

JACKSON, [John] *of Clements-lane; Wine-merchant, F. A. S. (an Quacker.)*
See Gentleman's Magaz. Y. 1794. March. p. 286.

*JACKSON, [John] *Jun.*
*History of the city and county of Lichfield. 1795. 8. (2 sh. 6 d.)

*JACKSON, [Joseph]
The reign of liberty, a poetical sketch. 1797. 4. (1 sh.)

*JACKSON, [Randle] *Esq.*
The substance of a speech delivered at the India house Jan. 21. 1795. 8.

JACKSON,

JACKSON, [Robert] *M. Dr. Physician at Stockton in the county of Durham.*

On the fevers of Jamaica, with some observations on the intermittent fevers of America and an appendix, containing some hints on the means of preserving the health of soldiers in hot climates. 1791. 8. (6 sh. 6 d.) übers. von *Kurt Sprengel*. Leipz. 1795. 8. Observations on the treatment of gun-shot wounds. (London M. J. Vol. II. p. 363.) An outline of the history and cure of fever, endemic and contagious; more expressly the contagious fever of jails, ships and hospitals; the concentrated endemic, vulgarly the yellow fever of the West-Indies: to which is added an explanation of the principles of military discipline and economy, with a scheme of medical arrangement for armies. 1798. 8. (7 sh.) übers. Stuttgart. 1804. 8. Remarks on the constitution of the medical department of the British army; with a detail of hospital management and an attempt to explain the action of causes in producing fever and the operation of remedies in effecting cure. 1803. 8. (7 sh. 6 d.)

JACKSON, [Seguin Henry] *M. Dr. M. R. S. Edinb. Physician to the Westminster General Dispensary and to the Infirmary of St. George's, Hannover-Square, London.*

Derma-pathologia, or practical observations, from some new thoughts on the pathology and proximate cause of the diseases of the true skin and its emanations the rete mucosum and cuticle. With an appendix containing further observations on the influence of the perspirable fluid in the production of animal heat and remarks on the late theories of scurvy. 1792. 8. (7 sh. 6 d.) übers. Erfurt. 1794. 8. Cautions to women respecting the state of pregnancy, the progress of labour and delivery, the confinement of child-bed and some constitutional diseases; —. 1798. 8. (4 sh. 6 d.)

*JACKSON, [W....] *Practical Chemist.*

A synopsis of the chemical characters, adapted to the new nomenclature, systematically arranged. 1799. (2 sh. coloured 2 sh. 6 d.)

*JACKSON, [W....]
Of the breeding, rearing and fattening of poultry. (Comm. and Agric. Magaz. Y. 1802. p. 183.)

*JACKSON, [William] *M. Dr. Phyſician at Islington.*
Cautions reſpecting ſome errors and abuſes in medicine. 17..

JACKSON, [William] *Organiſt in Exeter.*
born at Exeter 1730. in May.
See Public Characters of 1798 and 1799. p. 225. Thirty letters on various ſubjects. Ed. 3. with conſiderable additions. 1795. 8. (4 ſh.) Obſervations on the preſent ſtate of muſic in London. 1791. 8. (1 ſh.) The four ages, together with eſſays on various ſubjects. 1798. 8. (7 ſh.)

*JACKSON, [W.... F....] *Rev. (a priſoner in the new priſon Dublin on a charge of high treaſon.)*
born .... died 1798. Apr. 23.
See Gentleman's Magaz. Y. 1795. May. p. 443. Obſervations in anſwer to *Thomas Paine's* age of reaſon. 1795. 8. (2 ſh.) Sermons on practical and important ſubjects. 1795. 8. (4 ſh.)

JACOB, [John] *Esq.*
Obſervations on the beſt method of deſtroying vermin and preventing the deſtruction of young turnips by the fly. (Bath Agricult. Soc. Vol. 1. p. 223.) On the ſcab in ſheep. (*Young's* A. of Agr. Vol. 24. p. 389.)

*JAMES, [.....] *of Stockwell.*
— and *Malcolm*, on the fattening oxen and hogs by the diſtillers. (*Young's* A. of Agr. Vol. 23. p. 52.)

JAMES, [Charles] *Esq. late Captain in the weſtern regiment of Middleſex militia, and now Captain in the North York.*
Hints founded on facts, or, a curſory view of our ſeveral military eſtabliſhments; — 1791. 8. (2 ſh.) Suicide rejected, a poem, with a refutation of the doctrine inculcated on principles of chriſtianity: to which is added, time vanquiſhed by eternity, an ode. 1791. 4. (1 ſh. 6 d.) Poems. 1792. 8. (1 L. 1 ſh.) Audi alteram partem, or, an extenuation of the conduct of the french revolutioniſts from the 14 July 1789 until the 10 Aug. and the 2 and 3 Sept. 1792. being a curſory anſwer
to

to the manifold misrepresentations industriously circulated to injure the general character and principles of a long oppressed people. Ed. 2. 1792. 8. (1 sh.) A new edition. 1793. 8. (3 sh.) The extenuation and desultory sketch of abuses — . 17.. Proposed plan for the better regulating of the militia of Great-Britain, being an appendix to the desultory sketch of abuses in that establishment. 1794. 8. (1 sh. 6 d.) A comprehensive view of some existing cases of probable misapplication in the distribution of contingent allowances, particularly in the militia of Great-Britain; shewing the wisdom and propriety of a more general consolidation than has hitherto taken place. 1797. 8. (2 sh. 6 d.) The regimental companion; containing the relative duties of every officer in the British army and rendering the principles of system and responsibility familiar. 1799. 12. (5 sh.) A new and enlarged military dictionary. 1802. 4. (2 sh.)

°JAMES, [E.... M....]

A selection from the annals of virtue of Mad. *de Silling*, translated. 1795. 8. (5 sh.)

°JAMES, [Henry]

A short account of Smith's air-pump vapour-bath. (*Tilloch's* Phil. Magaz. Vol. 14. p. 293.)

°JAMES, [Isaac]

Providence displayed, or, the remarkable adventures of *Alexander Selkirk*, of Largo, in Scotland; — 1800. 12. (3 sh.) An essay on the sign of the prophet Jonah, — 1802. 8. (1 sh. 6 d.)

°JAMES, [S....] *Schoolmaster, formerly of Christ's Hospital.*

Dilworth improved, or, a new guide to the english tongue wherein the orthography is rendered analogous to the pronunciation. 1799. 12. (1 sh.)

°JAMES, [Samuel] *Surgeon.*

Observations on the bark of a particular species of willow; showing its superiority to the peruvian and its singular efficacy in the cure of agues, intermittent fevers, fluor albus, abscesses, hemorrhages — illustrated with cases. 1792. 8. (2 sh.)

*JAMES, [William] *at Garraway.*
On the multiplication of wheels in carriages. (*Young's* A. of Agr. Vol. 21. p. 516.)

*JAMESON, [Macmillan] *Surgeon: of Port Royal in the Island of Jamaica.*
Two dissections, (Mem. of M. S. of L. Vol. 3. p. 573.)

*JAMESON, [Robert] *M. R. Med. and Nat. Hist. Soc. Edinb. and L. S. London.*
An outline of the mineralogy of the Shetland islands and the island of Arran, illustrated with copper plates. With an appendix, containing observations on peat, kelp and coal. 1798. 8. (7 sh.) Mineralogy of the Scottish isles, with mineralogical observations made in a tour through different parts of the mainland of Scotland and dissertations upon peat and kelp. Vol. 1. 2. 1801. 4. (1 L. 12 sh.) übers. von *H. W. Meuder.* Leipz. 1802. 4. Observations on kelp. (Tr. of Highland Soc. Vol. 1. p. 43.) Examination of the supposed igneous origin of the rocks of the trapp-formation. (*Nicholson's* Journal Y. 1802. Oct. p. 111.) Observations and experiments on various saponaceous compounds, particularly the fish soap of Sir *John Dalrymple.* (Ibid. Vol. 3. p. 108.) On granite. (Ibid. Y. 1802. Aug. p. 225.) On the supposed existence of mechanical deposits and petrefactions in the primitive mountains and an account of petrefactions which have been discovered in the newest flötz trapp-formation. (Ibid. Y. 1802. Sept. p. 13.)

*JAMESON, [T....] *M. Dr.*
A geographical chart of Europe: containing the territorial and political state of Europe with the new constitutions of France and Poland — 1799. (7 sh. 6 d. in sheets and 15 sh. on canvas with rollers.)

JAMES, [Thomas] *Surgeon in Bloomsbury.*
Two cases of hydrocephalus. (Mem. of M. S. of L. Vol. 3. p. 414.)

JAMISON, [John] *D. D. F. A. S. Scot. Minister of the Gospel at Farfar.*
An alarm to Britain; or, an inquiry into the causes of the rapid progress of infidelity, in the present

fent age. 1795. 12. (2 sh. 6 d.) A vindication of the doctrine of scripture and of the primitive faith concerning the deity of Christ; in reply to Dr. *Priestley's* history of early opinions —. Vol. 1. 2. 1795. 8. (14 sh.) Eternity, a poem, addressed to free-thinkers and philosophical christians. 1798. 8. (1 sh.) Remarks on *Rowland Hill's* journal — including reflections on itinerant and lay preaching. Ed. 2. 1799. 8. (1 sh.) The use of sacred history, especially as illustrating and confirming the great doctrines of revelation. Vol. 1. 2. 1803. 8. (12 sh.)

*J'ANS, [Wrey] *Esq.*

Prices of corn &c, reduced from various measures to the Winchester standard. (*Young's* A. of Agr. Vol. 34. p. 268.) Letter to Lord *Dunstanville*. (Ib. Vol. 35. p. 113.)

*JANSON, [Baldwin] *Professor and Translator of the Dutch and French languages.*

Pocket dictionary of the dutch and english languages; in two parts. 1793. 4. (6 sh.)

*JAQUES, [William] *at Ampthill, Bedforshire.*

Produce of milk. (*Young's* A. of Agr. Vol. 32. p. 142.) Necessity of farmer's keeping accounts. (Ibid. Vol. 32. p. 305.)

JARDINE, [Alexander] *Esq. Major of the Artillery; Consul for Galicia.*

°Letters from Barbary, France, Spain, Portugal, by an English officer. Ed. 2. corrected. Vol. 1. 2. 1794. 8. (12 sh.)

*JARDINE, [B.....] *D. D. Minister at the Unitarian Chapel, Bath.*

The unpurchased love of god in the redemption of the world by Jesus Christ, a great argument for christian benevolence, illustrated in 3 discourses. To which are added, remarks on the discourses of the late *Caleb Evans* D. D. entitled: Christ crucified; and a letter to *David Bogue* of Gosport on his sermon, entitled, the great importance of having right sentiments in religion. 1792. 8. (2 sh. 6 d.)

*JARDINE, [David] *Pastor of the Unitarian Congregation at Pickwick near Bath.*
born .... died 1797. March 10.
See Gentleman's Magaz. Y. 1797. Apr. p. 352.
Monthly Magaz. Y 1797. April. p. 330.
Seasonable reflections on religious fasts, in a discourse delivered. 1794. (1 sh.) Sermons — published from the original manuscripts by *John Prior Estlin.* Vol. 1. 2. 1798. 8. (14 sh.)

*JARDINE, [L.... J....] *M. Dr.*
A letter from Pennsylvania to a friend in England, containing valuable information with respect to America. 1795. 8. (1 sh.)

*JARMAN, [James] *Rev.*
A concise view of christianity, or, a short catechism, explaining some of the principal doctrines of the christian religion, suited to young people. 1792. 8. (4 d.)

*JARMAN, [Nathaniel]
Letter on a root of rhubarb. (Tr. of the Soc. for the E. of A. Vol. 3. p. 174.)

*JARROLD, [Thomas] *from Essex; Student of Medicine at Edinburgh.*
Observations on a case of diabetes insipidus, with an account of some experiments on the urine. (*Duncan's* A. of Med. Y. 1801. p. 390.)

*JARRY, [.....] *General, Commander of the Roy. Military College at High Wycombe.*
Instructions concerning the duties of light infantry in the field. 1803. 12. (4 sh.)

*JAY, [John] *at New-York*
Letter on salt as a manure and a particular species of apple. (Comm. to the B. of Agr. Vol. 1. p. 361.) Address — on the subject of the proposed federal constitution. (American Museum Y. 1788. June. p. 554.)

*JAY, [William] *Dissenting Preacher at Bath.*
Sermons. 1802. 8. (8 sh.)

*JAZEWEL, [William] *M. Dr.*
Vademecum medicum, in duas partes divisum, quarum prior, nosologiam Cullinaeam, posterior compendium materiae medicae et pharmacopoea exhibet. Philad. 1798. 8.

IBBET-

IBBETSON, [James] *Esq. Barrister at Law;* born .... died 1790. March 26.

See Gentleman's Magaz. Y. 1790. Apr. p. 373. May. p. 473.

***JEANS**, [Thomas] *M. Dr.*

Treatise on the gout, wherein is delivered a new idea of its proximate cause and consequent means of relief; —. 1792. 8. (2 sh.) übers. Breslau u. Hirschberg. 1794. 8.

***JEANS**, [Thomas]

Potatoes mixed with meal. (*Young's* A. of Agr. Vol. 25. p. 533.)

***JEBB**, [Richard] *Esq.*

A reply to a pamphlet, entitled, arguments for and against an union. 1799. 8. (1 sh. 6 d.)

***JEE**, [George] *at Rotherham.*

Description of his invented mangle. (Tr. of the Soc. for the E. of A. Vol. 16. p. 303. *Tilloch's* Philos. Magaz. Vol. 2. p. 419.)

JEFFERSON, [Joseph] *A Dissenting Minister of Basingstoke.*

The ruins of a temple, a poem; to which is prefixed an account of the antiquity and history of holy-ghost chapel, Basingstoke, Hants. 1793. 4. (1 sh.) The young evangelist; exemplified in a view of the life of the late Rev. *John Savage;* with occasional reflections. To which is added a selection of his letters. 1798. 12. (1 sh. 6 d.)

JEFFERSON, [Thomas] *Vice-President of the United States of America.*

See Public Characters of 1800 and 1801. p. 193. Columbian Magaz. Y. 1787. July. p. 555.

Notes on the state of Virginia. Ed. 2. Philad. 1794. 8. Ed. 2. with an apppendix in which a candid and faithfull statement of facts is given relative to the murder of *Logan's* family. London. 1800. 8. Manuel of parliamentary practice for the use of the senate of the United States. 1800. Extracts from his notes on Virginia. (Columbian Magaz. Y. 1787. Aug. p. 573.) A memoir on the discovery of certain bones of a quadruped of the clawed kind in the western parts of Virginia. (Tr. of A. S. Vol. 4. p. 246. *Nicholson's* Journ. Vol. 4. p. 42. 66.) The description of a mould-beard of the

the least resistence, and of the easiest and most certain construction; (Ibid. Vol. 4. p. 313.) A description of the natural bridge, called in Virginia, Rocky bridge — (Columbian Magaz. Y. 1787. Sept. p. 617.) Opinion upon the establishment of an American naval force. (Ibid. Y. 1787. Nov. p. 767.) An account of an Indian barrow, or repository of the dead. (Ibid. Y. 1788. Febr. p. 75.) The state of religion in Virginia. (Ibid. Y. 1788. Febr. p. 86.) A comparative view of the faculties of memory, reason and imagination of Negroes. (Ibid. Y. 1788. March. p. 141.) Letter to Dr. *David Ramsay*. (American Museum Y. 1787. July. p. 83.) Notes on the olive tree. (Massachusetts Magaz. Y. 1792. June. p. 353.) See *Alex. Hamilton*.

*JEFFERYS, [John]
The pleasures of retirement, in 3 cantos with other poems. 1800. 8. (2 sh. 6 d.)

*JEKYLL, [Joseph] *Esq. M. P.*
Letters of the late *Ignatius Sancho*, an African, with memoirs of his life. 1803. 8. (7 sh.)

*JENKINS, [Herbert] *Rev. at Stourbridge.*
Grammatical cards of the English language, constructed for very young persons —. 1803. (2 sh. 6 d.)

JENKINS, [Joseph] *D. D. A Baptist Minister.*
A defence of the baptists against the aspersions and misrepresentations of *Peter Edwards*, late pastor of the baptist church at Portsea, Hants, in his book entitled, candid reasons for renouncing the principles of antipaedobaptism; in a series of letters. 1795. 12. (2 sh.) (Several single sermons.)

JENKINSON, [Charles] Earl of *Liverpool*, Lord HAWKESBURY.
See Public Characters of 1798 and 1799. p. 65. Discourse on the establishment of a national and constitutional force in England. 1794. (2 sh.) Discourse on the conduct of the government of Great-Britain with respect to neutral nation. 1794. 8. (2 sh. 6 d.) Collection of all the treaties of peace, alliance and commerce, between Great-Britain and other powers from the year 1648 to 1783: to which is prefixed a discourse on the conduct of the government

ment of Great-Britain in respect to neutral nations. Vol. 1-3. 1785. 8. (18 sh.) Speech in the British house of commons on the incorporation of the parliaments of Great-Britain and Ireland. 1800. 8. (1 sh.)

*JENKINSON, [John] *of Yealand, near Lancaster.* On the culture of waste land, with observations by *A. Young.* (*Young's* A. of Agr. Vol. 3. p. p. 89-93.) On the mildew. (Ibid. Vol. 3. p. 318.) On the inclosure of wastes. (Ibid. Vol. 3. p. 373.) Reply to Mr *Holmes's* queries on lime. (Ibid. Vol. p. 214.) Queries on inclosures. (Ibid. Vol. 6. p. 247.) On the proposed embankment of the sea, in Lancashire. (Ibid. Vol. 12. p. 273.) Crop of corn, 1790 at Yealand. (Ibid. Vol. 14. p. 437.) On the late season 1791. (Ibid. Vol. 17. p. 57.) On the present season. 1792. (Ibid. Vol. 18. p. 376.) State of Lancashire. (Ibid. Vol. 35. p. 33.)

*JENKS, [Jacquetta Agneta Mariana] *of Bellegrove priory in Wales.* Azemia, a descriptive and sentimental novel, interspersed with pieces of poetry. Vol. 1. 2. 1797. 8. (7 sh.)

*JENNER, [Edward] *Surgeon at Berkeley.* A process for preparing pure emetic tartar by re-crystallization. (Transact. of Med. and Chir. Soc. Y. 1793. p. 30.)

*JENNER, [Edward] *M. Dr. F. R. S: F. L. S. Surgeon at Berkley in Gloucestershire.*
born at Oxford. 1749.
See Public Characters of 1802 and 1803. p. 17. *Tilloch's* Phil. Magaz. Vol. 13. p. 266.
An inquiry into the causes and effects of the variolae vaccinae, a disease discovered in some of the western counties of England, particularly Gloucestershire and known by the name of cowpox. 1798. 4. (7 sh. 6 d.) Further observations on the variolae vaccinae or cowpox. 1799. 4. (2 sh. 6 d.) übers. von *G. F. Ballhorn.* Hannover. 1799. 8. 1800. 8. A continuation of facts and observations relative to the variolae vaccinae or cowpox. 1800. 4. (2 sh. 6 d.) An appendix to the treatises on the cow-pox, being a continuation of facts and observations relating to that disease. 1800.

(2 sh.

*JESSOP, [William] *Esq.*
On the fubject of inland navigation and public roads. (Comm. to the B. of Agr. Vol. 1. p. 176.)

*ILBERT, [William] *Esq. of Bowringsleigh.*
Account of planting fcotch cabbage. (Tr. of the Soc. for the E. of A. Vol. 2. p. 72.)

*ILIFF, [Edward Henry] *late of the Theatre Royal of Haymarket.*
Angelo, a novel founded on melancholy facts. Vol. 1-2. 1796. 8. (5 fh.)

*ILLINGWORTH, [William] *Of the Inner-Temple.*
An inquiry into the laws, antient and modern, refpecting foreftalling, regrating and ingroffing: together with adjudged cafes, copies of original records and proceedings in parliament relative to thofe fubjects. 1800. 8. (7 fh. 6 d.)

*IMBERT, [....]
All for the want of knowing one another. (New-York Magaz. Y. 1792. Jan. p. 50.) Rofetta, a tale. (Maffachufetts Magaz. Y. 1796. July. p. 389. Aug. p. 425.)

*IMLAY, [George] *Esq. Captain in the American Army during the late war and a Commiffioner for laying out lands in the back fettlements.*
A topographical defcription of the weftern territory of North-America; containing a fuccinct account of its climate, natural hiftory, population, agriculture, manners and cuftoms. 1792. 8. (4 fh.) überf. von *Zimmermann*. 1793. Ed. 2. with confiderable additions 1793. 8. (7 fh.) The emigrants or the hiftory of an expatriated family, being a delineation of englifh manners, drawn from real characters written in America. Vol. 1-3. 1793. 12. (9 fh.) The difcovery, fettlement and ftate of Kentuky and an effay towards the topography and natural hiftory of that important country. Ed. 3. 1797. 8. (9 fh.) Settlements in Kentucky, with obfervat. by *A. Young*. (*Young's* A. of Agr. Vol. 18. p. 550.)

IMPEY, [John] *Esq. of the Inner-Temple.*
The new inftructor clericalis, ftating the authority, jurisdiction and modern practice of the court of common pleas — Ed. 4. with confiderable additions. 1794. 8. (10 fh. 6 d.) Ed. 6. with many material

material alterations and confiderable additions including all the cafes in practice to the end of laft term. 1796. 8. (10 fh. 6 d.) The practice of the courts of king's bench and common pleas — 17.. The office of fheriff —. Ed. 2. 1800 8. (12 fh.) The modern pleader; containing the feveral forms of declarations in all actions, with notes —. 1794. 8. (7 fh.)

IMRIE, [.....] *Major.*

Mineralogical defcription of the mountain of Gibraltar. (Tr. of E. S. Vol. 4. P p. 191. *Nicholfon's* Journal. Vol. 2. p. 185. 219.)

NCHBALD, [Elizabeth] *Mrs. (Daughter of Mr. Simpfon, formerly a farmer near Bury St. Edmunds, in Suffolk.)*

See Public Characters of 1799 and 1800. p. 341. Animal magnetifm; 17.. A fimple ftory. Vol. 1.-4. 1791. (12 fh.) überf. von *Marianne Forkel.* Th. 1. 2. Leipz. 1792. 8. Next door neighbours, a comedy, in 3 acts, from the french drama l'indigent and le diffipateur. 1791. 8. (1 fh. 6 d.) Every one has his fault, a comedy. Ed. 3. 1793. 8. (1 fh. 6 d.) The wedding day, a comedy. 1794. 8. (1 fh.) Nature and art. Vol. 1. 2. 1796. 8. (7 fh.) überf. Leipz. 1797. 8. Wives as they were and maids as they are. 1797. 8. (2 fh.) Lover's vows; a play, in 5 acts, from the German of *Kotzebue.* 1798. 8. (2 fh.) The wife man of the eaft, from the German of *Kotzebue*, a play, in 5 acts. 1799. 8. (2 fh.)

INCLEDON, [Benjamin] *Esq.*

Account of the hofpital of St. Margaret, at Pilton in Devonfhire. (Arch. Vol. 12. p. 211.)

INGERSOL, [Charles Jared]

Edwy and Elgiva, a tragedy in 5 acts. 1802.

INGLIS, [Henry David] *One of the Paftors of the Baptift Church in Edinburgh.*

Two letters to the public, illuftrating the doctrine of the grace of God and exemplifying it in the late cafe of *William Mills.* 1791. 12. (8 d.) Sermon, proving from the word of God, the all important doctrine of the Godhead of Jefus Chrift. 1792. 8. (6 d.)

*INGLIS, [Hugh] *Esq.*
Economical food for the poor. (*Young's* A. of Agr. Vol. 26. p. 213.) Experiments in transplanting wheat. (Ibid. Vol 27. p. 497.)

*INGRAHAM, [Duncan] *Jun.*
* Extract of his letter upon his return from Niagara Aug. 8. 1792. (Coll. of Massachusetts H. S. Y. 1792. p. 284.)

*INGRAM, [Alexander]
The elements of *Euclid*, viz. the first six books with the XI and XII. 1801. 8. (6 sh.)

INGRAM, [Dale] *Surgeon to Christ's Hospital, London.*
born .... died 1793. Apr. 5. in a very advanced age.
See Gentleman's Magaz. Y. 1793. April. p. 380.

INGRAM, [Robert Acklom] *B. D: Curate of Boxted, in Essex, Fellow and formerly Tutor of Queen's College, Cambridge.*
Accounts of the ten tribes of Israel in America, originally published by *Manasseh* ben *Israel*, with observations thereon and extracts from sacred and prophane —. 1792. 8. (1 sh.) Enquiry into the present condition of the lower classes and the means of improving it, including some remarks on Mr. *Pitt's* bill for the better support and maintenance of the poor. 1797. 8. (2 sh. 6 d.) A syllabus or abstract of a system of political philosophy; to which is prefixed a dissertation, recommending that the study of political economy be encouraged in the universities and that a course of public lectures be delivered on that subject. 1799. 8. (2 sh.) An essay on the importance of schools of industry and religious instruction; in which the necessity of promoting the good education of poor girls its particularly considered. 1801. 12. (1 sh.)
(Several single sermons.)

INNES, [James Dunbar] *A. M. Surgeon in London.*
born ..... died 178. (?)

INNES, [John] *Prosector at Edinburgh.*
born .... died 1777. Jan. 12.

*JOBSON, [W....] *at Turwelaws.*
Account of some interesting experiments on the various

various modes of raising turnips. (Comm. to the B. of Agr. Vol. 2. p. 168.)

DRELL, [Sir Paul] *Knight*, *M. Dr. F. R. S.*
A widow and no widow, a comedy. 1780. 8. (1 sh. 6 d.) The knight and friars; an historic tale, 1785. 4. (2 sh.) *Seeing is believing, a comedy. 1786. 8. (1 sh.) Select dramatic pieces — 1787. 8. (6 sh.)

DRELL, [Richard Paul] *M. P. F. R. S.*
Illustrations of Euripides, on the Jon and the Bacchae. 1781. 8. (10 sh.) The persian Heroine; a tragedy. 1786. 4. (6 sh.) 8. (3 sh.) Illustrations of Euripides, on the Alcestis. 1790. 8. (7 sh.)

OHANSEN, [Andrew]
Geographical and historical account of the island of Bulam with observations on its climate, production — 1794. 8. (1 sh. 6 d.)

OHNES, [Thomas] *Esq. M P.*
Memoirs of the life of *Froissart*, with an essay on his works and a criticism on his history. Translated from the french of Mr. *De la Curne de St. Palaye.* 1802. 8. (5 sh. 6 d.) Crops and state of the poor Wales. (*Young's* A. of Agr. Vol. 34. p. 162.)

HNSON, [A.... M....] *Mrs.*
Monmouth, a tale. 1790.

HNSON, [Alexander] *M. Dr.*
born 1716. died 1799. Aug. in Charlotte-street, Portland-place, London.
See Gentleman's Magaz. Y. 1799. Sept. p. 820. Allg. Litt. Zeit. J. 1800. ItBl. S. 622.
Relief from accidental death, or summary instructions. 1793. 8. On the production and application of myrabolans, and their use as a substitute for Aleppo galls. (Tr. of the Soc. for the E. of A. Vol. 19. p. 343.)

JOHNSON, [Benjamin] *Rev.*
Original poems. 1799. 8. (5 sh.)

JOHNSON, [C.... W....]
Considerations on the case of the confined debtors in this kingdom. 1793. 8. (1 sh. 6 d.)

*JOHNSON, [J....] *Esq. (a fictitious name.)*
A guide for gentlemen studying medecine at the university of Edinburgh. 1792. 8. (1 sh. 6 d.)

*JOHNSON, [James] *Esq.*
A serious address to the people of England, on the subject of a reform, and the necessity of zeal and unanimity in defence of their country. 1798. 8. (1 sh. 6 d.)

JOHNSON, [James] *Surgeon at Lancaster.*
An account of the poisonous effects of the seeds of the datura stramonium, Linn. (*Simmons's* Med. Facts and Observ. Vol. 5. p. 78.)

*JOHNSON, [John] *A. M. formerly of Oriel-College, Oxford.*
Triffles in verse. 1796. 8. (2 sh.)

*JOHNSON, [Joseph]
An experimental inquiry into the properties of carbonic acid gas or fixed air; its mode of operation, use in diseases and the most effectual method of relieving animals affected by it. Philadelphia. 1797. 8.

*JOHNSON, [Richard] *A. B. Chaplain to the Colonies.*
Address to the inhabitants of the colonies, established in New South Wales and Norfolk islands; written in the year 1792. 1794. 12. (1 sh.)

*JOHNSON, [Richard]
Description of his invented double-gibbed crane. (Tr. of the Soc. for the E. of A. Vol. 11. p. 170.)

JOHNSON, [Robert Wallace] *M. Dr. Physician at Brentford.*
Friendly cautions to the heads of families and others, necessary to be observed in order to preserve health and long life. 1793. 12. (3 sh.)
Some remarks on religious opinions and their effects submitted to the consideration of the most learned and impartial persons of every denomination. 1796. 8. (2 sh.)

*JOHNSON, [Samuel] *Second Master of the free school in Shrewsbury.*
born 1739. died 1798. Sept. 2.
See Gentleman's Magaz. Y. 1798. Nov. p. 994. Allg. Litt. Zeit. ItBl. J. 1800. S. 652. Brittischer Plutarch. B. 7. 8. S. 308.

Poems

Poems. 1768. Essay on education, a poem in two parts; 1) the pedant; 2) the preceptor. 1771.

*JOHNSON, [William] *Esq. Barrister at Law.*
Letter to *Joshua Spencer* Esq., on an union (with Ireland). 1798. 8. (6 d.)

*JOHNSON, [W.... B....] *M. B.*
History of the progress and present state of animal chemistry. Vol. 1-3. 1803. 8. (1 L. 4 sh.)

JOHNSTON, [Alexander] *Surgeon at Dunbar.*
History of a case of rabies canina: (*Duncans M. C.* Dec. 2. Vol. 10. p. 264.)

*JOHNSTON, [Bryce]
Remarks on waste lands in the county of Dumfries. (Bath Agric. Soc. Vol. 8. p. 154.)

*JOHNSTON, [Bryce] *D. D. Minister of the Gospel at Holywood.*
A commentary on the revelation of St. John. Vol. 1. 2. 1794. (10 sh.) An essay on the way to restore and perpetuate peace, good order and prosperity to the nations. 1801. 8. (4 sh.)

JOHNSTONE, [James] *M. Dr. Physician at Worcester, before Physician at Kidderminster, Worcestershire. (Father of James Johnstone and Edward Johnstone.)*
born at Annan 1730. died 1802. Apr. 28.
See Gentleman's Magaz. Y. 1802. May. p. 475. Monthly Magaz. Y. 1802. June. p. 463. Allg. Litter. Zeit. J. 1803. ItBl. Nro. 43. S. 366.
Dissert: De aeris factitii imperio in corpore humano. Edinb. 1750. On the malignant epidemical fever of 1756 with account of the malignant diseases prevailing since the Y. 1752. in Kidderminster. 1758. 8. (1 sh.) Changes of iron to copper accounted for. (Gentlemans Magaz. Y. 1754. p. 355.) On the appearances of the urine attended with a putrid state of the blood. (Med. Mus. Vol. 2. p. 511.) Two extraordinary cases of gall-stones. (Philos. Transact. Y. 1758. p. 543.) Three papers on the ganglions of the nerves. (Ibid. Y. 1764. p. 177. Y. 1767. p. 118. Y. 1770. p. 30.) On the use of the ganglions of the nerves. 1771. 8. (2 sh.) übers. Stettin. 1787. 8. Account of the Walton water near Tewkesbury with thoughts on the use and diseases of the lymphatic

 glands.

glands. 1787. 8. (1 sh. 6 d.) Extraordinary case of cardialgia chronica and singular appearances in the body of an epileptic boy. (Med. Observat. and Inq. Vol. 2. p. ....) Cases of hydrophobia — with reflections on the prevention and treatment of persons bitten by mad and hydrophobic animals. (Mem. of M. S. of L. Vol. 1. p. 243.) Case of angina pectoris from an unexpected disease in the heart. (Ibid. Vol. 1. p. 376.) Case of paralysis rheumatica, cured by tinct. guajac. volat. and the application of caustics. (*Duncan's* Med. Comm. Vol. 9. p. 388.) übers. Samml. für prakt. Aerzte. Th. 11. S. 418. Case of cynanche pharyngea, or, defect of deglutition from a straitening of the oesophagus. (Mem. of M. S. of L. Vol. 2. p. ....) Remarks on the angina and scarlet fever of 1778. (Ibid. Vol. 3. p. 355.) Case of calculi passing through the bladder into the rectum. (Ibid. Vol. 3. p. 536.) Case of an ulcer of the bladder communicating with the rectum. (Ibid. Vol. 3. p. 542.) Case of a rupture of the bladder opening into the pelvis. (Ibid. Vol. 3. p. 543.) Some account of a species of phthisis pulmonalis, peculiar to persons employed in pointing needles in the needle manufacture. (Ibid. Vol. 5. p. 89.) Account of the life and writings of the late Prof. *Gregory*, M. Dr. (Mem. of Manchester. Vol. 2. p. 80.) Medical essays and observations with disquisitions relating to the nervous system: and an essay on mineral poisons, by *John Johnstone*, M. B Physician in Birmingham. 1795. 8. (7 sh. 6 d.) übers. von C. F. *Michaelis*. Leipz. 1796. 8. On *W. Waldegrave's* experiments in economy. (*Young's* A. of Agr. Vol. 25. p. 327.)

*JOHNSTONE, [James] *M. Dr. Physician at Worchester. (Son to the precedent.)*

born 1750. died 1783. Sept. 17.

See Gentleman's Magaz. Y. 1783. Aug. Y. 1795. April. p. 301.

Diss. De angina maligna. Edinb. 1773. On the malignant angina, or putrid and ulcerous sore throat. 1779. 8. (1 sh. 6 d.) übers. Samml. prakt. Abhandl. Th. 5. S. 345.

*JOHN-

*JOHNSTONE, [John] *Esq. Member of the Bengal Council and Chief of the province of Midnapore.* born .... died 1795. Dec. 10. at Alva.

See Gentleman's Magaz. Y. 1795. Dec. p. 1059. Suppl. p. 1111.

Letter to the proprietors of East-India Stock. 1766. 8.

*JOHNSTONE, [John] *M. Dr. Physician at Birmingham.*

Medical jurisprudence; on madness with strictures on hereditary insanity, lucid intervals, and the confinement of maniacs. 1800. 8. (2 sh.) On mineral poisons —. See *James Johnstone.* An account of the discovery of the power of mineral acid vapours to destroy contagion. 1803. 8. (1 sh.)

*JOHNSTONE, [John] *Land-Surveyor.*

Account of the most approved mode of draining land, according to the system practised by *Joseph Elkington.* — 1797. 4. (1 L. 1 sh.) New Ed. 1800. 8. (7 sh. 6 d.) übers. von Graf v. *Podewil.* Berlin. 1799. 4.

*JOHNSTONE, [William]

J. Beckmann's history of the inventions and discoveries: translated from the German. Vol. 1-3. 1797. 8. (1 L. 1 sh.) A voyage to the East-Indies by Fra *Paolino da San Bartolomeo* — with notes and illustrations by *J. R. Forster* — translated from the German. 1800. 8. (8 sh.) Astenology, or, the art of preserving feeble life, and of supporting the constitution under the influence of incurable diseases by C. *Aug. Struve*, translated from the German. 1801. 8. (8 sh.)

*JOHNSTONE, [William]

A new introduction to *Enfield's* speaker, or, a collection of easy lessons, arranged on an improved plan —. 1800. 12. (1 sh. 6 d.)

*JOLLIFFE, [William] *Esq. M. P.*

Project of the cultivation of commonable lands, with observat. by *A. Young.* (*Young's* A. of Agr. Vol. 14. p. 306.)

*JOLLY, [T....] *Minister at Dunnet, near Thurso, Caithness.*

On the peculiar circumstances which tend to make the use of horses almost universal, in agricultural operations, in the highland districts of Scotland; with an inquiry, how far, and with what effects, oxen might be substituted in their room. (Tr. of Highland Soc. Vol. 1. p. 126.)

*JONAS, [Peter] *late Surveyor of Excise.*
A new abridgment of all the laws of excise to the present time, with an appendix containing precedents and tables, exhibiting the weight of spirituous liquors, with rules for calculating their strength and value. 1802. 8.

*JONES, [.....] *Miss.*
Analysis of education and plan of a seminary for young ladies. 1798. 4. (1 sh.)

JONES, [Abraham]
State of the country in the month of November 1794. 8. (1 sh. 6 d.)

JONES, [Daniel] *of Hindsdale.*
An account of west-river mountain and the appearance of there having been a volcano in it. (American Museum. Y. 1787. March. p. 230.)

*JONES, [Edmund] *Dissenting Minister at Trench, near Pontypool in Monmouthshire.*
born in the parish of Abersytwyth in the county of Monmouth April 1. 1702. died 1793. Nov. 26.
See Gentleman's Magaz. Y. 1793. Dec. p. 1153. Evangelical Magazine Y. 1794. May. p. 177.
Sermon on Noah's ark; 17.. Sermon on the light of gospel; 17.. Sermon on Sampsons hair; 17.. History of the parish of Abersytwyth; 17..

*JONES, [Edward] *Esq.*
The prevention of poverty, by beneficial clubs, with preliminary observations upon houses of industry and the poor laws. Ed. 2. 1796. 8. (1 sh.)

*JONES, [Edward] *Esq. of the Inner-Temple.*
Index to records, called the originalia and memoranda on the Lord treasurer's remembrancer's side of the exchequer. Vol. 1. 2. 1795. fol. (3 L. 3 sh.)

JONES, [Edward] *Bard to the Prince of Wales; (native of Henblas, Llandderval, Merionetshire.)*
Musical and poetical relicks of the welsh bards — a new edition doubly augmented and improved. 1795. fol. (1 L. 11 sh. 6 d.) The bardic museum

museum of primitive british literature and other admirable rarities, forming the second volume of the musical, poetical and historical relicks of the welsh bards and druids. 1802. fol. (1 L. 5 sh.)

*JONES, [Edward] *Esq. of Wepre-Hall, in Flintshire*

On the destruction of the grub of the cock-chafer. (*Nicholson's* Journal. Y. 1802. June. p. 73. Tr. of the Soc. for E. of A. Vol. 19. p. 175.)

JONES, [Edward] *Teacher of the Classics and Geography at Bromley, in Kent.*

The young geographer and astronomer's best companion. Ed. 2. 1792. 8. (3 sh. 6 d.)

*JONES, [Edward T....] *An Accomptant of Bristol.*

English system of book-keeping, by single or double entry, in which it is impossible for an error, of the most trifling account to be passed unnoticed; — 1796. 4. (1 L. 11 sh. 6 d.) Ed. 2. 17.. übers. von *Th. Martens*, Bremen. 1801. 4. übers. von *Andr. Wagner*. Leipzig. 1801. 8. Defence of the English system of book-keeping — 1797. 8. (2 sh.)

*JONES, [Frederic] *Captain.*

A brief account of the Tullagaum expedition from Bombay, and likewise of the sieges of Bassien, Arnoll, Callian and Cannanore, on the western side of India, during the course of the war, commenced on the 21 Nov. 1778. Extracted from the journal of an officer who was actually employed on those services (Capt. *Frederic Jones*) 1794. 4. (1 sh.) Copies of letters, merely intended for and by the desire of intimate friends. 1795. 4. (1 sh.)

*JONES, [Frederic Coningesby] *of Gray's-Inn.*

The attorney's new pocket book and conveyancer's assistant. Vol. 1. 2. 1794. 12. (7 sh. 6 d.) Ed. 2. with many material corrections, alterations and additions. Vol. 1. 2. 1798. 12. (10 sh. 6 d.)

*JONES, [H.... J....]

— — — and *T.... H.... Williams's* picturesque excursions in Devonshire; consisting of select views, with descriptions. Nrb. 1. 2. 1801. 8. (14 sh.)

*JONES, [J....] *Navy-Surgeon.*
The philantropist, a play. 1801. 8. (1 sh. 6 d.)

*JONES, [Jenkin]
Hobby horses, a poetic allegory in 5 parts. 1797. 12. (3 sh.)

*JONES, [John] *Esq. of Bolas-Heath, Newport, Shropshire.*
On fatting hogs on potatoes. (*Young's* A. of Agr. Vol. 17. p. 586.) Further remarks on the late failure in the apple crop. (Comm. and Agric. Mag. Y. 1802. Dec. p. 439.)

*JONES, [John]
A defence of the mosaic or revealed creation: proving the authenticity of the pentateuch; the consistency of Moses's description with the principles of natural philosophy now current; and the truth of scripture chronology. 1797. 8. (1 sh.) A vindication of the Lord Bish. of Landaff's apology for the bible, in a series of letters to *A. Macleod.* 1797. 8. (1 sh.) The epistle of Paul to the Romans analyzed, from a developement of the circumstances by which it was occasioned. 1802. 8. (5 sh.)

*JONES, [John] *M. B.*
Medical, philosophical and vulgar errors of various kinds considered and refuted. 1797. (4 sh.)

*JONES, [John]
The reason of man P. 1. 2. containing strictures on rights of man; with observations on Mr. *Erskine's* defence of Mr. *Paine* and thoughts on the war with France. 1793. 8. (1 sh.)

*JONES, [John] *M. Dr. of the College of Physicians of Philadelphia.*
born .... died .... (?)
— — and *Dav. Rittenhouse's* account of several houses in Philadelphia, struck with lightning on June 7. 1789. (Tr. of A. S. Vol. 3. p. 119.) Case of anthrax. (Tr. of Phys. of Philad. Vol. 1. P. 1. p. 207.) The surgical works of the late *John Jones,* — by *James Mease.* Philad. 1795. 8.

*JONES, [John] *LL. Dr.*
Travels in the french republic — by *Thomas Bugge,* translated from the Danish. 1801. 8. (6 sh.)

*JONES,

*JONES, [John Gale]

Sketch of a ſpeech delivered at the Weſtminſter forum — in Dec. 1794. on the following queſtion, which have proved themſelves the true friends of their king and country, thoſe perſons who have endeavoured to procure a conſtitutional reform in parliament, or thoſe who have oppoſed that meaſure as ill-timed and dangerous? 1795. 8. (1 ſh.) Sketch of a political tour through Rocheſter, Chatham, Maidſtone, Graveſend &c. including reflections on the tempers and diſpoſitions of the inhabitants of thoſe places and on the progreſs of the ſocieties inſtituted for the purpoſe of obtaining a parliamentary reform. Part 1. 1796. 8. (2 ſh. 6 d.) An oration, delivered Nov. 29. 1796. at the great room in Brewer-ſtreet, on the reſignation of Gen. *Waſhington*, including a ſhort review of his life, character and conduct. 1797. 8. (1 ſh.) Obſervations on the tuſſis convulſiva, or hooping cough — wherein the nature, cauſe and cure of this diſeaſe are endeavoured to be demonſtrated and the practice of exhibiting emetics, ſhewn to be pernicious and uſeleſs. 1798. 8. (1 ſh.)

*JONES, [L.... T....] *Captain of the* 14 *Regt.*

An hiſtorical journal of the Britiſh campaign on the continent in the year 1794, with the retreat through Holland in 1795. 1797. 4. (1 L. 1 ſh.)

*JONES, [Richard] *A Diſſenting Miniſter of Peckham, in Surry.*

born .... died 1800. Sept. at Greenwich, Kent.

See Gentleman's Magaz. Y. 1800. Oct. p. 1005. Allg. Litter. Zeit. J. 1801. ItBl. S. 838.

A ſermon, in contemplation of the then approaching anniverſary of the glorious revolution by King *William* and the preſervation of Engliſh liberty by that great and happy event. 1788. A ſermon, on the early love and purſuit of wiſdom. 1793. 8. (1 ſh.) A ſermon, on the influence of religion on human happineſs. 17.. A ſermon, on the final appearance of Jeſus Chriſt; 17.. Friendſhip with God; an eſſay on its nature and

and excellence. 1797. 12. (3 ſh. 6 d.) A faſt-ſermon. 17..

*JONES, [Samuel] *A. M.*

An inaugural diſſertation on hydrocele. Philadelphia. 1797. 8.

*JONES, [Stephen]

A new biographical dictionary, containing a brief account of the lives and writings of the moſt eminent perſons and remarkable characters in every age and nation. Ed. 2. 1796. 12. (5 ſh.) Ed. 4. corrected with conſiderable additions. 1802. An abridgement of the hiſtory of Poland. 17.. *Sheridan* improved; a general pronouncing and explanatory dictionary of the Engliſh language. 1796. 8. (3 ſh. 6 d.) Maſonic miſcellanies in poetry and proſe. 1797. 8. (3 ſh.) * The poetical works of *Thomas Gray*, LL. B. — with ſome account of his life and writings, the whole carefully reviſed and illuſtrated by notes, original and ſelected; to which are annexed poems written by, addreſſed to, or in memory of Mr. *Gray*; ſeveral of which were never before collected. 1799.

*JONES, [Theophilus] *of Cork-Abbey, near Bray, Ireland.*

Uſe of clover and potatoes for ſwine. (Ibid. Vol. 34. p. 50.)

*JONES, [Thomas] *M. A. Fellow and head Tutor of Trinity College, Cambridge.*

See Public Characters of 1802 and 1803. p. 238. A ſermon on duelling. 1792. 4. (1 ſh.)

*JONES, [Thomas]

Myſtery Babylon encompaſſed for utter deſtruction; or, Antinomianiſm unmaſked — (written by *Maria de Fleury*) anſwered. 1791. 8. (1 ſh.)

*JONES, [Thomas] *Esq. F. R. S. F. A. S. M. P.*

Subſtance of his ſpeech on his motion for peace, in the houſe of Commons, May 8. 1800. 8. (1 ſh. 6 d.) The dismiſſal of his Maj. miniſters conſidered as abſolutely neceſſary to avert the ruin of the nation. 1801. (1 ſh.)

*JONES, [Thomas] *at London.*

On the culture of rhubarb. (Tr. of the Soc. for the E. of A. Vol. 11. p. 113. Vol. 15. p. 164. Vol. 16. p. 213.) On opium. (Ib. Vol. 18. p. 161.)

*JONES,

*JONES, [W....] *of Foxdown-Hill.*

Obſervations on the uſes of the wood of the Spaniſh cheſnut tree. (Tr. of the Soc. for the E. of A. Vol. 7. p. 9.)

JONES, [Sir William] *Knight;* —

born 1746. at his father's reſidence in Wales, died at Bengal Apr. 27. 1794.

See Gentleman's Magaz. Y. 1794. Suppl. p. 1205. Y. 1795. Febr. p. 111. April. p. 347. Y. 1801. June p. 547. Allg. Litter. Zeit. J. 1801. ItBl. S. 819. Sir *John Shore's* eulogium on Sir *Will. Jones;* See *Thomas Maurice;* See *Will. Hayley; Eichhorn's* Allgem. Biblioth. der Bibl. Litteratur. B. 6. S. 1094. Deutſche Monathsſchrift. Leipzig. J. 1796. März. S. 230. *Millin* Magaz. Encycloped. An 9. T. 1. p. 525.

Latin oration, when at Harrow School. (Gentleman's Magaz. Y. 1798. May. p. 373.) Eſſay on the law of bailments Ed. 2. by *John Balmanno.* 1797. 8. (5 ſh.) Sacontala, or the fatal ring — überſ. von *G. Forſter.* Mainz u. Leipz. 1791. 8. Diſcourſe on the Arabs. (Aſiat. Reſ. Vol. 2. p. 1.) Diſcourſe on the Tartars. (Ibid. Vol. 2. p. 19.) Diſcourſe on the Perſians. (Ibid. Vol. 2. p. 43.) Remarks on the iſland of Hinzuan or Johanna. (Ibid. Vol. 2. p. 77.) On the chronology of the Hindus. (Ibid. Vol. 2. p. 111. 389.) On the Indian game of cheſs. (Ibid. Vol. 2. p. 159.) On the ſecond claſſical book of the Chineſe. (Ibid. Vol. 2. p. 195.) On the antiquity of the Indian zodiack. (Ibid. Vol. 2. p. 289.) The deſign of a treatiſe on the plants of India. (Ibid. Vol. 2. p. 345.) Diſcourſe on the Chineſe. (Ibid. Vol. 2. p. 365.) On the ſpikenard of the ancients. (Ibid. Vol. 2. p. 405. Vol. 4. p. 109. *Simmons's* Med. Facts and Obſervat. Vol. 4. p. 180.) überſ. Repertor. Chirurg. u. Mediz. Abhandl. B. 2. S. 493. On the borderers, mountaineers and iſlanders of Aſia. (Aſiat. Reſ. Vol. 3. p. 1.) A royal grant of land in Carnata, tranſlated from the Sanſcrit. (Ibid. Vol. 3. p. 39.) On the muſical modes of The Hindus. (Ibid. Vol. 3. p. 55.) On the myſtical poetry of the Perſians and Hindus. (Ibid. Vol. 3. p. 165.) The lunar year of the Hindus. (Ibid.

(Ibid. Vol. 3. p. 257.) On the origin and families of nations. (Ibid. Vol. 3. p. 479.) On Asiatick history, civil and natural. (Ibid. Vol. 4. p. 1.) On the loris, or slowpaced lemur. (Ibid. Vol. 4. p. 135.) On the philosophy of the Asiaticks. (Ibid. Vol. 4. p. 165.) A catalogue of Indian plants, comprehending the Sanscrit and as many of their Linnaean generic names as could with any degree of precision be ascertained. (Ibid. Vol. 4. p. 229.) Botanical observations on select Indian plants. (Ibid. Vol. 4. p. 237.) A hymn to Camdeo. (Asiatic Miscellany. p. 1.) A hymn to Narayena. (Ibid. p. 7.) Institutes of Hindu-law, or the ordonances of Menu according to the gloss of Calluca, comprising the Indian system of duties, religious and civil: verbally translated from the original Sanskrit. Calcutta. 1794. 4. reprinted London. 1796. 8. (6 sh.) übers. von *J. C. Hüttner.* Weimar. 1797. 8. Dissertations and miscellaneous pieces relating to the history and antiquities, the arts, sciences and litterature of Asia. Vol. 1-4. 1792-1798. 8. (2 L.) Works. Vol. 1-6. 1799. 4. (10 L. 10 sh. large paper 21 L.) Supplemental volumes — Vol. 1. 2. 1801. 4. (3 L. 3 sh.)

JONES, [William] *Surgeon at Birmingham.*

A case of haemoptysis. (M. P. of M. S. Nrb. 1. p. 123. *Duncan's* Med. Comm. Dec. 2. Vol. 1. p. . . . .)

JONES, [William] *M. A: F. R. S: Rector of Paston, Northamptonshire; Vicar of Stocke with the chapel of Nayland, Suffolk.*

born 1726. 30 Jul. died 1800. Jan. 6.

See Gentleman's Magaz. Y. 1800. Febr. p. 183. March. p. 231. May. p. 437. Allg. Litt. Zeit. ItBl. J. 1800. S. 1802.

Observations on a journey to Paris. 1777. 8. The religious use of botanical philosophy; a sermon. 1784. 4. (1 sh.) A course of lectures on the figurative language of the holy scripture and the interpretation of it from the scripture itself. 1787. 8. (6 sh.) Essay on the first principles of philosophy; 17.. Considerations on the nature and oeconomy of beasts and cattle, a sermon. 1785. 4. (1 sh.)

(1 ſh.) Memoirs of the life, ſtudies and writings of G. *Horne*, D. D. late Biſh. of Norwich. To which is added his Lordſhip's own collection of his thoughts on a variety of great and intereſting ſubjects. 1795. 8. (5 ſh.) Ed. 2. with a new preface on certain points in theology and philoſophy. 1799. 8. (1 ſh.) The man of ſin; a ſermon. 1796. The age of unbelief, a ſecond part to the man of ſin, a ſermon. 1796. 8. The uſe and abuſe of the world. 1796. A friendly admonition to the churchman on the ſenſe and ſufficiency of his religion, in two ſermons. 1796. 8. (1 ſh.) The nature, uſes, dangers, ſufferings and preſervation of the human imagination; a ſermon. 1797. Popular commotions conſidered as a ſign of the approaching end of the world, a ſermon. 1790. The difficulty and the reſources of the chriſtian miniſtry in the preſent time, a ſermon. 1791. Catholic doctrine of the trinity. 1795. Sermons on moral and religious ſubjects. Vol. 1. 2. 1790. 8. (12 ſh.) A diſcourſe on the uſe and intention of ſome remarkable paſſages of the ſcripture, not commonly underſtood. 1798. 8. (1 ſh.) Letter to the church of England pointing out ſome popular errors of conſequence. 1798. A letter to three converted jews, lately baptiſed and confirmed in the church of England. 1799. 8. (1 ſh.) The theological, philoſophical and miſcellaneous works: to which is prefixed a ſhort account of his life and writings. Vol. 1-12. 1801. 8. (5 L. 8 ſh.)

(Several ſingle ſermons.)

*JONES, [William]

Geometrical and graphical eſſays, containing a general deſcription of mathematical inſtruments, uſed in geometry, ſurveying — by the late G. *Adams*, corrected and enlarged, with illuſtrating plates. Ed. 2. Vol. 1. 2. 1798. 8. (14 ſh.) Lectures on natural and experimental philoſophy by the late G. *Adams*. Ed. 2. with additions. Vol. 1-5. 1799. 8. Six letters on electricity. 1800. 8. (2 ſh.) Aſtronomical and geographical eſſays — by the late G. *Adams*. Ed. 5. reviſed and improved. 1802. (10 ſh. 6 d.)

*JONES,

***JONES**, [William] *F. L. S.*
A new arrangement of papilios. (Transact. of L. S. Vol. 2. p. 63.)

***JONES**, [William] *Student of Harvard-College.*
A topographical defcription of the town of Concord. Aug. 20. 1792. (Coll. of Maffachufetts H. S. Y. 1792. p. 237.)

***JONES**, [William Langham] *Bart.*
Queries — with Mr. *Anderdon's* anfwers. (Bath Agricult. Soc. Vol. 2. p. 48.)

***JONES**, [William Todd] *Esq.*
Letter — upon the fubject of certain apprehenfions which have arifen from a propofed reftoration of catholic rights; — with the declaration of the catholic fociety of Dublin, and fome thoughts on the prefent politics of Ireland, by *Theobald M'Kenna*, M. D. 1792. 8. (2 fh.)

***JOSS**, [Torial]
born at Auck-Medden in Scotland 1731. Sept. 23. died 1797. Apr. 17.
See Evangelical Magaz. Y. 1797. Oct. p. 397.
The faint's entrance into peace of, a funeral fermon occafioned by the death of the Rev. *Thomas Adams*. 17..

***JOYCE**, [Jeremiah] *(23 weeks a clofe prifoner in the Tower.)*
Sermon on funday, Febr. 1794. to which is added an appendix containing an account of the author's arreft for treafonable practices — 1794. 8. (1 fh. 6 d.) An account of his arreft for treafonable practices, his examination before his Maj. — Council; his commitment to the tower and fubfequent treatment. Ed. 2. corrected and enlarged. 1795. 8. (1 fh. 9 d.) A complete analyfis or abridgment of *Adam Smith's* inquiry into the nature and caufes of the wealth of nations. 1797. 8. (5 fh.)

***JOYCE**, [Thomas]
A ftatement of an experimental procefs of manufacture, to afcertain the value of Englifh wool from fheep of a fpanifh mixture. (Bath Agric. Soc. Vol. 9. p. 344.)

*IREDELL,

IREDELL, [James] *One of the Associate Justices of the Supreme Court of the United States.*
Laws of the state of North-Carolina. Edenton. 1791. fol.

IRELAND, [John] *A. M. Vicar of Croydon, in Surry.*
*Baviad and Maeviad. 17.. Five discourses, containing certain arguments for and against the reception of christianity by the antient jews and greeks. 1796. 8. (3 sh. 6 d.)

IRELAND, [John] *formerly a watchmaker in Maiden-Lane.*
See Public Characters of 1800 and 1801. p. 338. Hogarth illustrated. Vol. 1-3. 1791-1798. (4 L. 8 sh. 6 d.)

IRELAND, [Samuel]
born .... died at London 1800. July.
See Gentleman's Magaz. Y. 1800. Sept. p. 901. Oct. p. 1000. Supplem. p. 1258. Allg. Litter. Zeit. J. 1801. ItBl. S. 796.
Picturesque views of the Severn and Warwickshire Avon; 17.. Picturesque views on the river Thames, with observations on the works of arts in its vicinity. Vol. 1. 2. 1792. 8. (2 L. 12 sh. 6 d.) Picturesque views on the river Medway, from the Nore to the vicinity of its source in Sussex; with observations on the public buildings and other works of art in its neighbourhood. 1793. 8. (1 L. 11 sh. 6 d.) Graphic illustrations of *Hogarth* from pictures drawings and scarce prints. Vol. 1. 2. 1794. 1799. 4. (2 L. 5 sh. large paper 4 L. 4 sh.) Miscellaneous papers and legal instruments under the hand and seal of *Will. Shakespeare*, including the tragedy of King Lear and a small fragment of Hamlet from the original MSS. 1796. fol. (4 L. 4 sh.) Vindication of his conduct respecting the publication of the supposed Shakespeare MSS. being a preface or introduction to a reply to the critical labour of Mr. *Malone*. 1796. 8. (1 sh. 6 d.) An investigation of Mr. *Malone's* claim to the character of a scholar or critick, being an examination of his „Enquiry into the authenticity of the *Shakspeare* MSS. 1797. Picturesque view on the

river Wye, from its source at Plinlimmon-hill, to its junction with the severn below Chepstow. 1797. 8. (1 L. 16 sh.) Picturesque view with an historical account of the inns of court in London and Westminster. 1800. 4. (4 L. 4 sh.) 8. (2 L. 2 sh.)

*IRELAND, [William Henry]

An authentic account of the Shakspearian manuscripts — 1796. 8. (1 sh.) The abbess, a romance; Vol. 1–4. 1799. (14 sh.) Rimualdo; or the castle of Badajos, a romance Vol. 1–4. 1800. 12. (14 sh.) Mutius Scaevola, or, the roman patriot, an historical drama. 1801. 8. (2 sh. 6 d.) Ballads, in imitation of the antient. 1801. 12. (5 sh.) Rhapsodies —; 1803. 8. (7 sh.)

*IRONSIDE, [Edward] *Esq.*

The history and antiquities of Twickenham, being the first part of parochial collections for the county of Middlesex, begun in 1780. 1797. 4. (10 sh. 6 d.) Account of a large tree in India. (*Tilloch's* Philos. Magaz. Vol. 4. p. 359.) Account of a Bonian tree in the province of Bahar. (Ibid. Vol. 4. p. 360.)

IRONSIDE, [G....] *Colonel.*

On the manner of hunting and sporting by the English in Bengal. (*Tilloch's* Philos. Magaz. Vol. 14. p. 319.)

*IRVINE, [Alexander] *Minister of Ranoch.*

An inquiry into the causes and effects of emigration from the highlands and western islands of Scotland, with observations on the means to be employed for preventing it. 1802. 8. (3 sh. 6 d.)

*IRVING, [David] *A. M.*

The life of *Robert Fergusson*, with a critique on his works. 1800. 12. (1 sh.) The elements of English composition. 1801. 8. (4 sh. 6 d.) *Homer's* notion of destiny. (Monthly Magaz. Y. 1799. Dec. p. 872.) Critique on the poems of *Falconer.* (Ibid. Y. 1800. Febr. p. 12.)

IRWIN, [Eyles] *Esq. M. R. J. A. In the service of East India Company at Calcutta.*

born 1751. died .... (?)

St. Thomas mount, a poem. 17.. The triumph of innocence, an ode; written on the deliverance of of Maria Theresa Charlotte, Princess royal of France, from the prison of the temple. 1796. 4. (2 sh. 6 d.) Inquiry into the feasibility of the supposed expedition of Buonaparte to the East. 1798. 8. (1 sh.) Buonaparte in Egypt: or, an appendix to the inquiry into his supposed expedition to the East. 1798. 8. (1 sh.) Nilus, an elegy, occasioned by the victory of Admir. Nelson over the french fleet on Aug. 1. 1798. 1798. 4. (1 sh.) The failure of the french crusade or the advantages to be derived by Great-Britain from the restoration of Egypt to the Turks. 1799. 8. (1 sh. 6 d.) An account of the game of chess, as played by the Chinese. (Tr. of J. A. Vol. 5. p. 53. c.)

*ISAAC, [J....] *Secretary to the Apiarian Society at Exeter.*

The general apiarian wherein a simple, humane and advantageous method of obtaining the produce of bees, without destroying them, is pointed out in a series of letters. 1799. 8. (2 sh. 6 d.)

*ISAACS, [Henry] *D. D.*

On the profit of bees. (Comm. and Agric. Mag. Y. 1800. p. 40.)

*JUSTAMOND, [J....] *A. M.*

First settlement of nova Scotia; translated from the Abbé *Raynal's* Philos. and Polit. history of the settlements and trade of the Europ: in the E. and W. Indies. (Massachusett's Magaz. Vol. 1. 1789. p. 147.)

*IVES, [Edward Otto] *late Resident at the Nawaub Vizier's Court.*

Remarks on a pamphlet entitled, „letters, political, military and commercial on the present „state and government of Oude and its dependencies„ — 1796. 4. (2 sh.)

*IVISON, [Ursula]

The retired penitent, a poem. 1794. 8. (1 sh.)

*IVORY, [James] *A. M.*

A new series for the rectification of the ellipsis, with observations on the evolution of a certain algebraic formula. (Tr. of R. S. Vol. 4. P. p. 177.) A new method of resolving cubic equations. (Ib. Vol. 5. Part I. p. 99.)

*KANMACHER, [Frederick] *F. L. S.*

Essays on the microscope — by the late *George Adams*, Ed. 2. with considerable additions and improvements. 1798. 4. (1 L. 8 sh.)

*KAST, [Thomas] *A. M: F. M. M. S. Physician at Boston.*

Account of an aneyrism in the thigh, perfectly cured by the operation and the use of the limb preserved. (M. P. of M. S. Nrb. 1. p. 96.)

*KAY, [George]

Remarks on waste lands in Flintshire. (Bath Agric. Soc. Vol. 8. p. 164.) Remarks on waste lands in Carnarvonshire. (Ibid. Vol. 8. p. 166.) Remarks on waste lands in Montgomeryshire. (Ibid. Vol. 8. p. 167.) Remarks on waste lands in Mezionetshire. (Ibid. Vol. 8. p. 169.) Remarks on waste lands in Denbighshire. (Ibid. Vol. 8. p. 170.)

KEARNEY, [Michael] *D. D: M. R. J: A. and of the Etruscan Academy of Corzona.*

Thoughts on the history of alphabetic writing. (Tr. of J. A. 1789. p. 5. b.) Observations on the power of painting to express mixed passions. (Ibid. Vol. 6. p. 87.)

*KEARSLEY, [.....]

Traveller's entertaining guide through Great-Britain. 1801. 8. (6 sh.) Ed. 2. 1803. 8. (7 sh.)

KEARSLEY, [George] *Bookseller in London.*

born .... died 17.. (?)

KEATE, [George] *F. R. S: F. A. S:*

born at Trowbridge about 1729 or 1730. died 1797. June 28.

See Gentleman's Magaz. Y. 1797. June. p. 535. July. p. 613. Sept. p. 796. Y. 1800. Sept. p. 897. Monthly Magaz. Y. 1797. Aug. p. 153. Allgem. Litterat. Zeit. J. 1797. ItBl. Dec. S. 1407.

Ancient and modern Rome, a poem; 1760. Epistle from Lady *Jane Grey* to Lord Guildford Dudley. 1762. The ruins of Netley-Abbey, a poem; Ed. 2. enlarged. 1769. The temple stu-

dent.

dent. 1765. Observations on the roman earthen ware found in the sea on the Kentish coast; (Archaeol. Vol. 6. p. 125.) A companion in a visit to Netley-Abbey; to which is annexed Netley-Abbey, an elegy. 1800. 12. (1 sh.)

KEATE, [William] *M. A: Rector of Laveston, co. Somerset and Prebendary of Wells.*

born .... died at Chelsea-hospital. 1795. March 14.

See Gentleman's Magaz. Y. 1795. April. p. 351. Oct. p. 876.

Published *Will. Bull's* address to the steward of the manor. 1790. A free examination of Dr. *Price's* and Dr. *Priestley's* sermons. 1790. The 109th, commonly called the imprecating psalm considered on a principle, by which the psalm explains itself, a sermon. 1794. 4.

*KEATINGE, [Maurice] *Esq.*

The true history of the conquest of Mexico: by Capt. Bernal Diaz del Castillo, one of the conquerors; written in the Y. 1568. Translated from the original spanish. 1802. 4. (1 L. 5 sh.)

*KEDINGTON, [Roger] *Rev. of Rougham, near Bury St. Edmund's, Suffolk.*

On the comparative utility of oxen and horses in husbandry. (Bath Agricult. Soc. Vol. 2. p. 275.) On the proper husbandry for a gentleman. (*Young's* A. of Agr. Vol. 6. p. 11.) Plan for a barn — comparison of horses and oxen &c. (Ib. Vol. 16. p. 1.)

*KEEFE, [John] *Actor in the Irish stage.*

The little hunch-back, or frolic in Bagdad. 1792. (1 sh.) The she-Gallant. 1767. altered under the title of the positive man. 17.. The dead alive, a farce; 17.. The agreeable surprise, a farce; 17.. The Banditti, a comic opera; 17.. Lord Mayor's day, a speaking pantomine; 17.. The maid the mistress, a burletta from the Italian of La Serva Padrona; 17.. The shamrock, a comic opera; 17.. The young Quacker, a comedy; 17.. The birth day, or the prince of Arragon; 17.. The poor soldier, a comic

mic opera; 17.. Friar Bacon, a pantomine; 17.. Peeping Tom, a musical farce; 17.. Fontainebleau, a comic opera; 17.. The blacksmith of Antwerp, a farce; 17.. A beggar on horseback, a dramatic proverb; 17.. Omai, a pantomine; 17.. Love in a camp, a comic opera; 17.. The siege of Curzola, a comic opera; 17.. The manmilliner, a farce; 17.. The farmer, a farce; 17.. Tantararara, a farce, from the french; 17.. The prisoner at large, a farce; 17.. A key to the lock, a farce; 17.. The highlandreel, a comic romance, 17.. The Czar, a comic opera; 17.. Modern antiques, a farce; 17.. The doldrum, a farce; 17.. The prisonner at large, a comedy. 1788. 8. The little hunchback, a farce; 1790. 8. Sprigs of Laurel, a comic opera, in 2 acts. 1793. 8. (1 sh.) The London Hermit, or rambles in Dorsetshire, a comedy, in 3 acts. 1793. 8. (1 sh. 6 d.) The world in a village, a comedy. 1793. 8. (1 sh. 6 d.) The castle of Andalusia, a comic opera. 1794. 8. (1 sh. 6 d.) Wild oats, or, the strolling gentleman, a comedy. 1794. 8. (1 sh. 6 d.) Life's vagaries, a comedy in 5 acts. 1795. 8. (2 sh.) Oatlands, or the transfer of the laurel, a poem. 1795. 4. (1 sh.) The irish mimic, or blunder's at Brighton, a musical entertainment, in 2 acts. 1795. 8. (1 sh.) Dramatic works. Vol. 1-4. 1798-1800. 8. (2 L. 2 sh.)

*KEEVE, [Joseph] *Rev.*

Miscellaneous poetry, in English and Latin. Ed. 2. 1794. 8.

KEIR, [Archibald]

Of the method of distilling as practised by the natives at Chatra in Ramgur —; (Asiat. Res. Vol. 1. p. 309. *Tilloch's* Phil. Magaz. Vol. 5. p. 7.)

KEIR, [James] *Esq.* —

Experiments and observations on the dissolution of metals in acids. (Phil. Transact. Y. 1790. p. 359.) übers. von *L. Lentin.* Gött. 1791. 8. * Account of the life and writings of *Thomas Day* Esq. 1791. 8. (2 sh. 6 d.) übers. von *J. J. C. Timaeus.* Leipzig. 1798. 8. Letter on fossil alkali. (Tr. of the Soc. for the E. of A. Vol. 6. p. 129.)

*KEIR,

*KEIR, [Peter] *Engineer.*
Description of an improvement in the steam engine, by means of which the boiler is constantly supplied with water already heated nearly to the point of ebullition. (*Nicholson's* Journal. Vol. 5. p. 147.) Section and plan of a moveable crane, capable of heaving four tons with four men —; (Ibid. Y. 1802. Oct. p. 124.)

KEITH, [Alexander] *Esq. F. R. S: F. A. S. Edinb.*
On an improvement of the mercurial level. (Tr. of E. S. Vol. 4. H. p. 17.) Description of a thermometer, with marks the greatest degree of heat and cold from one time of observation to another. (Ibid. Vol. 4. P. p. 203. *Nicholson's* Journal. Vol. 3. p. 266. *Tilloch's* Philos. Magaz. Vol. 2. p. 61.) Description of a barometer which marks the rise and fall of the mercury from two different times of observation. (Tr. of E. S. Vol. 4. P. p. 209. *Tilloch's* Philos. Magaz. Vol. 2. p. 65.)

KEITH, [George Skene] *M. A. Minister of Keith-Hall and Kinkell, Aberdeenshire.*
Tracts on weights, measures and coins. 1791. 4. (1 sh. 6 d.) Tracts on the corn laws of Great-Britain. 1792. 8. (1 sh. 6 d.) An impartial and comprehensive view of the present state of Great-Britain —. 1797. 8. (1 sh. 6 d.) Lectures on ecclesiastical history: to which is added, an essay on christian temperance and self-denial by the late *George Campbell* D. D: — with some account of the life and writings of the author. Vol. 1. 2. 1800. 8. (16 sh.) A particular examination of the new french constitution, which was offered to the people for their acceptance or rather imposed on them, in Dec. 1799. 1801. 8. (2 sh.)

*KEITH, [James] *of the loyal North Britons.*
The soldiers assistant to the manual and platoon exercise; with directions for the discipline of volunteer corps and figures of the positions. 1803. (6 d.) The volunteer's guide. Part 1. 2. 1804. (2 sh.)

KEITH, [Thomas] *Teacher of Mathematics.*
The complete practical arithmetician. Ed. 2. 1799. 12. (3 sh. 6 d.) The new schoolmaster's assistant.

 1796.

1796. (2 ſh.) An introduction to the theory and practice of plane and ſpherical trigonometry and the orthographic and ſterographic projections of the ſphere. 1801. (10 ſh. 6 d.)

*KEITH, [Sir William] *formerly Governour of Penſylvania.*
Thoughts on cenſure, family disagreement &c. (American Muſeum Y. 1790. Nov. p. 218.)

*KELD, [C....] *Esq. of Beverley.*
On the poor laws; 17.. (1 ſh.) A ſecond letter to Mr *Gilbert* on the poor laws. (*Young's* A. of Agr. Vol. 33. p. 547. Vol. 34. p. 21. 126. 238. 394.)

*KELLIE, [Alexander] *Student of Medicine in Edinburgh.*
Account of a rupture of the abdominal integuments, occaſioned by a fall and followed by gangrene of the omentum, terminating favourably. (*Duncan's* M. C. Dec. 2. Vol. 6. p. 306.)

KELLIE, [George] *Surgeon on board his Maj. Ship the Iris.*
An account of the effects of compreſſion by the tourniquet, in ſtopping the cold fit of intermittents. (*Duncan's* M. C. Dec. 2. Vol. 9. p. 271.) überſ. in Samml. für prakt. Aerzte. B. 17. S. 78. Obſervations on the medical effects of compreſſion by the tourniquet. Edinb. 1797. 8. Some obſervations on the anatomy of the ſhark. (*Duncan's* A. of Med. Y. 1796. p. 395.) On the effects of the nitrous acid in the cure of ſyphilis. (Ibid. Y. 1797. p. 254.) überſ. in Samml. für prakt. Aerzte. B. 19. S. 15. Letter reſpecting the extract of the rhus radicans. (Ibid. Y. 1800. p. 483.)

°KELLS, [John] *Esq. Barriſter at Law.* died (?)
A general index to the modern reporters, relative to the law occurring at trials by niſi prius, from the period of the revolution to the preſent times. Vol. 1. Dublin. 1797. 8. (9 ſh.)

*KELLY, [Elizabeth]
Eva. Vol. 1-3. 1799. (10 ſh. 6 d.)

*KELLY,

*KELLY, [John] *L. L. Dr.*

A practical grammar of the antient gaelic, or, language of the isle of Mann, usually called mank. 1804. 4. (6 sh.)

*KELLY, [Isabella] *Mrs.*

Joscelina, or, the rewards of benevolence, a novel. Vol. 1. 2. 1797. 12. (6 sh.) The ruins of Avondale priory. Vol. 1–3. 1796. 8. (9 sh.) The baron's daughter, a gothic romance. Vol. 1–4. 1802. 12. (16 sh.)

*KELLY, [E.... (P.... (?)] *Master of Tinsbury-square Academy.*

A practical introduction to spherical and nautical astronomy. 1796. 8. (6 sh.) Ed. 2. 1801. 8. (8 sh.) The elements of book-keeping, both by single and double entry —. 1801. 8. (5 sh.)

*KELSON, [T.... M....]

A few remarks on the nature and cure of colds. 1797. 8. (1 sh. 6 d.)

*KEMBLE, [Charles]

The point of honour; a play, in 3 acts; taken from the french. 1800. 8. (2 sh.)

KEMBLE, [John] *Manager and one of the proprietors of Drurylane Theater.*

Belisarius. 17.. Oh! its impossible! a comedy; 17.. New way to pay old debts, altered from *Massinger*. 17.. The farmhouse, a comedy. 1792. 8. (1 sh.) Lodoiska, an opera, in 3 acts. 1794. 8. (1 sh. 6 d.) King Henry 5. or, the conquest of France; a play, by *Shakespeare;* altered. 1804.

*KENDAL, [.....] *Mrs.*

Essays addressed to young women: intended to a guide to their entering into the marriage state. 1802. 24. (1 sh.)

*KENDALL, [A....]

*Derwent priory; 17.. Tales of the abbey, founded on historical facts. Vol. 1–3. 1800. 12. (10 sh. 6 d.)

*KENDALL, [Edward Augustus] *Esq.*

The crested wren, 1799. 12. (1 sh. 6 d.) The Indian cottage, by *J. H. Bernardin De St. Pierre*, translated. 1799. 8. (1 sh. 6 d.) The stories of

Nn 5 senex;

senex; or little histories of little people. 1800. 8. (2 sh.) A pocket encyclopaedia — Vol. 1-6. 1802. Travels in upper and lower Egypt — translated from the french by *Vivant Denon* — Vol. 1. 2. 1802. 8. (2 L. 2 sh.) Parental education; or, domestic lessons: a miscellany, intended for youth. 1803. 12. (4 sh.)

***KENDALL, [John]**

An abstract from the old and new testament, containing what is most especially instructive in the historical parts and the many edifying examples in those writings. Vol. 1. 2. 1800. 12. (7 sh.)

KENDALL, [William] *Esq.

The science of legislature, translated from the Italian of *Filangieri*. 1792. 8. (4 sh.) Poems, 1793. 8. (3 sh.)

***KENNEDY, [James]**

Treason!!! or not treason!!! alias the weaver's budget 1795. 8. (6 d.)

KENNEDY, [John] *Surgeon in the 3 battalion of native Infantry, in the service of the East India Company at Bengal.

Account of the good effects, in the cure of diseases, obtained in Bengal, from the use of the toon-tree bark. (*Duncan's* A. of Med. Y. 1796. p. 387.)

***KENNEDY, [P....]**

A short defence of the present men and present measures, with occasional strictures on some recent publications of democratic notoriety. 1797. 8. (2 sh. 6 d.) An answer to *Paine's* letter to Gen. *Washington* or *Mad. Tom*, convicted of the blackest ingratitude. Including some pages of gratuitous counsel to the author of the cause and consequences — 1797. 8. (1 sh.)

KENNEDY, [Robert] *M. Dr. F. R. S. F. A. S. Edin.

A chemical analysis of three species of whinstone and two of lava. (Tr. of E. S. Vol. 5. Part I. p. 76. *Nicholson's* Journal. Vol. 2. p. 289. Vol. 4. p. 407. 438.) Chemical analysis of an uncommon species of zeolite. (*Tilloch's* Philos. Magaz. Vol. 14. p. 310.)

*KENNEDY,

***KENNEDY**, [William] *M. Dr. Physician at Inverness.*

Letter in answer to inquiry respecting the vaccina as a disease of cows in Scotland. (*Duncans* A. of Med. Y. 1800. p. 458.) Account of a case in which the anus was wanting, successfully cured. (Ibid. Y. 1801. p. 351.)

***KENNEY**, [Edward] *Rev.*

A method of preparing a sulphureous medicinal water. (Tr. of J. A. Vol. 5. p. 83.)

***KENNEY**, [James]

Society, a poem, with other poems. 1803. 8. (4 sh.) Raising the wind, a farce in two acts; — 1803. 8. (1 sh. 6 d.)

KENRICK, [William] *L. L. Dr.*

born .... died 1779. June 9.

Lecture on the perpetual motion. P. 1. 2. 1770. 4. (5 sh.) *Millot's* elements of the history of England, from the invasions of the romans to the reign of George 2. translated. Vol. 1. 2. 1771. 8. (8 sh.)

KENT, [Nathaniel] *of Fulham, Middlesex.*

General view of the agriculture of the county of Norfolk; with observations for the means of its improvement — 1796. 8. (5 sh.) Account of the improvements made on the farm in the great park of his Majesty, the King, at Windsor. (Tr. of the Soc. for the E. of A. Vol. 17. p. 119. *Nicholson's* Journal. Vol. 3. p. 422. 429.) Remarks on waste lands in Norfolk. (Bath Agric. Soc. Vol. 8. p. 108.) On Norfolk turnips and fallowing. (*Young's* A. of Agr. Vol. 22. p. 24.) On Norfolk sheep. (Ibid. Vol. 22. p. 30.) Exported produce of Norfolk. (Ibid. Vol. 22. p. 34.) The great advantage of a cow to the family of a labouring man. (Ibid. Vol. 31. p. 21.) Ploughing on his Majesty's farm in Windsor park and at the Earl of Egremont's, at Petworth. (Ibid. Vol. 32. p. 154.)

***KENT**, [P....]

Remarks on the properties of Mr. *Peacey's* rye grass. (Comm. and Agric. Magaz. Y. 1802. Dec. p. 442.)

*KENTISH,

***KENTISH**, [Edward] *Surgeon. M. Dr.*

An essay on burns, especially upon those which happen to workmen in mines from the explosions of inflammable air, containing a view of the opinions of ancient and modern authors upon the subject of burns and a variety of cases conducted upon different principles. 1797. (3 sh. 6 d.) übers. in *Schreger's* u. *Harles* Annalen d. neuesten Franz. u. Engl. Chir. u. Geburtsh. B. 1. S. 175. Essay 2. on burns. 1800 8. (3 sh.) Cases of cancer, with observations on the use of carbonate of lime in that disease. 1802. 8. (1 sh.)

***KENTISH**, [John]

Letter to *James White*, Esq. of Exeter, on the late correspondance, between him and *Toulmin*, relative to the society of Unitarian christians, established in the west of England. 1794. 8. (1 sh.) The moral tendency of the genuine christian doctrine. 1796. 8. (1 sh.) A vindication of the principles upon which several unitarian christians have formed themselves into societies for the purpose of avowing and recommending their views of religious doctrine by the distribution of books. Ed. 2. 1800. 12. The nature and duties of the christian ministry and the co-operation of a christian society with the labours of its ministers. Two sermons —; 1803. (1 sh. 6 d.)

KENTISH, [Richard] *M. Dr. F. A. S. E.*

Advice to gouty persons — übers. von C. F. *Michaelis* — Leipz. 1792. 8. Observations on the effects of the guillotine, as an instrument of death; tending to shew that it is one of the most painful mortal punishments now used in any country where torture is abolished. (New London M. J. Vol. 2. p. 431.)

KENTON, [James] *P. B. of Charter-house.*

A familiar epistle, on the juvenile exercises of the young gentlemen in Charter-house. 1793. 8. (4 d.)

***KER**, [Andrew]

Report to Sir *John Sinclair*, of a sheep farming-tour. (*Young's* A. of Agr. Vol. 17. p. 284.)

*KER,

*KER, [Anne] *Mrs.*
Adeline St. Julian; or, the midnight hour. Vol. 1. 2. 1799. (8 sh.) The heiress of Montalde or the castle of Bezanto. Vol. 1. 2. 1799. (7 sh.)

*a KERLIE, [Margaretha]
Receipt for pot-ash cake. (Monthly Magaz. Y. 1799. Dec. p. 873.)

KERR, [Robert] *F. R. S: F. A. S. E. Surgeon to the orphan hospital Edinburgh.*
Lavoisier's elements of chemistry. Ed. 2. 1793. 8. The animal kingdom, or zoological system of *Charles Linnaeus.* Vol. 1. P. 1. 1792. 4. (10 sh. 6 d.) Vol. 1. P. 2. The natural history of oviparous quadrupeds and serpents — by *De la Cepede,* translated. Vol. 1-4. 1802. 8. (2 L. 2 sh.)

*KERR, [Simon]
Scottish poems, songs &c. 1802. 12. (5 sh.)

*KERRICH, [John]
Use of kiln-drying discoloured barley. (Monthly Magaz. Y. 1800. March p. 107.)

*KERRISON, [Robert] *Surgeon*
The elements of physiology — translated from the French of *A. Richerand.* 1803. 8. (9 sh.)

*KERSHAW, [Arthur]
On the word hitch. (Monthly Magaz. Y. 1799. Jan. p. 24.) Information relative to the character, manners, opinions &c. of the peasantry in the northern parts of Zealand. (Comm. and Agric. Mag. Y. 1799. Sept. p. 96.)

*KETT, [Henry] *M. A: B. D: Fellow and Tutor of Trinity-College, Oxford.*
Sermons at *Bampton's* lecture — 1791. 8. (5 sh.) Juvenile poems; 1793. 8. (2 sh.) * A representation of the conduct and opinions of the primitive christians with remarks on certain affections of Mr. *Gibbon* and Dr. *Priestley* in 8 sermons — 17.. History, the interpreter of prophecy, or, a view of scriptural prophecies and their accomplishment in the past and present occurrences of the world; with conjectures respecting their future completion. Vol. 1-3. 1799. 12. (10 sh. 6 d.) Elements of general knowledge, introductory to useful books in the principal branches of littera-

ture

ture and ſcience; —. Vol. 1. 2. 1802. 8. (15 ſh.) Ed. 2. 1802. Additions to the elements of general knowledge, inſerted in the ſecond edition. 1802. 8. (1 ſh.)

*KEY, [.....] *Surgeon in the Borough.*

Abſtract of a caſe of morbus niger. (Mem. of M. S. of L. Vol. 2. p. 554.)

*KEY, [Richard] *Esq. LL. D. of the Middle-Temple; Fellow of Magdalen-College, Cambridge.*

The captive monarch, a tragedy, in 5 acts. 1794. 8.

KEYES, [John] *of Beekall, near Pembroke.*

On bees. (Bath Agric. Soc. Vol. 5. p. 319. 324.) The ancient bee-maſter's farewell, or, full and plain directions for the management of bees to the greateſt advantage — illuſtrated with plates. 1796. 8. (5 ſh.)

*KEYSAL, [John] *Esq. of Morton-upon-Lugg, near Hereford.*

On draining land. (Tr. of the Soc. for the E. of A. Vol. 10. p. 112.)

*KIDDERSLAW, [Johanſon]

Swediſh myſteries, or, hero of the mines; a tale; translated from a Swediſh MSS. Vol. 1-3. 1801. 12. (13 ſh. 6 d.)

*Biſhop of KILLALUE, [Thomas]

Method of cultivating potatoes. (Bath Agric. Soc. Vol. 4. p. 232.)

*KIMPTON, [Edward] *Vicar of Rogate, Suſſex, and Morning Preacher at St. Matthew's Bethnal green.*

Univerſal hiſtory of the holy bible. 17.. The whole genuine and complete works of *Flavius Joſephus* translated from the original — by *Gr. Henry Maynard*, illuſtrated with marginal references and notes, hiſtorical, biographical, claſſical, critical, geographical, explanatory. — Nrb. 1-60. (à 6 d.)

*KINDERSLEY, [N.... E....] *Esq. of the Eaſt-India Company's civil ſervice on their Madras Eſtabliſhment.*

Specimens of Hindoos litterature — to which are prefixed introductory remarks on the mytho-

mythology, litterature — of the Hindoos. 1794. 8. (7 sh. 6 d.)

*KING, [.....]

Letter 1–3. to *Thomas Paine*, author of the rights of man. 1793. 8. (6 d.)

*KING, [.....] *Lord.*

Thoughts on the restriction of payments in specie at the banks of England and Ireland. 1803. 8. (2 sh. 6 d.)

*KING, [Alexander] *of Suffield, Connecticut. M. Dr.*

A case of canine madness, which terminated fatally at Suffield, in Connecticut on the 11 of Nov. 1797. (Med. Reposit. Vol. 1. p. 337.) Medical observations on the virtues and properties of the seeds of the datura stramonium. (Ibid. Vol. 2. p. 35.)

*KING, [Anthony] *Esq. LL. Dr.*

Thoughts on the expediency of adopting a system of national education, more immediately suited to the policy of this country: with certain brief remarks on that class of free schools commonly distinguished by the name of diocesan schools. 1795. 8. (2 sh. 6 d.)

*KING, [Charlotta] *Miss.*

— — and *Sophia* KING trifles from helicon. 1798. 8. (3 sh.)

KING, [Edward] *Esq. F. R. S. F. A. S. late President of the Soc. of Antiq.*

See *J. Acland.* Morsels of criticism — Part 2. 1803. 4. (1 L. 1 sh. or 3 Vols. 8vo 1 L. 7 sh.) Considerations on the utility of the national debt; and on the present alarming crisis — 1793. 8. (1 sh.) Remarks concerning stones said to have fallen from the clouds, both in these days and in ancient times. 1796. 4. (2 sh. 6 d.) Vestiges of Oxford castle; or, a small fragment of a work intended to be published speedily on the history of antient castles and on the progress of architecture. 1796. fol. (9 sh.) Hymns to the supreme being; new edition. 1798. (5 sh.) Remarks on the signs of the times. 1798. 4. (2 sh. 6 d.) Supplement. 1799. 4. (3 sh.) Munumenta antiqua, or observations on ancient castles, including remarks on the whole progress of architecture, ecclesiastical as well as mili-

military in Great-Britain — Vol. 1. 1799. fol. (3 L. 13 ſh. 6 d.) Vol. 2. 1801. (3 L. 13 ſh. 6 d.)

***KING, [John]**

An eſſay, intended to eſtabliſh a new univerſal ſyſtem of arithmetic, diviſion of the year, circle and hour, ſyſtem of ſtandard meaſures, wights and coins — 1802. 8.

***KING, [John]**

A treatiſe on the cow-pox, containing the hiſtory of vaccine inoculation and an account of the various publications which have appeared on that ſubject in Great-Britain and other parts of the world. P. 1. 1801. 8. (8 ſh.)

***KING, [Joſeph]** *Accountant at Liverpool.*

Tables of intereſt, calculated at 5 per cent. P. 1. 2. 1799. 1800. 8. (9 ſh.)

***KING, [Iſaac]** *Esq. of Wycombe, Bucks.*

Letters from France, written in the months of Aug. Sept. and Oct. 1802. —; 1803. 8. (5 ſh.) On the change of ſeed. (*Young's A.* of Agr. Vol. 4. p. 486.) Fallowing unneceſſary. (Ibid. Vol. 5. p. 476.) On the growth of trees. (Ibid. Vol. 6. p. 89.) Notes of a tour in ſome eaſtern counties. (Ibid. Vol. 35. p. 545.) Farming account. (Ibid. Vol. 37. p. 156.) Crops-bucks. (Ibid. Vol. 36. p. 218.) Curious farming memoir. (Ibid. Vol. 37. p. 441.)

***KING, [M.... P....]**

A general treatiſe on muſic, particularly on harmony or thorough-baſs and its application in compoſition — 1800. fol. (1 L. 1 ſh.)

***KING, [Nicholas]**

An improvement in boats, for river-navigation. (Tr. of A. S. Vol. 4. p. 298.)

***KING, [Philip]** *Esq.*

Extracts of letters from *Arthur Phillips* Esq. to Lord *Sidney*, to which is annexed a deſcription of Norfolk islands and an account of expences incurred in tranſporting convicts to New South Wales. 1791. 4. (2 ſh.)

***KING, [Samuel]**

An impartial inquiry into the ſtate of religion in England. 1789. 8. (1 ſh.)

KING,

KING, [Samuel Croker] *Esq. M. R. J. A. Surgeon.*
Description of an instrument for performing the operation of trepanning the skull, with more ease, safety and expedition than with those now in general use. (Tr. of J. A. Vol. 4. p. 119. *Simmon's* Med. Facts and Observat. Vol. 7. p 191.)

KING, [Sophia] *Miss.* See *Charlotta King.*
Waldorf, or, the dangers of philosophy, a philosophical tale. Vol. 1. 2. 1798. (6 sh.) Cordelia, or, a romance of real life. Vol. 1. 2. 1799. 12. (6 sh.) The victim of friendship, a german romance. Vol. 1. 2. 1801. 8. (7 sh.)

KING, [Thomas] *Actor at Drury-Lane Theater.*
See Public Characters of 1798 and 1799. p. 218.
A dramatic olio; 1762.

KING, [W....]
Britannia triumphant over the french fleet by Admiral Lord Nelson of the mouth of the Nile, a poem. 1799. 8. (1 sh.)

KING, [Walker] *D. D. F. A. S: Preacher to the Soc. of Gray's-Inn.*
Two sermons. 1793. 4. (1 sh. 6 d.)

KINGHORN, [Joseph]
Defence of infant baptism its best confutation, being a reply to *Peter Edwards* candid reasons for renouncing the principles of antipaedobaptism on his own ground. 1795. 12. (6 d.) Public worship considered and enforced. 1800. 12. (6 d.)

KINGSBURY, [Benjamin] *Formerly a Dissenting Minister at Warwick; at present a Perfumer in fleet-street London.*
Prayers for the use of families. 1790. 8. (2 sh. 6 d.) A recommendation of family religion, addressed to christians of all denominations. 1792. 8. (2 d.) A treatise on razors; in which, the weight shape and temper of a razor, the means of keeping it in order, and the manner of using it, are particularly considered — 1797. 8. (1 sh. 6 d.) übers. Leipz. 1800. 8. An answer to an address to the people of Great-Britain by the Bish. of Landaff (*Rich. Watson*) in an other address to the people. 1798. 8. (1 sh.) An address to the people of Great-Britain on the subject of Mr. *Pitt's* proposed tax on income, in which its partial ope-

ration, its rank injustice and its dreadful consequences, are demonstrated: together with the property of an early and a strenuous opposition to this unprecedented scheme, previous to it's passing into a law. 1798. 8. (1 sh.)

*KINGSBURY, [William] *A. M. a Dissenting Minister at Southampton.*

Sermon on the death of *Robert Sealy*, with some account of the deceased; 1778. 8. (6 d.) Sermon on the King's recovery; 1789. 8. (1 sh.) Sermon on the death of Mrs. *Mounsher*. 1789. 8. (6 d.) The manner in which the protestant dissenters perform prayer in public worship represented and vindicated; in a letter to *Richard Mant*, D. D. Rector of all Saints, Southampton. 1796. 8. An apology for village-preachers, or an account of the proceedings aud motives of protestant dissenters and serious christians of other denominations, in their attempts to suppress infidelity and vice and to spread vital religion country places. 1799. 8. (1 sh.)

*KINGSFORD, [William]

Observations on Governour *Pownall's* bill for regulating the mealing trade. (*Young's* A. of Agr. Vol. 12. p. 174.)

*KINNOUL, [.....] *Earl of*

Speech to the British society for fisheries, containing the statement of its progress. 1799. 8. (2 sh.)

*KIPLING, [Thomas] *D. D. Of St. John's College, Cambridge, and Deputy Regius Professor of Divinity in the University.*

The elementary parts of Dr. *Smith's* complete system of optics — and an account of the scarcity and expence of Dr. *Smith's* valuable book. 1778. Codex *Theodori Bezae* Cantabrigiensis, evangelia et apostolorum acta complectens, quadratis litteris graeco-latinis. Vol. 1. 2. Cantabrigiae. 1793. fol. (2 L. 2 sh.) The articles of the church of England proved not to be calvinist. 1802. 8. (3 sh.)

KIPPIS, [Andrew] *D. D. F. R. S. F. A. S.* born at Nottingham March 28. 1725. died 1795. Oct. 8.

See Gentleman's Magaz. Y. 1795. Oct. p. 803. 882. Nov. p. 913. The Annual Necrology for 1797. 1798. p. 209. Allg. Litter. Zeit. J. 1796. ItBl. N. 56. S. 460. On

On the advantages of religious knowledge; a fermon. 1756. Obfervations on the coronation, a fermon. 1760. A fermon at Salters hall, before the fociety for propagation chriftian knowledge. 1777. Sermon at the ordination of Meff. *Worthington* and *Jacomb*. 1778. Biographia Britannica. Ed. 2. Vol. 5. 1793. fol. (1 L. 11 fh. 6 d.) An addrefs delivered at the interment of the late Dr. *Richard Price* on the 26 Apr. 1791. 8. (1 fh.) Sermons on practical fubjects. 1791. 8. (6 fh.) Propofal or profpectus for publifhing a moft fuperb edition of Mr. *Hume's* hiftory of England. 1792. 4. Life of *P. Doddridge* D. D. prefixed to his family expofitor, or, a paraphrafe and verfion of the new teftament, with critical notes. 1792. 8. A courfe of lectures on the principal fubjects in pneumatology, ethics and divinity; with references to the moft confiderable authors on each fubject, by the late *Phil. Doddridge* D. D. Ed. 3. to which are now added, a great number of references and many notes of reference to the various writers, on the fame topics, who have appeared fince the doctor's deceafe. Vol. 1. 2. 1794. 8. (15 fh.) A collection of hymns and pfalms, for public and private worfhip felected and prepared by *A. Kippis*, *Abraham Rees*, *Thomas Jervis* and *Thomas Morgan*. 1795. 12. (3 fh. 6 d.) (Hiftory of the knowledge, learning and tafte in Great-Britain, prefixed to the New Annual Regifter Y. 1781 and follow.) Anfwer to the letters refpecting an error in his life of Capt. *Cook*. (Coll. of Maffachufetts H. S. Y. 1798. p. 5.) (Several fingle fermons.)

KIRBY, [Ephraim]

American reporter; or reports of cafes adjudged in the fuperiour court of the ftate of Connecticut. 17.. 8.

KIRBY, [John] *Esq. of Ipswich.*

On the culture of carrots. (Bath Agricult. Soc. Vol. 3. p. 79.) Experiments on potatoes. (*Young's* A. of Agr. Vol. 1. p. 284.) Artificial yeaft. (Ibid. Vol. 1. p. 285.)

KIRBY, [William] *B. A. Rector of Barham in Suffolk. F. L. S.*

Defcriptions of three new fpecies of hirudo, with

additional note by *George Shaw*. (Transact. of L. S. Vol. 2. p. 316. 319.) A history of three species of cassida. (Ibid. Vol. 3. p. 7.) Ammophila, a new genus of insects in the class hymenoptera, including the sphex sabulosa of *Linnaeus*. (Ibid. Vol. 4. p. 195.) History of tipula tritici and ichneumon tipulae, with some observations upon other insects that attend the wheat. (Ibid. Vol. 4. p. 230. Vol. 5. p. 96.) Observations upon certain fungi, which are parasitica of the wheat. (Ibid. Vol. 5. p. 112.) Some observations upon insects that prey upon timber, whit a short history of the cerambyx violaceus of Linnaeus. (Ibid. Vol. 5. p. 246.) Monographia apum Angliae — to which are prefixed some introductory remarks upon the class hymenoptera and a synoptical table of the nomenclature of the external parts of these insects illustrated with plates. Vol. 1. 2. 1802. 8. (1 L. 1 sh.)

*KIRKLAND, [John Thornton]

Answers to queries respecting the western Indians. (Coll. of Massachusetts H. S. Y. 1795. p. 67.) Remarks on Mr. *Jac. Bailey's* observat. and conjectures on the antiquities of America. (Ibid. Y. 1795. p. 105.)

KIRKLAND, [Thomas] *M. Dr.*

born 1721. died 1798. Jan. 17. at Ashby-de-la-Zouch, Leicestershire.

See Gentleman's Magaz. Y. 1798. Jan. p. 88. 62. March. p. 254. *Duncan's* Annals of Medic. Y. 1798. p. 472. Allgem. Litter. Zeit. ItBl. J. 1800. S. 649.

A commentary on apoplectic and paralytic affections and on diseases connected with the subject. 1792. 8. (3 sh.) übers. Leipzig. 1794. 8.

*KIRKMAN, [James Thomas] *Esq of Lincoln's-Inn.*

Memoirs of the life of *Charles Macklin*, Esq. principally compiled from his own papers and memorandums; which contain his criticisms on and characters and anecdotes of *Betterton*, *Booth*, *Wilks*, *Cibber*, *Garrick*, *Barry*, *Mossop*, *Sheridan*, *Foote*, *Quin*, and most of his contemporaries; together with his valuable observations on the drama, on the science of acting, and on various other subjects:

jects: the whole forming a comprehensive but succinct history of the stage, which includes a period of one hundred years. Vol. 1. 2. 1799. 8. (14 sh.)

KIRKPATRICK, [H.....]
Account of the manner in which potatoes are cultivated and preserved and the uses to which they are applied, in the counties of Lancaster and Chester, together with a description of a new variety of the potatoe, peculiarly convenient for forcing in hot-houses and frames. 1796. 8. (1 sh.) übers. von *G. F. Leonhardi*. Leipzig. 1797. 8.

KIRKPATRICK, [John]
The reason of faith, or, an answer to that enquiry, wherefore we believe the scripture to be the word of God, by *John Owen*, D. D. abridged. 1799. 12.

KIRKPATRICK, [Joseph]
Description of the construction and use of a new implement in husbandry, for transplanting turnips. (Bath Agricult. Soc. Vol. 4. p. 220.) On the use of plaister of Paris as a manure. (Ibid. Vol. 5. p. 225.)

KIRKPATRICK, [William] *Major.*
An ode from Khoosro. (Asiat. Miscell. p. 28.) Muinoon; or the distracted lover, a tale, in imitation of Jovini. (Ibid. p. 78.) Introduction to the institutes of Ghazan Khan. (New Asiat. Miscell. Nro. 2. p. 130.)

KIRWAN, [Richard] *Esq. L.L. D: F. R. S: F. J. A.*
Some account of *Rich. Kirwan*: See *Tilloch's* Philos. Magaz. Vol. 14. p. 353.
Estimate of the temperature of different latitudes. 1787. 8. (3 sh.) übers. von *Crell.* Berlin u. Stettin. 1788. 8. A comparative view of meteorological observations made in Ireland since the Y. 1788. with some hints towards forming prognostics of the weather. Dublin. 1794. 4. Elements of mineralogy. Ed. 2. with considerable improvements and additions. Vol. 1. 1794. Vol. 2. 1797. 8. (8 sh.) übers. von *Crell.* B. 1. 2. Berlin. 1796. 1801. 8. The manures most advantageously applicable to the various sorts of soils, and the causes of their beneficial effect in each particular instance. 1796. 8.

 (2 sh.)

(2 ſh.) überſ. von *A. G. L. Lentin*. Göttingen. 1796. 8. An eſſay on chemical nomenclature, by *Stephan Dickſon*, M. Dr. in which are compriſed obſervations on the ſame ſubject, by *Rich. Kirwan*. 1796. 8. (5 ſh.) Eſſay on the analyſis of mineral waters; 1799. 8. (7 ſh.) Geological eſſays. 1799. 8. (8 ſh.) Phyſiſch-chemiſche Schriften — von *Lor. Crell*. B. 4. 5. Berlin. 1801. 8. Obſervations on coal mines. (Tr. of J. A. 1788. p. 157. Ib. 1789. p. 49.) Experiments on the alkaline ſubſtances uſed in bleaching and on the colouring matter of linen-yarn. (Tr. of J. A. 1789. p. 3.) Of the ſtrenght of acids and the proportion of ingredients in neutral ſalts. (Ibid. Vol. 4. p. 3.) A comparative view of meteorological obſervations made in Ireland ſince the Y. 1788. with ſome hints towards forming prognoſtics of the weather. (Ib. Vol. 5. p. 3.) Reflections on meteorological tables, aſcertaining the preciſe ſignification of the terms wet, dry and variable. (Ibid. Vol. 5. p. 31.) State of the weather in Dublin from the 1 June 1791. to the 1 June 1793. (Ibid. Vol. 5. p. 39.) Examination of the ſuppoſed igneous origin of ſtony ſubſtances. (Ibid. Vol 5. p. 51.) Eſſay in anſwer to the following queſtion propoſed by the R. J. A. What are the manures moſt advantageouſly applicable to the various ſorts of ſoils and what are the cauſes of their beneficial effect in each particular inſtance? (Ibid. Vol. 5. p. 129. *Young's* A. of Agr. Vol. 23. p. 77.) Meteorological obſervations made in Ireland in the Y. 1793. (Ibid. Vol. 5. p. 227.) Experiments on a new earth found near ſtronthian in Scotland. (Ibid. Vol. 5. p. 243.) On the compoſition and proportion of carbon in bitumens and mineral coal. (Ibid. Vol. 6. p. 141. *Nicholſon's* Journal: Vol. I. p. 487.) Synoptical view of the ſtate of the weather in Dublin. (Ibid. Vol. 6. p. 169.) Thoughts on magnetiſm. (Ibid. Vol. 6. p. 177. *Nicholſon's* Journal Vol. 4. p 90. 133.) On the primitive ſtate of the globe and its ſubſequent cataſtrophe. (Tr. of J. A. Vol. 6. p. 233.) Synoptical view of the ſtate of the weather at Dublin in the Y. 1796. 1797. 1798. 1799. 1800. 1801. (Ibid. Vol. 6. p. 309.

309. 435. Vol. 7. p. 316. 358. Vol. 8. p. 203. 509.) Additional obſervations on the proportion of real acid in the three antient known mineral acids and on the ingredients in various neutral ſalts and other compounds. (Ibid. Vol. 7. p. 163. *Nicholſon's* Journal. Vol. 3. p. 210. 273.) Eſſay on human liberty. (Ibid. Vol. 7. p. 305.) A plan for the introduction and eſtabliſhment of the moſt advantageous management of mines in the kingdom of Ireland. (Tr. of Dublin Soc. Vol. 1. P. 1. p. 277.) A reply to Mr. *Playfair's* reflections on *Kirwan's* refutation of the Huttonian theory of the earth. (*Tilloch's* Phil. Mag. Vol. 14. p. 3.) An illuſtration and confirmation of ſome facts mentioned in an eſſay on the primitive ſtate of the globe. (Tr. of J. A. Vol. 8. Sc. p. 29. *Tilloch's* Philoſ. Magaz. Vol. 14. p. 14.) Of the ſtate of vapour ſubſiſting in the atmosphere. (Ibid. Vol. 14. p. 143. 251.) Obſervations on the proofs of the *Huttonian* theory of the earth adduced by Sir *James Hall*, Bart. (Tr. of J. A. Vol. 8. Sc. p. 3. *Nicholſon's* Journal. Vol. 4. p. 97. 153.) An eſſay on the declivities of mountains. (Tr. of J. A. Vol. 8. Sc. p. 35. *Tilloch's* Philoſ. Magaz. Vol. 8. p. 29.) On chymical and mineralogical nomenclature. (Tr. of J. A. Vol. 8. Sc. p. 53. *Tilloch's* Philoſ. Magaz. Vol. 8. p. 172. 202.) Remarks on ſome ſceptical poſitions in Mr. *Hume's* enquiry concerning the human underſtanding and his treatiſe of human nature. (Tr. of J. A. Vol. 8. Sc. p. 157.) On the variation of the atmosphere in Dublin. (Ibid. Vol. 8. Sc. p. 269.)

KITE, [Charles] *Surgeon at Graveſend in Kent.*
Caſe of an unuſually large abſceſs, ſeated between the peritonaeum and abdominal muſcles, from which the matter appeared to be diſcharged, ſometimes by the external opening and at other times by expectoration. (M. C. Vol. 2. p. 46.) On the ſubmerſion of animals; its effects on the vital organs; and the moſt probable method of removing them. (Mem. of M. S. of L. Vol. 3. p. 215.) An account of the medicinal effects of the reſin acaroides reſinifera, or yellow reſin from Botany-Bay. (Ibid. Vol. 4. p. 24.) An account of ſome anoma-

anomalous appearances consequent to the inoculation of the small pox. (Ibid. Vol. 4. p. 114.) A rupture of the gravid uterus terminating favourably. (Ibid. Vol. 4. p. 253.) Cases of several women who had the small pox during pregnancy; with an account of the manner in which the children appeared to have been affected. (Ibid. Vol. 4. p. 295.) Essays and observations physiological and medical, on the submersion of animals and on the resin of the acaroides resinifera, or yellow resin from Botany-Bay; to which are added select histories of diseases, with remarks. 1795. 8. (6 sh.)

*KNIGHT, [Edward]

Description of his new-constructed harrow. (Tr. of the Soc. for the E. of A. Vol. 14. p. 198.)

KNIGHT, [E.... Cornelia] *Miss.*

*Dinarbas. 1790. Marcus Flaminius; or, a view of the military political and social life of the Romans: in a series of letters from a patrician to his friend. Vol. 1. 2. 1792. 8. (10 sh. 6 d.) übers. Dresden und Leipzig. 1794. 8.

*KNIGHT, [J.... A....]

Reflections on the book of Ruth —; Ed. 2. 1798. 24. (2 d.)

*KNIGHT, [L....] *Miss.*

*KNIGHT, [M....] *Miss.*

Method of giving clay models the appearance of bronze and hardening casts in plaster. (Tr. of the Soc. for the E. of A. Vol. 17. p. 302.)

*KNIGHT, [Richard] *Member of the British mineralogical society*

A new and expeditious process for rendering platina malleable. (*Tilloch's* Philos. Magaz. Vol. 6. p. 1.)

*KNIGHT, [Richard Payne] *Esq. M. P.*

An account of the remains of the worship of priapus lately existing at Isernia, in the kingdom of Naples —; to which is added, a discourse on the worship of priapus and its connexion with the mystic theology of the ancients. London. 1786. 4. (NB. never published, but liberally distributed.) An analytical essay on the greek alphabet. 1791. 4.

4. (15 sh.) The landscape, a didactic poem, in 3 books. 1794. (7 sh. 6 d.) A review of the landscape, a didactic poem: also of an essay on the picturesque: together with practical remarks on rural ornament. 1795. 8. (6 sh.) The progress of civil society, a didactic poem, in 6 books. 1796. 4. (10 sh. 6 d.) See *Humphrey Marshall.*

*KNIGHT, [T....]

The honest thieves, a farce, in two acts, altered from the committee. 1797. 12. (1 sh.) The turnpike gate, a musical entertainment in two acts. 1799. 8. (1 sh. 6 d.)

*KNIGHT, [Thomas Andrew] *Esq. of Elton, near Ludlow.*

On the culture of the apple and pear and on the manufacture of cider and parry. 1797. 8. (2 sh. 6 d.) Some doubts relative to the efficacy of Mr. *Forsyth's* plaister in filling up the holes in trees. 1802. 4. (1 sh.) Observations on the grafting of trees. (Phil. Transact. Y. 1795. p. 290.) An account of some experiments on the fecundation of vegetables. (Ibid. Y. 1799. p. 195. *Nicholson's* Journal. Vol. 3. p. 458. Comm. and Agric. Magaz. Y. 1800. p. 245. *Tilloch's* Philos. Magaz. Vol. 7. p. 97.) Description of his drill-machine for sowing turnip-seed. (Tr. of the Soc. for the E. of A. Vol. 19. p. 123. Comm. and Agric. Magaz. Y. 1802. p. 82. *Tilloch's* Philos. Magaz. Vol. 12. p. 271.) On the destructive effects of the aphis and blights on fruit trees. (Ib. Vol. 19. p. 129. Comm. and Agric. Mag. Y. 1802. May. p. 332.) Account of some experiments on the ascent of the sap in trees. (Philos. Transact. Y. 1801. p. 333.) Account of Herefordshire breeds of sheep, cattle, horses and hogs. (Comm. to the B. of Agr. Vol. 2. p. 172.)

*KNIGHT, [Titus] *Rev. of Halifax.*

born 1719. Dec. 17. died 1793. March 2.

See Evangelical Magaz. Y. 1793. Vol. 1. p. 90. Sermons, with a treatise on the imputation of sin and righteousness. 1766. Amyntas and Philetus, or christian conversation illustrated in dialogues. 1770. The balm of Gilead. 17.. Queries and

Oo 5 obser-

observations on the divinity of Christ. 17.. Elegy on the death of Mr. *Whitefield*. 17..
(Several single sermons.)

*KNIGHT, [W.... W....] *Esq. of Ruscombe near Maidenhead, Berkshire.*
Account of a flock of sheep. (*Young's* A. of Agr. Vol. 10. p. 477. Vol. 11. p. 29.) An account of a sow and pigs. (Ibid. Vol. 14. p. 169.)

KNIPE, [Rest] *Rev. of Edinburgh.*
Wonderful thoughts. (Massachusetts Magaz. Y. 1790. Oct. p. 615.)

KNOT, [G.... C.... P....]
Reflections on the slave trade, with remarks on the policy of its abolition, in a letter to a clergyman in the county of Suffolk. 1791. 8. (1 sh. 6 d.)

*KNOWLES, [Sir Charles] *Admiral.*
*View of the naval force of Great-Britain; in which its present state, growth and conversion of timber; constructions of ships, docks and harbours; regulations of officers and men in each department: are considered and compared with other European powers, with observations and hints for the improvement of the naval service. By an officer of rank. 1791. 8.

*KNOWLES, [John]
Principles of english grammar — Ed. 3. 1794. 12. (1 sh. 6 d.) Ed. 4. 1796. 12. (1 sh. 6 d.)

KNOWLES, [Thomas] *D. D. Lecturer of St. Mary's, in Bury St. Edmund's, Prebendary of Ely, Rector of Ickworth and Chedburgh and Vicar of Winston in the county of Suffolk.*
born at Ely 1724. died 1802. Oct. 6.
See Gentleman's Magaz. Y. 1802. Oct. p. 980. Monthly Magaz. Y. 1802. Nov. p. 367. Dec. p. 457.
The scripture doctrine of the existence and attributes of god in 12 sermons, with a preface in answer to a pamphlet on thoughts concerning the argument a priori; 17.. Lord *Hervey's* and Dr. *Middleton's* letters on the roman senate. 17.. Observations on the tithe bill. 17.. Dialogue on the test act. 17.. Advice to a young clergyman, in 6 letters. 17.. The passion, a sermon on the observation of the sabbath. 17.. On charity-

rity-schools, on sunday-schools and a preparatory discourse on confirmation. 17..

*KNOX, [.....]
*Letters on the subject of the concert of princes, and the dismemberment of Poland and France, by a calm observer. 1793. 8. (5 sh.)

*KNOX, [.....] *M. Dr: of the Island of Tortola.*
A curious case of a lusus naturae. (*Duncan's* M. C. Dec. 2. Vol. 6. p. 291.)

°KNOX, [Alexander] *Esq.*
Essays on the political circumstances of Ireland: written during the administration of Earl *Camden*; with an appendix, containing thoughts on the will of the people and a postscript, now first published. 1799. 8. (5 sh.)

*KNOX, [George] *Representative in Parliament for the University of Dublin, in the House of Commons. M. R. J. A.*
Speech on the subject of an incorporate union of Great-Britain and Ireland. 1800. 8. (6 d.) Observations on calp. (Tr. of J. A. Vol. 8. Sc. p. 207.)

*KNOX, [Samuel] *of York county, Pennsylvania.*
A case of scrophula. (Columbian Magaz. Y. 1790. Jul. p. 15.)

°KNOX, [Samuel] *A. M. of Maryland.*
An essay on the best system of liberal education. 1799.

*KNOX, [T....] *A. M.*
Hints to public speakers, intended for young barristers students at law and all others who may wish to improve their delivery and attain a just and graceful elocution. 1797. 12. (2 sh. 6 d.)

*KNOX, [Thomas] *late Lieuten. Colonel, Commandant of the Fishguard Volunteers.*
Some account of the proceedings that book place on the landing of the french near Fishguard, in Pembrokeshire, on the 22 Febr. 1797. — 1797.

KNOX, [Vicesimus] *D. D. Master of Tunbridge school in Kent, and late Fellow of St. John's College, Oxford.*
Sketch of his life; See Massachusetts Mag. Y. 1794. May. p. 286. Winter evenings or lucubrations on life and letters. Vol. 1–3. 1788. 12. Ed. 2. Vol. 1. 2. 1792. 8. (13 sh.) Sermons, chiefly intended to

to promote faith, hope and charity. 1792. 8. (6 ſh.) *Perſonal nobility: or, letters to a young nobleman, on the conduct of his ſtudies and the dignity of the peerage. 1793. 12. (4 ſh.) überſ. Hamburg u. Lüneburg. 1799. 8. A narrative of the tranſactions relative to a ſermon, preached in the Pariſh church of Brighton Aug. 18. 1793. with ſhort extracts from the ſermon and occaſional remarks. 1793. 8. (1 ſh. 6 d.) Antipolemus; or the plea of reaſon, religion and humanity againſt war; a fragment: translated from *Eraſmus* and addreſſed to aggreſſors. 1794. 8. (3 ſh. 6 d.) Chriſtian philoſophy; or, an attempt to diſplay the evidence and excellence of revealed religion. Vol. 1. 2. 1795. 8. (6 ſh.) *Elegant extracts, in verſe and proſe; 17.. Elegant epiſtles. 17.. Family lectures; 17.. Conſiderations on the nature and efficacy of the Lord's ſupper. 1799. 12. (4 ſh.) Ed. 2. 1801. (2 ſh.)

*KNOX, [William] *Lord Biſhop of Killaloe.*
Two ſermons. 1799. 8. (1 ſh. 6 d.)

KNOX, [William] *late Under-Secretary of ſtate to Lord Hillsborough and to Lord George Germaine, during the American war.*
born .... died (?)
See Biogr. Liter. and Polit. Anecdotes —; Vol. 2. p. 112.
The controverſy between Great-Britain and her colonies reviewed; 17..

*KNOX, [William]
*Obſervations upon the liturgy, with a propoſal for its reform upon the principles of chriſtianity —. 1789. 8. *Extraofficial ſtate papers — for the preſervation of the conſtitution and promoting the proſperity of the Britiſh empire. 1789. A letter to the people of Ireland, upon the intended application of the roman catholics to parliament for the exerciſe of the elective franchiſe. 1792. 8. (1 ſh.) A friendly addreſs to the members of the ſeveral clubs, in the pariſh of St. Ann, Weſtminſter, aſſociated for the purpoſe of obtaining a reform in parliament. 1793. 8. (1 ſh.) Conſiderations on the ſtate of Ireland. 1777.

*KNOX,

*KNOX, [William] *Merchant in Gothenburg.*
Letter to Sir *John Sinclair*, respecting the important discovery lately made in Sweden of a method to extinguish fire, with an account of the process adopted for that purpose and hints of means for preserving timber used either in houses or in ship-building from that destructive element. 1793. 8. (1 sh. 6 d.)

*KOOPS, [Matthias] *Esq.*
Thoughts on a sure method of annually reducing the national debt of Great-Britain, without imposing additional burdens upon the people: and which at the same time will tend to diminish the number of poor persons and gradually annihilate the poor-rates. 1796. 8. (1 sh. 6 d.)

*KYD, [Steward] *Esq. Barrister at Law, of the Inner-Temple.*
On the laws of bills of exchange and promissory notes. 1790. 8. (3 sh. 6 d.) Ed. 3. 1796. 8. (5 sh.) On the laws of awards. 1791. 8. (5 sh. 3 d.) Ed. 2. with considerable additions. 1799. 8. (10 sh. 6 d.) *John Comyns*, digest of the laws of England Ed. 3. considerably enlarged and continued down to the present time. Vol. 1-6. 1792. 8. (3 L. 15 sh.) On the law of corporations. Vol. 1. 1793. 8. Vol. 2. 1794. 8. (13 sh.) The substance of the income act, in a methodical arrangement of all its clauses, transposed, as nearly as possible, according to their natural connection with each other. 1798. 8. (1 sh. 6 d.) Arrangement under distinct titles of all the provisions of the several acts of parliament relating to the assessed taxes. 1799. 8. (6 sh.) Postscript. 1801. 8. (1 sh.)

Gedruckt

bey Johann Friedrich Röwer

in Göttingen.